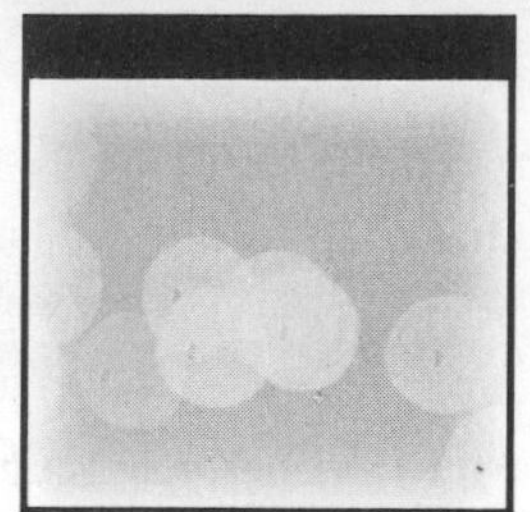

Mastering Enterprise JavaBeans™

Third Edition

Ed Roman
Rima Patel Sriganesh
Gerald Brose

Wiley Publishing, Inc.

Mastering Enterprise JavaBeans™, Third Edition
Published by
Wiley Publishing, Inc.
10475 Crosspoint Boulevard
Indianapolis, IN 46256
www.wiley.com

Published by Wiley Publishing, Inc., Indianapolis, Indiana
Published simultaneously in Canada
ISBN: 0-7645-7682-8
Manufactured in the United States of America
10 9 8 7 6 5 4 3 2 1

3B/RX/RR/QU/IN

For general information on our other products and services or to obtain technical support, please contact our Customer Care Department within the U.S. at (800) 762-2974, outside the U.S. at (317) 572-3993 or fax (317) 572-4002.

Wiley also publishes its books in a variety of electronic formats. Some content that appears in print may not be available in electronic books.

Library of Congress Control Number: 2004114268

To my wonderful wife, Christine, and to our boys, Johannes and Julius.

Rima wishes to dedicate this book to her dearest and loving husband Sriganesh, and her most wonderful parents.

Credits

Acquisitions Editor
Robert M. Elliott

Development Editor
Sydney Jones

Technical Editor
Floyd Marinescu

Copy Editor
Michael Koch

Editorial Manager
Kathryn Malm Bourgoine

Vice President & Executive Group Publisher
Richard Swadley

Vice President and Publisher
Joseph B. Wikert

Project Coordinator
Erin Smith

Graphics and Production Specialists
Sean Decker
Kelly Emkow
Jennifer Heleine

Quality Control Technician
Brian H. Walls

Proofreading and Indexing
TECHBOOKS Production Services

Contents

Acknowledgments

This book has been a project spanning several years. Many have commented that the first edition was one of the best technical books they ever read. What's made this book a reality are the many people who aided in its development.

As a special thanks, we'd like to acknowledge the great folks at John Wiley & Sons. They have been absolutely outstanding throughout this book's evolution. In particular, we thank Bob Elliott, Sydney Jones, and Kathryn Malm for their incredible efforts. We also thank Floyd Marinescu of The Middleware Company for his insightful technical reviews, and Jörg Bartholdt of Xtradyne Technologies for technical discussions. Finally, we thank Theserverside.com community for providing us with their very helpful reviews.

Introduction

This book is a tutorial on Enterprise JavaBeans (EJB). It's about EJB concepts, methodology, and development. This book also contains a number of advanced EJB topics, giving you a practical and real-world understanding of the subject. By reading this book, you will acquire a *deep* understanding of EJB.

Make no mistake about it—what you are about to read is *not* easy. EJB incorporates concepts from a wealth of areas, including distributed computing, databases, security, component-driven software, and more. Combining them is a magnificent stride forward for the Java community, but with that comes a myriad of concepts to learn and understand. This book will teach you the concepts and techniques for authoring reusable components in Java, and it will do so from the ground up. You need only to understand Java to understand this book.

While you're reading this book, you may want to download the EJB specification, available at http://java.sun.com/products/ejb/docs.html.

Goals for This Edition

The first edition of this book came out in 1999, and the second edition in 2002. We had to make some tough calls when writing the second and third editions, and we are confident you'll like them. Here were our goals:

- **To update the book for EJB 2.1.** EJB 2.1 has many new useful features that we detail throughout the book.
- **To be broad and also deep.** We do not regurgitate the complete EJB specification in this book, nor do we cover every last detail of EJB. Rather, we cover the most important parts of EJB, leaving room to discuss advanced issues. For a complete reference while you are coding,

search through the EJB specification using Adobe Acrobat. Readers who are looking for a well-written book that is interactive and fun to read and covers the basics through advanced subjects have come to the right place.

- **To be concise.** Your time as a reader is extremely valuable, and you're likely waiting to read a stack of books besides this one. Given that most people don't have time to read 1,000-plus–page books, we actually wanted to reduce the size of this book as much as possible. So we've tightened things up and eliminated redundant examples. This way, you can get to actually program with EJB, rather than read a book for months on end. The irony of this story is that it was harder for us to write a shorter book than a long book!
- **To be a book for developers.** This book is not intended for high-level businesspeople. This is a technical book for a technical audience.
- **To write a book the right way.** This book's primary author, Ed Roman, has taken his skills in training and knowledge transfer and applied them to this book. Thus, we've infused this book with the following attributes:
  - **A conversational style.** When you read this book, sometimes you'll feel like you're almost having a discussion with us. We think this is far superior to spending eons trying to re-read a formal writing style over and over again.
  - **Use of diagrams and bulleted lists.** The adage "a picture is worth a thousand words" applies here. These tactics are great for breaking up blocks of text. They keep things varied and make the book a much faster read.
  - **A consistent voice.** Even though several co-authors wrote this book, you'll hear one voice. This was done to combine best-of-breed knowledge from several expert co-authors while maintaining a uniform look and feel throughout the book.
- **To be an introductory book, but also to get quickly into advanced topics.** We figured that the average developer has had enough of books that merely skim the surface. We wanted to write a book that pushed beyond the basics. Our approach when writing this book was always to err on the side of being advanced. To achieve this, we did an immense amount of research. We participated in the mailing lists, performed many real-world projects, attended conferences and seminars, and networked with the top experts throughout the world.
- **To be vendor-neutral.** All vendor-specific deployment steps are externalized to the book's accompanying source code. This makes this book useful for any EJB server.

- **To add useful EJB information garnered from our instructor-led training classes.** Having taught EJB/J2EE for years, we have learned significantly from our students. We have interlaced this book with many of our own students' questions and answers in relevant sections.
- **To take all the source code and make it available online.** Because we've made the code available on the Web, you know it's the latest version. This will ensure that the code you receive works right the first time.

Organization of the Book

The text is organized into the following five parts:

- **Part One** is a whirlwind introduction to EJB programming. Part One serves as a great overview for people in a hurry. While Part One is essential information to EJB newcomers, veterans will also find nuggets of useful knowledge. The following chapters are covered:
  - **Chapter 1** is a tour of enterprise computing. We'll talk about components, service-oriented architectures, distributed computing frameworks, and containers. In this regard, we'll introduce EJB and J2EE.
  - **Chapter 2** moves on to the fundamentals of building an EJB system, including the tricky concept of request interception. We'll also look at the various source code files that make up an enterprise bean.
  - **Chapter 3** shows you how to put together a simple enterprise bean. We'll also learn how JNDI is used in EJB and see how to call that bean from a client.
- **Part Two** devotes exclusive attention to programming with EJB. We'll see how to use the triad of beans: entity beans, session beans, and message-driven beans. We'll cover the basics of writing each type of bean, including an example as well as detailed lifecycle diagrams.
  - **Chapter 4** introduces session beans. We'll look at the difference between stateful and stateless session beans, how to code a session bean, and what's going on behind the scenes with session beans.
  - **Chapter 5** shows how Web services can be implemented using EJB. In particular, we show how a stateless session bean can be made available as a Web service.
  - **Chapter 6** is a conceptual introduction to entity beans. We'll look at persistence concepts, what makes entity beans unique, and the files involved when building entity beans.

- **Chapter 7** covers bean-managed persistent (BMP) entity beans. We'll see how to program a BMP entity bean, and also look at what's happening behind the scenes with BMP.
- **Chapter 8** covers container-managed persistent (CMP) entity beans. We'll focus on the exciting features of EJB 2.*x* CMP, learn how to program a CMP entity bean, and look at what's happening behind the scenes with CMP.
- **Chapter 9** covers message-driven beans. We'll first review the Java Message Service (JMS), which is the messaging framework used mostly with message-driven beans. We'll then dive in and understand how to program with message-driven beans.
- **Chapter 10** discusses the EJB environment, along with services provided by the container. This includes environment properties, resource factories, references between beans, and handles.

- **Part Three**, the most exciting part of the book, covers advanced EJB concepts. The following chapters are included:
  - **Chapter 11** explains guidelines for using various Web application frameworks, model-driven development tools, and so on, in EJB applications. It also presents proven best practices for EJB design, development, and testing.
  - **Chapter 12** tackles transactions. Transactions are a crucial topic for anyone building an EJB application that involves state. We'll discuss transactions at a conceptual level followed by a discussion on how to apply them to EJB. We'll also learn about the Java Transaction API (JTA) as well as J2EE Extended Transaction concepts.
  - **Chapter 13** provides an in-depth treatment of EJB security and covers *Java Authentication and Authorization Service* (JAAS), secure interoperability, and Web Services security.
  - **Chapter 14** introduces the new EJB timer service that lets you schedule tasks for automatic execution.
  - **Chapter 15** covers relationships between entity beans. This is a critical concept for anyone performing complex persistence. We'll understand the concepts of cardinality, directionality, referential integrity, and cascading deletes. We'll also see how to code relationships for *both* CMP and BMP entity beans.
  - **Chapter 16** covers persistence best practices. You'll learn exciting concepts such as how to choose between entity beans and other persistence techniques, how to choose between BMP and CMP, and you'll survey a collection of persistence best practices that we've assembled from our knowledge and experience.

- **Chapter 17** covers integration to and from EJB platform in-depth. It provides introduction to the various styles of integration, followed by a discussion of various techniques for integrating EJB with the outside world. It explains the J2EE Connector Architecture, a predominant framework for integrating EJB with back-end enterprise applications, and discusses a connector example.
- **Chapter 18** covers EJB tips and techniques for designing and deploying EJB for better performance. You'll learn about design strategies that will help you make decisions such as when to choose between stateful versus stateless session beans, when to choose between local and remote interfaces, and so on. The chapter also focuses a great deal on providing performance tuning tips for different types of beans.
- **Chapter 19** discusses clustering in large-scale EJB systems. You'll learn about how clustering works behind the scenes and learn a few strategies for how containers might achieve clustering. This is a critical topic for anyone building a system that involves several machines working together.
- **Chapter 20** covers EJB project management. We'll talk about how to get your project started on the right foot. This includes guidelines on choosing between J2EE and .NET frameworks for your projects, building a first pass of your system, dividing your development team, and many such concepts.
- **Chapter 21** provides guidelines for choosing the right EJB server for your needs. We'll describe our methodology for how an organization can compare and contrast different vendors' offerings. We'll also list our set of criteria for what we would want in an EJB server.
- **Chapter 22** shows how to build a real-world J2EE system using EJB components. We'll see how the EJB components should be used *together* in an enterprise, as well as how to connect them with clients using Java servlets and JavaServer Pages (JSP) technology. We'll also demonstrate how to design an EJB object model using UML.

- **The Appendixes** are a collection of ancillary EJB topics. Some developers may want to read the appendices, while some may not need to do so.
  - **Appendix A** teaches you Java Remote Method Invocation over the Internet Inter-ORB Protocol (RMI-IIOP) and the Java Naming and Directory Interface (JNDI). These technologies are prerequisites for using EJB. If you're just starting down the EJB road, you must read this appendix first.
  - **Appendix B** discusses how to integrate EJB and CORBA systems. We'll learn about how EJB and CORBA are interoperable through

RMI-IIOP and see sample code for calling an EJB component from a CORBA client.

- **Appendix C** is a deployment descriptor reference guide. This will be useful for you later, when you're working with deployment descriptors and need a guide.
- **Appendix D** covers the EJB query language (EJB-QL) in detail.
- **Appendix E** is an API and diagram reference guide. This is useful when you need to look up the purpose of a method or class in EJB.

Throughout the book, this icon will signal a tip, note, or other helpful advice on EJB programming.

In a similar paradigm to our training courses, the content of this book is very interactive. We have taken our knowledge of adult learning and scattered boxes like this throughout the book. Each box asks you a question to get you thinking. The answers to the questions are posted on the book's accompanying Web site. What do you think are the benefits of this paradigm?

Illustrations in the Text

Almost all of the illustrations in this book are written in the Unified Modeling Language (UML). UML is the de facto standard methodology for illustrating software engineering concepts in an unambiguous way. If you don't know UML, pick up a copy of *The Unified Modeling Language User Guide* (Addison-Wesley, ISBN 0201571684), which illustrates how to effectively use UML in your everyday software. UML is a highly important achievement in object-oriented methodology. It's a common mechanism for engineers to communicate and design with, and it forces you to abstract your object model prior to implementation. We cannot stress its use enough.

The Accompanying Web Site

This book would not be complete without a way to keep you in touch after it was published. A Web site is available for resources related to this book. There you'll find:

- All of the source code you see in this book. The code comes complete with Ant scripts, ready to build and run. It should be deployed on any application server that is J2EE 1.4–compliant.
- Updates to the source code examples.

- Error corrections from the text.
- A PDF copy of this book

The Web site is at www.wiley.com/compbooks/roman.

Feedback

When you begin your EJB programming, we're sure you'll have many experiences to share with other readers. Feel free to e-mail examples, case studies, horror stories, or tips that you've found helpful in your experiences, and we'll post them on the Web site.

Send bug reports to books@middleware-company.com.

From Here

Now that we've gotten the logistics out of the way, let's begin our exploration of Enterprise JavaBeans.

About the Authors

Ed Roman is one of the world's leading authorities on high-end middleware technologies. He has been heavily involved with Sun Microsystems' enterprise Java solutions from their inception and has designed, built, and deployed a variety of enterprise applications, including architecting and developing complete application server products. He devotes a significant amount of time to influencing and refining Sun's enterprise specifications, contributes regularly to middleware interest mailing lists, and regularly speaks at middleware-related conferences.

Ed is the founder of The Middleware Company (which can be found on the Web at www.middleware-company.com). The Middleware Company offers the world's leading knowledge network for middleware professionals. The Middleware Company enables developers, technology vendors, and enterprises to implement, innovate, and communicate emerging technology offerings. The Middleware Company solutions include TheServerSide Communities, MiddlewareREACH, and MiddlewarePRO. TheServerSide Communities inform over half a million professionals monthly using an open forum to discuss and solve the most challenging middleware issues. Clients of The Middleware Company include the world's top software organizations including BEA Systems, Compuware, HP, IBM, Microsoft, Oracle, Sun Microsystems, and VERITAS Software. Ed also is the founder of TheServerSide.com, which is the de facto J2EE community Web site. Every day, thousands of developers get together on TheServerSide.com to share EJB design patterns, hear about the latest EJB news, ask and answer EJB development questions, and read articles. After you've read this book, visit TheServerSide.com to catch up on the latest EJB information. TheServerSide.com is a completely free service and is intended to help the community.

Rima Patel Sriganesh is a Member of Technical Staff presently working in the Technology Outreach group at Sun Microsystems, Inc. She specializes in Java, XML, and Integration platforms. Her areas of technology passion include Distributed Computing Models, Security and Trust Computing, Semantic web, Grid Computing, and Quantum Physics. She speaks regularly at premiere industry conferences such as JavaOne, Web Services Edge, SIGS 101, Sun Technology Days, and others. She also represents Sun at various security, choreography, and financial services technology standards.

Rima is a co-author of *Developing Java Web Services* (Wiley, 2002). She frequently publishes her take on technology and industry in the form of papers and blogs.

Rima graduated in Mathematics from M. S. University, Gujarat, India. She currently lives with her husband in the Greater Boston area.

To find out more about her work, use the Google queries "Rima Patel" Sun Microsystems or "Rima Patel Sriganesh."

Gerald Brose works as Security Software Architect at Xtradyne Technologies. Gerald is an expert in middleware security, including CORBA, J2EE, and Web Services. He is a regular speaker at international conventions and the author of several publications on middleware security and related issues. Gerald is a co-author of *Java Programming with CORBA* (Wiley, 2001).

As a member of the open source community, Gerald maintains JacORB, the most widely used Open Source ORB for Java, which is also part of the JBoss J2EE application server. Gerald holds a Ph.D. in computer science from Freie University, Berlin. He lives with his wife and two sons in Berlin, Germany.

PART One

Overview

In Part One, we introduce the server-side development platform, the *Java 2 Platform, Enterprise Edition* (J2EE), of which the *Enterprise JavaBeans* (EJB) component architecture is a vital piece. J2EE is a conglomeration of concepts, programming standards, and innovations—all written in the Java programming language. With J2EE, you can rapidly construct distributed, scalable, reliable, and portable secure server-side deployments.

- **Chapter 1** begins by exploring the need for server-side component architecture such as EJB. You'll see the rich needs of server-side computing, such as scalability, high availability, resource management, and security. We'll discuss how EJB architecture relates to the Service-oriented Architecture (SOA) paradigm. We'll also take a look at the J2EE server-side development platform.
- **Chapter 2** moves on to the fundamentals of Enterprise JavaBeans. We'll look at the concept of *request interception*, which is crucial for understanding how EJB works. We'll also look at the different files that go into a bean and how they work together.
- **Chapter 3** gets down and dirty with EJB programming. Here, we'll write our first simple bean. We'll explain how to code each of the files that compose the bean, and we'll also look at how to call that bean from clients.

CHAPTER

1

Overview

Enterprise JavaBeans (EJB) is a server-side component architecture that simplifies the process of building enterprise-class distributed component applications in Java. By using EJB, you can write scalable, reliable, and secure applications without writing your own complex distributed component framework. EJB is about rapid application development for the server side; you can quickly and easily construct server-side components in Java by leveraging a prewritten distributed infrastructure provided by the industry. EJB is designed to support application portability and reusability across any vendor's enterprise middleware services.

If you are new to enterprise computing, these concepts will be clarified shortly. EJB is a complicated subject and thus deserves a thorough explanation. In this chapter, we'll introduce EJB by answering the following questions:

- What plumbing do you need to build a robust distributed object deployment?
- What is EJB, and what value does it add?
- How does EJB relate to SOA?
- Who are the players in an EJB ecosystem?

Let's kick things off with a brainstorming session.

The Motivation for Enterprise JavaBeans

Figure 1.1 shows a typical business application. This application could exist in any vertical industry and could solve any business problem. Here are some examples:

- A stock trading system
- A banking application
- A customer call center
- A procurement system
- An insurance risk analysis application

Notice that this application is a *distributed system*. We broke up what would normally be a large, monolithic application and divorced each layer of the application from the others, so that each layer is completely independent and distinct.

Take a look at this picture, and ask yourself the following question based purely on your personal experience and intuition: *If we take a monolithic application and break it up into a distributed system with multiple clients connecting to multiple servers and databases over a network, what do we need to worry about now* (as shown in Figure 1.1)?

Take a moment to think of as many issues as you can. Then turn the page and compare your list to ours. Don't cheat!

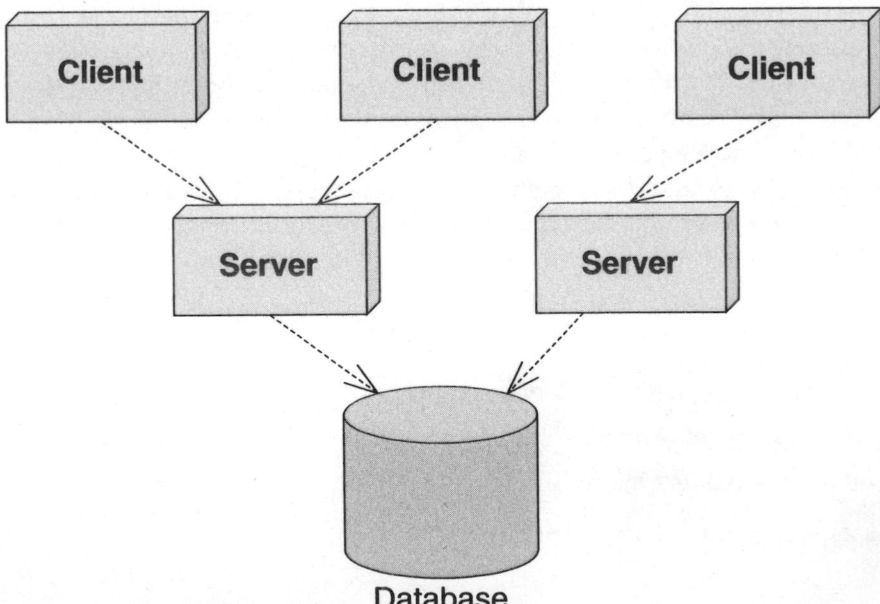

Figure 1.1 Standard multitier-only deployment.

In the past, most companies built their own middleware. For example, a financial services firm might build some of the middleware services above to help them put together a stock trading system.

These days, companies that build their own middleware risk setting themselves up for failure. High-end middleware is hideously complicated to build and maintain, requires expert-level knowledge, and is completely orthogonal to most companies' core business. Why not buy instead of build?

The *application server* was born to let you buy these middleware services, rather than build them yourself. Application servers provide you with common middleware services, such as resource pooling, networking, and more. Application servers enable you to focus on your application and not worry about the middleware you need for a robust server-side deployment. You write the code specific to your vertical industry and deploy that code into the runtime environment of an application server. You've just solved your business problem by *dividing and conquering*.

THINGS TO CONSIDER WHEN BUILDING LARGE BUSINESS SYSTEMS

By now you should have a decent list of things you'd have to worry about when building large business systems. Here's a short list of the big things we came up with. Don't worry if you don't understand all of them yet — you will.

- **Remote method invocations. We need logic that connects a client and server via a network connection. This includes dispatching method requests, brokering parameters, and more.**
- **Load balancing. Clients must be directed to the server with the lightest load. If a server is overloaded, a different server should be chosen.**
- **Transparent fail-over. If a server crashes, or if the network crashes, can clients be rerouted to other servers without interruption of service? If so, how fast does fail-over happen? Seconds? Minutes? What is acceptable for your business problem?**
- **Back-end integration. Code needs to be written to persist business data into databases as well as integrate with legacy systems that may already exist.**
- **Transactions. What if two clients access the same row of the database simultaneously? Or what if the database crashes? Transactions protect you from these issues.**
- **Clustering. What if the server contains state when it crashes? Is that state replicated across all servers, so that clients can use a different server?**
- **Dynamic redeployment. How do you perform software upgrades while the site is running? Do you need to take a machine down, or can you keep it running?**

(continued)

THINGS TO CONSIDER WHEN BUILDING LARGE BUSINESS SYSTEMS *(continued)*

- Clean shutdown. If you need to shut down a server, can you do it in a smooth, clean manner so that you don't interrupt service to clients who are currently using the server?
- Logging and auditing. If something goes wrong, is there a log that you can consult to determine the cause of the problem? A log would help you debug the problem so it doesn't happen again.
- Systems management. In the event of a catastrophic failure, who is monitoring your system? You want monitoring software that paged a system administrator if a catastrophe occurred.
- Threading. Now that you have many clients connecting to a server, that server is going to need the capability of processing multiple client requests simultaneously. This means the server must be coded to be multithreaded.
- Message-oriented middleware. Certain types of requests should be *message-based* where the clients and servers are very loosely coupled. You need infrastructure to accommodate messaging.
- Object life cycle. The objects that live within the server need to be created or destroyed when client traffic increases or decreases, respectively.
- Resource pooling. If a client is not currently using a server, that server's precious resources can be returned to a *pool* to be reused when other clients connect. This includes sockets (such as database connections) as well as objects that live within the server.
- Security. The servers and databases need to be shielded from saboteurs. Known users must be allowed to perform only operations that they have rights to perform.
- Caching. Let's assume there is some database data that all clients share and make use of, such as a common product catalog. Why should your servers retrieve that same catalog data from the database over and over again? You could keep that data around in the servers' memory and avoid costly network roundtrips and database hits.
- And much, much, *much* more.

Each of these issues is a separate service that needs to be addressed for serious server-side computing. These services are needed in any business problem and in any vertical industry. And each of these services requires a lot of thought and a lot of plumbing to resolve. Together, these services are called *middleware*.

Component Architectures

It has been a number of years since the idea of multitier server-side deployments surfaced. Since then, more than 50 application servers have appeared on the market. At first, each application server provided component services in a nonstandard, proprietary way. This occurred because there was no agreed definition of what a component should be or how it should be provided with services or how should it interact with the application server. The result? Once you bet on an application server, your code was locked into that vendor's solution. This greatly reduced portability and was an especially tough pill to swallow in the Java world, which promotes openness and portability.

What we need is an *agreement*, or set of interfaces, between application servers and components. This agreement will enable any component to run within any application server. This will allow components to be switched in and out of various application servers without having to change code or potentially even recompile the components themselves. Such an agreement is called *component architecture* and is shown in Figure 1.2.

If you're trying to explain components to a nontechie, try these analogies:

- **Any CD player can play any compact disc because of the CD standard. Think of an application server as a CD player and components as compact discs.**
- **In the United States, any TV set can tune into any broadcast because of the NTSC standard. Think of an application server as a TV set and components as television broadcasts.**

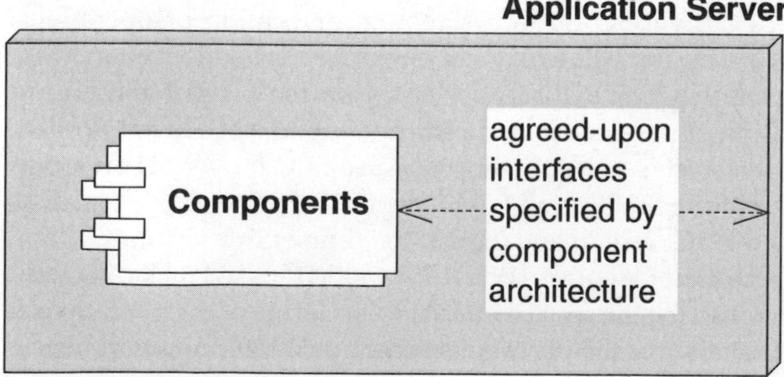

Figure 1.2 A component architecture.

Service-Oriented Architectures

At the core of a service-oriented architecture lies the concept of *service*. A simplistic definition of service is a group of related components that carry out a given business process function, for example transferring funds between banks or booking an itinerary. A *service-oriented architecture* (SOA) thus is a paradigm focusing on development of services rather than piecemeal components such that these services provide a higher level of abstraction from a functional standpoint. Of course, there are more properties to SOA than mere coarse-granularity. One such characteristic property of SOA is that they are autonomous in nature. These independent entities can interact with others in spite of differences in the way they have been implemented or the platform they have been deployed on. The notion of putting together (integrating) such autonomous and loosely coupled services to address the changing business needs has a huge value proposition and it is well on its way to realization with the emergence of various choreography, orchestration and collaboration technologies such as WS-BPEL, EbXML BPSS, and WS Choreography.

SOA and Web Services

The terms Web Services and SOA are often used interchangeably and wrongly so. SOA is a paradigm. There are many possible ways of building software so that it implements salient features of SOA, mainly coarse granularity and loose coupling. One such way is Web services. Web Services are a group of XML technologies, which can be used for implementing SOA. Core Web service technologies—mainly SOAP and WSDL—form the basis of most of these Web service implementations today.

Simple Object Access Protocol (SOAP) is an XML-based application-level protocol intended for exchanging information in a distributed network. SOAP supports both the models of distributed computing: RPC as well as document-style messaging. RPC style SOAP allows remote invocation of operations. Parameters and return in/out values of these operations are serialized in XML. Whereas, in document-style SOAP because an operation's input and output are XML, serialization of parameters and return value to XML is not needed. Although most of the Web service applications use SOAP over HTTP today, the standard does not preclude using SOAP over other IP protocols, such as SMTP. SOAP 1.2 is a W3C recommendation at the time of this writing.

Web Service Description Language (WSDL) is an XML-based metadata standard that is used to describe the service interface—in terms of the operations it supports, the parameters that the operations accept, and their return values in case of SOAP RPC, the XML schema that the input and output messages to the operations in case of document-style SOAP—as well as service binding information—in terms of the communication protocols, ports, service URL, and so on. At the time of this writing, WSDL 2.0 is well on its way to becoming a W3C standard.

Thus, Web Services present a powerful solution for distributed but loosely coupled, coarse-grained SOA wherein services are described using WSDL and accessed via SOAP. In fact, one of the main reasons for using Web Services to realize SOA is the ubiquitous support for XML, SOAP, and WSDL technologies on disparate platforms, ranging from mainframes to mobile devices. This is the main reason why Web Services provide a true solution for interoperability between applications deployed on these disparate platforms.

We will spend some more time explaining fundamental concepts in Chapter 5; however, explaining Web Services and related technologies in their entirety is outside the scope of this book. If you are new to Web Services, there are many books and online papers that you can refer to get started with Web Services conceptually. Given the solid adoption of this stack by the industry, we suggest that you familiarize yourself properly with Web services.

SOA and Component Architectures

SOA is *not* a replacement for component architecture; rather it neatly complements the component architecture. While component architectures enhance reusability at a finer grain level, SOA can enhance reusability at a coarser grained level. Hence, from an implementation standpoint, a given service might very well be developed using well-defined component frameworks such as EJB. The latest EJB standard, therefore, has in-built support for Web Services, the most popular stack for building SOA. So EJB is still very much in demand!

Chapter 5 covers Web Services support in EJB framework in detail.

Divide and Conquer to the Extreme with Reusable Services

We have been seeing a slow but steady shift in the "build-from-scratch" trend, for years now. More and more businesses want CIOs to stretch their IT dollars to the maximum. Naturally, this has led the IT departments to think of reuse; reuse in terms of systems as well as software. What better candidate than highly functional and autonomous services to fulfill this promise of reuse? SOA offers maximum reuse, especially when implemented using ubiquitous protocols such as those supported by Web services. Architects want to design their software as a composition of services such that these services can be used from any platform through well-defined service interfaces.

Why just stop at corporate ITs? Even ISVs are thinking of providing their software as services. Prime examples of "software as a service" include Salesforce.com and Siebel. Both these companies have made their enterprise software available to customers as hosted services. Many other businesses such as Amazon.com and Google provide their core business services, E-commerce, and Web searching, as reusable services to customers and end-users.

Reusable services are a very powerful concept, because:

- **Businesses can focus on strategic software development.** In cases where software functionality is horizontal and cuts across multiple business domains, it should be treated as commodity and hence procured from a specialized ISV in the form of services. For example, each business requires a corporate treasury management and cash management system. For such a commodity business need, it is best to acquire software from an outside vendor than to build it. This will relieve the IT staff from having to deal with complex treasury functions involving millions of regulations; it anyway does not have direct relevance to the business's core function.
- **The business processes can be assembled faster.** The autonomous and loosely coupled nature of services makes it easy to assemble them into business processes. This strength makes services the chosen paradigm for encapsulating business logic.
- **There is a lower total cost of ownership.** Businesses that build their software as services end up with a lower total cost of ownership in the long term because they are building software such that it can be easily reusable and assembled into business processes. This is a definite plus when businesses are required to adapt business processes to address the changing market demands or when they are required to support new customers and their IT systems. Businesses that sell software as services, on the other hand, can benefit their customers by offering flexible software licensing options, such as per-month billing or per-year billing, thereby enabling their customers to lower total cost of ownership.

Remember that these services can and should be built using components. Therefore, the component architectures are very much here to stay. Figure 1.3 depicts such a Treasury management service built using EJB components.

With this introduction to SOA and their relevance to EJB, let us further explore the EJB technology.

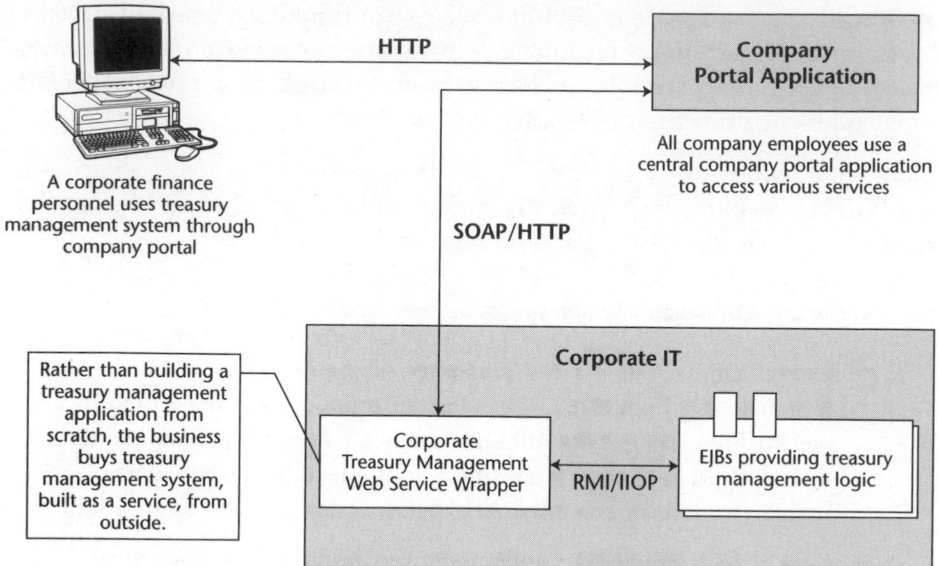

Figure 1.3 Reusable services built using EJB.

Introducing Enterprise JavaBeans

EJB is a standard for building server-side components in Java. It defines an agreement (contract) between components and application servers that enables any component to run in any application server. EJB components (called *enterprise beans*) are deployable, and can be imported and loaded into an application server, which hosts those components.

The top three propositions of EJB are as follows:

- **It is agreed upon by the industry.** Those who use EJB will benefit from its widespread use. Because everyone will be on the same page, in the future it will be easier to hire employees who understand your systems (since they may have prior EJB experience), learn best practices to improve your system (by reading books like this one), partner with businesses (since technology will be compatible), and sell software (since customers will accept your solution). The concept of "train once, code anywhere" applies.
- **Portability is easier.** The EJB specification is published and available freely to all. Since EJB is a standard, you do not need to gamble on a single, proprietary vendor's architecture. And although portability will never be free, it is cheaper than without a standard.

- **Rapid application development.** Your application can be constructed faster because you get middleware infrastructure services such as transactions, pooling, security, and so on from the application server. There's also less of a mess to maintain.

Note that while EJB does have these virtues, there are also scenarios in which EJB is overkill. See Chapters 11 and 16 for best practices and discussion surrounding the issue of when to (and when not to) use EJB.

Physically, EJB is actually two things in one:

- ***A specification.*** **This is a 640-plus-page Adobe Acrobat PDF file, freely downloadable from http://java.sun.com/products/ejb/docs.html. This specification lays out the rules of engagement between components and application servers. It constricts how you code enterprise beans to enable "write once, run anywhere" behavior for your EJB application.**
- ***A set of Java interfaces.*** **Components and application servers must conform to these interfaces. Since all components are written to the same interfaces, they all look the same to the application server. The application server therefore can manage anyone's components.**

Why Java?

EJB architecture has supported only the Java language thus far. Though this sounds a bit restrictive, the good news is that Java is one of the best-suited languages for building components for the following reasons.

- **Interface/implementation separation.** We need a language that supports clean separation between the interface and implementation mainly to keep the component upgrades and maintenance to minimum. Java supports this separation at a syntactic level through the *interface* and *class* keywords.
- **Safe and secure.** The Java architecture is much safer than traditional programming languages. In Java, if a thread dies, the application stays up. Pointers are no longer an issue. Memory leaks occur much less often. Java also has a rich library set, so that Java is not just the syntax of a language but a whole set of prewritten, debugged libraries that enable developers to avoid reinventing the wheel in a buggy way. This safety is extremely important for mission-critical applications. Sure, the overhead required to achieve this level of safety might make your application slower, but 90 percent of all business programs are glorified graphical user interfaces (GUIs) to databases. That database is going to be your number one bottleneck, not Java.

- **Cross-platform.** Java runs on any platform. Since EJB is an application of Java, this means EJB should also easily run on any platform. This is valuable for customers who have invested in a variety of powerful hardware, such as Win32, UNIX, and mainframes. They do not want to throw away these investments.

If you don't want to go the EJB route, you have two other choices:

- **Lightweight open source Java frameworks such as Spring. In Chapter 11 we discuss when to use EJB versus such non-standard frameworks.**
- **Microsoft .NET–managed components, part of the Microsoft .NET platform**

EJB as a Business Tier Component

The real difference between presentation tier components such as thick clients, dynamically generated Web pages, or Web Service clients and enterprise beans is the domain in which they operate. Presentation components are well suited to handle *client-side* operations, such as rendering GUIs, executing client-side validations, constructing appropriate SOAP messages to send them to Web Service, and so on. They deal directly with the end user or business partner.

Enterprise beans, on the other hand, are not intended for the client side; they are *server-side* components. They are meant to perform server-side operations, such as executing complex algorithms or performing high-volume business transactions. The server side has different kinds of needs than GUI clients do. Server-side components need to run in a highly available (24/7), fault-tolerant, transactional, and multiuser secure environment. The application server provides this high-end server-side environment for the enterprise beans, and it provides the runtime containment necessary to manage enterprise beans.

Specifically, EJB is used to help write logic that solves *business problems*. Typically, EJB components (enterprise beans) can perform any of the following tasks:

- **Perform business logic.** Examples include computing the taxes on the shopping cart, ensuring that the manager has authority to approve the purchase order, or sending an order confirmation e-mail using the *JavaMail API*.
- **Access a database.** Examples include submitting an order for books, transferring money between two bank accounts, or calling a stored procedure to retrieve a trouble ticket in a customer support system. Enterprise beans can achieve database access using the *Java Database Connectivity* (JDBC) *API*.

- **Access another system.** Examples include calling a high-performing *CICS* legacy system written in COBOL that computes the risk factor for a new insurance account, calling a legacy *VSAM* data store, or calling *SAP R/3*. Enterprise beans can integrate with an existing application through the *J2EE Connector Architecture* (JCA), which we will talk about in detail in Chapter 17.

Thus, EJB components are not presentation tier components; rather, they sit behind the presentation tier components (or clients) and do all the hard work. Examples of the clients that can connect to enterprise beans include the following:

- **Thick clients.** Thick clients execute on a user's desktop. They could connect through the network with EJB components that live on a server. These EJB components may perform any of the tasks listed previously (business logic, database logic, or accessing other systems). Thick clients in Java include applets and applications.
- **Dynamically generated Web pages.** Web sites that are transactional and personalized in nature need their Web pages generated specifically for each request. For example, the home page for Amazon.com is completely different for each user, depending on the user's profile. Core technologies such as Java servlets and JavaServer Pages (JSP) are used to dynamically generate such specific pages. Both servlets and JSPs live within a Web server and can connect to EJB components, generating pages differently based upon the values returned from the EJB layer.
- **Web Service clients.** Some business applications require no user interface at all. They exist to interconnect with other business partners' applications that may provide their own user interface. For example, consider a scenario where Dell Computer Corporation needs to procure Intel chips to assemble and distribute desktop computers. Here, Intel could expose an *Order Parts* Web Service that enables the Dell Web Service client to order chips. In this case, the Intel system does not provide a graphical user interface per se, but rather provides a Web Service interface. This scenario is shown in Figure 1.4.

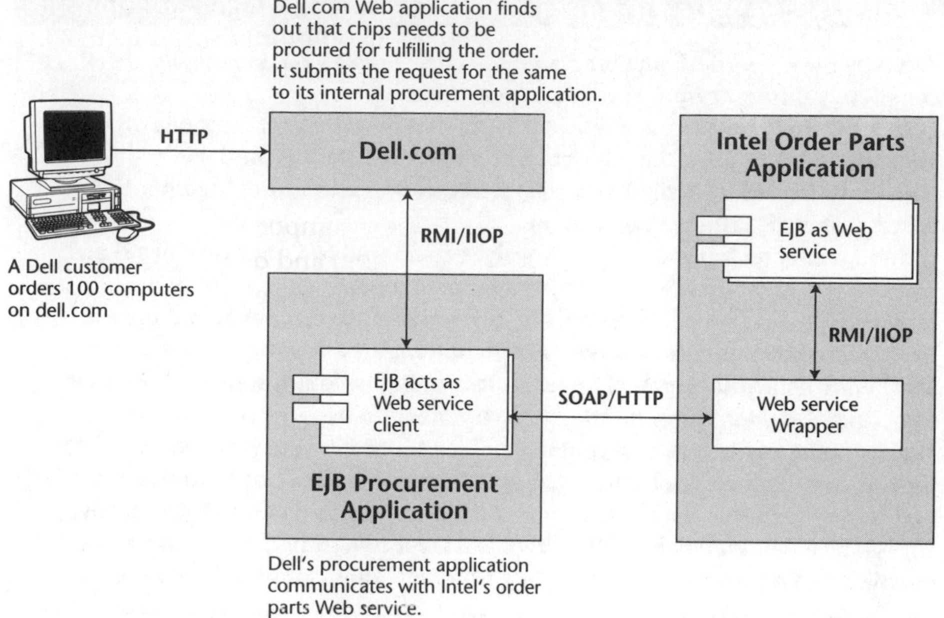

Figure 1.4 EJBs as Web Service clients.

The EJB Ecosystem

To get an EJB deployment up and running successfully, you need more than just an application server and components. In fact, EJB encourages collaboration of *more than six* different parties. Each of these parties is an expert in its own field and is responsible for a key part of a successful EJB deployment. Because each party is a specialist, the total time required to build an enterprise-class deployment is significantly reduced. Together, these players form the *EJB Ecosystem*.

Let's discuss who the players are in the EJB Ecosystem. As you read on, think about your company's business model to determine which role you fill. If you're not sure, ask yourself what the core competency of your business is. Also think about what roles you might play in upcoming projects.

The EJB Ecosystem is not for everyone. At my company, we've heard ghastly stories of businesses choosing EJB because everyone else is using it, or because it is new and exciting. Those are the wrong reasons to use EJB and can result in disappointing results. For best practices and a discussion surrounding the issue of when and when not to use EJB, see Chapters 11 and 16.

JAVABEANS VERSUS ENTERPRISE JAVABEANS

You may have heard of another standard called *JavaBeans*. JavaBeans are completely different from Enterprise JavaBeans.

In a nutshell, JavaBeans are Java classes that have *get/set* methods on them. They are reusable Java components with properties, events, and methods (similar to Microsoft *ActiveX controls*) that can be easily wired together to create (often visual) Java applications.

The JavaBeans framework is lightweight compared to Enterprise JavaBeans. You can use JavaBeans to assemble larger components or to build entire applications. JavaBeans, however, are development components and are not deployable components. You typically do not deploy a JavaBean; rather, JavaBeans help you construct larger software that is deployable. And because they cannot be deployed, JavaBeans do not need to live in a runtime environment and hence, in a container. Since JavaBeans are just Java classes, they do not need an application server to instantiate them, to destroy them, and to provide other services to them. An EJB application can use JavaBeans, especially when marshalling data from EJB layer to another, say to components belonging to a presentation tier or to a non-J2EE application written in Java.

The Bean Provider

The *bean provider* supplies business components, or enterprise beans. Enterprise beans are not complete applications, but rather are deployable components that can be assembled into complete solutions. The bean provider could be an internal department providing components to other departments.

The Application Assembler

The application assembler is the overall application architect. This party is responsible for understanding how various components fit together and writing the applications that combine components. An application assembler may even author a few components along the way. His or her job is to build an application from those components that can be deployed in a number of settings. The application assembler is the *consumer* of the beans supplied by the bean provider.

The application assembler could perform any or all of the following tasks:

- From knowledge of the business problem, decide which combination of existing components and new enterprise beans are needed to provide an effective solution; in essence, plan the application assembly.
- Supply a user interface (perhaps Swing, servlet or JSP, application or applet) or a Web Service.
- Write new enterprise beans to solve some problems specific to your business problem.

- Write the code that calls on components supplied by bean providers.
- Write integration code that maps data between components supplied by different bean providers. After all, components won't magically work together to solve a business problem, especially if different parties write the components.

An example of an application assembler is a systems integrator, a consulting firm, or an in-house programmer.

The EJB Deployer

After the application assembler builds the application, the application must be *deployed* (and go live) in a running operational environment. Some challenges faced here include the following:

- Securing the deployment with a hardware or software firewall and other protective measures.
- Integrating with enterprise security and policy repositories, which oftentimes is an LDAP server such as Sun Java System Directory Server (formerly Netscape Directory Server), Novell Directory Server, or Microsoft Active Directory.
- Choosing hardware that provides the required level of quality of service.
- Providing redundant hardware and other resources for reliability and fault tolerance.
- Performance-tuning the system.

Frequently the application assembler (who is usually a developer or systems analyst) is not familiar with these issues. This is where the EJB deployer comes into play. EJB deployers are aware of specific operational requirements and perform the tasks above. They understand how to deploy beans within servers and how to customize the beans for a specific environment. The EJB deployer has the freedom to adapt the beans, as well as the server, to the environment in which the beans are to be deployed.

An EJB deployer can be a staff person, an outside consultant, or a vendor.

The System Administrator

Once the deployment goes live, the system administrator steps in to oversee the stability of the operational solution. The system administrator is responsible for the upkeep and monitoring of the deployed system and may make use of runtime monitoring and management tools that the EJB server provides.

For example, a sophisticated EJB server might page a system administrator if a serious error occurs that requires immediate attention. Some EJB servers achieve this by developing hooks into professional monitoring products, such as Tivoli and Computer Associates. Others like JBoss are providing their own systems management by supporting the *Java Management Extension* (JMX) technology.

The Container and Server Provider

The container provider supplies an *EJB container* (the application server). This is the runtime environment in which beans live. The container supplies middleware services to the beans and manages them. There are about 20 Sun Microsystems–certified J2EE application servers. Although a complete list can be obtained from http://java.sun.com/j2ee/licensees.html, some of the popular J2EE application servers include BEA WebLogic, Sun Java System Application Server (formerly, Sun ONE Application Server), IBM WebSphere, Oracle Application Server, and of course JBoss open source application server.

The server provider is the same as the container provider. Sun has not yet differentiated these (and may never do so). We will use the terms *EJB container* and *EJB server* interchangeably in this book.

The Tool Vendors

To facilitate the component development process, there should be a standardized way to build, manage, and maintain components. In the EJB Ecosystem, there are several *integrated development environments* (IDEs) that assist you in rapidly building and debugging components. Some of the popular closed

QUALITIES OF SERVICE IN EJB

The monitoring of EJB deployments is not specified in the EJB specification. It is an optional service that advanced EJB users can provide. This means that each EJB server could provide the service differently.

At first blush you might think this hampers application portability. However, in reality, this service should be provided *transparently* behind the scenes, and should not affect your application code. It is a quality of service that lies beneath the application level and exists at the systems level. Changing application servers should not affect your EJB code.

Other transparent qualities of service not specified in the EJB specification include load balancing, transparent fail-over, caching, clustering, and connection pooling algorithms.

source and open source EJB development IDEs include Borland JBuilder, Oracle JDeveloper, BEA WebLogic Workshop, IBM WebSphere Studio Application Developer, Sun Microsystems Java Studio (formerly Forte for Java), NetBeans, and last but not least, Eclipse.

Most of these tools enable you to model components using unified modeling language (UML), which is the diagram style used in this book. You can also generate EJB code from these UML models. Some of the examples of specialized closed source products in this space include Borland Together and IBM Rational line of products. Also there are a bunch of open source code utilities and tools, which we discuss in Chapter 11, that can be used for UML modeling and code generation.

There are other tools as well, which you will need to develop your EJB applications rapidly and successfully. The categories mainly include testing tools (JUnit), build tools (Ant/XDoclet), and profilers (Borland OptimizeIt or Quest Software JProbe).

Summary of Roles

Figure 1.5 summarizes the interaction of the different parties in EJB.

You may be wondering why so many different participants are needed to provide an EJB deployment. The answer is that EJB enables companies or individuals to become experts in certain roles, and division of labor leads to best-of-breed deployments.

The EJB specification makes each role clear and distinct, enabling experts in different areas to participate in a deployment without loss of interoperability. Note that some of these roles could be combined as well. For example, the EJB server and EJB container today come from the same vendor. Or at a small startup company, the bean provider, application assembler, and deployer could all be the same person, who is trying to build a business solution using EJB from scratch. What roles do you see yourself playing?

For some of the parties EJB merely suggests possible duties, such as the system administrator overseeing the well being of a deployed system. For other parties, such as the bean provider and container provider, EJB defines a set of strict interfaces and guidelines that must be followed or the entire ecosystem will break down. By clearly defining the roles of each party, EJB lays a foundation for a distributed, scalable component architecture where multiple vendors' products can interoperate.

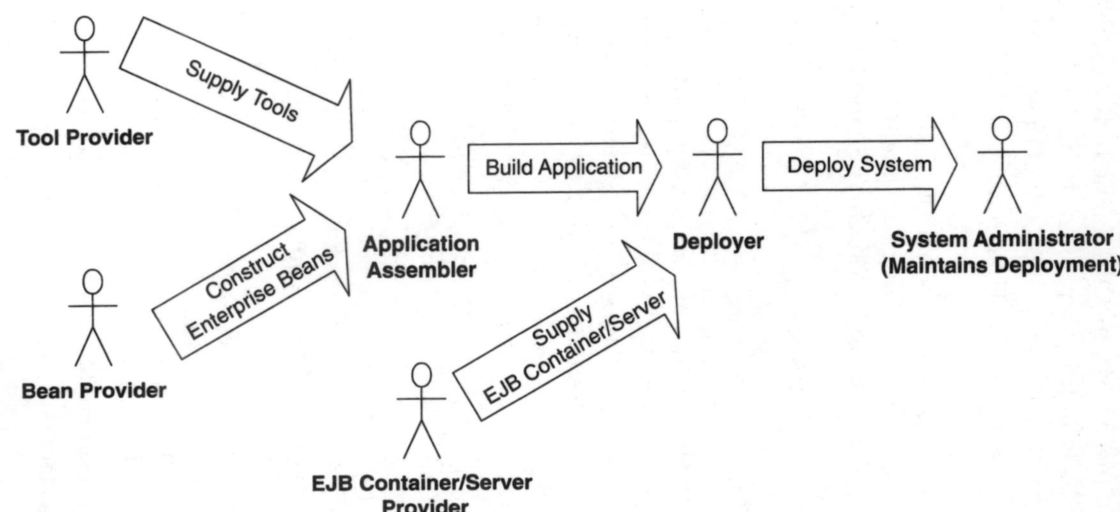

Figure 1.5 The parties of EJB.

The Java 2 Platform, Enterprise Edition (J2EE)

EJB is only a portion of a larger offering from the Java Community Process (a.k.a. JCP—a Java industry standards body) called the Java 2 Platform, Enterprise Edition (J2EE). The mission of J2EE is to provide a platform-independent, portable, multiuser, secure, and standard enterprise-class platform for server-side deployments written in the Java language.

J2EE is a specification, not a product. J2EE specifies the rules of engagement that people must agree on when writing enterprise software. Vendors then implement the J2EE specifications with their J2EE-compliant products.

Because J2EE is a specification (meant to address the needs of many companies), it is inherently not tied to one vendor; it also supports cross-platform development. This encourages vendors to compete, yielding best-of-breed products. It also has its downside, which is that incompatibilities between vendor products will arise—some problems due to ambiguities with specifications, other problems due to the human nature of competition.

J2EE is one of *three different* Java platforms. Each platform is a conceptual superset of the next smaller platform.

- **The Java 2 Platform, Micro Edition (J2ME)** is a development platform for applications running on mobile Java-enabled devices, such as Phones, Palm Pilots, Pagers, set-top TV boxes, and so on. This is a restricted form of the Java language due to the inherent performance and capacity limitations of small-form-factor wireless devices.
- **The Java 2 Platform, Standard Edition (J2SE)** defines a standard for core libraries that can be used by applets, applications, J2EE applications, mobile applications, and such. These core libraries span a much wider spectrum including input/output, graphical user interface facilities, networking, and so on. This platform contains what most people use in standard Java programming.
- **The Java 2 Platform, Enterprise Edition (J2EE)** is an umbrella standard for Java's enterprise computing facilities. It basically bundles together technologies for a complete enterprise-class server-side development and deployment platform in Java.

J2EE is significant because it creates a unified platform for server-side Java development. The J2EE stack consists of the following:

- **Specifications.** Each enterprise API within J2EE has its own specification, which is a PDF file downloadable from www.jcp.org. Each time there is a new version of J2EE, the J2EE Expert Group at JCP locks down the versions of each Enterprise API specification and bundles them together as the de facto versions to use when developing with J2EE. This increases code portability across vendors' products, because each vendor supports exactly the same API revision. This is analogous to a company such as Microsoft releasing a new version of Windows every few years: Every time a new version of Windows comes out, Microsoft locks down the versions of the technologies bundled with Windows and releases them together.

- **Test suite.** Sun provides a test suite (a.k.a. Test Compatibility Kit or TCK) for J2EE server vendors to test their implementations against. If a server passes the tests, Sun issues a J2EE compliance brand, alerting customers that the vendor's product is indeed J2EE-compliant. There are numerous J2EE-certified vendors, and you can read reviews of their products for free on TheServerSide.com.
- **Reference implementation.** To enable developers to write code against J2EE Sun provides its own free reference implementation for each version of J2EE. Sun is positioning it as a low-end reference platform, because it is not intended for commercial use. You can download the reference implementation for J2EE 1.4, the latest version of J2EE platform that includes EJB 2.1, the technology of focus in this book, from http://java.sun.com/j2ee/download.html.

The J2EE Technologies

J2EE is a robust suite of middleware services that make life very easy for server-side application developers. J2EE builds on the existing technologies in the J2SE. J2SE includes support for core Java language semantics as well as various libraries (.awt, .net, .io, and so on). Because J2EE builds on J2SE, a J2EE-compliant product must not only implement all of J2EE, but must also implement all of J2SE. This means that building a J2EE product is an absolutely *huge* undertaking. This barrier to entry has resulted in significant industry consolidation in the Enterprise Java space, with a few players emerging from the pack as leaders.

In this book, we will discuss EJB 2.1, an integral part of J2EE 1.4. Some of the major J2EE technologies are shown working together in Figure 1.6.

To understand more about the real value of J2EE, here are some of the important technologies and APIs that a J2EE 1.4-compliant implementation will support for you.

- **Enterprise JavaBeans (EJB).** EJB defines how server-side components are written and provides a standard contract between components and the application servers that manage them. EJB is the cornerstone for J2EE and uses several other J2EE technologies.

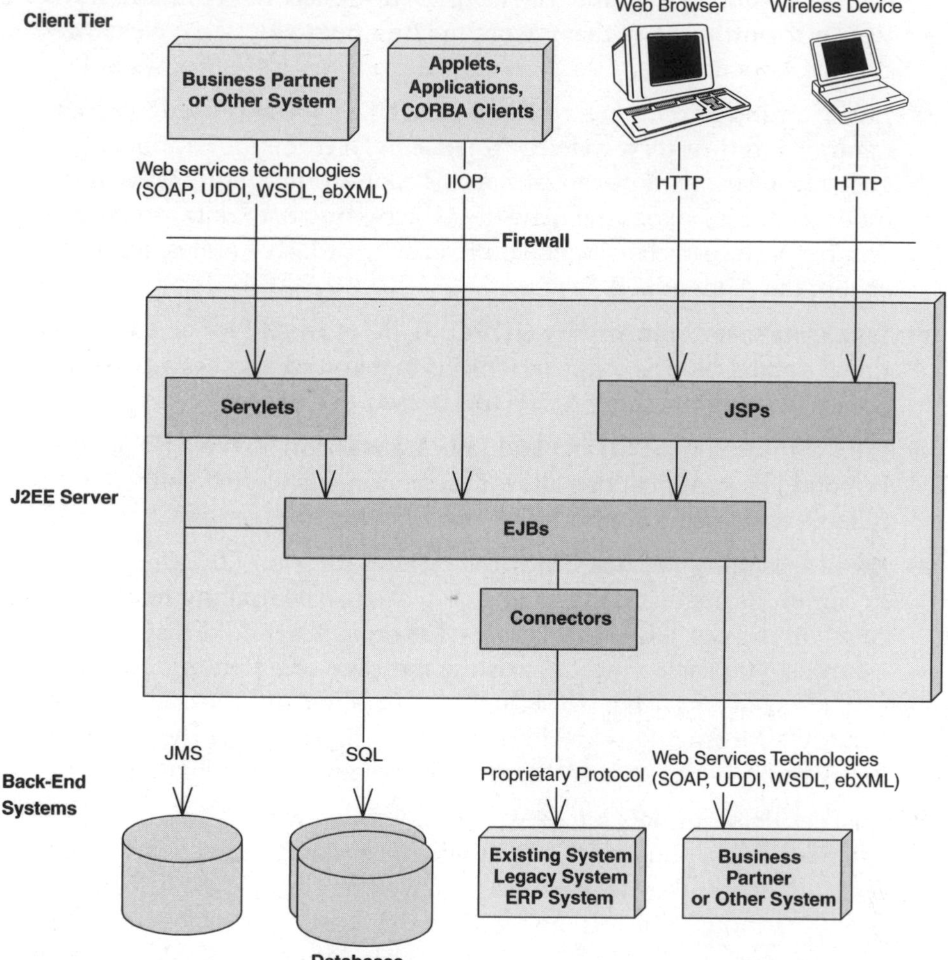

Figure 1.6 A J2EE deployment.

- **Java API for XML RPC (JAX-RPC).** JAX-RPC is the main technology that provides support for developing Web Services on the J2EE platform. It defines two Web Service endpoint models—one based on servlet technology and another based on EJB. It also specifies a lot of runtime requirements regarding the way Web Services should be supported in a J2EE runtime. Another specification called Web Services for J2EE defines deployment requirements for Web Services and uses the JAX-RPC programming model. Chapter 5 discusses support of Web Services provided by both these specifications for EJB applications.
- **Java Remote Method Invocation (RMI) and RMI-IIOP.** RMI is the Java language's native way to communicate between distributed objects, such as two different objects running on different machines. RMI-IIOP

is an extension of RMI that can be used for CORBA integration. RMI-IIOP is the official API that we use in J2EE (not RMI). We cover RMI-IIOP in Appendix A.

- **Java Naming and Directory Interface (JNDI).** JNDI is used to access naming and directory systems. You use JNDI from your application code for a variety of purposes, such as connecting to EJB components or other resources across the network, or accessing user data stored in a naming service such as Microsoft Exchange or Lotus Notes. JNDI is covered in Appendix A.
- **Java Database Connectivity (JDBC).** JDBC is an API for accessing relational databases. The value of JDBC is that you can access any relational database using the same API. JDBC is used in Chapter 7.
- **Java Transaction API (JTA) and Java Transaction Service (JTS).** The JTA and JTS specifications allow for components to be bolstered with reliable transaction support. JTA and JTS are explained in Chapter 12.
- **Java Messaging Service (JMS).** JMS allows for your J2EE deployment to communicate using messaging. You can use messaging to communicate within your J2EE system as well as outside your J2EE system. For example, you can connect to existing message-oriented middleware (MOM) systems such as IBM MQSeries or Microsoft Message Queue (MSMQ). Messaging is an alternative paradigm to RMI-IIOP, and has its advantages and disadvantages. We explain JMS in Chapter 9.
- **Java servlets.** Servlets are networked components that you can use to extend the functionality of a Web server. Servlets are request/response oriented in that they take requests from some client host (such as a Web browser) and issue a response back to that host. This makes servlets ideal for performing Web tasks, such as rendering an HTML interface. Servlets differ from EJB components in that the breadth of server-side component features that EJB offers, such as declarative transactions, is not readily available to servlets. Servlets are much better suited to handling simple request/response needs, and they do not require sophisticated management by an application server. We illustrate using servlets with EJB in Chapter 22.
- **JavaServer Pages (JSP).** JSP technology is very similar to servlets. In fact, JSP scripts are compiled into servlets. The largest difference between JSP scripts and servlets is that JSP scripts are not pure Java code; they are much more centered on look-and-feel issues. You would use JSP when you want the look and feel of your deployment to be physically separate and easily maintainable from the rest of your deployment. JSP technology is perfect for this, and it can be easily written and maintained by non–Java-savvy staff members (JSP technology

does not require a Java compiler). We illustrate using JSP with EJB in Chapter 22.

- **Java IDL.** Java IDL is the Sun Microsystems Java-based implementation of CORBA. Java IDL allows for integration with other languages. Java IDL also allows for distributed objects to leverage the full range of CORBA services. J2EE is thus fully compatible with CORBA, completing the Java 2 Platform, Enterprise Edition. We discuss CORBA interoperability in Appendix B.
- **JavaMail.** The JavaMail service enables you to send e-mail messages in a platform-independent, protocol-independent manner from your Java programs. For example, in a server-side J2EE deployment, you can use JavaMail to confirm a purchase made on your Internet e-commerce site by sending an e-mail to the customer. Note that JavaMail depends on the *JavaBeans Activation Framework* (JAF), which makes JAF part of J2EE as well. We do not cover JavaMail in this book.
- **J2EE Connector Architecture (JCA).** Connectors enable you to access existing enterprise information systems from a J2EE application. This could include *any* existing system, such as a mainframe system running high-end transactions (such as those deployed with IBM CICS, or BEA TUXEDO), Enterprise Resource Planning (ERP) systems, or your own proprietary systems. Connectors are useful because they automatically manage the details of middleware integration to existing systems, such as handling transactions and security concerns, life-cycle management, thread management, and so on. Another value of this architecture is that you can write a connector to access an existing system once, and then deploy it into any J2EE-compliant server. This is important because you only need to learn how to access an existing system once. Furthermore, the connector needs to be developed only once and can be reused in any J2EE server. This is extremely useful for independent software vendors (ISVs) such as SAP, Siebel, Peoplesoft and others who want their software to be accessible from within J2EE application servers. Rather than write a custom connector for each application server, these ISVs can write a standard J2EE connector. We discuss legacy integration in more details in Chapter 17.
- **The Java API for XML Parsing (JAXP).** There are many applications of XML in a J2EE deployment. For example, you might need to parse XML if you are performing B2B interactions (such as through Web Services), if you are accessing legacy systems and mapping data to and from XML, or if you are persisting XML documents to a database. JAXP is the de facto API for parsing XML documents in a J2EE application and is an implementation-neutral interface to XML parsing technologies such as DOM and SAX. You typically use the JAXP API from within servlets, JSP, or EJB components.

- **The Java Authentication and Authorization Service (JAAS).** JAAS is a standard API for performing security-related operations in J2EE. Conceptually, JAAS also enables you to plug in an authentication mechanism into a J2EE application server. See Chapter 13 for more details on security pertaining to EJB applications.

Summary

We've achieved a great deal in this chapter. First, we brainstormed a list of issues involved in a large, multitier deployment. We then understood that server-side component architecture enables us to write complex business applications without understanding tricky middleware services. We then dove into the EJB standard and fleshed out its value proposition. We investigated the different players involved in an EJB deployment and wrapped up by exploring J2EE.

The good news is that we're just getting started, and many more interesting and advanced topics lie ahead. The next chapter delves further into EJB fundamentals such as *request interception, various types of EJB,* and so on, which is the mental leap you need to make to understand EJB. Let's go!

CHAPTER

2

EJB Fundamentals

Chapter 1 introduced the motivation behind EJB. In this chapter, we'll dive into EJB in detail. After reading this chapter, you will understand the different types of enterprise beans. You'll also understand what an enterprise bean component is composed of, including the enterprise bean class, the remote interface, the local interface, the EJB object, the local object, the home interface, the home object, the deployment descriptor, and the Ejb-jar file.

EJB technology is based on two other technologies: Java RMI-IIOP and JNDI. Understanding these technologies is mandatory before continuing.

We have provided tutorials on each of these technologies in the appendixes of this book. If you don't yet know RMI-IIOP or JNDI, go ahead and read Appendix A now.

Enterprise Beans

An *enterprise bean* is a server-side software component that can be deployed in a distributed multitier environment. An enterprise bean can compose one or more Java objects because a component may be more than just a simple object. Regardless of an enterprise bean's composition, the clients of the bean deal with a single exposed component interface. This interface, as well as the enterprise bean itself, must conform to the EJB specification. The specification requires that your beans expose a few required methods; these required methods allow the EJB container to manage beans uniformly, regardless of which container your bean is running in.

Note that the client of an enterprise bean could be anything—a servlet, an applet, or even another enterprise bean. In the case of an enterprise bean, a client request to a bean can result in a whole chain of beans being called. This is a very powerful idea because you can subdivide a complex bean task, allowing one bean to call on a variety of prewritten beans to handle the subtasks. This hierarchical concept is quite extensible.

As a real-world example, imagine you go to a music store to purchase a compact disc. The cashier takes your credit card and runs it through a scanner. The scanner has a small Java Virtual Machine (JVM) running within it, which acts as a client of enterprise beans running on a central server. The central server enterprise beans perform the following tasks:

1. Contact American Express, a Web service that itself has an EJB-compliant application server containing a number of beans. The beans are responsible for conducting the credit card transaction on behalf of that client.
2. Call a product catalog bean, which updates inventory and subtracts the quantity the customer purchased.
3. Call an order entry bean, which enters the record for the customer and returns that record locator to the scanner to give to the customer on a receipt.

As you can see, this is a powerful, flexible model, which can be extended as needed.

Types of Beans

EJB 2.1 defines three different kinds of enterprise beans:

- **Session beans.** Session beans model business processes. They are like *verbs* because they perform actions. The action could be anything, such as adding numbers, accessing a database, calling a legacy system, or calling other enterprise beans. Examples include a pricing engine, a workflow engine, a catalog engine, a credit card authorizer, or a stock-trading engine.
- **Entity beans.** Entity beans model business data. They are like *nouns* because they are data objects—that is, Java objects that cache database information. Examples include a product, an order, an employee, a credit card, or a stock. Session beans typically harness entity beans to

achieve business goals, such as a stock-trading engine (session bean) that deals with stocks (entity beans). For more examples, see Table 2.1.

- **Message-driven beans.** Message-driven beans are similar to session beans in that they perform actions. The difference is that you can call message-driven beans only implicitly by sending *messages* to those beans (see Chapter 9 for a full description). Examples of message-driven beans include beans that receive stock trade messages, credit card authorization messages, or workflow messages. These message-driven beans might call other enterprise beans as well.

You may be wondering why the EJB paradigm offers these various kinds of beans. Why couldn't Sun come up with a simpler model? The *n*-tier vision advanced by Microsoft, for example, does not include the equivalent of entity beans—components that represent data in permanent storage.

The answer is that Sun is not the only company involved in constructing the EJB standard. Many companies have been involved, each with customers that have different kinds of distributed systems. To accommodate the needs of different enterprise applications, Sun allowed users the flexibility of each kind of bean.

Admittedly this increases the ramp-up time for learning EJB. It also adds an element of danger because some developers may misuse the intentions of each bean type. But it pays off in the long run with increased functionality. By including session beans, Sun provides a mechanism to model business processes in a distributed multitier environment. By including entity beans in the EJB specification, Sun has taken the first steps toward persistent, distributed objects usable by those business processes. And with message-driven beans, you can use messaging to access your EJB system.

Figure 2.1 illustrates some of the many possibilities of clients interacting with an EJB component system.

Table 2.1 Session Beans Calling Entity Beans

ENTITY BEAN	SESSION BEAN
Bank teller	Bank account
Credit card authorizer	Credit card
DNA sequencer	DNA strand
Order entry system	Order, Line item
Catalog engine	Product
Auction broker	Bid, Item
Purchase order Approval router	Purchase order

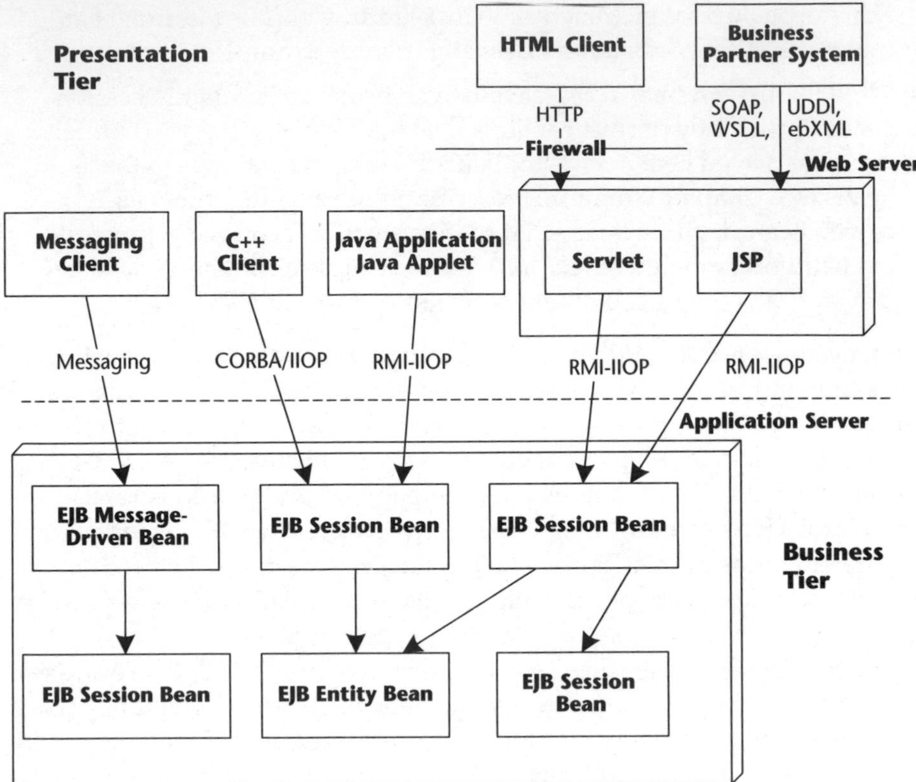

Figure 2.1 Clients interacting with an EJB component system.

Distributed Objects: The Foundation for EJB

Now that you've seen the different types of beans, let's dive into the technology behind them. EJB components are based on *distributed objects*. A distributed object is an object that is callable from a remote system. It can be called from an in-process client, an out-of-process client, or a client located elsewhere on the network.

Figure 2.2 shows how a client can call a distributed object. The following is an explanation of the diagram:

1. The client calls a *stub*, which is a *client-side proxy object*. This stub is responsible for masking network communications from the client. The stub knows how to call over the network using sockets, massaging parameters as necessary into their network representation.

2. The stub calls over the network to a skeleton, which is a server-side proxy object. The skeleton masks network communication from the distributed object. The skeleton understands how to receive calls on a socket. It also knows how to massage parameters from their network representations to their Java representations.
3. The skeleton delegates the call to the appropriate implementation object. This object does its work, and then returns control to the skeleton, which returns to the stub, which then returns control to the client.

A key point here is that both the stub and the server-side implementation object implement the same interface (called the *remote interface*). This means the stub clones the distributed object's method signatures. A client who calls a method on the stub *thinks* he is calling the distributed object directly; in reality, the client is calling an empty stub that knows how to go over the network. This is called *distribution transparency*. In fact, the distributed object is an abstraction that is created by the cooperation between the stub, skeleton, and implementation objects. No single entity in this scenario *is* the distributed object.

You can achieve distributed objects using many technologies, including CORBA (OMG), DCOM (Microsoft), and Java RMI-IIOP (Sun).

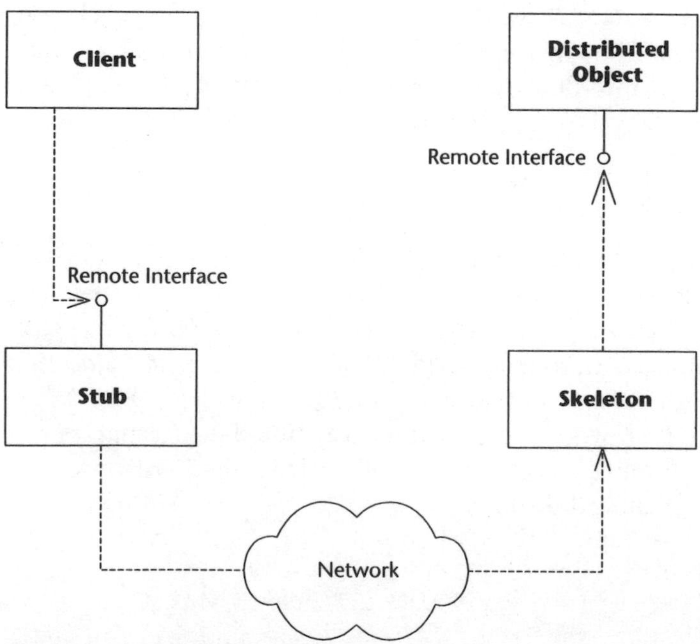

Figure 2.2 Distributed objects.

DISTRIBUTION TRANSPARENCY

Distribution transparency is the holy grail in distributed systems technology and very hard to achieve. Perfect distribution transparency would mean that a client never sees any differences between local and remote interactions. In the presence of the more complex failure modes of remote operations and network latency, this is not possible. Most of the time, the term distribution transparency is used rather loosely to mean that the syntax of the code making invocations is the same for both remote and local invocations. Even this is not always the case when you consider the different exceptions found in remote interfaces that in turn require different exception handling, and the subtle differences between the pass-by-reference and pass-by-value semantics that local and remote invocations sometimes exhibit.

For these reasons, most middleware systems settle for a less ambitious form of transparency, viz. location transparency. We will come back to location transparency in a moment.

Distributed Objects and Middleware

Distributed objects are great because they enable you to break up an application across a network. However, as a distributed object application gets larger, you'll need help from middleware services, such as transactions and security. There are two ways to get middleware: explicitly and implicitly. Let's investigate both approaches.

Explicit Middleware

In traditional distributed object programming (such as traditional CORBA), you can harness middleware by purchasing that middleware off the shelf and writing code that calls that middleware's API. For example, you could gain transactions by writing to a transaction API. We call this *explicit middleware* because you need to write to an API to use that middleware (see Figure 2.3).

The following example shows a bank account distributed object that knows how to transfer funds from one account to another. It is filled with pseudocode that illustrates explicit middleware.

```
transfer(Account account1, Account account2, long amount) {
// 1: Call middleware API to perform a security check
// 2: Call middleware API to start a transaction
// 3: Call middleware API to load rows from the database
// 4: Subtract the balance from one account, add to the other
// 5: Call middleware API to store rows in the database
// 6: Call middleware API to end the transaction
}
```

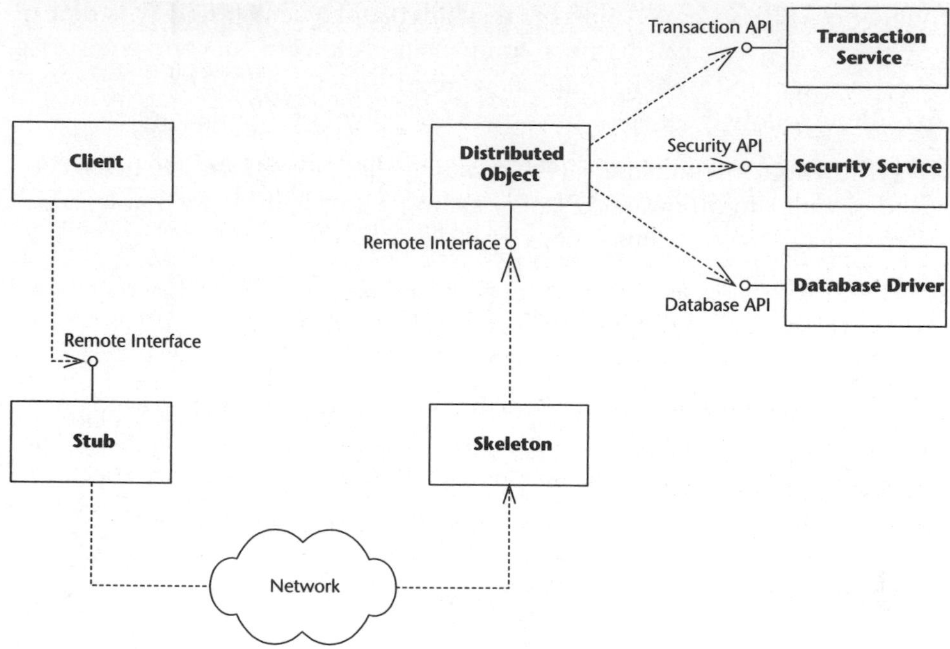

Figure 2.3 Explicit middleware (gained through APIs).

As you can see, we are gaining middleware, but our business logic is intertwined with the logic to call these middleware APIs, which is not without its downsides. This approach is:

- **Difficult to write.** The code is bloated. We simply want to perform a transfer, but it requires a large amount of code.
- **Difficult to maintain.** If you want to change the way you do middleware, you need to rewrite your code.
- **Difficult to support.** If you are an Independent Software Vendor (ISV) selling an application, or an internal department providing code to another department, you are unlikely to provide source code to your customers. This is because the source code is your intellectual property, and also because upgrading your customers to the next version of your software is difficult if those customers modify source code. Thus, your customers cannot change their middleware (such as changing how security works).

Implicit Middleware

The crucial difference between systems of the past (transaction processing monitors such as TUXEDO or CICS, or traditional distributed object technologies such as CORBA, DCOM, or RMI) and the newer, component-based technologies (EJB, CORBA Component Model, and Microsoft.NET) is that in this new world, you can harness complex middleware in your enterprise applications without writing to middleware APIs (see Figure 2.4).

In outline, follow these steps to harness the power of middleware:

1. Write your distributed object to contain *only business logic*. Do not write to complex middleware APIs. For example, this is the code that would run inside the distributed object:

```
transfer(Account account1, Account account2, long amount) {
    // 1: Subtract the balance from one account, add to the other
}
```

2. Declare the middleware services that your distributed object needs in a separate descriptor file, such as a plain text file. For example, you might declare that you need transactions, persistence, and a security check.

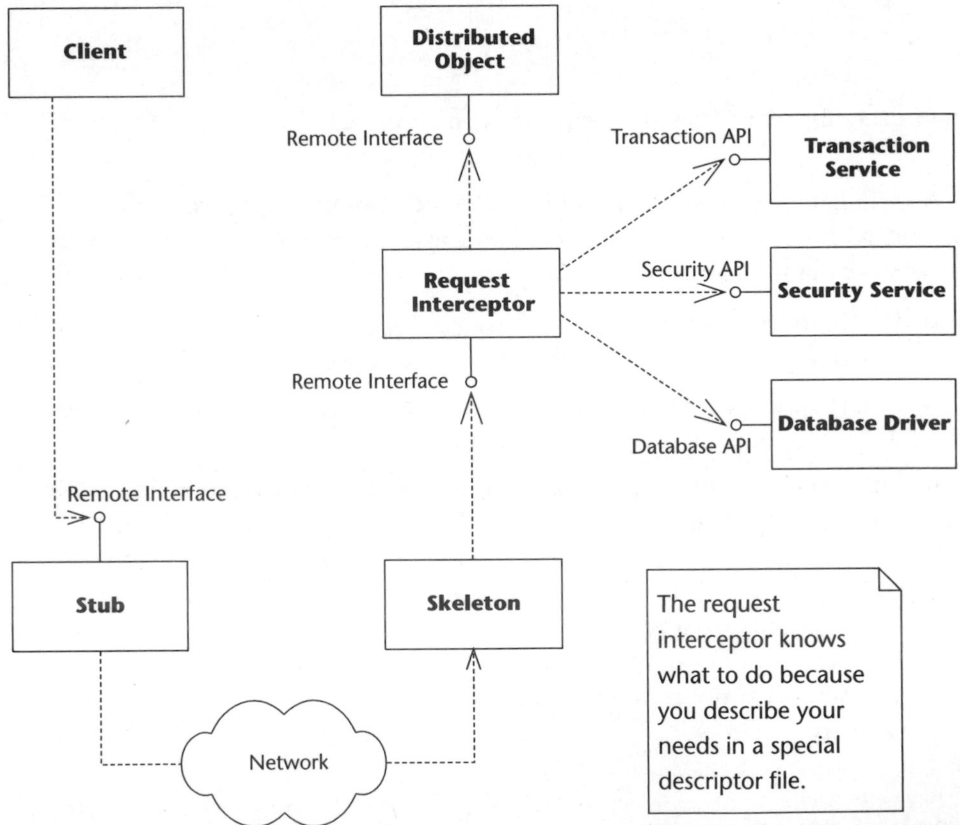

Figure 2.4 Implicit middleware (gained through declarations).

3. Run a command-line tool provided for you by the middleware vendor. This tool takes your descriptor file as input and generates an object that we'll call the *request interceptor*.
4. The request interceptor intercepts requests from the client, performs the middleware that your distributed object needs (such as transactions, security, and persistence), and then delegates the call to the distributed object.

The values of *implicit middleware* (also called *declarative middleware*) are:

- **Easy to write.** You don't actually write any code to middleware APIs; rather, you declare what you need in a simple text file. The request interceptor provides the middleware logic for you *transparently*. You focus away from the middleware and concentrate on your application's business code. This is truly divide and conquer!
- **Easy to maintain.** The separation of business logic and middleware logic is clean and maintainable. It is less code, which makes things simpler. Furthermore, changing middleware does not require changing application code.
- **Easy to support.** Customers can change the middleware they need by tweaking the descriptor file. For example, they can change the way a security check is performed without modifying source code. This avoids upgrade headaches and intellectual property issues.

What Constitutes an Enterprise Bean?

Now that you understand request interception, you are ready to dive in and see exactly what constitutes an enterprise bean. As you will see, an enterprise bean component is not a single monolithic file—a number of files work together to make up an enterprise bean.

The Enterprise Bean Class

The first part of your bean is the implementation itself, which contains the guts of your logic, called the *enterprise bean class*. This is simply a Java class that conforms to a well-defined interface and obeys certain rules. The rules are necessary for your beans to run in any EJB container.

An enterprise bean class contains implementation details of your component. Although there are no hard-and-fast rules in EJB, session bean, entity bean, and message-driven bean implementations are all very different from each other.

- **For session beans**, an enterprise bean class typically contains business process–related logic, such as logic to compute prices, transfer funds between bank accounts, or perform order entry.
- **For entity beans**, an enterprise bean class typically contains data-related logic, such as logic to change the name of a customer, reduce the balance of a bank account, or modify a purchase order.
- **For message-driven beans**, an enterprise bean class typically contains message-oriented logic, such as logic to receive a stock trade message and call a session bean that knows how to perform stock trading.

The EJB specification defines a few standard interfaces that your bean class can implement. These interfaces force your bean class to expose certain methods that all beans must provide, as defined by the EJB component model. The EJB container calls these required methods to manage your bean and alert your bean to significant events.

The most basic interface that *all* session, entity, and message-driven bean classes must implement is the *javax.ejb.EnterpriseBean* interface, shown in Source 2.1.

```
public interface javax.ejb.EnterpriseBean extends java.io.Serializable
{
}
```

Source 2.1 The javax.ejb.EnterpriseBean interface.

This interface serves as a *marker* interface; implementing this interface indicates that your class is indeed an enterprise bean class. The interesting aspect of *javax.ejb.EnterpriseBean* is that it extends *java.io.Serializable*. This means that all enterprise beans can be converted to a bit-blob and share all the properties of serializable objects (described in Appendix A). This will become important later.

Session beans, entity beans, and message-driven beans each have more specific interfaces that *extend* the *javax.ejb.EnterpriseBean* interface. All session beans must implement *javax.ejb.SessionBean*; all entity beans must implement *javax.ejb.EntityBean*; and all message-driven beans must implement *javax.ejb.MessageDrivenBean*. We'll discuss the details of these interfaces a bit later. For now, know that your enterprise bean class never needs to implement the *javax.ejb.EnterpriseBean* interface directly; rather, your bean class implements the interface corresponding to its bean type.

The EJB Object

Enterprise beans are not full-fledged remote objects. When a client wants to use an instance of an enterprise bean class, the client never invokes the method directly on an actual bean instance. Rather, the invocation is *intercepted* by the EJB container and then *delegated* to the bean instance. This is the concept of request interception that we touched on earlier. By intercepting requests, the EJB container can automatically perform implicit middleware. As a component developer, this means your life is simplified greatly because you can rapidly develop components without writing, debugging, or maintaining code that calls middleware APIs. Some of the services that you get at the point of interception include:

- **Implicit distributed transaction management.** Transactions enable you to perform robust, deterministic operations in a distributed environment by setting attributes on your enterprise beans. We'll get into the details of transactions and how you can use them effectively in Chapter 12. For now, know that the EJB container provides a *transaction service*—a low-level implementation of transaction management and coordination. The transaction service must be exposed through the Java Transaction API (JTA). The JTA is a high-level interface that you can use to control transactions, which we also cover in Chapter 12.
- **Implicit security.** Security is a major consideration for multitier deployments. The Java 2 Platform, Standard Edition yields a robust security service that can authorize and authenticate users, securing deployments from unwanted visitors. EJB adds to this the notion of transparent security, allowing components to reap the benefits of a secure deployment without necessarily coding to a security API.
- **Implicit resource management and component life cycle.** The EJB container implicitly manages resources for your enterprise beans, such as threads, sockets, and database connections. The life cycle of the enterprise beans themselves is also managed, allowing the EJB container to reuse the enterprise bean instances as necessary.
- **Implicit persistence.** Persistence is a natural requirement of any deployment that requires permanent storage. EJB offers assistance here by automatically saving persistent object data to an underlying storage and retrieving that data at a later time.
- **Implicit remote accessibility.** Your enterprise bean class cannot be called across the network directly because an enterprise bean class is not network enabled. Your EJB container handles networking for you by wrapping your bean in a network-enabled object. The network-enabled object receives calls from clients and delegates these calls to

instances of your bean class. This saves you from having to worry about networking issues (the container provides networking as a service to you). Thus EJB products automatically convert your standalone, networkless components into distributed, network-aware entities.

- **Implicit support.** EJB containers automatically handle concurrent requests from clients. EJB containers provide built-in thread support, instantiating multiple copies of your component as necessary by instantiating lots of instances of your enterprise bean and pushing one thread through each instance. If multiple clients simultaneously invoke methods on a bean, the invocations are *serialized*, or performed lock step. The container will allow only one client to call a bean at a time. The other clients are routed to other bean instances of the same class or are forced to wait. (Behind the scenes, the container might use Java thread synchronization to aid with this. The actual algorithm used is container-specific.) The value of threading is obvious—who enjoys writing multithreaded code?
- **Implicit component location transparency.** Clients of components are decoupled from the specific whereabouts of the component being used.
- **Implicit monitoring.** The EJB container can track which methods are invoked, display a real-time usage graph on a system administrator's user interface, gather data for intelligent load balancing, and more. An EJB container is not required to perform these tasks; however, high-end EJB containers perform these tasks at the point of interception.

Thus, the EJB container acts as a layer of indirection between the client code and the bean. This layer of indirection manifests itself as a single network-aware object called the *EJB object*. The EJB object is the request interceptor we alluded to earlier. As the old saying goes, a layer of indirection solves every problem in computer science.

The EJB object is a surrogate object that knows about networking, transactions, security, and more. It is an intelligent object that knows how to perform intermediate logic that the EJB container requires before a method call is serviced by a bean class instance. An EJB object is the request interceptor, or the glue, between the client and the bean. EJB objects replicate and expose every business method that the bean itself exposes. EJB objects delegate all client requests to beans. Figure 2.5 depicts EJB objects.

You should think of EJB objects as physical parts of the container; all EJB objects have container-specific code inside of them. (Each container handles middleware differently and provides different qualities of service.) Because each bean's EJB object is different, your container vendor *generates* the class file for your EJB objects automatically.

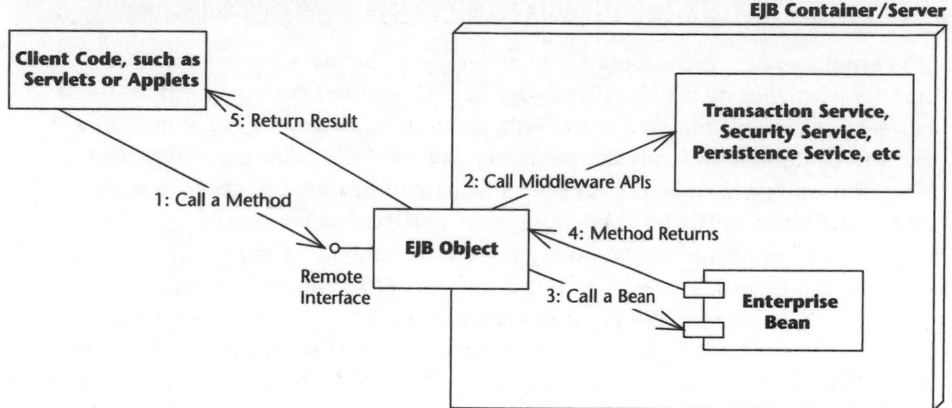

Figure 2.5 EJB objects.

Each EJB container ships with a suite of *glue-code tools*. These tools are meant to integrate beans into the EJB container's environment. The tools generate helper Java code—stubs, skeletons, data access classes, and other classes that this specific container requires. Bean providers do not have to think about the specifics of how each EJB container works because the container's tools generate its own proprietary Java code automatically.

The container's glue-code tools are responsible for transforming an enterprise bean into a fully managed, distributed server-side component. This involves logic to handle resource management, life cycle, state management, transactions, security, persistence, remote accessibility, and many other services. The generated code handles these services in the container's proprietary way.

The Remote Interface

As mentioned previously, bean clients invoke methods on EJB objects, rather than the beans themselves. Therefore, EJB objects must clone every business method that your bean classes expose. But how do the tools that autogenerate EJB objects know which methods to clone? The answer is in a special interface that a bean provider writes. This interface duplicates all the business logic methods that the corresponding bean class exposes. This interface is called the *remote interface*.

Remote interfaces must comply with special rules that the EJB specification defines. For example, all remote interfaces must derive from a common interface supplied by Sun Microsystems. This interface is called *javax.ejb.EJBObject*, and it is shown in Source 2.2.

THE EJB CONTAINER: YOUR SILENT PARTNER

EJB containers are responsible for managing your beans. Containers can interact with your beans by calling your beans' required management methods as necessary. These management methods are your beans' callback methods that the container, and only the container, invokes. The management methods allow the container to alert your beans when middleware events take place, such as when an entity bean is about to be persisted to storage.

The most important responsibility of an EJB container is to provide an environment in which enterprise beans can run. EJB containers house the enterprise beans and make them available for clients to invoke remotely. In essence, EJB containers act as invisible middlemen between the client and the beans. They are responsible for connecting clients to beans, performing transaction coordination, providing persistence, managing a bean's life cycle, and other tasks.

The key to understanding EJB containers is to realize that they are *abstract entities.* Neither the beans nor the clients that call beans ever explicitly code to the API of an EJB container. Rather, the container implicitly manages the overhead of a distributed component architecture. The container is analogous to a behind-the-scenes stage manager in a theater, providing the lighting and backdrop necessary for a successful stage performance by the actors on stage. Neither the actors nor the audience interact directly with the stage manager. The same is true for EJB containers. Clients that call the beans never code directly to an EJB container API.

javax.ejb.EJBObject lists a number of interesting methods. For now, don't worry about fully understanding the meanings—just know that these are required methods that all EJB objects must implement. And remember that *you* don't implement the methods—the EJB container does when it autogenerates the EJB objects for you.

```
public interface javax.ejb.EJBObject
extends java.rmi.Remote
{
    public javax.ejb.EJBHome getEJBHome()
       throws java.rmi.RemoteException;

    public java.lang.Object getPrimaryKey()
        throws java.rmi.RemoteException;

    public void remove()
         throws java.rmi.RemoteException,
        javax.ejb.RemoveException;

    public javax.ejb.Handle getHandle()
```

Source 2.2 A preview of the javax.ejb.EJBObject interface.

```
        throws java.rmi.RemoteException;

    public boolean isIdentical(javax.ejb.EJBObject)
        throws java.rmi.RemoteException;
}
```

Source 2.2 *(continued)*

The client code that wants to work with your beans calls the methods in *javax.ejb.EJBObject*. This client code could be standalone applications, applets, servlets, or anything at all—even other enterprise beans.

In addition to the methods listed in Source 2.2, your remote interface duplicates your beans' business methods. When a bean's client invokes any of these business methods, the EJB object delegates the method to its corresponding implementation, which resides in the bean itself.

Java RMI-IIOP and EJB Objects

You may have noticed that *javax.ejb.EJBObject* extends *java.rmi.Remote*. The *java.rmi.Remote* interface is part of Java Remote Method Invocation over the Internet Inter-ORB Protocol (RMI-IIOP). Any object that implements *java.rmi.Remote* is a *remote object* and is callable from a different JVM. This is how remote method invocations are performed in Java. (We fully describe this in Appendix A.)

Because the EJB object provided by the container implements your remote interface, it also indirectly implements *java.rmi.Remote*. Your EJB objects are fully networked RMI-IIOP objects, able to be called from other JVMs or physical machines located elsewhere on the network. Thus, EJB remote interfaces are really just RMI-IIOP remote interfaces—except that EJB remote interfaces must also be built to conform to the EJB specification.

EJB remote interfaces must conform to the RMI-IIOP remote interface rules. For example, any method that is part of a remote object callable across virtual machines must throw a special *remote exception*. A remote exception is a *java.rmi.RemoteException*, or (technically) a subclass of it. A remote exception indicates that something unexpected happened on the network while you were invoking across virtual machines, such as a network, process, or machine failure. Every method shown in Source 2.2 for *javax.ejb.EJBObject* throws a *java.rmi.RemoteException*.

Remote interfaces must conform to the RMI-IIOP parameter-passing conventions as well. Not everything can be passed over the network in a cross-VM method call. The parameters you pass in methods must be valid types for RMI-IIOP. This includes primitives, serializable objects, and RMI-IIOP remote objects. The full details of what you can pass are in Appendix A.

THE INSTANCE-POOLING CONCEPT

A multitier architecture's overall scalability is enhanced when an application server intelligently manages needed resources across a variety of deployed components. The resources could be threads, socket connections, database connections, and more. For example, database connections could be pooled by application servers and reused across heterogeneous components. In the EJB realm, the container is responsible for providing all resource management services behind the scenes.

In addition to resource management, the EJB container is responsible for controlling the life cycle of the deployed enterprise bean components. As bean client requests arrive, the EJB container dynamically instantiates, destroys, and reuses beans as appropriate. For example, if a client requests a certain type of bean that does not yet exist in memory, the EJB container may instantiate a new in-memory instance on behalf of the client. On the other hand, if a bean already exists in memory, it may not be appropriate to instantiate a new bean, especially if the system is low on memory. It might make more sense to reassign a bean from one client to another instead. It might also make sense to destroy some beans that are not being used anymore. This is called *instance pooling*.

The benefit of bean instance pooling is that the pool of beans can be much smaller than the actual number of clients connecting. This is due to client think time, such as network lag or human decision time on the client side. The classic example of this is an HTML (Web) client interacting with a human being. Web users often click a button that executes some business logic in a component, but then read text before initiating another action. While the user is waiting and reading, the application server could reuse that component to service other clients. While the client is thinking, the container can use the bean instances to service other clients, saving previous system resources.

The take-away point here is that the EJB container is responsible for coordinating the entire effort of resource management as well as managing the deployed beans' life cycle. Note that the exact scheme used is EJB container-specific.

The Home Object

As we've discussed, client code deals with EJB objects and never with beans directly. The next logical question is, how do clients acquire references to EJB objects?

The client cannot instantiate an EJB object directly because the EJB object can exist on a different machine than the one the client is on. Similarly, EJB promotes location transparency, so clients should never be aware of exactly where an EJB object resides.

LOCATION TRANSPARENCY

EJB inherits a significant benefit from RMI-IIOP. In RMI-IIOP, the physical location of the remote object you're invoking is masked from you. This feature spills over to EJB. Your client code is unaware of whether the EJB object it is using is located on a machine next door or a machine across the Internet. It also means the EJB object could be located on the same JVM as the client. This is called *location transparency*.

Why is location transparency beneficial? For one thing, you aren't writing your bean's client code to take advantage of a particular deployment configuration because you're not hard-coding machine locations. This is an essential part of reusable components that can be deployed in a wide variety of multitier situations.

Location transparency also enables container vendors to provide additional value-adds, such as the ability to take down a machine on the network temporarily to perform system maintenance, install new software, or upgrade components on that machine. During maintenance, location transparency allows another machine on the network to serve up components for a component's client because that client is not dependent on the hard locations of any components. If a machine that has components on it crashes due to hardware or software error, you may be able to reroute client invocations to other machines without the client even knowing about the crash, allowing for an enhanced level of fault tolerance.

To acquire a reference to an EJB object, your client code asks for an EJB object from an EJB object *factory*. This factory is responsible for instantiating (and destroying) EJB objects. The EJB specification calls such a factory a *home object*. The chief responsibilities of home objects are the following:

- Create EJB objects
- Find existing EJB objects (for entity beans, which we'll learn about in Chapter 6)
- Remove EJB objects

Just like EJB objects, home objects are proprietary and specific to each EJB container. They contain interesting container-specific logic, such as load-balancing logic, logic to track information on a graphical administrative console, and more. And just like EJB objects, home objects are physically part of the container and are autogenerated by the container vendor's tools.

The Home Interface

We've mentioned that home objects are factories for EJB objects. But how does a home object know how you'd like your EJB object to be initialized? For example, one EJB object might expose an initialization method that takes an integer as a parameter, and another EJB object might take a string instead. The container needs to know this information to generate home objects. You provide this information to the container by specifying a *home interface*. Home interfaces simply define methods for creating, destroying, and finding EJB objects. The container's home object *implements* your home interface (see Figure 2.6).

As usual, EJB defines some required methods that all home interfaces must support. These required methods are defined in the *javax.ejb.EJBHome* interface—an interface that your home interfaces must extend. Source 2.3 shows *javax.ejb.EJBHome*. You will learn about these methods later.

```
public interface javax.ejb.EJBHome extends java.rmi.Remote
{
    public EJBMetaData getEJBMetaData()
        throws java.rmi.RemoteException;

    public javax.ejb.HomeHandle getHomeHandle()
        throws java.rmi.RemoteException;

    public void remove(javax.ejb.Handle handle)
        throws java.rmi.RemoteException,
        javax.ejb.RemoveException;

    public void remove(Object primaryKey)
        throws java.rmi.RemoteException,
        javax.ejb.RemoveException;
}
```

Source 2.3 A preview of the javax.ejb.EJBHome interface.

Notice that the parent *javax.ejb.EJBHome* derives from *java.rmi.Remote*. This means your home interfaces do as well, implying that home objects are also fully networked Java RMI remote objects, which can be called across virtual machines. The types of parameters passed in the home interface's methods must be valid types for Java RMI-IIOP.

The Local Interfaces

One problem with the home interface is that creating beans through that interface is very slow. The same is true for calling beans through the remote interface. Just to give you an idea of what happens when you call an EJB object, the following steps may occur:

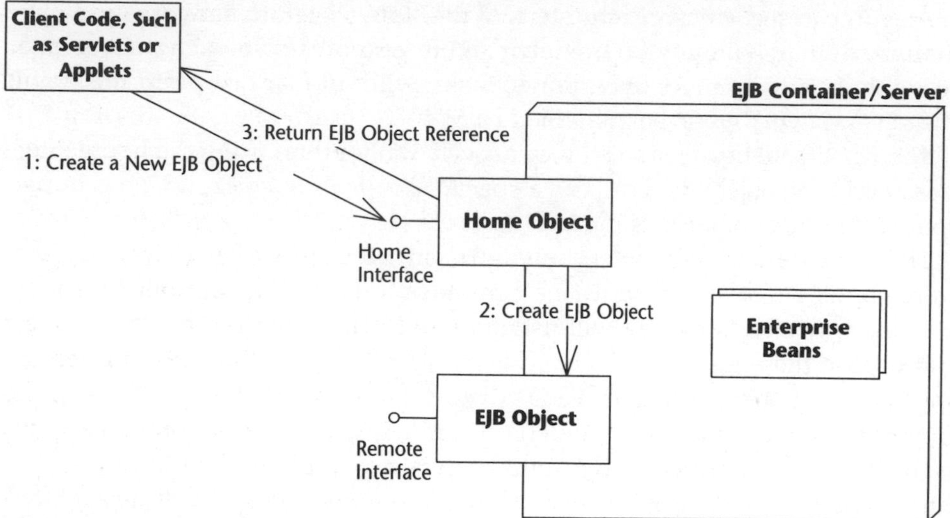

Figure 2.6 Home interfaces and objects.

1. The client calls a local stub.
2. The stub marshals parameters into a form suitable for the network.
3. The stub sends the parameters over a network connection to the skeleton.
4. The skeleton de-marshals parameters into a form suitable for Java.
5. The skeleton calls the EJB object.
6. The EJB object performs needed middleware, such as connection pooling, transactions, security, and life cycle services.
7. Once the EJB object calls the enterprise bean instance, and the bean does its work, each of the preceding steps must be repeated for the return trip home.

Ouch! That's a lot of overhead. Figure 2.4 shows this process.

Since version 2.0 of EJB, you can call enterprise beans in a fast, efficient way through their *local objects* rather than *EJB objects*. Local objects implement a *local interface* rather than a *remote interface*. The local objects are speed demons that enable you to make high-performance enterprise beans. The process works as follows:

1. The client calls a local object.
2. The local object performs needed middleware, such as connection pooling, transactions, security, and life cycle services.
3. Once the enterprise bean instance does its work, it returns control to the local object, which then returns control to the client.

As you can see, we avoid the steps of the stub, skeleton, network, and marshaling/demarshaling of parameters. This empowers us to write smaller beans that perform more fine-grained tasks, without fear of a performance hit at each and every cross-bean method call.

You can create beans in a fast way as well. Rather than using the home interface and home object, you can call a special *local home interface*, which is implemented by the container as the *local home object*.

These local interfaces are entirely optional; you can use them as a replacement or as a complement to the remote interfaces. For simplicity, in the remainder of this book, we will use the word EJB object to mean the request interceptor, the remote interface to mean the interface to the request interceptor, the home object to mean the factory, and the home interface to mean the factory interface. Unless it's pointed out explicitly, all information that applies to these remote interfaces and remote objects also apply to their local counterparts. Also note that the EJB specification has defined the term *component interface* to mean either the remote interface or local interface. We will occasionally use this term in this book.

EJB OBJECTS AND BEAN INSTANCES

One question we frequently are asked in our EJB training courses is "How many home objects are there for each bean?" The answer to this question is vendor-specific. Most containers will have a 1:N relationship between home objects and bean instances. This means that all clients use the same home object instance to create EJB objects. The home object will probably be written to be thread-safe so that it can service many client requests concurrently. It is perfectly fine for the container to do this because the container itself is multithreaded (only your beans are single-threaded).

Another question we typically get is "How many EJB object instances are there for each bean instance?" Some containers can have a 1:N relationship, where each EJB object is multithreaded (just like home objects). Other containers might have an M:N relationship, where M represents the number of EJB objects instantiated (and corresponds exactly to the number of clients currently connected), and N represents the number of bean instances in the pool. In this case, each EJB object is single-threaded.

None of this really matters to you as a bean provider because you should think of the container as a black box. However, it's sometimes fun to know what's going on behind the scenes in case low-level debugging is required.

When you write a local interface, you extend *javax.ejb.EJBLocalObject*, and when you write a local home interface, you extend *javax.ejb.EJBLocalHome*. Those interfaces are previewed in the following code, and are fully explained in Appendix E.

```
public interface javax.ejb.EJBLocalObject {
    public javax.ejb.EJBLocalHome getEJBLocalHome()
        throws javax.ejb.EJBException;

    public Object getPrimaryKey()
        throws javax.ejb.EJBException;

    public boolean isIdentical(javax.ejb.EJBLocalObject)
        throws javax.ejb.EJBException;

    public void remove()
        throws javax.ejb.RemoveException, javax.ejb.EJBException;
}

public interface javax.ejb.EJBLocalHome {
    public void remove(java.lang.Object)
        throws javax.ejb.RemoveException, javax.ejb.EJBException;
}
```

Local interfaces have two important side effects:

- **They only work when you're calling beans in the same process—for example, if you have a bank teller session bean that calls a bank account entity bean in the same application server. But there lies the rub. You cannot call a bean remotely if your code relies on the local interface. If you decide to switch between a local or remote call, you must change your code from using the local interface to using the remote interface. This is an inherent drawback to local interfaces.**
- **They marshal parameters by reference rather than by value. While this may speed up your application because parameters are not copied, it also changes the semantics of your application. Be sure that you're aware of this when coding your clients and beans.**

For a while, the primary author of this book (Ed Roman) has been pushing for Sun to adopt some kind of flag that enables you to switch between local and remote access to beans without changing code. The idea is that this flag would determine whether the container-generated interceptor object would behave as a local object or remote object. We think this is the best approach because (in reality) many developers will misjudge whether to use remote or local interfaces when designing their object models, and will have to rewrite parts of their code later in their projects.

The response so far from Sun is that this approach would not work because the semantics of the application change when switching between local interfaces and remote interfaces, due to the differences in pass-by-value versus pass-by-reference. It would be error-prone to allow developers to "flip a switch" in this respect.

Personally, we don't agree with Sun. We think developers are smart enough to avoid these mistakes, and the potential benefits outweigh the drawbacks. Many EJB server vendors disagree as well. They actually support this local/remote flag idea through proprietary container tools or vendor-specific files that are separate from your bean. Thus, if you want to, you may be able to still take advantage of these flags without sacrificing portability.

Deployment Descriptors

To inform the container about your middleware needs, you as a bean provider must *declare* your components' middleware service requirements in a *deployment descriptor* file. For example, you can use a deployment descriptor to declare how the container should perform lifecycle management, persistence, transaction control, and security services. The container inspects the deployment descriptor to fulfill the requirements that you lay out. The deployment descriptor is the key to implicit middleware.

For example, you can use a deployment descriptor to specify the following requirements of your bean:

- **Bean management and lifecycle requirements.** These deployment descriptor settings indicate how the container should manage your beans. For example, you specify the name of the bean's class, whether the bean is a session, entity, or message-driven bean, and the home interface that generates the beans.
- **Persistence requirements (entity beans only).** Authors of entity beans use the deployment descriptors to inform the container about whether the bean handles its persistence on its own or delegates the persistence to the EJB container in which it's deployed.
- **Transaction requirements.** You can also specify transaction settings for beans in deployment descriptors. These settings specify the bean requirements for running in a transaction, such as a transaction must start whenever anyone calls this bean, and the transaction must end after my bean completes the method call.
- **Security requirements.** Deployment descriptors contain *access control entries,* which the beans and container use to enforce access to certain operations. For example, you can specify who is allowed to use which

beans, and even who is allowed to use each method on a particular bean. You can also specify what security roles the beans themselves should run in, which is useful if the beans need to perform secure operations. For example only bank executives can call the method to create new bank accounts.

In EJB, a deployment descriptor is an XML file. You can write these XML files by hand, or (if you're lucky) your Integrated Development Environment (IDE) or EJB container will supply tools to generate the XML deployment descriptor. In the latter case, you simply might need to step through a wizard in a Java IDE to generate a deployment descriptor.

As a bean provider, you are responsible for creating a deployment descriptor. Once your bean is used, other parties can modify its deployment descriptor settings. For example, an application assembler who is piecing together an application from beans can tune your deployment descriptor. Similarly, a deployer who is installing your beans in a container in preparation for a deployment to go live can tune your deployment descriptor settings as well. This is all possible because deployment descriptors *declare* how your beans should use middleware, rather than you writing code that uses middleware. Declaring rather than programming enables people without Java knowledge and without source code access to tweak your components at a later time. This paradigm becomes an absolute necessity when purchasing EJB components from a third party because third-party source code is typically not available. By having a separate, customizable deployment descriptor, you can easily fine-tune components to a specific deployment environment without changing source code.

Vendor-Specific Files

Since all EJB server vendors are different, they each have some proprietary value-added features. The EJB specification does not touch these features, such as how to configure load-balancing, clustering, monitoring, and so on. Therefore, each EJB server vendor may require that you include additional files specific to that vendor, such as XML files, text files, or binary files.

Ejb-jar File

Once you've generated your bean classes, your home interfaces, your remote interfaces, and your deployment descriptor, it's time to package them into an *Ejb-jar file*. An Ejb-jar file is a compressed file that contains everything we have described, and it follows the .ZIP compression format. Jar files are convenient, compact modules for shipping your Java software. Figure 2.7 shows the Ejb-jar file creation process.

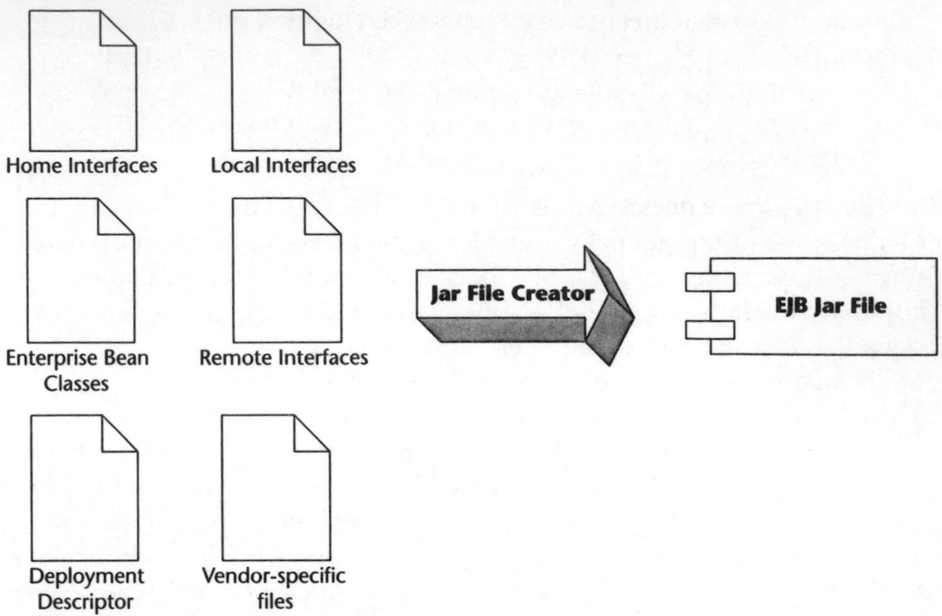

Figure 2.7 Creating an Ejb-jar file.

There are already a number of tools available to autogenerate Ejb-jar files, such as Java IDEs. You can also generate these files yourself—we'll show you how in Chapter 3.

Once you've made your Ejb-jar file, your enterprise bean is complete, and it is a deployable unit within an application server. When they are deployed (perhaps after being purchased), the tools that EJB container vendors supply are responsible for decompressing, reading, and extracting the information contained within the Ejb-jar file. From there, the deployer has to perform vendor-specific tasks, such as generating EJB objects, generating home objects, importing your bean into the container, and tuning the bean. Support for Ejb-jar files is a standard, required feature for all EJB tools.

Note that you can have more than one bean in an Ejb-jar file, allowing you to ship an entire product set of beans in a single jar file.

Summary of Terms

For your convenience, we now list the definitions of each term we've described so far. As you read future chapters, refer to these definitions whenever you need clarification. You may want to bookmark this page.

The **enterprise bean instance** is a Java object instance of an enterprise bean class. It contains business method implementations of the methods defined in the remote or local interface. The enterprise bean instance is networkless in that it contains no networked logic.

The **remote interface** is a Java interface that enumerates the business methods exposed by the enterprise bean class. In EJB, client code always goes through the remote or local interface and never interacts with the enterprise bean instance directly. The remote interface is network-aware in that the interface obeys the rules for Java RMI-IIOP.

The **local interface** is the high-performing version of the remote interface. Use the local interface when you are calling enterprise beans that live in the same process. Your calls will not undergo stubs, skeletons, network calls, or the marshaling/demarshaling of parameters.

The **EJB object** is the container-generated implementation of the remote interface. The EJB object is a network-aware intermediary between the client and the bean instance, handling necessary middleware issues. All client invocations go through the EJB object. The EJB object delegates calls to enterprise bean instances and implements the remote interface.

The **local object** is the high-performing version of the EJB object. The local object implements the local interface.

The **home interface** is a Java interface that serves as a factory for EJB objects. Client code that wants to work with EJB objects must use the home interface to retrieve them. The home interface is network-aware because clients use it across the network.

The **local home interface** is the high-performing version of the home interface.

The **home object** is the container-generated implementation of the home interface. The home object is also network-aware, and it obeys the RMI-IIOP rules.

The **local home object** is the high-performing version of the home object. The local home object implements the local home interface.

The **deployment descriptor** is an XML file that specifies the middleware requirements of your bean. You use the deployment descriptor to inform the container about the implicit middleware you want, such as how to manage your bean, your bean's life cycle needs, your transactional needs, your persistence needs, and your security needs.

The **vendor-specific files** enable you to take advantage of vendor-specific features. These files are not portable between application servers.

The **Ejb-jar file** is the finished, complete ZIP file that contains the above files. It is the unit of deployment and is given to the application server. The application server unpacks the Ejb-jar file and loads the bean.

Summary

In this chapter, we've taken a whirlwind tour of EJB. We started by looking at what a bean is, and then discussed the different kinds of beans, including session, entity, and message-driven beans.

We then took a bean apart into its constituent pieces, and examined each part: the enterprise bean class, remote interface, local interface, EJB object, local object, home interface, home object, deployment descriptor, and Ejb-jar file.

Now that you understand the high-level concepts, let's learn how to write and use each type of EJB component, starting with a simple Hello World example.

CHAPTER

3

Writing Your First Bean

In this chapter, we'll get down-and-dirty and write a real working EJB component. Our stateless session bean will be responsible for the mighty task of returning the string "Hello, World!" to the client. We'll see how to write each of the files that make up this bean and how to access it from clients.

This chapter is great for you if you want to discover how to get up and running with EJB quickly. While this may not be the most functional demonstration of the power of EJB, it illustrates the basics of EJB programming and is a useful template for building more complex beans. This will give you the necessary foundation to understand later chapters on entity beans, session beans, and message-driven beans. We encourage you to compile and execute the example code as we go along.

How to Develop an EJB Component

When building an EJB component, the following is a typical order of operations:

1. Write the .java files that compose your bean: the component interfaces, home interfaces, enterprise bean class file, and any helper classes you might need.
2. Write the deployment descriptor, or have it generated by your IDE or tools like XDoclet.
3. Compile the .java files from Step 1 into .class files.
4. Using the *jar* utility, create an Ejb-jar file containing the deployment descriptor and .class files.
5. Deploy the Ejb-jar file into your container in a vendor-specific manner, perhaps by running a vendor-specific tool or perhaps by copying your Ejb-jar file into a folder where your container looks to load Ejb-jar files.
6. Configure your EJB server so that it is properly configured to host your Ejb-jar file. You might tune things such as database connections, thread pools, and so on. This step is vendor-specific and might be done through a Web-based console or by editing a configuration file.
7. Start your EJB container and confirm that it has loaded your Ejb-jar file.
8. Optionally, write a standalone test client .java file and let vendor tools generate stub classes for remote access, if required. Compile that test client into a .class file. Run the test client from the command line and have it exercise your bean's APIs.

We will apply the preceding process to our Hello World example. The complete build scripts are available with the book's accompanying source code, which can be downloaded from our Web site.

Figure 3.1 shows the class diagram for our Hello World example and its base classes. In the following sections, we will first look at the client interfaces, both remote and local, then at the home interfaces, again remote and local, and finally at the bean class itself.

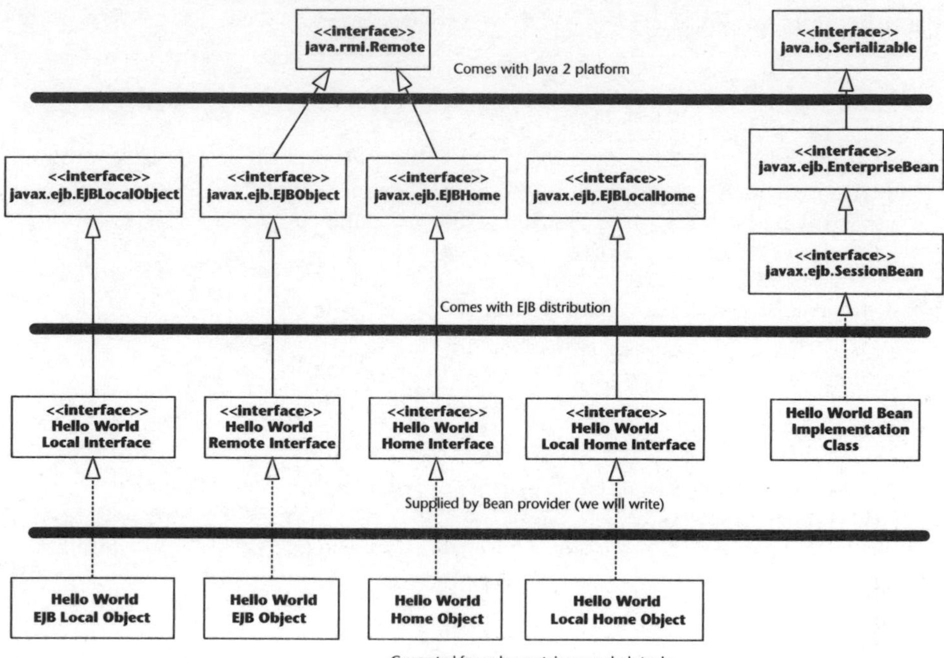

Figure 3.1 Our Hello world object model.

The Remote Interface

First, let's code up the remote interface. The remote interface supports every business method that our beans expose. The code is shown in Source 3.1.

Things to notice about our remote interface include the following:

- We extend *javax.ejb.EJBObject*. This means that the container-generated EJB object, which implements the remote interface, will contain every method that the *javax.ejb.EJBObject* interface defines. This includes a method to compare two EJB objects, a method to remove an EJB object, and so on.
- We have one business method—*hello()*—which returns the String "Hello, World!" to the client. We need to implement this method in our enterprise bean class. Because the remote interface is an RMI-IIOP remote interface (it extends *java.rmi.Remote*), it must throw a remote exception. This is the only difference between the remote interface's *hello()* signature and our bean's *hello()* signature. The exception indicates a networking or other critical problem.

```
package examples;

/**
 * This is the HelloBean remote interface.
 *
 * This interface is what clients operate on when
 * they interact with EJB objects.  The container
 * vendor will implement this interface; the
 * implemented object is the EJB object, which
 * delegates invocations to the actual bean.
 */
public interface Hello extends javax.ejb.EJBObject
{

  /**
   * The one method - hello - returns a greeting to the client.
   */
  public String hello() throws java.rmi.RemoteException;
}
```

Source 3.1 Hello.java.

The Local Interface

Local clients will use our local interface, rather than the remote interface, to call our beans' methods. It is shown in Source 3.2.

```
package examples;

/**
 * This is the HelloBean local interface.
 *
 * This interface is what local clients operate
 * on when they interact with EJB local objects.
 * The container vendor will implement this
 * interface; the implemented object is the
 * EJB local object, which delegates invocations
 * to the actual bean.
 */
public interface HelloLocal extends javax.ejb.EJBLocalObject
{

  /**
```

Source 3.2 HelloLocal.java.

```
     * The one method - hello - returns a greeting to the client.
     */
    public String hello();
}
```

Source 3.2 *(continued)*

As you can see, there are trivial differences between the local interface and the remote interface. We extend a different interface, and we don't throw remote exceptions.

The Home Interface

Next, let's put together the home interface. The home interface has methods to create and destroy EJB objects. The implementation of the home interface is the home object, which is generated by the container tools.

The code for our home interface is shown in Source 3.3.

```
/**
 * This is the home interface for HelloBean.  This interface
 * is implemented by the EJB Server's tools - the
 * implemented object is called the Home Object, and serves
 * as a factory for EJB Objects.
 *
 * One create() method is in this Home Interface, which
 * corresponds to the ejbCreate() method in HelloBean.
 */
public interface HelloHome extends javax.ejb.EJBHome
{

    /*
     * This method creates the EJB Object.
     *
     * @return The newly created EJB Object.
     */
    Hello create() throws java.rmi.RemoteException,
        javax.ejb.CreateException;
}
```

Source 3.3 HelloHome.java.

Notice the following about our home interface:

- The single *create()* is a factory method that clients use to get a reference to an EJB object. The *create()* method is also used to initialize a bean.

- The *create()* method throws two exceptions: *java.rmi.RemoteException* and *javax.ejb.CreateException*. Remote exceptions are necessary side effects of RMI-IIOP because the home object is a networked RMI-IIOP remote object. *CreateException* is also required in all *create()* methods. We explain this further in the Exceptions and EJB sidebar.
- Our home interface extends *javax.ejb.EJBHome*. This is required for all home interfaces. *EJBHome* defines a way to destroy an EJB object, so we don't need to write that method signature.

EXCEPTIONS AND EJB

Every networked object in EJB conforms to the RMI-IIOP standard and must throw a remote exception. Thus, every method in an EJB object and home object (such as our *hello()* method) must throw a remote exception. When such an exception is thrown, it indicates a special error condition—a network failure, machine failure, or other catastrophic failure.

But how can your beans throw exceptions that indicate regular, run-of-the-mill problems, such as bad parameters passed to a business method? EJB comes with some built-in exceptions to handle this, and it also allows you to define your own exception types.

More formally, EJB defines the following exception types:

- **A *system-level exception* is a serious error that involves some critical failure, such as a database malfunction.**
- **An *application-level exception* is a more routine exception, such as an indication of bad parameters to a method or a warning of an insufficient bank account balance to make a withdrawal. For example, in our "Hello, World!" home interface, we throw the standard exception *javax.ejb.CreateException* from the home interface's *create()* method. This is an example of a required application-level exception, indicating that some ordinary problem occurred during bean initialization.**

Why must we separate the concepts of system-level and application-level exceptions? The chief reason is that system-level exceptions are handled quite differently from application-level exceptions.

For example, system-level exceptions are not necessarily thrown back to the client. Remember that EJB objects—the container-generated wrappers for beans—are middlemen between a bean's client and the bean itself. EJB objects have the ability to *intercept* any exceptions that beans may throw. This allows EJB objects to pick and choose which exceptions the client should see. In some cases, if a bean fails, it may be possible to salvage the client's invocation and redirect it to another bean. This is known as *transparent fail-over*, a quality of service that some EJB container/server vendors provide. This is an easy service to provide for stateless beans because there is no lost state when a bean crashes. Some high-end EJB products even provide transparent fail-over for

stateful beans by routinely checkpointing the stateful bean's conversational state (see Chapter 19 for more). In case of a critical, unrecoverable problem, your EJB container may support professional monitoring systems, alerting a system administrator if a catastrophic error occurs.

By way of comparison, application-level exceptions should always be thrown back to the client. Application-level exceptions indicate a routine problem, and the exception itself is valuable data that the client needs. For example, we could notify a client of insufficient funds in a bank account by throwing an application-level exception. The client would always want to know about this because it is an application-level problem, not a system-level problem.

Besides correctly routing system-level and application-level exceptions, the EJB object is responsible for catching all *unchecked* exceptions (flavors of *java.lang.RuntimeException*) that your bean may throw, such as a *NullPointer* exception. These are typically not caught by the code. Exceptions that are unchecked in the bean could leave the bean in an abnormal state because the bean is not expecting to handle such an exception. In this scenario, the EJB container intercepts the exception and performs some action, such as throwing the exception back to the client as a remote exception. It also probably stops using that bean because the bean is in an undefined state.

The following two rules of thumb should help you with exceptions.

- **Application-level exceptions are always thrown back to the client. This includes any exception the bean defines. It also includes the exception *javax.ejb.CreateException* for creating beans (and *javax.ejb.FindException* for entity beans, which we'll discuss in Chapters 5 through 8).**
- **When system-level exceptions occur, the EJB container can do anything it wants: page a system administrator with an alert, send an e-mail to a third party, or throw the exception back to the client. Your bean can throw a system-level exception as either an RMI-IIOP remote exception or unchecked *RuntimeException*. If the exception is thrown to the client, it is always thrown as a remote exception or a subclass of it.**

Exceptions also have an impact on transactions. You'll learn more about this effect in Chapter 12.

The Local Home Interface

Our local home interface, the higher-performing home interface used by local clients, is in Source 3.4.

```
package examples;

/**
 * This is the local home interface for HelloBean.
```

Source 3.4 HelloLocalHome.java. *(continues)*

```
 * This interface is implemented by the EJB Server's
 * tools - the implemented object is called the
 * local home object, and serves as a factory for
 * EJB local objects.
 */
public interface HelloLocalHome extends javax.ejb.EJBLocalHome
{

    /*
     * This method creates the EJB Object.
     *
     * @return The newly created EJB Object.
     */
    HelloLocal create() throws javax.ejb.CreateException;
}
```

Source 3.4 *(continued)*

The differences between the remote interface and the local interface are as follows:

- The local home interface extends *EJBLocalHome* rather than *EJBHome*. The *EJBLocalHome* interface does not extend *java.rmi.Remote*. This means that the generated implementation will not be a remote object.
- The local home interface does not throw *RemoteExceptions*.

WHAT HAPPENS DURING CREATE() AND REMOVE()

As we've discussed, the container, rather than a client, creates and destroys your beans. But if the container is responsible for a bean life cycle, then why does the home interface and local home interface specify *create()* and *remove()* methods? What you must remember is that these methods are for creating and destroying *EJB objects.* This may not correspond to the actual creation and destruction of beans. The client shouldn't care whether the actual bean is created or destroyed—all the client code cares about is that the client has an EJB object to invoke. The fact that beans are pooled and reused behind the EJB object is irrelevant.

So when debugging your EJB applications, don't be alarmed if your bean isn't being created or destroyed when you call *create()* or *remove()* on the home object or local home object. Depending on your container's policy, your beans may be pooled and reused, with the container creating and destroying at will.

The Bean Class

Now let's look at the bean class itself. The code is shown in Source 3.5.

```
package examples;

/**
 * Demonstration stateless session bean.
 */
public class HelloBean implements javax.ejb.SessionBean {

    private SessionContext ctx;

    //
    // EJB-required methods
    //
    public void ejbCreate() {
        System.out.println("ejbCreate()");
    }

    public void ejbRemove() {
        System.out.println("ejbRemove()");
    }

    public void ejbActivate() {
        System.out.println("ejbActivate()");
    }

    public void ejbPassivate() {
        System.out.println("ejbPassivate()");
    }

    public void setSessionContext(javax.ejb.SessionContext ctx) {
        this.ctx = ctx;
    }

    //
    // Business methods
    //
    public String hello() {
        System.out.println("hello()");
        return "Hello, World!";
    }
}
```

Source 3.5 HelloBean.java.

This is just about the most basic bean class possible. Notice the following:

- Our bean implements the *javax.ejb.SessionBean* interface, which makes it a session bean. This interface defines a few required methods that you must fill in. The container uses these management methods to interact with the bean, calling them periodically to alert the bean to important events. For example, the container will alert the bean when it is being initialized and when it is being destroyed. These callbacks are not intended for client use, so you will never call them directly—only your EJB container will. We'll learn about the specifics of these management methods in the pages to come.
- The bean has an *ejbCreate()* method that matches the home object's *create()* method, and takes no parameters.
- We have one business method, *hello()*. It returns Hello, World! to the client.
- The *ejbActivate()* and *ejbPassivate()* methods do not apply to stateless session beans, and so we leave these methods empty. You'll learn what these methods mean and what to use them for in the next chapters.
- When we destroy the bean, there's nothing to clean up, so we have a very simple *ejbRemove()* method.

We also have a method called *setSessionContext()*. This method is explained in the following sidebar.

EJB CONTEXTS: YOUR GATEWAY TO THE CONTAINER

Since your enterprise beans live in a managed container, the container is free to call your EJB components' methods at its leisure. But what if your bean needs to query the container for information about its current status? For example, inside your bean, you may want to access the security credentials of the user currently calling your bean's method.

The container houses all of this information in one object, called an *EJB context object*. An EJB context object is your gateway to the container. EJB contexts are physical parts containers and can be accessed from within your beans. Thus, a context represents a way for beans to perform callbacks to the container. These callbacks help beans both ascertain their current status and modify their current status. This is shown in Figure 3.2.

The motivation behind a context is to encapsulate the bean's domain in one compact object. Note that a bean's status may change over the bean's life cycle, and thus this context object can dynamically change over time as well. At runtime, the container is responsible for changing the context to reflect any status changes, such as the bean becoming involved in a new transaction.

Here is what the *javax.ejb.EJBContext* interface looks like (thrown exceptions omitted):

```
public interface javax.ejb.EJBContext
{
 /*
  * Call these from within your bean to access
  * your own home object or local home object.
  *
  * You can use them to create, destroy, or
  * find EJB objects and EJB local objects
  * of your own bean class type.
  */
 public javax.ejb.EJBHome getEJBHome();
 public javax.ejb.EJBLocalHome getEJBLocalHome();
 /*
  * These are transaction methods - see Chapter 10
  */
 public boolean getRollbackOnly();
 public void setRollbackOnly();
 public javax.transaction.UserTransaction getUserTransaction();
 /*
  * These are security methods - see Chapter 13
  */
 public boolean isCallerInRole(java.lang.String);
 public java.security.Principal getCallerPrincipal();
}
```

An EJB context contains callbacks useful for session beans, entity beans, and message-driven beans. In comparison, a *session context, entity context,* and *message-driven context* are specific EJB contexts used only for session beans, entity beans, and message-driven beans.

The container associates your bean with a context by calling *setSessionContext, setEntityContext,* or *setMessageDrivenContext,* depending on your bean type. When you define each of these methods, you should store the context away in a member variable so the context can be queried later, as shown in Source 3.5.

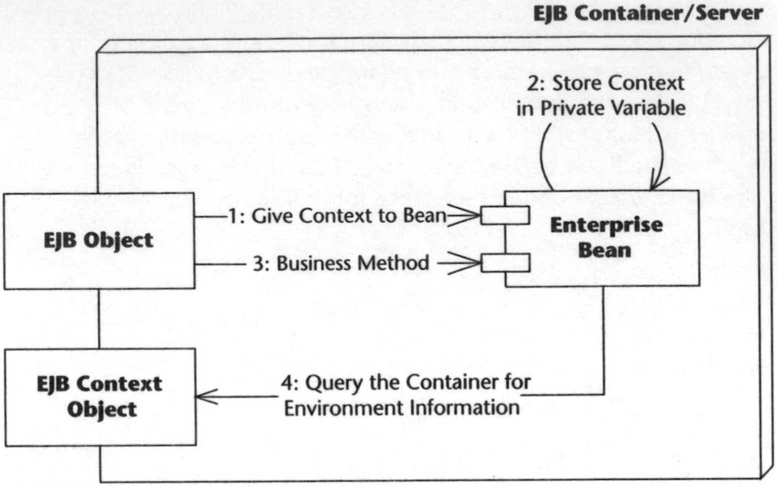

Figure 3.2 EJB contexts.

The Deployment Descriptor

Next, we need to generate a *deployment descriptor,* which describes our bean's middleware requirements to the container. Deployment descriptors are one of the key features of EJB because they enable you to *declaratively* specify attributes on your beans, rather than program this functionality into the bean itself.

Physically, a deployment descriptor is an XML document. Your EJB container, IDE environment, or other tool (such as a UML editor that can generate EJB code) should supply tools to help you generate such a deployment descriptor.

Our deployment descriptor is shown in Source 3.6.

Many different settings make up a deployment descriptor. For a full deployment descriptor reference, see Appendix C. For now, here is an explanation of our session bean descriptor:

<ejb-name> The nickname for this particular bean. Can be used later in the deployment descriptor to refer back to this bean to set additional settings.

<home> The fully qualified name of the home interface.

<remote> The fully qualified name of the remote interface.

<local-home> The fully qualified name of the local home interface.

<local> The fully qualified name of the local interface.

<ejb-class> The fully qualified name of the enterprise bean class.

<session-type> Whether the session bean is a stateful or stateless session bean.

<transaction-type> Ignore for now—see Chapter 12 for more details on transactions.

```
<!DOCTYPE ejb-jar PUBLIC "-//Sun Microsystems, Inc.//DTD Enterprise ⮐
JavaBeans 2.0//EN" " http://java.sun.com/dtd/ejb-jar_2_0.dtd">

<ejb-jar>
 <enterprise-beans>
  <session>
   <ejb-name>Hello</ejb-name>
   <home>examples.HelloHome</home>
   <remote>examples.Hello</remote>
   <local-home>examples.HelloLocalHome</local-home>
   <local>examples.HelloLocal</local>
   <ejb-class>examples.HelloBean</ejb-class>
   <session-type>Stateless</session-type>
   <transaction-type>Container</transaction-type>
  </session>
 </enterprise-beans>
</ejb-jar>
```

Source 3.6 ejb-jar.xml.

The Vendor-Specific Files

Next in our stateless session bean are vendor-specific files. These files exist because the EJB specification can't cover everything; vendors differentiate their products in areas such as instance pooling algorithms, clustering algorithms, and so on. The vendor-specific files are not portable and can use any file format, including XML, flat file, or binary. In fact, it may not even exist as files—the settings could be stored in some database with a GUI on top of it.

The source code that accompanies this book shows an example of a vendor-specific file.

The Ejb-jar File

Now that we've written all the necessary files for our component, we need to package all the files together in an Ejb-jar file. If you're using a development environment supporting EJB, the development environment may contain an automated way to generate the Ejb-jar file for you. We can generate it manually as follows:

```
jar cf HelloWorld.jar *
```

The asterisk indicates the files to include in the jar—the bean class, home interface, local home interface, remote interface, local interface, deployment descriptor, and possibly vendor-specific files (depending on your container's policy).

The folder structure within the Ejb-jar file looks as follows:

```
META-INF/
META-INF/MANIFEST.MF
examples/
examples/HelloBean.class
examples/HelloHome.class
examples/Hello.class
examples/HelloLocal.class
examples/HelloLocalHome.class
META-INF/ejb-jar.xml
```

The files must be in properly named subdirectories of the current directory. For example, our *Hello.class* file is located in *examples/ Hello.class,* below the current directory. You must store your classes in a directory corresponding to the package that the class belongs to, or the JVM will be unable to locate your classes when it searches your jar. The ejb-jar.xml file must be placed in the META-INF subfolder. The container consults that file first when opening the Ejb-jar file to figure out what beans are inside the jar.

The MANIFEST.MF file is a listing of the files within the Ejb-jar file. It is autogenerated by the *jar* utility. You don't need to worry about this file.

Deploying the Bean

Finally, we're ready to deploy our bean in an EJB container. This step varies from container to container. When you reach this point, consult your container's documentation about how to deploy a bean. This could involve anything from running a command-line tool on your Ejb-jar file to copying your Ejb-jar file into a well-known folder where your application server detects its presence. For an example of deploying a bean, see the source code accompanying this book.

When deploying an Ejb-jar file into a container, the following steps are usually performed:

- The Ejb-jar file is verified. The container checks that the enterprise bean class, the remote interface, and other items are valid. Any commercial tool should report intelligent errors back to you, such as, "You need to define an *ejbCreate()* method in your bean."
- The container tool generates an EJB object and home object for you.
- The container tool generates any necessary RMI-IIOP stubs and skeletons. (See Appendix A for more information about stubs and skeletons.)

Once you've performed these steps, start up your EJB container (if it isn't already running). Most products output a server log or have a GUI to view the beans that are deployed. Make sure that your container is indeed making your bean available. It should tell you it did so.

The Optional EJB Client JAR File

One common question deployers ask is, "Which classes do I need to deploy with my *client* applications that call enterprise beans?" EJB enables you to specify the exact classes you need with an *Ejb-client jar file*. An Ejb-client jar file is an archive of classes that must be deployed for any clients of a particular Ejb-jar file. You specify the name of the Ejb-client jar file in your XML deployment descriptor, as shown in Source 3.7.

```
...
<ejb-jar>

    <enterprise-beans>
    ...
    </enterprise-beans>

    <!--
    This is an optional instruction to the deployer that
    he must make the this jar file accessible to
    clients of these beans.  If this instruction does not
    exist, the deployer must make the entire Ejb-jar file
    accessible to clients.
    -->
    <ejb-client-jar>HelloClient.jar</ejb-client-jar>

</ejb-jar>
```

Source 3.7 Declaring an Ejb-client jar file within a deployment descriptor.

When you build an Ejb-client jar file, you should bundle only the files needed by the client. This typically includes interfaces, helper classes, and stubs.

You might find Ejb-client jar files useful for saving hard disk space, so you can avoid copying the entire Ejb-jar file onto the client machine. This might be useful if you're in an applet environment.

However, Ejb-client jar files are completely optional and most deployments will not make use of them. This is because hard disk space is usually not a problem, especially if the client of your application server is a Web server. Laziness will usually prevail.

Understanding How to Call Beans

We now take a look at the other half of the world—the client side. We are now customers of the beans' business logic, and we are trying to solve some real-world problem by using one or more beans together. There are two different kinds of clients.

- **Java RMI-IIOP–based clients.** These clients use the *Java Naming and Directory Interface* (JNDI) to look up objects over a network, and they use the *Java Transaction API* (JTA) to control transactions.
- **CORBA clients.** Clients can also be written to the CORBA standard. This would primarily be useful if you want to call your EJB components using another language, such as C++. CORBA clients use the *CORBA Naming Service* (COS Naming) to look up objects over the network, and they use CORBA's *Object Transaction Service* (OTS) to control transactions.

Whether you're using CORBA or RMI-IIOP, your client code typically breaks down like this:

1. Look up a home object.
2. Use the home object to create an EJB object.
3. Call business methods on the EJB object.
4. Remove the EJB object.

You're about to see how to call EJB components from RMI-IIOP clients. This is the paradigm we'll use throughout this book. If you're interested in CORBA clients, see Appendix B.

Looking up a Home Object

One of the goals of EJB is that your application code should be "write once, run anywhere." If you deploy a bean onto one machine and then switch it for a different machine, your code should not change because it is location transparent.

EJB achieves location transparency by leveraging *naming and directory services*. Naming and directory services are products that store and look up resources across a network. Some examples of directory service products are Directory Server (iPlanet), Active Directory (Microsoft), and Lotus Notes Domino Server (IBM).

Corporations traditionally have used naming and directory services to store user names, passwords, machine locations, printer locations, and so on. EJB servers exploit naming services to store location information for resources that your application code uses in an enterprise deployment. These resources could be EJB home objects, enterprise bean environment properties, database drivers, message service drivers, and other resources. By using naming services, you can write application code that does not depend on specific machine names or locations. This is all part of the EJB location transparency, and it keeps your code portable. If you decide later that resources should be located elsewhere, your code does not need to be rebuilt because the naming service can simply be updated to reflect the new resource locations. This greatly enhances maintenance of a multitier deployment that may evolve over time. This becomes absolutely necessary when purchasing prewritten software (such as enterprise beans), because your purchased components' source code will likely not be made available to you to change.

While naming and directory servers have typically run standalone, they can also run in the same process as the application server. Many containers are written in Java, and so their naming and directory services are just bunches of Java classes that run inside of the container.

Unless you're using CORBA, the de facto API used to access naming and directory services is JNDI, which we explain in Appendix A. JNDI adds value to your enterprise deployments by providing a standard interface for locating users, machines, networks, objects, and services. For example, you can use the JNDI to locate a printer on your corporate intranet. You can also use it to locate a Java object or to connect with a database. In EJB, JNDI is used to look up home objects. JNDI is also useful for locating resources across an enterprise deployment, including environment properties, database resources, and more; we'll show you how to leverage JNDI for these purposes in Chapter 10.

How to Use JNDI to Locate Home Objects

To achieve location transparency, EJB containers mask the specific locations of home objects from your enterprise beans' client code. Clients do not hard-code the machine names that home objects reside on; rather, they use JNDI to *look up* home objects. Home objects are physically located somewhere on the network—perhaps in the address space of an EJB container residing on machine #1, or perhaps on a container residing on machine #2. As a developer who writes client code to use beans, you don't care.

For clients to locate a home object, you must provide a JNDI *nickname* for your bean's home object. Clients will use this nickname to identify the home object they want. For example, our Hello World example might have a nickname *HelloHome*. You specify this nickname using the proprietary vendor-specific files that are bundled with your bean.

When you deploy your bean into the container, the container automatically *binds* the nickname *HelloHome* to the home object. Then any client on any machine across a multitier deployment can use that nickname to find home objects, without regard to physical machine locations. Clients use the JNDI API to do this. JNDI goes over the network to some naming service, or JNDI tree, to look for the home object, perhaps contacting one or more naming services in the process. Eventually the home object is found, and a reference to it is returned to the client (see Figure 3.3).

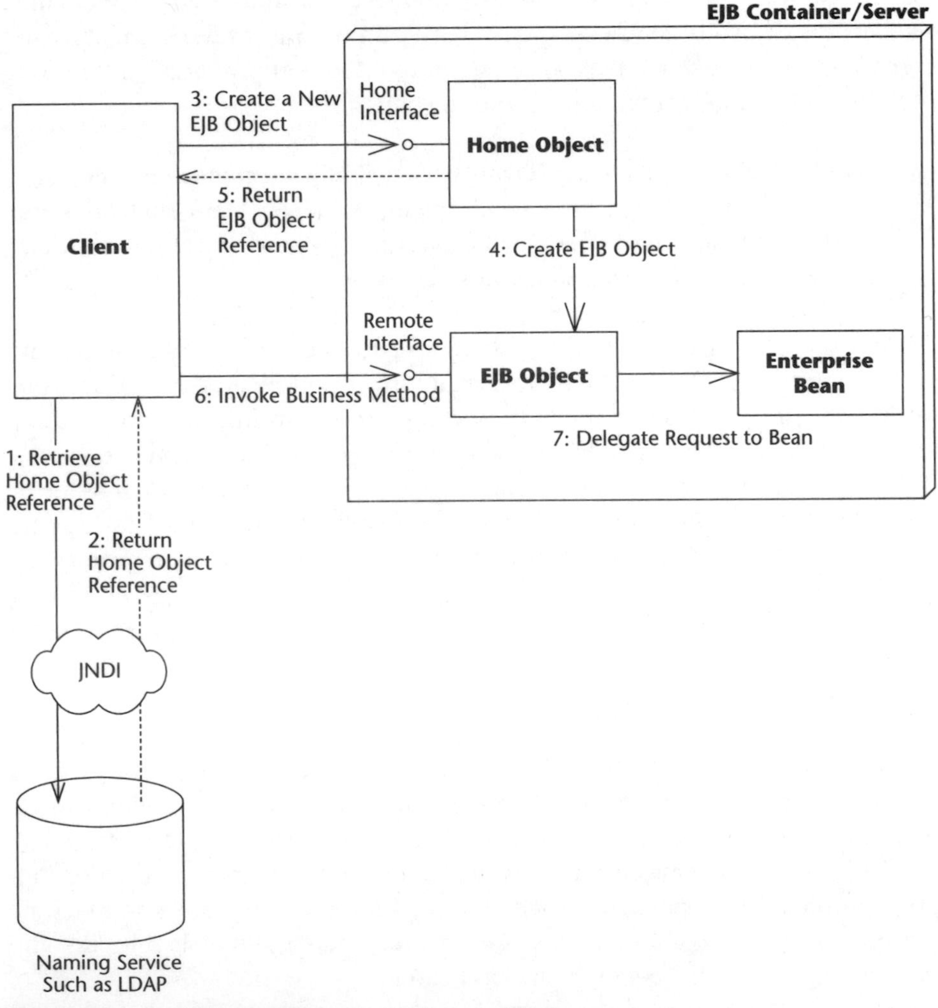

Figure 3.3 Acquiring a reference to a home object.

The complete client source code is shown in Source 3.8.

```
package examples;

import javax.naming.Context;
import javax.naming.InitialContext;
import java.util.Properties;

/**
 * This class is an example of client code that invokes
 * methods on a simple stateless session bean.
 */
public class HelloClient {

     public static void main(String[] args) throws Exception {
          /*
           * Setup properties for JNDI initialization.
           *
           * These properties will be read-in from
           * the command-line.
           */
          Properties props = System.getProperties();

          /*
           * Obtain the JNDI initial context.
           *
           * The initial context is a starting point for
           * connecting to a JNDI tree. We choose our JNDI
           * driver, the network location of the server, etc.
           * by passing in the environment properties.
           */
          Context ctx = new InitialContext(props);

          /*
           * Get a reference to the home object - the
           * factory for Hello EJB Objects
           */
          Object obj = ctx.lookup("HelloHome");


          /*
           * Home objects are RMI-IIOP objects, and so
           * they must be cast into RMI-IIOP objects
           * using a special RMI-IIOP cast.
           *
           * See Appendix A for more details on this.
           */
          HelloHome home = (HelloHome)
               javax.rmi.PortableRemoteObject.narrow(
```

Source 3.8 HelloClient.java. *(continued)*

```
                    obj, HelloHome.class);

            /*
             * Use the factory to create the Hello EJB Object
             */
            Hello hello = home.create();

            /*
             * Call the hello() method on the EJB object.  The
             * EJB object will delegate the call to the bean,
             * receive the result, and return it to us.
             *
             * We then print the result to the screen.
             */
            System.out.println(hello.hello());

            /*
             * Done with EJB Object, so remove it.
             * The container will destroy the EJB object.
             */
            hello.remove();
    }
}
```

Source 3.8 *(continued)*

The client code is self-explanatory.

Running the System

To try the deployment, you first must bring up the application server. This step varies depending on your vendor. Again, since we want to keep this book vendor-neutral, please see the book's accompanying source code for an example.

Next, run the client application. When running the client, you need to supply the client with JNDI environment information. As we explain in Appendix A, JNDI requires a minimum of two properties to retrieve an initial context:

- The name of the initial context factory. Examples are *com.sun.jndi.ldap.LdapCtxFactory* for an LDAP JNDI context, and *com.sun.jndi.cosnaming.CNCtxFactory* for a CORBA Naming Service context.
- The provider URL, indicating the location of the JNDI tree to use. Examples are *ldap://louvre:389/o5Airius.com* and *corbaloc::raccoon:3700/NameService.*

The actual parameters you need should be part of your EJB container's documentation. See the book's accompanying source code for examples of this.

For your EJB client code to work, you must take care to distribute the correct class files on the right machines. If remote client code uses home interfaces and remote interfaces, then you must deploy those class files and the necessary client stub classes in your client environment. And because clients never directly access your bean implementation, you should not deploy your bean classes in your client environment.

The Server-Side Output

When we run the client, our container shows the following debug log. (Debug logs are great for seeing what your enterprise beans are doing.)

```
setSessionContext()
ejbCreate()
hello()
ejbRemove()
```

As you can see, the container associated our bean with a session context, called *create()*, delegated a business method to the bean, and then called *remove()*. Note that some containers may give slightly different output than others—it's all implementation-specific and part of EJB product differentiation. Keep this in mind when debugging your beans.

The Client-Side Output

After running the client, you should see the following output:

```
Hello, World!
```

Implementing Component Interfaces

We wrap up this chapter with a quick design strategy. As you probably noticed, our enterprise bean class does not implement its own component interface (either remote interface or local interface). But why not? Doesn't the component interface seem like a natural fit for the interface to your bean? After all, the component interface defines every business method of the bean. Implementing your component interface would be a nifty way to perform compile-time checking to make sure your bean's method signature matches your component interface's signature.

There are two good reasons not to implement your bean's component interface:

- **Reason 1.** Component interfaces extend interfaces defined by Sun, such as *javax.ejb.EJBObject* or *javax.ejb.EJBLocalObject*. These superinterfaces define additional methods intended for client use, and you'd therefore have to provide no-op implementations of those methods in your bean. Those methods have no place in your bean class.
- **Reason 2.** Let's assume your enterprise bean wants to call a method on a *different* enterprise bean, and you want to pass a reference to your bean as a parameter to the other bean's method (similar to passing the *this* parameter in Java). How can you do this in EJB?

Remember that all clients call methods on EJB objects, not beans. Thus, if your bean calls another bean, you must pass a reference to your bean's EJB object, rather than a reference to your bean. The other bean should operate on your EJB object, and not your bean, because the other bean is a client, just like any other client, and all clients must go through EJB objects.

The danger here is if your enterprise bean class implements your EJB object's remote interface. You could accidentally pass a reference to the bean itself, rather than pass a reference to the bean's EJB object. Because your bean implements the same interface as the EJB object, the compiler would let you pass the bean itself as a *this* parameter, which is an error.

A Solution

There is an alternative way to preserve compile-time checks of your method signatures. The approach is to contain your bean's business method signatures within a common superinterface that your remote interface extends and your bean implements. You can think of this superinterface as a *business interface* that defines your business methods and is independent of EJB. The following example illustrates this concept:

```
// Business interface
public interface HelloBusinessMethods {
    public String hello() throws java.rmi.RemoteException;
}
// EJB remote interface
public interface HelloRemote extends javax.ejb.EJBObject,
HelloBusinessMethods {
}
// EJB local interface
public interface HelloLocal extends javax.ejb.EJBLocalObject,
HelloBusinessMethods {
}
```

```
// Bean implementation
public class HelloBean implements SessionBean, HelloBusinessMethods {
    public String hello() {
        return "Hello, World!";
    }
    <...define other required callbacks...>
}
```

The only problem with this approach is that the local interface throws *remote exceptions*. If you can live with that, then this design strategy works.

Summary

In this chapter, you learned how to write the component interfaces, home interface, enterprise bean class, deployment descriptor, and Ejb-jar file. You also saw how to call beans using JNDI and RMI-IIOP. Congratulations are in order: It took a while, but you've successfully completed your first Enterprise JavaBeans deployment!

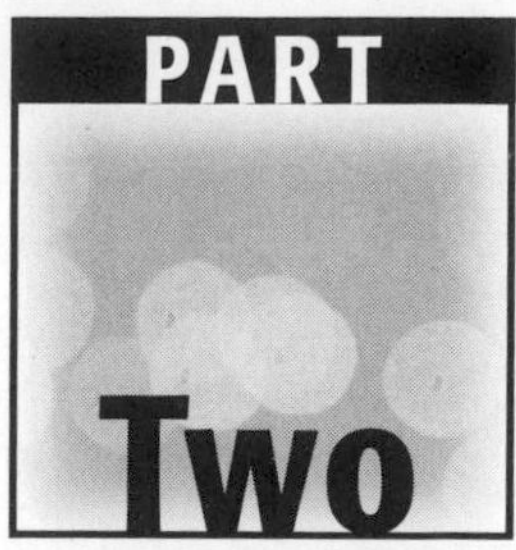

PART Two

The Triad of Beans

In Part Two of this book, we'll focus on the development details for implementing an EJB application. We'll discuss the three types of enterprise beans: session beans (Chapter 4), entity beans (Chapter 6), and message-driven beans (Chapter 9). We'll also explore their subtypes: stateless session beans, stateful session beans, session beans as Web Services (Chapter 5), bean-managed persistent entity beans (Chapter 7), and container-managed persistent entity beans (Chapter 8). Not only will we cover each of these conceptually, but we'll also write an example for each bean type. We'll end Part Two with a discussion of container-provided services (Chapter 10), such as security, the environment, and calling beans from other beans.

Part Two is essential for those of you who are ready to delve into EJB programming fundamentals. It is essential groundwork to prepare yourself for the more advanced topics, such as transactions and EJB design strategies, which are coming in Part Three.

CHAPTER

4

Introduction to Session Beans

A *session bean* represents work being performed for client code that is calling it. Session beans are business process objects that implement business logic, business rules, algorithms, and workflow. For example, a session bean can perform price quoting, order entry, video compression, banking transactions, stock trades, database operations, complex calculations, and more. They are reusable components that contain logic for business processes.

Let's examine the characteristics of session beans in detail and then code up a stateful session bean.

Session Bean Lifetime

A key difference between session beans and other bean types is the scope of their lives. A session bean instance is a relatively short-lived object. It has roughly the lifetime equivalent of a *session* or of the client code that is calling the session bean. Session bean instances are not shared between multiple clients.

For example, if the client code contacted a session bean to perform order entry logic, the EJB container is responsible for creating an instance of that session bean component. When the client later disconnects, the application server may destroy the session bean instance.

A client's session duration could be as long as a browser window is open, perhaps connecting to an e-commerce site with deployed session beans. It could also be as long as your Java applet is running, as long as a standalone application is open, or as long as another bean is using your bean.

The length of the client's *session* generally determines how long a session bean is in use—that is where the term *session bean* originated. The EJB container is empowered to destroy session beans if clients time out. If your client code is using your beans for 10 minutes, your session beans might live for minutes or hours, but probably not weeks, months, or years. Typically session beans do not survive application server crashes, nor do they survive machine crashes. They are in-memory objects that live and die with their surrounding environments.

In contrast, entity beans can live for months or even years because entity beans are *persistent objects*. Entity beans are part of a durable, permanent storage, such as a database. Entity beans can be constructed in memory from database data, and they can survive for long periods of time.

Session beans are *nonpersistent*. This means that session beans are not saved to permanent storage, whereas entity beans are. Note that session beans *can* perform database operations, but the session bean *itself* is not a persistent object.

Session Bean Subtypes

All enterprise beans hold *conversations* with clients at some level. A conversation is an interaction between a client and a bean, and it is composed of a number of method calls between the client and the bean. A conversation spans a business process for the client, such as configuring a frame-relay switch, purchasing goods over the Internet, or entering information about a new customer.

The two subtypes of session beans are *stateful session beans* and *stateless session beans*. Each is used to model different types of these conversations.

Stateful Session Beans

Some business processes are naturally drawn-out conversations over several requests. An example is an e-commerce Web store. As a user peruses an online e-commerce Web site, the user can add products to the online shopping cart. Each time the user adds a product, we perform another request. The consequence of such a business process is that the components must track the user's state (such as a shopping cart state) from request to request.

Another example of a drawn-out business process is a banking application. You may have code representing a bank teller who deals with a particular client for a long period of time. That teller may perform a number of banking transactions on behalf of the client, such as checking the account balance, depositing funds, and making a withdrawal.

A *stateful session bean* is a bean that is designed to service business processes that span multiple method requests or transactions. To accomplish this, stateful session beans *retain state* on behalf of an individual client. If a stateful session bean's state is changed during a method invocation, that same state will be available to that same client upon the following invocation.

Stateless Session Beans

Some business processes naturally lend themselves to a single request conversation. A single request business process is one that does not require state to be maintained across method invocations.

A *stateless session bean* is a bean that holds conversations that span a single method call. They are stateless because they do not hold multimethod conversations with their clients. After each method call, the container may choose to destroy a stateless session bean, or recreate it, clearing itself out of all information pertaining to past invocations. It also may choose to keep your instance around, perhaps reusing it for all clients who want to use the same session bean class. The exact algorithm is container specific. The takeaway point is this: Expect your bean to forget everything after each method call, and thus retain no conversational state from method to method. If your bean happens to hang around longer, then great—but that's your container's decision, and you shouldn't rely on it.

For a stateless session bean to be useful to a client, the client must pass all client data that the bean needs as parameters to business logic methods. Alternatively, the bean can retrieve the data it needs from an external source, such as a database.

***Stateless* really means no *conversational* state. Stateless session beans *can* contain state that is not specific to any one client, such as a database connection factory that all clients would use. You can keep this around in a private variable. So long as you're willing to lose the data in your private variable at any time, you'll be fine.**

An example of a stateless session bean is a high-performance engine that solves complex mathematical operations on a given input, such as compression of audio or video data. The client could pass in a buffer of uncompressed data, as well as a compression factor. The bean returns a compressed buffer and is then available to service a different client. The business process spanned one method request. The bean does not retain any state from previous requests.

Another example of a stateless session bean is a credit card verification component. The verifier bean takes a credit card number, expiration date, cardholder's name, and dollar amount as input. The verifier then returns a yes or no answer, depending on whether the card holder's credit is valid. Once the bean completes this task, it is available to service a different client and retains no past knowledge from the original client.

Because stateless session beans hold no conversational state, all instances of the same stateless session bean class are equivalent and indistinguishable to a client. It does not matter who has called a stateless session bean in the past, since a stateless session bean retains no state knowledge about its history. This means that *any* stateless session bean can service *any* client request because they are all exactly the same. In fact, stateless session beans can be pooled, reused, and swapped from one client to another client on *each method call!* We show this in Figure 4.1.

Since EJB 2.1, stateless session beans can also provide Web Services interfaces to clients. We will examine this important new option in details in Chapter 5.

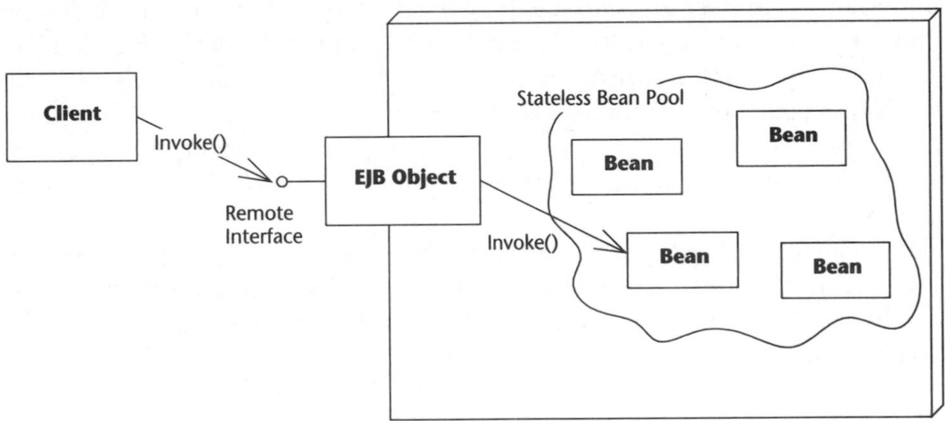

Figure 4.1 Stateless session bean pooling.

Special Characteristics of Stateful Session Beans

So far, we've seen session beans in general. We also coded up a simple stateless session bean in Chapter 3. Now let's look at the trickier flavor, stateful session beans.

Achieving the Effect of Pooling with Stateful Beans

With stateful session beans, pooling is not as simple as with stateless session beans. When a client invokes a method on a bean, the client is starting a *conversation* with the bean, and the conversational state stored in the bean must be available for that same client's next method request. Therefore, the container cannot easily pool beans and dynamically assign them to handle arbitrary client method requests, since each bean is storing state on behalf of a particular client. But we still need to achieve the effect of pooling for stateful session beans so that we can conserve resources and enhance the overall scalability of the system. After all, we only have a finite amount of available resources, such as memory, database connections, and socket connections. If the conversational state that the beans are holding is large, the EJB server could easily run out of resources. This was not a problem with stateless session beans because the container could pool only a few beans to service thousands of clients.

This problem should sound quite familiar to operating systems gurus. Whenever you run an application on a computer, you have only a fixed amount of physical memory in which to run. The operating system still must provide a way for many applications to run, even if the applications take up more aggregate memory than is available physically. To provide for this, operating systems use your hard disk as an extension of physical memory. This effectively extends your system's amount of *virtual memory*. When an application goes idle, its memory can be *swapped out* from physical memory and onto the hard disk. When the application becomes active again, any needed data is *swapped in* from the hard disk and into physical memory. This type of swapping happens often when switching between applications (called *context switching*).

EJB containers exploit this very paradigm to conserve stateful session bean resources. To limit the number of stateful session bean instances in memory, the container can *swap out* a stateful bean, saving its conversational state to a hard disk or other storage. This is called *passivation*. After passivating a stateful bean, the conversational state is safely stored away, allowing resources like memory to be reclaimed. When the original client invokes a method, the passivated conversational state is *swapped in* to a bean. This is called *activation*. This bean now resumes the conversation with the original client. Note that the bean that receives the activated state may not be the original bean instance. But that's all right because the new instance resumes its conversation from the point where the original instance was passivated.

Thus, EJB does indeed support the *effect* of pooling stateful session beans. Only a few instances can be in memory when there are actually many clients. But this pooling effect does not come for free—the passivation/activation steps could entail an input/output bottleneck. Contrast this to stateless session beans, which are easily pooled because there is no state to save.

How does the container decide which beans to activate and which beans to passivate? The answer is specific to each container. Most containers employ a *Least Recently Used* (LRU) passivation strategy, which simply means to passivate the bean that has been called the least recently. This is a good algorithm because remote clients have the habit of disconnecting from the network, leaving beans stranded without a client, ready to be passivated. If a bean hasn't been invoked in a while, the container writes it to disk.

Passivation can occur at any time, as long as a bean is not involved in a method call. It's up to the container to decide when passivation makes sense. There is one exception to this rule: Any bean involved in a *transaction* (see Chapter 12) cannot be passivated until the transaction completes.

To activate beans, most containers commonly use a *just-in-time* algorithm. Just in time means that beans should be activated on demand, as client requests come in. If a client request comes in, but that client's conversation has been passivated, the container activates the bean on demand, reading the passivated state back into memory.

In general, passivation and activation are not useful for stateless session beans. Stateless beans do not have any state to passivate/activate, so the container can simply destroy stateless beans arbitrarily.

The Rules Governing Conversational State

More rigorously, the *conversational state* of a bean follows the rules laid out by *Java object serialization*. At passivation time the container uses object serialization (or an equivalent protocol) to convert the bean's conversational state to a bit-blob and write the state out to disk. This safely tucks the state away. The bean instance (which still exists) can be reassigned to a different client, and can hold a brand-new conversation with that new client.

Activation reverses the process: A serialized blob that had been written to storage is read back into memory and converted to in-memory bean data. What makes this whole process work is that the *javax.ejb.EnterpriseBean* interface *extends java.io.Serializable*, and every enterprise bean class indirectly implements this interface.

For every Java object that is part of a bean's conversational state, the previous algorithm is reapplied recursively on those objects. Thus, object serialization constructs an entire graph of data referred to by the main bean. Note that while your beans must follow the rules for object serialization, the EJB container itself does not necessarily need to use the default serialization protocol; it could use a custom protocol to allow for flexibility and differentiation between container vendors.

More concretely, every member variable in a bean is considered to be part of the bean's conversational state if one of the following is true:

- The member variable is a nontransient primitive type.
- The member variable is a nontransient Java object (extends *java.lang.Object*).

Your bean might also hold references to container-implemented objects. The container must preserve each of the following upon passivation/activation:

- EJB object references
- Home object references
- EJB context references (see Chapter 10)
- JNDI naming contexts

For example, let's say you have the following stateful session bean code:

```
public class MySessionBean implements javax.ejb.SessionBean
{
    // State variables
    private Long myLong;
    private MySessionBeanRemoteInterface ejbObject;
    private MySessionBeanHomeInterface homeObject;
    private javax.ejb.SessionContext mySessionContext;
    private javax.naming.Context envContext;
    // EJB-required methods (fill in as necessary)
    public void setSessionContext(SessionContext ctx) { }
    public void ejbCreate() { }
    public void ejbPassivate() { }
    public void ejbActivate() { }
    public void ejbRemove() { }
    // Business methods
    ...
}
```

The container must retain the values of the preceding member variables across passivation and activation operations.

Activation and Passivation Callbacks

Let's now look at what actually happens to your bean during passivation and activation. When an EJB container passivates a bean, the container writes the bean's conversational state to secondary storage, such as a file or database. The container informs the bean that it's about to perform passivation by calling the bean's required *ejbPassivate()* callback method. *ejbPassivate()* is a warning to the bean that its held conversational state is about to be swapped out.

It's important that the container inform the bean using *ejbPassivate()* so that the bean can relinquish held resources. These held resources include database connections, open sockets, open files, or other resources that it doesn't make sense to save to disk or that can't be transparently saved using object serialization. The EJB container calls the *ejbPassivate()* method to give the bean a chance to release these resources or deal with the resources as the bean sees fit. Once the container's *ejbPassivate()* callback method into your bean is complete, your bean must be in a state suitable for passivation. For example:

```
import javax.ejb.*;
public class MyBean implements SessionBean {
    public void ejbPassivate() {
        <close socket connections, etc...>
    }
    ...
}
```

The passivation process is shown in Figure 4.2. This is a typical stateful bean passivation scenario. The client has invoked a method on an EJB object that does not have a bean tied to it in memory. The container's pool size of beans has been reached. Thus, the container needs to passivate a bean before handling this client's request.

Exactly the opposite process occurs during the activation process. The serialized conversational state is read back into memory, and the container reconstructs the in-memory state using object serialization or the equivalent. The container then calls the bean's required *ejbActivate()* method. *ejbActivate()* gives the bean a chance to restore the open resources it released during *ejbPassivate()*. For example:

```
import javax.ejb.*;
public class MyBean implements SessionBean {
    public void ejbActivate() {
        <open socket connections, etc...>
    }
    ...
}
```

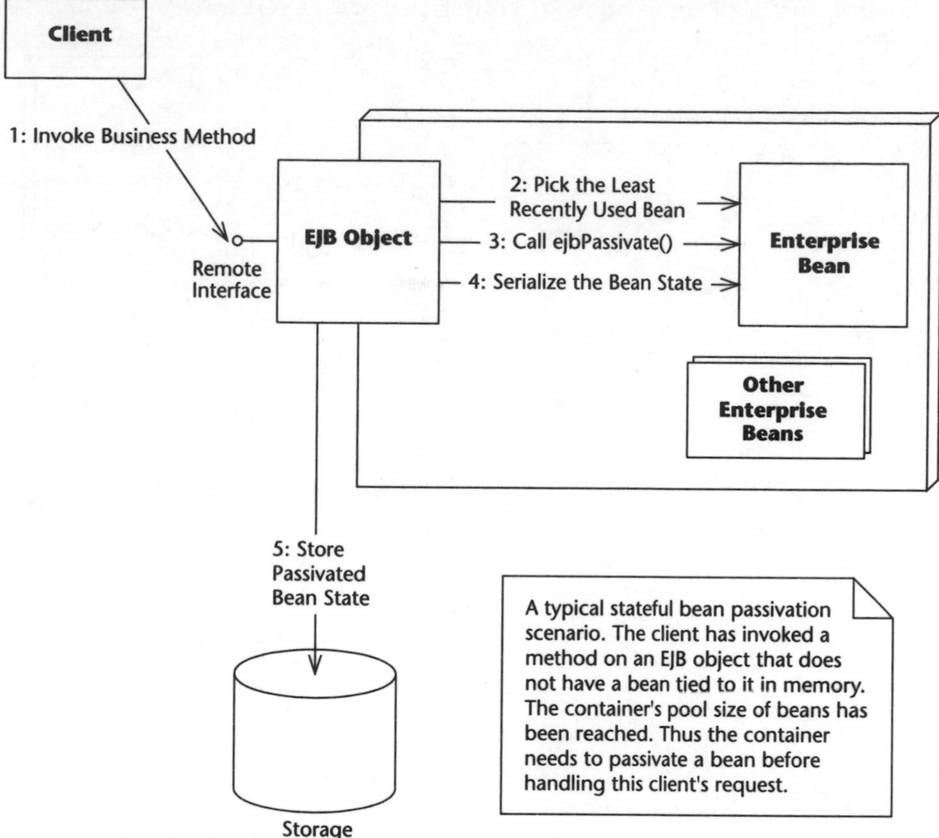

Figure 4.2 Passivation of a stateful bean.

The activation process is shown in Figure 4.3. This is a typical just-in-time stateful bean activation scenario. The client has invoked a method on an EJB object whose stateful bean had been passivated.

You probably don't need to worry about implementing *ejbPassivate()* and *ejbActivate()* unless you are using open resources, such as socket connections or database connections, that must be reestablished after activation. In most cases, you can simply leave these methods empty.

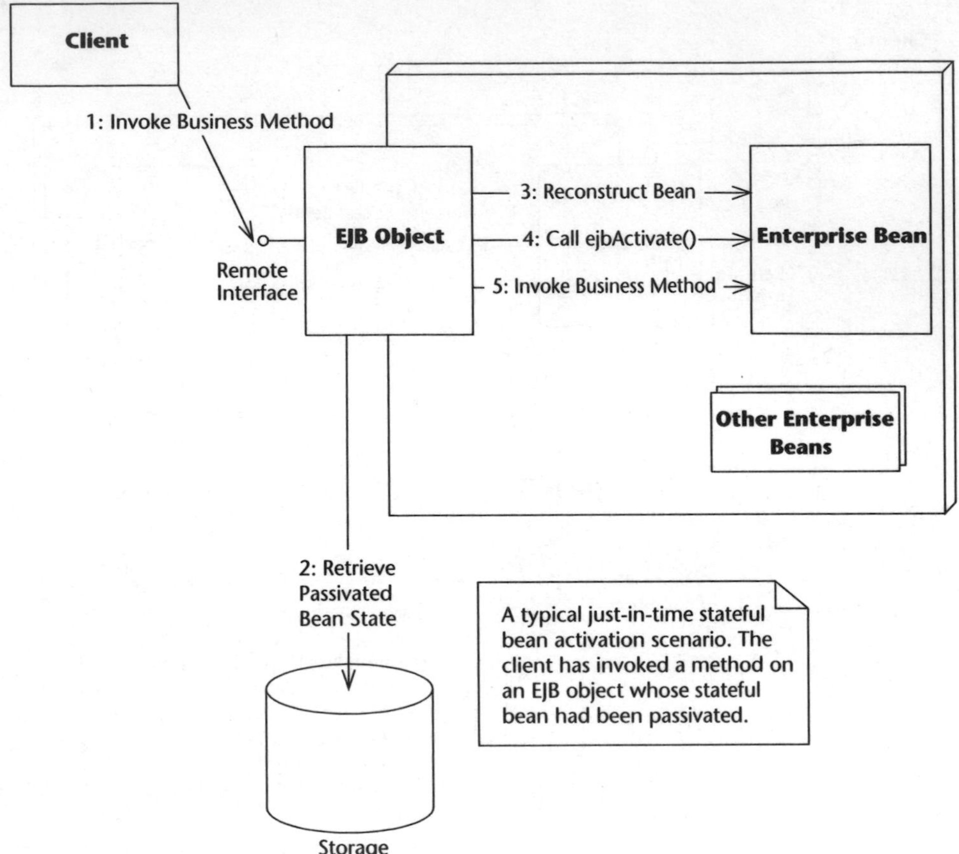

Figure 4.3 Activation of a stateful bean.

Method Implementation Summary

Table 4.1 summarizes how to develop session bean classes.

A Simple Stateful Session Bean

Let's put our stateful session bean knowledge to use by programming a simple stateful bean. Our bean will be a counter bean, and it will be responsible for simply counting up one by one. The current count will be stored within the bean and will increment as client requests arrive. Thus, our bean will be stateful and will hold a multimethod conversation with a particular client.

Table 4.1 Required Methods for Session Bean Classes

METHOD	DESCRIPTION	TYPICAL IMPLEMENTATION (STATELESS SESSION BEANS)	TYPICAL IMPLEMENTATION (STATEFULL SESSION BEANS)
setSessionContext (SessionContext ctx)	Associates your bean with a session context. Your bean can query the context about its current transactional state, its current security state, and more.	Store the context away in a member variable so the context can be queried later.	Store the context away in a member variable so the context can be queried later
ejbCreate()	Initializes your session.	Perform any initialization your bean needs, such as setting member variables to the argument values passed in. Note: You can define several *ejbCreate()* methods, and each can take different arguments. You must provide at least one *ejbCreate()* method in your session bean.	Perform any initialization your bean needs, such as setting member variables to the argument values passed in. Note: You can define only a single empty *ejbCreate()* method with no parameters. If it had parameters, and the bean initialized itself to those parameters, the bean would never remember what it initialized itself to upon subsequent calls, since it is stateless!
ejbPassivate()	Called immediately before your bean passivated (swapped out to disk because there are too many instantiated beans).	Release any resources your bean may be holding.	Unused because there is no conversational state; leave empty.
ejbActivate()	Called immediately before your bean is activated (swapped in from disk because a client needs your bean).	Acquire any resources your bean needs, such as those released during *ejbPassivate()*.	Unused because there is no conversational state; leave empty.
ejbRemove()	Called by the container immediately before your bean is removed from memory.	Prepare your bean for destruction Free all resources you may have allocated.	Prepare your bean for destruction. Free all resources you may have allocated.

The Count Bean's Remote Interface

First let's define our bean's remote interface. The code is shown in Source 4.1.

```
package examples;

import javax.ejb.*;
import java.rmi.RemoteException;

/**
 * These are CountBean's business logic methods.
 *
 * This interface is what clients operate on when they
 * interact with EJB objects. The container vendor will
 * implement this interface; the implemented object is
 * the EJB object, which delegates invocations to the
 * actual bean.
 */
public interface Count extends EJBObject {

    /**
     * Increments the int stored as conversational state
     */
    public int count() throws RemoteException;
}
```

Source 4.1 Count.java.

Our remote interface defines a single business method, *count()*, which we will implement in the enterprise bean class.

The Count Bean

Our bean implementation has one business method, *count()*, which is responsible for incrementing an integer member variable, called *val*. The conversational state is the *val* member variable. Source 4.2 shows the code for our counter bean.

```
package examples;

import javax.ejb.*;

/**
 * Demonstration Stateful Session Bean.  This Bean is initialized
 * to some integer value, and has a business method which
```

Source 4.2 CountBean.java.

```
 * increments the value.
 *
 * This example shows the basics of how to write a stateful
 * session bean, and how passivation/activation works.
 */
public class CountBean implements SessionBean {

     // The current counter is our conversational state.
     public int val;

     //
     // Business methods
     //

     /**
      * Counts up
      */
     public int count() {
          System.out.println("count()");
          return ++val;
     }

     //
     // EJB-required methods
     //

     public void ejbCreate(int val) throws CreateException {
          this.val = val;
          System.out.println("ejbCreate()");
     }

     public void ejbRemove() {
          System.out.println("ejbRemove()");
     }

     public void ejbActivate() {
          System.out.println("ejbActivate()");
     }

     public void ejbPassivate() {
          System.out.println("ejbPassivate()");
     }

     public void setSessionContext(SessionContext ctx) {
     }
}
```

Source 4.2 *(continued)*

Note the following about our bean:

- The bean implements *javax.ejb.SessionBean* (described fully in Appendix E). This means the bean must define all methods in the *SessionBean* interface. By looking at the bean, you can see we've defined them but kept them fairly trivial.
- Our *ejbCreate*() initialization method takes a parameter, *val*. This method customizes our bean to the client's needs. Our *ejbCreate()* method is responsible for beginning a conversation with the client. It uses *val* as the starting state of the counter.
- The *val* member variable obeys the rules for conversational state because it is serializable. Thus, it lasts across method calls and is automatically preserved during passivation/activation.

Notice, too, that our code has a *setSessionContext()* method. This associates our bean with a *session context*, which is a specific EJB context used only for session beans. Our bean can call back to the container through this object. The session context interface looks like this:

```
public interface javax.ejb.SessionContext
    extends javax.ejb.EJBContext
{
 public javax.ejb.EJBLocalObject getEJBLocalObject();
 public javax.ejb.EJBObject getEJBObject();
}
```

Notice that the *SessionContext* interface extends the *EJBContext* interface, giving session beans access to all the methods defined in *EJBContext* (see Chapter 3 or Appendix E).

Specific to session beans, the *getEJBObject()* and *getEJBLocalObject()* methods are useful if your bean needs to call another bean and if you want to pass a reference to your own bean. In Java, an object can obtain a reference to itself with the *this* keyword. In EJB, however, a bean cannot use the *this* keyword and pass it to other beans because all clients invoke methods on beans indirectly through a bean's EJB object. Thus, a bean can refer to itself by using a reference to its EJB object, rather than the *this* keyword.

The Count Bean's Home Interface

To complete our stateful bean code, we must define a home interface. The home interface details how to create and destroy our Count EJB object. The code for our home interface is in Source 4.3.

```
package examples;

import javax.ejb.*;
import java.rmi.RemoteException;

/**
 * This is the home interface for CountBean.  This interface
 * is implemented by the EJB Server's glue-code tools - the
 * implemented object is called the Home Object, and serves
 * as a factory for EJB Objects.
 *
 * One create() method is in this Home Interface, which
 * corresponds to the ejbCreate() method in the CountBean file.
 */
public interface CountHome extends EJBHome {

    /*
     * This method creates the EJB Object.
     *
     * @param val Value to initialize counter to
     *
     * @return The newly created EJB Object.
     */
  Count create(int val) throws RemoteException, CreateException;
}
```

Source 4.3 CountHome.java.

Because we implement *javax.ejb.EJBHome,* our home interface gets the *remove()* destroy method for free.

The Count Bean's Deployment Descriptor

Now that we have all our Java files for our bean, we need to define the deployment descriptor to identify the bean's settings to the container. The deployment descriptor settings we use are listed in Source 4.4.

```
<!DOCTYPE ejb-jar PUBLIC
    "-//Sun Microsystems, Inc.//DTD Enterprise JavaBeans 2.0//EN"
    "http://java.sun.com/dtd/ejb-jar_2_0.dtd">

<ejb-jar>
  <enterprise-beans>
    <session>
      <ejb-name>Count</ejb-name>
      <home>examples.CountHome</home>
```

Source 4.4 ejb-jar.xml. *(continued)*

```
      <remote>examples.Count</remote>
      <ejb-class>examples.CountBean</ejb-class>
      <session-type>Stateful</session-type>
      <transaction-type>Container</transaction-type>
    </session>
  </enterprise-beans>
</ejb-jar>
```

Source 4.4 *(continued)*

Note that our bean's stateful nature is defined declaratively in the deployment descriptor. We never introduce the notion of a bean being stateful in the bean code itself. This enables us to easily switch from the stateful to the stateless paradigm and back.

The Count Bean's Proprietary Descriptor and Ejb-jar File

To complete our component, we need to write any proprietary files that our application server may require and package those files and our bean together into an Ejb-jar file. These steps are similar to our Hello, World! example.

One special setting we will try to make (which is vendor specific) is to force the container to limit the number of bean instances that it will keep active to two beans. Note that this may or may not be possible with your particular application server. We will then create three beans and observe how the container passivates instances to service requests.

To save space, in future examples we'll consider that the proprietary descriptors, the Ejb-jar file, and the deployment itself are implied steps. If you're really curious about how this is achieved, take a look at the source code accompanying the book.

The Count Bean's Client Code

Now that our bean is deployed, we can write some Java code to test our beans. Our client code performs the following steps:

1. We acquire a JNDI initial context.
2. We locate the home object using JNDI.
3. We use the home object to create three different Count EJB objects. Thus, we are creating three different conversations and are simulating three different clients.
4. We limited the number of active bean instances to two beans, so during the previous step some of the three beans must have been passivated. We print out a message during the *ejbPassivate()* callback to illustrate this.

5. We call *count()* on each EJB object. This forces the container to activate the instances, restoring the conversations to memory once again. We print out a message during the *ejbActivate()* callback to illustrate this.
6. Finally, all the EJB objects are removed.

The code appears in Source 4.5.

```
package examples;

import javax.ejb.*;
import javax.naming.*;
import java.util.Properties;

/**
 * This class is a simple example of client code.
 *
 * We create 3 EJB Objects in this example, but we only allow
 * the container to have 2 in memory.  This illustrates how
 * beans are passivated to storage.
 */
public class CountClient {

     public static void main(String[] args) {

          try {
               /*
                * Get System properties for JNDI initialization
                */
               Properties props = System.getProperties();

               /*
                * Get a reference to the Home Object - the
                * factory for EJB Objects
                */
               Context ctx = new InitialContext(props);
               CountHome home = (CountHome)
                 javax.rmi.PortableRemoteObject.narrow(
                   ctx.lookup("CountHome"), CountHome.class);

               /*
                * An array to hold 3 Count EJB Objects
                */
               Count count[] = new Count[3];

               int countVal = 0;

               /*
                * Create and count() on each member of array
```

Source 4.5 CountClient.java. *(continued)*

```
         */
        System.out.println("Instantiating beans...");
        for (int i=0; i < 3; i++) {
             /*
              * Create an EJB Object and initialize
              * it to the current count value.
              */
             count[i] = home.create(countVal);

             /*
              * Add 1 and print
              */
             countVal = count[i].count();

             System.out.println(countVal);

             /*
              * Sleep for 1/2  second
              */
             Thread.sleep(500);
        }

        /*
         * Let's call count() on each EJB Object to
         * make sure the beans were passivated and
         * activated properly.
         */
        System.out.println("Calling count() on beans...");
        for (int i=0; i < 3; i++) {

             /*
              * Add 1 and print
              */
             countVal = count[i].count();

             System.out.println(countVal);

             /*
              * Sleep for 1/2  second
              */
             Thread.sleep(500);
        }

        /*
         * Done with EJB Objects, so remove them
         */
        for (int i=0; i < 3; i++) {
             count[i].remove();
        }
```

Source 4.5 *(continued)*

```
            }  catch (Exception e) {
                e.printStackTrace();
            }
        }
    }
```

Source 4.5 *(continued)*

Running the Client

To run the client, you need to know the parameters your JNDI service provider uses. This should also be part of your container's documentation. See the book's accompanying source code for scripts.

Client-Side Output

After running the client, we see the following output:

```
Instantiating beans...
1
2
3
Calling count() on beans...
2
3
4
```

We first created three beans and then called *count()* on each. As expected, the beans incremented their values by one each during the second pass, so output is as expected. But were our beans really passivated and activated? Let's check the server log.

Server-Side Output

If the container log yields the following results:

```
ejbCreate()
count()
ejbCreate()
count()
ejbCreate()
ejbPassivate()
count()
ejbPassivate()
ejbActivate()
count()
ejbPassivate()
ejbActivate()
```

```
count()
ejbPassivate()
ejbActivate()
count()
ejbPassivate()
ejbActivate()
ejbRemove()
ejbActivate()
ejbRemove()
ejbRemove()
```

Then, as you can see from the passivation/activation messages in the log, the container is indeed passivating and activating beans to conserve system resources. Because the client-side output is correct, each of our beans' conversational state was retained properly. However, not all containers enable you to control their internal bean caching at the granularity of a single bean instance. If your actual application server product does not trigger passivation with the small number of beans in this example, you may have to increase the number of session bean instances to see the effects of activation and passivation.

Life Cycle Diagrams for Session Beans

Now that we've written a complete stateless session bean (in Chapter 3) and a complete stateful session bean (in this chapter), let's see what's happening behind the scenes.

Figure 4.4 shows the life cycle of a stateless session bean inside the container. Note that in this diagram, the client is not calling methods on the bean, since the client never accesses a bean directly. (The client always goes through the container.) In the diagram, the container (that is, the home object and EJB objects) is calling methods on our bean.

Let's walk through this diagram.

1. At **first, the bean instance does not exist.** Perhaps the application server has just started up.
2. **The container decides it wants to instantiate a new bean.** When does the container decide it wants to instantiate a new bean? It depends on the container's policy for *pooling* beans. The container may decide to instantiate 10 beans all at once when the application server first starts because you told the container to do so using the vendor-specific files that you ship with your bean. Each of those beans are equivalent (because they are stateless) and they can be reused for many different clients.

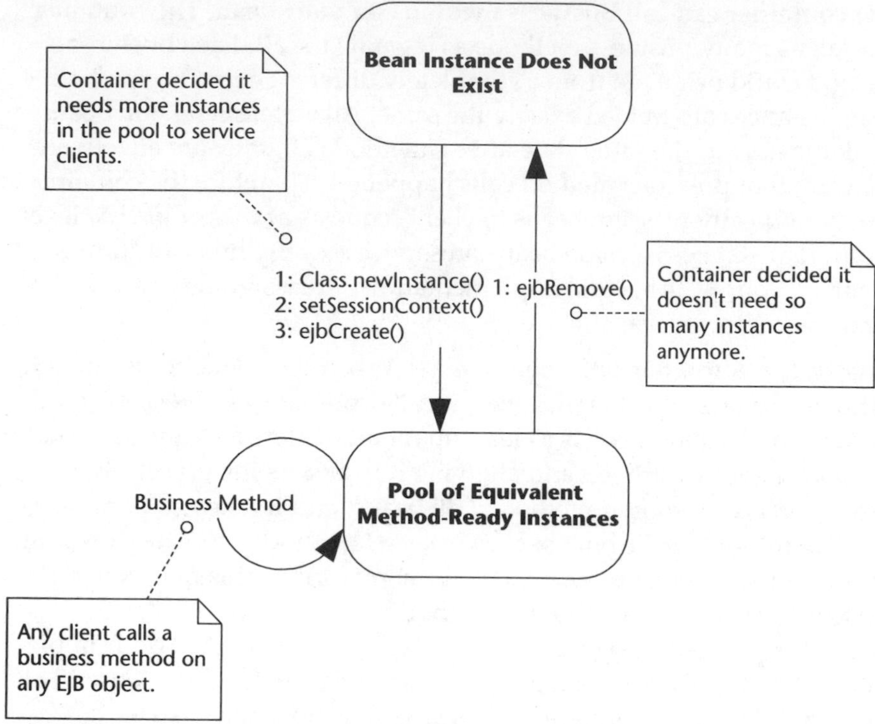

Figure 4.4 The life cycle of a stateless session bean.

3. **The container instantiates your bean.** The container calls *Class.newInstance("HelloBean.class")* on your session bean class, which is the dynamic equivalent of calling *new HelloBean()*. The container does this so that the container is not hard-coded to any specific bean name; the container is generic and works with any bean. This action calls your bean's default constructor, which can do any necessary initialization.
4. **The container calls setSessionContext().** This associates you with a context object, which enables you to make callbacks to the container (see Chapter 9 for some examples of these callbacks).
5. **The container calls ejbCreate().** This initializes your bean. Note that because stateless session beans' *ejbCreate()* methods take no parameters, clients never supply any critical information that bean instances need to start up. EJB containers can exploit this and pre-create instances of your stateless session beans. In general when a client creates or destroys a bean using the home object, that action might not necessarily correspond with literally creating or destroying in-memory bean objects, because the EJB container controls their life cycles to allow for pooling between heterogeneous clients.

6. **The container can call business methods on your bean.** The container can call as many business methods as it wants to call. Each business method could originate from a completely different client because all bean instances are treated exactly the same. All stateless session beans think they are in the same state after a method call; they are effectively unaware that previous method calls happened. Therefore the container can dynamically reassign beans to client requests at the *per-method* level. A different stateless session bean can service *each* method call from a client. Of course, the actual implementation of reassigning beans to clients is container-specific.

7. **Finally, the container calls *ejbRemove()*.** When the container is about to remove your session bean instance, it calls your bean's *ejbRemove()* callback method. *ejbRemove()* is a clean-up method, alerting your bean that it is about to be destroyed and allowing it to end its life gracefully. *ejbRemove()* is a required method of all beans, and it takes no parameters. Therefore there is only one *ejbRemove()* method per bean. This is in stark contrast to *ejbCreate()*, which has many forms. This makes perfect sense: Why should a destructive method be personalized for each client? (This is an analogous concept to destructors in C11.) Your implementation of *ejbRemove()* should prepare your bean for destruction. This means you need to free all resources you may have allocated.

Figure 4.5 shows the life cycle of a stateful session bean. Remember that in the diagram, the container (not the client) is calling methods on our bean instance.

The life cycle for stateful session beans is similar to that of stateless session beans. The big differences are as follows:

- There is no pool of equivalent instances because each instance contains state.
- There are transitions for passivating and activating conversational state.

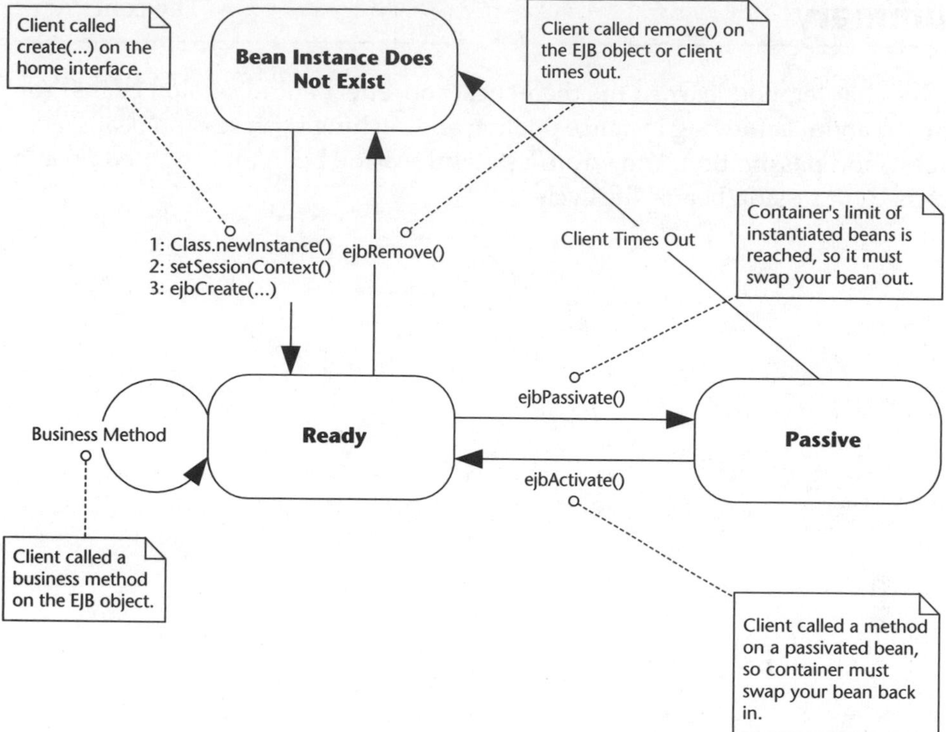

Figure 4.5 Life cycle of a stateful session bean.

DON'T RELY ON EJBREMOVE()

Your container can call *ejbRemove()* at any time, even if the container decides that the bean's life has expired (perhaps due to a very long timeout). Note that the container may *never* call your bean's *ejbRemove()* method, for example if the container crashes or if a critical exception occurs. You must be prepared for this contingency. For example, if your bean performs shopping cart operations, it might store temporary shopping cart data in a database. Your application should provide a utility that runs periodically to remove any abandoned shopping carts from the database because otherwise the database resources associated with the abandoned shopping carts will never be freed.

Summary

In this chapter, you learned the theoretical concepts behind session beans. You learned about achieving instance pooling and caching with session beans, activation, and passivation. You wrote a stateful session bean that counted up and touched on session beans' life cycle.

CHAPTER

5

Writing Session Bean Web Services

One of the most important enhancements of EJB 2.1 over its predecessors is the support it offers for Web Services. Web Services are a way to build and integrate large-scale systems within and between companies by sending XML messages to well-defined, modular interfaces.

In this chapter, we will discuss central Web Services concepts and then explain how EJB supports the writing of Web Service implementations and Web Services clients. We will show how EJB enables you to build Web Services from stateless session beans and take a closer look at the *Java API for XML-based RPC* (JAX-RPC) that enables you to access Web Services from Java clients.

Web Services Concepts

Let's take a quick look again at some fundamental concepts. As mentioned in Chapter 1, Web Services are a way of building a *Service-Oriented Architecture* (SOA). SOA is an architectural approach to structuring large-scale, distributed applications that integrate heterogeneous applications behind *service* interfaces. Figure 5.1 shows the basic model of a lookup in a service-oriented architecture as supported by Web Services technologies.

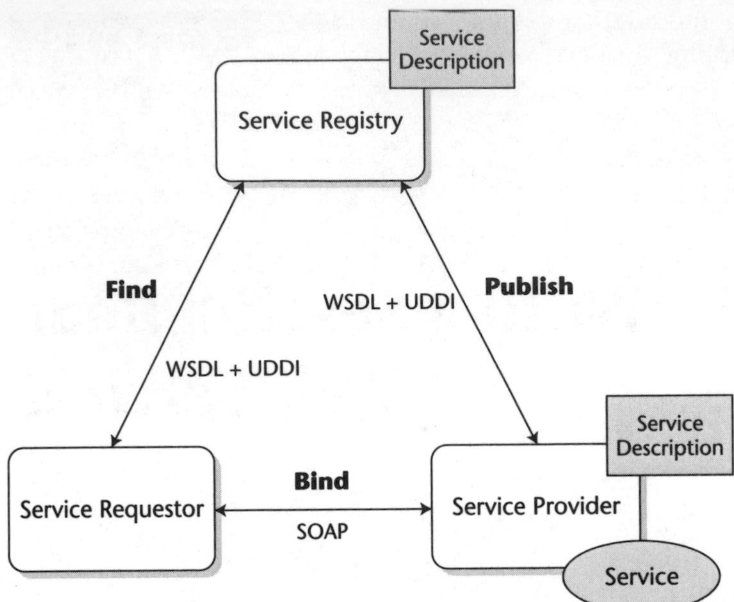

Figure 5.1 Service-oriented architecture with Web Services.

A service provider creates an abstract service definition that it publishes in a service registry. With Web Services, the description is a *Web Services Definition Language* (WSDL) file, and the registry follows the *Universal Description, Discovery, and Integration* (UDDI) standard. A service requestor can find the service description, possibly using a set of selection criteria to query the registry. If a suitable description is found, the requestor can bind to the service. You can find simple examples of Web Services collected on Web sites such xmethods.org, for example a service to determine if a given Internet domain name is taken, or to convert temperature values from Fahrenheit to Celsius. More realistic Web Services are built today in larger-scale, in-house architectures that interconnect existing, heterogeneous applications, for example, a billing application and a report generator.

A service interface is similar to an object or bean interface, but the contract between the interface and its clients is more flexible and the client and the service implementation are less closely coupled than in EJB or other distribution platforms. This looser coupling allows client and service implementations to run on very different platforms, for example, a Microsoft .NET client could access a service running in a J2EE application server. Also, services are generally coarser-grained entities than objects are. From a client perspective, their life cycles are more static because services don't just pop up and go away but stay around longer than your average object, even if services are implemented using object technology.

SOAs emphasize modularity through standardized interfaces, flexibility through looser coupling, and extensibility through using XML. All of this is important in the B2B scenarios, which are the primary targets of Web Services. Web Services are not just another RPC mechanism for your intranet applications but rather a great help in settings where no single middleware platform is applicable. As an example, consider the B2B relationships between a car manufacturer and its suppliers. Each of these companies has its own IT infrastructure and set of applications, such as payroll, inventory, order processing, and so on. Also, each supplier builds parts for more than just a single car manufacturer, and each manufacturer buys parts from different suppliers. In a situation like this, it is highly unlikely that any of the involved parties will be able to switch to a specific middleware for the sake of the business relationship with just a single partner. For any given supplier, building a middleware X adapter (for example CORBA) to its order processing application to interoperate with customer A, and then building another adapter Y (say, MQSeries) to interoperate with customer B, and so on is going to be too much effort and too expensive.

This is what standardization efforts in the past (such as EDI) tried but failed to tackle on a larger scale. Web Services can thus be seen as a new attempt at building universally agreed upon standards that hide the differences behind standardized interfaces. This time, the standards are going to be based on XML and on established Internet protocols. So why do we talk about integration and interoperability so much in the context of Web Services? Aren't EJBs interoperable already, thanks to the standardization of the RMI/IIOP protocol and the container and bean APIs? EJBs are interoperable in the sense of vendor and platform independence: there are J2EE/EJB products from many different vendors that run on different platforms and still talk to each other. These containers can host your beans no matter which product they were written for, so you also get portability. But there is language dependency: EJBs are coded in Java and nothing else, so you cannot create interoperate bean implementations written in different languages.

On the one hand, this is great because of Java's portability (write once run anywhere). On the other hand, portability is not always an issue, and you may actually need a specific language for your project if you wanted to leverage, say, a large amount of C++ or COBOL code for business objects that your company has investments in. With EJB, a common approach is to build wrapper beans that talk to an adapter in C++, most likely based on CORBA. Another way of putting this is to say that EJBs prescribe not only the component interfaces and client contracts, but also an implementation model. With Web Services, there is no single implementation framework; a contract with a Web Service involves only its interface. Web Services interfaces are defined in *the Web Services Description Language* (WSDL). Web Services can be implemented in any language. Of course, we will be building them with EJB in this book, so they will be written in Java.

Web Services Standards

The set of de-facto standards that make up Web Services today can be summarized in a simple equation:

Web Services = WSDL + SOAP + UDDI

Let's take a quick look at WSDL and SOAP. We won't cover UDDI here because it is not necessarily required: Note that the actual service usage in Figure 5.1 does not depend on the existence of UDDI. The requestor may actually have known the service and its endpoint address without the registry. Also note that the registry is not simply a naming service but supports queries for services that obey a given predicate. At this stage in the life of Web Services, however, it is unclear whether dynamic service lookups in UDDI registry will ever happen on a larger scale than within enterprises. It did not happen with similar concepts that were available earlier, such as CORBA Trading Service.

If you have been around in distributed computing for a while some of the technology in the Web Services arena will appear like a déja vu. Figure 5.1, for example, looks a lot like the RM-ODP trader and later CORBA Trading Service. Many aspects that Web Services address are not new per se but have simply not been solved on a larger scale.

WSDL

To give you a first impression of a service description in WSDL, here is the definition of the HelloWorld component that we used in Chapter 3:

```
<?xml version="1.0" encoding="UTF-8"?>
<definitions name="HelloWorldWS" targetNamespace="urn:examples">
<types/>
   <message name="HelloInterface_hello"/>
   <message name="HelloInterface_helloResponse">
      <part name="result" type="xsd:string"/>
   </message>
   <portType name="HelloInterface">
      <operation name="hello">
         <input message="tns:HelloInterface_hello"/>
         <output message="tns:HelloInterface_helloResponse"/>
      </operation>
   </portType>
   <binding name="HelloInterfaceBinding" type="tns:HelloInterface">
      <soap:binding transport="http://schemas.xmlsoap.org/soap/
http" style="rpc"/>
      <operation name="hello">
         <soap:operation soapAction=""/>
```

```
            <input>
               <soap:body
encodingStyle="http://schemas.xmlsoap.org/soap/encoding/"
                          use="encoded" namespace="urn:examples"/>
            </input>
            <output>
               <soap:body
encodingStyle="http://schemas.xmlsoap.org/soap/encoding/"
                          use="encoded" namespace="urn:examples"/>
            </output>
         </operation>
      </binding>
      <service name="HelloWorldWS">
         <port name="HelloInterfacePort"
binding="tns:HelloInterfaceBinding">
            <soap:address location="http://localhost:8080/HelloBean"/>
         </port>
      </service>
</definitions>
```

Some good news first before we look at some of the details: Relax, you don't have to write this XML document yourself. This interface description was automatically generated from a Java interface using a generator tool: the *wscompile* tool that comes with the J2EE SDK.

A number of things are worth noting about the HelloWorld WSDL:

- **The number of language concepts used here is larger than in Java.** We have a *service* that provides one or more *ports* at an address. Ports represent the service interfaces and have *bindings* to protocols.
- **The service description includes an endpoint address.** The WSDL is thus like a Java interface and an object reference joined together. In other words, Web Services do not have distinct identities. They are not objects and must be viewed as modules. There is no client-visible state, and you cannot compare two references for equality!
- **Operations are specified in terms of input and output messages rather than parameters and return values.** These have to be represented as elements ("parts") of input and output messages. Here, there is only the part that is actually transferred inside a message: the *result* part of type *xsd:string* in the *HelloInterface_helloResponse* message.
- **The binding for the service is a SOAP binding.** There can be other bindings in theory, but in practice SOAP is the only available option today. Also note that the *soap:binding* has an attribute *style="rpc"*, so there must be other possible styles. Currently, the only other style for exchanging SOAP messages is document-style, which means that there is no specific representation of a called operation in the SOAP message's body.

SOAP

The SOAP protocol defines an XML message format for Web Services and their clients. Until version 1.1, SOAP was an acronym for Simple Object Access Protocol, but it was turned into a proper name for version 1.2 of the standard. That SOAP starts with the three letters SOA is sheer coincidence. As we just mentioned, the targets of SOAP messages (both services and clients) are not objects in the object-oriented sense, so the acronym was a misnomer anyway.

The SOAP message format is very simple. In a message exchange between a client and the HelloWorld service, the request message would look like this:

```
POST /HelloBean HTTP/1.1
Content-Type: text/xml; charset="utf-8"
Content-Length: 398
SOAPAction: ""
Host: falcon:8080

<?xml version="1.0" encoding="UTF-8"?>
<env:Envelope xmlns:env="http://schemas.xmlsoap.org/soap/envelope/">
   <env:Body>
      <ans1:hello xmlns:ans1="urn:examples"/>
   </env:Body>
</env:Envelope>
```

This is an actual message as sent over the wire. As you can see, the message has two parts, an *HTTP POST* request header, and an XML document in the HTTP payload. This XML document is a SOAP envelope, which represents a request. The envelope contains a body element, which in turn contains the hello element that represents the operation call.

The reply message is just as simple:

```
HTTP/1.1 200 OK
SOAPAction: ""
Content-Type: text/xml;charset=utf-8
Transfer-Encoding: chunked

<?xml version="1.0" encoding="UTF-8"?>
<env:Envelope xmlns:env="http://schemas.xmlsoap.org/soap/envelope/"
 xmlns:xsi="http://www.w3.org/2001/XMLSchema-instance"
 xmlns:ns0="urn:examples">
   <env:Body>
      <ns0:helloResponse>
         <result xsi:type="xsd:string">Hello, World!</result>
      </ns0:helloResponse>
   </env:Body>
</env:Envelope>
```

Again, there is the HTTP header and an XML document that contains a SOAP envelope. This time, the SOAP body represents the result of the operation call, which is a single result element of type string.

The two messages reproduced here serve to illustrate another key term that is often used in the context of Web Services. The SOAP protocol is extremely *lightweight* in the sense that it is very simple to use and does not make many assumptions about the behavior of clients and services. The SOAP protocol is not lightweight in terms of compactness and high performance. If uncompressed, there is a large transmission overhead when compared to binary representations, for example in CORBA's IIOP protocol. The XML parsing required to marshal and demarshal messages can also become CPU-intensive for larger messages. But this is beside the point: Web Services are not designed to deliver hitherto unknown performance but to enable integration where high-performance middleware is much less useful than lightweight protocols that can be implemented easily by simple scripts. (For an interesting discussion of scripting languages as middleware, refer to Steve Vinoski's article on *Middleware Dark Matter* available at www.iona.com/hyplan/vinoski/.)

XML Artifacts and Platform Independence

Web Services help with the integration of heterogeneous, distributed systems by using standardized XML documents for many different aspects of service design, deployment, lookup, and usage that leverages a broad array of open standards and sophisticated tools that are widely available. Many of the tools, like Apache Axis SOAP, IBM WSDL4J toolkit, and JBoss Application Server, are also in the open source arena.

In a sense, the XML usage that we just looked at is perhaps the biggest technological advantage here because many of the practical virtues, like loose coupling and platform independence, follow from XML itself and the way the different XML technologies are combined. XML documents are also *self-describing* in that they contain a description of their structure in their markup tags. This does not mean that you will be able to understand arbitrary documents without any prior knowledge. What it does mean is that you can easily skip parts of a message that you are not concerned with and don't understand, and just deal with those parts that do concern you. This may sound trivial at first, but it has important consequences in that this enables the decoupling of applications and middleware.

To understand this point, recall that clients of your beans have to use a fixed component interface. If that interface changes because a parameter is added to a method signature, you will have to rebuild, reassemble, and redeploy not only your beans, but your clients will also have to be recompiled. This is not loose coupling because you cannot develop the different components of your application individually. If one piece changes, the others have to change, too.

Applications are not as flexibly extensible as we would like. With IIOP-based request messages, all parties must have complete type information because they are not able to demarshal messages otherwise. There is no skipping of unknown parts of a message in IIOP. These restrictions do not exist with interfaces written in XML and with XML messages.

XML also enables you to write *extensible* specifications (after all, that's the X in XML): data types in interface definitions can contain extensibility points from the outset. These extensibility points make use of a wildcard *any* type and, optional elements in sequences, and so on. Future versions of a service, while still servicing the clients written to the original interface, may fill in complex data records in these places for the benefit of more current client applications. If your end of the application does not rely on it, you don't need to care.

To summarize this approach more generally, you could say that Web Services leave many details open for mutual agreement between the parties that will be actually involved whereas other middleware systems, such as CORBA, have sought to define stricter, inherent semantics as part of their models. This means that to use Web Services successfully in practice, you have to fill in these details. It also means that there is more room for refinement and thus wider applicability.

Implementing a Web Service

The J2EE model for Web Services provides a seamless Java perspective on Web Services, both for the service implementations and its clients. The model is relatively simple to use and allows you to deal with SOAP in the same way you deal with RMI or RMI/IIOP, which is to entrust all the details to the lower transport layers and happily ignore them for your business logic. The first thing to note is that your Web Services, like your beans, are managed for you completely by the container.

The JSR 921 specification *Implementing Enterprise Web Services* defines the programming model for Web Services. This specification uses the term *port component* for the server-side view of a Web Service. A port component is a portable Java implementation of a service interface (a port) and comprises a Java mapping of the service interface and an implementation bean. Port components are deployed into and live in containers. Writing a Web Service using EJB requires creating one or more port components as stateless session beans. This involves writing (and generating) some more XML descriptors. A big advantage of the way the Web Services programming model is defined is that you can also expose existing session beans as Web Services. This is what we will do in the remainder of this chapter. To leverage the large investments that we made in Chapter 3, we will take our HelloWorld session bean and make it available as a Web Service at no extra cost.

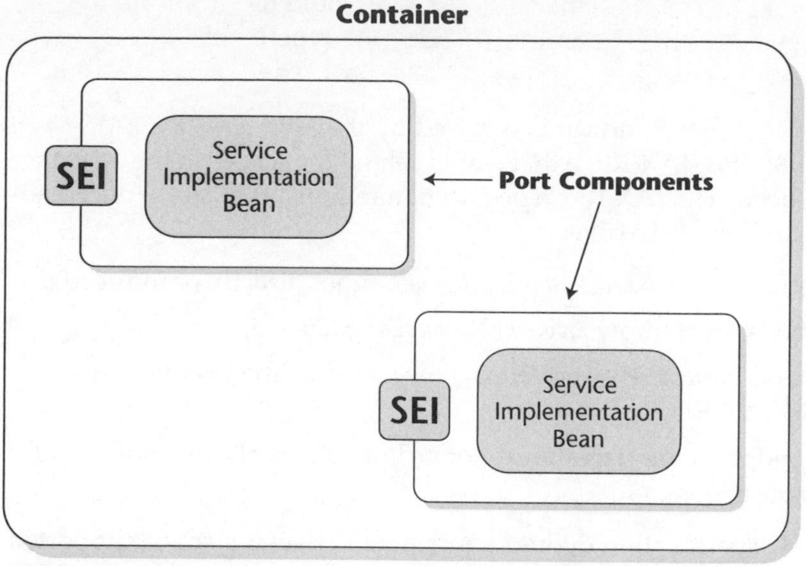

Figure 5.2 EJB container with port components.

The great news is that (almost) no additional coding is required. The only thing that our session bean is missing is a slightly different form of remote interface, which we will add. After that, exposing the bean as a Web Service requires only repackaging and redeploying the application, which now contains a port component. The EJB container will know how to dispatch incoming SOAP messages to our bean implementation and how to map incoming XML data types to Java. The same will happen on the way back: The container just knows how to map our Java return values back into XML, how to build a SOAP response message, and where to send it. Figure 5.2 depicts the additional ports that the container now supports.

The JAX-RPC Service Endpoint Interface

The simple convention that we mentioned previously is to provide a Java interface to your bean that lists all the business methods supported by the bean. This interface is called the *Service Endpoint Interface* (SEI) and shown in the following block of code. The remaining HelloBean implementation does not have to be changed to actually implement this interface. All that is required is that the HelloBean support business methods with the same name and signature as those in the remote interface, as shown in the following example:

```
package examples;
/** This is the Hello service endpoint interface. */
public interface HelloInterface extends java.rmi.Remote
```

```
{
  public String hello() throws java.rmi.RemoteException;
}
```

The service endpoint interface is required by the Java *APIs for XML-based Remote Procedure Calls* (JAX-RPC) that works behind the scenes in the container to invoke the bean. The JAX-RPC specification requires that the service endpoint interface follow these rules:

- The interface must extend *java.rmi.Remote* either directly or indirectly.
- All methods must throw *java.rmi.RemoteException*.
- The method parameters and return types must be the Java types supported by JAX-RPC.
- Service endpoint interfaces must not include constants (as public final static declarations).

The JAX-RPC specification defines a mapping between a set of supported Java types and WSDL/XML types. The Java types directly supported by JAX-RPC are the primitive types *boolean*, *byte*, *double*, *float*, *int*, *long*, *short*, and arrays of these types. In addition, the following non-primitive types are directly supported by JAX-RPC:

java.lang.Boolean

java.lang.Byte

java.lang.Double

java.lang.Float

java.lang.Integer

java.lang.Long

java.lang.Short

java.lang.String

java.math.BigDecimal

java.math.BigInteger

java.net.URI

java.util.Calendar

java.util.Date

JAX-RPC also provides hooks for customized type mappers that extend the standard type mapping provided by JAX-RPC. In our HelloWorld example, the only data type that is transmitted is *java.lang.String*, which is mapped to the XML string type without additional effort.

WSDL and the XML/Java Mapping

You have seen the WSDL description of the HelloWorld Web Service already. If you are building new Web Services, you can start with a WSDL description of your service and write WSDL directly and then use a WSDL compiler to generate the service endpoint interface in Java. Alternatively, almost all Web Services platforms and SOAP toolkits provide tools to derive WSDL descriptions automatically from Java endpoint interfaces. See the source code for this book for examples of generating WSDL from Java.

Packaging and Deploying a Web Service Session Bean

The packaging of a Web Service implementation as a stateless session bean is an extension of the packaging for regular stateless session beans, that is, an *ejb-jar* archive. This file contains the usual set of Java classes, plus the service endpoint interface class.

The EJB server requires extra information to be able to dispatch incoming SOAP messages to an implementation of the service endpoint interface. First, it needs to know the Java class that will handle these calls. Additionally, it needs the WSDL file with the endpoint address that it should listen on. The WSDL file is provided in the META-INF directory of the *ejb-jar* archive.

The other information is provided in an additional descriptor file, the webservices.xml file, which is also added to the *ejb-jar* archive's META-INF directory. Your specific J2EE product may provide vendor-specific deployment tools to generate this file. The webservices.xml file for our HelloWorld service is reproduced here:

```
<?xml version="1.0" encoding="UTF-8"?>
<webservices xmlns="http://java.sun.com/xml/ns/j2ee" version="1.1"
 xmlns:xsi="http://www.w3.org/2001/XMLSchema-instance"
 xsi:schemaLocation="http://java.sun.com/xml/ns/j2ee
 http://www.ibm.com/webservices/xsd/j2ee_web_services_1_1.xsd">
  <webservice-description>
    <display-name>HelloWorldWS</display-name>
    <webservice-description-name>HelloWorldWS</webservice-
description-name>
    <wsdl-file>META-INF/wsdl/HelloWorldWS.wsdl</wsdl-file>
    <jaxrpc-mapping-file>META-INF/wsdl/mapping.xml</jaxrpc-mapping-file>
    <port-component>
      <display-name>HelloWS</display-name>
      <port-component-name>HelloWS</port-component-name>
      <wsdl-port xmlns:wsdl-port_ns__="urn:examples">wsdl-port_ns__:
HelloInterfacePort</wsdl-port>
      <service-endpoint-interface>examples.HelloInterface</
service-endpoint-interface>
```

```
      <service-impl-bean>
        <ejb-link>HelloBean</ejb-link>
      </service-impl-bean>
    </port-component>
  </webservice-description>
</webservices>
```

The webservices.xml file tells the container where to look for the WSDL file in the package in the *<wsdl-file>* element. Likewise, it specifies the location of the JAX-RPC mapping file. Finally, the webservices.xml file defines the Web Service implementation package, the port component. The port component definition lists the fully qualified Java class name of the service endpoint interface and the name of the implementation bean. The simple name is sufficient here as the container already knows the bean details from the ejb-jar.xml file. The port component is linked to the Web Service's port using the *<wsdl-port>* element, which gives the name of the port that this port component implements.

With this, we're actually done! The container now has all the information that it needs to link the abstract concept of a Web Service as defined in WSDL to the port component that we have just defined by adding a service endpoint interface to our existing HelloBean.

Implementing a Web Service Client

Web Services clients in J2EE are very similar to regular bean clients. They come in two flavors:

- Standalone JAX-RPC clients without JNDI access for service lookup
- J2EE clients (both Web clients and standalone) that can access client-side JNDI contexts

Standalone clients without JNDI access, such as remote Java clients not running inside an application server, can be coded using one of two approaches. The first approach is called *static stub* and relies on statically generated SOAP client stubs, much like RMI stubs. The second approach is called *dynamic proxy* and retrieves a WSDL description at runtime to generate the dynamic proxy from it. Both approaches rely on the client's knowledge of the service endpoint address URL and not just a symbolic lookup name as with JNDI. These approaches are functionally equivalent.

Actually, there is a third option that relies on a dynamic invocation interface (DII) to create call objects at runtime, which allows you to build dynamic bridges and to live without any prior knowledge of a service's WSDL. We do not cover this style of programming here as it is low-level and cumbersome to use, and beneficial only in limited cases. With the DII approach, your client code has to create SOAP call objects and explicitly embed parameters before sending them.

The following example shows the code for a standalone, remote client to our simple HelloWorld Web Service and uses both approaches:

```
package examples;

import java.net.URL;
import javax.xml.rpc.Service;
import javax.xml.rpc.JAXRPCException;
import javax.xml.rpc.ServiceFactory;
import javax.xml.rpc.Stub;
import javax.xml.namespace.QName;

/**
 * This class is an example of a standalone JAX-RPC client code which
 * uses both the static stub and the dynamic proxy approach to get
 * a reference to the remote Web Service
 */
public class HelloClient
{
    static String host = "localhost";
    static String serviceURL = "HelloBean";
    static String nameSpaceUri = "urn:examples";
    static String serviceName = "HelloWorldWS";
    static String serviceEndpointAddress = "http://" + host + ":
8080/" + serviceURL;

    public static void main(String[] args)
        throws Exception
    {
        // the static stub approach: get the port reference
        HelloInterface hello = getStaticStub();
        // call hello()
        System.out.println("Static stub: " + hello.hello());

        // the dynamic proxy approach:
        // a) Specify the location of the WSDL file
        URL url = new URL(serviceEndpointAddress + "?WSDL");

        // b) Create an instance of a service factory
        ServiceFactory serviceFactory = ServiceFactory.newInstance();

        // c) Create a service object to act as a factory for proxies.
        Service helloService =
            serviceFactory.createService(url,
                                         new QName(nameSpaceUri,
serviceName));
```

```
        // d) get the port reference
        hello = (examples.HelloInterface)
                   helloService.getPort(examples.HelloInterface
.class);
        // Call the hello() method
        System.out.println("Dynamic proxy: " + hello.hello());
    }

    /** convenience method to retrieve the port reference though a
static stub */
    private static HelloInterface getStaticStub()
    {
        // the HelloWorldWS_Impl class is generated by the
JAX-RPCstub compiler
        Stub stub =
            (Stub)(new HelloWorldWS_Impl().getHelloInterfacePort());
        // tell the stub where the endpoint is
        stub._setProperty(javax.xml.rpc.Stub.ENDPOINT_ADDRESS_PROPERTY,
                          serviceEndpointAddress);
        return (HelloInterface)stub;
    }
}
```

J2EE client code that is running in a client container, for example a servlet, can be shielded from the actual service endpoint address by using JNDI lookups instead. The client container's local JNDI context provides the binding from the service endpoint address to a service name according to the client's deployment descriptor. The configuration of the client container is vendor-specific, but after everything is set up properly, the following code can be used to retrieve the service reference:

```
    InitialContext ctx = new InitialContext();
    Service helloService =
       (Service)ctx.lookup("java:comp/env/services/HelloWorldWS");
    HelloInterface hello =
       (examples.HelloInterface)helloService.getPort(examples
.HelloInterface.class);
```

This concludes our simple programming example for Web Services in EJB. While the example itself is far from realistic or even prototypical for a Web Service, it is useful to show how you can turn something into a Web Service after it has been coded, and how EJB supports generating the necessary XML scaffolding without you having to worry about it. You will see another example of a Web Service in action in Chapter 22.

Summary

In this chapter we provided a basic overview of the concepts and technologies required to use and build Web Services with EJB. This completes our introduction to session beans. We have covered a lot of ground, going from stateless to stateful session beans and back again to stateless beans that implement Web Services.

In the next chapters, you'll learn about the more complex (and also quite interesting) entity bean. Turn the page and read on!

CHAPTER

6

Introduction to Entity Beans

One of the key benefits of EJB is that it gives you the power to create *entity beans*. Entity beans are *persistent objects* that you place in permanent storage. This means you can model your business's fundamental, underlying data as entity beans.

In this chapter, we'll cover the basic concepts of persistence. We'll give you a definition of entity beans from a programmer's perspective. You'll learn the features that entity beans offer and entity bean programming concepts.

This chapter is relatively theoretical, and it is meant to give you a solid foundation in entity bean programming concepts. Make sure you've read and understood the previous chapters in this book; our discussion of entity beans will build on the knowledge you've acquired so far. We'll use these concepts with hands-on code in later chapters.

Persistence Concepts

Because entity beans are persistent objects, our discussion begins with a quick look at popular ways to persist objects.

Object-Relational Mapping

Another popular way to store Java objects is to use a traditional relational database, such as Oracle, Microsoft SQL Server, or MySQL. Rather than serialize each object, we could decompose each object into its constituent parts and store each part separately. For example, for a bank account object, the bank account number could be stored in one relational database field and the bank account balance in another field. When you save your Java objects, you would use JDBC to *map* the object data into a relational database. When you want to load your objects from the database, you would instantiate an object from that class, read the data in from the database, and then populate that object instance's fields with the relational data read in. This is shown in Figure 6.1.

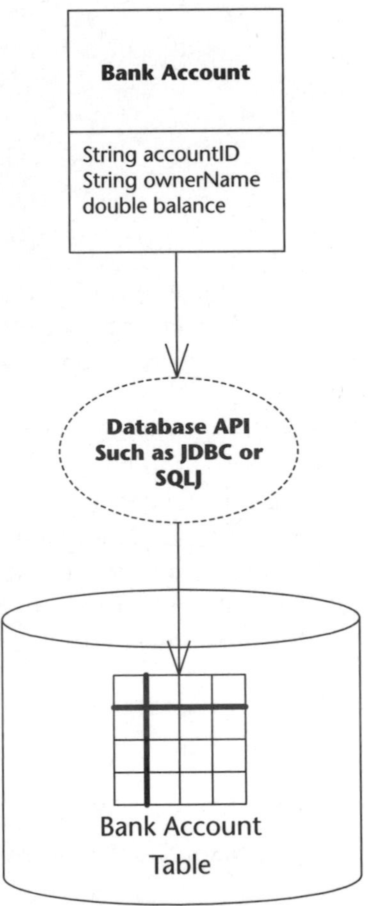

Figure 6.1 Object-relational mapping.

This mapping of objects to relational databases is a technology called *object-relational mapping*. It is the act of converting and unconverting in-memory objects to relational data. An object-relational (O/R) mapper may map your objects to any kind of relational database schema. For example, a simple object-relational mapping engine might map a Java class to a SQL table definition. An instance of that class would map to a row in that table, while fields in that instance would map to individual cells in that row. This is shown in Figure 6.2. You'll see more advanced cases of mapping data with *relationships* to other data in Chapter 11.

Object-relational mapping is a much more sophisticated mechanism of persisting objects than the simple object serialization offered by the Java language. By decomposing your Java objects as relational data, you can issue arbitrary queries for information. For example, you can search through all the database records that have an account balance entry greater than $1,000 and load only the objects that fulfill this query. More advanced queries are also possible. You can also visually inspect the database data because it is not stored as bit-blobs, which is great for debugging or auditing.

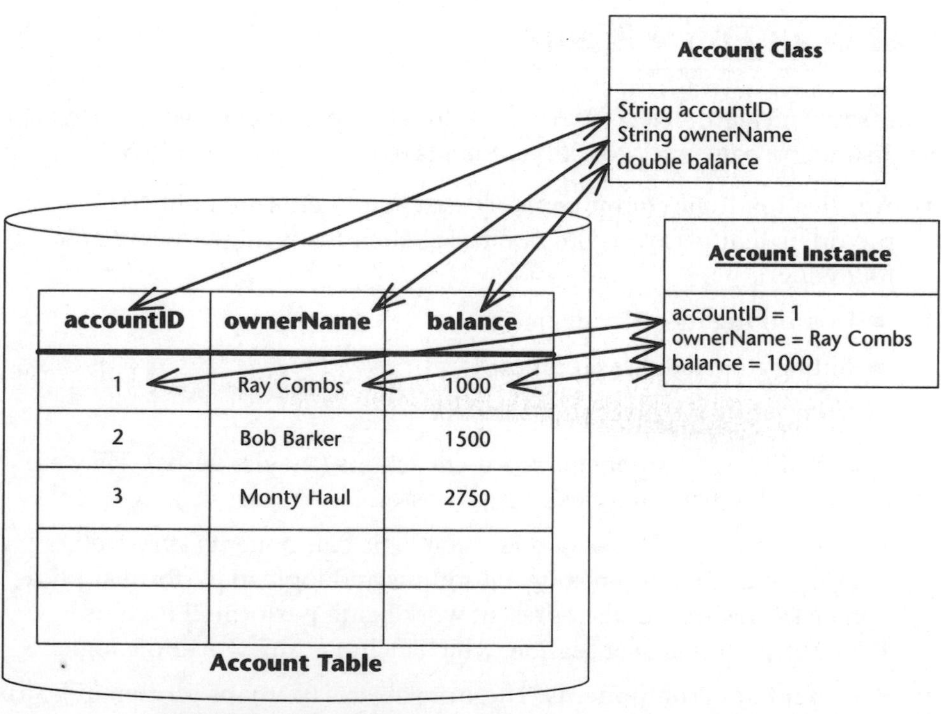

Figure 6.2 An example of object-relational mapping.

Mapping objects to relational data can be done in two ways. You can either handcraft this mapping in your code or use an object-relational mapping product, such as Oracle TopLink, or open source tools, such as Hibernate, to automate or facilitate this mapping. These tools have become increasingly popular. Handcrafted mappings using a database access API such as JDBC are becoming less frequently used because the cost of developing and maintaining an object-relational mapping layer is significant.

The Sun *Java Data Objects* (JDO) specification, available as JSR 12 from the *Java Community Process* (JCP) Web site at www.jcp.org, defines portable APIs to a persistence layer that is conceptually neutral to the database technology used to support it. It can thus be implemented by vendors of relational and object-oriented databases. According to recent announcements, future versions of the EJB specification are going to be more closely aligned with container-independent persistence mechanisms, such as Hibernate, TopLink, and JDO.

Now that we've whetted your appetite with persistence mechanisms, let's take a look at how entity bean persistent objects are used in an EJB multitier environment.

What Is an Entity Bean?

In any sophisticated, object-oriented multitier deployment, we can draw a clear distinction between two different kinds of components deployed.

- **Application logic components.** These components are method providers that perform common tasks. Their tasks might include the following:
  - Computing the price of an order
  - Billing a customer's credit card
  - Computing the inverse of a matrix

  Note that these components represent actions (they're verbs). They are well suited to handling business processes.

  Session beans model these application logic components very well. They often contain interesting algorithms and logic to perform application tasks. Session beans represent work being performed for a user. They represent the user session, which includes any workflow logic.

- **Persistent data components.** These are objects (perhaps written in Java) that know how to render themselves into persistent storage. They use some persistence mechanism, such as serialization, O/R mapping to a relational database, or an object database. These kinds of objects represent *data*—simple or complex information that you'd like saved. Examples here include:

- Bank account information, such as account number and balance
- Human resources data, such as names, departments, and salaries of employees
- Lead tracking information, such as names, addresses, and phone numbers of prospective customers that you want to keep track of over time

Note that these components represent people, places, and things (they're nouns). They are well suited to handling business data.

The big difference between session beans and entity beans is that entity beans have an identity and client-visible state, and that their lifetime may be completely independent of the client application's lifetime. For entity beans, having an identity means that different entity beans can be distinguished by comparing their identities. It also means that clients can refer to individual entity bean instances by using that identity, pass handles to other applications, and actually share common entities with other clients. All this is not possible with session beans.

You might question the need for such persistent data components. Why should we deal with our business data as objects, rather than deal with raw database data, such as relational rows? It is handy to treat data as objects because they can be easily handled and managed and because they are represented in a compact manner. We can group related data in a unified object. We associate some simple methods with that data, such as compression or other data-related activities. We can also use implicit middleware services from an application server, such as relationships, transactions, network accessibility, and security. We can also cache that data for performance.

Entity beans are these persistent data components. Entity beans are enterprise beans that know how to persist themselves permanently to a durable storage, such as a database or legacy system. They are physical, storable parts of an enterprise. Entity beans store data as fields, such as bank account numbers and bank account balances. They also have methods associated with them, such as *getBankAccountNumber()* and *getAccountBalance()*. For a full discussion of when to (and when not to) use entity beans, see Chapter 16.

In some ways, entity beans are analogous to serializable Java objects. Serializable objects can be rendered into a bit-blob and then saved into a persistent store; entity beans can persist themselves in many ways, including Java serialization, O/R mapping, or even an object database persistence. Nothing in the EJB 2.*x* specification dictates any particular persistence mechanism, although O/R mappings are the most frequently used mechanism in practice.

Entity beans are different from session beans. Session beans model a process or workflow (actions that are started by the user and that go away when the user goes away). Entity beans, on the other hand, contain core business data—product information, bank accounts, orders, lead tracking information, customer information, and more. An entity bean does not perform complex tasks or workflow logic, such as billing a customer. Rather, an entity bean *is* the customer itself. Entity beans represent persistent state objects (things that don't go away when the user goes away).

For example, you might want to read a bank account data into an entity bean instance, thus loading the stored database information into the in-memory entity bean instance's fields. You can then play with the Java object and modify its representation in memory because you're working with convenient Java objects, rather than bunches of database records. You can increase the bank account balance in-memory, thus updating the entity bean's in-memory bank account balance field. Then you can save the Java object, pushing the data back into the underlying store. This would effectively deposit money into the bank account.

The term *entity bean* is not always used stringently. Sometimes it refers to an in-memory Java object instance of an entity bean class, and sometimes it refers to database data that an in-memory Java object instance represents. To make the distinction clear, we will use the following two terms:

***The entity bean instance* is the in-memory view into the database. It is an instance of your entity bean class.**

***The entity bean data (or data instance)* is the physical set of data, such as a bank account record, stored in the database.**

In summary, you should think of an entity bean instance as the following:

- An in-memory Java representation of persistent data that knows how to read itself from storage and populate its fields with the stored data
- An object that can then be modified in-memory to change the values of data
- Persistable, so that it can be saved back into storage again, thus updating the database data

About the Files That Make Up an Entity Bean

An entity bean contains the standard set of files that all EJB components have, including the remote and/or local interface, the home and/or local home interface, the enterprise bean class, and the deployment descriptor.

There are several noteworthy differences between entity bean files and other types of EJB components.

- **The entity bean class** maps to an entity definition in a database schema. For example, an entity bean class could map to a relational table definition. In this case, an entity bean instance of that class would map to a row in that table. Your entity bean class can expose simple methods, such as a method to decrease a bank account balance, to manipulate or access that data. Like a session bean class, EJB also requires that an entity bean class must fill in some standard callback methods. The EJB container will call these methods appropriately to manage the entity bean.

- **The primary key class** makes every entity bean different. For example, if you have one million bank account entity beans, each bank account needs to have a unique ID (such as a bank account ID string) that can never be repeated in any other bank account. A primary key is an object that may contain any number of attributes. This could be any data necessary to identify uniquely an entity bean data instance. In some advanced cases, when the entity bean represents a complex relationship, the primary key might be an entire object. EJB gives you the flexibility to define what your unique identifier is by including a primary key class with your entity bean. The one rule is that your primary key class must be serializable and follow the rules for Java object serialization. The rules for object serialization are covered in Appendix A.

Features of Entity Beans

Let's take a look at the features of entity beans.

Entity Beans Survive Failures

Entity beans are long lasting. They survive critical failures, such as application servers crashing, or even databases crashing. This is because entity beans are just representations of data in a permanent, fault-tolerant, underlying storage. If a machine crashes, the entity bean can be reconstructed in memory. All we need to do is read the data back in from the permanent database and instantiate an entity bean Java object instance with fields that contain the data read in from the database.

This is a huge difference between session and entity beans. Entity beans have a much longer life cycle than a client's session, perhaps years long, depending on how long the data sits in the database. In fact, the database records representing an object could have existed before the company even decided to go with a Java-based solution, because a database structure can be language independent. This makes sense—you definitely would want your bank account to last for a few years, regardless of technology changes in your bank.

Entity Bean Instances Are a View into a Database

When you load entity bean data into an in-memory entity bean instance, you read in the data stored in a database so that you can manipulate the data within a Java Virtual Machine. However, *you should think of the in-memory object and the database itself as one and the same*. This means if you update the in-memory entity bean instance, the database should automatically be updated as well. You should *not* think of the entity bean as a separate version of the data in the database. The in-memory entity bean is simply a *view* or *lens* into the database.

Of course, in reality there are multiple physical copies of the same data: the in-memory entity bean instance and the entity bean data itself stored in the database. Therefore, there must be a mechanism to transfer information back and forth between the Java object and the database. This data transfer is accomplished with two special methods that your entity bean class must implement, called *ejbLoad()* and *ejbStore()*.

- *ejbLoad()* reads the data in from the persistent storage into the entity bean's in-memory fields.
- *ejbStore()* saves your bean instance's current fields to the underlying data storage. It is the complement of *ejbLoad()*.

So who decides when to transfer data back and forth between the in-memory bean and the database? That is, who calls *ejbLoad()* and *ejbStore()*? The answer is your EJB container. *ejbLoad()* and *ejbStore()* are callback methods that the container invokes. They are management methods required by EJB. The container worries about the proper time to call *ejbLoad()* and *ejbStore()*—this is one of the value-adds of the container. This is shown in Figure 6.3.

Your beans should be prepared to accept an *ejbLoad()* or *ejbStore()* call at almost any time (but not during a business method). The container automatically figures out when each of your instances needs to be refreshed depending on the current transactional state (see Chapter 12). This means that you never explicitly call your own *ejbLoad()* or *ejbStore()* methods. This is one of the advantages of EJB: You don't have to worry about synchronizing your objects with the underlying database. The EJB black box handles it for you. That is why you can think of the entity bean and the database as the same; there should never be a time when the two are transactionally out of sync.

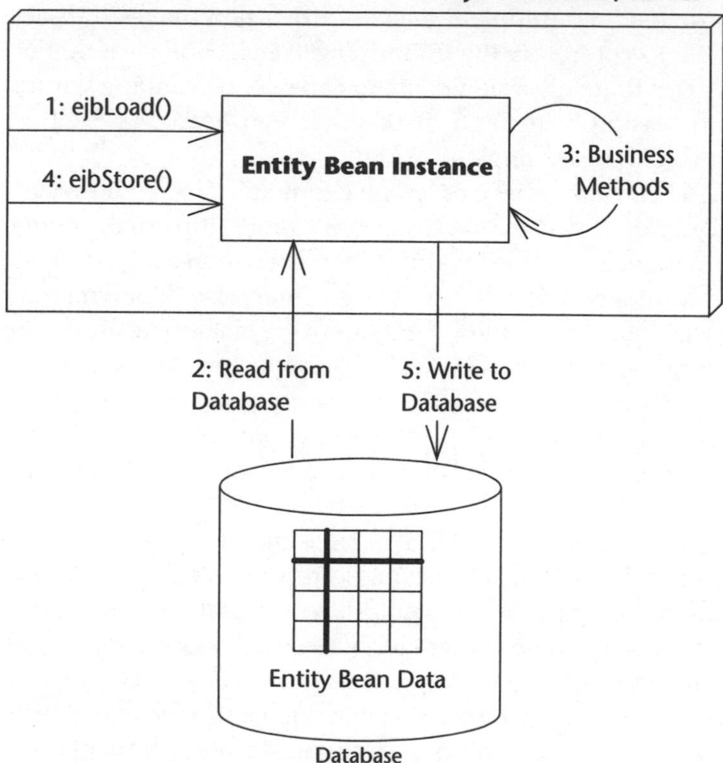

Figure 6.3 Loading and storing an entity bean.

Several Entity Bean Instances May Represent the Same Underlying Data

Let's consider the scenario in which many threads of execution want to access the same database data simultaneously. In banking, interest might be applied to a bank account, while at the same time a company directly deposits a check into that same account. In e-commerce, many different client browsers may be simultaneously interacting with a catalog of products.

To facilitate many clients accessing the same data, we need to design a high-performance access system to our entity beans. One possibility is to allow many clients to share the same entity bean instance; that way, an entity bean could service many client requests simultaneously. While this is an interesting idea, it is not very appropriate for EJB, for two reasons. First, if we'd like an entity bean instance to service many concurrent clients, we'd need to make that instance thread-safe. Writing thread-safe code is difficult and error-prone. Remember that the EJB value proposition is rapid application development. Mandating that component vendors produce stable thread-safe code does not encourage this. Second, having multiple threads of execution makes transactions almost impossible to control by the underlying transaction system. For these reasons, EJB dictates that only a single thread can ever be running within a bean instance. With session beans and message-driven beans, as well as entity beans, all bean instances are single-threaded.

Mandating that each bean can service only one client at a time could result in performance bottlenecks. Because each instance is single-threaded, clients need to effectively run in lockstep, each waiting their turn to use a bean. This could easily grind performance to a halt in any large enterprise deployment.

To boost performance, we could allow containers to instantiate multiple instances of the same entity bean class. This would allow many clients to interact concurrently with separate instances, each representing the same underlying entity data. Indeed, this is exactly what EJB allows containers to do. Thus, client requests do not necessarily need to be processed sequentially, but rather concurrently.

Having multiple bean instances represent the same data now raises a new problem: data corruption. If many bean instances are representing the same underlying data through caching (see Chapter 19), we're dealing with multiple in-memory cached replicas. Some of these replicas could become stale, representing data that is not current.

To achieve entity bean instance cache consistency, each entity bean instance needs to be routinely synchronized with the underlying storage. The container synchronizes the bean with the underlying storage by calling the bean's *ejbLoad()* and *ejbStore()* callbacks, as described in the previous section.

The frequency with which beans are synchronized with an underlying storage is dictated by *transactions*, a topic we cover in Chapter 12. Transactions enable each client request to be isolated from every other request. They enable clients to *believe* they are dealing with a single in-memory bean instance, when in fact many instances are behind the scenes. Transactions give clients the illusion that they have exclusive access to data when in fact many clients are touching the same data.

Entity Bean Instances Can Be Pooled

Let's say you've decided to author your own EJB container/server. Your product is responsible for instantiating entity beans as necessary, with each bean representing data in an underlying storage. As clients connect and disconnect, you could create and destroy beans as necessary to service those clients.

Unfortunately this is not a scalable way to build an application server. Creation and destruction of objects is expensive, especially if client requests come frequently. How can we save on this overhead?

One thing to remember is that an entity bean class describes the fields and rules for your entity bean, but it does not dictate any specific data. For example, an entity bean class may specify that all bank accounts have the following fields:

- The name of the bank account owner
- An account ID
- An available balance

That bean class can then represent any distinct instance of database data, such as a particular bank account record. The class itself, though, is not specific to any particular bank account.

To save precious time-instantiating objects, entity bean instances are therefore recyclable objects and may be pooled depending on your container's policy. The container may pool and reuse entity bean instances to represent different instances of the same type of data in an underlying storage. For example, a container could use a bank account entity bean instance to represent different bank account records. When you're done using an entity bean instance, that instance may be assigned to handle a different client's request and may represent different data. The container performs this by dynamically assigning the entity bean instance to different client-specific EJB objects. Not only does this save the container from unnecessarily instantiating bean instances, but this scheme also saves on the total amount of resources held by the system. We show this in Figure 6.4.

Instance pooling is an interesting optimization that containers may provide, and it is not at all unique to entity beans. However, complications arise when reassigning entity bean instances to different EJB objects. When your entity bean is assigned to a particular EJB object, it may be holding resources such as socket connections. But when it's in the pool, it may not need that socket. Thus, to allow the bean to release and acquire resources, your entity bean class must implement two callback methods:

- *ejbActivate()* is the callback that your container will invoke on your bean instance when transitioning your bean *out of* a generic instance pool. This process is called *activation*, and it indicates that the container is associating your bean with a specific EJB object and a specific primary key. Your bean's *ejbActivate()* method should acquire resources, such as sockets, that your bean needs when assigned to a particular EJB object.

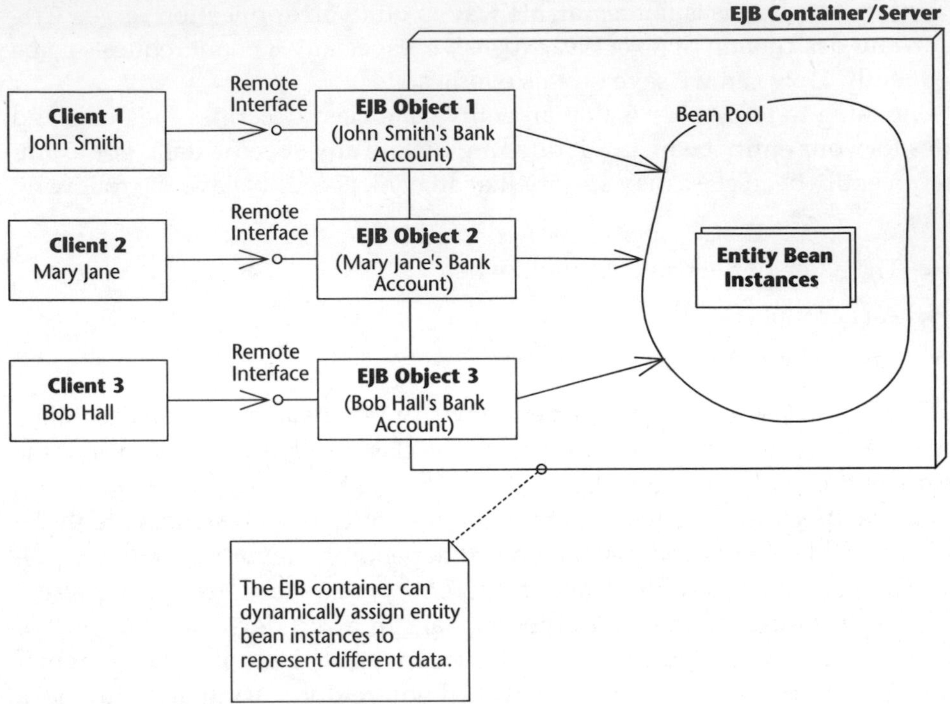

Figure 6.4 EJB container pooling of entity beans.

- *ejbPassivate()* is the callback that your container will invoke when transitioning your bean *into* a generic instance pool. This process is called *passivation*, and it indicates that the container is disassociating your bean from a specific EJB object and a specific primary key. Your bean's *ejbPassivate()* method should release resources, such as sockets, that your bean acquired during *ejbActivate()*.

When an entity bean instance is passivated, it must not only release held resources but also save its state to the underlying storage; that way, the storage is updated to the latest entity bean instance state. To save the instance's fields to the database, the container invokes the entity bean's *ejbStore()* method prior to passivation. Similarly, when the entity bean instance is activated, it must not only acquire any resources it needs but also load the most recent data from the database. To load data into the bean instance, the container invokes the entity bean's *ejbLoad()* method after activation. This is shown in Figure 6.5.

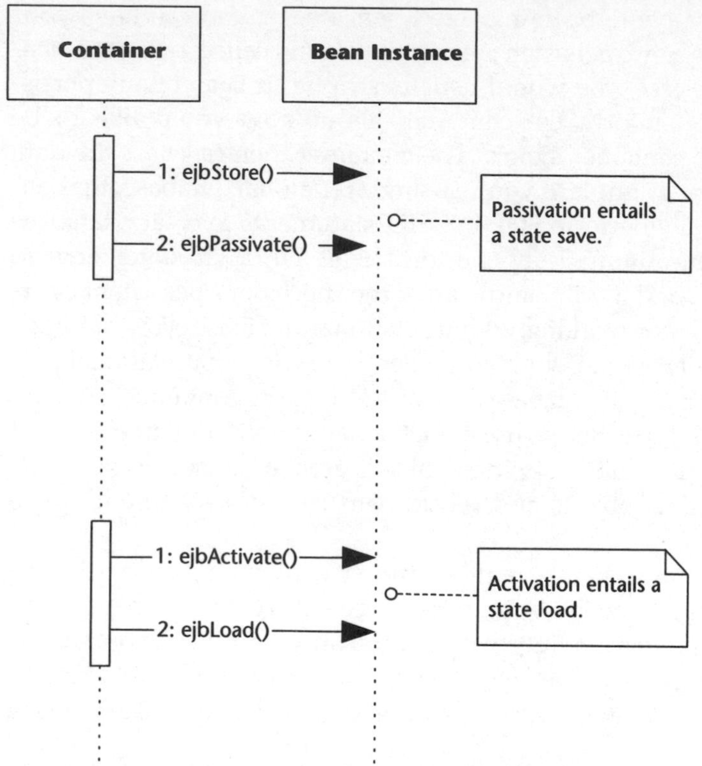

Figure 6.5 Passivation of entity beans entails a state save, and activation entails a state load.

There Are Two Ways to Persist Entity Beans

Since entity beans map to storage, someone needs to write the database access code.

A *bean-managed persistent entity bean* is an entity bean that must be persisted by hand. In other words, you as the component developer must write code to translate your in-memory fields into an underlying data store, such as a relational database or an object database. You handle the persistent operations yourself—including saving, loading, and finding data—within the entity bean. Therefore, you must write to a persistence API, such as JDBC. For example, with a relational database, your entity bean could perform a SQL INSERT statement via JDBC to stick some data into a relational database. You could also perform an SQL DELETE statement via JDBC to remove data from the underlying store.

EJB offers an alternative to bean-managed persistence: You can have your EJB container perform your persistence for you. This is called *container-managed persistence*. In this case, you would usually strip your bean of any persistence logic. Then, you inform the container about how you'd like to be persisted by using the container's tools. The container then *generates* the data access code for you. For example, if you're using a relational database, the container may automatically perform SQL INSERT statements to create database data. Similarly, it will automatically perform SQL DELETE statements to remove database data, and it will handle any other necessary persistent operations. Even if you are not working with a relational database, you can have your container persist for you. If your container supports a nonrelational persistent store, such as an object database or a VSAM file, the container will generate the appropriate logic as necessary. In fact, you can wait until deployment time before you set up the O/R mapping, which is great because you can write storage-independent data objects and reuse them in a variety of enterprise environments.

Container-managed persistence reduces the size of your beans tremendously because you don't need to write JDBC code—the container handles all the persistence for you. This is a huge value-add feature of EJB. Of course, it is still evolving technology. Once we've written a few entity beans, we'll review the trade-offs of bean-managed versus container-managed persistence (see Chapter 16).

Creation and Removal of Entity Beans

As we mentioned earlier, entity beans are a view into a database, and you should think of an entity bean instance and the underlying database as one and the same (they are routinely synchronized). Because they are one and the same, the initialization of an entity bean instance should entail initialization of database data. Thus, when an entity bean is initialized in memory during *ejbCreate()*, it makes sense to create some data in an underlying database that correlates with the in-memory instance. That is exactly what happens with entity beans. When a bean-managed persistent entity bean's *ejbCreate()*

method is called, the *ejbCreate()* method is responsible for creating database data. Similarly, when a bean-managed persistent entity bean's *ejbRemove()* method is called, the *ejbRemove()* method is responsible for removing database data. If container-managed persistence is used, the container will modify the database for you, and you can leave these methods empty of data access logic.

Let's look at this in more detail.

Understanding How Entity Beans Are Created and Destroyed

In EJB, remember that clients do not directly invoke beans—they invoke an EJB object proxy. The EJB object is generated through the home object. Therefore, for each *ejbCreate()* method signature you define in your bean, you must define a corresponding *create()* method in the home interface. The client calls the home object's *create()* method, which delegates to your bean's *ejbCreate()* method.

For example, let's say you have a bank account entity bean class called *AccountBean*, with a remote interface *Account*, home interface *AccountHome*, and primary key class *AccountPK*. Given the following *ejbCreate()* method in *AccountBean*:

```
public AccountPK ejbCreate(String accountID, String owner) throws...
```

you must have this *create()* method in your home interface (notice there is no "ejb" prefix):

```
public Account create(String accountID, String owner) throws ...
```

Notice that there are two different return values here. The bean instance returns a primary key (*AccountPK*), while the home object returns an EJB object (*Account*). This makes sense—the bean returns a primary key to the container (that is, to the home object) so that the container can identify the bean. Once the home object has this primary key, it can generate an EJB object and return that to the client. We show this process more rigorously with the sequence diagram in Figure 6.6.

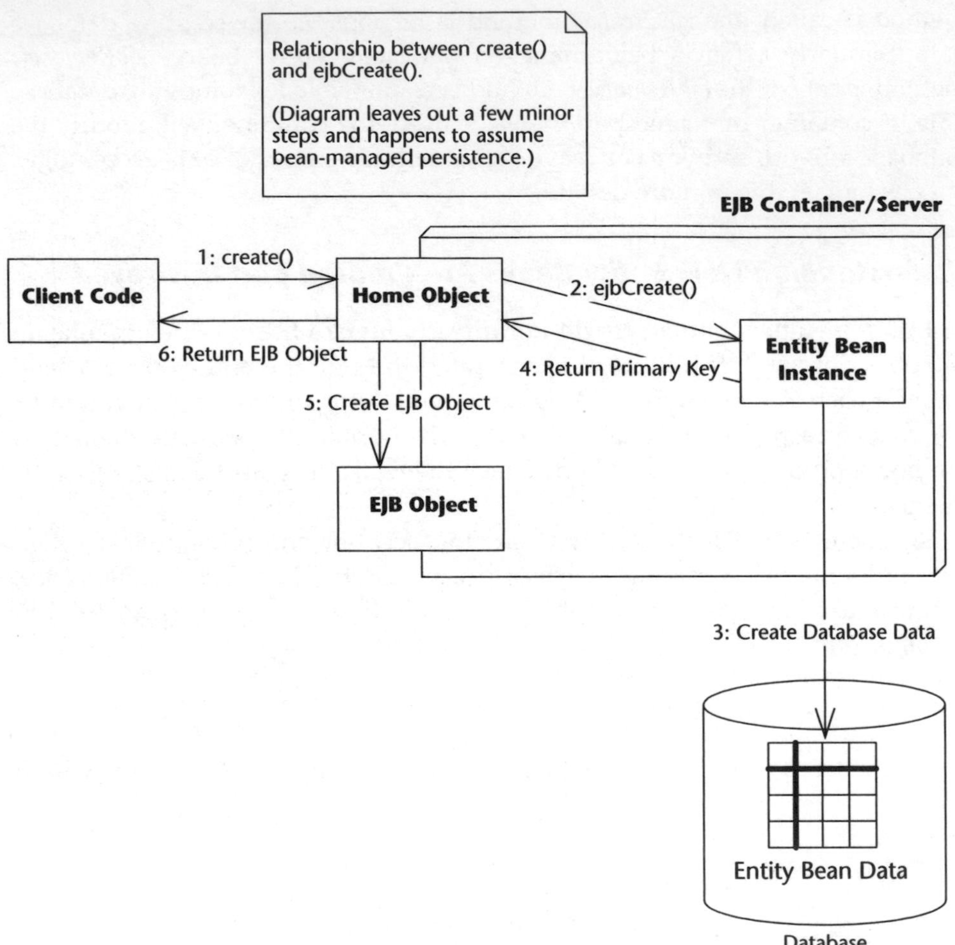

Figure 6.6 Creating an entity bean and EJB object.

To destroy an entity bean's data in a database, the client must call *remove()* on the EJB object or home object. This method causes the container to issue an *ejbRemove()* call on the bean. Figure 6.7 shows the relationship between *remove()* and *ejbRemove()*. Note that *remove()* can be called on either the home object or the EJB object. Figure 6.7 happens to assume bean-managed persistence.

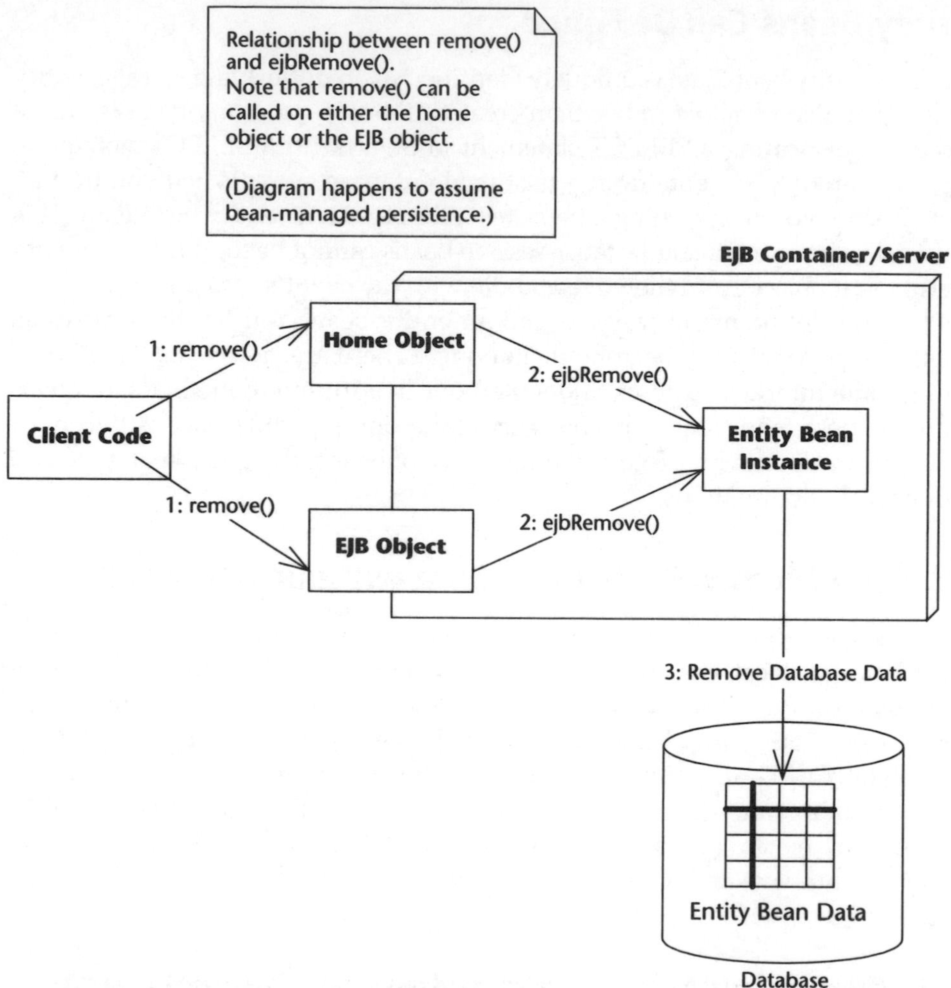

Figure 6.7 Destroying an entity bean's data representation.

Note that *ejbRemove()* does not mean the in-memory entity bean instance is actually going to be destroyed; *ejbRemove()* destroys only database data and makes the entity bean inaccessible to the client. The bean instance can be recycled by the container to handle a different database data instance, such as a bank account bean representing different bank accounts.

ejbRemove() is a required method of all entity beans, and it takes no parameters. There is only one form of *ejbRemove()*. With entity beans, *ejbRemove()* is not called if the client times out because the lifetime of an entity bean is longer than the client's session.

Entity Beans Can Be Found

Because entity bean data is uniquely identified in an underlying storage, entity beans can also be *found* rather than created. Finding an entity bean is analogous to performing a SELECT statement in SQL. With a SELECT statement, you're searching for data from a relational database store. When you find an entity bean, you're searching a persistent store for some entity bean data. This differs from session beans because session beans cannot be found: They are not permanent objects, and they live and die with the client's session.

You can define many ways to find an entity bean. You list these ways as methods in your entity bean home interface. These are called *finder* methods. Your home interface exposes finder methods in addition to methods for creating and destroying entity beans. This is the one big difference between an entity bean's home interface and other types of beans; the other bean types do not have finder methods.

You Can Modify Entity Bean Data without Using EJB

Usually you will create, destroy, and find entity bean data by using the entity bean's home object. But you can interact with entity beans another way, too: by directly modifying the underlying database where the bean data is stored. For example, if your entity bean instances are being mapped to a relational database, you can simply delete the rows of the database corresponding to an entity bean instance (see Figure 6.8). You can also create new entity bean data and modify existing data by directly touching the database. This may be necessary if you have an investment in an existing system that touches a database directly.

These external database updates could raise cache consistency issues if you're choosing to cache your entity beans. See Chapter 19 for more details.

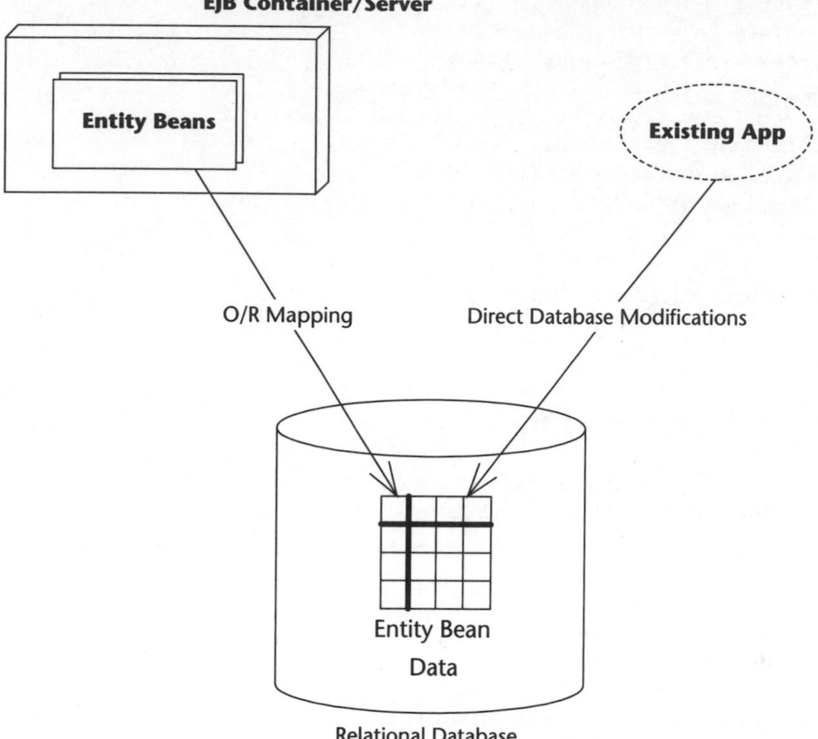

Figure 6.8 Modifying an entity bean's database representation manually.

Entity Contexts

As you learned in Chapter 3, all enterprise beans have a *context object* that identifies the environment of the bean. These context objects contain environment information that the EJB container sets. Your beans can access the context to retrieve all sorts of information, such as transaction and security information. For entity beans, the interface is *javax.ejb.EntityContext*.

We provide a refresher of the *javax.ejb.EJBContext* methods in Source 6.1. Appendix E explains the meaning of each method.

Entity contexts add the methods in Source 6.2 on top of the generic EJB context.

```
public interface javax.ejb.EJBContext {
    public javax.ejb.EJBHome getEJBHome();
    public javax.ejb.EJBLocalHome getEJBLocalHome();
    public java.security.Principal getCallerPrincipal();
    public boolean isCallerInRole(java.lang.String);
    public void setRollbackOnly();
    public boolean getRollbackOnly();
}
```

Source 6.1 The javax.ejb.EJBContext interface.

```
public interface javax.ejb.EntityContext
 extends javax.ejb.EJBContext {
    public javax.ejb.EJBLocalObject getEJBLocalObject();
    public javax.ejb.EJBObject getEJBObject();
    public java.lang.Object getPrimaryKey();
}
```

Source 6.2 The javax.ejb.EntityContext interface.

Let's look at each of these methods in more detail.

getEJBLocalObject() / getEJBObject()

Call the *getEJBObject()* method to retrieve the current, client-specific EJB object that is associated with the entity bean. Remember that clients invoke on EJB objects, not on entity beans directly. Therefore, you can use the returned EJB object as a way to pass a reference to yourself, simulating the *this* argument in Java. *getEJBLocalObject()* is the same, except it gets the more optimized EJB local object.

getPrimaryKey()

*getPrimaryKey()*retrieves the primary key that is currently associated with this entity bean instance. Primary keys uniquely identify an entity bean. When an entity bean is persisted in storage, the primary key can be used to uniquely retrieve the entity bean because no two entity bean database data instances can ever have the same primary key.

Why would you want to call *getPrimaryKey()?* You call it whenever you want to figure out with which database data your instance is associated. Remember that entity bean instances can be reused and pooled, as shown in Figure 6.4. When the container wants to switch an entity bean instance from one data instance to another, the container needs to passivate and activate that entity bean instance. When this happens, your bean instance may switch to a different data instance and thus a different primary key. But your entity bean instance is never told this explicitly when it is activated. Rather, your entity bean must perform a *getPrimaryKey()* callback to the entity context to figure out what data it should be dealing with.

Thus, when you have an entity bean that's performing any persistent work (with bean-managed persistence), you should be calling *getPrimaryKey()* whenever you need to figure out what data your bean is associated with. This is very useful, for example, in the following methods:

- *ejbLoad()*. Recall that *ejbStore()* and *ejbLoad()* are bean callbacks to synchronize a bean instance with an underlying storage. *ejbStore()* saves data to storage, and *ejbLoad()* reads data from storage. When the container calls *ejbStore()*, your bean knows exactly what data to save because the bean instance has the data in memory. But when the container calls *ejbLoad()*, how does your bean know what data to load? After all, bean instances are pooled and can be dynamically assigned to different data. The answer is to use *getPrimaryKey()*; it will tell you what primary key you should be looking for in the underlying storage when loading database data.
- *ejbRemove()*. Recall that *ejbCreate()* and *ejbRemove()* are callbacks for creating and removing data from an underlying storage, respectively. When the container calls *ejbCreate()*, your bean knows exactly what data to create in the database because your bean has received information in the parameters of *ejbCreate()*. But when the container calls *ejbRemove()*, how does your bean know what data to remove? Because bean instances are pooled and dynamically assigned to handle different data instances, you might be deleting the wrong data. Thus, you must call *getPrimaryKey()* to figure out what data, keyed on the primary key, your bean should remove from the database.

It is important to consider bean pooling when writing your enterprise beans, and *getPrimaryKey()* is the key to knowing what data your bean is representing.

Summary

In this chapter, we've taken the first steps toward developing with entity beans. We started by discussing various persistence mechanisms, including object serialization, object/relational mapping, and persistence to pure object databases. We then looked at what an entity bean is, and we listed the files included with an entity bean component. After surveying their features, we took a look at entity contexts.

But the best is yet to come. In the coming chapters, you'll learn hands-on about entity bean programming. Chapter 7 explains bean-managed persistent entity beans and guides you through the steps in developing them using JDBC. Chapter 8 continues with container-managed persistent entity beans. In Chapter 15 you'll learn how to program entity beans that require relationships. By the time you're through, you'll be armed to create your own entity beans in enterprise deployments.

CHAPTER

7

Writing Bean-Managed Persistent Entity Beans

In this chapter, we'll demonstrate how to program *bean-managed persistent entity beans*, the first of two flavors of entity beans. When you code these types of entity beans, you must provide your own data access logic. You are responsible for providing the implementation to map your entity bean instances to and from storage. To do this, you typically use a database API, such as JDBC, or an O/R mapping framework, such as TopLink or Hibernate. This contrasts with container-managed persistent entity beans, which have their data access handled for them by the EJB container. Bean-managed persistence is typically used only when the container-managed persistence (CMP) provided by your application server and database does not deliver satisfactory performance. In this case, you may need to exercise tight control over each and every data access for improving the performance of your entity beans. For more details on performance issues please refer to Chapters 16 and 18.

This chapter explains the basics of bean-managed persistence (BMP) and shows you how to build a simple bean-managed entity bean using JDBC.

Entity Bean Coding Basics

To write an entity bean class, you write a Java class that implements the *javax.ejb.EntityBean* interface. This interface defines a number of required methods that your entity bean class must implement. Most of these methods are management methods called by your EJB container. The following code (Source 7.1 and Source 7.2) details *javax.ejb.EntityBean,* as well as its parent, *javax.ejb.EnterpriseBean* (exceptions are omitted).

The *javax.ejb.EnterpriseBean* interface defines no methods—it is simply a marker interface. The *javax.ejb.EntityBean* interface defines callback methods that your bean must implement. The container will call these methods whenever it wishes.

```
public interface javax.ejb.EnterpriseBean
implements java.io.Serializable {
}
```

Source 7.1 The javax.ejb.EnterpriseBean interface.

```
public interface javax.ejb.EntityBean
 extends javax.ejb.EnterpriseBean {
     public void setEntityContext(javax.ejb.EntityContext);
     public void unsetEntityContext();
     public void ejbRemove();
     public void ejbActivate();
     public void ejbPassivate();
     public void ejbLoad();
     public void ejbStore();
}
```

Source 7.2 The javax.ejb.EntityBean interface.

JAVA DATABASE CONNECTIVITY

This chapter uses Java Database Connectivity (JDBC). JDBC is a standard Java extension that enables Java programmers to access relational databases. By using JDBC, Java programmers can represent database connections, issue SQL statements, process database results, and more in a relatively portable way. Clients program to the unified JDBC API, which is implemented by a *JDBC Driver,* an adapter that knows how to talk to a particular database in a proprietary way (see Figure 7.1). JDBC is similar to the Open Database Connectivity (ODBC) standard, and the two are quite interoperable through JDBC-ODBC bridges. JDBC contains built-in support for database connection pooling, further enhancing the database independence of your application code.

All entity bean classes, both bean-managed persistent and container-managed persistent, must implement the *javax.ejb.EntityBean* interface. This interface defines callback methods that the container invokes on your beans. There are additional methods you also may define, such as methods to create and find your entity beans.

Finding Existing Entity Beans: Finder Methods

As shown in Table 7.1, we have methods labeled *ejbFind()*. These finder methods are defined on the local and remote home interfaces and implemented by your bean implementations to find an existing entity bean in storage. Finder methods do not create new database data—they simply load old entity bean data.

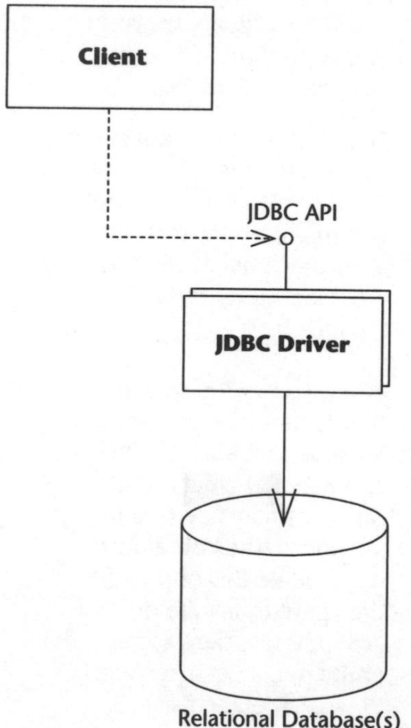

Figure 7.1 Java Database Connectivity.

Table 7.1 Descriptions and Implementation Guidelines for Bean-Managed Persistent Entities

TYPICAL IMPLEMENTATION	METHOD	EXPLANATION
setEntityContext()	Stick the entity context somewhere, such as in a member variable. You can access the context later to acquire environment information, such as security information, from the container. You should also request any resources you will need regardless of what data the bean manages.	If the container wants to increase its pool size of bean instances, it will instantiate a new entity bean instance. Next, the container calls the instance's *setEntityContext()* method. Once this method is called, the bean can access information about its environment. *The bean is now in a pool, does not have any specific database data inside of it, and is not bound to any particular EJB object.*
ejbFind<...>(<...>)	While your bean instance is still in the pool, the container can use your bean to service a *finder* method. Finder methods locate one or more existing entity bean data instances in the underlying persistent store. You must define a least one finder method—*ejbFindByPrimaryKey().*	Search through a data store using a storage API such as JDBC or SQL/J. For example, you might perform relational query such as "SELECT id FROMaccounts WHERE balance > 0." When you've found some data, return the primary keys for that data back to the container by creating one or more primary key Java object instances. The container will then create EJB objects for the client to invoke on and possibly associate some entity bean instances with those EJB objects. *Those entity bean instances are no longer in the pool—they now have specific database data inside of them, and they are bound to particular EJB objects.*

Table 7.1 *(continued)*

TYPICAL IMPLEMENTATION	METHOD	EXPLANATION
ejbHome<...>(<...>)	Sometimes you need methods on an entity bean that are not specific to any given data instance (or row). For example, counting the total number of accounts in a table. You can write home methods to perform these operations. The home methods are special business methods because they are called from a bean in the pool, before the bean is associated with any specific data. Clients call home methods from the home interface or local home interface.	Perform your global operations, such as counting the rows in a database using JDBC, and return the result to the client.
ejbCreate(<...>) Note: You do not need to write any *ejbCreate()* methods if you don't want EJB clients to be able to create new database data. Instead, you could mandate that all data is created through other means, such as through direct database inserts or batch files.	When a client calls the *create()* method on a home object, the container calls *ejbCreate()* on a pooled bean instance. *ejbCreate()* methods are responsible for creating new database data and for initializing your bean. Each *ejbCreate()* method you define gives clients a different way to create your entity beans, such as methods to create a checking account and a savings account.	Make sure the client's initialization parameters are valid. Explicitly create the database representation of the data through a storage API like JDBC or SQL/J, typically through a SQL INSERT. Then return a primary key to the container, so that the container can identify which data your instance represents. Your entity bean instance is no longer in the pool–it now has specific database data inside of it. The container will bind your instance to a particular EJB objects.

(continued)

Table 7.1 *(continued)*

TYPICAL IMPLEMENTATION	METHOD	EXPLANATION
ejbPostCreate(<...>)	Your bean class must define one *ejbPostCreate()* for each *ejbCreate()*. Each pair must accept the same parameters. The container calls *ejbPostCreate()* right after *ejbCreate()*.	The container calls *ejbPostCreate()* after it has associated your bean instance with an EJB object. You can now complete your initialization by doing anything you need to that requires that EJB object, such as passing your bean's EJB object reference to other beans. You might also use this method to reset certain transaction-related parameters. For example, you could keep a data status flag in the bean to indicate whether a field has been changed. Because the bean instance may have been used before, these fields might have dirty data.
ejbActivate()	When a client calls a business method on an EJB object, but no entity bean instance is bound to the EJB object, the container needs to take a bean from the pool and transition it into a ready state. This is called *activation*. Upon activation, the *ejbActivate()* method is called by the EJB container.	Acquire any resources, such as socket connections, that your bean needs to service a particular client when it is moved into the ready state. Note that you should *not* read the entity bean data from the database in this method. That is handled by a separate method, *ejbLoad()*, which is called right after *ejbActivate()*.
ejbLoad()	The EJB container calls this method to load database data into your bean instance (typically a SQL SELECT), based on the current transactional state.	First, your bean instance must figure out what data it should load. Call the *getPrimaryKey()* method on the entity context; that will tell your bean what data it should be loading. Next, read database data into your bean using a storage API such as JDBC or SQL/J.

Table 7.1 *(continued)*

TYPICAL IMPLEMENTATION	METHOD	EXPLANATION
ejbStore()	The EJB container calls this method to update the database to the new values of your in-memory fields, thus synchronizing the database. The current transactional state dictates when this method is called. This method is also called during passivation, directly before *ejbPassivate()*.	Explicitly update the database representation of the data via a storage API like JDBC. Typically, you'll write a number of your member variable fields out to disk through a SQL UPDATE.
bPassivate()	The EJB container calls this method when it wants to return your entity bean to the pool. This is called *passivation* and is the opposite of activation. On passivation, the *ejbPassivate()* method is called by the EJB container.	Release any resources, such as socket connections, that you allocated in *ejbActivate()* and that bean was holding during the ready state for a particular client. You should not save the entity bean data into the database in this method. That is handled by a separate method, *ejbStore()*, which is called right before *ejbPassivate()*.
ejbRemove()	Destroys database data. It is not used to destroy the Java object; the object can be pooled and reused for different data.	First, figure out what data you should destroy using the *getPrimaryKey()* method on the *EntityContext* field. Then explicitly delete the database representation of the data using a storage API like JDBC, typically through a SQL DELETE.
unsetEntityContext()	This method disassociates a bean from its environment. The container calls this right before your entity bean instance is destroyed when it wants to reduce the pool size.	Release any resources you allocated during *setEntityContext()*, and get ready to be garbage collected.

You define finder methods only when you use bean-managed persistence. With container-managed persistence (CMP), these method implementations are generated for you.

As with *ejbCreate()*, clients do not invoke your finder methods on the bean instance itself. A finder method is just like any other method on your entity bean class—clients never directly call any of your bean's methods. Rather, clients invoke finder methods on home objects, implemented by the EJB container, that delegate to your bean. Therefore, for each finder method you define in your bean class, you should define a corresponding finder in the local home interface. Clients call your local home object's finder methods, which delegate to your bean's finders.

For example, given the following finder method in the local home interface:

```
public AccountLocal findBigAccounts(int minimum) throws FinderException;
```

here is the finder implementation in your bean class (notice the *ejb* prefix):

```
public AccountPK ejbFindBigAccounts(int minimum)
 throws FinderException {  ... }
```

As with *ejbCreate()*, the home signature and the bean class signature have a couple of differences:

- The entity bean instance returns a primary key to the container, whereas the home object returns an EJB object to the client.
- The bean class signature is the same as the home signature, except for an extra, mandatory ejb prefix and that the first letter in the word *Find* is capitalized.

These signature differences between the home and bean are valid because the bean does not implement the local home interface. Rather, the local home object *delegates* to the bean, so strict signature matching is not needed.

You can have many different finder methods, all of which perform different operations. Here are some examples of finder methods in an entity bean class:

```
/**
 * Finds the unique bank account indexed by primary key
 */
public AccountPK ejbFindByPrimaryKey(AccountPK key)
 throws FinderException {  ... }


/**
 * Finds all the product entity beans.  Returns a Collection
 * of primary keys.
```

```
  */
public Collection ejbFindAllProducts()
 throws FinderException {  ... }


/**
 * Finds all Bank Accounts that have at least a minimum balance.
 * Returns a Collection of primary keys.
 */
public Collection ejbFindBigAccounts(int minimum)
 throws FinderException {  ... }


/**
 * Finds the most recently placed order
 */
public OrderPK ejbFindMostRecentOrder()
 throws FinderException {  ... }
```

Another interesting aspect of finders is that they can return collections. Your database search may turn up more than one result and therefore more than one entity bean. Here is the local home interface signature:

```
public Collection findAllProducts() throws FinderException;
```

And here is the bean implementation signature:

```
public Collection ejbFindAllProducts()
 throws FinderException {  ... }
```

The finder process works as follows:

- When the client invokes the home object's finder, the home object asks a bean to find all primary keys matching the client's criteria. The bean then returns a *collection* of those primary keys to the container.
- When the container receives the collection of keys from the entity bean instance, *it creates a collection of EJB objects*, one for each primary key, and returns those EJB objects in its own collection to the client. The client can then invoke methods on the EJB objects: Each EJB object represents its own instance of data within the entity bean's database storage.

In summary, here are some of the rules about finder methods:

- All finder methods must begin with *ejbFind*. This is simply a syntactic rule.
- You must have at least one finder method, called *ejbFindByPrimaryKey*. This method finds one unique entity bean instance in the database

based on its unique primary key. Because every entity bean has an associated primary key, it makes sense that every entity bean class supports this method.

- You can have many different finder methods, each with different names and different parameters. This allows you to find using different semantics, as illustrated by the examples above.
- A finder method must return either the primary key for the entity bean it finds or a collection of primary keys if it finds more than one. Because you could find more than one data instance in the database, finder methods can return collections of primary keys.

Bean-Managed Persistence Example: A Bank Account

Our first example is a simple bank account entity bean. This bank account bean can be used to represent and manipulate real bank account data in an underlying relational database. Figure 7.2 details the class diagram for our bank account.

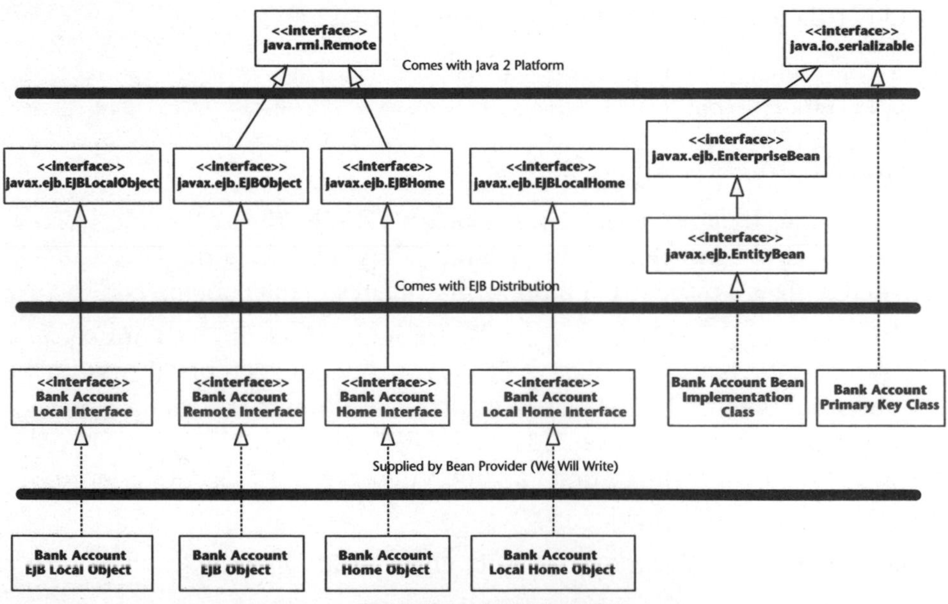

Figure 7.2 The bank account class diagram.

Notice that we're developing both local and remote interfaces. When this bean is used in production, the local interfaces will be used, because this entity bean will be accessed by other beans that run in-process. However, for testing purposes, and to help you understand entity beans easily, we don't want to introduce other beans. Rather, we will connect to this bean from a standalone application. Since a standalone application is remote, we thus need to use its remote interface. This is a common issue with EJB programming—to test beans on an individual basis in this manner, you need to code its remote interface even though you only plan to use the local interface in production. The good news is that the code is almost identical for the local interface—see the book's accompanying source code (the e-commerce example) for examples of calling entity beans through their local interfaces. Now let's take a look at each of the files that we must create for our entity bean component.

Account.java

Account.java is our entity bean's remote interface—what remote clients use to call our bean's methods. The interface is shown in Source 7.3.

```
package examples.bmp;

import javax.ejb.*;
import java.rmi.RemoteException;

/**
 * This is the remote interface for AccountBean.
 *
 * Client interact with beans through this interface.
The container will implement
 * this interface. The implemented object is called the EJB object,
which delegates
 * invocations to the actual bean.
 */
public interface Account
      extends EJBObject {
      /**
       * Deposits amt into account.
       */
      public void deposit(double amt)
          throws AccountException, RemoteException;

      /**
       * Withdraws amount from bank account.
       * @throw AccountException thrown if amount > available balance
```

Source 7.3 Account.java. *(continued)*

```
     */
    public void withdraw(double amount)
        throws AccountException, RemoteException;

    // Getter/setter methods on Entity Bean fields

    public double getBalance() throws RemoteException;

    public String getOwnerName() throws RemoteException;
    public void setOwnerName(String name) throws RemoteException;

    public String getAccountID() throws RemoteException;
    public void setAccountID(String id) throws RemoteException;
}
```

Source 7.3 *(continued)*

Notice that the account remote interface extends *javax.ejb.EJBObject*, which all remote interfaces must do. Our interface exposes a number of methods for manipulating entity beans, such as for making deposits and withdrawals. All of our methods throw remote exceptions to signal system-level catastrophic failures, as is required for methods in the remote interface. Notice that in our withdrawal method, we also throw our own custom application-level exception, *AccountException*. We'll define that exception later.

A final word on the use of remote interfaces: Generally, a remote client should call an entity bean directly only when you are writing small test applications to exercise your entity bean's API, as in this example. Otherwise you should use the local interface for performance reasons, and access entity beans through additional session beans (see Chapter 11).

AccountLocal.java

AccountLocal.java is our entity bean's local interface—what local clients use to call our bean's methods. The interface is shown in Source 7.4.

```
package examples.bmp;

import javax.ejb.*;

/**
 * This is the local interface for AccountBean.
 *
 * Local clients interact with beans through this interface. The
container will
```

Source 7.4 AccountLocal.java.

```
 * implement this interface; the implemented object is called the ⮐
local object,
*  which delegates invocations to the actual bean.
 */
public interface AccountLocal
     extends EJBLocalObject {
     /**
      * Deposits amt into account.
      */
     public void deposit(double amt) throws AccountException;

     /**
      * Withdraws amt from bank account.
      * @throw AccountException thrown if amt > available balance
      */
     public void withdraw(double amt) throws AccountException;

     // Getter/setter methods on Entity Bean fields

     public double getBalance();

     public String getOwnerName();
     public void setOwnerName(String name);

     public String getAccountID();
     public void setAccountID(String id);
}
```

Source 7.4 *(continued)*

AccountHome.java

Our home interface is specified in *AccountHome.java,* shown in Source 7.5.

```
package examples.bmp;

import javax.ejb.*;
import java.util.Collection;
import java.rmi.RemoteException;

/**
 * This is the home interface for Account. This interface is
implemented by the EJB
*  container's tools - the implemented object is called the home
object, which
```

Source 7.5 AccountHome.java. *(continued)*

```
 * is a factory for EJB objects.
 */
public interface AccountHome
    extends EJBHome {
   /**
    * We define a single create() method in this home interface,
    * which corresponds to the ejbCreate() method in AccountBean.
    * This method creates the local EJB object.
    *
    * Notice that the local home interface returns a local interface,
    * whereas the bean returns a Primary Key.
    *
    * @param accountID The number of the account (unique)
    * @param ownerName The name of the person who owns the account
    * @return The newly created local object.
    */
   Account create(String accountID, String ownerName)
       throws CreateException, RemoteException;

   /**
    * Finds an Account by its primary Key (Account ID)
    */
   public Account findByPrimaryKey(AccountPK key)
       throws FinderException, RemoteException;

   /**
    * Finds all Accounts under an owner name
    */
   public Collection findByOwnerName(String name)
       throws FinderException, RemoteException;

   /**
    * This home business method is independent of any particular
    * account. It returns the total of all accounts in the bank.
    */
   public double getTotalBankValue()
      throws AccountException, RemoteException;
}
```

Source 7.5 *(continued)*

We provide one *create()* method to create a new account. This will create new database data representing a bank account. It returns an EJB object to the client so the client can manipulate that newly created account. Notice that we throw the application-level *javax.ejb.CreateException*, which all *create()* methods must throw.

We also have two finder methods. *findByPrimaryKey()* searches the database for a bank account that already exists; it searches by the account ID, which we will define in *AccountPK.java*. We also have a custom finder method, *findByOwnerName()*, which searches the database for all bank accounts that have the same owner's name. Because we're using bean-managed persistence, we need to implement both of these finder methods in our entity bean implementation. (If we were using container-managed persistence, the container would search the database for us.) As with our *create()* method, both finders return EJB objects so the client can manipulate the newly found bank accounts. We throw the application-level *javax.ejb.FinderException*, which all finders must throw.

Finally, we have a business method, *getTotalBankValue()*. This business method is an operation applied to the entire table rather than to an individual row. Thus it is a global method that is independent of any particular entity bean instance. This business method will be implemented in the bean class as an *ejbHome()* method, as previously described in Table 7.1.

AccountLocalHome.java

Our local home interface, the home interface used by local clients, is specified in *AccountLocalHome.java*, shown in Source 7.6.

The only differences between the local home interface and the home interface are that the local home interface does not throw remote exceptions, and extends a different parent interface.

```
package examples.bmp;

import javax.ejb.*;
import java.util.Collection;

/**
 * This is the local home interface for Account.  This
 * interface is implemented by the EJB container's tools - the
 * implemented object is called the local home object, which
 * is a factory for local EJB objects.
 */
public interface AccountLocalHome
    extends EJBLocalHome {
   /**
     * We define a single create() method in this home interface,
     * which corresponds to the ejbCreate() method in AccountBean.
     * This method creates the local EJB object.
     *
     * Notice that the local home interface returns a
     * local interface, whereas the bean returns a PK.
     *
     * Notice we don't throw RemoteExceptions because we are local
not remote.
```

Source 7.6 AccountLocalHome.java. *(continued)*

```
     *
     * @param accountID The number of the account (unique)
     * @param ownerName The name of the person who owns the account
     * @return The newly created local object.
     */
    public AccountLocal create(String accountID, String ownerName)
        throws CreateException;

    /**
     * Finds an Account by its primary Key (Account ID)
     */
    public AccountLocal findByPrimaryKey(AccountPK key)
        throws FinderException;

    /**
     * Finds all Accounts under an owner's name
     */
    public Collection findByOwnerName(String name)
       throws FinderException;

    /**
     * This home business method is independent of any particular
     * account instance.  It returns the total of all the bank
     * accounts in the bank.
     */
    public double getTotalBankValue()
       throws AccountException;
}
```

Source 7.6 *(continued)*

AccountPK.java

Our entity bean's primary key class is defined by *AccountPK.java,* detailed in Source 7.7.

```
package examples.bmp;

/**
 * Primary Key class for Account.
 */
public class AccountPK implements java.io.Serializable {
  public String accountID;

  public AccountPK(String id) {
     this.accountID = id;
```

Source 7.7 AccountPK.java.

```
    }

    public AccountPK() {
    }

    public String toString() {
        return accountID;
    }

    public int hashCode() {
        return accountID.hashCode();
    }

    public boolean equals(Object account) {
        if (!(account instanceof AccountPK))
            return false;
        return ((AccountPK)account).accountID.equals(accountID);
    }
}
```

Source 7.7 *(continued)*

Notice the following:

- Our primary key contains a simple String—the account ID string. For example, an account ID string could be "ABC-123-0000." This string must be unique to its bank account; we rely on the client code that constructs our account ID to make sure it is unique. The primary key is used to identify each bank account uniquely. More advanced entity beans that map to more than one table may have primary key classes that have several fields inside of them, each representing the primary key of a table in the database.
- There is a required *toString()* method. This container calls this method to retrieve a String value of this primary key. For simple primary keys, we just return the stored field. For more advanced primary keys, we need somehow to combine the various fields in the primary key class to form a String.
- There is a required *hashCode()* method. By supplying this method, our primary key class can be stored in a Hashtable. The container needs this because inside of the container it may use a Hashtable or similar structure to store a list of all entity beans it has in memory, keyed on their primary keys.
- There is a required *equals()* method. The container calls this to compare this primary key to others when determining internally if two cached entity beans (which each have a primary key) are representing the same database data.

AccountBean.java

Next we have our entity bean implementation class, *AccountBean.java*. Our bean implementation code is quite lengthy and is divided into several sections.

- **Bean-managed state fields.** These are the persistable fields of our entity bean class. Our bean instance will load and store the database data into these fields.
- **Business logic methods.** These methods perform services for clients, such as withdrawing or depositing into an account. They are exposed by the remote interface, *Account*.
- **EJB-required methods.** These are methods that the container calls to manage our bean. They also include our create and find methods defined in the home interface.

The code is presented in Source 7.8 through Source 7.10. We divide it into three parts because the code is extremely cumbersome, even for a simple bank account. This is an unfortunate drawback of bean-managed persistence because you must provide all data access code.

```
package examples.bmp;

import java.sql.*;
import javax.naming.*;
import javax.ejb.*;
import java.util.*;

/**
 * Demonstration Bean-Managed Persistent Entity Bean. This Entity Bean
 * represents a Bank Account.
 */
public class AccountBean implements EntityBean {

     protected EntityContext ctx;

     //
     // Bean-managed state fields
     //

     private String accountID;      // PK
     private String ownerName;
     private double balance;

     public AccountBean() {
```

Source 7.8 AccountBean.java (Part 1 of 3).

```
        System.out.println("New Bank Account Entity Bean Java
Object created by EJB Container.");
    }

    ... methods continue ...
```

Source 7.8 *(continued)*

The first part of our bean is straightforward. We have our bean's fields (one of which is the primary key field), and a default constructor. We keep an *EntityContext* field around so that we can query the container from our bean as necessary (however, *EntityContext* is not a persistent field).

The next part of our bean is the business logic methods, shown in Source 7.9.

```
    ... continued ...

    //
    // Business Logic Methods
    //

    /**
     * Deposits amt into account.
     */
    public void deposit(double amt) throws AccountException {
        System.out.println("deposit(" + amt + ") called.");

        balance += amt;
    }

    /**
     * Withdraws amt from bank account.
     * @throw AccountException thrown if amt > available balance
     */
    public void withdraw(double amt) throws AccountException {
        System.out.println("withdraw(" + amt + ") called.");

        if (amt > balance) {
            throw new AccountException("Your balance is " +
            balance + "!  You cannot withdraw "
            + amt + "!");
        }

        balance -= amt;
```

Source 7.9 AccountBean.java (Part 2 of 3).*(continued)*

```
    }

    // Getter/setter methods on Entity Bean fields

    public double getBalance() {
        System.out.println("getBalance() called.");
        return balance;
    }

    public void setOwnerName(String name) {
        System.out.println("setOwnerName() called.");
        ownerName = name;
    }

    public String getOwnerName() {
        System.out.println("getOwnerName() called.");
        return ownerName;
    }

    public String getAccountID() {
        System.out.println("getAccountID() called.");
        return accountID;
    }

    public void setAccountID(String id) {
        System.out.println("setAccountID() called.");
        this.accountID = id;
    }

    /**
     * This home business method is independent of any
     * particular account instance.  It returns the total
     * of all the bank accounts in the bank.
     */
    public double ejbHomeGetTotalBankValue() throws AccountException {
        PreparedStatement pstmt = null;
        Connection conn = null;

        try {
            System.out.println("ejbHomeGetTotalBankValue()");

            /* Acquire DB connection */
            conn = getConnection();

            /* Get the total of all accounts */
            pstmt = conn.prepareStatement(
              "select sum(balance) as total from accounts");
```

Source 7.9 *(continued)*

```
                ResultSet rs = pstmt.executeQuery();

                /* Return the sum */
                if (rs.next()) {
                    return rs.getDouble("total");
                }
            }
            catch (Exception e) {
              e.printStackTrace();
              throw new AccountException(e);
            }
            finally {
                /*
                 * Release DB Connection for other beans
                 */
                try {  if (pstmt != null) pstmt.close(); }
                catch (Exception e) { }
                try {  if (conn != null) conn.close(); }
                catch (Exception e) { }
            }

            throw new AccountException("Error!");
        }

        /**
         * Gets JDBC connection from the connection pool.
         *
         * @return The JDBC connection
         */
        public Connection getConnection() throws Exception {
            try {
                Context ctx = new InitialContext();
                javax.sql.DataSource ds =

    (javax.sql.DataSource)ctx.lookup("java:comp/env/jdbc/ejbPool");
                return ds.getConnection();
            }
            catch (Exception e) {
                System.err.println("Couldn't get datasource!");
                e.printStackTrace();
                throw e;
            }
        }
    }
```

Source 7.9 *(continued)*

Our withdraw and deposit methods simply modify the in-memory fields of the entity bean instance. If the client tries to withdraw more money than is available in the account, we throw our custom application-level exception, *AccountException*.

The *ejbHomeGetTotalBankValue()* business method implementation adds the total of all bank account balances in the database. It retrieves a JDBC connection using the *getConnection()* helper method. In that *getConnection()* method we look up the database connection using JNDI (see Chapter 10 for a full description of this process).

Notice, too, that we close each connection after every method call. This allows our EJB container to pool JDBC connections. When the connection is not in use, another bean can use our connection. This is the standard, portable way for *connection pooling*. The connection pooling is built into the JDBC 2.0 specification and happens automatically behind the scenes.

The final part of our bean demonstrates the various EJB callback methods, shown in Source 7.10.

```
... continued ...

//
// EJB-required methods
//

/**
 * Called by Container.  Implementation can acquire
 * needed resources.
 */
public void ejbActivate() {
     System.out.println("ejbActivate() called.");
}

/**
 * Removes entity bean data from the database.
 * Corresponds to when client calls home.remove().
 */
public void ejbRemove() throws RemoveException {
     System.out.println("ejbRemove() called.");

     /*
      * Remember that an entity bean class can be used to
      * represent different data instances.  So how does
      * this method know which instance in the database
      * to delete?
      *
      * The answer is to query the container by calling
      * the entity context object.  By retrieving the
      * primary key from the entity context, we know
      * which data instance, keyed by the PK, that we
      * should delete from the DB.
```

Source 7.10 AccountBean.java (Part 3 of 3).

```
         */
        AccountPK pk = (AccountPK) ctx.getPrimaryKey();
        String id = pk.accountID;

        PreparedStatement pstmt = null;
        Connection conn = null;
        try {
             /*
              * 1) Acquire a new JDBC Connection
              */
             conn = getConnection();

             /*
              * 2) Remove account from the DB
              */
             pstmt = conn.prepareStatement(
             "delete from accounts where id = ?");
             pstmt.setString(1, id);

             /*
              * 3) Throw a system-level exception if something
              * bad happened.
              */
             if (pstmt.executeUpdate() == 0) {
                  throw new RemoveException(
                  "Account " + pk +
                  " failed to be removed from the database");
             }
        }
        catch (Exception ex) {
             throw new EJBException(ex.toString());
        }
        finally {
             /*
              * 4) Release the DB Connection
              */
             try {  if (pstmt != null) pstmt.close(); }
             catch (Exception e) { }
             try {  if (conn != null) conn.close(); }
             catch (Exception e) { }
        }
   }

   /**
    * Called by Container.  Releases held resources for
    * passivation.
    */
   public void ejbPassivate() {
        System.out.println("ejbPassivate () called.");
```

Source 7.10 *(continued)*

```
    }

    /**
     * Called by the container.  Updates the in-memory entity
     * bean object to reflect the current value stored in
     * the database.
     */
    public void ejbLoad() {
        System.out.println("ejbLoad() called.");

        /*
         * Again, query the Entity Context to get the current
         * Primary Key, so we know which instance to load.
         */
        AccountPK pk = (AccountPK) ctx.getPrimaryKey();
        String id = pk.accountID;

        PreparedStatement pstmt = null;
        Connection conn = null;
        try {
            /*
             * 1) Acquire a new DB Connection
             */
            conn = getConnection();

            /*
             * 2) Get account from the DB, querying
             *    by account ID
             */
            pstmt = conn.prepareStatement(
            "select ownerName, balance from accounts "
            + "where id = ?");
            pstmt.setString(1, id);
            ResultSet rs = pstmt.executeQuery();
            rs.next();
            ownerName = rs.getString("ownerName");
            balance = rs.getDouble("balance");
        }
        catch (Exception ex) {
            throw new EJBException(
            "Account " + pk
            + " failed to load from database", ex);
        }
        finally {
            /*
             * 3) Release the DB Connection
             */
            try {  if (pstmt != null) pstmt.close(); }
            catch (Exception e) { }
```

Source 7.10 *(continued)*

```
            try {  if (conn != null) conn.close(); }
            catch (Exception e) { }
        }

    }

    /**
     * Called from the Container.  Updates the database
     * to reflect the current values of this in-memory
     * entity bean instance.
     */
    public void ejbStore() {
        System.out.println("ejbStore() called.");

        PreparedStatement pstmt = null;
        Connection conn = null;
        try {
            /*
             * 1) Acquire a new DB Connection
             */
            conn = getConnection();

            /*
             * 2) Store account in DB
             */
            pstmt = conn.prepareStatement(
            "update accounts set ownerName = ?, balance = ?"
            + " where id = ?");
            pstmt.setString(1, ownerName);
            pstmt.setDouble(2, balance);
            pstmt.setString(3, accountID);
            pstmt.executeUpdate();

        }
        catch (Exception ex) {
            throw new EJBException("Account " + accountID +
                                   " failed to save to
database", ex);
        }
        finally {
            /*
             * 3) Release the DB Connection
             */
            try {  if (pstmt != null) pstmt.close(); }
            catch (Exception e) { }
            try {  if (conn != null) conn.close(); }
            catch (Exception e) { }
        }
```

Source 7.10 *(continued)*

```
    }

    /**
     * Called by the container.  Associates this bean
     * instance with a particular context.  We can query
     * the bean properties that customize the bean here.
     */
    public void setEntityContext(EntityContext ctx) {
         System.out.println("setEntityContext called");
         this.ctx = ctx;
       }

    /**
     * Called by Container.  Disassociates this bean
     * instance with a particular context environment.
     */
    public void unsetEntityContext() {
         System.out.println("unsetEntityContext called");
         this.ctx = null;
       }

    /**
     * Called after ejbCreate().  Now, the Bean can retrieve
     * its EJBObject from its context, and pass it as
     * a 'this' argument.
     */
    public void ejbPostCreate(String accountID, String ownerName) {
    }

    /**
     * This is the initialization method that corresponds to the
     * create() method in the Home Interface.
     *
     * When the client calls the Home Object's create() method,
     * the Home Object then calls this ejbCreate() method.
     *
     * @return The primary key for this account
     */
    public AccountPK ejbCreate(String accountID, String ownerName)
      throws CreateException {

         PreparedStatement pstmt = null;
         Connection conn = null;
         try {
              System.out.println("ejbCreate() called.");
              this.accountID = accountID;
              this.ownerName = ownerName;
              this.balance = 0;
```

Source 7.10 *(continued)*

```
            /*
             * Acquire DB connection
             */
            conn = getConnection();

            /*
             * Insert the account into the database
             */
            pstmt = conn.prepareStatement(
            "insert into accounts (id, ownerName, balance)"
            + " values (?, ?, ?)");
            pstmt.setString(1, accountID);
            pstmt.setString(2, ownerName);
            pstmt.setDouble(3, balance);
            pstmt.executeUpdate();

            /*
             * Generate the Primary Key and return it
             */
            return new AccountPK(accountID);
        }
        catch (Exception e) {
            throw new CreateException(e.toString());
        }
        finally {
            /*
             * Release DB Connection for other beans
             */
            try {  if (pstmt != null) pstmt.close(); }
            catch (Exception e) { }
            try {  if (conn != null) conn.close(); }
            catch (Exception e) { }
        }
    }

    /**
     * Finds a Account by its primary Key
     */
    public AccountPK ejbFindByPrimaryKey(AccountPK key)
      throws FinderException {
        PreparedStatement pstmt = null;
        Connection conn = null;
        try {
            System.out.println("ejbFindByPrimaryKey("
                                   + key + ") called");

            /*
             * Acquire DB connection
             */
```

Source 7.10 *(continued)*

```
            conn = getConnection();

            /*
             * Find the Entity in the DB
             */
            pstmt = conn.prepareStatement(
            "select id from accounts where id = ?");
            pstmt.setString(1, key.toString());
            ResultSet rs = pstmt.executeQuery();
            rs.next();

            /*
             * No errors occurred, so return the Primary Key
             */
            return key;
        }
        catch (Exception e) {
            throw new FinderException(e.toString());
        }
        finally {
            /*
             * Release DB Connection for other beans
             */
            try {  if (pstmt != null) pstmt.close(); }
            catch (Exception e) { }
            try {  if (conn != null) conn.close(); }
            catch (Exception e) { }
        }
    }

    /**
     * Finds Accounts by name
     */
    public Collection ejbFindByOwnerName(String name)
      throws FinderException {
        PreparedStatement pstmt = null;
        Connection conn = null;
        Vector v = new Vector();

        try {
            System.out.println(
              "ejbFindByOwnerName(" + name + ") called");

            /*
             * Acquire DB connection
             */
            conn = getConnection();

            /*
```

Source 7.10 *(continued)*

```
             * Find the primary keys in the DB
             */
            pstmt = conn.prepareStatement(
            "select id from accounts where ownerName = ?");
            pstmt.setString(1, name);
            ResultSet rs = pstmt.executeQuery();

            /*
             * Insert every primary key found into a vector
             */
            while (rs.next()) {
                String id = rs.getString("id");
                v.addElement(new AccountPK(id));
            }

            /*
             * Return the vector of primary keys
             */
            return v;
        }
        catch (Exception e) {
            throw new FinderException(e.toString());
        }
        finally {
            /*
             * Release DB Connection for other beans
             */
            try { if (pstmt != null) pstmt.close(); }
            catch (Exception e) { }
            try { if (conn != null) conn.close(); }
            catch (Exception e) { }
        }
    }
}
```

Source 7.10 *(continued)*

Source 7.10 is quite long because of the enormous amount of JDBC coding required to write even a simple bean-managed persistent entity bean. The bulk of the code occurs in the methods that perform CRUD operations (Create, Read, Update, Delete). These are namely *ejbCreate()*, *ejbFind()* and *ejbLoad()*, *ejb-Store()*, and *ejbRemove()*. The code is self-documenting and you should be able to understand it if you cross-reference Table 7.1. If you're still stuck, we will further explain these methods later in this chapter when we discuss the life cycle of a bean-managed persistent entity bean.

When a statement is sent to a database, the container's installer JDBC driver parses it, determines the best way to execute the statement based on statistics that it maintains, and then executes the statement. Parsing and determining an execution strategy can be computationally expensive. The good news is that JDBC is smart—when an instance of *PreparedStatement* is executed on a connection, it first checks its cache to see whether this statement has been executed previously; if so, it reuses the previously prepared version, thus improving performance. For more information, refer to Billy Newport's article "How Prepared Statements Greatly Improve Performance," posted at www.ejbinfo.com.

AccountException.java

Our custom exception class is *AccountException.java,* displayed in Source 7.11. It simply delegates to the parent *java.lang.Exception* class. It is still useful to define our own custom exception class, however, so that we can distinguish between a problem with our bank account component and a problem with another part of a deployed system.

```
package examples.bmp;

/**
 * Exceptions thrown by Accounts
 */
public class AccountException extends Exception {

     public AccountException() {
          super();
     }

     public AccountException(Exception e) {
          super(e.toString());
     }

     public AccountException(String s) {
          super(s);
     }
}
```

Source 7.11 AccountException.java.

Client.java

Our last Java file is a simple test client to exercise our bean's methods. It is shown in Source 7.12.

```
package examples.bmp;

import javax.ejb.*;
import javax.naming.*;
import java.rmi.*;
import javax.rmi.*;
import java.util.*;

/**
 * Sample client code that manipulates a Bank Account Entity Bean.
 */
public class AccountClient {

     public static void main(String[] args) throws Exception {

          Account account = null;

          try {
               /*
                * Get a reference to the Account Home Object - the
                * factory for Account EJB Objects
                */
               Context ctx =
                 new InitialContext(System.getProperties());

               Object obj = ctx.lookup("AccountHome");
               AccountHome home = (AccountHome)
                 PortableRemoteObject.narrow(
                   obj, AccountHome.class);

               System.err.println(
                "Total of all accounts in bank initially = "
                + home.getTotalBankValue());

               /* Use the factory to create the Account EJB Object */
               home.create("123-456-7890", "John Smith");

               /* Find an account */
               Iterator i = home.findByOwnerName(
                 "John Smith").iterator();
               if (i.hasNext()) {
                    account =
                        (Account)javax.rmi.PortableRemoteObject.narrow(
                            i.next(), Account.class);
```

Source 7.12 Client.java. *(continued)*

```
            }
            else {
                throw new Exception("Could not find account");
            }

            /* Call the balance() method, and print it */
            System.out.println("Initial Balance = " +
account.getBalance());

            /* Deposit $100 into the account */
            account.deposit(100);

            /* Retrieve the resulting balance. */
            System.out.println(
              "After depositing 100, account balance = "
              + account.getBalance());

            System.out.println(
              "Total of all accounts in bank now = "
              + home.getTotalBankValue());

            /* Retrieve the Primary Key from the EJB Object */
            AccountPK pk = (AccountPK) account.getPrimaryKey();

            /*
             * Release our old EJB Object reference.  Now call
             * find() again, this time querying on Account ID
             * (i.e. the Primary Key).
             */
            account = null;
            account = home.findByPrimaryKey(pk);

            /* Print out current balance */
            System.out.println(
              "Found account with ID " + pk + ".  Balance = "
              + account.getBalance());

            /* Try to withdraw $150 */
            System.out.println(
              "Now trying to withdraw $150, which is more "
            + "than is currently available.  This should "
            + "generate an exception..");
            account.withdraw(150);

        }
        catch (Exception e) {
            System.out.println("Caught exception!");
            e.printStackTrace();
        }
```

Source 7.12 *(continued)*

```
            finally {
                /*
                 * Destroy the Entity permanently
                 */
                try {
                    System.out.println("Destroying account..");
                    if (account != null) {
                        account.remove();
                    }
                }
                catch (Exception e) {
                    e.printStackTrace();
                }
            }
        }
}
```

Source 7.12 *(continued)*

The client code is fairly self-explanatory. We perform some bank account operations in the *try* block. We have a *finally* clause to make sure our bank account is properly deleted afterward, regardless of any exceptions that may have been thrown.

The Deployment Descriptor

Now, let's take a look at our deployment descriptor, shown in Source 7.13.

```
<?xml version="1.0" encoding="UTF-8"?>

<ejb-jar xmlns="http://java.sun.com/xml/ns/j2ee" version="2.1"
         xmlns:xsi="http://www.w3.org/2001/XMLSchema-instance"
         xsi:schemaLocation="http://java.sun.com/xml/ns/j2ee
http://java.sun.com/xml/ns/j2ee/ejb-jar_2_1.xsd">
  <display-name>AccountJAR</display-name>
  <enterprise-beans>
    <entity>
      <ejb-name>AccountEJB</ejb-name>
      <home>examples.bmp.AccountHome</home>
      <remote>examples.bmp.Account</remote>
      <ejb-class>examples.bmp.AccountBean</ejb-class>
      <persistence-type>Bean</persistence-type>
      <prim-key-class>examples.bmp.AccountPK</prim-key-class>
      <reentrant>false</reentrant>
      <resource-ref>
        <res-ref-name>jdbc/bmp-account</res-ref-name>
```

Source 7.13 The Account Bean's ejb-jar.xml deployment descriptor. *(continued)*

```
        <res-type>javax.sql.DataSource</res-type>
        <res-auth>Container</res-auth>
        <res-sharing-scope>Shareable</res-sharing-scope>
      </resource-ref>
    </entity>
  </enterprise-beans>
  <assembly-descriptor>
    <container-transaction>
      <method>
        <ejb-name>AccountEJB</ejb-name>
        <method-intf>Remote</method-intf>
        <method-name>*</method-name>
      </method>
     <method>
        <ejb-name>AccountEJB</ejb-name>
        <method-intf>Local</method-intf>
        <method-name>*</method-name>
      </method>
      <trans-attribute>Required</trans-attribute>
    </container-transaction>
  </assembly-descriptor>
</ejb-jar>
```

Source 7.13 *(continued)*

Notice the following features of our deployment descriptor that are different from session beans:

- The *persistence-type* element indicates whether we are bean-managed persistent (set it to "Bean") or container-managed persistent (set it to "Container").
- The *prim-key-class* element specifies our primary key class.
- The *reentrant* element dictates whether our bean can call itself through another bean. A given bean A is reentrant if bean A calls bean B, which calls back on bean A. This is a special case of multithreading because it is really only one path of execution that happens to loop back on itself. If we would like to support this reentrant behavior, we should set this setting to *True* so that the container will allow two threads to run inside of bean A at once. Since our bean doesn't call itself through another bean, we set it to *False*, which is usually what you'll want to do to avoid unintended multithreading issues.
- The *resource-ref* element sets up our JDBC driver and makes it available at the proper JNDI location (see Chapter 10 for a full description of this process).
- The *assembly-descriptor* associates transactions with our bean. We will describe transactions fully in Chapter 12.

The Container-Specific Deployment Descriptor

Finally, we have our container-specific deployment descriptor, which configures our bean in ways specific to a particular EJB server. We will not show this file because we want the code in this book to remain vendor-neutral. Typically, you would use this proprietary descriptor to associate the home interface, local home interface, and JDBC driver with JNDI locations. For an example descriptor, see the book's accompanying source code.

Setting up the Database

Lastly, we need to create the appropriate database table and columns for our bank accounts. You can do this through your database's GUI or command-line interface. The book's included source code includes installation scripts that will do this for you for the J2EE SDK's database. If you're using a different database, you should enter the following SQL *Data Definition Language* (DDL) statements in your database's SQL interface:

```
drop table accounts;
create table accounts (id varchar(64), ownername varchar(64), balance
numeric(18));
```

This creates an empty table of bank accounts. The first column is the bank account ID (the primary key), the second column is the bank account owner's name, and the third column is the bank account balance.

Running the Client Program

To run the client program, type a command similar to the following (depending on what your EJB container's Java Naming and Directory Interface [JNDI] connection parameters are—see your container's documentation):

```
java -Djava.naming.provider.url=corbaloc::localhost:3700/NameService
     -Djava.naming.factory.initial=com.sun.jndi.cosnaming.CNCtxFactory
     examples.bmp.AccountClient
```

The initialization parameters are required by JNDI to find the home object, as we learned in Chapter 3.

Server-Side Output

When you run the client, you should see something *similar* to the following output on the server side. Note that your particular output may vary, because of variances in EJB container behavior.

```
New Bank Account Entity Bean Java Object created by EJB Container.
setEntityContext called.
ejbHomeGetTotalBankValue() called.
ejbCreate() called.
ejbStore() called.
New Bank Account Entity Bean Java Object created by EJB Container.
setEntityContext called.
ejbFindByOwnerName(John Smith) called.
ejbLoad() called.
getBalance() called.
ejbStore() called.
ejbLoad() called.
deposit(100.0) called.
ejbStore() called.
ejbLoad() called.
getBalance() called.
ejbStore() called.
ejbHomeGetTotalBankValue() called.
ejbFindByPrimaryKey(123-456-7890) called.
ejbLoad() called.
getBalance() called.
ejbStore() called.
ejbLoad() called.
withdraw(150.0) called.
ejbStore() called.
ejbLoad() called.
ejbRemove() called.
```

Notice what's happening here:

- When our client code called *create()* on the home object, the container created an entity bean instance. The container first called *newInstance()* and *setEntityContext()* to get the entity bean into the available pool of entity beans. The container then serviced our client's home business method and used the bean in the pool. Then the client called *create()*, which caused the container to take the bean out of the pool and call the bean's *ejbCreate()* method, which created some new database data, and returned control back to the container. Finally, the container associated the bean instance with a new EJB object and returned that EJB object to the client.

- To service our finder method, the container instantiated another entity bean. The container called *newInstance()* and then *setEntityContext()* to get that new bean instance into the available pool of entity beans. It then used the bean in the pool to service our finder method. Note that the bean instance is still in the pool and could service any number of finder methods.
- In addition to the methods that the client calls, our EJB container inserted a few *ejbStore()* and *ejbLoad()* calls to keep the database in synch.

Client-Side Output

Running the client program yields the following client-side output:

```
Total of all accounts in bank initially = 1200000.0
Initial Balance = 0.0
After depositing 100, account balance = 100.0
Total of all accounts in bank now = 1200100.0
Found account with ID 123-456-7890.  Balance = 100.0
Now trying to withdraw $150, which is more than is currently
available. This should generate an exception..
Caught exception!
examples.AccountException: Your balance is 100.0!  You cannot
withdraw 150.0!
Destroying account..
```

Our table already had $1,200,000 from previous records in the database. We then created an entity bean, deposited into it, and tried to withdraw more than we had. The entity bean correctly threw an application-level exception, indicating that our balance had insufficient funds.

Putting It All Together: Walking through a BMP Entity Bean's Life Cycle

Let's wrap up this chapter by examining the big picture and understanding exactly how a container interacts with a BMP entity bean. The state machine diagram in Figure 7.3 illustrates the life cycle of a BMP entity bean.

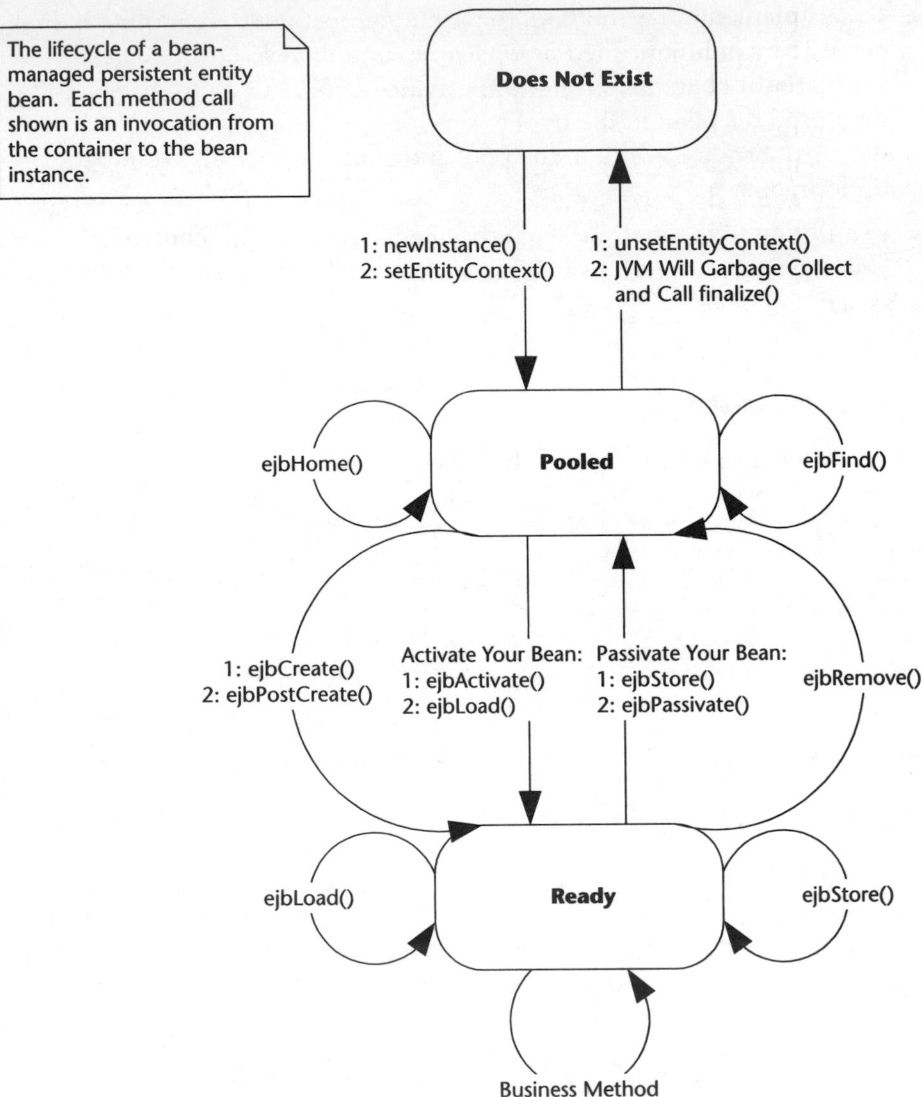

Figure 7.3 The BMP entity bean life cycle.

Here is what's going on in this diagram:

1. The *does not exist* state represents entity bean instances that have not been instantiated yet.
2. To create a new instance, the container calls the *newInstance()* method on the entity bean class. This calls your entity bean's default constructor, bringing a new instance into memory. Next, the container associates your entity bean with an entity context object through a callback that

you implement, called *setEntityContext(EntityContext ctx)*. Note that this step occurs only when the container wants to increase the available pool of entity bean instances, not necessarily when a client connects.

3. Next, your entity bean is in a pool of other entity beans. At this point your entity bean does not have any entity bean database data loaded into it, and it does not hold any bean-specific resources, such as socket connections. Your bean instance can be used in this mode to find entity data in the database, by servicing a *finder* method on behalf of a client. Your bean instance can also perform operations not dependent on a particular data instance by servicing an *ejbHome()* method on behalf of a client. If the container wants to reduce its pool size, it can destroy your bean. The container signals your bean instance that it is about to be destroyed by calling the *unsetEntityContext()* method on your bean. Once this is done, the container releases any references to your bean, and eventually, the Java garbage collector cleans up the memory your instance had been using. Therefore your *unsetEntityContext()* method should prepare your bean to be cleaned up, perhaps by releasing any resources your bean had claimed during *setEntityContext()*.

4. When the client wants to create some new database data (say, a new order for goods placed over the Internet), it calls a *create()* method on your entity bean's home object. The container then grabs an entity bean instance from the pool, and the instance's *ejbCreate()* method is called. *ejbCreate()* initializes the entity bean to a specific data set. For example, if a client calls a *create()* method to create a bank account, it might pass the bank account holder's name and the initial balance as parameters. Your entity bean's *ejbCreate()* method would populate its member variables with these parameters. It would also create the corresponding database representation (if you're using bean-managed persistence). Now your bean is in the "ready" state.

5. While your bean is in the ready state, it is tied to specific data and hence a specific EJB object. If there are other entity bean instances that are views into the same database data, the container may occasionally need to synchronize your bean instance with the underlying database, so that you will always be working with the most recent data. The *ejbLoad()* and *ejbStore()* methods do this; the container calls them as appropriate, based on how you define your transactions (see Chapter 11).

6. Your entity beans can be kicked back into the pool in two ways. If a client calls *remove()* on the home object, the container will call your instance's *ejbRemove()*. The underlying database data is destroyed and so, of course, your entity bean instance will become disassociated with the client's EJB object to which it was bound.

7. The second way your bean can return to the pool is if the EJB container decides that your client has timed out, if the container needs to use your bean to service a different client, or if the container is simply running out of resources. At this point, your bean is passivated, and the container calls your *ejbStore()* method to ensure the database has the most recent version of your in-memory data. Next the container calls your *ejbPassivate()* method, allowing your bean instance to release held resources. Your bean instance then enters the pool.
8. When the container wants to assign you to an EJB object again, your bean instance must be activated. The container calls your bean's *ejbActivate()* method, allowing your bean to acquire resources. The container then calls your instance's *ejbLoad()* method to load the database data into your bean.

Note that there are a few other minor steps in this process, such as transactional synchronization. Overall, these stages are the essence of a BMP entity bean instance's life cycle. The next step is for you to look at Figure 7.3 again and make sure you fully grasp it. Do you understand how a single Java object instance can be pooled and reused, going back and forth through various transitions between the pooled and ready state, perhaps representing different database data each time? If so, congratulations. This is a crucial step toward fully understanding EJB.

Summary

In this chapter, you've seen how to write bean-managed persistent (BMP) entity beans. Table 7.1 is provided for your reference and summarizes what you should implement in each method in your entity bean when using bean-managed persistence. You should refer to it when rereading the code in this chapter or when programming your own entity bean classes.

Bean-managed persistent entity beans are useful if you need to control the underlying database operations yourself. From a developer's perspective, the real advantage of EJB comes from *container-managed persistent* entity beans. Container-managed persistent (CMP) entity beans can be developed much more rapidly because the container handles all data access logic for you. The next chapter covers the EJB container-managed persistence model.

CHAPTER

8

Writing Container-Managed Persistent Entity Beans

In the previous chapters, we learned the basics of entity beans and wrote a bean-managed persistent entity bean that represented a bank account. In this chapter, we'll see how things change when we move to a container-managed persistent (CMP) model. With container-managed persistence, you don't implement any persistence logic (such as JDBC) in the entity bean itself; rather, the EJB container performs storage operations for you. As you will see, this greatly simplifies bean development.

Features of CMP Entity Beans

We'll kick things off by looking at the major differences between CMP and bean-managed persistence (BMP). Before reading this, you should be familiar with the entity bean concepts we covered in the previous two chapters.

CMP Entity Beans Are Subclassed

Imagine that you are a bean provider who writes beans that others will consume, such as an independent software vendor (ISV) or a department that writes components that other departments reuse. You need to write your beans to be database-independent because you don't know what storage the consumers of your bean will use. You certainly don't want to allow the consumers of your beans to access your source code, because it violates your intellectual property rights. Furthermore, if they modify the code, it makes future upgrades to new versions of your components difficult.

To answer this need, the authors of the EJB specification tried to make a clean separation between an entity bean and its persistent representation—that is, a separation between the business methods, such as logic in your entity bean to add two fields together, and the data access layer. This separation is valuable because you can modify the persistent representation of an entity bean (for example, to change from a relational database to an object database) without affecting the entity bean logic. This is a crucial feature for bean providers.

To achieve this clean separation, you write your CMP entity bean class without any persistence logic. The container then *generates* the data access code by *subclassing* your entity bean class. The generated subclass inherits from your entity bean class. Thus, all CMP entity beans actually comprise two classes: the superclass, which you write and which contains the entity bean business logic; and the subclass, which the container generates and which contains the persistence logic. These two classes achieve a clean separation of entity bean logic and persistent representation. The actual entity bean is a combination of the superclass and the subclass. This is shown in Figure 8.1.

Entity beans are very different between EJB 1.1 and EJB 2.x. EJB 1.1 entity beans do not require the use of subclassing. EJB 2.x containers must support both the old EJB 1.1 style and the EJB 2.x style of entity beans.

CMP Entity Beans Have No Declared Persistent Fields

Another issue with CMP is that the container might have additional fields or logic that are part of your persistent representation but are container-specific. As a bean developer, you should be oblivious to this information. Here are two examples:

- A container might keep around a bit vector that tracks which of your entity bean fields have been modified (that is, are dirty) and need to be written to storage. Then when your bean is stored, the container persists only the part of your bean that has changed.
- Your bean might hold references to other beans. The container must preserve the referential integrity of those relationships, as described in Chapter 12.

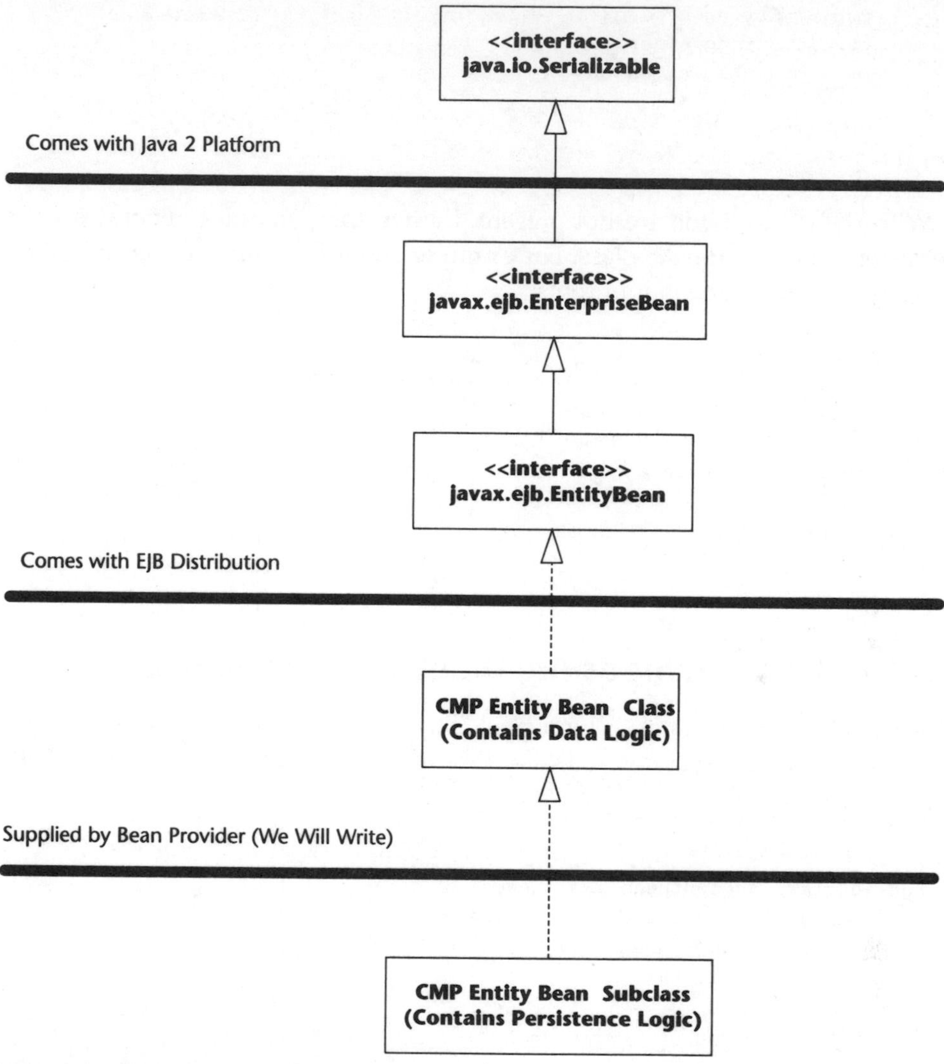

Figure 8.1 The subclassing concept.

Since every container has its own proprietary way of dealing with your persistent representation, your persistent fields are kept in the subclass, not the superclass. This is another paradigm shift with container-managed persistent entity beans: You don't declare any persistent fields in your bean. For example, take a look at the following snippet of code from the BMP bank account entity bean class that we wrote in Chapter 7:

```
// BMP
public class AccountBean implements EntityBean {
```

```
    public String accountID;      // PK
    public String ownerName;
    public double balance;

    ...methods...
}
```

With CMP, the fields are not present. Rather, the container generates your persistent fields in the subclass. For example, the following subclass might be generated from the container tools:

```
// CMP Subclass
public class AccountBeanSubClass extends AccountBean {
    public String accountID;      // PK
    public String ownerName;
    public double balance;

    ...methods...
}
```

CMP Get/Set Methods Are Defined in the Subclass

One corollary of the subclass paradigm is that the subclass, not the superclass, implements the get/set methods. For example, here is that BMP bank account again:

```
// BMP
public class AccountBean implements EntityBean {
    public String accountID;      // PK
    public String ownerName;
    public double balance;

    public String getOwnerName() {
        return ownerName;
    }

    public void setOwnerName(String ownerName) {
        this.ownerName = ownerName;
    }

    ...other methods...
}
```

With CMP, the get/set methods would appear in the subclass, since that is where the fields exist and thus the only place they can be accessed. Here is what the container-generated subclass looks like.

```
// CMP subclass
public class AccountBeanSubClass extends AccountBean {
     public String accountID;      // PK
     public String ownerName;
     public double balance;

     public String getOwnerName() {
          return ownerName;
     }
     public void setOwnerName(String ownerName) {
          this.ownerName = ownerName;
     }

     ...other methods...
}
```

So what does the superclass look like? First, realize that the superclass cannot possibly implement the get/set methods because it doesn't have access to the fields. However, the superclass *does* need to *call* those get/set methods. For example, let's say you have a shopping cart entity bean that contains a *subtotal* field and a *taxes* field on the contents in the shopping cart. One useful method you might want to write is a *getTotal()* method, which returns the subtotal 1 taxes. That is more than just a simple get/set method and thus cannot be generated automatically by the container in the subclass. Therefore you need to write that method in the superclass yourself. But what would that *getTotal()* method look like? With BMP, it could look like this:

```
// BMP
public class CartBean implements EntityBean {
     ...

     public float getTotal() {
          return this.getSubtotal() + this.getTaxes();
     }

     ...
}
```

This code works well with BMP because we can define the *getSubtotal()* and *getTaxes()* methods. But with CMP, the simple get/set methods *getSubtotal()* and *getTaxes()* are defined in the subclass, so how can we access those get/set methods? The answer is to declare your get/set methods as *abstract* methods in the superclass. An abstract method is a method whose implementation is deferred to a subclass; yet by defining a method as abstract you can call it from the superclass. For example, a CMP shopping cart bean would look like this:

```
// CMP superclass
public abstract class CartBean implements EntityBean {
```

```
        // no fields

        // abstract get/set methods
        public abstract float getSubTotal();
        public abstract float getTaxes();

        // other business methods
        public float getTotal() {
            return this.getSubtotal() + this.getTaxes();
        }

        // EJB required methods follow
}
```

The subclass for this bean is the subclass we showed earlier. As another example, a CMP account bean would look like this:

```
// CMP superclass
public abstract class AccountBean implements EntityBean {
     // no fields

     // abstract get/set methods
     public abstract String getOwnerName();
     public abstract void setOwnerName(String ownerName);

     // EJB required methods follow
}
```

CMP Entity Beans Have an Abstract Persistence Schema

So far, we've discussed how the container generates JDBC code, persistent fields, and get/set method implementations. One lurking question is how does the container know what to generate? The answer is that you *declare it* in your bean's deployment descriptors. The EJB container inspects the deployment descriptors to figure out what to generate. This definition of how you'd like to be persisted is called your *abstract persistence schema*. For example, here is a snippet from an Account deployment descriptor:

```
...
   <cmp-version>2.x</cmp-version>

   <abstract-schema-name>AccountBean</abstract-schema-name>

   <cmp-field>
    <field-name>accountID</field-name>
```

```
    </cmp-field>

    <cmp-field>
     <field-name>ownerName</field-name>
    </cmp-field>

    <cmp-field>
     <field-name>balance</field-name>
    </cmp-field>

    <primkey-field>accountID</primkey-field>
...
```

Here is a brief explanation of this deployment descriptor snippet.

- The *cmp-version* must be 2.*x* if you want to take advantage of EJB 2.0 CMP. If you are on the older EJB 1.1 specification, you should define this to be 1.*x*. We do not cover EJB 1.1 CMP in this book; see your application server's documentation and samples for details.
- The *abstract-schema-name* is the nickname you want to give this abstract persistence schema. It can have any value you want. We recommend naming it after your bean, or using other, consistent naming schemes. Later we will reference this nickname when doing queries. The abstract schema is not to be confused with the concrete database schema. A mapping between the abstract and the concrete schema is defined using platform tools, for example by generating a database-specific mapping file from the abstract schema.
- The *cmp-field* elements are your container-managed persistent fields. Each field is a persistent field that the container will generate in the subclass. The names of these fields must match the names of your abstract get/set methods, except the first letter is not capitalized. For example, if your abstract get/set methods are *getOwnerName()* and *setOwnerName()*, your cmp-field should be called *ownerName*. The container derives the types of these fields from the get/set methods as well.

We will see a complete example of an abstract persistence schema later in this chapter.

CMP Entity Beans Have a Query Language

Another piece of our CMP entity bean puzzle is addressing how to query entity beans. To enable clients of your bean to find you, you must define *finder methods*. For example, in BMP, you'd define this method in your home interface:

```
public Collection findBigAccounts(int minimum);
```

The home object would delegate this call to your bean. The implementation would be:

```
public Collection ejbFindBigAccounts(int minimum) {
     // Perform JDBC, and return primary keys for
     // all accounts whose balance is greater
     // than the minimum passed in
}
```

With CMP, the container generates JDBC code for us. However, we need a way to tell the container how to generate the data access code, because the container can't magically know what *find big accounts* means. We want to specify how to generate the persistence code in a portable way so that we don't have to rewrite completely the definitions of these finder methods every time we port our bean to a new container.

The solution to this challenge is the *EJB Query Language* (EJB-QL). EJB-QL is an object-oriented SQL-like syntax for querying entity beans. It contains a SELECT clause, a FROM clause, and optional WHERE and ORDER_BY clauses. You write the EJB-QL code in the deployment descriptor, and the container should be able to generate the corresponding database logic (such as SQL), perhaps with some help from the container tools. This is a similar concept to the Object Query Language (OQL) described in Chapter 6.

Here is an example of EJB-QL that finds all accounts:

```
SELECT OBJECT(a)
FROM Account AS a
WHERE a.accountID IS NOT NULL
```

If you are using a relational database, at deployment time and with the help of the container's tools that you use, the container will inspect this code and generate the appropriate JDBC code.

Here is another example that satisfies the *findBigAccounts()* home method:

```
SELECT OBJECT(a)
FROM Account AS a
WHERE a.balance > ?1
```

In the preceding code, *?1* means the first parameter passed in, which in this case is the variable *minimum*.

We will see more EJB-QL in the example later in this chapter. For the details, refer to the EJB-QL reference in Appendix D.

Not all fields within the bean have to be managed by the container. You might be pulling data manually from a secondary source, or you might have calculated fields. The EJB container automatically notifies your bean class during persistent operations, allowing you to manage these fields.

In general, containers are not responsible for persisting any data in the superclass, such as entity context references or environment naming contexts used for JNDI lookups. You never store these persistently as container-managed fields because they contain runtime EJB-specific information, and they do not represent persistent business data.

The complete process of developing and deploying a CMP entity bean is shown in Figure 8.2.

CMP Entity Beans Can Have ejbSelect() Methods

The final major difference between BMP and CMP entity beans is that CMP entity beans can have special *ejbSelect()* methods. An *ejbSelect()* method is a query method (like a finder method) but is not directly exposed to the client in the home interface or component interface. Rather, *ejbSelect()* is used internally within an entity bean as a helper method to access a storage. *ejbSelect()* is useful when you have entity beans in relationships with external data, such as other entity beans.

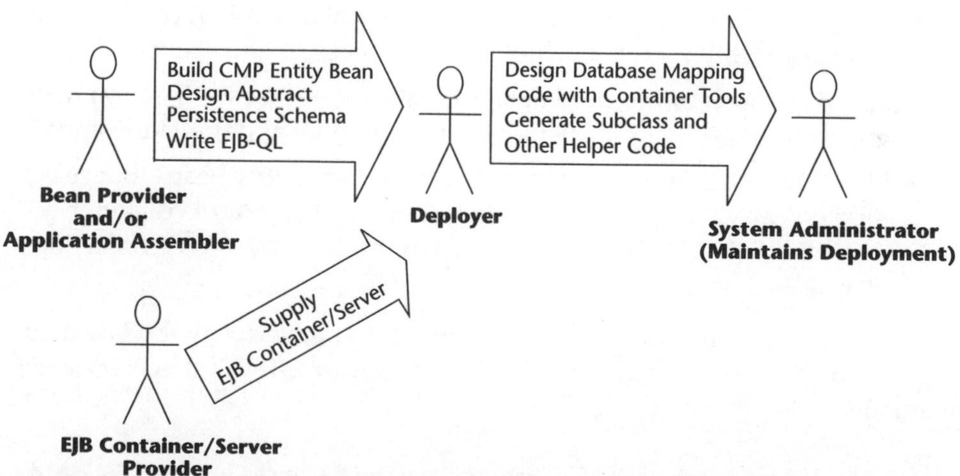

Figure 8.2 The process of developing and deploying a CMP entity bean.

For example, in our bank account example from the previous chapter, we defined a method called *ejbHomeGetTotalBankValue()*, which added the total of all bank accounts in the bank table by performing a SQL SELECT statement using JDBC. With CMP, you shouldn't be writing this JDBC code—rather, the container should generate it for you in an *ejbSelect()* method, and you should call that *ejbSelect()* method from the *ejbHomeGetTotalBankValue()* method. You then tell the container how to write the *ejbSelect()* method just like you do for a finder method—by using the EJB Query Language (EJB QL) described earlier.

For example, you might define the following method in your entity bean:

```
public abstract double ejbSelectAllAccountBalances()
throws FinderException;

public double ejbHomeGetTotalBankValue() throws Exception {

     // Get a collection of bank account balances
     Collection c = this.ejbSelectAllAccountBalances();

     // Loop through collection and return sum
}
```

ejbSelect() methods are not exposed to end clients via the remote interface or local interface. They *must* be called from within your bean, either from a business method or a home business method.

The value of *ejbSelect()* methods are threefold:

- Select methods can perform fine-grained database operations that your bean needs, but that you do not want to expose to end clients.
- Select methods can retrieve data from other entity beans that you have relationships with. (See Chapter 12 to learn more about relationships.)
- Like finder methods, select methods can return entity beans. But select methods are more powerful because they can also return container-managed fields, such as our previous example—it returns a collection of *double* values.

You tell the container about how to implement your select method by defining an EJB-QL query string. For more details on how EJB-QL affects *ejbSelect()* methods, see Appendix D.

As you may have noticed by now, the major differences between CMP and BMP lie in the entity bean class and the deployment descriptors. The remote, local, home, local home interfaces, and primary key class remain basically the same. This means it is possible to switch between CMP and BMP without changing the clients who call your beans, which is a nice side effect.

Implementation Guidelines for Container-Managed Persistence

Now that we've explored CMP entity beans in theory, let's see how to build CMP entity beans. The method implementations of your BMP entity beans should be different for CMP. No longer are you controlling the routine persistent operations of your beans, and so many of the methods can be left empty—the container will do it for you. Table 8.1 summarizes what you should implement in each method, assuming your entity bean's persistence is container managed. Take a quick glance at the table for now. As you can see, many of the database-intensive operations have been reduced in scope significantly. You should refer to the table when reading through the code in this chapter or when programming your own entity bean classes.

Table 8.1 Descriptions and Implementation Guidelines for Container-Managed Persistent Entity Beans

METHOD	EXPLANATION	TYPICAL IMPLEMENTATION
setEntityContext() (same as BMP)	If the container wants to increase its pool size of bean instances, it instantiates a new entity bean instance. Following this, the container calls the instance's *setEntityContext()* method. This method associates a bean with *context information*—information about the bean's environment. Once this method is called, the bean can access information about its environment.	Stick the entity context somewhere, such as in a member variable. You can access the context later to acquire environment information, like security information, from the container. You should also request any resources your instance will need regardless of what data the bean represents. *The bean is now in a pool, does not have any specific database data inside of it, and is not bound to any particular EJB object.*

(continued)

Table 8.1 *(continued)*

METHOD	EXPLANATION	TYPICAL IMPLEMENTATION
ejbFind,....(,....) (new for CMP)	*You do not write finder methods for container-managed beans.* The EJB container will handle *all* issues related to finding data for you. But how does the EJB container know what kinds of finder methods you want in your bean? After all, an infinite variety of ways exist to find data in a database. The answer is that your EJB container ships with tools for this purpose. You use EJB-QL and the container tools to tell the container what logic to execute when the client performs a finder method on the home object.	You should not implement these methods for CMP entity beans.
ejbSelect,....(,....) (new for CMP)	*ejbSelect()* methods are helper methods that perform queries internally by your bean but are not accessible to clients of your bean.	Define this method as abstract. Then write EJB-QL in the deployment descriptor to set up the query.

Table 8.1 *(continued)*

METHOD	EXPLANATION	TYPICAL IMPLEMENTATION
ejbHome,....(,....) (new for CMP)	Sometimes you need methods on an entity bean that are not specific to any given data instance (or row)—for example, counting up the total number of accounts in a table. You can write *ejbHome* methods to perform these operations. The *ejbHome* methods are special business methods because they are called from a bean in the pool before the bean is associated with any specific data. Clients call these methods from the home interface or local home interface.	Perform your global operations, such as counting up the rows in a database and returning the results to the client. The fast-and-easy way to achieve this is to use JDBC. The cleaner (but lower-performing if you're not careful) way is to call *ejbSelect()* and perhaps other entity bean methods.
ejbCreate(,....) (new for CMP) *Note: You do not need to write any ejbCreate() methods if you don't want EJB clients to be able to create new database data. Some systems may allow creation of data to occur via direct database inserts through batch files or other means.*	When a client calls *create()* on a home object, the container then calls *ejbCreate()* on a pooled bean instance. *ejbCreate()* methods are responsible for creating new database data and initializing your bean.	*Do not create database data in this method.* Rather, validate the client's initialization parameters. Call your abstract *set()* methods to initialize the generated bean subclass to the parameters passed in. The container will then use these values in the subclass to create the database data for you. Your entity bean instance is then no longer in the pool—it now has specific database data inside it. The container will bind your instance to a particular EJB objects.

(continued)

Table 8.1 *(continued)*

METHOD	EXPLANATION	TYPICAL IMPLEMENTATION
ejbPostCreate(,....) (same as BMP)	There is one *ejbPostCreate(...)* for each *ejbCreate(...)*. Each pair has the same parameters. The container calls your bean instance's *ejbPostCreate(...)* method following *ejbCreate(...)*.	The container calls *ejbPostCreate()* after it has associated your bean instance with an EJB object. You can now complete your initialization by doing anything you need to that requires that EJB object, such as passing your bean's EJB object reference to other beans. *Note:* By now the EJB container will have created your primary key object, so you can retrieve and use it.
ejbActivate() (same as BMP)	When a client calls a business method on an EJB object, but no entity bean instance is bound to the EJB object, the container needs to take a bean from the pool and transition it into a ready state. This is called *activation*. On activation, the *ejbActivate()* method is called by the EJB container.	Acquire any bean-specific resources, like socket connections, that your bean needs to service a particular client when it is moved into the ready state.
ejbLoad() (new for CMP)	The EJB container calls this method to load database data into your bean instance, based on the current transactional state.	*Do not read data from the database in this method.* Rather, the EJB container will read in data from the database for you automatically right *before* calling your *ejbLoad()* method. It does this by setting your container-managed fields to the data it reads from the database. In this method, you should perform any utilities you need to work with the read-in data, such as decompressing a text field.

Table 8.1 *(continued)*

METHOD	EXPLANATION	TYPICAL IMPLEMENTATION
ejbStore() (new for CMP)	The EJB container calls this to update the database to the new values of your in-memory fields, thus synchronizing the database. The current transactional state dictates when this method is called. This method is also called during passivation, directly before *ejbPassivate()*.	*Do not update the database in this method.* Rather, the EJB container will update the database for you automatically right *after* calling your *ejbStore()* method. It does this in the subclass by writing your container-managed fields to the database. In method, you should prepare your container-managed fields to be written to the database. For example, you can compress the text of your fields if necessary by calling your own abstract *set()* methods.
ejbPassivate() (same as BMP)	The EJB container calls this method when it wants to return your entity bean to the pool. This is called *passivation* and is the opposite of activation. On passivation, the *ejbPassivate()* method is called by the EJB container.	Release any resources, such as socket connections, that you allocated in *ejbActivate()* and that your bean was holding during the ready state for a particular client.
ejbRemove() (new for CMP)	The client calls the home object's *remove()* method to destroy database data *remove()*, then calls your *ejbRemove()*. Note that this does not destroy the Java object because the object can be pooled and reused for different data.	*Do not destroy database data in this method.* Rather, simply perform any operations that must be done before the data in the database is destroyed. The EJB container will destroy the data for you right after *ejbRemove()* is called.
unsetEntityContext() (same as BMP)	This method disassociates a bean from its environment. The container calls this right before your entity bean instance is destroyed (when it wants to reduce the pool size).	Release any resources you allocated during *setEntityContext()*, and get ready for garbage collection.

> **Note:** **Looking to see how BMP and CMP method implementations compare? Appendix E has a table comparing them.**

Container-Managed Persistence Example: A Product Line

Let's see a quick demonstration of CMP in action, applied to the concept of a product line.

If you work for a product-based company, your company's product line is the suite of products that your company offers. For example, if you're an appliance company, you might offer a dishwasher, a stove, and a dryer. If you're a computer hardware company, you might offer memory, hard disks, and processors. We're going to model a generic product as an entity bean that uses CMP.

Figure 8.3 details the class diagram for our product line.

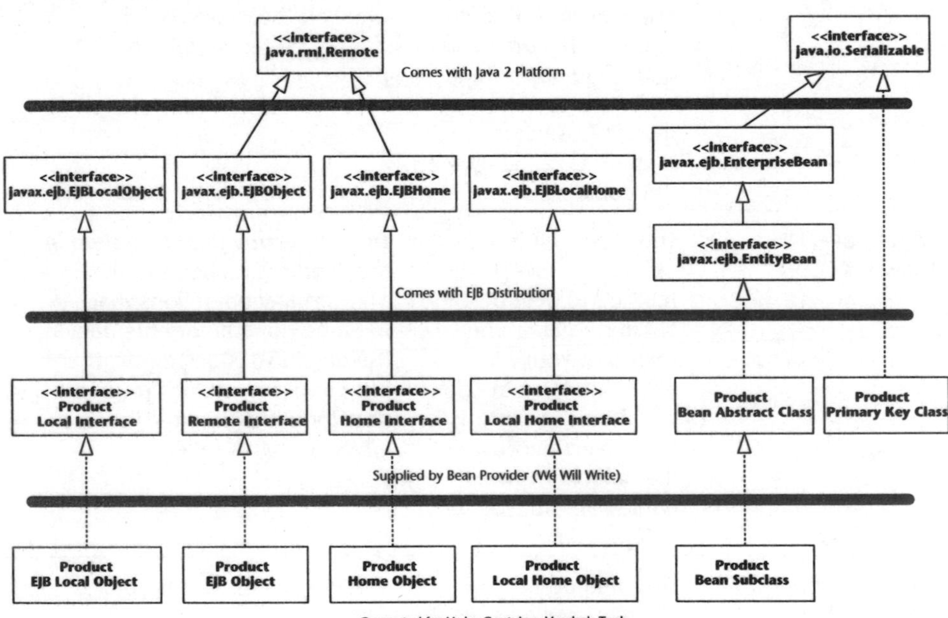

Figure 8.3 The class diagram for the product line example.

Let's take a look at each of the files that we must create for our entity bean component.

Product.java

Remote clients will call our remote interface. The only case in which a remote client should call an entity bean is when you are writing small test applications to exercise your entity bean's API, as we will do in this example. Otherwise you should use the local interface for performance reasons, and wrap your entity beans with session beans (see Chapter 13). The remote interface is shown in Source 8.1.

```
package examples.cmp;

import javax.ejb.*;
import java.rmi.RemoteException;

/**
 * These remote interface with public business methods of ProductBean.
 *
 * This interface is what remote clients operate on when they interact
 * with beans. The EJB Server vendor will implement this interface;
 * the implemented object instance is called the EJB Object, which
 * delegates invocations to instances of the ProductBean class.
 */
public interface Product
    extends EJBObject
{
    // Getter/setter methods for Entity Bean fields

    public String getName() throws RemoteException;
    public void setName(String name) throws RemoteException;

    public String getDescription() throws RemoteException;
    public void setDescription(String description) throws
RemoteException;

    public double getBasePrice() throws RemoteException;
    public void setBasePrice(double price) throws RemoteException;

    public String getProductID() throws RemoteException;
}
```

Source 8.1 Product.java.

Our remote interface is quite simple. It has methods to modify the entity bean instance's fields and throws remote exceptions to indicate system-level errors.

ProductLocal.java

Our local interface is our business interface called by local clients, such as session beans or other entity beans. It is shown in Source 8.2.

```
package examples.cmp;

import javax.ejb.*;

/**
 * These are the public business methods of ProductBean.
 *
 * This local interface is what local clients operate
 * on when they interact with our bean. The container
 * will implement this interface; the implemented object
 * is called the EJB local object, which delegates
 * invocations to instances of the entity bean class.
 */
public interface ProductLocal extends EJBLocalObject {

  public String getName();
  public void setName(String name);

  public String getDescription();
  public void setDescription(String description);

  public double getBasePrice();
  public void setBasePrice(double price);

  public String getProductID();
}
```

Source 8.2 ProductLocal.java.

The local interface is trivially different than the remote interface. The only differences are the lack of thrown *RemoteExceptions* and the fact that we extend *EJBLocalObject* rather than *EJBObject*.

ProductHome.java

Next, we have the product's home interface, which is shown in Source 8.3. As with the remote interface, this home interface should be used only by remote clients, such as a standalone application.

```
package examples.cmp;

import javax.ejb.*;
import java.rmi.RemoteException;
import java.util.Collection;

/**
 * This is the home interface for Product.  This interface
 * is implemented by the EJB container.  The implemented
 * object is called the Home Object, and serves as a
 * factory for EJB Objects.
 *
 * One create() method is in this Home Interface, which
 * corresponds to the ejbCreate() method in the bean class.
 */
public interface ProductHome extends EJBHome {

     /*
      * Creates a product
      *
      * @param productID The number of the product (unique)
      * @param name The name of the product
      * @param description Product description
      * @param basePrice Base Price of product
      *
      * @return The newly created EJB Object.
      */
     Product create(String productID, String name, String description,
double basePrice) throws CreateException, RemoteException;

     // Finder methods.  These are implemented by the
     // container.  You can customize the functionality of
     // these methods in the deployment descriptor through
     // EJB-QL and container tools.

     public Product findByPrimaryKey(ProductPK key) throws
FinderException, RemoteException;

     public Collection findByName(String name) throws FinderException,
RemoteException;

     public Collection findByDescription(String description) throws
FinderException, RemoteException;

     public Collection findByBasePrice(double basePrice) throws
FinderException, RemoteException;
```

Source 8.3 ProductHome.java. *(continued)*

```
    public Collection findExpensiveProducts(double minPrice) throws
FinderException, RemoteException;

    public Collection findCheapProducts(double maxPrice) throws
FinderException, RemoteException;

    public Collection findAllProducts() throws FinderException,
RemoteException;
}
```

Source 8.3 *(continued)*

Our home interface defines a single *create()* method to create a new product in the database. It returns a Product EJB object so the client can manipulate the entity bean data and throws a *javax.ejb.CreateException* to indicate an application-level problem.

We also expose all sorts of finder methods to find existing products. One of the finders returns a single EJB object, while others return a *java.util.Collection* of multiple EJB objects. This is needed if the finder methods find more than one matching object. Note that *findByPrimaryKey()* should never return a collection, because primary keys must be unique.

ProductLocalHome.java

Our entity bean's local home interface is the more optimized (see Chapter 2) home interface that session beans or other entity beans should use. The code is in Source 8.4.

```
package examples.cmp;

import javax.ejb.*;
import java.util.Collection;

/**
 * This is the local home interface for Product.
 * This interface is implemented by the EJB container.
 * The implemented object is called the local home object,
 * and serves as a factory for EJB local objects.
 *
 * One create() method is in this Home Interface, which
 * corresponds to the ejbCreate() method in the bean class.
 */
public interface ProductLocalHome extends EJBLocalHome {

    /*
     * Creates a product
```

Source 8.4 ProductLocalHome.java.

```
     *
     * @param productID The number of the product (unique)
     * @param name The name of the product
     * @param description Product description
     * @param basePrice Base Price of product
     *
     * @return The newly created EJB local Object.
     */
    ProductLocal create(String productID, String name, String
description, double basePrice) throws CreateException;

    // Finder methods.  These are implemented by the
    // container.  You can customize the functionality of
    // these methods in the deployment descriptor through
    // EJB-QL and container tools.

    public ProductLocal findByPrimaryKey(ProductPK key) throws
FinderException;

    public Collection findByName(String name) throws FinderException;

    public Collection findByDescription(String description) throws
FinderException;

    public Collection findByBasePrice(double basePrice) throws
FinderException;

    public Collection findExpensiveProducts(double minPrice) throws
FinderException;

    public Collection findCheapProducts(double maxPrice) throws
FinderException;

    public Collection findAllProducts() throws FinderException;
}
```

Source 8.4 *(continued)*

ProductPK.java

Our primary key class is defined by *ProductPK.java,* shown in Source 8.5. This unique identifier uses a *productID* that could represent the product's SKU number.

```
package examples;

import java.io.Serializable;

/**
 * Primary Key class for our 'Product' Container-Managed
 * Entity Bean
 */
public class ProductPK implements java.io.Serializable {

     /*
      * Note that the primary key fields must be a
      * subset of the container-managed fields.
      * The fields we are marking as container-managed in
      * our Bean are productID, name, desc, and basePrice.
      * Therefore our PK fields need to be from that set.
     */
     public String productID;

     public ProductPK(String productID) {
          this.productID = productID;
     }

     public ProductPK() { }

     public String toString() {
          return productID.toString();
     }

     public int hashCode() {
           return productID.hashCode();
     }

     public boolean equals(Object prod) {
           return ((ProductPK)prod).productID.equals(productID);
     }
}
```

Source 8.5 ProductPK.java.

As with BMP, CMP dictates that your primary key class must be serializable. Because the EJB container is persisting for you, it may need to query the primary key class and manipulate or compare its fields with the fields in your bean. Thus, an important restriction with CMP is that the fields you have in your primary key class must come from the container-managed fields defined in your deployment descriptor.

In our example, the *ProductPK* class is valid because it is serializable and because its public fields come from our container-managed fields, which we will define shortly in the deployment descriptor.

ProductBean.java

Next, we have our container-managed entity bean implementation, *ProductBean.java*, shown in Source 8.6.

```
package examples.cmp;

import javax.ejb.*;

/**
 * Entity Bean that demonstrates Container-Managed persistence.
 *
 * This is a product that's persistent.  It has an ID #, a name,
 * a description, and a base price.
 */
public abstract class ProductBean implements EntityBean {

     protected EntityContext ctx;

     public ProductBean() {
     }

     //----------------------------------------------
     // Begin abstract get/set methods
     //----------------------------------------------

     public abstract String getName();
     public abstract void setName(String name);
     public abstract String getDescription();
     public abstract void setDescription(String description);
     public abstract double getBasePrice();
     public abstract void setBasePrice(double price);
     public abstract String getProductID();
     public abstract void setProductID(String productID);

     //----------------------------------------------
     // End abstract get/set methods
     //----------------------------------------------

     //----------------------------------------------
     // Begin EJB-required methods.  The methods below
     // are called by the Container, and never called
     // by client code.
     //----------------------------------------------

     /**
      * Called by Container.
      * Implementation can acquire needed resources.
      */
```

Source 8.6 ProductBean.java. *(continued)*

```
public void ejbActivate() {
     System.out.println("ejbActivate() called.");
}

/**
 * EJB Container calls this method right before it
 * removes the Entity Bean from the database.
 * Corresponds to when client calls home.remove().
 */
public void ejbRemove() {
     System.out.println("ejbRemove() called.");
}

/**
 * Called by Container.
 * Releases held resources for passivation.
 */
public void ejbPassivate() {
     System.out.println("ejbPassivate () called.");
}

/**
 * Called from the Container.  Updates the entity bean
 * instance to reflect the current value stored in
 * the database.
 *
 * Since we're using Container-Managed Persistence, we
 * can leave this method blank.  The EJB Container will
 * automatically load us in the subclass.
 */
public void ejbLoad() {
     System.out.println("ejbLoad() called.");
}

/**
 * Called from the Container.  Updates the database to
 * reflect the current values of this in-memory Entity Bean
 * instance representation.
 *
 * Since we're using Container-Managed Persistence, we can
 * leave this method blank.  The EJB Container will
 * automatically save us in the subclass.
 */
public void ejbStore() {
     System.out.println("ejbStore() called.");
}

/**
 * Called by Container.  Associates this Bean instance with
```

Source 8.6 *(continued)*

```
     * a particular context.  Once done, we can query the
     * Context for environment info
     */
    public void setEntityContext(EntityContext ctx) {
         System.out.println("setEntityContext called");
         this.ctx = ctx;
    }

    /**
     * Called by Container.  Disassociates this Bean instance
     * with a particular context environment.
     */
    public void unsetEntityContext() {
         System.out.println("unsetEntityContext called");
         this.ctx = null;
    }

    /**
     * Called after ejbCreate().  Now, the Bean can retrieve
     * its EJBObject from its context, and pass it as a 'this'
     * argument.
     */
    public void ejbPostCreate(String productID, String name, String
description, double basePrice) {
         System.out.println("ejbPostCreate() called");
    }

    /**
     * This is the initialization method that corresponds to the
     * create() method in the Home Interface.
     *
     * When the client calls the Home Object's create() method,
     * the Home Object then calls this ejbCreate() method.
     *
     * We need to initialize our Bean's fields with the
     * parameters passed from the client, so that the Container
     * can create the corresponding database entries in the
     * subclass after this method completes.
     */
    public String ejbCreate(ProductPK productID, String name,
      String description, double basePrice)
      throws CreateException {
         System.out.println("ejbCreate() called");

         setProductID(productID);
         setName(name);
         setDescription(description);
```

Source 8.6 *(continued)*

```
            setBasePrice(basePrice);

            return new ProductPK(productID);
        }

        // No finder methods
        // (they are implemented by Container)

        //-----------------------------------------------
        // End EJB-required methods
        //-----------------------------------------------
}
```

Source 8.6 *(continued)*

This bean is more complex than our bank account example. We've defined many finder methods, and we have more persistent fields. Yet even though we've added this complexity, our bean is less than 40 percent of the size of our Bank Account bean. This is an amazing reduction in code complexity. And because our bean has no database code in it, we have reduced the chance for bugs in our bean due to user error working with JDBC code. This is a huge savings in development and testing time.

We do not have any fields, since the container declares them in the subclass. We have a few abstract get/set methods, which the container also implements in the subclass. The only really interesting method is *ejbCreate()*, which takes the parameters passed in from the client and calls the bean's own abstract *set()* methods to populate the bean with the initialization data. The container then performs a SQL INSERT in the subclass once *ejbCreate()* concludes.

The rest of our bean is just empty EJB-required methods and comments. In fact, if we took the comments, whitespace, and printlns out, the bean would just be this:

```
package examples.cmp;
import javax.ejb.*;

public abstract class ProductBean implements EntityBean {
     protected EntityContext ctx;

     public abstract String getName();
     public abstract void setName(String name);
     public abstract String getDescription();
     public abstract void setDescription(String description);
     public abstract double getBasePrice();
     public abstract void setBasePrice(double price);
     public abstract String getProductID();
     public abstract void setProductID(String productID);

     public void ejbActivate() { }
```

```
    public void ejbRemove() { }
    public void ejbPassivate() { }
    public void ejbLoad() { }
    public void ejbStore() { }
    public void setEntityContext(EntityContext ctx) {
        this.ctx = ctx;
    }
    public void unsetEntityContext() {  this.ctx = null; }

    public void ejbPostCreate(String productID, String name,
      String description, double basePrice) { }

    public String ejbCreate(String productID, String name,
      String description, double basePrice) {
        setProductID(productID);
        setName(name);
        setDescription(description);
        setBasePrice(basePrice);
        return productID;
    }
}
```

The Deployment Descriptor

We now need to inform our container about our entity bean, including our container-managed fields and our EJB-QL. The deployment descriptor that now plays a primary role in the entire ensemble is shown in Source 8.7.

```
<?xml version="1.0"?>

<ejb-jar xmlns="http://java.sun.com/xml/ns/j2ee" version="2.1"
        xmlns:xsi="http://www.w3.org/2001/XMLSchema-instance"
        xsi:schemaLocation="http://java.sun.com/xml/ns/j2ee
http://java.sun.com/xml/ns/j2ee/ejb-jar_2_1.xsd">

  <display-name>Product</display-name>

  <enterprise-beans>
    <entity>
      <ejb-name>Product</ejb-name>
      <home>examples.cmp.ProductHome</home>
      <remote>examples.cmp.Product</remote>
      <ejb-class>examples.cmp.ProductBean</ejb-class>
      <persistence-type>Container</persistence-type>
      <prim-key-class>java.lang.String</prim-key-class>

      <reentrant>false</reentrant>

       <cmp-version>2.x</cmp-version>
```

Source 8.7 ejb-jar.xml. *(continued)*

```
      <abstract-schema-name>PRODUCTS</abstract-schema-name>

      <cmp-field>
        <field-name>productID</field-name>
      </cmp-field>
      <cmp-field>
        <field-name>name</field-name>
      </cmp-field>
      <cmp-field>
        <field-name>description</field-name>
      </cmp-field>
      <cmp-field>
        <field-name>basePrice</field-name>
      </cmp-field>

      <primkey-field>productID</primkey-field>

      <query>
        <query-method>
          <method-name>findByName</method-name>
          <method-params>
            <method-param>java.lang.String</method-param>
          </method-params>
        </query-method>
        <ejb-ql>SELECT DISTINCT OBJECT(p) FROM PRODUCTS p WHERE p.name = ?1
        </ejb-ql>
      </query>

      <query>
        <query-method>
          <method-name>findByDescription</method-name>
          <method-params>
            <method-param>java.lang.String</method-param>
          </method-params>
        </query-method>
        <ejb-ql>SELECT DISTINCT OBJECT(p) FROM PRODUCTS p WHERE p.description =
?1
        </ejb-ql>
      </query>

      <query>
        <query-method>
          <method-name>findByBasePrice</method-name>
          <method-params>
            <method-param>double</method-param>
          </method-params>
        </query-method>
        <ejb-ql>SELECT DISTINCT OBJECT(p) FROM PRODUCTS p WHERE p.basePrice =
?1</ejb-ql>
      </query>

      <query>
```

Source 8.7 *(continued)*

```
        <query-method>
          <method-name>findExpensiveProducts</method-name>
          <method-params>
            <method-param>double</method-param>
          </method-params>
        </query-method>
        <ejb-ql><![CDATA[SELECT DISTINCT OBJECT(p) FROM PRODUCTS p WHERE
p.basePrice > ?1]]></ejb-ql>
      </query>

      <query>
        <query-method>
          <method-name>findCheapProducts</method-name>
          <method-params>
            <method-param>double</method-param>
          </method-params>
        </query-method>
        <ejb-ql><![CDATA[SELECT DISTINCT OBJECT(p) FROM PRODUCTS p WHERE
p.basePrice < ?1]]></ejb-ql>
      </query>

      <query>
        <query-method>
          <method-name>findAllProducts</method-name>
          <method-params>
          </method-params>
        </query-method>
        <ejb-ql>SELECT DISTINCT OBJECT(p) FROM PRODUCTS p WHERE p.productID IS
NOT NULL</ejb-ql>
      </query>

    </entity>
  </enterprise-beans>

  <assembly-descriptor>
    <container-transaction>
      <method>
        <ejb-name>Product</ejb-name>
        <method-intf>Remote</method-intf>
        <method-name>*</method-name>
      </method>
      <method>
        <ejb-name>Product</ejb-name>
        <method-intf>Home</method-intf>
        <method-name>*</method-name>
      </method>
      <trans-attribute>Required</trans-attribute>
    </container-transaction>
  </assembly-descriptor>

</ejb-jar>
```

Source 8.7 *(continued)*

Our deployment descriptor begins by identifying the name of the bean, then the bean class, and so on, which is the same as BMP. We then define the container-managed fields, which must match the abstract get/set methods in the enterprise bean class.

The bulk of the descriptor following this is the code for our queries. For example, the *findExpensiveProducts()* finder method locates all products that are more expensive than the *double* parameter passed in. To instruct the container on how to implement this finder functionality, we define our EJB-QL as follows:

```
<![CDATA[SELECT OBJECT(p) FROM PRODUCTS p WHERE p.basePrice > ?1]]>
```

When the container interprets this EJB-QL, it generates database access code (such as JDBC) to find all of the expensive products whose *basePrice* column is greater in value than the double passed in, represented by the *?1*. Whenever a client wants to execute a finder method on the home object, the container automatically runs the database access code.

Notice also the word *CDATA*. This instructs the container's XML parser that reads the descriptor to treat the text *SELECT OBJECT(a) FROM ProductBean AS a WHERE basePrice . ?1* as unstructured character data. This is important because the container's XML parser may think that the text inside the CDATA section does not comply with the XML standard; it may think the > character is actually the closing of an XML tag, rather than a less-than sign. Thus, all EJB-QL that contains < or > must be enclosed in CDATA sections. Alternatively, < and > can be written as the escape sequences *'<'* and *'>'*, so the previous example could also be written as:

```
SELECT OBJECT(p) FROM PRODUCTS p WHERE p.basePrice &gt; ?1
```

We recommend enclosing queries in CDATA sections, however, so that the whole query remains readable.

The end of our descriptor associates transactions with our entity bean, which we'll discuss in Chapter 11.

The Container-Specific Deployment Descriptor

In addition to the deployment descriptor, we need to tell the container exactly how to perform persistent operations. This is one trade-off of CMP—you still need to declare persistent rules, even if you don't code them into your bean using JDBC.

If you're using a relational data store, you need to define exactly how your entity bean's public fields map to that database. Thus, we must define a series

WHEN TO USE CUSTOM PRIMARY KEY CLASSES

In our bean we've declared a custom primary key class, *ProductPK*. We then have this element in our deployment descriptor:

```
<prim-key-class>examples.ProductPK</prim-key-class>
```

This is not strictly necessary, however. You can choose not to invent a custom primary key class and just use one of your container-managed fields as the primary key. For example, we could use the *productID* String field as the primary key, rather than wrapping it in another primary key wrapper class. Then we would declare the primary key class to be a *java.lang.String*, and we would have this element after we declare the container-managed fields:

```
<primkey-field>productID</primkey-field>
```

When should you use a custom primary key class, and when should you use one of your fields? In our opinion, you should avoid using your own fields as primary key classes. The reason is because having a primary key class wrapper isolates you from changes to how you'd like to be uniquely represented in an underlying storage. Having a primary key class wrapper makes it much easier to change how you'd like to be uniquely identified without breaking code.

of object-relational mapping entries. These entries map entity bean fields to relational database column names. The EJB container uses this mapping when storing or retrieving our container-managed fields from the database. Note that this is very EJB container-specific! Some EJB containers support object databases and thus do not have a mapping into a two-dimensional relational database. Consult your EJB container's documentation for more information. Our product line bean's persistent entries for a relational database are shown in Table 8.2. See the book's accompanying source code for the actual descriptor.

Table 8.2 Sample Persistent Settings for ProductBean

OBJECT/RELATIONAL SETTING (ENTITY BEAN FIELD = RELATIONAL COLUMN NAME)
productID=productid
name=name
description=description
basePrice=basePrice

Client.java

Our client code is a simple suite of test cases to try out our bean, as shown Source 8.8.

```
package examples.cmp;

import javax.ejb.*;
import javax.naming.*;
import java.rmi.*;
import javax.rmi.PortableRemoteObject;
import java.util.*;

/**
 * Client test application on a CMP Entity Bean, Product.
 */
public class ProductClient {

  public static void main(String[] args) throws Exception {

    ProductHome home = null;

    try {
      /*
       * Get a reference to the Product Home Object - the
       * factory for Product EJB Objects
       */
      Context ctx = new InitialContext(System.getProperties());
      home = (ProductHome) PortableRemoteObject.narrow(
        ctx.lookup("ProductHome"), ProductHome.class);

      /*
       * Use the factory to create the Product EJB Object
       */
      home.create("123-456-7890", "P5-350", "350 Mhz Pentium", 200);
      home.create("123-456-7891", "P5-400", "400 Mhz Pentium", 300);
      home.create("123-456-7892", "P5-450", "450 Mhz Pentium", 400);
      home.create("123-456-7893", "SD-64", "64 MB SDRAM", 50);
      home.create("123-456-7894", "SD-128", "128 MB SDRAM", 100);
      home.create("123-456-7895", "SD-256", "256 MB SDRAM", 200);

      /*
       * Find a Product, and print out its description
       */
      Iterator i = home.findByName("SD-64").iterator();
      System.out.println("These products match the name SD-64:");
      while (i.hasNext()) {
```

Source 8.8 Client.java. *(continued)*

```
        Product prod = (Product) PortableRemoteObject.narrow(
          i.next(), Product.class);
        System.out.println(prod.getDescription());
      }

      /*
       * Find all products that cost $200
       */
      System.out.println("Finding all products that cost $200");
      i = home.findByBasePrice(200).iterator();

      while (i.hasNext()) {
        Product prod = (Product) PortableRemoteObject.narrow(
          i.next(), Product.class);
        System.out.println(prod.getDescription());
      }
    }
    catch (Exception e) {
      e.printStackTrace();
    }
    finally {
      if (home != null) {
        System.out.println("Destroying products..");

        /*
         * Find all the products
         */
        Iterator i = home.findAllProducts().iterator();
        while (i.hasNext()) {
          try {
            Product prod = (Product) PortableRemoteObject.narrow(
              i.next(), Product.class);
            if (prod.getProductID().startsWith("123")) {
              prod.remove();
            }
          }
          catch (Exception e) {
            e.printStackTrace();
          }
        }
      }
    }
  }
}
```

Source 8.8 *(continued)*

Because this standalone application runs in a separate process from the application server, for testing purposes, this client calls through the bean's remote interface rather than a local interface. However, in a real-world scenario, we would wrap this entity bean with a session bean and call it through its local interface.

The client performs a JNDI lookup to acquire the home object and create some entity bean data. We then try out a couple of finder methods. We can loop through the finders' returned collection and call business methods on each EJB object. We then destroy all the EJB objects we created in a *finally{ }* clause.

Running the Client Program

To run the client program, type a command similar to the following (depending on your EJB container's JNDI initialization parameters):

```
java -Djava.naming.factory.initial=com.sun.jndi.cosnaming.CNCtxFactory
 -
Djava.naming.provider.url=corbaloc::raccoon:3700/NameServiceexamples.cmp
.ProductClient
```

The initialization parameters are required by JNDI to find the home object, as we learned in Chapter 3.

When we run the client, we first create a few products and then perform a *find* for all products that cost $200. Indeed, multiple entity beans were returned in our collection, as shown here:

```
These products match the name SD-64:
64 MB SDRAM
Finding all products that cost $200
350 Mhz Pentium
256 MB SDRAM
Destroying products..
```

The Life Cycle of a CMP Entity Bean

Now that we've seen a complete CMP entity bean example, you should be able to understand Figure 8.4, which illustrates how the container interacts with CMP entity beans.

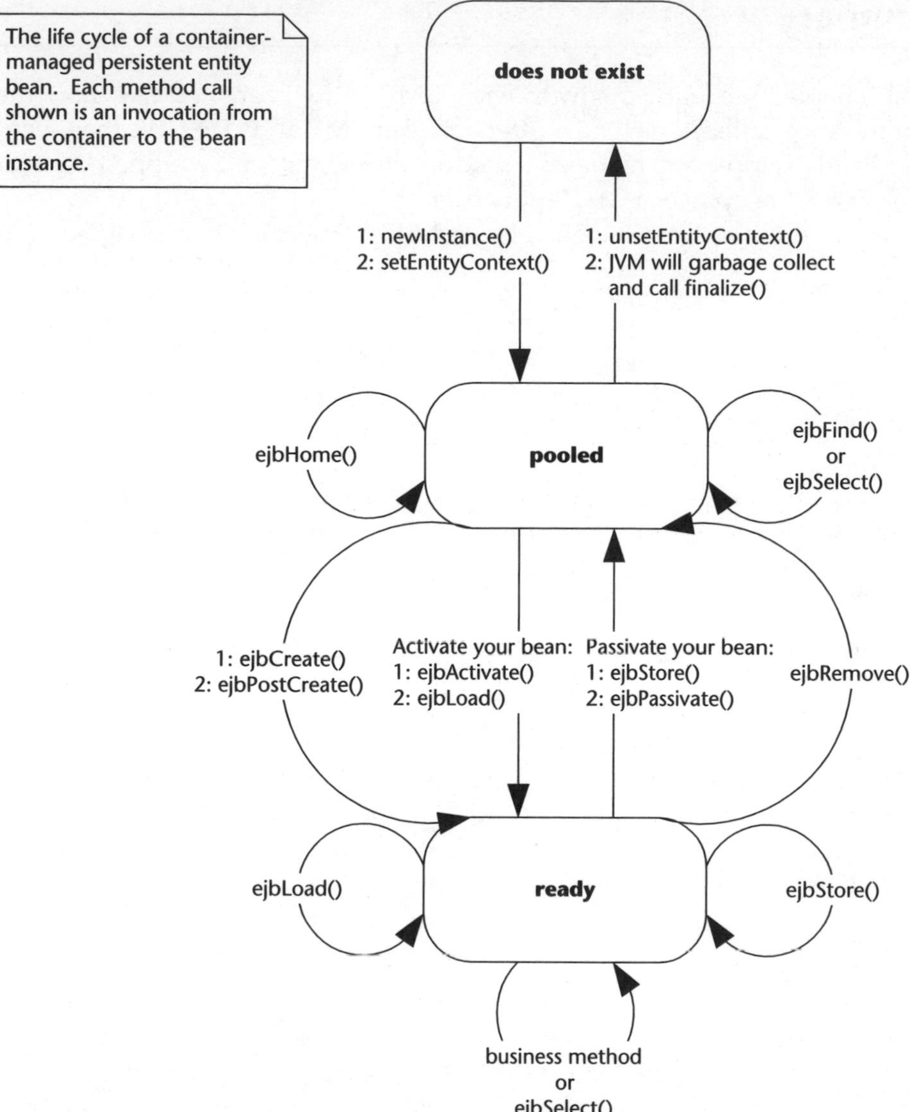

Figure 8.4 The CMP entity bean life cycle.

The life cycle of a CMP entity bean is exactly the same as that of a BMP entity bean, which we fully described at the end of the previous chapter. The only differences are that *ejbSelect()* methods can be called from the pooled state or ready state.

Summary

In this chapter, we learned how to write CMP entity beans. We saw how the bean instance callback methods differ between BMP and CMP. We then went through an example that modeled a product line. Finally, we wrapped up with a look at the life cycle of a CMP entity bean.

In the next chapter, we'll look at the last EJB 2.0 bean type, message-driven beans.

CHAPTER

9

Introduction to Message-Driven Beans

In this chapter, we will learn about *messaging*, which is a lightweight vehicle for communications. Messaging is more appropriate than RMI-IIOP in numerous scenarios. We'll also learn about *message-driven beans*, special beans that can be accessed via messaging. Message-driven beans were added in the 2.0 release of the EJB specification.

Specifically, you'll learn about the following:

- How to implement messaging, including an overview of asynchronous behavior and message-oriented middleware (MOM)
- How to use Java Message Service (JMS), the underlying MOM framework for JMS-based message-driven beans
- What the features of message-driven beans are
- How message-driven beans compare with entity and session beans
- How to develop message-driven beans
- How to work with message-driven beans, including advanced topics, such as gotchas and possible solutions

Motivation to Use Message-Driven Beans

In previous chapters, you learned how to code session and entity beans—distributed components that are accessed using RMI-IIOP. RMI-IIOP is a traditional, heavyweight way to call components. While RMI-IIOP may be useful in many scenarios, several other areas are challenging for RMI-IIOP. Here are just four examples:

- **Performance.** A typical RMI-IIOP client must wait (or block) while the server performs its processing. Only when the server completes its work does the client receive a return result, which enables it to continue processing.
- **Reliability.** When an RMI-IIOP client calls the server, the latter has to be running. If the server crashes or the network crashes, the client cannot perform its intended operation.
- **Support for multiple senders and receivers.** RMI-IIOP limits you to a single client talking to a single server at any given time. There is no built-in functionality for multiple clients to broadcast *events* to multiple servers.
- **Integration with other MOM systems.** When you have enterprise systems that communicate through messages, message-driven beans coupled along with J2EE connectors can integrate these different message-driven enterprise systems.

Messaging is an alternative to remote method invocations (see Figure 9.1). The idea behind messaging is that a *middleman* sits between the client and the server. (A layer of indirection solves every problem in computer science.) This middleman receives messages from one or more *message producers* and broadcasts those messages to one or more *message consumers*. Because of this middleman, the producer can send a message and then continue processing. He can optionally be notified of the response later when the consumer finishes. This is called *asynchronous* programming.

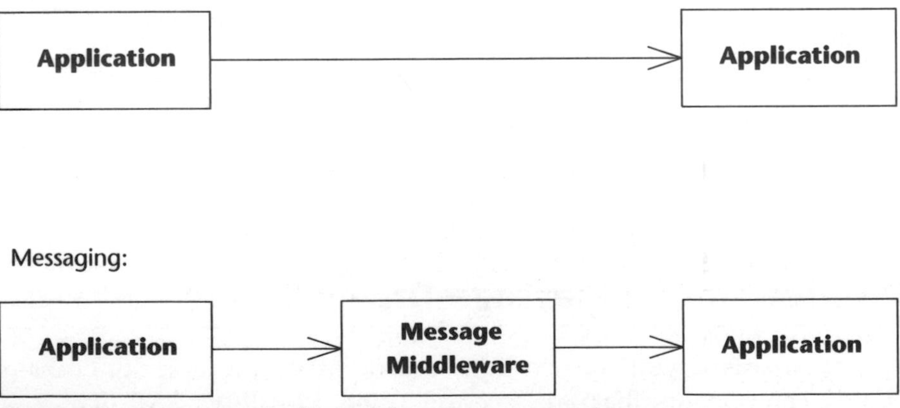

Figure 9.1 Remote method invocations versus messaging.

Messaging addresses the three previous concerns with RMI-IIOP as follows:

- **Non-blocking request processing.** A messaging client does not need to block when executing a request. As an example, when you purchase a book using the Amazon.com one-click order functionality, you can continue browsing the site without waiting to see if your credit card authorizes. Unless something goes wrong, Amazon.com sends you a confirmation e-mail afterwards. This type of fire-and-forget system could easily be coded using messaging. When the user clicks to buy the book, a message is sent that results in credit card processing later. The user can continue to browse.
- **Reliability.** If your message-oriented middleware supports *guaranteed delivery*, you can send a message and know for sure that it will reach its destination, even if the consumer is not available. You send the message to the MOM middleman, and that middleman routes the message to the consumer when he comes back alive again. With RMI-IIOP, this is not possible because there is no middleman. If the server is down, an exception is thrown.
- **Support for multiple senders and receivers.** Most message-oriented middleware products can accept messages from many senders and broadcast them to many receivers. This enables you to have multinary communications.

Note that messaging also has many disadvantages. Performance, for one, can be slower in many circumstances due to the overhead of having the messaging middleman. For a complete comparison of when to (and when not to) use messaging, see Chapter 18.

Message-oriented middleware (MOM) is a term used to refer to any infrastructure that supports messaging. A variety of products are considered to have a MOM-based architecture. Examples include Tibco Rendezvous, IBM WebSphere MQ, BEA Tuxedo/Q, Sun Java System Messaging Server, Microsoft MSMQ, Sonic Software SonicMQ, and FioranoMQ. These products can give you a whole host of value-added services, such as guaranteed message delivery, fault tolerance, load balancing of destinations, subscriber throttling of message consumption, inactive subscribers, support for SOAP over JMS, and much, much more. By allowing the MOM server to address these infrastructure issues, you can focus on the business task at hand.

The Java Message Service

Over the years, MOM systems have evolved in a proprietary way. Each product has its own API, which creates vendor lock-in because code is not portable to other messaging systems. It also hurts developers, because they need to relearn each messaging product's proprietary API.

HOW DOES GUARANTEED MESSAGE DELIVERY WORK?

With guaranteed message delivery, the MOM system persists your messages to a file, database, or other store. Your message resides in the persistent store until it's sent to a message consumer, *and* the message consumer acknowledges the consumption of the message. If the acknowledgment of a message is not received in a reasonable amount of time, the message remains on the persistent store and is redelivered.

This feature is beneficial when the message consumer is brought down on a regular basis for maintenance, and lost messages are unacceptable. This is especially true in industries, such as financial services, where messages represent securities changing hands.

A variation on the guaranteed message delivery theme is certified message delivery. Certified message delivery not only ensures the delivery of a message from a producer to a consumer, but also generates a consumption receipt that is delivered to the message originator, indicating a successful consumption of the message. Certified message delivery is used by producers to better manage communication with consumers.

Another variation of guaranteed message delivery is called store and forward. Store and forward enables a message producer to successfully send a message to an inactive MOM system. The producer transparently spools the message to a local store until the MOM system is reactivated, at which point the message is delivered to the MOM system and forwarded to any available consumers. Guaranteed message delivery without the store-and-forward option requires producers to send messages to active MOM systems, but consumers do not have to be active. Store and forward with guaranteed message delivery allows messages to be sent whether MOM systems or consumers are active or inactive.

The Java Message Service (JMS) is a messaging standard, designed to eliminate many of the disadvantages that MOM-based products faced over past years. JMS has two parts: an API, for which you write code to send and receive messages, and a Service Provider Interface (SPI) where you plug in JMS providers. A JMS provider knows how to talk to a specific MOM implementation. The JMS promise is that you can learn the JMS API once and reuse your messaging code with different plug-and-play MOM implementations (an idea similar to the other J2EE APIs, such as JNDI or JDBC).

Let's explore the JMS API and see how to write a simple JMS program that publishes messages.

Messaging Domains

When you perform messaging, you need to choose a *domain.* A domain is a fancy word for style of messaging. The types of domains are:

- **Publish/subscribe (pub/sub).** Publish/subscribe is analogous to watching television. Many TV stations broadcast their signals, and many people listen to those broadcasts. Thus, with publish/subscribe, you can have *many* message producers talking to *many* message consumers. In this sense, the pub/sub domain is an implementation of a distributed event-driven processing model. Subscribers (listeners) register their interest in a particular event *topic*. Publishers (event sources) create messages (events) that are distributed to all of the subscribers (listeners). Producers aren't hard-coded to know the specific consumers interested in receiving its messages; rather, the MOM system maintains the subscriber list.

- **Point-to-point (PTP).** Point-to-point is analogous to calling a toll-free number and leaving a voice mail. Some person will listen to your voice mail and then delete it. Thus, with point-to-point, you can have only a single consumer for *each* message. Multiple consumers can grab messages off the queue, but any given message is consumed exactly once. In this sense, point-to-point is a degenerate case of publish/subscribe. Multiple producers can send messages to the queue, but each message is delivered only to a single consumer. The way this works is that publishers send messages directly to the consumer or to a centralized *queue*. Messages are typically distributed off the queue in a first-in, first-out (FIFO) order, but this isn't assured.

Figure 9.2 shows the difference between publish/subscribe and point-to-point.

Publish/Subscribe:

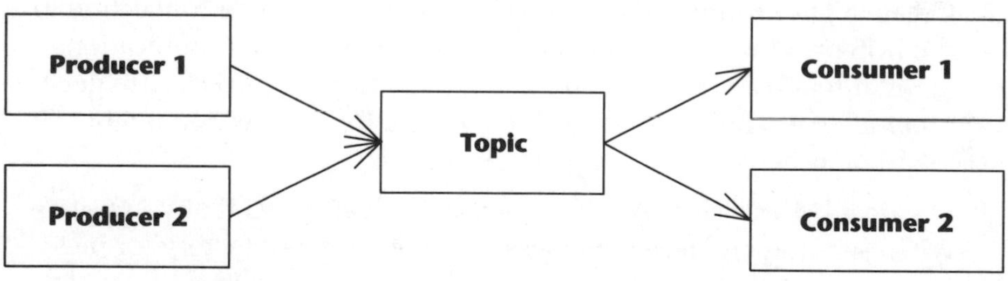

Point-to-Point:

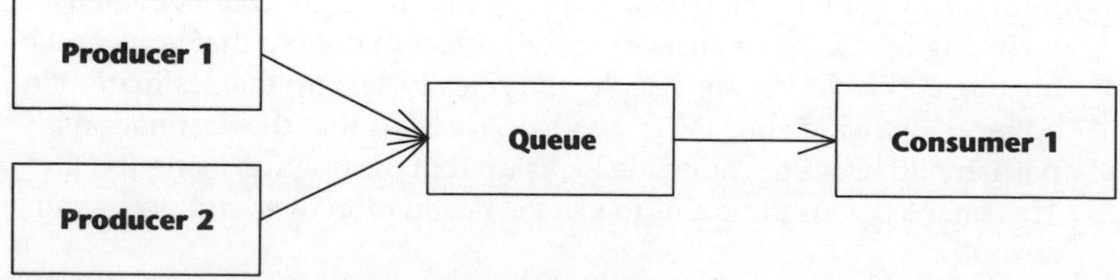

Figure 9.2 Publish/subscribe versus point-to-point.

Another domain called request/reply is less broadly used than the others. The request/reply domain is analogous to RMI-IIOP. It requires any producer that generates a message to receive a reply message from the consumer at some later point in time. Typically, most MOM architectures implement a request/reply paradigm asynchronously using the technologies supplied in the point-to-point and publish/subscribe domains.

The JMS API

The JMS API is more involved than RMI-IIOP. You need to become familiar with many different interfaces to get going. Despite the complexities involved in working with each of these interfaces, low-level topology issues, such as networking protocol, message format and structure, and server location, are mostly abstracted from the developer.

The JMS programming model is shown in Figure 9.3. It is explained in the list that follows:

1. **Locate the JMS Provider ConnectionFactory instance.** You first need to get access to the JMS provider of the particular MOM product you're using. For this, you need to establish a connection using a *ConnectionFactory* instance. You can get hold of *ConnectionFactory* by *looking it up* in JNDI. An administrator will typically create and configure the *ConnectionFactory* for the JMS client's use.
2. **Create a JMS connection.** A JMS *Connection* is an active connection to the JMS provider, managing the low-level network communications (similar to a JDBC connection). You use the *ConnectionFactory* to get a *Connection*. If you're in a large deployment, this connection might be load-balanced across a group of machines.
3. **Create a JMS session.** A JMS *Session* is a helper object that you use when sending and receiving messages. It serves as a factory for message consumers and producers, and also enables you to encapsulate your messages in transactions. You use the *Connection* to get a *Session*.
4. **Locate the JMS destination.** A JMS *Destination* is the channel to which you're sending or from which you're receiving messages. Locating the right destination is analogous to tuning into the right channel when watching television or answering the correct phone, so that you get the messages you desire. Your deployer typically sets up the destination in advance by using your JMS provider's tools, so that the destination is permanently set up. Your code looks up that destination using JNDI. This enables your programs to use the destination over and over again at runtime.

5. **Create a JMS producer or a JMS consumer.** If you want to send messages, you need to call a JMS object to pass it your messages. This object is called *producer.* To receive messages, you call a JMS object and ask it for a message. This object is called the *Consumer* object. You use the *Session* and *Destination* to get a hold of a *Producer* or a *Consumer* object.

6. **Send or receive your message.** If you're producing, you first need to put your message together. There are many different types of messages, such as text, bytes, streams, objects, and maps. After you instantiate your message, you send it using the *Producer* object. If, on the other hand, you're receiving messages, you first receive a message using the *Consumer* object, and then crack it open (depending on the message type) and see what is in it.

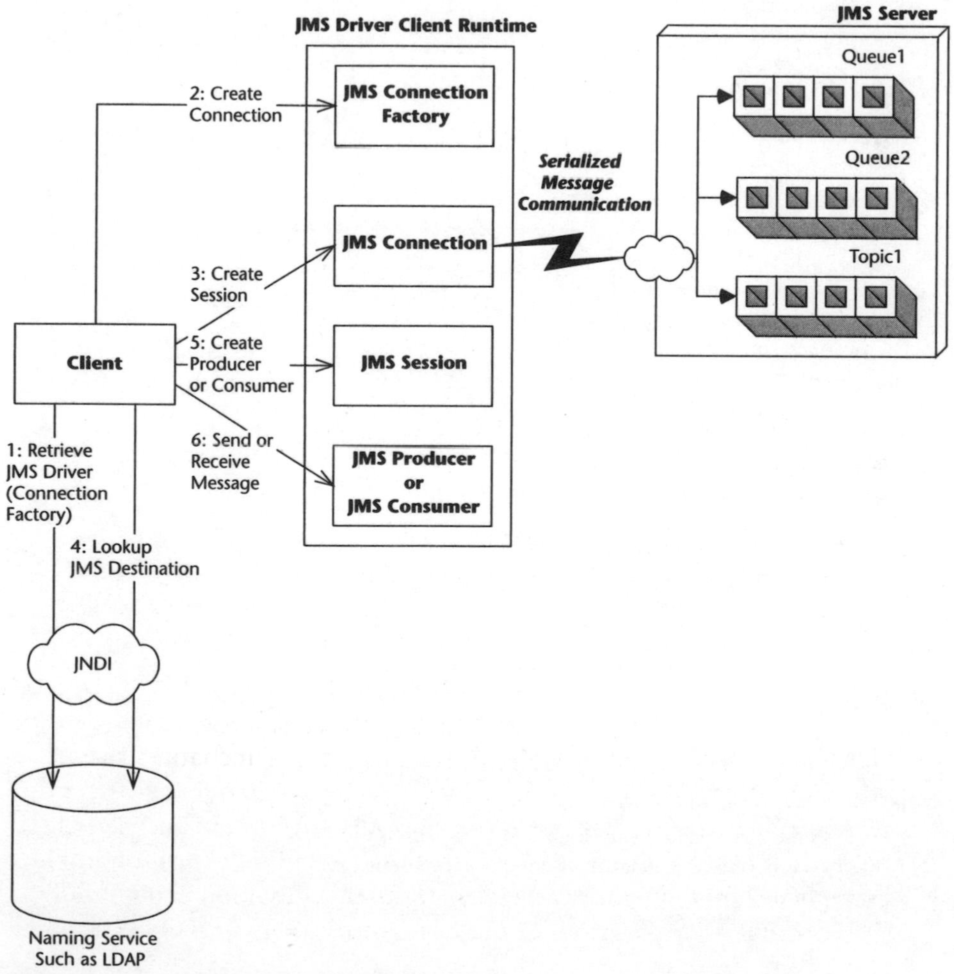

Figure 9.3 Client view of a JMS system.

Everything we just learned applies to both publish/subscribe and point-to-point messaging. The words in *italics* in the preceding process represent actual JMS interface names. There are two different flavors of those interfaces, and the flavor you use depends on if you're using publish/subscribe or point-to-point. See Table 9.1 for a list.

As you can see from Table 9.1, point-to-point has two types of message consumers: a receiver and a browser. What do you think these are for? And why does publish/subscribe have only one type of consumer?

As an example, the code for a client application that publishes a *TextMessage* to a topic using publish/subscribe is provided in Source 9.1.

```
import javax.naming.*;
import javax.jms.*;
import java.util.*;

public class Client {

 public static void main (String[] args) throws Exception {

  // Initialize JNDI
  Context ctx = new InitialContext(System.getProperties());

  // 1: Lookup ConnectionFactory via JNDI
  TopicConnectionFactory factory =
      (TopicConnectionFactory)
       ctx.lookup("TopicConnectionFactory");

  // 2: Use ConnectionFactory to create JMS connection
  TopicConnection connection =
  factory.createTopicConnection();

  // 3: Use Connection to create session
  TopicSession session = connection.createTopicSession(
   false, Session.AUTO_ACKNOWLEDGE);

  // 4: Lookup Destination (topic) via JNDI
  Topic topic = (Topic) ctx.lookup("testtopic");

  // 5: Create a Message Producer
  TopicPublisher publisher = session.createPublisher(topic);

  // 6: Create a text message, and publish it
  TextMessage msg = session.createTextMessage();
  msg.setText("This is a test message.");
  publisher.publish(msg);
 }
}
```

Source 9.1 TopicClient.java.

Table 9.1 The Two Flavors of JMS Interfaces

PARENT INTERFACE	POINT-TO-POINT	PUB/SUB
ConnectionFactory	*QueueConnectionFactory*	*TopicConnectionFactory*
Connection	*QueueConnection*	*TopicConnection*
Destination	*Queue*	*Topic*
Session	*QueueSession*	*TopicSession*
MessageProducer	*QueueSender*	*TopicPublisher*
MessageConsumer	*QueueReceiver, QueueBrowser*	*TopicSubscriber*

Most of Source 9.1 is self-explanatory. Here are the answers to a few questions you might have:

- The parameters to *InitialContext* should be your JNDI provider information. If your JMS provider is integrated into your EJB server, the JNDI parameters should be the same as those when you look up an EJB home. You specify this via the command line using the *-D* switch to the *java* runtime. See the book's accompanying source code for example scripts.
- Our JNDI name for the *TopicConnectionFactory* is *TopicConnectionFactory* but it could be anything—it depends on your container's policy and also where you choose to place it using your container's tools.
- When we create a Session, we pass two parameters: *false,* which indicates that we don't want to use transactions (see Chapter 12 for more on transactions), and *Session.AUTO_ACKNOWLEDGE*, which indicates how we should acknowledge messages that we receive. Since our code is sending (not receiving) messages, this parameter doesn't matter. If you're curious about how message acknowledgment works, see Table 9.3 later in this chapter.

Note that this example does not illustrate point-to-point. The point-to-point code is basically the same, except we use the point-to-point interfaces listed in Table 9.1. We'll leave the point-to-point example as an exercise for you.

Note, too, that this example does not demonstrate any consumption logic. Although message consumption is an important concept, it's not relevant to our discussion, because message-driven beans effectively act as our message consumers.

You should now know enough about JMS to be productive with message-driven beans. If you want to learn more about JMS, a free tutorial is available at http://java.sun.com/products/jms/tutorial/1_3_1-fcs/doc/jms_tutorialTOC.html. Rather than repeating this free information, let's cover some more interesting topics—JMS-EJB integration, advanced message-driven bean topics, and gotchas.

SINGLE-THREADED VERSUS MULTITHREADED BEANS

One great benefit of EJB is you don't need to write thread-safe code. You design your enterprise beans as single-threaded components and never need to worry about thread synchronization when concurrent clients access your component. In order to service concurrent client requests, your EJB container automatically instantiates multiple instances of your component.

The container's thread services can be both a benefit and a restriction. The benefit is that you don't need to worry about race conditions or deadlock in your application code. The restriction is that some problems lend themselves well to multithreaded programming, and that class of problems cannot be easily solved in an EJB environment.

So why doesn't the EJB specification allow for multithreaded beans? EJB is intended to relieve the component developers' worry about threads or thread synchronization. The EJB container handles those issues for you by load-balancing client requests to multiple instances of a single-threaded component. An EJB server provides a highly scalable environment for single-threaded components.

If the EJB specification allowed for beans to control threads, a Pandora's box of problems would result. For example, an EJB container would have a *very* hard time controlling transactions if beans were randomly starting and stopping threads, especially because transaction information is often associated with a thread.

The bottom line is that EJB was not meant to be a Swiss army knife, solving every problem in existence. It was designed to assist with server-side *business problems*, which are largely single-threaded. For applications that absolutely must be multithreaded, EJB may not be the correct choice of distributed object architectures.

Integrating JMS with EJB

JMS-EJB integration is a compelling idea. It would allow EJB components to benefit from the value proposition of messaging, such as non-blocking clients and multinary communications.

To understand the motivations behind introducing a completely different type of bean to consume messages in an EJB application, let us contemplate for a moment what other approaches could we have taken and whether they would have worked:

- **Using a Java object that receives JMS messages to call EJB components.** Rather than coming up with a whole new type of bean, the Java community could have promoted the idea of a Java object that can receive messages and in turn call the appropriate EJB components, such as session beans and entity beans. The problems with this approach are as follows:

- You'd need to write special code to register yourself as a listener for JMS messages. This is a decent amount of code (as we demonstrated previously).
- To increase the throughput of message consumption, you would have to write the multithreading logic such that you can listen to the messages on multiple threads. However, writing multithreaded applications is not a trivial task for a business application developer.
- Your Java object that listens to messages would need some way of starting up, since it wrapped your other EJB components. If the class ran within the container, you would need to use an EJB server-specific *startup class* to activate your Java object when the EJB server came up. This is not portable because EJB specification does not define a standard way of activating a given logic.
- Your plain Java object wouldn't receive any services from an EJB container, such as automatic life cycle management, clustering, pooling, and transactions. You would need to hard-code this yourself, which is difficult and error-prone.
- You would need to hard-code the JMS destination name in your Java object. This hurts reusability, because you couldn't reuse that Java object with other destinations. If you get the destination information from a disk (such as with property files), this is a bit clunky.

- **Reuse an existing type of EJB component somehow to receive JMS messages.** Another option could have been to shoehorn session beans or entity beans into receiving JMS messages. Problems with this approach include:
  - **Threading.** If a message arrives for a bean while it's processing other requests, how can it take that message, given that EJB does not allow components to be multithreaded?
  - **Life cycle management.** If a JMS message arrives and there are no beans, how does the container know to create a bean?

What Is a Message-Driven Bean?

A *message-driven bean,* introduced in EJB 2.0, is a special EJB component that can receive JMS messages as well as other types of messages. See the sidebar *Pluggable Message Providers* to find out more about how message-driven beans can be used to consume messages other than JMS. A message-driven bean is invoked by the container upon arrival of a message at the destination or endpoint that is serviced by message-driven bean. A message-driven bean is decoupled from any clients that send messages to it. *A client cannot access a message-driven bean through a component interface.* You will have to use message provider–specific API, such as JMS, to send messages from clients, which in turn would be received by the message-driven beans (see Figure 9.4).

PLUGGABLE MESSAGE PROVIDERS

A message-driven bean can be defined to consume messages of a given messaging type in accordance with the message listener interface it employs, that is JMS-based message-driven beans will implement the *javax.jms.MessageListener* interface and so on. In EJB 2.0, message-driven beans supported consumption of JMS messages only. You could not receive non-JMS messages, such as asynchronous enterprise information system–specific message. This has changed in EJB 2.1 standard so that the message-driven bean can employ different listener interfaces to consume different message types in addition to JMS.

This is achieved with the help of J2EE Connector Architecture 1.5. Connector architecture defines message inflow contracts to enable resource adapters to asynchronously deliver messages to message endpoints residing in the application server independent of the specific messaging type or messaging semantics. So in practice, we can write resource adapters that act as message providers. Resource adapters are standard J2EE components and hence, can be plugged into any J2EE compliant application server. As a result, resource adapters capable of delivering messages to message endpoints, such as message-driven beans, can be plugged into any J2EE-compliant application server as well. This is widely known as message provider pluggability.

For example, imagine a scenario where you want your EJB application to receive EbXML messages. Using JAX-RPC is not a choice here since it supports only SOAP 1.1 messages. Besides, JAX-RPC does not support asynchronous messaging. In this case, connector architecture–based message providers/resource adapters can be extremely handy. We can write an EbXML message provider using connector architecture such that it provides a specific messaging listener interface say, *com.xyz.messaging.EbXMLMessageListener*, which can be implemented by message-driven beans so as to enable their receiving EbXML messages.

This is a powerful concept—any enterprise information system can effectively send any type of messages to a message-driven bean endpoint via J2EE connector architecture-based resource adapter. All message providers from EJB 2.1 onwards, regardless of whether they consume JMS messages or not, are resource adapters based on J2EE Connector Architecture 1.5. In Chapter 17 we discuss J2EE connector architecture and provide guidance toward developing resource adapters that consume messages.

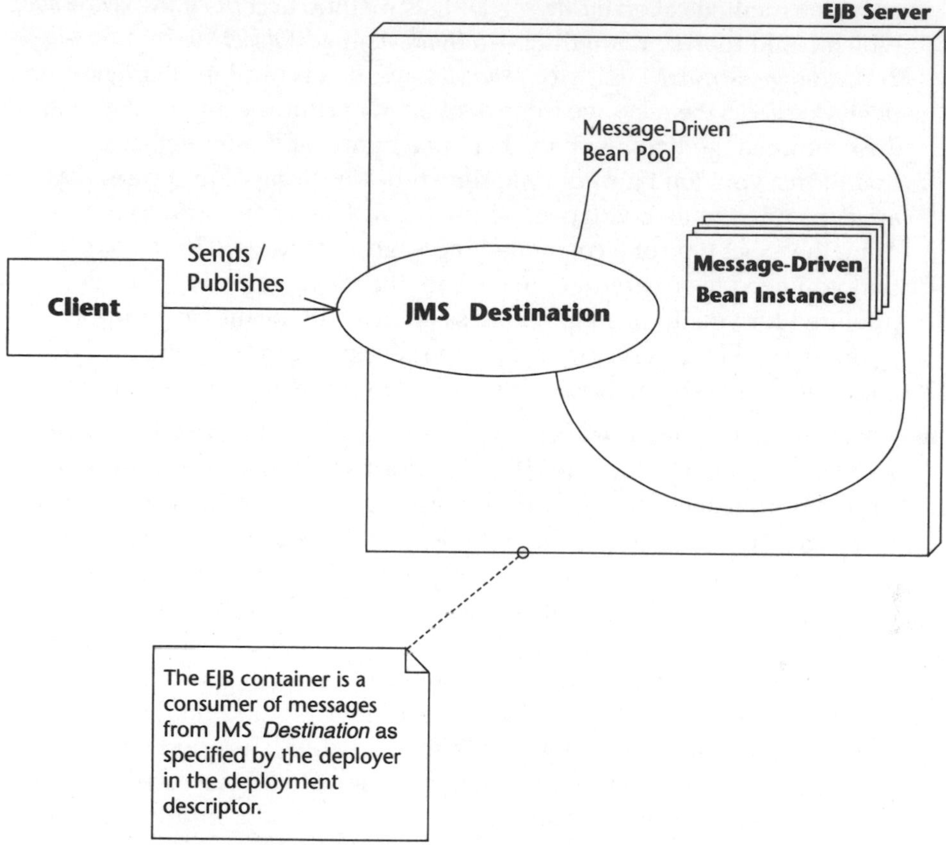

Figure 9.4 A client calling JMS message-driven beans.

The following are some major characteristics of message-driven beans.

- **A message-driven bean does not have a home interface, local home interface, remote interface, or a local interface.** You do not call message-driven beans using an object-oriented remote method invocation interface. The reason is that message-driven beans process messages, and those messages can come from any messaging client, such as an MQSeries client, an MSMQ client, a message provider/resource adapter, or a J2EE client using the JMS API. Message-driven beans, along with appropriate message providers, can thus consume any valid message.
- **Message-driven beans have weakly typed business method.** Message-driven beans are merely receiving messages from a destination or a resource adapter and they do not know anything about what's inside the messages. The listener interface implemented by message-driven beans typically has a method (or methods) called by an EJB container upon arrival of a message or by the resource adapter (via application server). JMS message listener interface, *javax.jms.MessageListener* has

only one method called *onMessage()*. This method accepts a JMS *Message*, which could represent anything—a *BytesMessage*, *ObjectMessage*, *TextMessage*, *StreamMessage*, or *MapMessage*. In a typical implementation of *onMessage()*, the message is cracked open at runtime and its contents are examined, perhaps with the help of a bunch of *if* statements. In formal terms, you don't get compile-time type-checking of messages that are consumed; rather, you need to use the *instanceof* operator to determine the exact type of a consumed message at runtime. This also means that you need to be careful to make sure the message you receive is intended for you. In comparison, session or entity beans can support strongly typed business methods. Type checking can be performed at compile time to ensure that clients are properly using a given interface.

- **Message-driven bean listener method(s) might not have any return values.** Although EJB 2.1 specification does not restrict a message-driven bean listener method from returning a value to the client, certain messaging types might not be suitable for this. For example, consider the listener interface of a messaging type that supports asynchronous messaging, such as JMS. In this case, due to the asynchronous interaction between message producers and consumers, the message producers don't wait for your message-driven bean to respond. As a result, it doesn't make sense for the *onMessage()* listener method on the *javax.jms.MessageListener* interface to return value. The good news is that using several design patterns, it is possible to send a response to an asynchronous message producer. We discuss this later in this chapter.
- **Message-driven beans might not send exceptions back to clients.** Although, EJB 2.1 does not restrict message-driven bean listener interface methods from throwing application exceptions, certain messaging types might not be able to throw these exceptions to the clients. Again consider the example of a listener interface of a messaging type that supports asynchronous messaging, such as JMS. In this case, message producers won't wait for your message-driven bean to send a response because the interaction is asynchronous. Therefore clients can't receive any exceptions. All message listener interfaces, however, can generate system exceptions regardless of the messaging semantics (synchronous versus asynchronous) because the container (rather than the client) handles system exceptions.
- **Message-driven beans are stateless.** Message-driven beans hold no conversational state. It would be impossible to spread messages across a cluster of message-driven beans if a message-driven bean held state. In this sense, they are similar to stateless session beans because the container can similarly treat each message-driven bean instance as equivalent to all other instances. All instances are anonymous and do not have an identity that is visible to a client. Thus, multiple instances of the bean can process multiple messages from a JMS destination or a resource adapter concurrently.

JMS MESSAGE-DRIVEN BEANS AND DURABLE-NONDURABLE SUBSCRIBERS

A *durable* subscription to a topic means that a JMS subscriber receives all messages, even if the subscriber is inactive. If a message is sent to a topic that has an inactive durable subscriber, the message is persisted and delivered when the durable subscriber is once again active. A *non-durable* subscription to a topic means the subscriber receives only messages that are published while the subscriber is active. Any messages delivered while the subscriber is inactive are lost. Since a JMS message-driven bean is essentially a consumer, it can register itself as a durable or non-durable subscriber to messages published to a topic. Durability allows persistent messages to be sent to a topic even though the application server hosting the JMS message-driven bean consumer has crashed. The messages will persist until the crashed application server restarts and the durable subscriber message-driven bean container positively acknowledges consumption of all of the stored messages.

Developing Message-Driven Beans

Let's now take a look at what's involved with developing message-driven beans. In the subsequent sections, we will focus on JMS message-driven beans. To a great extent, the programming model for developing other types of message-driven beans will be quite similar to that for JMS message-driven beans.

The Semantics

JMS message-driven beans are classes that implement two interfaces: *javax.jms.MessageListener* and *javax.ejb.MessageDrivenBean*. Additionally, every JMS message-driven bean implementation class must provide an *ejbCreate()* method that returns *void* and accepts no arguments. Here is what the *javax.jms.MessageListener* interface looks like:

```
public interface javax.jms.MessageListener {
    public void onMessage(Message message);
}
```

Here is what the *javax.ejb.MessageDrivenBean* interface looks like:

```
public interface javax.ejb.MessageDrivenBean
 extends javax.ejb.EnterpriseBean {

 public void ejbRemove()
  throws EJBException;

 public void setMessageDrivenContext(MessageDrivenContext ctx)
  throws EJBException;
}
```

We summarize the methods that must be provided in every message-driven bean implementation class in Table 9.2.

Table 9.2 Methods to Be Implemented in JMS Message-Driven Beans

METHOD	DESCRIPTION
onMessage(Message)	This method is invoked for each message that is consumed by the bean. The input parameter of the method is the incoming JMS message that is being consumed. The container is responsible for serializing messages to a single message-driven bean. A single message-driven bean can process only one message at a time. It is the container's responsibility to provide concurrent message consumption by pooling multiple message-driven bean instances. A single instance cannot concurrently process messages, but a container can. This method does not have to be coded for reentrancy and should not have any thread synchronization code contained within.
ejbCreate()	This method is invoked when a message-driven bean is first created and added to a pool. Application server vendors can implement an arbitrary algorithm that decides when to add message-driven bean instances from the pool. Beans are typically added to the pool when the component is first deployed or when the load of messages to be delivered increases. Bean developers should initialize variables and references to resources needed by the bean, such as other EJBs or database connections. Bean developers should initialize only references to resources that are needed for every message that is consumed by the bean, as opposed to gaining access and releasing the resource every time a message is consumed.
ejbRemove()	This method is invoked when a message-driven bean is being removed from a pool. Application server vendors can implement an arbitrary algorithm that decides when to remove message-driven bean instances from the pool. Beans are typically removed from the pool when the component is being undeployed or when a load of messages to be delivered by an application server decreases, thereby requiring the application server to remove idle instances to free up system resources. Bean developers should use this method to clean up any dangling resources that are used by the bean.

Table 9.2 *(continued)*

METHOD	DESCRIPTION
SetMessageDrivenContext (MessageDrivenContext)	This method is called as part of the event transition that a message-driven bean goes through when it is being added to a pool. This method is called before the *ejbCreate()* method is invoked. The input parameter for this method is an instance of the *MessageDrivenContext* interface. The input parameter gives the bean access to information about the environment that it executes within. The only methods on the *MessageDrivenContext* that are accessible by the message-driven bean are transaction related methods. Other methods, such as *getCallerPrincipal()*, cannot be invoked in this method because message-driven beans do not have home, local home, remote, or local interface, and do not have a visible client security context.

Given this simple description, you can see that developing JMS message-driven beans is significantly less complicated than developing session or entity beans. The number of methods that have to be implemented is less than with session or entity beans.

The life cycle of a message-driven bean is also very straightforward. Figure 9.5 illustrates the life cycle of a message-driven bean.

A message-driven bean is in either the *does not exist* state or in the *pooled* state. When a container decides to add another instance to its pool, it creates a new instance, passes the instance its *MessageDrivenContext* object describing the domain and then calls *ejbCreate()*, allowing the bean to initialize itself. That application server will likely create an initial pool of beans at boot time and then increase the size of the pool as the quantity of messages increases. A container will remove an instance from the pool and destroy it at system shutdown or when the container decides it needs to decrease the size of the pool to conserve cache space. If the container decides to take an instance out of the bean pool, it calls the bean's *ejbRemove()* method.

A Simple Example

Now that we've learned the theory behind message-driven beans, let's apply our knowledge to construct a simple bean that logs text messages to the screen. In the future, you could generalize this bean and make it into a generic logging facility, where you have different log levels depending on the urgency of the log.

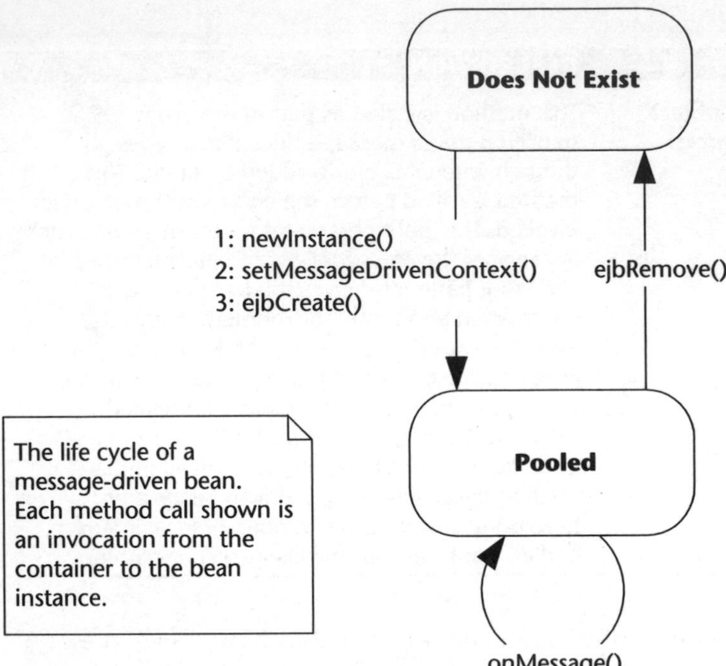
Does Not Exist
1: newInstance()
2: setMessageDrivenContext()
3: ejbCreate()
ejbRemove()
Pooled
The life cycle of a message-driven bean. Each method call shown is an invocation from the container to the bean instance.
onMessage()

Figure 9.5 Life cycle of a message-driven bean.

This is a trivial example and not demonstrative of real-world systems. It is, however, a good template to use when writing your own beans. If you want to see a real-world message-driven bean in action that uses other EJB components, see Chapter 22, along with the book's accompanying source code. As we will see when writing this bean, the rules for writing JMS message-driven beans are trivial.

The Bean Implementation Class

Since message-driven beans do not have home, component, local home, or local interfaces associated with them, we can completely skip designing the public interface to our bean. We can get right to the heart of development of this bean and write the implementation class. The code for the implementation class is shown in Source 9.2.

```
package examples;

import javax.ejb.*;
import javax.jms.*;

/**
```

Source 9.2 LogBean.java.

```
 * Sample JMS Message-Driven Bean
 */
public class LogBean implements MessageDrivenBean, MessageListener {

 protected MessageDrivenContext ctx;

 /**
  * Associates this Bean instance with a particular context.
  */
 public void setMessageDrivenContext(MessageDrivenContext ctx) {
  this.ctx = ctx;
 }

 /**
  * Initializes the bean
  */
 public void ejbCreate() {
  System.err.println("ejbCreate()");
 }

 /**
  * Our one business method
  */
 public void onMessage(Message msg) {

  if (msg instanceOf TextMessage) {
   TextMessage tm = (TextMessage) msg;

   try {
    String text = tm.getText();
    System.err.println("Received new message : " + text);
   }
   catch(JMSException e) {
    e.printStackTrace();
   }
  }
 }

 /**
  * Destroys the bean
  */
 public void ejbRemove() {
  System.err.println("ejbRemove()");
 }
}
```

Source 9.2 *(continued)*

This is the most basic message-driven bean. Notice the following:

- Our bean implements the *javax.ejb.MessageDrivenBean* interface that makes it a message-driven bean.
- Our bean implements the *javax.jms.MessageListener* interface that provides the methods necessary for JMS message consumption.
- The *setMessageDrivenContext()* method associates a bean with an environment. We store the context as a member of the implementation class so that other methods of the bean can make use of it.
- The bean is stateless and does not contain any client-specific state that spans messages. Therefore each bean is identical and has an identical initialization method—a simple *ejbCreate()* that takes no arguments.
- The *onMessage()* method receives a message, checks to make sure that the passed-in message is of type *TextMessage* by using the *instanceof* operator, and then downcasts appropriately. If the passed-in message is not a *TextMessage*, the method just returns. *TextMessage* is a particular type of JMS message that has methods for getting and setting the text as the body of the message. After down-casting the input parameter, the method prints out the content of the message, if any exists.
- When the bean is being destroyed, there is nothing to clean up so we have a very simple *ejbRemove()* method.

Notice that you don't hard-code JMS message-driven beans for a specific queue or topic. Your JMS message-driven bean code is independent of destination. The deployment descriptor determines whether a topic or a queue is consumed, as we will see.

A message-driven bean can register itself with the EJB timer service for time-based notifications by implementing the *javax.ejb.TimedObject* interface apart from the message listener and *javax.ejb.MessageDrivenBean* interfaces. The container will invoke the bean instance's *ejbTimeout()* method upon timer expiration.

The Deployment Descriptor

Message-driven beans have only a couple of deployment descriptor tags applicable to them. The portion of the deployment descriptor relevant to our simple JMS message-driven bean is shown in Source 9.3.

```
<?xml version="1.0" encoding="UTF-8"?>

<ejb-jar xmlns="http://java.sun.com/xml/ns/j2ee"
         xmlns:xsi="http://www.w3.org/2001/XMLSchema-instance"
         xsi:schemaLocation=http://java.sun.com/xml/ns/j2ee
         http://java.sun.com/xml/ns/j2ee/ejb-jar_2_1.xsd"
         version="2.1">
 <enterprise-beans>

  <!--
   For each message-driven bean that is located in an
   ejb-jar file, you have to define a <message-driven> entry
   in the deployment descriptor.
  -->
  <message-driven>

   <!-- The nickname for the bean could be used later in DD -->
   <ejb-name>Log</ejb-name>

   <!-- The fully qualified package name of the bean class -->
   <ejb-class>examples.LogBean</ejb-class>
   <messaging-type>javax.jms.MessageListener</messaging-type>

   <!-- The type of transaction supported (see Chapter 12) -->
   <transaction-type>Container</transaction-type>

   <!-- Whether I'm listening to a topic or a queue -->
   <message-destination-type>javax.jms.Topic</message-destination-type>

   <!-- Provide further details on message-driven bean activation -->
   <activation-config>
    <activation-config-property>
     <activation-config-property-name>
      destinationType
     </activation-config-property-name>
     <activation-config-property-value>
      javax.jms.Topic
     </activation-config-property-value>
    </activation-config-property>
  </message-driven>
 </enterprise-beans>
</ejb-jar>
```

Source 9.3 ejb-jar.xml for the simple bean.

Table 9.3 contains definitions for additional deployment descriptor tags that are unique to JMS message-driven beans. Just glance over it now—it's not important to fully understand them if you're just starting to learn message-driven beans. See Appendix C for a complete deployment descriptor reference.

EJB 2.1 introduced new *<activation-config-property>* elements in the deployment descriptors, specifically to configure message-driven beans. These elements are meant to represent operational information pertaining to message-driven beans, JMS or others, in the deployment descriptors. In the case of JMS message-driven beans, these elements are used to specify their specific operational requirements, such as type of subscription to topics, type of destination, and so on.

Table 9.3 Optional Sub-Elements for the <message-driven> Tag

FUNCTIONALITY	DESCRIPTION	EXAMPLE
Destination type	Destination type setting advises the deployer as to whether a JMS message-driven bean will consume messages from a queue or a topic. The bean developer should provide this setting in the deployment descriptor even though deployer can override it.	<activation-config-property> <activation-config-property-name>destinationType</activation-config-property-name> <activation-config-property-value>javax.jms.Topic</activation-config-property-value> </activation-config-property>
Message selector	A message selector filters, or limits, which messages are sent to your bean. Message selectors are very powerful; they increase overall performance by reducing the number of messages delivered to clients that have no interest in the message. To use message selectors, first your JMS client sets up header fields	<activation-config-property> <activation-config-property-name>messageSelector</activation-config-property-name> <activation-config-property-value>JMSType='log' AND logLevel='severe' </activation-config-property-value>

Table 9.3 *(continued)*

FUNCTIONALITY	DESCRIPTION	EXAMPLE
Message selector *(continued)*	on JMS messages using the JMS API. For example, the JMS client might call *message.setStringProperty ("logLevel", "severe")* before sending the message. When the JMS destination receives the message, the container applies the message selector criteria defined in the deployment descriptor. Only messages with headers that match the selector are delivered.	</activation-config-property> Note: You can use the more complicated SQL-like functionality here as well, such as arithmetic, logical operators (AND/OR/NOT), and more. If you use greater than (>) or less than (<) signs then you need to wrap this in a CDATA section, to avoid XML parsing confusion, as we described in Chapter 8. See the JMS specification at http://java.sun.com/ for complete rules for message selector syntax, which is a subset of the SQL 92 standard.
Message acknowledgment	If you let the container handle transactions (called *container-managed transactions* described in Chapter 12), then the container delivers the message to you in a transaction. There is no need for message acknowledgment then, because if the transaction rolls back the message is automatically put back on the queue. If you program your own transactions (called *bean-managed transactions*), the transaction occurs within your bean, and begins and ends after the message has been delivered to your bean; thus the consumption of the message occurs outside the transaction.	<activation-config-property> <activation-config-property-name>acknowledgeMode</activation-config-property-name> <activation-config-property-value>Auto-acknowledge</activation-config-property-value> </activation-config-property>

(continued)

Table 9.3 *(continued)*

FUNCTIONALITY	DESCRIPTION	EXAMPLE
Message acknowledgment *(continued)*	Therefore, if you are using bean-managed transactions, you need to tell the container to *acknowledge* messages. *Auto-acknowledge* setting forces the container to acknowledge a message when the JMS message-driven bean's *onMessage()* method has successfully returned. The Dups-ok-acknowledge setting allows the container to acknowledge a message when it feels like doing so and when it finds the required resources and processing time. Since it may not acknowledge the messages fast enough, you run the risk of the JMS destination sending you a duplicate message. You should use this only if you can tolerate duplicate messages.	
Message durability	JMS message-driven beans that consume messages from topic can be either of durable type or nondurable type. We discuss durable and nondurable subscriptions in the sidebar, "*JMS Message-Driven Beans and Durable-Nondurable Subscriptions.*"	<activation-config-property> <activation-config-property-name>subscription Durability</activation-config-property-name> <activation-config-property-value>NonDurable</activation-config-property-value> </activation-config-property>

As you can see, developing the deployment descriptor for JMS message-driven beans is simple. In addition to the characteristics that are definable for all message-driven beans, application server vendors can provide value-add extensions in an application server–specific deployment descriptor. For example, an application server vendor may provide a deployment descriptor parameter that defines the maximum size of the message-driven bean pool or another parameter that defines its initial size.

A question that you may be asking now is, "Exactly how does the application server bind a JMS message-driven bean container to a specific topic or queue?" If you look closely at the deployment descriptor provided in Source 9.3, the *<message-driven-destination>* tag specifies whether the bean should consume queue or topic messages; however, it never indicates which topic or queue the JMS message-driven bean container should bind to. This is done purposely to make JMS message-driven beans portable across application servers. Since the names of actual topics and queues deployed into a JMS server are application server-specific, the mapping of a bean's container to a specific JMS server destination has to be done in an application server-specific deployment descriptor. Most EJB vendors are expected to have a custom deployment descriptor that binds the bean to a specific destination.

The Client Program

The client application for our simple JMS message-driven bean example is the JMS client we developed earlier in this chapter in Source 9.1. This shows you the power of message-driven beans—our client is solely a JMS client, and the application is never the wiser that a JMS message-driven bean is consuming the messages.

If you'd like to try this example yourself, see the book's accompanying source code for compilation and deployment scripts.

Advanced Concepts

So far, we have discussed the mechanics of developing JMS message-driven beans. Now let's take a closer look at the support containers can give for JMS message-driven beans. We'll see how they might integrate with transactions, provide advanced JMS features, and behave in a clustered environment.

Transactions

JMS message-driven beans do not run in the same transaction as the producer who sends the message, because there are typically two transactions associated with every durable JMS message (one transaction for the producer to put the message on the queue, and another transaction for the JMS message-driven bean to get the message off the queue). It is theoretically impossible for the JMS message-driven bean to participate in the same transaction (and hence the same unit of work) as the producer, because until the producer commits the transaction, the message wouldn't even appear on the queue!

For a complete discussion of transactions and how they apply to JMS message-driven beans, see Chapter 12.

Security

JMS message-driven beans do not receive the security identity of the producer who sends the message, because there is no standard way to stick security information into a JMS message. Therefore you cannot perform EJB security operations (described in Chapter 13) with JMS message-driven beans.

Load-balancing

Clustering message-driven beans is quite different than clustering session or entity beans (see Chapter 19). With session and entity beans, your requests are *load-balanced* across a group of containers. The load-balancing algorithm *guesses* which server is the least-burdened server and pushes requests out to that server. It's guessing because the client's RMI-IIOP runtime can never know for sure which server is the least burdened, because all load-balancing algorithms are approximation algorithms based on imperfect historical data. This is called a *push model* because we are pushing requests out to the server, and the server has no say about which requests it receives.

With JMS message-driven beans, producers put messages onto a destination. The messages reside in the destination until a consumer takes the messages off of the destination, or (if the messages are nondurable) the server hosting the destination crashes. This is a *pull model,* since the message resides on the destination until a consumer asks for it. The containers contend (fight) to get the next available message on the destination.

Thus, JMS message-driven beans feature an *ideal* load-balancing paradigm and distribute the load more smoothly than session or entity beans do. The server that is the least burdened and asks for a message gets the message. The trade-off for this optimal load-balancing is that messaging has extra overhead because a destination "middleman" sits between the client and the server.

Duplicate Consumption in a Cluster

Since JMS topics use the publish/subscribe model, it's possible that a message sent to a JMS topic will be delivered to more than one consumer. Many containers will create a pool of many message-driven beans instances to process multiple messages concurrently, so some concern can arise around message-driven bean containers that subscribe to JMS topics.

In particular, if a JMS message-driven bean container has pooled five instances of its message-driven bean type and is subscribed to the *DogTopic*, how many consumers will consume a message sent to the *DogTopic* topic? Will the message be consumed by each JMS message-driven bean instance in the container or just once by a single JMS message-driven bean? The answer is simple: A container that subscribes to a topic consumes any given message only once. This means that for the five instances that the container created to concurrently process messages, only one of the instances will receive any particular message freeing up the other instances to process other messages that have been sent to the *DogTopic*.

Be careful, though. *Each* container that binds to a particular topic will consume a JMS message sent to that topic. The JMS subsystem will treat each JMS message-driven bean container as a separate subscriber to the message. This means that if the same JMS message-driven bean is deployed to many containers in a cluster, then *each* deployment of the JMS message-driven bean will consume a message from the topic it subscribes to. If this is not the behavior you want, and you need to consume messages exactly once, you should consider deploying a queue instead of a topic.

For JMS message-driven beans that bind to a queue, the JMS server will deliver any message on the queue to only one consumer. Each container registers as a consumer to the queue, and the JMS server load-balances messages to consumers based on availability. JMS message-driven beans that bind to queues that are deployed in a cluster are ideal for scalable processing of messages. For example, if you have two servers in your cluster and 50 messages on a queue, each server will consume on average 25 messages—as opposed to a single server responsible for consuming 50 messages.

JMS message-driven beans in a cluster are shown in Figure 9.6. Notice that many JMS message-driven beans process the same JMS message from Topic #1. Also notice that only a single bean processes any given message from Queue #1.

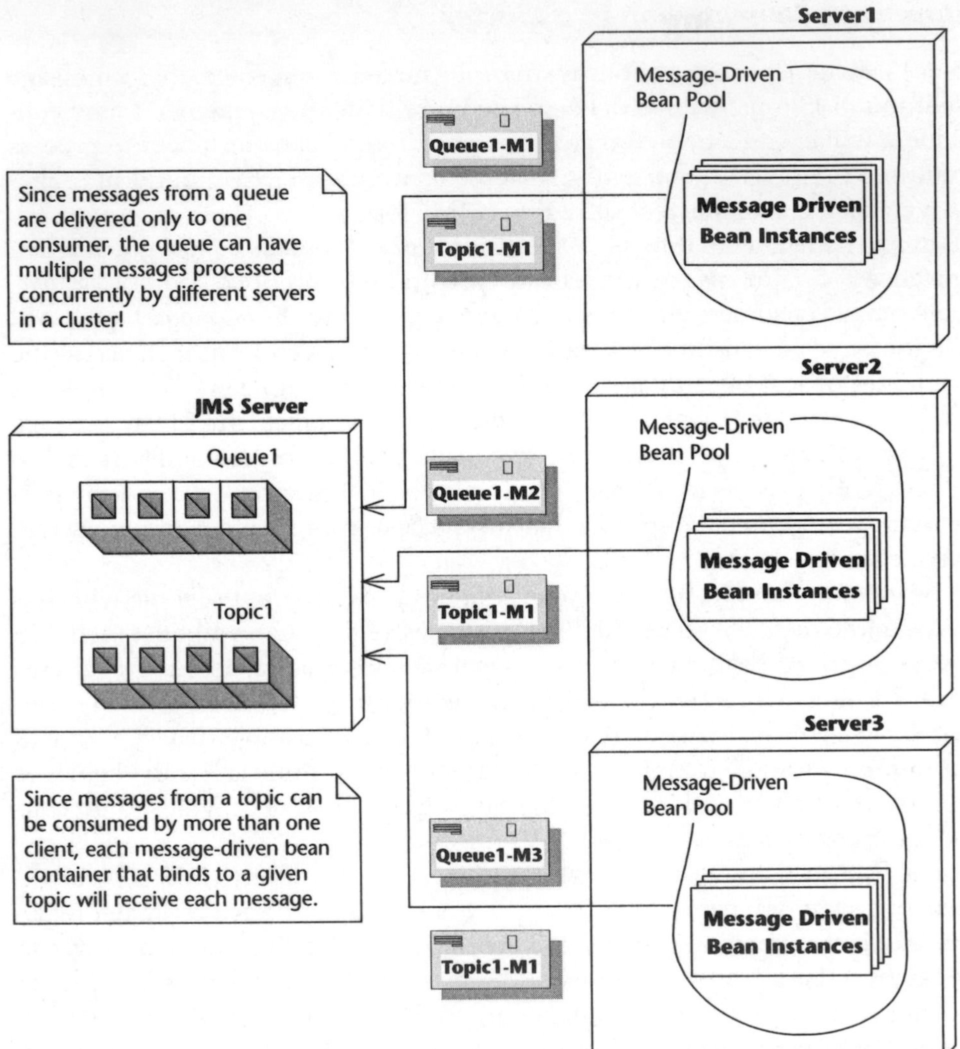

Figure 9.6 JMS message-driven beans in a cluster.

JMS Message-Driven Bean Gotchas

Although developing JMS message-driven beans is a straightforward process, many dark corners and caveats can be encountered unknowingly. In this section we uncover some of these JMS message-driven demons and suggest solutions to help speed you on your way to successful implementation.

Message Ordering

A JMS server does not guarantee delivery of messages to a pool of JMS message-driven beans in any particular order. The container likely attempts to deliver messages in an order that doesn't impact the concurrency of message processing, but there is no guarantee as to the order that the beans actually process the message. Therefore JMS message-driven beans should be prepared to process messages that are not in sequence. For example, a message adding a second hamburger to a fast food order might be processed before the message indicating that a new fast food order with a hamburger should be created. Bean developers must take these scenarios into account and handle them appropriately.

Missed ejbRemove() Calls

As with session and entity beans, you are not guaranteed that the container will call your *ejbRemove()* method when your bean is destroyed. In particular, if there is a system crash or a crash from within the EJB container, any active message-driven bean instances are destroyed without going through the proper life cycle shutdown. Additionally, for any method that throws a system exception, such as *EJBException*, the *ejbRemove()* method is not invoked. Developers should be alert to this fact and perform any relevant cleanup before throwing a system exception.

Developers should also be aware that the *ejbRemove()* method is invoked by the container only when the container no longer needs that instance. Many containers pool the necessary number of message-driven bean instances needed to handle concurrently multiple messages. The limits on the minimum and maximum size of the message-driven bean pool are typically set in an application-server specific deployment descriptor. A container adds and removes message-driven bean instances to and from the pool as appropriate. However, since message-driven beans are extremely lightweight objects, a container generally destroys a message-driven bean instance *only* when the EJB itself is being undeployed (the whole EJB component is being undeployed). For most systems, the only time container undeployment occurs is at system shutdown or when an administrator decides to undeploy the component. The important point here is that message-driven bean containers are rarely undeployed and therefore message-driven instances are rarely destroyed. As a general rule of thumb, the *ejbRemove()* method is rarely invoked.

USING QUEUES TO PARTITION BUSINESS PROCESSING IN A CLUSTER

Suppose you have two clusters of machines: One cluster is configured for a development and test environment, and the other cluster is configured for a production environment. You need to make sure that traffic coming from test clients is sent to the development cluster, while traffic coming from real clients is sent to the production cluster.

As one solution, you could set up your JMS server with two queues: *DevelopmentQueue* and *ProductionQueue*. You could deploy a series of JSPs or front-end stateless session beans that analyze each incoming request, format it into a JMS message, and then place requests onto one of the queues. Requests that come from an internal development machine could be placed onto the *DevelopmentQueue*, and all other requests could be placed on the *ProductionQueue*.

On the back end, you could configure two clusters: One cluster has JMS message-driven beans bound to the *DevelopmentQueue*, and the other cluster has JMS message-driven beans bound to the *ProductionQueue*. The logic for each of these beans can vary based on the needs of the system. For example, the behavior of the JMS message-driven beans bound to the *DevelopmentQueue* can mimic those bound to the *ProductionQueue* but add on debugging statements. You can also tune each cluster independently based on load to the system. Since the *ProductionQueue* will likely have more load than the *DevelopmentQueue*, you could independently grow the size of the cluster servicing the *ProductionQueue* without impacting the cluster servicing the *DevelopmentQueue*.

This illustrates a general paradigm of using queues to partition business logic processing. Rather than the servers pulling messages off a single queue, you pre-choose which machines get the messages by splitting the queue into two queues. This is an artificial way to achieve controlled load-balancing in a JMS system.

Poison Messages

When using container-managed transactions (see Chapter 12) with a JMS message-driven bean, it is easy to code yourself into a situation that causes the generation of *poison messages*. A poison message is a message that is continually retransmitted by a JMS destination to the consumer because the consumer continuously fails to acknowledge the consumption of the message. Any time your JMS message-driven bean does not acknowledge messages to the JMS destination, you have a situation with the potential to create poison messages. See Figure 9.7 to see a diagram indicating how poison messages can inadvertently be generated.

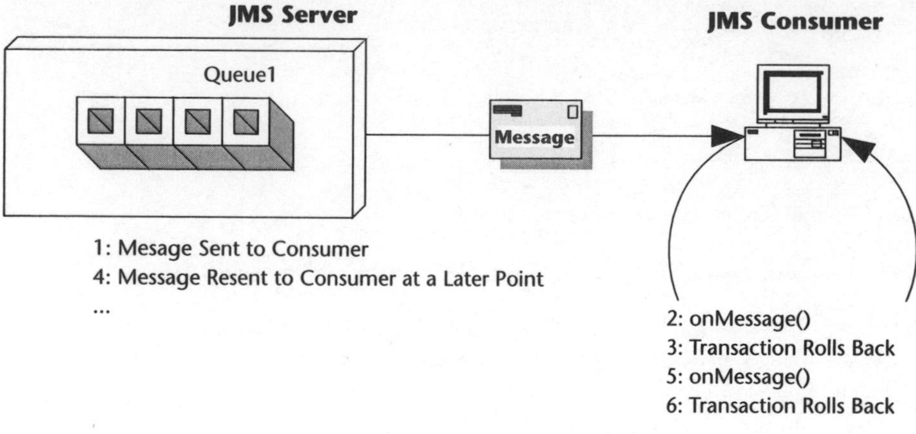

Figure 9.7 How JMS message-driven beans can cause poison messages.

For example, suppose you have a stock-quoting JMS message-driven bean that accepts a text message, which represents the stock ticker symbol to be quoted. Your bean cracks open that message. If the string contained within the message matches a stock symbol, the bean retrieves the value of that symbol and sends a response message. Otherwise, the bean throws a system exception or calls *MessageDrivenContext.setRollbackOnly()*. This causes the transaction to be rolled back, which means the message acknowledgment will never be sent to the JMS destination. The JMS destination eventually resends the same message to the container, causing this same process to occur.

See Source 9.4 for an example of a JMS message-driven bean implementation class that will cause a poison message scenario. Note that our abuse of threading is for illustrative purposes only!

```
package examples;

import javax.ejb.*;
import javax.jms.*;

public class PoisonBean
 implements MessageDrivenBean, MessageListener {

 private MessageDrivenContext ctx;

 public void setMessageDrivenContext(MessageDrivenContext ctx) {
  this.ctx = ctx;
```

Source 9.4 PoisonBean.java. *(continued)*

```
    }

    public void ejbCreate() { }

    public void ejbRemove() { }

    public void onMessage(Message msg)  {
     try {
      System.out.println("Received msg " + msg.getJMSMessageID());

      // Let's sleep a little bit so that we don't
      // see rapid fire re-sends of the message.
      Thread.sleep(3000);

      // We could either throw a system exception here or
      // manually force a rollback of the transaction.
      ctx.setRollbackOnly();
     }
     catch (Exception e) {
      e.printStackTrace();
     }
    }
}
```

Source 9.4 *(continued)*

You can use any of the following strategies to resolve poison messages:

- Make sure to not throw any system exceptions for any business logic-related error conditions. System exceptions like *EJBException* are intended to indicate system or container failure. If this were a session or entity bean, the ideal solution would be to generate an application exception and throw it (especially since application exceptions do not force transactions to be rolled back). However, the EJB specification discourages application exceptions from being thrown from the *onMessage()* method of a JMS message-driven bean. The ideal solution to this problem would likely involve logging the business error message and then quietly returning.
- Consider using bean-managed transactions instead of container-managed transactions. Message consumption and acknowledgment is not part of the transaction if bean-managed transactions are used. A bean-managed transaction can be rolled back and the message is acknowledged anyway.
- Some application servers enable you to configure a poison message queue. Messages that are redelivered a certain number of times are flagged as poison messages, removed from their primary queue, and

placed into a poison message queue. Typically, any message that is redelivered from three to five times can be considered a poison message. You can then bind special consumers or JMS message-driven beans to the poison message queue to handle any unexpected error conditions.

- Some application servers place a retry count value as a property of any redelivered messages. Each redelivery of a message incrementally increases the retry count. Your JMS message-driven bean could check the value of a retry count (if it exists) to see if it has repeatedly consumed the same message.
- Some application server vendors provide a *redelivery delay* feature that administrators can configure to determine how long the JMS destination delays the redelivery of a message after it receives a negative acknowledgment. This way, your system doesn't grind to a halt in case of rapid-fire poison messages.

How to Return Results Back to Message Producers

The EJB specification does not outline any mechanism that allows a JMS message-driven bean to propagate a response back to the client that originally generated the message. So we need to build those facilities ourselves. Figure 9.8 shows how this could be accomplished.

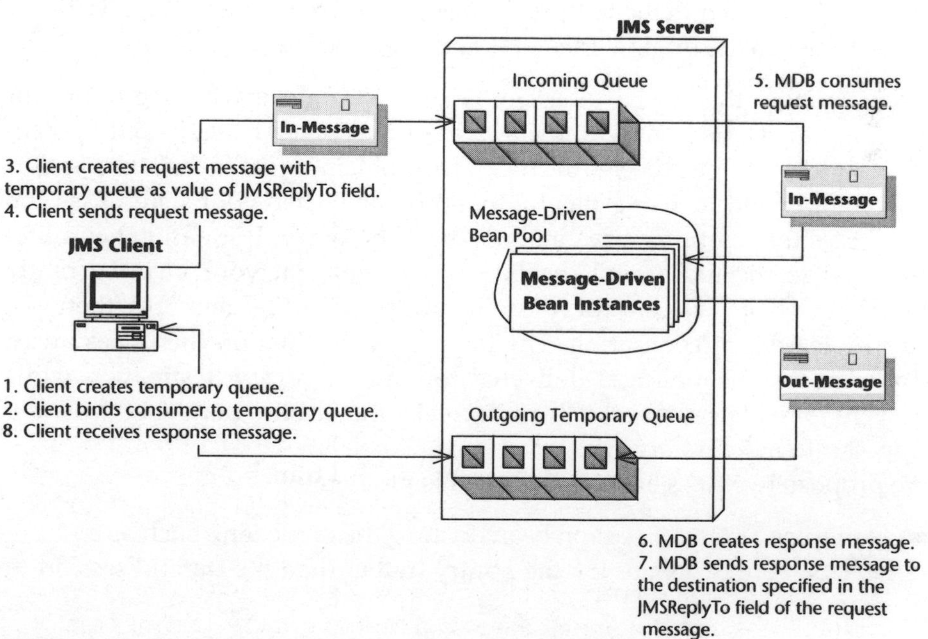

Figure 9.8 A simple JMS request/response paradigm solution.

Here is an explanation of Figure 9.8:

1. The client that generates a JMS message for consumption creates a *temporary destination* associated with its *Connection* object. The JMS server temporarily creates a *Topic* or *Queue* object and that object exists for the lifetime of the *Connection* object.
2. The request message that the client sends contains extra information, so the receiving JMS message-driven bean knows how to reply correctly. Specifically, the client sticks the name of the temporary queue in the *JMSReplyTo* header field of the request message. The JMS message-driven bean can harness this field to reply on the correct queue. The client also has a unique identifier of the original message in the *JMSCorrelationID* header field of the original message. When the JMS message-driven bean replies, it embeds this original identifier, so the client knows to which original message he's receiving a reply.
3. The client creates a new *Session* object and registers a *MessageListener* object to consume messages sent to the temporary destination that was just created.
4. The client sends the message.
5. After consuming the message, the JMS message-driven bean formats a response and sends it using the *JMSReplyTo* and *JMSCorrelationID* attribute of the received message.
6. The client's *MessageListener* class asynchronously consumes the message that is sent to the temporary destination, recognizes that it is a response to the original message, and processes it.

Even though this scenario seems like a straightforward solution for responding to clients from within a JMS message-driven bean, it could potentially lead to some unexpected results. The problem arises if the *client itself* is an EJB component, such as a stateful session bean. When your stateful session bean creates the temporary destination, that temporary destination has a lifespan equal to the lifespan of the JMS connection that your bean currently holds. If your bean is *passivated* (meaning swapped out of memory), then you need to release that connection. The temporary destination then goes away, and you've lost all messages delivered to that temporary destination while you were passivated, even if you recreate the destination after you are swapped into memory again.

We propose two possible solutions to this problem:

- Don't use a stateful session bean. Instead the end client, such as a servlet, application, or JSP tag library (rather than the stateful session bean), creates a temporary queue that all response messages are sent to. The stateful session bean is therefore not holding onto a connection, eliminating any danger of the destination going away because of passivation. See the book's accompanying source code for an implementation of this solution.

The advantages of using this architecture include:

- **Ease of implementation.** Creating temporary queues doesn't require any extra configuration from an administrator, whereas setting up a dedicated response topic requires management on the part of the administrator and your application.
- **Security.** Since temporary queues are bound to a particular connection, malicious clients cannot bind to a temporary queue and intercept response messages.
- **Immediate client notification.** Since the remote client creates and manages the receiving logic for the temporary queue, the client is notified immediately when a response message is generated, rather than having to wait for a middleman session bean to respond.

The disadvantages of this architecture include:

- **No persistent messages.** Temporary queues cannot have persistent stores associated with them and therefore cannot support guaranteed message delivery. If the system fails while a response message is located on the temporary queue, the message will be lost.
- **Poor abstraction.** Since temporary queues are associated with a *Connection* object, a stateful session EJB cannot perform middle-tier management of the request/response process. It might be more natural to abstract away the JMS request/response logic from the client.

- A *permanent* response *topic* is configured and deployed in the JMS server. All response messages are delivered to the same response topic for all clients. Clients filter out the messages that belong to them by registering a message selector with the JMS server. Any request message that is sent has a custom application property called *ClientName*=MyID where *MyID* varies for each client. The JMS message-driven bean that consumes the request message takes the application property from the request message and inserts the same property in the response message. All response messages are sent to the same response topic irrespective of the client. Figure 9.9 illustrates this scenario, and the book's accompanying source code has its implementation.

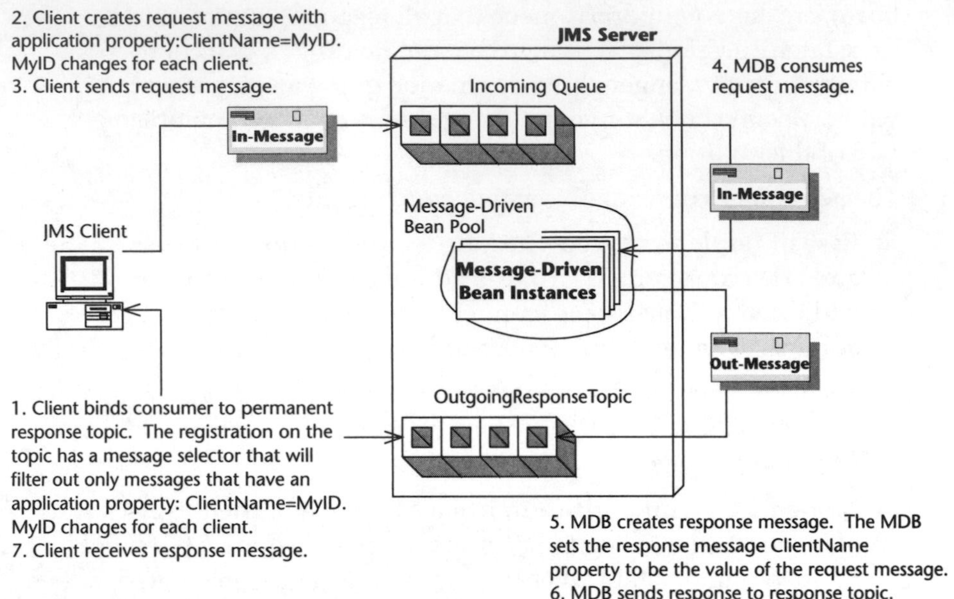
2. Client creates request message with
application property:ClientName=MyID.
MyID changes for each client.
3. Client sends request message.
JMS Server
Incoming Queue
4. MDB consumes
request message.
In-Message
In-Message
Message-Driven
Bean Pool
JMS Client
Message-Driven
Bean Instances
Out-Message
OutgoingResponseTopic
1. Client binds consumer to permanent
response topic. The registration on the
topic has a message selector that will
filter out only messages that have an
application property: ClientName=MyID.
MyID changes for each client.
7. Client receives response message.
5. MDB creates response message. The MDB
sets the response message ClientName
property to be the value of the request message.
6. MDB sends response to response topic.

Figure 9.9 Another JMS request/response paradigm solution.

The advantages of using this architecture include:

- **Better fault tolerance.** Because this architecture proposes that a permanent topic be set up for all outgoing messages, the response topic could be associated with a persistent store. All outgoing messages could then be sent persistently with guaranteed message delivery. Temporary topics and queues cannot have persistent messages delivered to them. This could be ideal for a data retrieval system. For example, suppose you had a remote client that randomly connected to the central server requesting a download of the latest market data as it pertains to that client. The data could be anywhere from 1K to 1MB. Let's also suppose that for situations where a large amount of data needs to be retrieved for the client, you want to break up the data chunks into 100K messages. If the client needed to retrieve 1MB of data, you would need to send 10 response messages. All of the response messages could be sent with guaranteed message delivery. If the remote client application were to fail during the download process, it could easily resume from the last response message that it received instead of having to restart the entire download process.
- **Better filtering.** You can add additional filtering of response messages through the message selector that the client registers with the JMS server. In the example provided with this book, the client registers to receive messages that have an application property

ClientName=MyID. You could conceivably add application properties about the response message that the client filters on. These properties could be message size, message importance, and so on.

The disadvantages are as follows:

- **Lack of security.** The main disadvantage of this architecture is lack of security. Since the JMS specification does not have any security restrictions on which clients can bind which message selectors, any client can register any message selector. This presents the opportunity for a malicious client to register for consumption of response messages that are destined for another client. This malicious behavior is not possible with temporary destinations. Of course, if you're secured by a firewall, security probably isn't an issue. Also, it would take a pretty snazzy developer to actually figure out that you're sending messages and register a message listener.
- **Intermediary EJB.** This approach allows a session EJB to act as a mediator between the client and the back-end system, as mentioned in the actual description of the problem. By using an intermediary session EJB, security can be improved, because the topic that response messages are delivered to can be made available only internally by simply not exposing it to a client or blocking the message server using a firewall or other security measure. The session EJB can be coded to filter out messages based upon the logged-in user name.

An Alternative Request/Response Paradigm

If you don't feel like writing your own request/response code as we've just described, you can tap into the JMS facilities to help you. JMS has two special classes, *javax.jms.QueueRequestor* and *javax.jms.TopicRequestor*, that implement a simple request/response paradigm. You call a method called *request()* that takes as input the request message and returns the response message. This is implemented in the book's accompanying source code.

The downsides to this approach are:

- **You need to block when waiting for a response.** You can't continue processing and do other things, which is one of the major advantages of messaging in the first place.
- **You can't use transactions.** If you did, the outgoing message would be *buffered* until the transaction committed. Since the *QueueRequestor* class doesn't commit right away, but instead blocks until it receives a response message, it will block indefinitely. The outgoing request message will wait forever to be flushed from the buffer. See Chapter 12 for more on transactions.

The Future: Asynchronous Method Invocations

One of the downsides to JMS message-driven beans is that you need to learn a whole new API, JMS, to call them. This API is highly procedural in nature, because you are not invoking lots of different business methods on your JMS message-driven bean; rather, you are sending messages using the JMS API, and the server has a single method to crack the message open and then call the intended method using a giant *if* statement.

An *asynchronous method invocation* is a real method invocation executed in an asynchronous fashion. You are actually calling business methods on the server, such as *logMessage()* or *quoteStock()*. You can choose whether you want to block and wait for an asynchronous response or to return immediately and not wait for a response. Furthermore, the server can take on the context information of the client.

Asynchronous RMI and Microsoft Queued Components are asynchronous method invocation infrastructures. JAX-RPC supports one-way RPC over SOAP. CORBA also has some support for this, with a slightly different definition of deferred synchronous invocations: "A request where the client does not wait for completion of the request, but does intend to accept results later."

We hope a future EJB specification supports asynchronous method invocations. Until then, you'll have to build such facilities on top of JMS yourself, perhaps by writing a code generator.

Summary

In this chapter, we've learned about developing JMS message-driven beans and the pitfalls associated with doing asynchronous development with EJBs. We started by learning about the various benefits of developing asynchronous components and how message-driven beans compare to their session and entity bean counterparts. We also learned about the key difference between message-driven beans of EJB 2.0 and those of EJB 2.1. We looked at how to build a JMS message-driven bean and deploy it. Next we looked at how a JMS message-driven bean behaves in its environment, including how it interacts with transactions. Finally, we took a look at the common pitfalls of using message-driven beans and proposed some solutions.

CHAPTER

10

Adding Functionality to Your Beans

In previous chapters, you learned the fundamentals of EJB programming. In this chapter, we'll build on that knowledge and cover a slew of essential topics, including:

- How to call beans from other beans
- How to use environment properties to customize your beans and access those environment properties at runtime
- How to access resource factories (such as JDBC or JMS drivers) from your bean
- How to use EJB object handles and EJB home handles

This knowledge is key for building nontrivial EJB deployments. So let's get to it!

Calling Beans from Other Beans

Any nontrivial EJB object model has *layers* of beans calling other beans. For example, a bank teller bean might call a bank account bean, or a customer bean might call a credit card bean. In this chapter, we'll use the following examples:

- A pricing engine that computes prices of products, using all sorts of interesting rules, such as discounts, taxes, and shipping costs
- A catalog engine that is a catalog for products, retrieving products from the database as necessary

The pricing engine calls the catalog engine. For simplicity, we'll assume that both of these beans are stateless session beans, since that's what you've learned so far.

Default JNDI Lookups

For your bean to call another bean, you must go through the same process that any other client would go through. Your bean might:

1. Look up the other bean's home object via JNDI
2. Call *create()* on the home object
3. Call business methods on the EJB object
4. Call *remove()* on the EJB object

As we mentioned earlier, to look up a home object using JNDI, you first need to supply *JNDI initialization parameters*, such as the JNDI driver you're using, which differs from container to container. But if you're writing a bean that calls another bean, how do you know which JNDI service provider to use? After all, your beans should be container-independent. Hard-coding that JNDI information into your bean would destroy portability.

The good news is that if you're looking up a bean from another bean, you don't need to supply *any* JNDI initialization parameters. You simply acquire a *default* JNDI initial context. The container sets the default JNDI initial context before your bean ever runs. For example, the following code snippet is taken from a bean calling another bean:

```
// Obtain the DEFAULT JNDI initial context by calling the
// no-argument constructor
Context ctx = new InitialContext();

// Look up the home interface
Object result = ctx.lookup("java:comp/env/ejb/CatalogHome");

// Convert the result to the proper type, RMI-IIOP style
CatalogHome home = (CatalogHome)
    javax.rmi.PortableRemoteObject.narrow(
        result, CatalogHome.class);

// Create a bean
Catalog c = home.create(...);
```

The preceding code is portable because nobody ever needs to supply container-specific JNDI initialization parameters.

Understanding EJB References

Notice from the previous section that we looked up a bean in *java:comp/env/ejb*. This is the JNDI context that the EJB specification recommends (but does not require) you to put your beans' names that are referenced from other beans.

Unfortunately, you cannot guarantee that the JNDI location you've specified will be available. It could be unavailable if your bean has a conflict with another bean or if the deployer has a funky JNDI tree that is spread out across multiple domain boundaries.

Thus, your code will break if the JNDI location changes at deployment time. And often, the deployer is unable to modify your code, because it comes to him as *.class* files only. This could happen for example, if you are an independent software vendor that ships beans, and you want to protect your intellectual property and make future upgrades easier by preventing customers from seeing source code.

EJB resolves this situation with *EJB references*. An EJB reference is a *nickname* for the JNDI location that you want to look up a bean. This nickname may not correspond to the actual JNDI location the deployer sticks your bean into. Your code looks up a home via its nickname, and the deployer then binds that nickname to the JNDI location of its choice, perhaps using symbolic links (an advanced JNDI feature not covered in this book—see the JNDI specification for more). Once again, a layer of indirection solves every problem in computer science.

EJB references are declared in the deployment descriptor. Source 10.1 illustrates references.

```
...
<enterprise-beans>


    <!--
    Here, we define our Catalog bean.  Notice we use the
    "Catalog" ejb-name.  We will use this below.
    -->
    <session>
        <ejb-name>Catalog</ejb-name>
        <home>examples.CatalogHome</home>
        ...
```

Source 10.1 Declaring an EJB reference. *(continued)*

```
    </session>

    <session>

        <ejb-name>Pricer</ejb-name>
        <home>examples.PricerHome</home>
        ...

        <ejb-ref>
            <description>
    This EJB reference says that the Pricing Engine
    session bean (Pricer) uses the Catalog Engine
    session bean (Catalog)
            </description>

            <!--
                The nickname that Pricer uses to look
                up Catalog.  We declare it so the deployer
                knows to bind the Catalog home in
                java:comp/env/ejb/CatalogHome.  This may not
                correspond to the actual location to which the
                deployer binds the object via the container
                tools.  The deployer may set up some kind of
                symbolic link to have the nickname point to the
                real JNDI location.
            -->
            <ejb-ref-name>ejb/CatalogHome</ejb-ref-name>

            <!-- Catalog is a Session bean -->
            <ejb-ref-type>Session</ejb-ref-type>

            <!-- The Catalog home interface class -->
            <home>examples.CatalogHome</home>

            <!-- The Catalog remote interface class -->
            <remote>examples.Catalog</remote>

            <!-- (Optional) the Catalog ejb-name -->
            <ejb-link>Catalog</ejb-link>
        </ejb-ref>
    </session>

</enterprise-beans>
...
```

Source 10.1 *(continued)*

Programming with EJB references is straightforward. Our pricer bean is using a catalog bean, so inside the pricer bean we simply list all the necessary information about the catalog bean in an EJB reference. The deployer then knows that our pricer bean uses exactly one other enterprise bean—catalog—and no other. This is useful, because the deployer now knows which class files the pricer bean depends on and which JNDI location needs to be bound. Similarly, the container's tools can easily inspect the deployment descriptor and verify that the deployer has done his job.

Note that while this example declares the catalog bean within our deployment descriptor, we didn't have to do this. The catalog bean could have been in its own Ejb-jar file with its own deployment descriptor.

You can also access EJB components from other EJB components through their local interfaces rather than through their remote interfaces. To do this, our deployment descriptor would be almost exactly the same—except instead of calling the element *<ejb-ref>*, we would call it *<ejb-local-ref>*, instead of *<home>* we would use *<local-home>*, and instead of *<remote>* we would use *<local>*. The JNDI code to look up the bean would change as well; it would look up the local home interface rather than the home interface, and call the local interface rather than the remote interface:

```
// Obtain the DEFAULT JNDI initial context by calling the
// no-argument constructor
Context ctx = new InitialContext();

// Look up the home interface
Object result = ctx.lookup("java:comp/env/ejb/CatalogLocalHome");

// Convert the result to the proper type.  No RMI-IIOP cast
// required since local interfaces are being used.
CatalogLocalHome home = (CatalogLocalHome) result;

// Create a bean
CatalogLocal c = home.create(...);
```

Resource Factories

Our next topic is how to perform callouts to external resources from an EJB component. A *resource factory* is a provider of resources. Examples include a Java Database Connectivity (JDBC) driver, a Java Message Service (JMS) driver, or a J2EE Connector Architecture (JCA) resource adapter. A resource factory is the driver that gives you connections, such as a JDBC driver giving you a database connection.

CONNECTION POOLING

Connection pooling is the reuse of sockets. If a client isn't using a socket, a different client can harness the socket. This increases the scalability of a system. Connection pooling is built into most containers. JDBC specifies standard interfaces for connection pooling, further enhancing your code portability. The connection pooling typically happens completely behind the scenes, and your bean code is oblivious to it.

To begin using a resource factory, you need to locate it. EJB mandates that you use JNDI to look up a resource factory. This is very nice, because you merely need to learn a single API—JNDI—and you can look up JDBC drivers, JMS drivers, JCA drivers, and so on. In fact, you already know how to perform this lookup. It's the same JNDI code you use to look up an EJB home object:

```
// Obtain the initial JNDI context
Context initCtx = new InitialContext();

// Perform JNDI lookup to obtain resource factory
javax.sql.DataSource ds = (javax.sql.DataSource)
    initCtx.lookup("java:comp/env/jdbc/ejbPool");
```

Notice that we're using *java:comp/env/jdbc*. While this is the EJB-suggested location for your JDBC resources, you must specify your resource factory's JNDI location in the deployment descriptor. When your bean is deployed, the deployer binds a real resource factory to that JNDI location. The corresponding deployment descriptor is shown in Source 10.2.

```
...
<enterprise-beans>

    <session>

        <ejb-name>Catalog</ejb-name>
        <home>examples.CatalogHome</home>
        ...

        <!--
        This element indicates a resource factory reference
        -->
        <resource-ref>

            <description>
            This is a reference to a JDBC driver used within
            the Catalog bean.
```

Source 10.2 Declaring a resource factory reference within a deployment descriptor.

```
            </description>

            <!--
            The JNDI location that Catalog uses to look up
            the JDBC driver.
            We declare it so the deployer knows to bind the
            JDBC driver in java:comp/env/jdbc/ejbPool.
            -->
            <res-ref-name>jdbc/ejbPool</res-ref-name>

            <!--
            The resource factory class
            -->
            <res-type>javax.sql.DataSource</res-type>

            <!--
            Security for accessing the resource factory.
            Can either be "Container" or "Application".
            -->
            <res-auth>Container</res-auth>

            <!--
            Whether connections should be shared with other
            clients in the different transactions
            -->
            <res-sharing-scope>Sharable</res-sharing-scope>
        </resource-ref>

    </session>
</enterprise-beans>
...
```

Source 10.2 *(continued)*

Source 10.2 is fairly self-explanatory, except for the *res-auth* entry. To understand it, realize that when you acquire a connection to a database or other resource, that resource may require authorization. For example, you may need to specify a user name and password when obtaining a JDBC connection. EJB gives you two choices for authenticating yourself to a resource:

- **Perform the authentication yourself in the bean code.** Call the resource factory with the appropriate sign-on information, such as a login name and password. In this case, set the deployment descriptor's *res-auth* element to *Application*.
- **Let the deployer handle authentication for you.** The deployer specifies all sign-on information in the deployment descriptor. In this case, set the deployment descriptor's *res-auth* element to *Container*.

The second choice is the most useful, especially when you are writing beans for resale or reuse by other companies, because only the deployer will know which sign-on credentials are needed to access a particular resource.

Environment Properties

Our next tidbit of essential EJB knowledge is how to *customize* our beans at runtime. What does customization mean? Well, our pricing bean might have several different pricing algorithms it could apply. We'd like the consumers of our bean to be able to select their preferred algorithm.

Your bean's *environment properties* are application-specific properties that your beans read in at runtime. These properties can be used to customize your bean and make your beans data-driven. It's a quick-and-dirty alternative to storing information in a database.

The first step to using environment properties is to declare them in the deployment descriptor. The container reads in this deployment descriptor and makes the environment properties available for your bean to access at runtime. An example is shown in Source 10.3.

```
...
<enterprise-beans>

    <session>

        <ejb-name>Pricer</ejb-name>
        <home>examples.PricerHome</home>
        ...

        <!--
        This element contains a single environment property.
        The property is only accessible from the Pricer.
        -->
        <env-entry>

            <description>
            The algorithm for this pricing engine.
            </description>

            <!--
            The JNDI location that Pricer uses to look up
            the environment property.  We declare it so the
            container knows to bind the property in
            java:comp/env/PricerProperties/algorithm.
            -->
```

Source 10.3 Declaring environment properties within an EJB deployment descriptor.

```
            <env-entry-name>Pricer/algorithm</env-entry-name>

            <!-- The type for this environment property -->
            <env-entry-type>java.lang.String</env-entry-type>

            <!-- The environment property value -->
            <env-entry-value>NoTaxes</env-entry-value>
        </env-entry>
    </session>
</enterprise-beans>
. . .
```

Source 10.3 *(continued)*

The environment property declared in Source 10.3 tells our pricing engine to use an algorithm that gives all customers no taxes, due to the Internet tax moratorium that we all love.

You use JNDI to access the environment from your bean. The following code illustrates this.

```
// 1: Acquire the initial context
Context initCtx = new InitialContext();

// 2: Use the initial context to look up
//    the environment properties
String taxAlgorithm = (String)
initCtx.lookup("java:comp/env/Pricer/algorithm");

// 3: Do what you want with the properties
if (!taxAlgorithm.equals("NoTaxes")) {
  // add tax
}
```

Notice that we look up environment properties under the JNDI name *java:comp/env*. All EJB environment properties *must* be somewhere beneath this naming context.

Understanding Handles

Our final topic in this chapter is the subject of handles. Many EJB applications require that clients be able to disconnect from beans and reconnect later to resume using that bean. For example, if you have a shopping cart that you'd like to save for a later time, and a stateful session bean manifests that shopping cart, you'd want your shopping cart state maintained when you reconnect later.

EJB provides for this need with *EJB object handles*. An EJB object handle is a long-lived proxy for an EJB object. If for some reason you disconnect from the EJB container/server, you can use the EJB object handle to reconnect to your EJB object, so that you don't lose your conversational state with that bean. An EJB object handle is an essentially persistent reference to an EJB object. The following code demonstrates using EJB object handles:

```
// First, get the EJB object handle from the EJB object.
javax.ejb.Handle myHandle = myEJBObject.getHandle();

// Next, serialize myHandle, and then save it in
// permanent storage.
ObjectOutputStream stream = ...;
stream.writeObject(myHandle);

// time passes...

// When we want to use the EJB object again,
// deserialize the EJB object handle
ObjectInputStream stream = . . .;
Handle myHandle = (Handle) stream.readObject();

// Convert the EJB object handle into an EJB object
MyRemoteInterface myEJBObject = (MyRemoteInterface)
      javax.rmi.PortableRemoteObject.narrow(
           myHandle.getEJBObject(), MyRemoteInterface.class);

// Resume calling methods again
myEJBObject.callMethod();
```

The *getHandle()* method is available only in remote interfaces, not in local ones. The EJB specification does not require that handles have the ability to be saved in one environment and then restored in a different environment. This means handles are not guaranteed to be portable across EJB containers, nor across machines.

Home Handles

A variant on EJB object handles are the EJB home handles. These are simply persistent references to home objects, rather than persistent references to EJB objects. The following code shows how to use home handles:

```
// First, get the EJB home handle from the home object.
javax.ejb.HomeHandle homeHandle = myHomeObject.getHomeHandle();

// Next, serialize the home handle, and then save it in
// permanent storage.
```

```
ObjectOutputStream stream = ...;
stream.writeObject(homeHandle);

// time passes...

// When we want to use the home object again,
// deserialize the home handle
ObjectInputStream stream = ...;
javax.ejb.HomeHandle homeHandle =
 (HomeHandle) stream.readObject();

// Convert the home object handle into a home object
MyHomeInterface myHomeObject = (MyHomeInterface)
    javax.rmi.PortableRemoteObject.narrow(
        homeHandle.getHomeObject(), MyHomeInterface.class);

// Resume using the home object
myHomeObject.create();
```

Home handles may be useful because you can acquire a reference to a home object, persist it, and then use it again later without knowledge of the home object's JNDI location. But in our opinion, home handles are not going to benefit most applications a tremendous amount. We have never seen any organization make use of them (e-mail us and be the first!).

Summary

In this chapter, we learned a great deal about how to make our beans more robust. We learned how to call beans from other beans, how to use resource factories, how to access environment properties, and how to use handles. Most nontrivial EJB deployment will make use of some of these concepts.

This completes Part Two. You've now covered the fundamentals and should have a strong foundation for learning about advanced concepts. Let's now move on to Part Three, which begins with transactions.

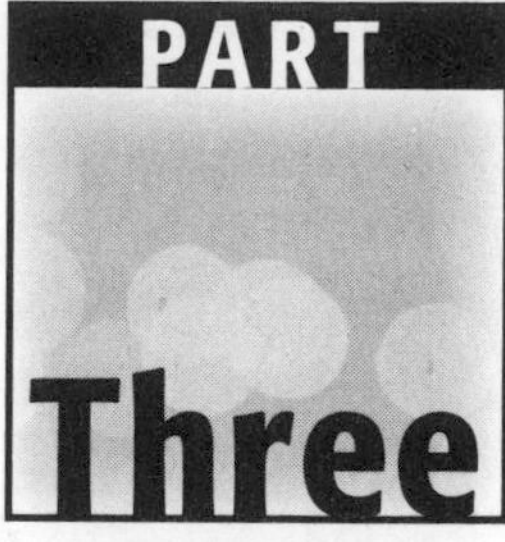

Advanced Enterprise JavaBeans Concepts

If you've read to this point, you should be quite familiar with the basics of Enterprise JavaBeans development. In Part Three, we raise the bar by moving on to more advanced concepts. These include the following:

- **EJB best practices.** Chapter 11 covers a lot of best practices pertinent to EJB such as when to use EJB, how to choose the right Web application framework when working with EJB applications that have Web clients, how to apply aspect-oriented programming concepts with EJB, and many more best practices/guidelines.
- **Transactions.** Chapter 12 shows you how to harness transactions to make your EJB deployments reliable. We'll discuss transactions at a conceptual level and how to apply them to EJB. We'll also learn about the Java Transaction API (JTA).
- **EJB Security.** Chapter 13 provides an in-depth coverage of techniques and best practices surrounding EJB application security. It covers how to enable authentication and authorization declaratively and programmatically in EJB applications. Also the chapter showcases enabling JAAS-based authentication for EJB applications.
- **EJB Timers.** Chapter 14 focuses on building EJB timers. It covers how to write and deploy code that uses the timer service provided by containers.

- **BMP and CMP relationships.** Chapter 15 covers how to build *relationships* between entity beans, both BMP and CMP. This is an essential EJB 2.0 topic for anyone performing persistent operations with entity beans.
- **Persistence best practices.** In Chapter 16, you'll learn about some of the critical tradeoffs when building a persistence layer—how to choose between session beans and entity beans, how to choose between BMP and CMP—and survey a collection of persistence best practices that we've assembled from our knowledge and experience.
- **EJB-based integration.** Chapter 17 covers various approaches to integrating disparate applications with EJB. Here you will learn how various technologies, such as J2EE Connectors and Web Services, could be used to integrate EJB applications with the outside world.
- **EJB performance optimizations.** Chapter 18 covers tips and techniques for boosting EJB performance. You'll learn about best practices for boosting performance of stateless session beans, stateful session beans, entity beans, and message-driven beans. Also, a lot of miscellaneous design and development tips are presented in this chapter.
- **Clustering.** Chapter 19 shows you how EJBs are clustered in large-scale systems. You'll learn how clustering works behind the scenes and a few strategies for how containers might achieve clustering. This is a critical topic for anyone building a system that involves several machines working together.
- **Starting your EJB project on the right foot.** Chapter 20 shows you how to get your project off in the right direction. This includes how to choose between J2EE and .NET, how to staff your project team, how to determine the important investment areas to ensure project success, and so on.
- **How to choose an EJB server.** In Chapter 21, we'll describe our methodology for how an organization can compare and contrast different vendors' offerings. We'll also list our criteria for what we would want in an EJB server.
- **EJB-J2EE integration: Building a complete application.** Chapter 22 shows how each of the EJB components can work together to solve a business problem, as well as how EJB and J2EE can be integrated through Java servlets and JavaServer Page (JSP) technology.

These are extremely interesting middleware topics; indeed, many books could be written on each subject alone. To understand these concepts, we highly recommend you read Part One and Part Two first. However, if you're already well versed in EJB, please join us to explore these advanced issues.

CHAPTER

11

EJB Best Practices

In this chapter, we will discuss best practices in terms of design, development, building, testing, and working with EJB. These guidelines will help in answering some of the dilemmas you face in real-world EJB projects. By being aware of these best practices, you will avoid common pitfalls that others have experienced when building EJB systems.

Note that persistence-related best practices and various performance optimizations are covered in Chapter 16 and Chapter 18, respectively.

Let us begin now with various design, development, testing, debugging, and deployment strategies.

We do not discuss lower-level EJB design patterns in this chapter since there are many resources in terms of books, papers, and so on that already focus on that. Besides, discussing lower-level EJB design patterns itself warrants a whole book. Our recommendation is that you read *EJB Design Patterns* (ISBN: 0-471-20831-0) published by John Wiley & Sons as a guide for EJB design patterns.

When to Use EJB

The cost of not making a correct go or no-go decision for EJB can be very high. It can range from a project getting delayed to a project getting scrapped. Hence, we would like to take a few moments to address this very crucial design point in the very beginning.

In our opinion, you should think of using EJB in the following design situations:

- **Remoting is required.** Gone are the days when everybody used to think of distributed systems as a panacea. Modeling an application's functionality into various tiers composed of reusable components is surely a way to achieve a clean and manageable design. However, deploying these components on separate boxes just for the heck of it does not necessarily result in the best systems. Do not confuse the need for componentization by way of distribution of these components on multiple systems. Both are quite different and both have different costs associated with them.

  With that said, once you determine the need for distributed components in your application, consider EJB as your first alternative. Their sole purpose is to provide a programming model to build managed and distributed components in Java platform.

- **Distributed transactions are required.** Transaction semantics are beautifully defined by the EJB standard. A protocol as complicated as the two-phase commit—one of the most widely used distributed transactions protocols in enterprise applications today—is neatly supported by the EJB architecture. Although, non-standard frameworks such as Spring and Hibernate do support distributed transactions, the level of support of these in EJB containers is one of the best. It probably has to do with maturity gained by EJB server vendors on account of implementing distributed transactions for years. Hence, for large-scale distributed transactional systems, leveraging EJB makes a lot of sense.

One of the common complaints against the EJB transaction model is its lack of support for nested transactions and long-running transactions. Well, this will not remain the case for long. JSR 095 (J2EE Activity Service for Extended Transactions) defines a low-level framework for creating various transaction models. At the time of this writing, JSR 095 is in proposed final draft stage. Hopefully, it shall become part of J2EE 1.5 platform.

- **Component-security is required.** EJB architecture defines a standard fine-grained security model for the components. Although, EJB architecture does not provide support for fancy security schemes, such as Single Sign-On or Biometric authentication, as yet, it does provide a basic framework for authentication and access control that is more than enough to meet security needs of 85 percent of enterprise applications. So if you have a requirement for access control at the application-component level (and not just at the Web level), then you should consider using EJB.

- **Persistence is required.** Much has been said—both, good and bad—about the persistence functionality as defined by the EJB standard. Although there are numerous ways to achieve persistence in EJB applications these days, ranging from the de facto open source frameworks, such as Hibernate, to de jure frameworks, such as Java Data Objects (JDO), an important point to remember here is that EJB persistence, especially CMP, can come in very handy for systems that are extremely transactional and time sensitive. Chapter 16 covers various persistence-related best practices.
- **Integration with legacy applications is required.** More recently, this has become one of the main selling points of EJB architecture. EJB provides multiple elegant models through. J2EE Connector Architecture, EJB Web Services, and JMS for integrating with legacy/non-legacy applications deployed on heterogeneous platforms. Thus, if your application requires integration with another application, you should consider using the EJB framework for this integration. Chapter 17 covers these EJB integration programming models and related best practices in depth.
- **Scalability is required.** EJB technology was designed with scalability in mind. The idea is to make scaling up of applications seamless, for example without re-architecting and reprogramming, so that it simply becomes a matter of throwing more hardware at an application. J2EE enables you to scale your EJB and Web tiers separately. Remoting allows you to keep both of these tiers on separate boxes and scale these boxes as needed. For example, in an application that involves a simple Web interface but complex middle-tier processing, throwing more resources at systems on which an EJB application is deployed just makes more sense.

In conclusion, if you are going to need transactions, remoting, security, persistence, application integration, and other such infrastructure-oriented facilities in your application, consider leveraging the time-tested EJB framework in your project. Working with EJB can get complex if not done right. However, there are thousands of ways to deal with this complexity. But, creating your own framework is definitely not one of them.

IS USING A POJO + FRAMEWORK COMBINATION ALWAYS A GOOD IDEA?

The recent wave in enterprise Java computing is to replace all or some parts of the EJB framework with frameworks, such as Spring, Hibernate, and so on. Spring framework (springframework.org) is a J2EE framework. Spring applications can be built using EJB or Plain Old Java Object (POJO). In case you choose POJO, Spring can provide declarative local transactions for POJO without relying on the EJB container. Similarly, Spring supports data access via JDBC and O/R mapping frameworks such as Hibernate. Thus, Spring is unique in the sense that it makes using heavyweight EJB containers a matter of choice and not necessity in some respects. It provides a lightweight framework alternative for writing business tier objects.

Hibernate (hibernate.org) is another popular O/R framework whose biggest value proposition is ease of use. It is a POJO-driven lightweight transactional persistence and data access framework. One of the interesting features it provides is the modeling of inheritance relationships of data.

Like always, we would like to maintain that just as EJB is not a sure shot way of building robust and scalable applications, using POJO frameworks is not a sure shot way of simplifying business tier development and deployment. Think of using POJOs only when the architectural benefits are substantial. Note that ease of development is not always equipped with highly transactional enterprise functionality. For instance, if distributed transactions are a must for your application, Spring + POJO would not work.

The safest route is to stick to EJBs and trust the Java Community Process (JCP) to evolve the standard, and evolve it they will. EJB 3.0 entity beans from the draft specification seem to have borrowed many concepts from Hibernate. If the direction taken by EJB 3.0 tells us anything, it is that JCP is open to gain from the experiences of the community.

How to Choose a Web Application Framework to Work with EJB

Model 2 Web application frameworks have very much become a part of infrastructure software these days and rightly so. Working with such frameworks guarantees a lot of functionality related to localization, error handling, validation of form data, and so on out of the box. Many of these functions would otherwise need to be coded when working with raw Web components, such as servlets and Java Server Pages (JSP).

You can choose from dozens of Web application frameworks, both open source and closed source. Choosing a Web application framework is an important decision for you as an architect. Here are some of the factors that you should consider while deciding on a Web application framework for your EJB project:

- **Integration with EJB technology.** In EJB projects one of the obvious requirements for your Web application framework would be how well it integrates with EJB technology. EJB integration basically implies the support for EJB design patterns, EJB entity beans handling, and so on from within the framework components. For instance, the Struts community has made it quite simple to work with EJB via the StrutsEJB project (http://strutsejb.dev.java.net). The StrutsEJB project provides base classes and patterns (mainly—Service Locator, Business Delegate, DTO, and Session Façade patterns) to build a Struts Web application that uses EJB in the business tier.
- **Tools support.** Tools enable Rapid Application Development (RAD) thereby increasing productivity. Most of the framework communities and vendors provide some kind of IDE plug-in technology-based tools to help in development. However, usually this plug-in support is limited to one or two IDE at most. So if you are using an IDE the plug-in doesn't support, you might have no tools available for the framework.

  For instance, although Tapestry is a powerful framework, Spindle, a plug-in that provides IDE support for Tapestry, is available only for the Eclipse IDE. As a result, developers of projects that use other IDEs, such as NetBeans, have to develop and deploy the framework components manually.

  On the other hand, mature frameworks, such as Struts, have good tools support in the form of IDE plug-ins (Struts Console plug-in for NetBeans, Eclipse and Struts Tools for IBM WSAD, and so on) and standalone GUI tools (Struts Console and Struts Studio).
- **Small device support.** Generating content in a markup language so that it can be rendered on small devices is a very real requirement of today's business applications. If your application falls in this category, then you should select an application framework that provides a comparatively painless way of generating markup content for small device browsers. Most of the device browsers today support WML, HDML, cHTML, or XHTML markup languages. Frameworks, such as Cocoon, SOFIA, and Struts, provide tag libraries for generating device markups, such as WML, HDML, and XHTML.

If your candidate framework does not provide a tag library for the needed markup language, then you should think about developing a new tag library. Developing a tag library is a non-trivial task and hence, should be considered only when other options are not available.

- **Standards support.** View technology leveraged by these Web application frameworks should be standards-based simply because you do not want to trade innovation from the wider JCP community for innovation from your specific Web application framework community. Although, all the Web application frameworks are based on standards, watch out for those proprietary hooks.
- **Learning curve and availability of expertise.** If you are planning on using your existing staff for application development, then you should consider the learning curve required for them in order to efficiently develop using the candidate Web application framework. Make sure that proper help and documentation is available for the candidate framework, regardless of whether it is open or closed sourced, to speed up the learning. On the other hand, if you are planning to hire new people for your project, then select a framework that is popular and widely used so that finding the right talent is possible.
- **Open source versus closed source.** At the end of the day, if most of your requirements in the areas mentioned previously are met by a given application framework, we'd like to say it does not matter whether it is closed source or open source. However, in the real world, both cost and a sense of control over your own destiny are important concerns. We have witnessed quite a few projects where open source Web application frameworks were chosen because they were "good enough" and were "free." In some other projects, open source Web application frameworks were chosen simply because their source was made available for tweaking; whereas in a select few cases, customers went for closed-source application frameworks from vendors because of a well-defined product support model.

  Whatever your reasons might be for choosing an open or closed source Web application framework, we recommend that you select a framework that meets most of the criteria given in this section.

A very interesting project named Wafer (www.waferproject.org) is under way. Wafer aims at comparing some of the popular Web application frameworks using a common application. The criteria for comparison include support for localization, form validation, documentation, error handling, tools, integration with other technologies, small devices, and so on. At the time of writing, Wafer was evaluating only open source Web application frameworks.

Applying Model Driven Development in EJB Projects

Middle Driven Development (MDD) is becoming more and more popular within the developer community lately because of its promise of increased productivity over the traditional code-centric development approach. MDD is a development methodology wherein a model is at the core of development. In this context, model typically represents an entity in the problem domain and applicable business logic that needs to be performed on this domain entity. For example, in a typical order processing system, a customer model will represent appropriate data attributes and business operations applicable to a customer entity. Thus, if such an order processing system is developed using the MDD paradigm, a given MDD tool will take the customer model as input and generate application code from it, thereby establishing a close link between the model and its system implementation.

Here is an obvious question: "What is the difference between the modeling tools such as Together or Rational Rose and MDD tools?" After all, modeling tools have been generating skeleton implementation code from models for years.

Well, the difference is in how far the tool can take you with a model. Any modeling tool these days can generate Java classes from a corresponding UML class diagram. However, is that enough? No. Because even after the tool generates a Java class, we are still required to write code for utilizing persistence, security, logging, transactions, and other such services of the underlying EJB/JDO/JDBC/XYZ framework. Similarly, we still need to write code for accessing other services, implemented as POJO, EJB, or Web services, from our Java class.

On the other hand, an MDD tool will generate most of these relevant artifacts from a given model and also potentially adhere to the industry best practices of the underlying platform, say Java, J2EE, or .NET. Thus, MDD tools translate the domain model to code not just based on technical specifications, but also based on best practices and design patterns. For example, application code generated by Compuware OptimalJ or open source AndroMDA MDD tools can implement the core J2EE design patterns, such as Command, DAO, and so on, with discretion from the architect, of course. Thus, MDD tools are capable of generating highly functional and quality code.

Evidently tools play a crucial role in the MDD paradigm. We believe that a natural evolution for modeling tools today would be toward supporting MDD. Now, MDD tools can be categorized as follows:

- **Tools that follow standards.** Tools such as Compuware OptimalJ, Infer-Data Model Component Compiler (MCC), Interactive Objects ArcStyler, and open source tools, such as AndroMDA and OpenMDX, and so on, support Model Driven Architecture (MDA), an OMG vendor-neutral standard of building platform-independent models for consumption by MDD tools. MDA makes extensive use of UML and XMI (XML Meta-Data Interchange) to achieve its goal of platform independence.
- **Tools that do not follow standards.** Tools such as IBM Rational Rapid Developer (RRD) do not support any specific standard for MDD, but rather follow their own paradigm. For example, RRD is based on proprietary MDD methodology named Architectured Rapid Application Development (ARAD).

Here are some suggestions for those considering MDD for EJB projects:

- **Begin with a proof of concept.** Start with developing a small application using both traditional code-centric and MDD approaches to verify whether MDD does in fact bring productivity gains to your team. Also in our opinion, it is easier to apply the MDD approach to new application development than to existing application development or maintenance. This is because, at present not many tools provide a sound strategy for migrating existing applications developed using a code-centric approach to MDD.
- **Consider using standards-based tools.** Using tools that follow standards, such as MDA, protects you from vendor lock-in. A healthy ecosystem of tools around a given standard enables migration of platform-independent domain models from one tool to another in future.
- **Consider MDD tool integration with an existing infrastructure.** Consider how well your candidate MDD tool integrates with the existing platform infrastructure products used in your shop. For instance, if using JBoss, an obvious question should be whether MDD would generate packaging and deployment artifacts specific to JBoss.

  Similarly, not all MDD tools (for example, OpenMDX) provide modeling facilities. As a result, you will have to make sure that the MDD tool you choose integrates with your existing modeling tool.
- **Leverage existing research.** The Middleware Company has done extensive research on MDD methodology and published reports comparing traditional code-centric application development with MDD. They have also compared two prevalent MDD tools—OptimalJ and RRD—in terms of how they support MDD. Our suggestion is to leverage this research in your decision-making. These reports are available for free at middlewareresearch.com/endeavors/031126MDDCOMP/endeavor.jsp.

Applying Extreme Programming in EJB Projects

Extreme Programming (XP) is a software engineering discipline whose core practices revolve around an underlying assumption: Change in requirements and hence software design will inevitably occur during the course of software development. As almost all software development methodology pundits agree, XP's underlying assumption is not far from reality. After all, how many projects have you worked on where the design was frozen before writing a single line of code so that it never had to change? None.

This pragmatic approach that XP takes makes it extremely alluring to architects and development team leaders. There are almost a dozen practices defined by the original thinker of XP, Kent Beck. However, we do not think that you need to understand and implement all of them in your EJB projects as long as you follow a couple of core practices strictly.

One of the great advantages of using XP is the availability of a wide variety of tools that can be used for functions ranging from unit testing XP code to managing XP projects to continually integrating components developed using XP methodology. Even better, most of these tools are highly functional, time tested, and open source.

In our opinion, here is how the core principles of XP should be followed in EJB projects:

- **Iterative development.** In iterative development, the development team is given a certain target to meet per iteration. These iterations can last one week, two weeks, or more; whatever seems reasonable to code your requirements. Each such successful iteration will lead the system toward its final form. You will need to divide your EJB projects into such iterations. What has worked very well for us in the past is subdividing a given iteration into three subphases.
- **EJB subphase.** This is when we develop, build, and deploy the EJB—session beans, message-driven beans, or entity beans—on development systems.
- **Testing subphase.** This is when we build the unit test clients that follow simple test cases such as checking the getters/setters, mocking the calls to beans, checking whether the data in the database gets added/updated/deleted properly. Various strategies for unit testing EJB are discussed in the best practice section titled "How to Test EJB."
- **User subphase.** In this phase, we present the work we have done in the given iteration to the actual users. These users might be people from other business units who in turn will be using your application, or from your customer. The clients define various acceptance tests that they

would use in this subphase to make sure that their requirements, defined during the iteration planning, are met.

An important factor for the success of iterative development is setting and meeting deadlines. To meet deadlines, you should refrain from adding new functionality in the middle of the iteration. The idea is to keep your iterations short and yet meaningful.

- **Continuous integration.** Continuous integration is about keeping various application components in sync with each other so that the system is fully integrated most of the time. The motivation behind this practice is to avoid integration nightmares, which usually arise when you take a piecemeal approach to application development and do not stop to check that various pieces work with each other. Frequently checking that the different parts of application fit nicely leads to fewer surprises during the testing subphase. Continuous integration is achieved by typically building the system at least once a day; however, the exact period between consequent builds will mostly depend on how long your iteration is. But the idea is not to defer integration of application components until last moment.
- **Refactoring.** Refactoring is a process of continuously improving the design of existing code without affecting the code behavior. Refactoring usually involves the restructuring of code so as to remove the redundant code, reduce coupling in the code, introduce better naming conventions in the code, or organize the code more cohesively and consistently.

  An example of a good refactoring candidate would be an EJB application where one EJB, say *SavingsBean*, has a method named *calculateInterest()* that accepts parameters in this order: *accountId* and *interestRate*. While another EJB, say *MortgageBean*, has a method named *calculateMortgage()* that accepts parameters in this order: *interestRate* and *accountId*. Here, one of the bean methods takes the *accountId* parameter first; whereas the other bean method takes *interestRate* first. This is a clear example of inconsistency in code design and hence, a good candidate for refactoring.

  Thus, each cycle of refactoring transforms your code into a more evolved structure. A good practice to follow is to keep the changes during refactoring small and have multiple refactoring cycles. Each refactoring cycle should be followed with continuous integration and then testing to ensure that your code evolution has not introduced any new bugs.

  Martin Fowler's book *Refactoring: Improving the Design of Existing Code* (ISBN: 0201485672) is a good resource in that it discusses various techniques for code refactoring such that the underlying behavior is retained. Also http://industriallogic.com/xp/refactoring/catalog.html maintains a catalog of patterns to be used during code design to achieve maximum refactoring. Most of the J2EE/EJB IDEs these days support refactoring transformations of code. Some tools such as Eclipse also enable you to preview the changes resulting from a refactoring action before actually carrying them out. They also can let you know the potential problems refactoring might lead to in the functioning of your code.

- **Test-driven development.** XP focuses largely on testing and thereby requires obtaining feedback from customers at various logical points (end of iteration cycles) in the development life cycle. Also XP style test-driven development encourages doing a lot of unit testing of new or modified code. A typical XP project will maintain a set of unit test cases that a developer will run whenever new or modified code is released. Quite a lot of emphasis is put on the automation of these tests to make XP even more efficient. We talk about EJB testing best practices in the next section.

XP development, thus, is lightweight and flexible as compared to more formal development methodologies such as Rational Unified Process or even some of the obsolete development models such as the waterfall model. We think that applying XP to your EJB projects can provide good benefits regardless of the project complexity given that core principles of XP are followed strictly.

Testing EJB

Of the three types of testing—code testing, regression and functional testing, and load testing—we will focus on the techniques for code testing using unit tests because that is an area where you can automate a lot and thereby make code testing easier and more efficient. Code testing is about ensuring that the given code behaves the way a developer intended it to behave; a code unit test is a piece of code that checks the behavior of the target code. Whereas code unit testing leads to acceptance of a piece of code, functional unit testing leads to acceptance of a subsystem of application. The quality assurance team does functional testing at the use-case level, and it is often composed of customers.

EJB Unit Testing

You can write code unit tests for your EJB to see if your beans are doing the *right* things. For example a code unit test for a BMP account entity bean can determine whether the bean's *ejbCreate()* method is inserting the account data in the database properly. Similarly, a code unit test for a mortgage session bean might check whether its *calculateMortgage()* method is calculating the mortgage payment right. Thus, a code unit test is always about testing the piece of code and its localized behavior. Another important reason to unit test your EJB code is that it helps you catch the inconsistencies and difficulties in using the EJB interfaces early on.

The tricky thing about unit testing EJB code is that it cannot be tested as you would test a plain Java class. An EJB composed of three Java classes has to be tested in a holistic manner; for example, you have to deploy the EJB first and then write a client that can talk to the EJB. This means that our unit tests must encompass deployment and probably redeployment of EJB. The good news is that we can automate deployment. Another consideration while creating EJB code unit tests is about whether to use a test client that sits within the container versus outside the container. Also testing EJB as a standalone component might not make much sense in certain scenarios. For example, consider a design in which a stateless session bean is acting as a façade to other session beans and entity beans. In that case, you should also deploy these other beans in order to unit test the façade stateless session beans. Similarly for entity beans that have relationships with other entity beans, you have to ready all the relationship beans to unit test the original entity bean.

You will need to deploy and redeploy various beans during the testing process. Deploying EJB is a tedious step; it requires a lot of parameters to be specified. Hence, it is best to automate the deployment process for your beans. Pretty much all EJB servers provide command line tools for deploying EJB. You can use these tools in combination with Ant scripts to automate the deployment. You can also automate redeployment as a two-step process: undeploy the existing EJB and deploy the newer version again.

Use Frameworks for EJB Unit Testing

Using a framework will greatly help reduce the effort involved in unit testing. Let us see some of the commonly used frameworks for EJB unit testing.

The JUnit Framework

For instance, a unit test framework such as JUnit will make it easier to create unit tests by extending unit test cases from the framework base classes. JUnit also provides the facility to create a test suite made up of tests that you want to run. Hence, you can combine several unit tests in a test suite to enable regression testing. Graphical test runners based on Swing are made available by JUnit. Test runners are responsible for running JUnit tests and collecting, summarizing, and formatting their results.

JUnit also integrates with Ant so that you can run various tests as part of the build process. For this you will have to insert the *<junit>* Ant task in the Ant script. The *<junit>* Ant task can also create a file consisting of the status of each test. This integration with Ant is very useful because you can bundle not just the test cases but also the configuration needed to run them as part of your Ant scripts. Another benefit of using JUnit and Ant together is that it enables the generation of HTML test reports by using the *<junitreport>* task. This task uses XSLT technology to transform XML test results to HTML.

JUnit is a widely adopted framework with great support tools. It integrates with IDEs such as Eclipse, Netbeans, Oracle JDeveloper, IntelliJ IDEA, Borland JBuilder, and so on. Also, several modeling tools such as Borland TogetherJ support the generation of test cases based on JUnit framework.

Another test framework of interest could be Apache Cactus. Cactus is an extension of JUnit and it specifically caters to testing enterprise Java applications. You can unit test EJB using classic JUnit framework itself; however, you should use Cactus if your EJB clients also run in a J2EE environment, as is the case when servlets or JSP use your beans. This is a requirement for more than half of the EJB applications and Cactus comes in handy for testing such applications because it unit tests these client J2EE components as well, apart from EJB. With Cactus you get an end-to-end framework for unit testing EJB applications with a Web front end. Cactus allows for writing three types of test case classes based on the *ServletTestCase*, *JspTestCase*, and *FilterTestCase* classes also known as redirectors. Hence, your test case classes will extend any one of these, depending on which client model you use, and get a home reference to your EJB, create an instance, call the method on it, and assert the test results.

Like the *<junit>* Ant task, the *<cactus>* Ant task provides Cactus integration with Ant. In fact, *<cactus>* extends the *<junit>* task to enable in-container testing. It deploys the WAR/EAR file containing Cactus classes and related deployment information into the target container, starts the container if it is not started, and runs the Cactus tests. It supports most of the Web and EJB containers including Apache Tomcat, JBoss, Orion, Resin, WebLogic. Also if your container is not supported explicitly by Cactus, then you can use a generic Cactus container, which lets you specify Ant targets to be executed to start up and shut down your container.

Mock Object Frameworks

Using Mock objects could be another approach to unit testing EJB. A mock is a dummy placeholder object instead of a real object such that

- It acts as a false implementation of an interface or a class mimicking the external behavior of their true implementation.
- It observes how other objects interact with its methods and compares this with preset expectations. If a discrepancy occurs, the mock object interrupts the test and reports about it.

Expectations, a terminology often used in the mock object world, consist of a set of conditions that we want our code to meet. For example, we might *expect* our code to close a database connection after using it. A mock object can be told to expect conditions such as these so that it can let us know when our expectations are not met.

You should use mock objects when unit testing complex logic that has dependencies on other objects and you want to test the interaction among these objects. The mock object will show you whether the tested code calls the right methods on the mocked object with the correct parameters. There are a number of mock object based unit testing frameworks such as MockObjects. There are also quite a few mock object code generation utilities such as MockMaker and MockDoclet. Both these code generation tools rely on the doclet tags embedded within the Javadocs of the class being mocked, which are referred to as *target objects*. These doclet tags are read during the preprocessing in order to generate mocks. It is a good idea to use mock object code generation utilities when the target object has a frequently changing API. Another genre of mock object code generation consists of utilities such as EasyMock and jMock (previously Dynamocks). Both of them use the dynamic proxy approach to generate mock objects. Hence, you can generate mock objects only for target objects that implement interfaces using these utilities unless you apply patches to enable mock object code generation for target objects that do not implement interfaces. Hence, mocking objects is a good solution to unit testing although it cannot and should not be used for integration tests since during integration tests you are supposed to test your entire application end to end.

Thus, by using such frameworks developers can test their EJB code and make design changes, if necessary, before the code moves to QA.

Implementing Client-Side Callback Functionality in EJB

Imagine a scenario wherein an EJB has to place a callback to the client. How would you implement this scenario? There is no provision for implementing client-side callback in the EJB standard. As a result, developers find themselves in a tough spot when faced with this requirement. The three viable strategies for implementing client-side callbacks in EJB are presented in the following sections. Note that all these strategies have their own pros and cons and should be applied under specific situations.

JMS

In this strategy, the client uses JMS temporary destinations (queue or topic, depending on your need) to receive callback notifications from EJB server components. The reason we want to a use temporary JMS destination for each client is because we do not want multiple clients popping messages from the same JMS destination; we want EJB server components to have unique *ReplyTo* addresses for all our clients.

Before calling a given method on EJB, the client will create a temporary JMS destination from which it will later receive messages. The client passes the JNDI name of the temporary JMS destination to the bean during the method call. The client starts listening, on a separate thread, to the temporary destination that it created earlier. On the EJB side, the bean will send a JMS message when it needs to call back the client. The client JMS listener receives the message and notifies the application upon receipt. Finally, the client deletes the temporary destination and closes the JMS connection.

As far as we know, this is the simplest way to achieve client-side callback functionality in EJB today. However, creating a temporary destination for each client does consume resources. You should do enough load testing to ensure that this model scales up to your needs.

Remote Method Invocation

This strategy is particularly useful with application clients. The idea here is to create RMI remote object on the client side that implements the *java.rmi.Remote* interface and registers it with the EJB. After registering this remote object, the client can continue doing its work, until the server calls a method on the registered RMI Remote object.

Implementing this strategy is fairly straightforward. You will need to provide the callback object stubs to the EJB.

Web Service

This strategy is useful in order to make callbacks happen across the firewalls or when the client is a J2EE Web application. Here, the client implements a JAX-RPC service endpoint to which the EJB will send a SOAP message in case of a callback. The bean will use Dynamic Invocation Interface (DII) to keep the callback Web Service client code generic. On the client side, you can use either a document model or RPC model for implementing such a callback Web Service.

One of the major drawbacks associated with this strategy is the lack of reliability. The SOAP message sent by the bean might never reach the client-side callback Web Service, because SOAP over HTTP is inherently unreliable and the industry is still working toward defining the semantics of reliable SOAP over HTTP. We will eventually get there once OASIS finalizes the Web Services Reliable Messaging standard (oasis-open.org/committees/tc_home.php?wg_abbrev=wsrm).

Choosing Between Servlets and Stateless Session Beans as Service Endpoints

J2EE Web services are based on three main technologies: JAX-RPC, servlet, and stateless session beans. As you know by now, a J2EE Web Service endpoint can be implemented either as a stateless session bean or as a servlet. So then, which component model should you use for your Web Services? A servlet or stateless session bean? Here are some guidelines that should help you in choosing between the two.

Use a servlet as Web Service endpoint if:

- The business logic of the service is within a Web tier, because in this case the endpoint and Web Service's business implementation will reside in the same tier.
- You need a lightweight Web Service container viz. servlet container.
- You need to execute some logic that resides on the Web tier before invoking Web Services.
- You do not mind writing logic for synchronizing multithreaded access to your service. This is required since the servlet container does not synchronize concurrent requests to the servlet instance and hence, in this case, to your Web Service endpoint.

Use a stateless session bean as Web Service endpoint if:

- The business logic of the service is within an EJB tier, because in this case both the endpoint and the Web Service's business implementation will reside in the same tier.
- You need the Web Service implementation to avail the transaction and component-level security services from the container.
- Before invoking Web Services, you need to execute some logic that resides on the EJB tier.
- You want the container to take care of synchronizing concurrent access to your service.

Considering the Use of Aspect-Oriented Programming Techniques in EJB Projects

There has been a lot of discussion lately about using aspect-oriented programming or AOP with EJB. Here are some of the concepts that are worth understanding about AOP before we continue our discussion on when you should use AOP in EJB projects.

Aspect-Oriented Programming

AOP techniques are not new. They have been around for close to a decade; in fact, Microsoft Transaction Server is one of the early implementations that employed AOP techniques followed by EJB servers.

So what is AOP? Obviously, *aspect* forms the core of AOP. Aspects are *reusable* services that are quintessentially crosscutting to your application. In the context of a business application, services that provide user authentication, user authorization, logging of access to the system, and persistence of application data are examples of crosscutting services or *concerns* for a business application developer—*concerns* because a developer cannot write robust applications without taking care of them. Hence, AOP can be defined as a programming platform that facilitates the development of *aspects* to mitigate *concerns* so that aspects can be *reused* by all the living objects within a given environment. Note the emphasis placed on reuse here.

With this in mind, come back to the EJB world and think about whether it uses AOP techniques or not—of course it does. All the services that our beans get are aspects; for example, persistence, life cycle management, transaction management, security, and dozens of other things are concerns that we, the business application developers, care about. EJB containers implement these crosscutting concerns and provide reusable aspects so that all the beans deployed within the container can offload these concerns on the container aspects. So yes, it is very much an aspects-oriented implementation.

However, here is the caveat: The EJB programming model does not allow you to develop new aspects to take care of concerns that are not supported by the EJB container, not today at least. Therefore EJB, and J2EE for that matter, is not an AOP platform even though EJB technology uses AOP techniques.

When to Use AOP in EJB Applications

In order to use AOP in EJB, you will need to use tools such as AspectJ, Spring AOP, or tools provided by your application server. Quite a few application server vendors such as JBoss Group and IBM already support or have declared the intent to support AOP in their products. The only thing you have to be wary of when going the AOP route is that standard Java platform does not provide inherent support in terms of APIs and compilers for AOP, and that you are embedding AOP in your application at the risk of losing portability.

We present some of the scenarios here to consider use of AOP with EJB.

Support Custom Concerns

The EJB container does provide implementation of some of the very common infrastructure concerns such as transaction management, security, persistence, and so on. However, EJB designers have kept the implementation of these aspects transparent to the EJB developers. Meaning, developers cannot customize the behavior of aspects beyond what deployment descriptor configuration parameters allow nor can they create new aspects using EJB programming model. As a result, if you want to support a concern that is crosscutting across your application components but is not provided by the EJB container, then you need more than EJB can provide, and should use AOP for developing aspects to address your concerns.

Supply Aspects to the World Outside the EJB Container

Almost all of us have worked in EJB projects where we had to use POJOs in order to get around constraints imposed by the EJB standard—for example, to do things like access file systems or read/write static fields. We might also end up reusing these POJOs outside the EJB container, for example, in a Web application or a Swing application. In this scenario, it might be better to write reusable aspects to address concerns relevant to your POJOs. For example, consider a POJO that reads and writes to a file. Here you might need to log the timestamp of the last updating of the file. In which case, you would create an aspect to address the logging concern. This way you can use the Logging aspect no matter whether your POJO is being used within an EJB container or within a Web container or in a vanilla Java Swing application.

IS AOP DIFFERENT THAN OOP?

We see this question many times and the simple answer to it is—yes. One of the common traits of both OOP and AOP platforms is their support for reusability. However, OOP instills reusability via inheritance. This means that in order to reuse the behavior encapsulated in an object, say A, some object B will have to *inherit* A. Inheritance is the key word here. B is able to reuse A's behavior only if it expects to build a long-lasting relationship with A, such as a parent-child relationship. This works well if B does not mind A's sub-imposed behavior as a side effect of reuse and direct effect of inheritance.

However, OOP does not work when behavior needs to be reused horizontally, owing to the behavior's crosscutting nature. Now why would you need to reuse behavior horizontally? Because you do not want your business object, for example a ShoppingCart, to inherit the behavior pertaining to transactions, since these behaviors are unrelated; you do not want an apple to inherit grape-like qualities; rather you want to mix apples and grapes to prepare a margarita drink. This is where AOP comes into picture.

AOP and OOP are not competing but complementary technologies. Consider, for example, an EJB server where crosscutting aspects are provided to your object-oriented beans. In conclusion, OOP and AOP co-exist.

A word of caution: Do not use aspects for the sake of it. Especially, do not replace EJB services with your aspects, unless you are sure of what you are doing. After all, EJB vendors have pre-written these aspects to keep you out of implementing them mainly because implementing them is a humungous task. And finally, do not think that AOP is going to replace OOP!

Reflection, Dynamic Proxy, and EJB

When you call EJB, you write code that essentially takes the binding information of the EJB home object in JNDI, gets the home object, creates an EJB object, and finally invokes methods on an EJB object. This style of invocation is usually referred to as *static* invocation where the information about the interface and methods to invoke on its object are known at the compile time. Although there are advantages to other styles of invocation models, such as dynamic proxy and dynamic invocation interface (DII), EJB programming APIs support only static invocation.

In the dynamic proxy approach, a proxy class implements a list of interfaces specified by the client at runtime. Hence, this approach provides a type-safe invocation on interfaces wherein proxy is generated dynamically during runtime rather than at compile time. Any method invocation on an instance of a dynamic proxy object, for example, the *java.lang.reflect.Proxy* object, is dispatched to a single method, *invoke()*, in the instance's invocation handler object; *invoke()* accepts method information via the *java.lang.reflect.Method* object as well as method arguments via an object array. Dynamic proxy invocation is slightly different than reflective invocation in that the former provides a generic API for implementing methods of a class manufactured at runtime; whereas the latter provides a generic API for dynamic invocation of *already* implemented methods. Combining dynamic proxies with reflective invocation leads to a powerful generic object that is capable of intercepting methods from the clients on *any* server object.

Hence, you may want to use dynamic proxies for EJB method invocation in order to:

- Dynamically invoke methods on EJB in scenarios where the client does not have a priori knowledge of interfaces implemented by EJB.
- Write interceptors that can provide additional services during invocation such as security services, logging services, and so on.

Before making a decision to invoke your EJB using dynamic proxies, always remember that reflective invocation is slower than direct method invocation even with all the reflection-oriented performance enhancements in JDK 1.4. Besides this, debugging dynamic proxy stack trace is generally trickier than static invocation stack.

Deploying EJB Applications to Various Application Servers

Deploying EJB applications can be trickier than you think especially when you are trying to package EJB applications to be deployed on multiple application servers. Multiple application server deployment is a common requirement for commercial applications written using the EJB framework. In spite of the standardization of most of the EJB application metadata in the form of deployment descriptors, a lot of deployment information still remains in application server specific deployment descriptors. A good example of this is the metadata for mapping CMP data attributes to database schema, which is normally kept in a deployment descriptor specific to the target application server.

ATTRIBUTE-ORIENTED PROGRAMMING

Attribute-oriented programming is a technique that revolves around the notion of using attributes aka metadata aka annotations within the source to instruct the underlying framework to perform a certain action upon encountering an attribute while parsing the source. This "action" might be about generating programming artifacts—for example, skeleton code for EJB home, remote and bean classes—or might be about providing crosscutting functionality—for example, security or logging—at a certain juncture in the source.

Two interesting JSR efforts in this area are JSR 175 and JSR 181. JSR 175 defines the Java programming language syntax for supplying metadata information for classes, interfaces, methods, and fields, as well as an API that can be used by tools and libraries to access the metadata information within the source and act on it. JSR 181 defines metadata/annotations that can be used to simplify development of Java Web Services.

EJB 3.0 (for J2EE 1.5 platform) is planning on using metadata to greatly simplify the EJB development and deployment kind of similar to the way the JBoss IDE uses XDoclet today for generating EJB code from a single source.

THE J2EE DEPLOYMENT API

The J2EE Deployment API (JSR-88) aims to address the problem of J2EE application deployment on multiple J2EE application servers rather interestingly. It defines an API, and the deployment of the API, which should be implemented by all application servers so that tools can use this API to send J2EE application deployment and undeployment requests to the application server. The Deployment API standard is part of J2EE 1.4 platform. Therefore, all J2EE 1.4 application servers will have to implement such a *Deployment* service.

This facility provides the utmost benefit to tools vendors. Tool vendors would not have to write proprietary plug-ins for automating deployment tasks for application servers they support. This will increase productivity and lessen product development cost for tools vendors. It benefits the application developers as well. They no longer have to worry about their IDE's integration with their application server. They can take it for granted.

So then does the J2EE Deployment API eliminate the need for XDoclet-like frameworks? Not, exactly. If you are in the business of selling packaged applications, your setup application has to be able to deploy J2EE components to the customer's application server naturally without using tools. In this case you have two options: either build your own client that uses J2EE deployment service of your customer's application server, or simply use XDoclet. Obviously using XDoclet and the like in such scenarios will provide an easier solution for automated deployment than using the J2EE Deployment API will, simply because the former comes in handy; whereas you will have to write a client for the latter.

Thus, in situations where you are required to automate deployment of your EJB applications on multiple application servers, your obvious choice should be to use the open source XDoclet framework. XDoclet is a powerful, attribute-oriented, open source code generation engine. Using XDoclet, a developer can generate practically anything—XML descriptors, such as deployment descriptors, source code and so on—by inserting attributes (metadata) within the JavaDoc for their source. For instance, while generating code for EJB, it can generate code for value classes, primary key classes, a struts action form based on Entity EJB, and home and remote interfaces. Finally, when the XDoclet engine parses the source file it generates the code necessary for supporting the semantics of attributes. Note that apart from generating code for standard frameworks such as EJB, Servlet, JDO and others, XDoclet is also capable of generating code for non-standard but popular frameworks such as Hibernate, Castor, and Struts.

XDoclet can generate server-specific deployment descriptors, apart from standard deployment descriptors (ejb-jar.xml), for all major application servers including JBoss, IBM WebSphere, BEA WebLogic, Sun Java System Application Server, Pramati, etc., with the help of their respective attributes. For example, *@jboss.persistence datasource java:comp/env/jdbc/employeeDB* specifies the JNDI name used to look up the data source. Also, integration of XDoclet with Ant through *ejbdoclet* tasks makes it an even more powerful framework for deployments.

Debugging EJB

As EJB technology is evolving quickly, the containers are evolving as well. The containers or their tools often have small oddities. In addition, users may introduce bugs that are difficult to debug. How do you debug with EJB?

Unfortunately, true debugging is a problem with EJB. Because your beans run under the hood of a container, you'd have to load the container itself into a debugger. But for some containers, this is impossible because you don't have access to the container's source code, or the source code has been obfuscated. For these situations, you may need to use the tried-and-true debugging method of logging.

An even more serious debugging problem occurs if exceptions are being thrown from the EJB container, rather than from your beans. This can happen for a number of reasons:

- **Your EJB container's generated classes are incorrect**, because your interfaces, classes, or deployment descriptor haven't fully complied with the EJB specification. Your EJB container's tools should ship with compliance checkers to help resolve this. But know that not everything can be checked. Often because of user error, your deployment descriptor will not match your interfaces. This type of problem is extremely difficult to target, especially if your container tools crash!
- **Your EJB container has a real bug.** This is a definite possibility that you must be prepared to encounter. In the future, however, this should not happen very often because EJB containers that comply with J2EE must test their implementations against the Sun Microsystems J2EE Compatibility Toolkit (J2EE TCK).
- **A user error occurs within the EJB container.** Probably the most frustrating part of an application is doing the database work. Punctuation errors or misspellings are tough to debug when performing JDBC. This is because your JDBC queries are not compiled—they are interpreted at runtime, so you don't get the nifty things like type checking that the Java language gives you. You are basically at the mercy of the JDBC driver. It may or may not give you useful error description. For example,

let's say that you're modeling a product, and you use the word *desc* rather than *description* to describe your products. Unfortunately, the keyword *desc* is a SQL reserved keyword. This means that your JDBC driver would throw an exception when trying to execute any database updates that involved the word *desc*. These exceptions might be cryptic at best, depending on your JDBC driver. And when you try to figure out why JDBC code is acting up, you will run into a roadblock: With container-managed persistence, the JDBC code won't be available because your bean does not perform its own data access! What do you do in this situation?

When you're faced with grim situations like these, contacting your EJB vendor is probably not going to be very helpful. If you are operating with a deadline, it may be too late by the time your vendor comes up with a solution. If you could only somehow get access to the JDBC code, you could try the query yourself using the database's tools.

You can try several options here:

- Some EJB containers support IDE debugging environments, allowing you to step through your code in real time to pinpoint problems. This is something you should look for when choosing a container.
- Check your database's log file to view a snapshot of what is really happening. This is especially useful when you are using CMP.
- Use a JDBC driver wrapper that logs all SQL statements such as P6Spy driver from Provision6, Inc.
- Your EJB container tools may have an option to keep generated Java files, rather than to delete them when compiling them into classes. For example, you can do this with BEA WebLogic with the *keepgenerated* option to its EJB compiler tool. This is analogous to the way you can use the *keepgenerated* option to keep generated proxies with Java RMI's *rmic* compiler.
- As a last resort, you may have to decompile the offending classes to see what's going on. A good decompiler is *Jad* by Pavel Kouznetsov (see the book's accompanying Web site wiley.com/compbooks/roman for a link). Of course, decompiling may be illegal, depending on your container's license agreement.

Inheritance and Code Reuse in EJB

Our next best practice addresses the challenge of developing reusable components. This may be important, for example, if you're developing beans to be reused by other business units within your organization or if you are shipping a product assembled as EJB components and your customers want to customize your product. There can be many such situations.

First, let's do a reality check—don't believe anyone who tells you that enterprise beans are reusable by definition because that is *not true*, at least not today. You need to design your beans correctly if you want them to be reusable. You need to consider the different applications, domains, and users of your enterprise beans, and you need to develop your beans with as much flexibility as possible. Developing a truly reusable set of beans will likely require many iterations of feedback from customers using your beans in real-world situations.

Roughly speaking, bean reusability can fall into three different levels:

- **Reuse as given.** The application assembler uses the acquired bean *as is* to build an application. The bean functionality cannot be tailored to fit the application. Most projects will have a difficult time reusing these components because of their inflexibility.
- **Reuse by customization.** The application assembler configures the acquired bean by modifying the bean properties to fit the specific needs of the application. Bean customization typically occurs during deployment time. To allow for a more flexible maintenance environment, some bean providers allow runtime bean customization.
- **Reuse by extension (subclass).** This is the kind of reuse that is not possible, not in a straightforward way, in EJB simply because EJB does not support component-level inheritance. By component-level inheritance, we mean extending EJB component A to enable its reuse by another EJB component B. This level of reusability is generally more powerful but not available in EJB. Hence, you will have to use a technique to enable reuse by extension of EJB components—put all the bean logic in a POJO and make your bean class inherit this POJO. However, this hack does not present a good solution for EJB reuse by extension in the case of entity beans because it does not take into consideration complexities around reuse of entity beans such as, what the relationship between the primary keys of the two entities would look like when one entity inherits another. The good news is EJB 3.0 seems to address these issues around entity reuse at the component level. Check out its early draft specification at http://java.sun.com/products/ejb/docs.html.

The more reusability levels that a bean can provide, the more useful a bean becomes. By leveraging pre-built beans, organizations can potentially lessen the development time of building enterprise applications.

Many organizations have tried—and failed—to truly reuse components. Because of this, it is a perfectly valid strategy to not attempt *true* reuse at all. Rather, you can shoot for a *copy-and-paste reuse* strategy, which means to make the source code for components available in a registry to other team members or other teams. They can take your components' code and change them as necessary to fit their business problem. While this may not be true reuse, it still offers some benefits. The Middleware Company offers a service to help organizations re-architect their applications in this manner.

Writing Singletons in EJB

A *singleton* is a very useful design pattern in software engineering. In a nutshell, a singleton is a single instantiation of a class with one global point of access. You would normally create a singleton in Java by using the *static* keyword when defining a class. However, one restriction of EJB is that you cannot use static fields in your beans. This precludes the use of the singleton design pattern. But if you still have to use a singleton, then here are a couple of strategies:

- **Limit the pool size.** If your EJB product lets you finely tune the EJB bean instance pool, then you can limit the size of the bean instances to 1, by setting both the initial and maximum size to 1. This is not truly a singleton, although it simulates singleton behavior, because although the container guarantees that at any given point in time there would only be one instance of bean in the pool, it does not guarantee that it would always be the same bean instance in the pool. The container might destroy the bean instance if it remains inactive for a certain period of time.
- **Use RMI-IIOP and JNDI.** You can use JNDI to store arbitrary objects to simulate the singleton pattern. If all your objects know of a single, well-known place in a JNDI tree where a particular object is stored, they can effectively treat the object as a single instance. You can perform this by binding an RMI-IIOP stub to a JNDI tree. Any client code that accessed the JNDI tree would get a copy of that remote stub, and each copy would point back to the same RMI-IIOP server object. The downside to this pattern is you are leaving the EJB sandbox and downgrading to vanilla RMI-IIOP, and thus you lose all the services provided by EJB.

When to Use XML with EJB

XML is a popular buzzword these days, and so we should discuss the appropriateness of XML in an EJB deployment. XML is useful in the following scenarios:

- **For data-driven integration.** If you have a large number of legacy systems, or even if you have one big hairy legacy system, you'll need a way to view the data that you send and receive from the legacy system. XML can help you here. Rather than sending and receiving data in proprietary structures that the legacy system might understand, you can invent an XML façade to the legacy systems. The façade takes XML input from your EJB components and maps that XML to the proprietary structures that the legacy system supports. When the legacy system returns data to your EJB application, the XML façade transforms the legacy data into XML data that your EJB application can understand.

- **As a document persistence mechanism.** If you are persisting large documents (news reports, articles, books, and so on), representing those documents using XML may be appropriate. This will help to translate the XML documents into various markups supported by client devices.
- **As a Web Service interface.** As described in Chapter 5, EJB components can also be accessed as a Web Service, in which case XML becomes the on-the-wire data format sent between Web Services.

The one important scenario that XML is not useful for is as an on-the-wire format for communication *between* EJB components.

The idea is that rather than application components sending proprietary data to each other, components could interoperate by passing XML documents as parameters. Because the data is formatted in XML, each component could inspect the XML document to determine what data it received.

Although several J2EE-based workflow solutions use this approach, XML is often inappropriate for EJB-EJB communications because of performance. Parsing XML documents takes time, and sending XML documents over the wire takes even longer. For high-performance enterprise applications, using XML at runtime for routine operations is costly. The performance barrier is slowly becoming less important, however, as XML parsers become higher performing and as people begin to use several techniques, such as XML compression, before sending XML documents over the wire. However, it still remains the bottleneck in many systems.

Another important reason not to use XML is because it's often simply not needed. Assuming that a single organization writes all your EJB applications, there is less need for data mapping between these various systems, since you control the object model.

When to Use Messaging Versus RMI-IIOP

Another hot topic when designing an EJB object model is choosing when (and when not) to use messaging, rather than RMI-IIOP.

The following advantages of messaging provide reasons why you might want to use it:

- **Database performance.** If you are going to perform relational database work, such as persisting an order to a database, it may be advantageous to use messaging. Sending a message to a secondary message queue to be processed later relieves stress on your primary database during peak hours. In the wee hours of the morning, when site traffic is low, you can process messages off the message queue and insert the orders into the database. Note that this works only if the user doesn't need immediate confirmation that his operation was a success. It would not work, for example, when checking the validity of a credit card.

- **Quick responses.** A client may not want to block and wait for a response that it knows does not exist. For methods that return *void,* the only possible return values are nothing or an exception. If a client never expects to receive an exception, why should it block for a response? Messaging allows clients to process other items when they would otherwise be blocking for the method to return.
- **Smoother load balancing.** In Chapter 9, we discuss how message-driven beans distribute load more smoothly than session or entity beans do. With session and entity beans, a load-balancing algorithm makes an educated *guess* about which server is the least burdened. With messaging, the server that is the least burdened will *ask* for a message and get the message for processing. This also aids in upgrading your systems in terms of capacity because all you need to do is detect when your queue size reaches a threshold. When the queue size reaches threshold value, it indicates that the number of consumers is not enough to meet the messaging load and that you need to add new machines.
- **Request prioritization.** Asynchronous servers can queue, prioritize, and process messages in a different order than they the in which they arrive into the system. Some messaging systems allow message queues to be prioritized to order messages based upon business rules. For example, in a military battle tank, if all requests for the system sent to a centralized dispatch queue are made asynchronously, disaster could result if a fire control message was queued up behind 100 communication messages that had to be processed first. In a military system, it would be advantageous to process any fire control and safety messages before communication messages. A prioritized queue would allow for the reordering of messages on the queue to account for the urgency of fire control in a battle tank.
- **Rapid integration of disparate systems.** Many legacy systems are based on message-oriented middleware and can easily interact with your J2EE system through messaging. Messaging provides a rapid development environment for systems that have distributed nodes that perform business processing and must communicate with one another.
- **Loosely coupled systems.** Messaging enables loose coupling between applications. Applications do not need to know about each other at compile time. This empowers you to have *dynamic consumption* of applications and services, which may be useful in a rapidly changing, service-oriented business environment.

- **Geographically disperse systems.** Messaging is very useful when you have applications communicating over the Internet or a wide-area network. The network is slow and unreliable, and RMI-IIOP is not intended for such broad-range communications. Messaging along with guaranteed message delivery adds an element of safety to your transactions.
- **Parallel processing.** Messaging is a way to perform pseudo-threading in an EJB deployment. You can launch a series of messages and continue processing, which is the distributed equivalent of launching threads.
- **Reliability.** Messaging can be used even if a server is down. System-level problems (such as a database crashes) typically do not affect the success of the operation, because when you're using *guaranteed message delivery* the message remains on the queue until the system-level problem is resolved. Even if the message queue fails, message producers can spool messages and send them when the queue comes back up (called *store and forward*). By combining guaranteed message delivery with store-and-forward, the system will not lose any requests unless a complete system failure happens at all tiers (extremely unlikely).
- **Many-to-many communications.** If you have several parties communicating together, messaging is appropriate since it enables many producers and many consumers to collaborate, whereas RMI-IIOP is a single-source, single-sink request model.

The following are scenarios in which you *might not* want to use messaging:

- **When you're not sure if the operation will succeed.** RMI-IIOP systems can throw exceptions, whereas message-driven beans cannot.
- **When you need a return result.** RMI-IIOP systems can return a result immediately because the request is executed immediately. Not so for messaging. You can return results eventually with messaging, but it's clunky—you need to send a separate return message and have the original client listen for it.
- **When you need an operation to be part of a larger transaction.** When you put a message onto a destination, the receiving message-driven bean does not act upon that message until a future transaction. This is inappropriate when you need the operation to be part of a single, atomic transaction that involves other operations. For example, if you're performing a bank account transfer, it would be a bad idea to deposit money into one bank account using RMI-IIOP and then withdraw money using messaging, because the deposit and withdrawal operations will not occur as part of a single transaction and hence, the failure in the latter will not roll back the former.

- **When you need to propagate the client's security identity to the server.** Since messaging does not propagate the client's security identity to the receiving message-driven bean, you cannot easily secure your business operations.
- **When you are concerned about request performance.** Messaging is inherently slower than RMI-IIOP because there's a middleman (the JMS destination) sitting between the sender and the receiver.
- **When you want a strongly-typed, OO system.** You send messages using a messaging API such as JMS. This is a flat API and is not object-oriented. If you want to perform different operations, the server needs to crack open the message or filter it somehow. In comparison, RMI-IIOP allows you to call different business methods depending on the business operation you want to perform. This is much more intuitive. It's also easier to perform compile-time semantic checking.
- **When you want a tighter, more straightforward system.** Synchronous development tends to be more straightforward than messaging is. You have great freedom when sending data types, and the amount of code you need to write is minimal compared to messaging. Debugging is also much more straightforward. When using services that are completely synchronous, each client thread of control has a single execution path that can be traced from the client to the server and vice versa. The effort to trace any bugs in the system is thus minimal.

Summary

We covered so many best practices in this chapter—and we aren't even half done with best practices yet! We will talk about persistence best practices in Chapter 16 and performance-related best practices and tuning tips in Chapter 18. Also, we have woven the discussion of best practices related to integration to and from the EJB world in the next chapter. So there is a lot more to come.

CHAPTER

12

Transactions

Many middleware services are needed for secure, scalable, and reliable server-side development. This includes resource pooling services, security services, remoting services, persistence services, and more.

A key service required for robust server-side development is *transactions*. Transactions, when used properly, can make your mission-critical operations run predictably in an enterprise environment. Transactions are an advanced programming paradigm that enables you to write robust code. Transactions are also very useful constructs when performing persistent operations such as updates to a database.

In the past, transactions have been difficult to use because developers needed to code directly to a transaction API. With EJB, you can gain the benefits of transactions without writing any transaction code.

In this chapter, we'll discuss some of the problems that transactions solve. We'll also discuss how transactions work and show how they're used in EJB. Because transactions are at the very core of EJB and are somewhat difficult to understand, we'll provide extensive background on the subject. To explain transactions properly, we'll occasionally get a bit theoretical. If the theory presented in this chapter piques your interest, many tomes written on transactions are available for further reading. See the book's accompanying Web site, www.wiley.com/compbooks/roman, for links to more information.

Motivation for Transactions

We begin our discussion with a few motivational problems that transactions address.

Atomic Operations

Imagine that you would like to perform multiple discrete operations yet have them execute as one contiguous, large, *atomic* operation. Take the classic bank account example. When you transfer money from one bank account to another, you want to withdraw funds from one account and deposit those funds into the other account. Ideally, both operations will succeed. But if an error occurs, you would like *both* operations to always fail; otherwise, you'll have incorrect funds in one of the accounts. You never want one operation to succeed and the other to fail, because both operations are part of a single atomic transaction.

One simplistic way to handle this is to perform exception handling. You could use exceptions to write a banking module to transfer funds from one account to another, as in the following pseudo-code:

```
try {
     // Withdraw funds from account 1
}
catch (Exception e) {
     // If an error occurred, do not proceed.
return;
}
try {
     // Otherwise, deposit funds into account 2
}
catch (Exception e) {
     // If an error occurred, do not proceed,
     // and redeposit the funds back into account 1.
return;
}
```

This code tries to withdraw funds from account 1. If a problem occurs, the application exits and no permanent operations occur. Otherwise, we try to deposit the funds into account 2. If a problem occurs here, we redeposit the money back into account 1 and exit the application.

There are many problems with this approach:

- The code is bulky and unwieldy.
- We need to consider every possible problem that might occur at every step and code error-handling routines to consider how to roll back our changes.
- Error handling gets out of control if we perform more complex processes than a simple withdrawal and deposit. It is easy to imagine, for example, a 10-step process that updates several financial records. We'd need to code error-handling routines for each step. In the case of a problem, we need to code facilities to undo each operation. This gets tricky and error-prone to write.
- Testing this code is yet another challenge. You would have to simulate logical problems as well as failures at many different levels.

Ideally, we would like a way to perform *both* operations in a single, large, atomic operation, with a guarantee that both operations, either always succeed or always fail.

Network or Machine Failure

Let's extend our classic bank account example and assume our bank account logic is distributed across a multitier deployment. This may be necessary to achieve necessary scalability, and modularization. In a multitier deployment, any client code that wants to use our bank account application must do so across the network via a remote method invocation (see Figure 12.1).

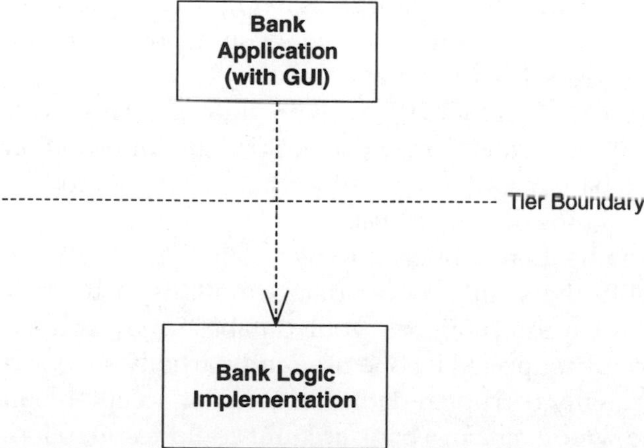

Figure 12.1 A distributed banking application.

Distributing our application across the network introduces failure and reliability concerns. For example, what happens if the network crashes during a banking operation? Typically, an exception (such as a Java RMI *RemoteException*) is generated and thrown back to the client code—but this exception is quite ambiguous. The network may have failed *before* money was withdrawn from an account. It's also possible that the network failed *after* we withdrew the money. There's no way to distinguish between these two cases—all the client code sees is a network failure exception. Thus, we can never know for sure how much money is in the bank account.

The network may not be the only source of problems. In dealing with bank account data, we're dealing with persistent information residing in a database. It's entirely possible that the database itself could crash. The machine on which the database is deployed could also crash. If a crash occurs during a database write, the database could be in an inconsistent, corrupted state.

None of these situations is acceptable for a mission-critical enterprise application. Big iron systems, such as mainframes or mid-frames, do offer preventive measures, such as system component redundancy and hot swapping of failed components to handle system crashes more graciously. But in reality, nothing is perfect. Machines, processes, or networks will always fail. There needs to be a recovery process to handle these crashes. Simple exception handling such as *RemoteException* is not sufficient for enterprise-class deployments.

Multiple Users Sharing Data

In any enterprise-level distributed system, you will see the familiar pattern of multiple clients connecting to multiple application servers, with those application servers maintaining some persistent data in a database. Let's assume these application servers all share the same database, as in Figure 12.2. Because each server is tied to the same database image, servers could potentially be modifying the *same* set of data records within that database.

For example, you might have written a tool to maintain your company's catalog of products in a database. Your catalog may contain product information that spans more than one database record. Information about a single product could span several database records or even tables.

Several people in your organization may need to use your tool simultaneously. But if two users modify the same product data simultaneously, their operations may become interleaved. Therefore, your database may contain product data that's been partially supplied by one user and partially supplied by another user. This is essentially corrupted data, and it is not acceptable in any serious deployment. The wrong data in a bank account could result in loss of millions of dollars to a bank or the bank's customers.

Thus, there needs to be a mechanism to deal with multiple users concurrently modifying data. We must guarantee data integrity even when many users concurrently update the data.

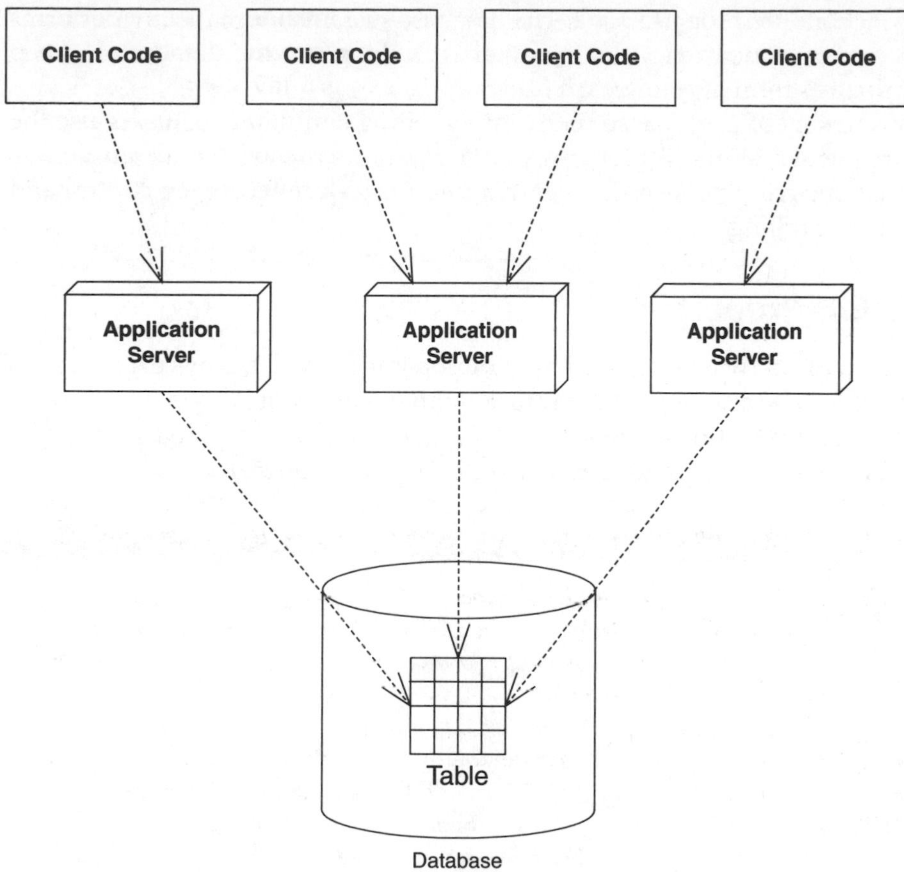

Figure 12.2 Application servers tied to a single database.

Benefits of Transactions

The problems raised in the previous sections can lead to catastrophic errors. You can avoid these problems by properly using *transactions*.

A transaction is a series of operations that appear to execute as one large, atomic operation. Transactions guarantee an all-or-nothing value proposition: Either all of your operations will succeed, or none of them will. Transactions account for network or machine failure in a graceful, reliable way. Transactions allow multiple users to share the same data and guarantee that any set of data they update will be completely and wholly written, with no interleaving of updates from other clients.

By using transactions properly, you can force multiuser interactions with databases (or other resources) to occur independently. For example, two clients reading and writing from the same database will be mutually exclusive if transactions are properly used. The database system automatically performs the necessary concurrency control (that is, locking) on the database to keep client threads from affecting each other.

Transactions offer far more than simply letting simultaneous users use the same persistent stores. By having your operations run within a transaction, you are effectively performing an advanced form of concurrency control and exception handling.

The ACID Properties

When you properly use transactions, your operations will always execute with a suite of four guarantees. These four guarantees are well known as the *ACID properties* of transactions. The word ACID stands for *atomicity*, *consistency*, *isolation*, and *durability*. The following list explains each property.

TRANSACTION VOCABULARY

Before we get into the specifics of transactions, let's establish a vocabulary. There are several types of participants in a transaction: *transactional objects, transaction managers, resources,* and *resource managers.* Let's take a look at each of these parties in more detail.

A transactional object (or transactional component) **is an application component, such as a banking component, that is involved in a transaction. This could be an enterprise bean, a Microsoft .NET–managed component, a CORBA component, and so on. These components perform operations that need to execute in a robust fashion, like database interactions.**

A transaction manager **is responsible for managing the transactional operations of the transactional components. It manages the entire overhead of a transaction, running behind the scenes to coordinate things (similar to the way a conductor coordinates a symphony).**

A resource **is a persistent storage from which you read or write. A resource could be a database, a message queue, or other storage.**

A resource manager **manages a resource. An example of a resource manager is a driver for a relational database, object database, message queue, or other store. Resource managers are responsible for managing all state that is permanent. The most popular interface for resource managers is the *X/Open XA* resource manager interface. Most database drivers support this interface. Because *X/*Open *XA* is the de facto standard for resource managers, a deployment with heterogeneous XA resource managers from different vendors can interoperate.**

- **Atomicity** guarantees that many operations are bundled together and appear as one contiguous *unit of work*. In our banking example, when you transfer money from one bank account to another, you want to add funds to one account and remove funds from the other account, and you want both operations to occur or neither operation to occur. Atomicity guarantees that operations performed within a transaction undergo an *all-or-nothing paradigm*—either all the database updates are performed, or nothing happens if an error occurs at any time. Many different parties can participate in a transaction, such as an enterprise bean, a CORBA object, a servlet, and a database driver. These transaction participants can force the transaction to result in *nothing* due to any malfunction. This is similar to a voting scheme: Each transaction participant votes on whether the transaction should be successful, and if any of the participants votes no, the transaction fails. If a transaction fails, all the partial database updates are automatically undone. In this way, you can think of transactions as a robust way of performing error handling.
- **Consistency** guarantees that a transaction leaves the system's state to be *consistent* after a transaction completes. What is a consistent system state? A bank system state could be consistent if the rule *bank account balances must always be positive* is always followed. This is an example of an invariant set of rules that define a consistent system state. During the course of a transaction, these rules may be violated, resulting in a temporarily inconsistent state. For example, your enterprise bean component may temporarily make your account balance negative during a withdrawal. When the transaction completes, the state is consistent once again; that is, your bean never leaves your account at a negative balance. And even though your state can be made inconsistent temporarily, this is not a problem. Remember that transactions execute *atomically* as one contiguous unit of work (from the atomicity property discussed previously). Thus, to a third party, it appears that the system's state is always consistent. Atomicity helps enforce that the system *always* appears to be consistent.
- **Isolation** protects concurrently executing transactions without seeing each other's incomplete results. Isolation allows multiple transactions to read or write to a database without knowing about each other because each transaction is isolated from the others. This is useful for multiple clients modifying a database at once. It appears to each client that he or she is the only client modifying the database at that time. The transaction system achieves isolation by using low-level synchronization protocols on the underlying database data. This synchronization isolates the work of one transaction from that of another. During a transaction, locks

on data are automatically assigned as necessary. If one transaction holds a lock on data, the lock prevents other concurrent transactions from interacting with that data until the lock is released. For example, if you write bank account data to a database, the transaction may obtain locks on the bank account record or table. The locks guarantee that, while the transaction is occurring, no other concurrent updates can interfere. This enables many users to modify the same set of database records simultaneously without concern for interleaving of database operations.

- **Durability** guarantees that updates to managed resources, such as database records, survive failures. Some examples of failures are machines crashing, networks crashing, hard disks crashing, or power failures. Recoverable resources keep a transactional log for exactly this purpose. If the resource crashes, the permanent data can be reconstructed by reapplying the steps in the log.

Transactional Models

Now that you've seen the transaction value proposition, let's explore how transactions work. We begin by taking a look at *transactional models,* which are the different ways you can perform transactions.

There are many different models for performing transactions. Each model adds its own complexity and features to your transactions. The two most popular models are *flat transactions* and *nested transactions.*

To use a particular transaction model, your underlying transaction service must support it. And unfortunately, not all of the vendors who crafted the EJB specification currently implement nested transactions in their products. Hence, Enterprise JavaBeans mandate flat transactions but do not support nested transactions. Note that this may change in the future based on industry demands. In the interim, however, J2EE Activity Service, discussed in a later section, can lend a way of implementing nested transactions in an EJB application.

Flat Transactions

A *flat transaction* is the simplest transactional model to understand. A flat transaction is a series of operations that are performed atomically as a single *unit of work.* After a flat transaction begins, your application can perform any number of operations. Some may be persistent operations, and some may not. When you decide to end the transaction, there is always a binary result: either success or failure. A successful transaction is *committed,* while a failed transaction is *aborted*. When a transaction is committed, all persistent operations become permanent changes; that is, all updates to resources, such as databases, are made durable into permanent storage only if the transaction ends with a *commit*. If the transaction is aborted, none of the resource updates are made durable, and thus all changes are *rolled back*. When a transaction aborts, all persistent operations that your application may have performed are automatically undone by the underlying system. Your application can also be notified in case of an abort, so that your application can undo in-memory changes that occurred during the transaction.

This is the *all-or-nothing* proposition we described preciously. The flat transaction process is outlined in Figure 12.3.

A transaction might abort for many reasons. Many components can be involved in a transaction, and any one component could suffer a problem that would cause an abort. These problems include the following:

- **Invalid parameters passed to one of the components.** For instance, a banking component may be called with a null argument when it was expecting a bank account ID string.
- **An invariant system state was violated.** For example, if an ongoing transactional operation can cause the bank account to reach a negative balance, your banking component can force the transaction to abort, undoing all associated bank account operations.
- **Hardware or software failure.** If the database that your component is using crashes, the transaction is rolled back and all permanent changes are undone. Similarly, if there is a software failure (such as a JVM crash) the transaction is rolled back.

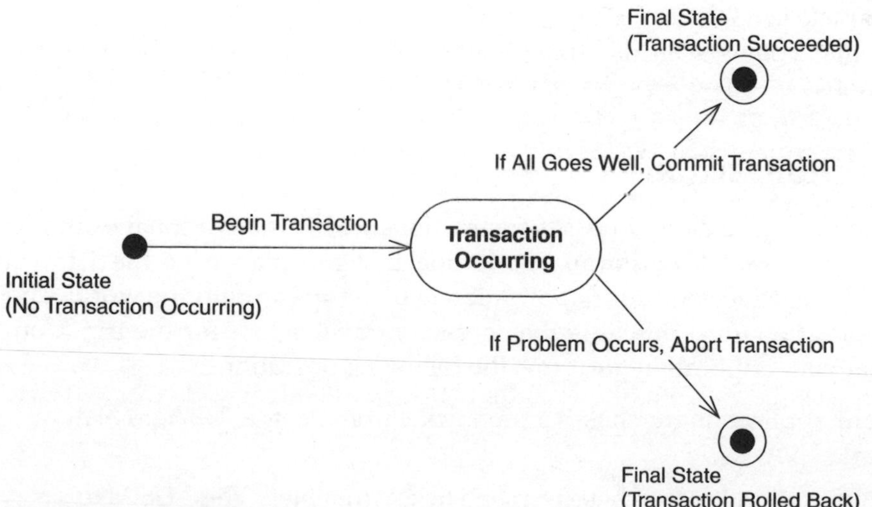

Figure 12.3 The flat transaction.

Any of these problems can cause a transaction to abort. But when an abort occurs, how is the transactional state rolled back? That is the topic of the next section.

How Transactional State Is Rolled Back

Let's assume you're performing a flat transaction that includes operations on physical, permanent resources, such as databases. After the transaction begins, one of your business components requests a connection to a database. This database connection is automatically enlisted in the transaction in which your component is involved. Next, your component performs some persistent operations, such as database updates. But when this happens, your database's resource manager does not permanently apply the updates to the database—your persistent operations are not yet durable and permanent. The resource manager waits until a *commit* statement has been issued. A commit is issued only when the transaction is complete, meaning when all your business components have finished performing all of the operations under that transaction. If the resource is told to commit, it persists the data permanently. If the transaction aborts, the data is not persisted at all.

The take-away point from this discussion is that your business components typically do not perform any rollback of permanent state; if there's an *abort*, the resource (such as a database) does not make your database updates permanent. Your components don't have any *undo* logic for permanent data inside of them; rather, the underlying system does it for you behind the scenes. Your components control the transaction and tell the transaction to abort, but the persistent state rollback is performed for you automatically. Thus, when your business components perform operations under a transaction, each component should perform all persistent operations assuming that the transaction will complete properly.

Now that you've seen flat transactions, let's take a quick look at nested transactions.

Nested Transactions

We begin our discussion of nested transactions with a motivational example. Let's say you need to write an application that can plan trips for a travel agency. You need to code your application to plan trips around the world, and your application must purchase the necessary travel tickets for the trip. Consider that your application performs the following operations:

1. Your application purchases a train ticket from Boston, USA, to New York, USA.
2. Your application purchases a plane ticket from New York, USA, to London, England.

3. Your application purchases a balloon ride ticket from London, England, to Paris, France.
4. Your application finds out that there are no outgoing flights from France.

This is the famous *trip-planning problem*. If this sequence of bookings were performed under a flat transaction, your application would have only one option: to roll back the transaction. Thus, because there are no outgoing flights from France, your application has lost all of its bookings! But it may be possible to use another means of transportation out of France, allowing you to salvage the train ticket, plane ticket, and balloon ride. Thus, a flat transaction is insufficient. The all-or-nothing proposition is shooting us in the foot, and we need a more comprehensive transactional model.

A nested transaction solves this problem. A *nested transaction* enables you to embed atomic units of work within other units of work. The unit of work that is nested within another unit of work can roll back without forcing the entire transaction to roll back. Therefore the larger unit can attempt to retry the embedded unit of work. If the embedded unit can be made to succeed, the larger unit can succeed. If the embedded unit of work cannot be made to work, it will ultimately force the entire unit to fail.

You can think of a nested transaction as a *tree* of transactions, all spawning off one *root-* or *top-level transaction*. The root transaction is the *main* transaction: In our trip-planning example, the root transaction is the overall process of booking tickets around the world. Every other transaction in the tree is called a *subtransaction*. The subtransactions can be flat or nested transactions (see Figure 12.4).

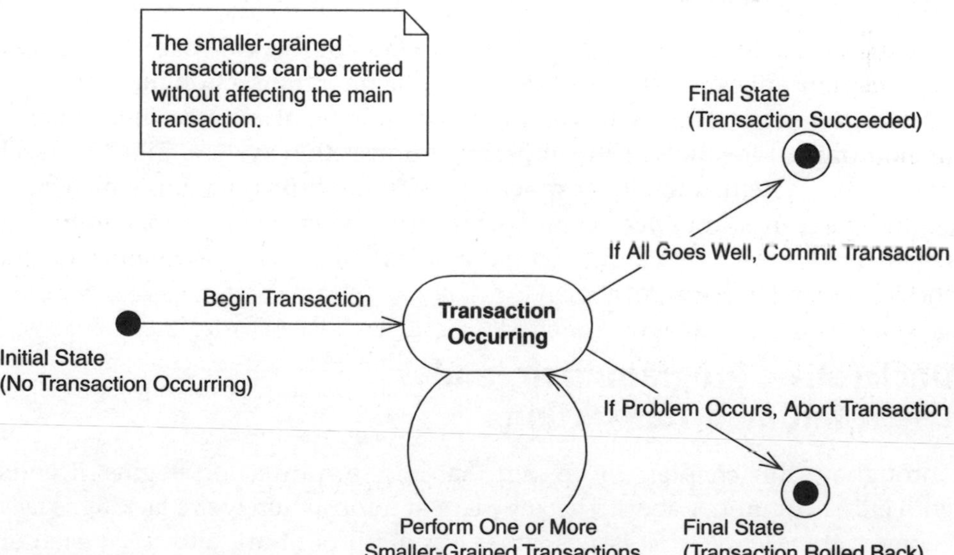

Figure 12.4 The nested transaction.

What's special about nested transactions is that subtransactions can independently roll back without affecting higher transactions in the tree. That's a very powerful idea, and it solves our trip-planning problem: If each individual booking is a nested transaction, we can roll back any one booking without canceling all our other reservations. But in the end, if the nested transaction cannot be committed, the entire transaction will fail.

Other Transactional Models

This concludes our discussion of transactional models. There are other models as well, such as *chained transactions* and *sagas*, but we will not address these subjects here because the EJB specification does not support them. And because the EJB specification does not currently mandate support for nested transactions, for the rest of this chapter we'll assume that our transactions are flat.

Enlisting in Transactions with Enterprise JavaBeans

Let's apply what we've learned so far about transactions to the EJB world.

Enterprise beans can be transactional in nature. This means they can fully leverage the ACID properties to perform reliable, robust server-side operations. Thus, enterprise beans are ideal modules for performing mission-critical tasks.

Underlying Transaction System Abstraction

In EJB, your code never gets directly involved with the low-level transaction system. Your enterprise beans never interact with a transaction manager or a resource manager. You write your application logic at a much higher level, without regard for the specific underlying transaction system. The low-level transaction system is totally abstracted out by the EJB container, which runs behind the scenes. Your bean components are responsible for simply voting on whether a transaction should commit or abort. If things run smoothly, you should commit; otherwise, abort.

Declarative, Programmatic, and Client-Initiated Transactions

Throughout this chapter, we've said that once a transaction begins, it ends with either commit or abort. The key piece of information we're lacking is *who* begins a transaction, *who* issues either a commit or abort, and *when* each of these steps occurs. This is called *demarcating transactional boundaries*. You can demarcate transactions *programmatically*, *declaratively*, or *client-initiated*.

Programmatic Transactions

Most existing systems demarcate transactional boundaries *programmatically*. When using programmatic transactions, you are responsible for programming transaction logic into your application code. That is, *you* are responsible for issuing a *begin* statement and either a *commit* or an *abort* statement.

For example, an EJB banking application might have an enterprise bean that acts as a bank teller. A teller bean would expose a method to transfer funds from one bank account to another. With programmatic transactions, the teller bean is responsible for issuing a *begin* statement to start the transaction, performing the transfer of funds, and issuing either a *commit* or *abort* statement. This is the traditional way to perform transactions, and it is shown in Figure 12.5.

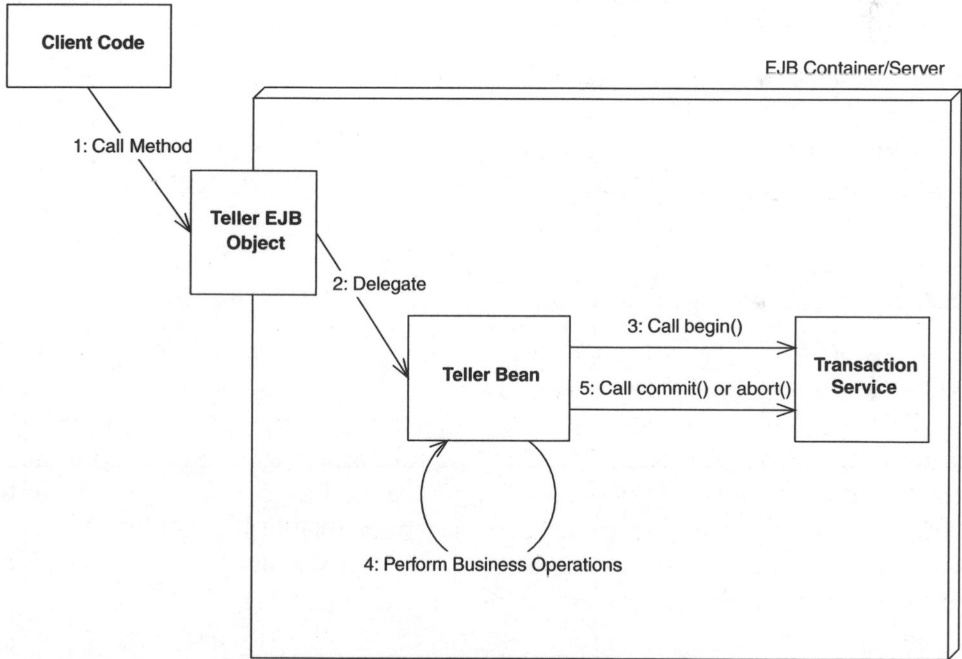

Figure 12.5 Beans with programmatic transactions.

Declarative Transactions

Declarative transactions allow for components to *automatically* be enlisted in transactions. That is, your enterprise beans never explicitly issue a *begin, commit,* or *abort* statement. The EJB container performs it for you.

Let's take our bank teller example again, and assume some client code has called our teller bean to transfer funds from one account to another. With declarative transactions, the EJB container *intercepts* the request and starts a transaction automatically on behalf of your bean. That is, the container issues the *begin* statement to the underlying transaction system to start the transaction. The container then delegates the invocation to your enterprise bean, which performs operations in the scope of that transaction. Your bean can do anything it wants to, such as perform logic, write to a database, send an asynchronous message, or call other enterprise beans. If a problem occurs, the bean can signal to the container that the transaction must abort. When the bean is done, it returns control to the container. The container then issues either a *commit* or *abort* statement to the underlying transaction system, depending on whether a problem occurred. This is a very simple model, and it is shown in Figure 12.6.

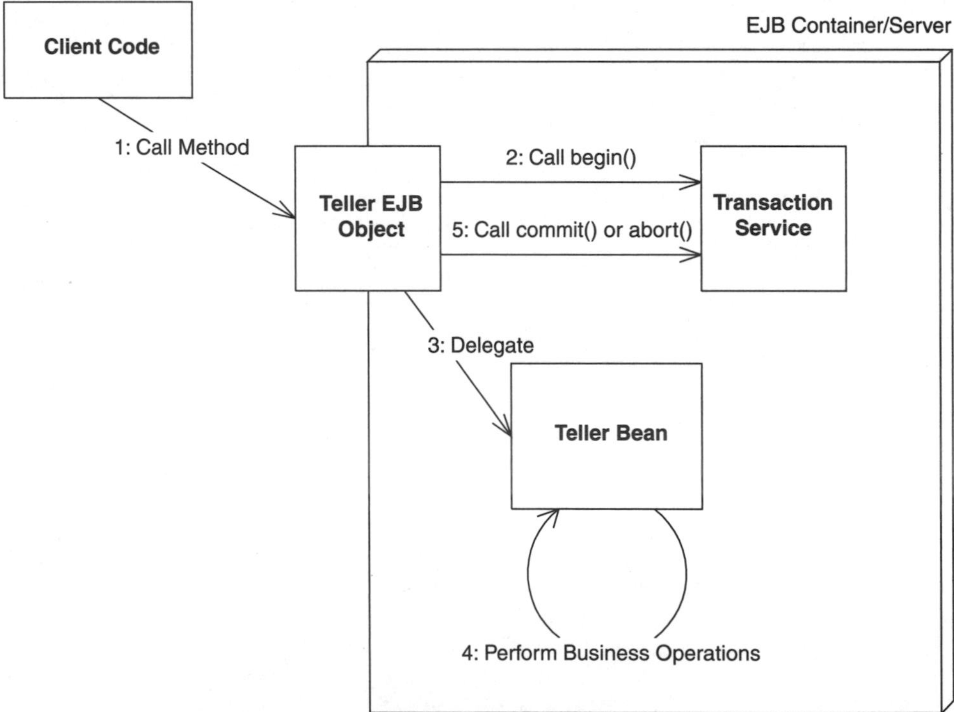

Figure 12.6 Beans with declarative transactions.

EJB declarative transactions add huge value to your deployments because your beans may not need to interact with any transaction API. In essence, your bean code and your client are not even really aware of transactions happening around them.

So how do you instruct the container about whether your bean is using declarative or programmatic transactions? EJB enables you to specify how your enterprise bean is enrolled in a transaction through the deployment descriptor, as follows:

```
<?xml version="1.0" encoding="UTF-8"?>

<ejb-jar xmlns=http://java.sun.com/xml/ns/j2ee
         xmlns:xsi=http://www.w3.org/2001/XMLSchema-instance
         xsi:schemaLocation="http://java.sun.com/xml/ns/j2ee
         http://java.sun.com/xml/ns/j2ee/ejb-jar_2_1.xsd"
         version="2.1">
 <enterprise-beans>
  <session>
   <ejb-name>Hello</ejb-name>
   <home>examples.HelloHome</home>
   <remote>examples.Hello</remote>
   <ejb-class>examples.HelloBean</ejb-class>
   <session-type>Stateless</session-type>
   <transaction-type>Container</transaction-type>
  </session>
 </enterprise-beans>
</ejb-jar>
```

The preceding deployment descriptor chooses container-managed (declarative) transactions. If instead of *Container* we chose *Bean*, then we would use bean-managed (programmatic) transactions.

Client-Initiated Transactions

The final way to perform transactions is to write code to start and end the transaction from the client code outside of your bean. For example, if you have a servlet, JSP tag library, application, applet, CORBA client, or other enterprise bean as a client of your beans, you can begin and end the transaction in that client. This is shown in Figure 12.7.

Note that the enterprise bean the client calls would still need to be written to use either programmatic or declarative transactions.

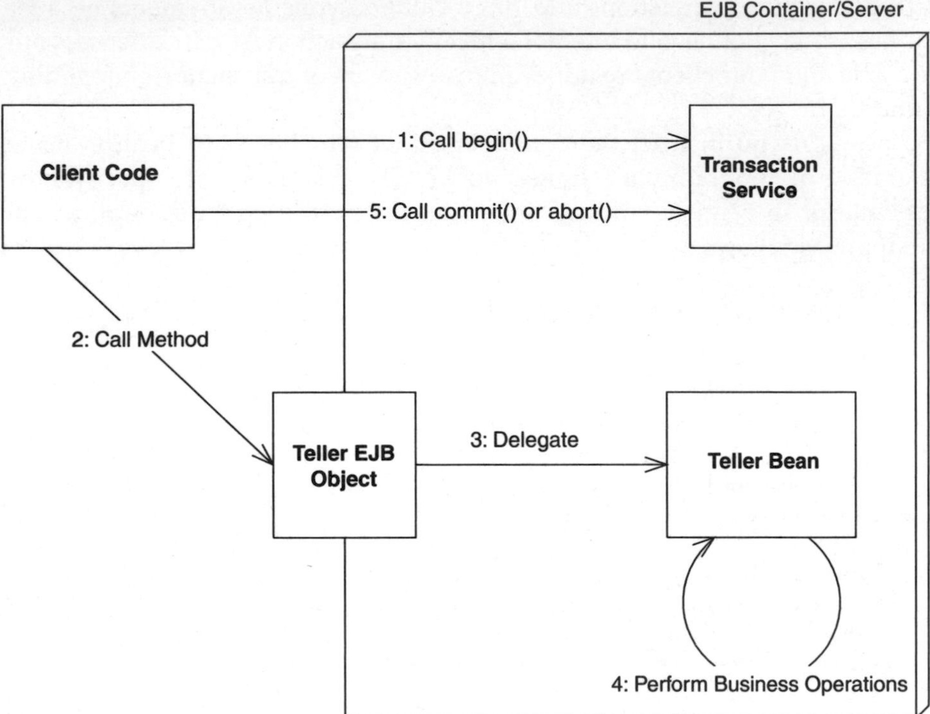

Figure 12.7 Beans with client-initiated transactions.

Choosing a Transaction Style

One question that students often ask in our EJB training classes is "Should I use declarative, programmatic, or client-controlled transactions?"

The benefit of programmatic transactions is that your bean has full control over transactional boundaries. For instance, you can use programmatic transactions to run a series of mini-transactions within a bean method. In comparison, with declarative or client-initiated transactions, your entire bean method must either run under a transaction or not run under a transaction.

The benefit of declarative transactions is that they are simpler. You don't need to write transactional logic into your bean class, which saves coding time and enables you to tune transactions without having access to source code. Also, by having transactions automatically start up and end, you keep client code from misusing your beans. If you're a component vendor, this will reduce a great number of headaches down the line.

TRANSACTIONS AND ENTITY BEANS

Perhaps one of the most misunderstood concepts in EJB is how transactions relate to entity beans. Let's explore this concept.

When you call an entity bean in a transaction, the first action that happens is the entity bean needs to load database data through the *ejbLoad()* method, which acquires locks in the database and ensures the entity bean cache is consistent. Then one or more business methods are called. When the transaction is committed, the entity bean's *ejbStore()* method is called, which writes all updates to the database and releases the locks. A transaction should thus span the *ejbLoad()* business methods, and the final *ejbStore()*, so that if any one of those operations fail, they all fail.

If we were to use bean-managed transactions, we would write code to perform *begin()* and *commit()* methods inside our bean (perhaps around the JDBC code). Perhaps we would start the transaction in *ejbLoad()*, and then commit the transaction in *ejbStore()*. The problem, though, is that you do not call your own *ejbLoad()* or *ejbStore()* methods—the container does. The bean cannot enforce that these methods happen in this order, if at all. Therefore if you started a transaction in *ejbLoad()*, the transaction may never complete.

Because of this, bean-managed transactions are illegal for entity beans. Entity beans *must* use declarative transactions. Session beans or message-driven beans can use bean-managed transactions because a session bean can load database data, perform operations on that data, and then store that data; all in a single method call, and thus is in direct control over the transaction.

A corollary of this discussion is that entity beans do not load and store their data on every method call; rather, they load and store their data on every transaction. If your entity beans are not performing well, it could be because a transaction is happening on each method call, and thus a database read/write is happening on every get/set method. The solution is to make sure your transactions begin earlier and end later, perhaps encompassing many entity bean method calls. By properly controlling the duration of your transactions with transaction attributes (as we will see later in this chapter), you can control when database reads and writes happen with entity beans.

To understand the benefit of client-controlled transactions, consider the following scenario in which we *don't* use client-controlled transactions. Imagine that a non-transactional remote client calls an enterprise bean that performs its own transactions (either programmatically or declaratively). The bean succeeds in the transaction, but the network or application server crashes before the result is returned to a remote client. The remote client would receive a Java RMI *RemoteException* indicating a network error, but would not know whether the transaction that took place in the enterprise bean was a success or a failure. The remote client would then have to write code to check the state of the resources to find out whether they were updated successfully by the transaction. This code places an additional burden on the application developer.

With client-controlled transactions, you do not need to worry about this scenario, because the transaction is defined in the client code. If anything goes wrong, the client will know about it. The downside to client-controlled transactions is that for distributed applications, the chances of client-initiated transaction rollbacks are more due to the fact that the transaction is occurring over a network and hence, network failures can cause the transaction to roll back more often. Because of this, use client-transactions sparingly—especially if the client is far away.

TRANSACTIONS AND JMS MESSAGE-DRIVEN BEANS

When using JMS message-driven beans, your choice of transaction style has a big impact on your bean. Only the *Required* and *NotSupported* transaction attributes can be applied to JMS message-driven bean listener method *onMessage()*.

***If you use container-managed transactions,* your JMS message-driven bean will read a message off the destination in the same transaction as it performs its business logic. If something goes wrong, the transaction will roll back and the message acknowledgment will occur.**

***If you use bean-managed transactions,* the transaction begins and ends *after* your JMS message-driven bean receives the message. You can then use deployment descriptor *acknowledgment modes* to instruct the container about when to acknowledge messages (see Chapter 9).**

***If you don't support transactions at all,* the container will acknowledge the message at some later time, perhaps when your bean's method completes. The timing is not guaranteed, however.**

So which style do you use? If you don't use container-managed transactions, you can't cause the JMS messages to remain on the original destination if something goes wrong, because your bean has no way to indicate a problem.

In general, we recommend using container-managed transactions with JMS message-driven beans. If you want to perform many smaller transactions, consider breaking up your JMS message-driven bean into several other beans, with each bean having a granularity of a single transaction.

Note that there is a huge caveat with using container-managed transactions with JMS message-driven beans in a certain scenario. Let's say you have an EJB component (any type of component) that sends *and then* receives a message all within one big container-managed transaction. In this case, the send operation will never get its message on the queue, because the transaction doesn't commit until after the receive operation ends. Thus, you'll be waiting for the receive operation to complete forever. This is called the *infinite block* problem, also known as the *halting problem* in computer science.

An easy solution to this problem is after sending the request message, you can call *commit()* on the JMS *Session*, which is your JMS transaction helper object. This causes the outgoing message buffer to be flushed. Hence, the receive operation does not have to wait forever for the transaction to commit to get a message.

Container-Managed Transactions

Let's now assume that we are using container-managed transactions and understand how to implement them. Although we're not writing any code that starts and stops transactions, we still need to provide instructions to the container for how we'd like our transactions to operate. For example, how can we choose whether a bean always runs in a transaction, or whether a bean never runs in a transaction?

A *transaction attribute* is a setting that you give to a bean to control how your bean is enlisted in container-managed transactions. You can specify a different transaction attribute on each bean in your system, no matter how many beans are working together.

The transactional attribute is a required part of each bean's deployment descriptor. The container knows how transactions should be handled with a bean by reading that bean's transaction attribute from its deployment descriptor. Note that you can specify transaction attributes for entire beans or for individual bean methods. If both are specified, then method-level attributes take precedence. See Source 12.1 for transaction attributes within a deployment descriptor.

```
<assembly descriptor>

    <!--
    This demonstrates setting a transaction attribute
    on every method on the bean class.
    -->
    <container-transaction>

        <method>
            <ejb-name>Employee</ejb-name>
            <method-name>*</method-name>
        </method>

        <!--
        Transaction attribute.  Can be "NotSupported",
        "Supports", "Required", "RequiresNew",
        "Mandatory", or "Never".
        -->
        <trans-attribute>Required</trans-attribute>

    </container-transaction>

    <!--
    You can also set transaction attributes on individual methods.
    -->
```

Source 12.1 Declaring transaction attributes in the deployment descriptor. *(continued)*

```
    <container-transaction>

        <method>
            <ejb-name>Employee</ejb-name>
            <method-name>setName</method-name>
        </method>

        <trans-attribute>Required</trans-attribute>

    </container-transaction>

    <!--
    You can even set different transaction attributes on
    methods with the same name that take different parameters.
    -->
    <container-transaction>

        <method>
            <ejb-name>Employee</ejb-name>
            <method-name>setName</method-name>
            <method-param>String</method-param>
        </method>

        <trans-attribute>Required</trans-attribute>

    </container-transaction>

</assembly-descriptor>
```

Source 12.1 *(continued)*

You must specify transaction attributes on all business methods for your beans. Furthermore, with entity beans you must specify transaction attributes that cover home interface methods, because the home interface creation methods insert database data and thus need to be transactional.

EJB Transaction Attribute Values

Every enterprise bean must have a transaction attribute setting. The following subsections explain the possible values for the transaction attribute in the deployment descriptor.

TRANSACTIONS AND J2EE CONNECTORS

The J2EE Connector Architecture defines a standard contract between Resource Adapters (RA) and application servers such that RA can leverage the container services for supporting transactions. This standard contract enables an application server to provide the infrastructure and runtime environment for transaction management of RA components. RA can support either a local transaction, which is managed internally by the resource manager, or it can support a distributed transaction, whose coordination does involve external transaction managers. If RA that supports local transactions, the client component, such as an EJB, will have to acquire the common client interface API object, such as *javax.resource.cci.LocalTransaction* or an equivalent from the resource adapter to demarcate the transactions. If RA supports distributed transactions, the container will automatically enlist the client in the transaction context, if the client wants to work within a distributed transaction.

J2EE Connector Architecture 1.5 supports the inflow of transactions from Enterprise Information System (EIS) to the J2EE environment. This is a powerful addition because it enables the J2EE applications to participate in transactions initiated by backend EIS. For example, you can make your stateless session bean participate in a transaction that was initiated in the Tuxedo environment, given that the underlying RA supports this contract. Chapter 17 explains J2EE Connector Architecture in more details.

Required

You should use the *Required* mode if you want your bean to *always* run in a transaction. If a transaction is already running, your bean joins in on that transaction. If no transaction is running, the EJB container starts one for you.

For example, say you write a credit card component that performs operations on credit cards, such as charging a credit card or refunding money on a credit card. Let's assume you ship the component with the *Required* transaction attribute. You then sell that component to two customers.

- **Customer 1** deploys our component in its customer service center, using the component to refund money when an angry customer calls. The customer writes some code to call your bean as necessary. When the client code calls your bean, the container automatically starts a transaction by calling *begin* and then delegating the call to your bean. When your method completes, the container issues either a *commit* or *abort* statement, depending on whether a problem occurred.
- **Customer 2** uses our billing component as part of a complete workflow solution. The customer wants to use the credit card component to charge a user's credit card when a user purchases a product from a Web site. The customer then wants to submit an order to manufacture that

> product, which is handled by a separate component. Thus, the customer has two separate components running but both of them run under the same transaction. If the credit card cannot be charged, the customer doesn't want the order to be submitted. If the order cannot be submitted, the customer doesn't want the credit card charged. Therefore the customer produces his or her own workflow bean, which first calls our credit card–charging bean and then calls the bean to generate a manufacturing order. The workflow bean is deployed with *Required*, so a transaction automatically starts up. Because your credit card bean is also deployed with *Required*, you *join* that transaction, rather than start your own transaction. If the order submission component is also deployed with *Required*, it joins the transaction as well. The container commits or aborts the transaction when the workflow bean is done.

Thus, *Required* is a flexible transaction attribute that enables you to start your own transaction or join existing ones, depending on the scenario.

RequiresNew

You should use the *RequiresNew* attribute if you always want a *new* transaction to begin when your bean is called. If a transaction is already under way when your bean is called, that transaction is suspended during the bean invocation. The container then launches a new transaction and delegates the call to the bean. The bean performs its operations and eventually completes. The container then commits or aborts the transaction and finally resumes the old transaction. Of course, if no transaction is running when your bean is called, there is nothing to suspend or resume.

RequiresNew is useful if your bean needs the ACID properties of transactions but wants to run as a single unit of work without allowing other external logic to also run in the transaction.

Supports

When a bean is called with *Supports*, it runs in a transaction only if the client had one running already. If the client does not have a transaction, the bean runs with no transaction at all.

Supports is similar in nature to *Required*, with the one exception: *Required* enforces that a new transaction is started if one is not running already. Because *Supports* will sometimes not run within a transaction, you should be careful when using this attribute. Mission-critical operations should be encapsulated with a stricter transaction attribute (like *Required*).

Mandatory

Mandatory mandates that a transaction *must be already running* when your bean method is called. If a transaction isn't running, the *javax.ejb.TransactionRequiredException* exception is thrown back to the caller (or *javax.ejb.Tranasction-RequiredLocalException* if the client is local).

Mandatory is a safe transaction attribute to use. It guarantees that your bean should run in a transaction. There is no way your bean can be called if a transaction isn't already running. However, *Mandatory* relies on a third party to start the transaction before your bean is called. The container will *not* automatically start a transaction; rather, an exception is thrown back to the caller. This is the chief difference between *Mandatory* and *Supports*. *Mandatory* is useful if your component is designed to run within a larger system, such as a workflow system, where your bean is only part of a larger suite of operations, and you want to mandate that the larger operations start a transaction before calling your bean.

NotSupported

If you set your bean to use *NotSupported*, then your bean *cannot* be involved in a transaction at all. For example, assume we have two enterprise beans, A and B. Let's assume bean A begins a transaction and then calls bean B. If bean B is using the *NotSupported* attribute, the transaction that A started is suspended. None of B's operations are transactional, such as reads/writes to databases. When B completes, A's transaction is resumed.

You should use *NotSupported* if you are certain that your bean operations do not need the ACID properties. This should be used only if your beans are performing non–mission-critical operations, where you are not worried about isolating your bean's operations from other concurrent operations. An example here is an enterprise bean that performs rough reporting. If you have an e-commerce Web site, you might write a bean that routinely reports a rough average number of e-commerce purchases per hour by scanning a database. Because this is a low-priority operation and you don't need exact figures, *NotSupported* is an ideal, low-overhead mode to use.

Never

The *Never* transaction attribute means that your bean cannot be involved in a transaction. Furthermore, if the client calls your bean in a transaction, the container throws an exception back to the client (*java.rmi.RemoteException* if remote, *javax.ejb.EJBException* if local).

This transaction attribute is useful when you want to make sure all clients that call your bean do not use transactions. This can help reduce errors in client code, because a client will not be able to call your bean erroneously in a transaction and expect your bean to participate in the ACID properties with other transaction participants. If you are developing a system that is not transactional in nature and would like to enforce that behavior, consider using the *Never* attribute.

Transaction Attribute Summary

Table 12.1 is a summary of the effects of each transaction attribute. In the chart, T1 and T2 are two different transactions. T1 is a transaction passed with the client request, and T2 is a secondary transaction initiated by the container.

Table 12.1 is important because you can use this information to control the length of your transaction. For example, let's say you want to perform a transfer between two bank accounts. To achieve this, you might have a bank teller session bean that calls into two bank account entity beans. If you deploy all three of these beans with the *Required* transaction attribute, they will all be involved in a single transaction, as shown in Figure 12.8.

In this example, assume all three beans are deployed with the *Required* attribute. Notice that

- Transactions always begin and end in the same place. In this case, the Teller EJB object.
- Both Account beans automatically enlist in the Teller's transaction. Thus, we have created a transaction spanning three beans by merely using transaction attributes.

Table 12.1 The Effects of Transaction Attributes

TRANSACTION ATTRIBUTE	CLIENT'S TRANSACTION	BEAN'S TRANSACTION
Required	none T1	T2 T1
RequiresNew	none T1	T2 T2
Supports	none T1	none T1
Mandatory	none T1	error T1
NotSupported	none T1	none none
Never	none T1	none error

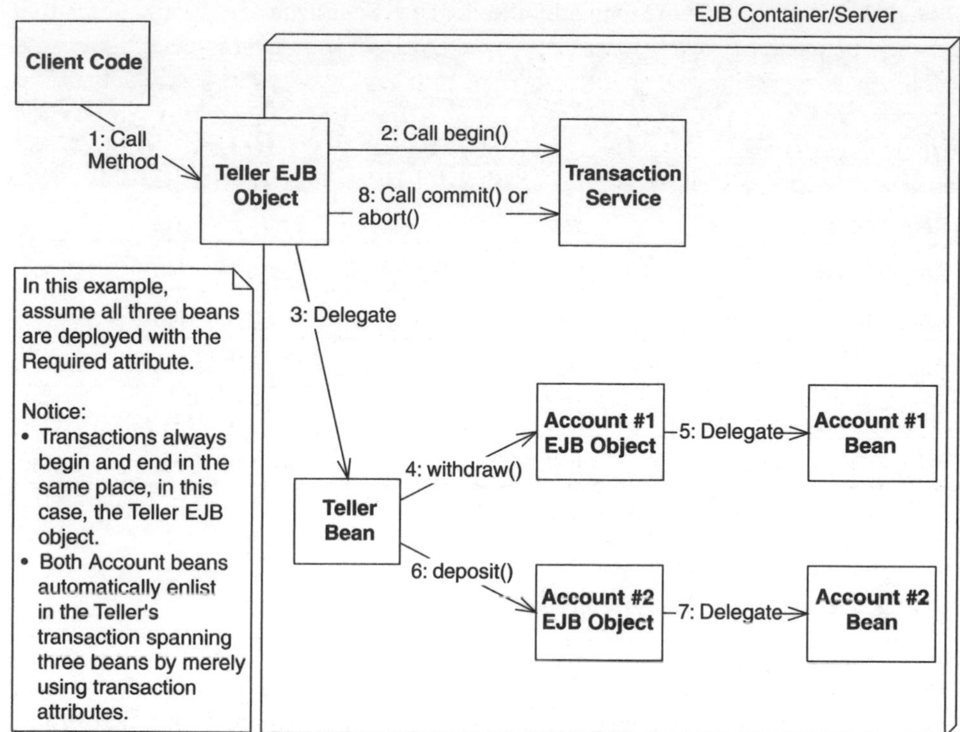

Figure 12.8 Using transaction attributes to control a transaction's length.

Finally, you should note that not all transaction attributes are available for use on all beans. Table 12.2 shows which are permissible.

Here is a brief explanation of why certain transaction attributes are disallowed. Entity beans and stateful session beans with *SessionSynchronization* must use transactions. The reason is that both of these types of beans are inherently transactional in nature. Entity beans perform database updates, and stateful session beans with *SessionSynchronization* (which we describe later in this chapter) are also transactional. Therefore you normally can't use the following attributes: *Never, NotSupported, Supports*. Note that the EJB specification *does* allow for containers to *optionally* support these attributes for stateful session beans and entity beans—but only if you're using non-transactional data stores—and with the warning that if you use this, your beans will not be portable, and you may find that you receive inconsistent results.

A client does not call a message-driven bean directly; rather, message-driven beans read messages off a message queue in transactions separate from the client's transaction. There is no client, and therefore transaction attributes that deal with the notion of a client's transaction make no sense for message-driven beans—namely *Never, Supports, RequiresNew,* and *Mandatory*.

Table 12.2 Permissible Transaction Attributes for Each Bean Type

TRANSACTION ATTRIBUTE	STATELESS SESSION BEAN	STATEFUL SESSION BEAN IMPLEMENTING SESSION SYNCHRONIZATION	ENTITY BEAN	MESSAGE-DRIVEN BEAN
Required	Yes	Yes	Yes	Yes
RequiresNew	Yes	Yes	Yes	No
Mandatory	Yes	Yes	Yes	No
Supports	Yes	No	No	No
NotSupported	Yes	No	No	Yes
Never	Yes	No	No	No

Programmatic Transactions in EJB

Next let's discuss how you can control transactions programmatically in EJB. Programmatic transactions allow for more advanced transaction control than declarative transactions do, but they are trickier to use. To control transaction boundaries yourself, you must use the Java Transaction API (JTA). We begin by taking a look at how the JTA was established.

CORBA Object Transaction Service

When we described the ACID properties earlier in this chapter, we mentioned that many parties, such as an enterprise bean and a database driver, could participate in a transaction. This is really an extension to the basic ACID properties, and it's the primary reason that Object Management Group (OMG) developed a standardized *Object Transaction Service* (OTS) as an optional CORBA service. OTS improved on earlier transaction systems that didn't support multiple parties participating in a transaction.

OTS is a suite of well-defined interfaces that specify how transactions can run behind the scenes—interfaces that the transaction manager, resource manager, and transactional objects use to collaborate. OTS is decomposed into two parts: *CosTransactions* and *CosTSPortability*.

- **The *CosTransactions* interfaces** are the basic interfaces that transactional objects or components, resources, resource managers, and transaction managers use to interoperate. These interfaces ensure that any combination of these parties is possible.

- **The *CosTSPortability* interface** offers a portable way to perform transactions with many participants.

The inner workings of OTS are not relevant to the development of enterprise beans. As an EJB programmer, you need to think only about writing your application, not about low-level transaction services. This is how EJB achieves rapid application development; you can write a distributed server-side application without understanding complex middleware APIs. EJB shields you from transaction services, such as OTS.

The Java Transaction Service

The Java community realized that you, as an application developer, should not care about most of OTS. Only system-level vendors need to be concerned with the inner workings of OTS. Part of OTS is very applicable to you, however, because it enables you to demarcate transaction boundaries programmatically. Hence, Sun has split up OTS into two sub-APIs: the *Java Transaction Service* (JTS) and the *Java Transaction API* (JTA).

The *Java Transaction Service* (JTS) is a Java mapping of CORBA OTS for system-level vendors. JTS defines the interfaces used by transaction managers and resource managers behind the scenes. It is used to enable transaction interoperability across various vendor products. It also defines various objects passed around and used by transaction managers and resource managers. As an application programmer, you should not care about most of OTS, and you should not care about JTS at all. What you should care about is the Java Transaction API (JTA).

The Java Transaction API

The *Java Transaction API* (JTA) is a transaction API used by component and application developers. You can use the JTA in your client and bean code to programmatically control transactional boundaries. The JTA package is a standard Java extension, so the package is automatically downloaded if needed.

You can do very useful things with the JTA, such as start a transaction inside your bean, call other beans that also are involved in a transaction, and control whether things commit or abort. Non-EJB applications can use the JTA as well—the client code that calls your beans can use the JTA to control transaction boundaries in a workflow scenario, where the client code is calling multiple beans and wants each bean to participate in one transaction.

JTA consists of two sets of interfaces: one for *X/Open XA* resource managers (which we don't need to worry about) and one that we will use to support programmatic transaction control. The interface you use to programmatically control transactions is *javax.transaction.UserTransaction*.

javax.transaction.UserTransaction

The *javax.transaction.UserTransaction* interface enables you to programmatically control transactions. Here is what the *javax.transaction.UserTransaction* interface looks like:

```
public interface javax.transaction.UserTransaction {
    public void begin();
    public void commit();
    public int getStatus();
    public void rollback();
    public void setRollbackOnly();
    public void setTransactionTimeout(int);
}
```

As you can see, six methods are exposed by the *UserTransaction* interface. Three of them—*begin*, *commit*, and *rollback*—are used to begin a new transaction, commit a transaction permanently, and roll back a transaction in case some problem occurred, respectively. The JTA methods are in Table 12.3.

Table 12.3 The *javax.transaction.UserTransaction* Methods for Transactional Boundary Interaction

METHOD	DESCRIPTION
begin()	Begins a new transaction. This transaction becomes associated with the current thread.
commit()	Runs the two-phase commit protocol on an existing transaction associated with the current thread. Each resource manager will make its updates durable.
getStatus()	Retrieves the status of the transaction associated with this thread.
rollback()	Forces a rollback of the transaction associated with the current thread.
setRollbackOnly()	Calls this to force the current transaction to roll back. This will eventually force the transaction to abort.
setTransactionTimeout(int)	The transaction timeout is the maximum amount of time that a transaction can run before it's aborted. This is useful to avoid deadlock situations, when precious resources are being held by a transaction that is currently running.

JTA also defines a number of constants that indicate the current status of a transaction. You might see these constants when you call the *UserTransaction .getStatus()* method:

```
public interface javax.transaction.Status {
    public static final int STATUS_ACTIVE;
    public static final int STATUS_NO_TRANSACTION;
    public static final int STATUS_MARKED_ROLLBACK;
    public static final int STATUS_PREPARING;
    public static final int STATUS_PREPARED;
    public static final int STATUS_COMMITTING;
    public static final int STATUS_COMMITTED;
    public static final int STATUS_ROLLING_BACK;
    public static final int STATUS_ROLLEDBACK;
    public static final int STATUS_UNKNOWN;
}
```

Table 12.4 explains the values of those constants.

Table 12.4 The *javax.transaction.Status* Constants for Transactional Status

CONSTANT	MEANING
STATUS_ACTIVE	A transaction is currently happening and is active.
STATUS_NO_TRANSACTION	No transaction is currently happening.
STATUS_MARKED_ROLLBACK	The current transaction will eventually abort because it's been marked for rollback. This could be because some party called *UserTransaction.setRollbackOnly()*.
STATUS_PREPARING	The current transaction is preparing to be committed (during Phase One of the two-phase commit protocol).
STATUS_PREPARED	The current transaction has been prepared to be committed (Phase One is complete).
STATUS_COMMITTING	The current transaction is in the process of being committed right now (during Phase Two).
STATUS_COMMITTED	The current transaction has been committed (Phase Two is complete).
STATUS_ROLLING_BACK	The current transaction is in the process of rolling back.
STATUS_ROLLEDBACK	The current transaction has been rolled back.
STATUS_UNKNOWN	The status of the current transaction cannot be determined.

Declarative versus Programmatic Transactions Example

We now show you how to write an enterprise bean in two equivalent ways: using programmatic (or bean-managed) transactions and using declarative (or container-managed) transactions. To illustrate this, we'll use a bank account example. This example has a method called *deposit()* that deposits funds into an account. We'll make this method transactional.

The following code illustrates a deposit method using declarative transactions:

```
/**
 * Deposits amt into account.
 */
public void deposit(double amt) throws AccountException {
    System.out.println("deposit(" + amt + ") called.");

    balance += amt;
}
```

A bean using the preceding method relies on the EJB container to demarcate transactional boundaries. Therefore, the bean's deployment descriptor should use a transaction attribute that provides this (such as *Required*, *Mandatory*, or *RequiresNew*). We showed the code for such a deployment descriptor earlier in this chapter.

The following code illustrates the same method using programmatic transactions:

```
/**
 * Deposits amt into account.
 */
public void deposit(double amt) throws AccountException {

 javax.transaction.UserTransaction userTran = null;

 try {
  System.out.println("deposit(" + amt + ") called.");

  userTran = ctx.getUserTransaction();

  userTran.begin();
  balance += amt;
  userTran.commit();
 }
 catch (Exception e) {
  if (userTran != null) userTran.rollback();
  throw new AccountException("Deposit failed because of " +
  e.toString());
 }
}
```

DOOMED TRANSACTIONS

Dooming a transaction means to force a transaction to abort. You may need to doom a transaction if something goes wrong, such as a database being unavailable or the client sending you bad parameters.

If you're performing programmatic or client-initiated transactions, you are calling the *begin()* and *commit()* methods. You can easily doom a transaction by calling *rollback()* on the JTA, rather than *commit()*. But how can you doom a transaction if you are participating in a transaction that someone else started? This can occur in one of two cases:

- Your transaction participant is an EJB component using declarative transactions. The container then starts and ends transactions on your behalf. To instruct the container to abort the transaction, your first instinct might be to throw an exception and expect the container to abort the transaction. But this approach will not work in all cases, because if you are throwing your own custom exception classes, the container has no way of knowing whether the exception is critical enough to indicate a failed transaction and will not abort the transaction. The best way to doom a transaction from a bean with container-managed transactions is to call *setRollbackOnly()* on your *EJB context* object, which we introduced in Chapter 3.
- Your transaction participant is not an EJB component, such as a Java object. You can doom a transaction by looking up the *UserTransaction* object in JNDI and calling its *setRollbackOnly()* method, as shown in the code listed in the section *Transactions from Client Code*.

Dooming transactions brings up an interesting side discussion. Imagine you have 10 beans in a chain executing in the same transaction, and bean 2 decides to doom the transaction by calling *setRollbackOnly()*. Why should beans 3 through 10 perform their work if the transaction is doomed to failure anyway? After all, those beans might be performing CPU- or database-intensive operations, and this work will all be wasted when the transaction aborts. The solution is that your beans can *detect* doomed transactions and avoid performing work when a doomed transaction exists. You can detect doomed transactions as follows:

- Container-managed transactional beans can detect doomed transactions by calling the *getRollbackOnly()* method on the EJB context object. If this method returns *true*, the transaction is doomed.
- Other participants, such as bean-managed transactional beans, can get hold of the *UserTransaction* object from the JNDI and call its *getStatus()* method.

You should write code to detect doomed transactions if you expect a good number of transactions to roll back and are performing intensive operations.

Here, we are controlling the transactional boundaries explicitly in code. We first retrieve the JTA from our bean's EJB context object. Then, rather than relying on the EJB container to *begin* and *commit* transactions, we perform these steps ourselves. A bean using the preceding method should be deployed with the deployment descriptor, transaction-type of *Bean*, because the bean is performing its own transaction boundary demarcation.

Take a look at the size difference between the two sets of source code. Bean-managed transactions clutter your source code because you need to write to a transaction API. Container-managed transactions enable you to write application code elegantly and externalize all transaction logic to the container. This is analogous to the way we saw entity beans with container-managed persistence as much smaller than those with bean-managed persistence in Chapter 8.

When using programmatic transactions, always try to complete your transactions in the same method in which you began them. Doing otherwise results in spaghetti code where it is difficult to track the transactions; the performance decreases because the transaction is held open longer, and the behavior of your system may be odd. See the EJB specification for more details about what the container will do if your transaction is left open.

Transactions from Client Code

The last way you can control transactions is from client code (with the word *client* here meaning anything that calls your beans, even other enterprise beans). You use the Java Transaction API (JTA) to control transactions from client code.

To control transactions from client code, you must look up the JTA *UserTransaction* interface with the *Java Naming and Directory Interface* (JNDI). JNDI is a generic lookup facility for looking up resources across a network, and it is fully described in Appendix A. The following code illustrates looking up the JTA *UserTransaction* interface from client code using JNDI:

```
try {
    /*
     * 1: Set environment up.  You must set the JNDI Initial
     *    Context factory, the Provider URL, and any login
     *    names or passwords necessary to access JNDI.  See
     *    your application server product's documentation for
     *    details on their particular JNDI settings.
     */
    java.util.Properties env = ...

    /*
```

```
         * 2: Get the JNDI initial context
         */
        Context ctx = new InitialContext(env);

        /*
         * 3: Look up the JTA UserTransaction interface
         *    via JNDI.  The container is required to
         *    make the JTA available at the location
         *    java:comp/UserTransaction.
         */
        userTran = (javax.transaction.UserTransaction)
            ctx.lookup("java:comp/UserTransaction");

        /*
         * 4: Execute the transaction
         */
        userTran.begin();

        // perform business operations

        userTran.commit();
    }
    catch (Exception e) {
        // deal with any exceptions, including ones
        // indicating an abort.
    }
```

When you demarcate transactional boundaries in client code, you should be *very* careful. Always strive to keep your transactions as short in duration as possible. Longer-lived transactions result in multiuser performance grinding to a halt. If you need a long transaction (that lasts for minutes, hours, or days) use a distributed locking mechanism, such as the CORBA locking service. Unfortunately, no distributed locking service equivalent currently exists in the Java 2 Platform, Enterprise Edition. However, J2EE Activity Service standard, discussed in a later section, can be used to create an HLS that supports long-running transactions.

Transactional Isolation

Now that you've seen how to enlist enterprise beans in transactions, let's discuss the *I* in ACID: *isolation*. Isolation is the guarantee that concurrent users are isolated from one another, even if they are touching the same database data. Isolation is important to understand because it does not come for free. As we'll see, you can control how isolated your transactions are from one another. Choosing the right level of isolation is critical for the robustness and scalability of your deployment.

The underlying transaction system achieves isolation by performing *concurrency control* behind the scenes. We elaborate on this concept in the following section.

The Need for Concurrency Control

Let's begin our isolation discussion with a motivational example. Imagine there are two instances of the same component executing concurrently, perhaps in two different processes or two different threads. Let's assume that the component wants to update a shared database using a database API such as JDBC or SQL/J. Each of the instances of the component performs the following steps:

1. Read an integer *X* from a database.
2. Add 10 to *X*.
3. Write the new value of *X* to the database.

If each these three steps executes together in an atomic operation, everything is fine. Neither instance can interfere with the other instance's operations. Remember, though, that the thread-scheduling algorithm being used in the background does not guarantee this. If two instances are executing these three operations, the operations could be interleaved. The following order of operations is possible:

1. Instance A reads integer *X* from the database. The database now contains X = 0.
2. Instance B reads integer *X* from the database. The database now contains X = 0.
3. Instance A adds 10 to its copy of *X* and persists it to the database. The database now contains *X* = 10.
4. Instance B adds 10 to its copy of *X* and persists it to the database. The database now contains *X* = 10.

What happened here? Due to the interleaving of database operations, instance B is working with a stale copy of X: The copy before instance A performed a write. Thus, instance A's operations have been lost! This famous problem is known as a *lost update*. It is a very serious situation—instance B has been working with stale data and has overwritten instance A's write. How can transactions avoid this scenario?

The solution to this problem is to use *locking* on the database to prevent the two components from reading data. By locking the data your transaction is using, you guarantee that your transaction and only your transaction has access to that data until you release that lock. This prevents interleaving of sensitive data operations.

In our scenario, if our component acquired an exclusive lock before the transaction began and released that lock after the transaction, then no interleaving would be possible.

1. Request a lock on X.
2. Read an integer X from a database.
3. Add 10 to X.
4. Write the new value of X to the database.
5. Release the lock on X.

If another component ran concurrently with ours, that component would have to wait until we relinquished our lock, which would give that component our fresh copy of X. We explore locking further in the Isolation and Locking sidebar.

ISOLATION AND LOCKING

During a transaction, a number of *locks* are acquired on the resource being updated. These locks are used to ensure isolation: Multiple clients all updating the same data set cannot interfere with each other. The locks are implicitly retrieved when you interact with resource managers—you do not have to worry about obtaining them yourself.

By intelligently acquiring locks on the resource being used, transactions guarantee a special property: *serializability*. Serializability means that a suite of concurrently executing transactions behaves as if the transactions were executing one after another (non-concurrently). This is guaranteed no matter how scheduling of the transactions is performed.

The problem with locking is that it physically locks out other concurrent transactions from performing their database updates until you release your locks. This can lead to major performance problems. In addition, a *deadlock* scenario (not specific to databases, by the way) can arise. Deadlock causes the entire system to screech to a dead stop. An example of deadlock occurs when two concurrent transactions are both waiting for each other to release a lock.

To improve performance, transactions distinguish between two main types of locks: *read locks* and *write locks*. Read locks are nonexclusive, in that any number of concurrent transactions can acquire a read lock. In comparison, write locks are exclusive—only one transaction can hold a write lock at any time.

Locking exists in many circles: databases, Version Control Systems, and the Java language itself (through the *synchronized* keyword). The problems experienced in locking are common to all arenas. EJB abstracts concurrency control away from application developers via *isolation levels*.

If you would like more details about locking and transactions, check out *Principles of Databases Systems* by Jeffrey D. Ullman (Computer Science Press, 1980). This classic, theoretical book on databases forms the basis for many database systems today.

It's important to understand why *dirty reads*, *unrepeatable reads*, and *phantoms* occur, or you won't be able to use transactions properly in EJB. This section gives you the information you need to make an intelligent isolation level choice when programming with transactions.

The Dirty Read Problem

A dirty read occurs when your application reads data from a database that has not been committed to permanent storage yet. Consider two instances of the same component performing the following:

1. You read integer X from the database. The database now contains X = 0.
2. You add 10 to X and save it to the database. The database now contains X = 10. You have not issued a *commit* statement yet, however, so your database update has not been made permanent.
3. Another application reads integer X from the database. The value it reads in is X = 10.
4. You *abort* your transaction, which restores the database to X = 0.
5. The other application adds 10 to X and saves it to the database. The database now contains X = 20.

The problem here is the other application reads your update before you committed. Because you aborted, the database data has erroneously been set to 20; your database update has been added in despite the abort! This problem of reading uncommitted data is a *dirty read*. (The word *dirty* occurs in many areas of computer science, such as caching algorithms. A dirty cache is a cache that is out of sync with the main source.)

READ UNCOMMITTED

Dirty reads can occur if you use the weakest isolation level, called *READ UNCOMMITTED*. With this isolation level, if your transaction is executing concurrently with another transaction, and the other transaction writes some data to the database *without* committing, your transaction will read that data in. This occurs regardless of the isolation level being used by the other transaction.

READ UNCOMMITTED experiences the other transactional problems as well: unrepeatable reads and phantoms. We'll describe those problems in the pages to come.

When to Use READ UNCOMMITTED

This isolation level is dangerous to use in mission-critical systems with shared data being updated by concurrent transactions. It is inappropriate to use this mode in sensitive calculations, such as in a debit/credit banking transaction. For those scenarios, it's better to go with one of the stricter isolation levels we detail later.

This level is most appropriate if you know beforehand that an instance of your component will be running only when there are no other concurrent transactions. Because there are no other transactions to be isolated from, this isolation level is adequate. But for most applications that use transactions, this isolation level is insufficient.

The advantage of this isolation level is performance. The underlying transaction system doesn't have to acquire any locks on shared data in this mode. This reduces the amount of time that you need to wait before executing, and it also reduces the time concurrent transactions waste waiting for you to finish.

READ COMMITTED

The *READ COMMITTED* isolation level is very similar to *READ UNCOMMITTED*. The chief difference is that your code will read committed data only when running in *READ COMMITTED* mode. When you execute with this isolation level, you will *not* read data that has been written but is uncommitted. This isolation level thus solves the dirty read problem.

Note that this isolation level does not protect against the more advanced transactional problems, such as unrepeatable reads and phantoms.

When to Use READ COMMITTED

This isolation level offers a step up in robustness from the *READ UNCOMMITTED* mode. You aren't going to be reading in data that has just been written but is uncommitted, which means that any data you read is going to be consistent data.

One great use for this mode is for programs that read data from a database to report values of the data. Because reporting tools aren't in general mission-critical, taking a snapshot of committed data in a database makes sense.

When you run in *READ COMMITTED* mode, the underlying concurrency control system needs to acquire additional locking. This makes performance slower than with *READ UNCOMMITTED*. *READ COMMITTED* is the default isolation level for most databases, such as Oracle or Microsoft SQL Server.

The Unrepeatable Read Problem

Our next concurrency control problem is an *Unrepeatable Read*. Unrepeatable reads occur when a component reads some data from a database, but upon rereading the data, the data has been changed. This can arise when another concurrently executing transaction modifies the data being read. For example:

1. You read a data set X from the database.
2. Another application overwrites data set X with new values.
3. You reread the data set X from the database. The values have magically changed.

Again, by using transactional locks to lock out those other transactions from modifying the data, we can guarantee that unrepeatable reads will never occur.

REPEATABLE READ

REPEATABLE READ guarantees yet another property on top of *READ COMMITTED*: Whenever you read committed data from a database, you will be able to reread the same data again at a later time, and the data will have the same values as the first time. Hence, your database reads are *repeatable*. In contrast, if you are using the *READ COMMITTED* mode or a weaker mode, another concurrent transaction may commit data between your reads.

When to Use REPEATABLE READ

Use *REPEATABLE READ* when you need to update one or more data elements in a resource, such as one or more records in a relational database. You want to read each of the rows that you're modifying and then be able to update each row, knowing that none of the rows are being modified by other concurrent transactions. If you choose to reread any of the rows at any time later in the transaction, you'd be guaranteed that the rows still have the same data that they did at the beginning of the transaction.

The Phantom Problem

Finally, we have the phantom problem. A phantom is a *new* set of data that magically appears in a database between two read operations. For example:

1. Your application queries the database using some criteria and retrieves a data set.
2. Another application inserts new data that would satisfy your query.
3. You perform the query again, and *new* sets of data have magically appeared.

The difference between the unrepeatable read problem and the phantom problem is that unrepeatable reads occur when existing data is changed, whereas phantoms occur when *new* data that didn't exist before is inserted. For example, if your transaction reads a relational record, and a concurrent transaction commits a new record to the database, a new *phantom record* appears that wasn't there before.

SERIALIZABLE

You can easily avoid phantoms (as well as the other problems described earlier) by using the strictest isolation level: *SERIALIZABLE*. *SERIALIZABLE* guarantees that transactions execute serially with respect to each other, and it enforces the isolation ACID property to its fullest. This means that each transaction truly appears to be independent of the others.

When to Use SERIALIZABLE

Use *SERIALIZABLE* for mission-critical systems that absolutely must have perfect transactional isolation. You are guaranteed that no data will be read that has been uncommitted. You'll be able to reread the same data again and again. And mysterious committed data will not show up in your database while you're operating due to concurrent transactions.

Use this isolation level with care because serializability does have its cost. If all of your operations execute in *SERIALIZABLE* mode, you will quickly see how fast your database performance grinds to a halt. (A personal note: Because transactional errors can be very difficult to detect, due to scheduling of processes, variable throughput, and other issues, we subscribe to the view that it's better to be safe than sorry.)

Transaction Isolation Summary

The various isolation levels and their effects are summarized in Table 12.5.

Table 12.5 The Isolation Levels

ISOLATION LEVEL	DIRTY READS?	UNREPEATABLE READS?	PHANTOM READS?
READ UNCOMMITTED	Yes	Yes	Yes
READ COMMITTED	No	Yes	Yes
REPEATABLE READ	No	No	Yes
SERIALIZABLE	No	No	No

Isolation and EJB

Now that you understand isolation in theory, let's see how to set up isolation in an EJB environment.

- **If your bean is managing transactions,** you specify isolation levels with your resource manager API (such as JDBC). For example, you could call *java.sql.Connection.SetTransactionIsolation()*.
- **If your container is managing transactions,** there is no way to specify isolation levels in the deployment descriptor. You need to either use resource manager APIs (such as JDBC) or rely on your container's tools or database's tools to specify isolation.

If you're using different resource managers within a single transaction, each resource manager can have a different isolation level, yet all run together under a single transaction. Note that any particular resource manager running under a transaction usually requires a single isolation level for the duration of that transaction. This new model has some drawbacks as well, as described in the "Isolation Portability Issues" sidebar.

ISOLATION PORTABILITY ISSUES

Unfortunately, there is no way to specify isolation for container-managed transactional beans in a portable way—you are reliant on container and database tools. This means if you have written an application, you cannot ship that application with built-in isolation. The deployer now needs to know about transaction isolation when he uses the container's tools, and the deployer might not know a whole lot about your application's transactional behavior. This approach is also somewhat error-prone, because the bean provider and application assembler need to communicate isolation requirements informally to the deployer, rather than specifying it declaratively in the deployment descriptor.

When we queried Sun on this matter, Mark Hapner, coauthor of the EJB specification, provided this response: "Isolation was removed because the vendor community found that implementing isolation at the component level was too difficult. Some felt that isolation at the transaction level was the proper solution; however, no consensus was reached on specific replacement semantics."

"This is a difficult problem that unfortunately has no clear solution at this time...The best strategy is to develop EJBs that are as tolerant of isolation differences as possible. This is the typical technique used by many optimistic concurrency libraries that have been layered over JDBC and ODBC."

Pessimistic and Optimistic Concurrency Control

The two basic object concurrency control strategies that EJBs may follow, pessimistic and optimistic, are summarized in Table 12.6. Pessimistic concurrency control is the algorithm we've been assuming throughout this chapter—you acquire a lock for the data for the duration of the transaction, ensuring that nobody messes with your data.

With optimistic concurrency control, your EJB component does not hold the lock for the duration of the transaction. Instead, you *hope* everything will be okay. Then if the database detects a collision, the transaction rolls back. The basic assumption behind optimistic concurrency is that because it is unlikely that separate users will access the same object simultaneously, it is better to handle the occasional collision than to limit the request-handling throughput of your system.

Table 12.6 Comparing Pessimistic and Optimistic Concurrency Control Strategies

STRATEGY	ADVANTAGES	DISADVANTAGES
Pessimistic—Your EJB locks the source data for the entire time it needs the data, not allowing anything greater (at least anything greater than read/view access) to potentially update the data systems until it completes its transaction.	• Brute force approach • Provides reliable access to data • Suitable for small scale systems • Suitable for systems simultaneous access where concurrent access is rare	• Does not scale well because it blocks simultaneous access to common resources
Optimistic—Your EJB implements a strategy to detect whether a system change has occurred to the source data between the time it was read and the time it now needs to be updated. Locks are placed on the data only for the small periods of time the EJB interacts with the database	• Suitable for large system • Suitable for systems requiring significant concurrent access	• Requires complex code to be written to support collision detection and handling

Distributed Transactions

Now that we've concluded our discussion of isolation levels, we'll shift gears and talk about *distributed transactions*, which are transactions spanning multiple tiers of deployments with several transaction participants.

The most basic flat transaction occurs with a single application server tied to a single database. Depending on the functionality of your application server's transaction service, you may be able to perform *distributed flat transactions* as well. Distributed flat transactions obey the same rules as simple flat transactions: If one component on one machine aborts the transaction, the entire transaction is aborted. But with distributed flat transactions, you can have many different types of resources coordinating in a single transaction across the network. Here are some possible cases for which you may need distributed flat transactions.

- You have multiple application servers coordinating in the same transaction.
- You have updates to different databases in the same transaction.
- You are trying to perform a database update and send or receive a JMS message from a message queue in the same transaction.
- You are connecting to a legacy system as well as one or more other types of storage (such as databases, message queues, or other legacy systems) in the same transaction.

Each of these scenarios requires multiple processes or machines to collaborate, potentially across a network, to solve a business problem. Distributed flat transactions allow multiple transaction participants, *written by different vendors*, to collaborate under one transactional hood.

Durability and the Two-Phase Commit Protocol

One important ACID property is durability. Durability guarantees that all resource updates that are committed are made permanent. Durability is easy to implement if you have just one storage into which you are persisting. But what if multiple resource managers are involved? If one of your resources undergoes a catastrophic failure, such as a database crash, you need to have a recovery mechanism. How do transactions accomplish this?

One way would be to log all database operations before they actually happen, allowing you to recover from a crash by consulting the log and reapplying the updates. This is exactly how transactions guarantee durability. To accomplish this, transactions complete in two *phases*.

- **Phase One** begins by sending a *before commit* message to all resources involved in the transaction. At this time, the resources involved in a transaction have a final chance to abort the transaction. If any resource involved decides to abort, the entire transaction is cancelled and no resource updates are performed. Otherwise, the transaction proceeds on course and cannot be stopped, unless a catastrophic failure occurs. To prevent catastrophic failures, all resource updates are written to a transactional log or journal. This journal is persistent, so it survives crashes and can be consulted after a crash to reapply all resource updates.
- **Phase Two** occurs only if Phase One completed without an abort. At this time, all of the resource managers, which can all be located and controlled separately, perform the actual data updates.

The separation of transaction completion into two phases is called the *two-phase commit protocol* or *2PC*. The two-phase commit protocol is useful because it allows for many transaction managers and resource managers to participate in a transaction across a deployment. If any participant votes that the transaction should abort, all participants must roll back.

In the distributed two-phase commit, there is one master transaction manager called the *distributed transaction coordinator*. The transaction coordinator runs the show and coordinates operations among the other transaction managers across the network. The following steps occur in a distributed two-phase commit transaction:

1. The transaction coordinator sends a *prepare to commit* message to each transaction manager involved.
2. Each transaction manager may propagate this message to the resource managers that are tied to that transaction manager.
3. Each transaction manager reports back to the transaction coordinator. If everyone agrees to commit, the commit operation that's about to happen is logged in case of a crash.
4. Finally, the transaction coordinator tells each transaction manager to commit. Each transaction manager in turn calls each resource manager, which makes all resource updates permanent and durable. If anything goes wrong, the log entry can be used to reapply this last step.

This process is shown in Figure 12.9.

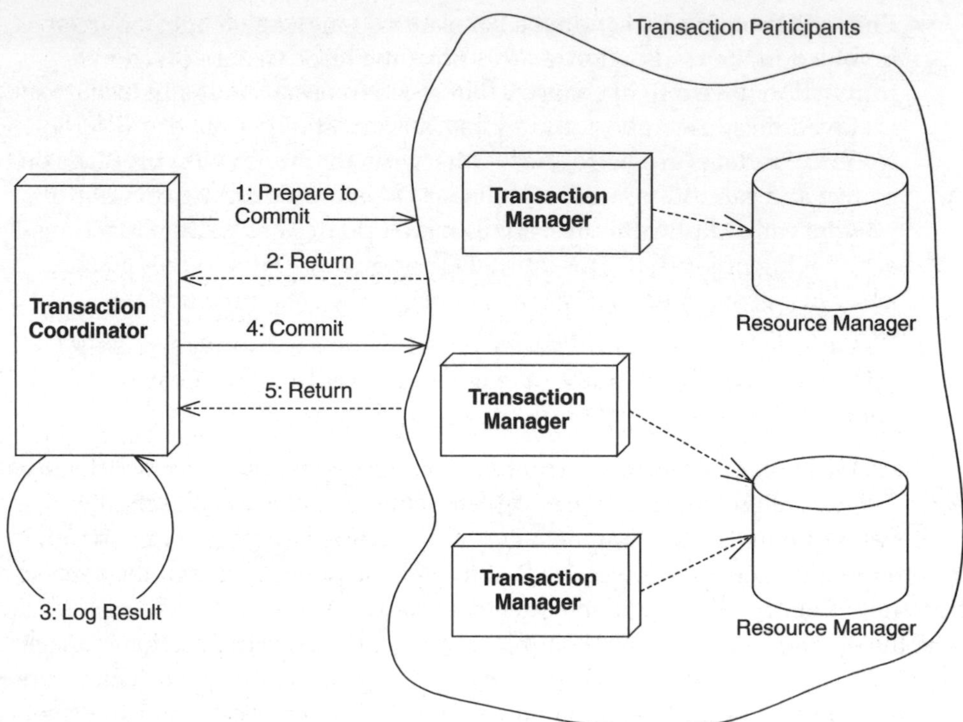

Figure 12.9 A distributed flat transaction using a two-phase commit protocol.

The Transactional Communications Protocol and Transaction Contexts

A distributed two-phase commit transaction complicates matters, because the transaction managers must all agree on a standard mechanism of communicating. Remember that each of the participants in a distributed transaction may have been written by a different vendor, such as is the case in a deployment with heterogeneous application servers. The communication mechanism used is called the *transactional communications protocol*. An example of such a protocol is the *Internet Inter-ORB Protocol* (IIOP), which we describe in Appendix B.

The most important piece of information sent over the transactional communications protocol is the *transaction context*. A transaction context is an object that holds information about the system's current transactional state. It is passed around among parties involved in transactions. By querying the transaction context, you can gain insight into whether you're in a transaction, what stage of a transaction you are at, and other useful data. For any component to be involved in a transaction, the current thread in which the component is executing must have a transaction context associated with it.

The EJB specification suggests, but does not require, that application server vendors support on-the-wire transaction context interoperability. If an application server does support interoperable transactions, EJB requires that it leverage the transaction context propagation facilities built into CORBA Object Transaction Service (OTS) and the Internet Inter-ORB Protocol (IIOP). Application servers that use these technologies should be interoperable and run in a distributed two-phase commit transaction.

Since the EJB specification does not require this level of interoperability, application servers from different vendors cannot be guaranteed to work together and participate in a distributed two-phase commit transaction, because they may not be able to communicate in a standard way.

For most users, this is acceptable because a distributed two-phase commit transaction has poor performance. And more to the point, most organizations struggle enough as it is with a single application server vendor.

It's important to understand which communications protocol your application server uses. If you want to perform a distributed two-phase commit transaction, the transaction participants must agree on a standard protocol.

Designing Transactional Conversations in EJB

In this chapter, we've seen that a transactional abort entails an automatic rollback of database updates that were performed during the transaction. But database updates are only half of the picture. Your application code needs to consider the impacts of a failed transaction as well.

When a transaction aborts, your application code has several choices. You can abort your business process and throw an exception back to the client, or you can attempt to retry the transaction several times. But unfortunately, your application cannot sit in a loop retrying transactions forever, as that would yield horrible performance for concurrent threads of execution. If the transaction cannot eventually be made to succeed, you should consider aborting your business process.

For a stateless session bean, aborting a business process is a simple task—simply throw an exception back to the client. But for a stateful session bean, things are a bit trickier. Stateful session beans represent business processes that span multiple method calls and hence have in-memory *conversational state*. Tossing away that conversation and throwing an exception to the client could entail a significant amount of lost work.

Fortunately, a well-designed stateful session bean can salvage its conversations in the case of failed transactions. The key is to design your beans to be aware of changes to conversational state and to be smart enough to undo any of those changes if a transactional abort occurs.

Because this process is highly application-specific, your application server cannot automate this task for you. Your application server *can* aid you in determining when a transaction failed, enabling you to take application-specific steps. If your session bean needs to be alerted to transaction status (like failed transactions), your enterprise bean class can implement an optional interface called *javax.ejb.SessionSynchronization*, shown in the following code:

```
public interface javax.ejb.SessionSynchronization
{
     public void afterBegin();
     public void beforeCompletion();
     public void afterCompletion(boolean);
}
```

You should implement this interface in your enterprise bean class and define your own implementations of each of these methods. The container will call your methods automatically at the appropriate times during transactions, alerting you to important transactional events. This adds to the existing arsenal of alerts that your session beans receive already—life-cycle alerts via *ejbCreate()* and *ejbRemove()*, passivation alerts via *ejbActivate()* and *ejbPassivate()*, and now transactional alerts via *afterBegin()*, *beforeCompletion()*, and *afterCompletion()*.

Here's what each of the *SessionSynchronization* methods do:

- *afterBegin()* is called by the container directly after a transaction begins.
- *beforeCompletion()* is called by the container right before a transaction completes.
- *afterCompletion()* is called by the container directly after a transaction completes.

The key method that is most important for rolling back conversations is *afterCompletion()*. The container calls your *afterCompletion()* method when a transaction completes either in a commit *or* an abort. You can figure out whether a commit or an abort happened by the Boolean parameter that gets passed to you in *afterCompletion()*: True indicates a successful commit, false indicates an abort. If an abort happened, you should roll back your conversational state to preserve your session bean's conversation.

Here's an example of *afterCompletion()* in action:

```
public class CountBean implements SessionBean, SessionSynchronization {

 public int val;
 public int oldVal;

 public void ejbCreate(int val) {
  this.val=val;
  this.oldVal=val;
```

```
}

public void afterBegin() {  oldVal = val;}
public void beforeCompletion() { }
public void afterCompletion(boolean b) {  if (b == false) val = oldVal;
}

public int count() {  return ++val; }
public void ejbRemove() { }
public void ejbActivate() { }
public void ejbPassivate() { }
public void setSessionContext(SessionContext ctx) { }
}
```

This is a new version of our count bean from Chapter 4. The conversational state is *val,* an integer that increases incrementally whenever *count()* is called. We also keep a backup copy of *val,* called *oldVal,* which we revert to in case of a transactional rollback. Here is what's going on:

1. When our bean is first initialized in *ejbCreate(),* or when a transaction first begins in *afterBegin(), val* and *oldVal* are set to the same value.
2. One or more *count()* business methods are called, incrementing *val.*
3. If the transaction fails, the *afterCompletion()* method is called when the transaction completes. If the transaction failed (that is, if a *false* value was passed into *afterCompletion()*), we roll back our conversational state by reverting back to *oldVal.*

Note that for this to work, we must make *count()* transactional in the deployment descriptor using transaction attributes that we described earlier in this chapter.

SessionSynchronization is also useful when your stateful session bean caches database data in memory during a transaction. You can use *SessionSynchronization* to track when to cache and when not to cache data as follows.

- When the container calls *afterBegin(),* the transaction has just started. You should read in any database data you want to cache in your stateful session bean.
- When the container calls *beforeCompletion(),* the transaction has ended. Write out any database data you've cached.

You can implement *SessionSynchronization only* if you're using a stateful session bean with declarative (container-managed) transactions. If your bean is using programmatic (bean-managed) transactions, you are already in control of the transaction because you issue the *begin(), commit(),* and *abort()* statements. Stateless session beans do not hold conversations and hence do not need these callbacks.

J2EE Transaction Service and Extended Transactions

As we discussed earlier, J2EE provides good support for flat transactions, both local and distributed. However, there are times when flat transactions might not be the best model for transactions as in the trip-planning problem that we saw earlier. In such situations, we need to extend the concept of ACID transactions as is defined in J2EE to suit our requirements. That is where J2EE Activity Service and Extended Transactions standard come into picture.

J2EE Activity Service and the Extended Transactions specification (JSR 095) defines a framework for developing and deploying extended transaction models—such as nested transactions, long-running transactions, and so on—that are not presently supported by the classic J2EE architecture. Its primary purpose is to integrate a wide variety of transaction models with J2EE application server such that these extended transaction services can be managed by the application server and are portable across application servers.

The two main components in a J2EE activity service are:

- ***High-Level Service (HLS)***, which is an implementation of a specific unit of work (UOW) model. An HLS sits in an application server, and much like J2EE Resource Adapters (Connectors), can communicate with application server through well-defined interfaces. Interfaces between the HLS and J2EE application are specific to the HLS and are not defined by the J2EE Activity Service specification.
- ***Activity service***, which is the facilitator of communication between HLS' transaction context and other transaction contexts maintained by Java Transaction Service. In fact, Activity service maintains the transaction context of HLS on its behalf.

Figure 12.10 shows the pluggable HLS architecture.

Each HLS has to implement the *javax.coordination.ServiceManager* interface. HLS also provides various signals that it supports via the implementation *SignalSet* interface. *ActivityCoordinator*, implemented by the Activity service, gets *SignalSet* via HLS *ServiceManager*. *ActivityCoordinator* is responsible for producing signals and distributes them to registered *Actions*. *ActivityCoordinator* also distributes the resulting *outcomes* of these *actions* to the HLS via *SignalSet*. Thus, *SignalSet* provides a finite state machine that produces signals and accepts outcomes to those signals to influence state transitions. The semantics of HLS are thus encapsulated mainly in *SignalSet* and *Action* implementations.

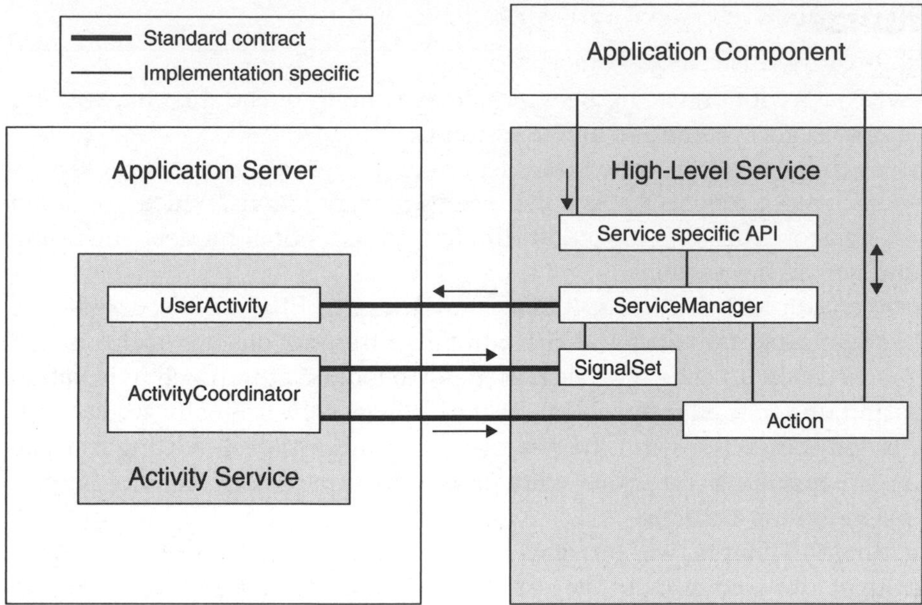

Figure 12.10 Pluggable HLS architecture.

Signals are events that are broadcast to interested parties, such as *Actions*. *Signals* could indicate to the interested parties to start performing a certain action in response, for example a rollback or a commit. *Actions* usually would implement the logic of compensating an activity. The result of an *Action* is encapsulated in *Outcome* object.

The specification itself is well written and provides good examples of implementing extended transactions with the Activity service. The specification is in its final stages. We believe that J2EE activity service will be made an integral part of J2EE 1.5.

We believe that the application server vendors will provide support for other transaction models, such as long-running transactions or nested transactions as HLS. An average developer will be required to use the appropriate APIs supported by the HLS to work with these extended transactions. The J2EE activity service work can evolve further to support declarative extended transactions to J2EE applications. That would be awesome!

Summary

Whew! That's a lot of data to digest. You may want to reread this chapter later to make sure you've grasped all the concepts.

In this chapter, we discussed transactions and how they can make a server-side deployment robust. We saw the virtues of transactions, which are called the ACID properties. We looked at different transactional models, including flat and nested transactions.

We then applied this transactional knowledge to EJB. We discussed how declarative, programmatic, and client-initiated transactions are useful in EJB and learned how to code with each model. We looked at transaction isolation levels and understood the problems that each level solves. Finally, we covered distributed transactions and the two-phase commit protocol, writing transactional conversations. We ended with an introduction to J2EE Activity Service and extended transactions.

Reading this chapter will prove well worth the effort, because now you have a wealth of knowledge about the importance and usefulness of transactions in EJB. You should definitely return to this chapter frequently when you're creating transactional beans.

CHAPTER

13

Security

This chapter introduces and explains EJB security in detail. Let's start with a fundamental observation: when building systems based on enterprise middleware, you typically want to integrate important business resources. Because *important* also means *critical*, security can be one of the most important aspects of your EJB application architecture. To build a secure system, you need to make informed and *balanced* decisions about placing security controls. Without understanding the fundamental risks in your application and its environment, you won't be able to make these decisions. Balancing your decisions is important because security comes at a price, such as increased cost or complexity, reduced performance, maintainability, or functionality, and so on.

An introduction to important security concepts is given in the introductory section. We will then take a look at Web application security in J2EE as a prelude to introducing the two basic security approaches in EJB—declarative and programmatic security. We provide information on security interoperability aspects that are important for applications that span different EJB vendor's platforms and communicate across individual networks. Finally, we explain the latest and greatest in security technology for Web Services.

Introduction

Security is often a nebulous thing. It can be difficult and costly, and dealing with it is often avoided until very late in a project. In large-scale projects involving enterprise middleware like EJB, however, the risks of a badly or altogether unprotected infrastructure can be enormous. For example, loosing the customer data in your enterprise database because someone drilled a hole into the backend with an unprotected EJB application can put you out of business very quickly.

Being secure means that no harmful events can happen to you and your assets (data, processes, infrastructure, whatever). What makes security sometimes hard to grasp is that it spans a wide variety of technologies, such as networks, operating systems, databases, application servers, EJBs, and so on. Moreover, security is not confined to information technology but also involves physical controls like door locks and alarms. It also depends to a great degree on appropriate human behavior, such as correct operations, proper monitoring of systems, swift responses to alarms, and users not sharing passwords or keys with others. Security books abound with anecdotes about successful social engineering attacks, where attackers simply exploit people's good will and trust in others. To complete the story, it can sometimes be very hard to say exactly (and completely) what must be considered secure or insecure. This last issue is the domain of security policy design. In a broader sense, then, security is the process that aims at securing systems rather than the idealized state of absolute security itself.

One word of caution before we start getting into details: don't roll your own security systems! Don't start designing new exciting crypto algorithms, authentication protocols, or access control systems. This is a discipline that takes years of experience, and you need to understand the faults and sidetracks of the past in order to avoid repeating them. At best, it is a waste of time and money. At worst, the false sense of security created by homegrown technology will cloud up the enormous risks created by the subtle or not so subtle design flaws in your protections.

For further reading on EJB and enterprise security with many more details than we are able to cover in this one chapter, please refer to Bret Hartman et al., *Enterprise Security with EJB and CORBA* (2001; ISBN: 0471401315), published by Wiley. For in-depth treatment of security as an engineering discipline, we recommend Ross Anderson's *Security Engineering* (2001; ISBN 0471389226), also published by Wiley.

Violations, Vulnerabilities, and Risk

Let's quickly define a handful of terms that we need on the following pages. Feel free to jump ahead and skip this and the following section if you are familiar with these terms. The events that you would like to avoid are often called security breaches or *violations*, for example an intruder reading files that you would prefer to remain confidential. A security violation is possible if there are no safeguards that protect against them, in other words no file system protection. Alternatively, violations are possible if the system has weaknesses that allow users to circumvent security, for example, where a user can obtain another user's privileges and thus get access. Both these deficiencies are called *vulnerabilities*, which can be exploited by those who find them. Another example of a vulnerable system is one that has its default administrator password unchanged after installation and is thus open to anyone who can read the installation documentation, or a program using libraries that are ridden with buffer overflow bugs.

Because the list of potential vulnerabilities is open-ended and increases with every piece of hardware or software that is added to a system, complete protection is not a realistic goal. Also, it may be very expensive to protect even against all known vulnerabilities. As there is no perfect security anyway, it has become common practice to try to *reduce the overall risks* to an acceptable level instead. To reduce risks, however, we first need to know them, meaning that we need to perform a *risk assessment* before we can decide how much and what needs to be done.

In the simplest definition, risk is a product of two factors: *probability of the occurrence* of a violation, and the *estimated damage* caused by this event. This may sound a bit like insurance business, and in fact it is very similar. The probability of occurrence is a function of your system's vulnerabilities and the attacker's resources, and the potential damage is a function of the value of your assets. In other words, if you have a complex system with weak protections and a resourceful enemy, then the probability of a successful attack is high. Don't let your hair turn gray yet; given our definition of risk, we may not have to worry about this: if the system is just a gaming console that does not represent any business value (and the resourceful attackers are students doing an internship at your company) then the actual risk is low!

Controls

By eliminating or reducing the vulnerabilities in your systems, risks are reduced, ideally down to zero. (The obvious other measure, reducing the value of your assets, is not a desirable option in most cases.) This is done by placing security *controls* in the right places.

ATTACKER MODEL

As we saw, risk assessment should include a model of your potential adversary, such as foreign intelligence services, determined criminals, or bored high-school students. The motivation for defining who to defend against is that the different levels of skills, determination, and resources that are associated with the different model attackers shed a different light on the concept of vulnerability. A password that is hard to crack for some people using their limited attacker toolbox and computing resources may be very easy to crack for others using off-line attacks with terabytes of precomputed passwords that are indexed for faster lookup. A bored teenager will not be sufficiently motivated to spend more than the weekend to analyze messages encrypted with even low-grade cryptography, but a foreign intelligence service may be. Defining your model attacker is a more precise way of estimating your vulnerabilities by establishing additional context.

As we saw, it is important to understand the risks in a system before you start setting up arbitrary controls. Without such an understanding, you may be spending an enormous amount of time and resources protecting against relatively harmless events that may not be more than a nuisance—while not paying attention to the others that will ruin your company. For example, the actual risk associated with an attacker observing the *update()* method calls in an MVC pattern may not even warrant the use of SSL/TLS protection, with the associated performance hit at connection setup time and the administrative overhead of distributing credentials such as public key certificates.

The term *control* is generally translated to one or more of the following, canonic security functions:

- **Authentication.** Verifying the authenticity of user information. In most cases this means verifying that the other side is who it claims to be. The authenticated entity is called *principal*. Authentication can mean checking a provided user ID and password against a database, or it can involve verifying a digital signature on a public key certificate to establish trust in the holder of that key.
- **Authorization.** Controlling principals' accesses to resources. This usually involves checking access privileges to find out who is authorized.
- **Data integrity protection.** Preventing or at least detecting modifications of data. Data integrity mishaps can be prevented by controlling all write accesses to that data. When data is communicated over an open transport channel, such as a WLAN, access to that data cannot be prevented at all times. In these cases, integrity protection usually means applying a cryptographic hash and later recomputing that hash to determine whether the data has been modified in transit.

- **Data confidentiality protection.** Preventing unauthorized disclosure of information. As with data integrity, data confidentiality can be protected by controlling read access to data, or by encrypting the data on the wire so that it can be read only by receivers with the correct cryptographic keys.

To conclude this introductory section before taking a dive into the security technologies that are relevant for EJB, let's take a minute to think about the security of the EJB infrastructure itself. This chapter is about protecting applications using EJB security, but this obviously hinges on the security of the system that provides it, meaning your application server. We need not go as far as looking for programming errors in the software; all the security that we are about to introduce now can be turned off again just like that if administrator access is not adequately controlled. This means that choosing a good password and protecting it is a prerequisite for any higher-level security. Protecting the application server is necessarily a product-specific task, and you should take the time to consult your product documentation to find out what needs to be done.

In addition, consider the security of the services that the EJB container provides to applications and that may be externally accessible. Most importantly, this means the *Java Naming and Directory Service* (JNDI). Can anyone other than your expected clients connect to your container's JNDI contexts, for example by using RMI over IIOP (RMI/IIOP) applications? With most application servers, this is possible by default. If there is no protection for the JNDI, then your application may think it is retrieving a particular bean reference, but in fact it is receiving an object reference to a carefully crafted *man-in-the-middle* bean at *hacker.org* that was skillfully bound to the very name of the bean that you expected to use. This bean can then intercept and inspect any application traffic and may actually forward it to the appropriate server so that its existence can remain concealed for a while. Rebinding a name in JNDI is simple, so you must make sure that only trusted clients may bind or rebind names.

Web Application Security

In J2EE applications with a Web tier, the first point of interaction with a client is the Web container and the JSP files or servlets it hosts, as shown Figure 13.1. Clients send Hypertext Transfer Protocol (HTTP) requests, and the servlets or JSP files would call bean instances in the EJB containers using RMI-IIOP or SOAP.

Web application security is not covered by the EJB specifications but rather by the *Java Servlet Specification* and the *J2EE Platform Specification* version 1.4. The general security concepts used by J2EE for both servlets and EJB are very similar, but if you are building complex Web applications, we recommend that you consult the *Java Servlet Specification* that is available at http://java.sun.com/products/servlet/.

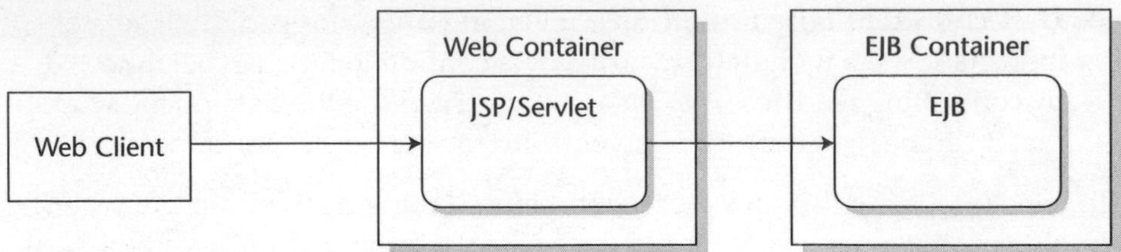

Figure 13.1 Web applications.

Authentication in Web Applications

Web applications are accessed by sending HTTP request messages to the servlet container. The servlet specification does not define any additional authentication mechanisms beyond the ones that are available in HTTP, so the actual authentication is done by the general Web server component. These mechanisms are as follows:

- **HTTP Basic and Digest authentication.** A user ID and password mechanism, where both the user name and password are transmitted in a special header field of the HTTP request. With basic authentication, the password is transmitted in base64 encoding, but unencrypted. This is insecure and only appropriate in combination with SSL (HTTPS), or in relatively trusted environments. With digest authentication, the password is transmitted in encrypted form. Digest authentication is not in widespread use, and hence not required to be available in all products.
- **Form-based authentication.** Another form of user ID and password authentication. The user information is sent in the request message body as part of HTML form input data. Like basic authentication, this data is unprotected unless additional mechanisms (HTTPS) are used.
- **HTTPS Client authentication.** A strong authentication mechanism based on public key certificates exchanged in the Secure Socket Layer (SSL/TLS) underneath HTTP. HTTPS client authentication requires clients to provide a public key certificate in X.509 format. When client authentication is required, the SSL layer performs a handshake procedure as part of the connection establishment process. In this process, the SSL layer will transmit the client's public key certificate and use the corresponding private key to prove possession of the public key. These keys may reside in a Java keystore file at the client.

Authentication requirements for Web applications can be specified in the Web application's deployment descriptor (the web.xml file) using the *login-config* element. To require HTTP basic authentication for a servlet, the *login-config* element would look like this, where *realm-name* refers to an authentication realm (a set of users) that is known to the servlet container:

```
<login-config>
  <auth-method>BASIC</auth-method>
  <realm-name>basic-file</realm-name>
</login-config>
```

Other valid content for the *login-config* element is *DIGEST*, *FORM*, or *CLIENT-CERT*, as in the following example:

```
<login-config>
  <auth-method>CLIENT-CERT</auth-method>
  <realm-name>basic-file</realm-name>
</login-config>
```

Authorization

There are two options for authorization checking for a J2EE Web application:

- **Declarative security.** The servlet container checks access to Web resources based on access rules in deployment descriptors.
- **Programmatic security.** The servlet performs its own access checks based on internal state, hard-coded access rules, and the authentication information provided by the container. The security context API provided by the servlet container is similar to the one provided by EJB containers, which we explain later in this section. Servlets can use the *isUserinRole* and the *getUserPrincipal* methods to make authorization decisions. Refer to the servlet specification for details.

To specify access rules declaratively, the servlet specification uses the *security-constraint* element of the deployment descriptor, which defines constraints for a collection of Web resources. Here is an example:

```
<security-constraint>
  <web-resource-collection>
    <web-resource-name>basic security test</web-resource-name>
    <url-pattern>/*</url-pattern>
  </web-resource-collection>
  <auth-constraint>
    <role-name>staffmember</role-name>
  </auth-constraint>
</security-constraint>
```

The preceding descriptor snippet specifies that all HTTP requests that apply to the URL pattern /*, in other words to all URLs in the Web application, are to be constrained to the listed role *staffmember*, meaning only users that are members of that role are allowed access. An *auth-constraint* with empty content would be taken as denial. How users are mapped to roles is vendor-specific. Typically, application servers will use an additional descriptor file with a *role-mapping* element for this purpose.

Confidentiality and Integrity

Confidentiality and integrity protection for Web applications is based entirely on secure transport, meaning on HTTPS. A Web application's requirements are again expressed in the deployment descriptor, as in the following example:

```
<security-constraint>
   <web-resource-collection>
      <web-resource-name>wholesale</web-resource-name>
      <url-pattern>/acme/wholesale/*</url-pattern>
      <http-method>GET</http-method>
      <http-method>POST</http-method>
   </web-resource-collection>
   <auth-constraint>
      <role-name>CONTRACTOR</role-name>
   </auth-constraint>
   <user-data-constraint>
      <transport-guarantee>CONFIDENTIAL</transport-guarantee>
   </user-data-constraint>
</security-constraint>
```

Here, the *user-data-constraint* contains a *transport-guarantee* element that requires confidentiality protection from the transport layer. Other values for the *transport-guarantee* are *INTEGRAL* and *NONE*, where *NONE* means that no requirements exist. Note that *CONFIDENTIAL* implies *INTEGRAL* because any encrypted data is implicitly protected against modifications: modified encrypted data simply does not correctly decrypt on the receiver side.

The confidentiality and integrity protections for Web applications are relatively coarse-grained in that there is no way for the deployment descriptor to express requirements on the cryptographic strength of the protection through the choice of SSL/TLS cipher suite. When you deploy a Web application, you must trust the container that its provision of a *CONFIDENTIAL* transport is confidential enough.

Understanding EJB Security

There are two security measures that clients must pass when you add security to an EJB system: authentication and authorization. Authentication must be performed before any EJB method is called. Authorization, on the other hand, occurs at the beginning of each EJB method call.

Authentication in EJB

In earlier versions of EJB (1.0 and 1.1), there was no portable way to achieve authentication. The specific way your client code became associated with a security identity was left to the discretion of your application and your EJB container. This meant each EJB container could handle authentication differently.

The good news is that since EJB 2.0, authentication is now portable and robust. You can call authentication logic through the *Java Authentication and Authorization Service* (JAAS), a separate J2EE API. Let's now take a mini-tutorial of JAAS and see how it can be used in an EJB environment.

JAAS Overview

JAAS is a portable interface that enables you to authenticate and authorize users in Java. In a nutshell, it allows you to log into a system without knowing about the underlying security system being used. Behind the scenes in JAAS, the implementation (such as an application server) then determines if your credentials are authentic. Moreover, JAAS enables you to write your own customized authentication modules that can then be plugged in without the need to change client code.

The power of JAAS lies in its ability to use almost any underlying security system. Some application servers allow you to set up user names and passwords in the application server's properties, which the application server reads in at runtime. More advanced servers support complex integration with existing security systems, such as a list of user names and passwords stored in an LDAP server, database, or custom security system. Other systems support certificate-based authentication. Regardless, the integration is performed behind the scenes by the container and does not affect your application code.

There are two likely candidate scenarios when you may want to use JAAS from your code, shown in Figure 13.2.

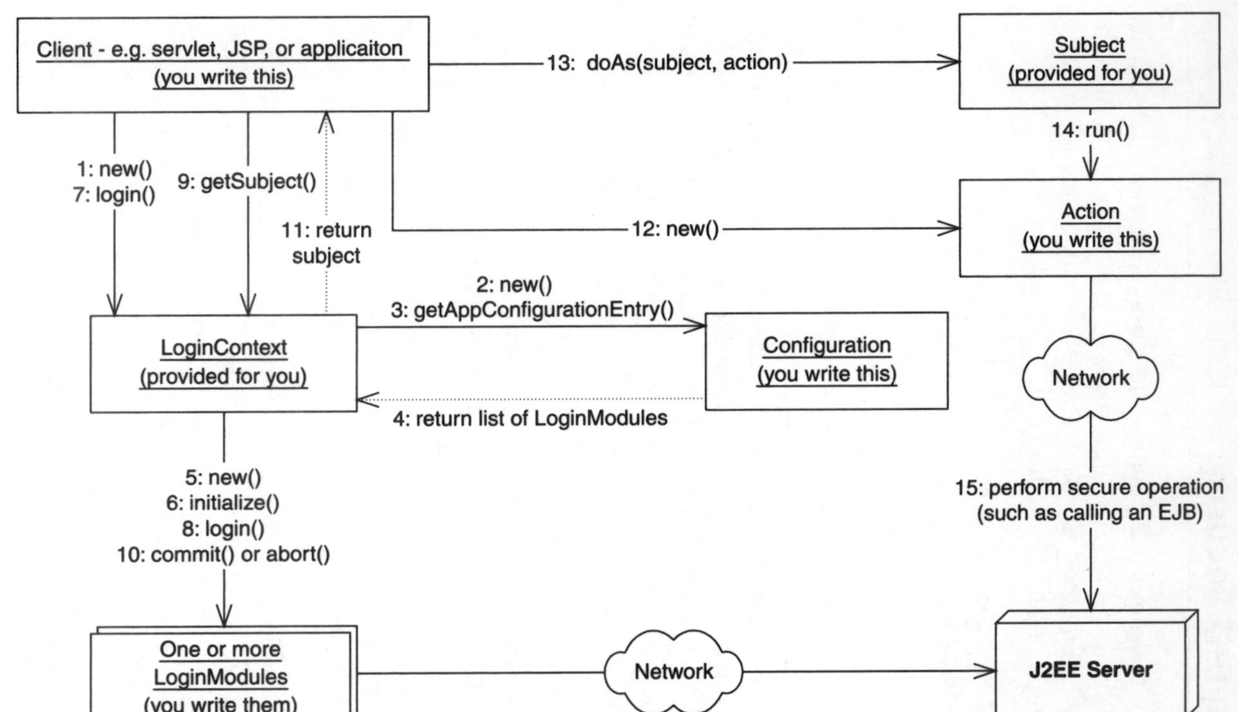

Figure 13.2 JAAS overview.

- When you have a standalone application connecting to a remote EJB system, the user would supply credentials to the application (or perhaps the application would retrieve the credentials from a file or other system). The standalone application would then use the JAAS API to authenticate the user prior to calling the EJB components residing within the application server. The application server would verify the user's credentials. Once the user has been authenticated via JAAS, the client can call EJB methods securely, and the user's security identity will be propagated to the server upon method invocations.
- When you have a Web browser client connecting to a servlet or JSP layer, the Web browser user supplies credentials to a servlet/JSP layer, and the servlet or JSP layer could use JAAS to authenticate the user. The Web browser could supply the credentials in one of the four ways that we discussed in the section on Web application security. To recap, these were:
  - Basic authentication
  - Form-based authentication
  - Digest authentication
  - Certificate authentication

As with standalone applications, once the user has been authenticated via JAAS, the client can call EJB methods securely, and the user's security identity will be propagated to the server upon method invocations.

The JAAS Architecture

JAAS has a flexible design, but can be surprisingly complicated for what you think would be a simple function. We have distilled JAAS down into a simple procedure to make it easier for you to understand.

Figure 13.3 shows the basics of a JAAS authentication procedure.

The JAAS authentication procedure breaks down as follows (follow along with the picture as we review each step):

1. The client instantiates a new login context. This is a container-provided class. It's responsible for coordinating the authentication process.
2. The login context retrieves a configuration object. The configuration object knows about the type of authentication you want to achieve by consulting a configuration file that lists the login modules. For example, your configuration object might know that you want to perform both password-based authentication and certificate-based authentication.
3. The login context asks the configuration object for the list of authentication mechanisms to use (such as password-based and certificate-based).

4. The configuration object returns a list of authentication mechanisms. Each one is called a login module. A login module knows how to contact a specific security provider and authenticate in some proprietary way.
5. The login context instantiates your login modules. You can have many login modules if you want to authenticate across several different security providers. In the example we're about to show, we will use only one login module, and it will know how to authenticate using a user name and password combination to a J2EE server.
6. The login context initializes the login modules.
7. The client code tries to log in by calling the *login()* method on the login context.
8. The login context delegates the *login()* call to the login modules, since only the login modules know how to perform the actual authentication.
9. The login modules (written by you) authenticate you using a proprietary means. In the example we're about to show, our user name and password login module will perform a local authentication only that always succeeds because the authentication data is not checked on the client side at all. After the login succeeds, the login module is told to *commit()*. It can also *abort()* if the login process fails. This is not a very critical step to understand—read the JAAS docs if you're curious to understand more.
10. Authentication information is kept in a subject. You can use this subject to perform secure operations or just have it sit in the context.
11. Your client code calls remote operations (such as in an EJB component) and the logged-in security context is automatically propagated along with the method call. If you are curious: for RMI/IIOP clients the machinery to pass this context is based on the CSIv2 standard that we will explain later in this chapter. The EJB server can now perform the actual authentication using the authentication data that is passed in the security context. The server can then perform authorization based on the authenticated client identity.

What's neat about JAAS is that the login modules are separate from the configuration, which means you can chain together different login modules in interesting combinations by specifying different configurations in the local configuration file. Another thing to note in the sequence outlined above is that the authentication may succeed on the client side, but fail on the server side. If the password is incorrect, this will result in the server rejecting the invocation with a *NO_PERMISSION* exception.

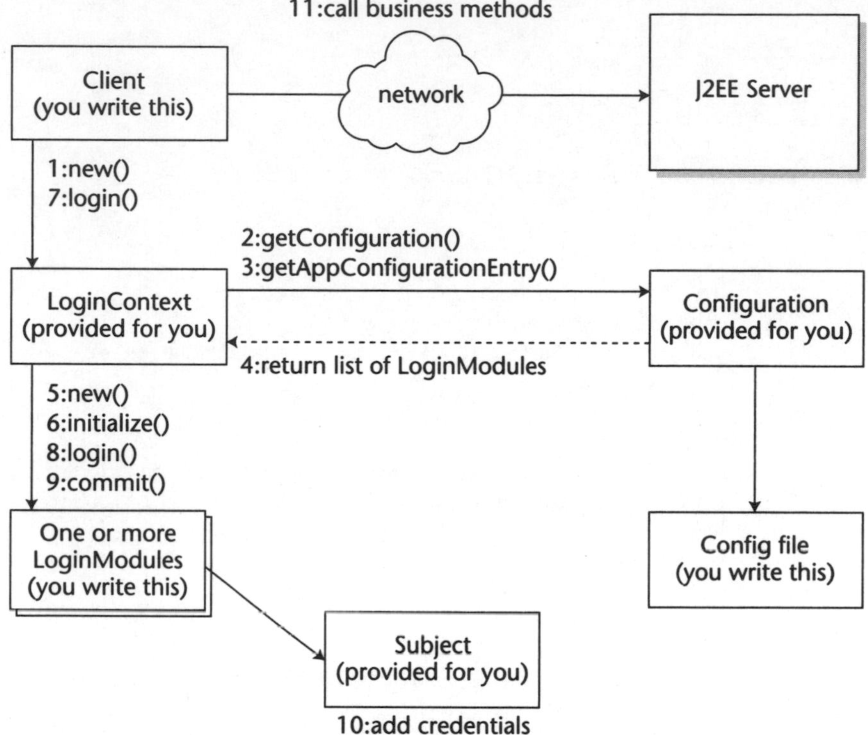

Figure 13.3 JAAS authentication in detail.

JAAS Sample Code

Let's show a simple JAAS example. The code will authenticate and then call a "Hello, World" method on a bean. If the password is right, then the invocation succeeds. If not, then the server throws an exception. The example shows both the use of the JAAS client API and how a custom *LoginModule* is plugged in.

The code is in Source 13.1 through 13.3 and is fairly self-documenting. By reviewing Figure 13.3, this sample code, and the process we laid out earlier, you should be able to get a feeling for what this code is doing.

```
package examples.security;

import java.util.*;
import javax.security.auth.*;
import javax.security.auth.login.*;
import javax.naming.*;

import javax.rmi.PortableRemoteObject;
```

Source 13.1 HelloClient.java *(continued)*

```
/**
 * A client program that uses JAAS to authenticate
 */
public class HelloClient
{
    public static void main(String[] args)
    {
        try
        {
            /* Authenticate via JAAS */
            LoginContext loginContext =
                new LoginContext("HelloClient", new CallbackHandler());
            loginContext.login();

            /* Get a bean */
            Context ctx = new InitialContext(System.getProperties());
            Object obj = ctx.lookup("JAASHelloHome");
            HelloHome home =
                (HelloHome)PortableRemoteObject.narrow(obj,
HelloHome.class);
            Hello hello = home.create();

            /* Call a business method, propagating the security context */
            String result = hello.hello();

            /* Print the return result from the business logic */
            System.out.println(result);
        }
        catch (Exception e)
        {
            e.printStackTrace();
        }
    }
}
```

Source 13.1 HelloClient.java *(continued)*

```
package examples.security;

import java.util.*;
import java.io.IOException;

import javax.security.auth.*;
import javax.security.auth.callback.*;
import javax.security.auth.login.*;
```

Source 13.2 PasswordLoginModule.java

```
import javax.security.auth.spi.*;

import com.sun.enterprise.security.auth.login.PasswordCredential;

/**
 * A login module that performs password authentication.
 *
 * The purpose of this class is to actually use a callback handler
 * to collect authentication information and add it to the subject
 */

public class PasswordLoginModule
    implements LoginModule
{
    private Subject subject;
    /** the callback handler is the mechanism to collect authentication
data */
    private javax.security.auth.callback.CallbackHandler callbackHandler;

    /** credentials: username and password */
    private String username;
    private char[] password;

    /**
     * Initializes us with a particular subject to which we will later
     * add the collected password data.
     */

    public void initialize(Subject subject,
                           javax.security.auth.callback.CallbackHandler
callbackHandler,
                           Map sharedState,
                           Map options)
    {
        this.subject = subject;
        this.callbackHandler = callbackHandler;
    }

    /**
     * Authenticate the user by prompting for a username and password.
     * It is called when the client tries to login in.
     *
     * @return    true in all cases since this <code>LoginModule</code>
     *            should not be ignored.
     * @exception FailedLoginException if the authentication fails.
     * @exception LoginException if this <code>LoginModule</code> is
unable to
```

Source 13.2 *(continued)*

```
     *            perform the authentication.
     */

    public boolean login()
        throws LoginException
    {
        // prompt for a username and password
        if (callbackHandler == null)
        {
            throw new LoginException("Error: No CallbackHandler
available to collect authentication information");
        }

        // set up a name callback and a password callback
        Callback[] callbacks = new Callback[2];
        callbacks[0] = new NameCallback("username: ");
        callbacks[1] = new PasswordCallback("password: ", false);

        try
        {
            // let handler handle these
            callbackHandler.handle(callbacks);

            // get authentication data
            username = ((NameCallback)callbacks[0]).getName();
            if(username == null)
            {
                throw new LoginException("No user specified");
            }

            char[] tmpPassword =
((PasswordCallback)callbacks[1]).getPassword();

            if (tmpPassword == null)
            {
                // treat null password as an empty password
                tmpPassword = new char[0];
            }
            password = new char[tmpPassword.length];
            System.arraycopy(tmpPassword, 0, password, 0,
tmpPassword.length);
            ((PasswordCallback)callbacks[1]).clearPassword();
        }
        catch (java.io.IOException ioe)
        {
            throw new LoginException(ioe.toString());
        }
        catch (UnsupportedCallbackException uce)
        {
```

Source 13.2 *(continued)*

```
            throw new LoginException("Error: No Callback available to
collect authentication data :"  +
                                            uce.getCallback().toString());
        }
        catch( Exception e )
        {
            e.printStackTrace();
        }

        // The client side login module will always succeed. The
        // actual login will take place on the server side when the
        // security context is passed.
        return true;
    }

    /**
     * This method is called if the overall authentication succeeds
     * after potentially many login modules had their way. In our
     * simple case, we always succeed. The important part here is
     * adding the newly authenticated principal to the security
     * context.
     *
     * @return true if this method executes properly
     */

    public boolean commit()
        throws LoginException
    {
        // add the user name and password as credentials to the
        // security context, i.e., the Subject
        PasswordCredential pc =
            new PasswordCredential(username,
                                   new String(password),
                                   "fileRealm");

        subject.getPrivateCredentials().add(pc);

        username = null;
        password = null;
        return true;
    }

    /**
     * This method is called if the overall authentication failed
     * (even if this particular login module succeeded).  This cannot
     * happen int our simple examples.
     *
     * @return true if this method executes properly
```

Source 13.2 *(continued)*

```
     */

    public boolean abort()
        throws LoginException
    {
        return true;
    }

    /**
     * Logout the user and clean up.
     *
     * @return true if this method executes properly
     */
    public boolean logout()
        throws LoginException
    {
        username = null;
        password = null;
        return true;
    }
}
```

Source 13.2 *(continued)*

```
package examples.security;

import java.io.*;
import java.util.*;
import javax.security.auth.login.*;
import javax.security.auth.*;
import javax.security.auth.callback.*;

/**
 * Implements the CallbackHandler that gathers uid/pw input from
 * System.in.
 */
public class CallbackHandler
    implements javax.security.auth.callback.CallbackHandler
{
    /**
     * @param callbacks an array of <code>Callback</code> objects
     *
     * @exception java.io.IOException
     * @exception UnsupportedCallbackException if the
<code>callbacks</code>
     *          parameter contains unknown callback objects
     */
    public void handle(Callback[] callbacks)
```

Source 13.3 CallbackHandler.java

```
        throws IOException, UnsupportedCallbackException
    {
      for (int i = 0; i < callbacks.length; i++)
        {
          if (callbacks[i] instanceof NameCallback)
            {
            // prompt user for name
            NameCallback nc = (NameCallback)callbacks[i];
            System.out.print(nc.getPrompt());
                String name =
                    (new BufferedReader(new
InputStreamReader(System.in))).readLine();
            nc.setName(name);
          }
            else if (callbacks[i] instanceof PasswordCallback)
            {
             // prompt user for password
            PasswordCallback pc = (PasswordCallback)callbacks[i];
            System.out.print(pc.getPrompt());
                String pwLine =
                    (new BufferedReader(new
InputStreamReader(System.in))).readLine();
            pc.setPassword( pwLine.toCharArray());
       }
            else
            {
            throw new UnsupportedCallbackException(callbacks[i],
"Unrecognized Callback");
         }
     }
    }
}
```

Source 13.3 *(continued)*

Finally, here is the content of a client-side configuration file that specifies that the *PasswordLoginModule* is used both as the default login module and for applications that provide the name "HelloClient" as the parameter to the *LoginContext* constructor.

```
certificate {
  com.sun.enterprise.security.auth.login.ClientCertificateLoginModule
required debug=false;
};

default {
   examples.security.PasswordLoginModule required debug=false;
```

```
};

HelloClient {
    examples.security.PasswordLoginModule required debug=false;
};
```

Authorization in EJB

After the client has been authenticated, it must pass an authorization test to call methods on your beans. The EJB container enforces authorization by defining *security policies* for your beans. Again, there are two ways to perform authorization with EJB:

- **With *programmatic authorization*, you hard-code security checks into your bean code.** Your business logic is interlaced with security checks.
- **With *declarative authorization*, the container performs all authorization checks for you.** You declare how you'd like authorization to be achieved through the deployment descriptor, and the container *generates* all necessary security checks. You are effectively delegating authorization to the EJB container.

Security Roles

Regardless of whether you're performing programmatic or declarative authorization, you need to understand the concept of *security roles*. A security role is a collection of client identities. For a client to be authorized to perform an operation, its security identity must be in the correct security role for that operation. The EJB deployer is responsible for associating the identities with the correct security roles *after* you write your beans.

The advantage to using security roles is that you do not hard-code specific identities into your beans. This is necessary when you are developing beans for deployment in a wide variety of security environments, because each environment will have its own list of identities. This also enables you to modify access control without recompiling your bean code.

Specifying security roles in EJB is application server-specific but should not affect portability of your code. Table 13.1 shows some sample mappings.

Table 13.1 Sample Security Roles

SECURITY ROLE	VALID IDENTITIES
employees	EmployeeA, EmployeeB
managers	ManagerA
administrators	AdminA

Performing Programmatic Authorization

Let's discuss how to authorize programmatically. Then we'll see how to authorize declaratively and compare the two approaches.

Step 1: Write the Programmatic Security Logic

To perform explicit security authorization checks in your enterprise beans, you must first get information about who is calling your bean's method. You can get this information by querying the container through the EJB context object. (Refer to Chapter 3 if you need to refresh your memory.)

The EJB context object has the following relevant security methods:

```
public interface javax.ejb.EJBContext
{
    ...
    public java.security.Principal getCallerPrincipal();
    public boolean isCallerInRole(String roleName);
    ...
}
```

isCallerInRole(String role) checks whether the current caller is in a particular security role. When you call this method, you pass the security role that you want the caller compared against. For example:

```
public class EmployeeManagementBean implements SessionBean {

          private SessionContext ctx;

...

    public void modifyEmployee(String employeeID)
   throws SecurityException
    {
        /*
         * If the caller is not in the 'administrators'
         * security role, throw an exception.
         */
        if (!ctx.isCallerInRole("administrators")) {
            throw new SecurityException(...);
        }

        // else, allow the administrator to modify the
        // employee records
        // ...
    }
}
```

The preceding code demonstrates how to perform different actions based on the security role of the client. Only if the caller is in the *administrators* role (defined in Table 13.1, and setup using your container's tools) does the caller have administrator access.

The other programmatic security method, *getCallerPrincipal()*, retrieves the current caller's security principal. You can use that principal for many purposes, such as retrieving the caller's distinguished name from it to use this name in a database query. This might be handy if you're storing your security information in a database. Here is sample code that uses *getCallerPrincipal()*:

```
import java.security.Principal;

...

public class EmployeeManagementBean implements SessionBean {

private SessionContext ctx;

...

   public void modifyEmployee() {
        Principal id = ctx.getCallerPrincipal();
        String name = id.getName();
        // Query a database based on the name
        // to determine if the user is authorized
   }
}
```

Step 2: Declare the Abstract Security Roles Your Bean Uses

Next you must declare all the security roles that your bean code uses, such as an *administrators* role, in your deployment descriptor. This signals to others (like application assemblers and deployers) that your bean makes the security check *isCallerInRole (administrators)*. This is important information for the deployer, because he or she needs to fulfill that role, just like the deployer fulfills EJB references, as mentioned in Chapter 10. Source 13.4 demonstrates this.

```
. . .
<enterprise-beans>

    <session>

        <ejb-name>EmployeeManagement</ejb-name>
        <home>examples.EmployeeManagementHome</home>
```

Source 13.4 Declaring a Bean's required security roles.

```
    . . .

   <!--
    This declares that our bean code relies on
    the administrators role; we must declare it here
    to inform the application assembler and deployer.
    -->
    <security-role-ref>

        <description>
        This security role should be assigned to the
        administrators who are responsible for
        modifying employees.
        </description>

        <role-name>administrators</role-name>

    </security-role-ref>

    . . .
  </session>

  . . .

</enterprise-beans>
. . .
```

Source 13.4 *(continued)*

Step 3: Map Abstract Roles to Actual Roles

Once you've written your bean, you can ship it, build it into an application, or make it part of your company's internal library of beans. The consumer of your bean might be combining beans from all sorts of sources, and each source may have declared security roles a bit differently. For example, we used the string *administrators* in our previous bean, but another bean provider might use the string *sysadmins* or have completely different security roles.

The deployer of your bean is responsible for generating the *real* security roles that the final application will use (see Source 13.5).

```
. . .
<enterprise-beans>

    <session>

        <ejb-name>EmployeeManagement</ejb-name>
        <home>examples.EmployeeManagementHome</home>
        ...

        <security-role-ref>

            <description>
            This security role should be assigned to the
            administrators who are responsible for
            modifying employees.
            </description>

            <role-name>administrators</role-name>
            <!--
            Here we link what we call "administrators" above, to
            a real security-role, called "admins", defined below
            -->
            <role-link>admins</role-link>

        </security-role-ref>

        . . .
    </session>

    <assembly-descriptor>

        . . .

        <!--
        This is an example of a real security role.
        -->
        <security-role>

            <description>
            This role is for personnel authorized to perform
            employee administration.
            </description>

            <role-name>admins</role-name>
```

Source 13.5 Mapping abstract roles to actual roles.

```
            </security-role>

            . . .

        </assembly-descriptor>

    </enterprise-beans>
    . . .
```

Source 13.5 *(continued)*

Once you've completed your application, you can deploy it in a wide variety of scenarios. For example, if you write a banking application, you could deploy that same application at different branches of that bank, because you haven't hard-coded any specific principals into your application. The deployer of your application is responsible for mapping principals to the roles you've declared using proprietary container APIs and tools.

Performing Declarative Authorization

Now that we've seen programmatic authorization, let's move on to declarative authorization. The primary difference between the two models is that with declarative authorization, you *declare* your bean's authorization requirements in your deployment descriptor. The container enforces these requirements at runtime.

Step 1: Declare Method Permissions

You first need to declare permissions on the bean methods that you want to secure. The container takes these instructions and *generates* security checks in your EJB objects and EJB home objects (see Source 13.6).

```
...

<assembly-descriptor>

    . . .

    <!--
    You can set permissions on the entire bean.

    Example: Allow role "administrators"
    to call every method on the bean class.
    -->
    <method-permission>
```

Source 13.6 Declaring a bean's security policies. *(continued)*

```
        <role-name>administrators</role-name>

        <method>
            <ejb-name>EmployeeManagement</ejb-name>
            <method-name>*</method-name>
        </method>
    </method-permission>

    <!--
    You can set permissions on a method level.

    Example: Allow role "managers" to call method
             "modifySubordinate()" and "modifySelf()".
    -->
    <method-permission>
        <role-name>managers</role-name>

        <method>
            <ejb-name>EmployeeManagement</ejb-name>
            <method-name>modifySubordinate</method-name>
        </method>

        <method>
            <ejb-name>EmployeeManagement</ejb-name>
            <method-name>modifySelf</method-name>
        </method>
    </method-permission>

    <!--
    If you have multiple methods with the same name
    but that take different parameters, you can even set
    permissions that distinguish between the two.

    Example: allow role "employees" to call method
             "modifySelf(String)" but not "modifySelf(Int)"
    -->
    <method-permission>
        <role-name>employees</role-name>

        <method>
            <ejb-name>EmployeeManagement</ejb-name>
            <method-name>modifySelf</method-name>
            <method-params>String</method-params>
        </method>
    </method-permission>

    <!--
    This is the list of methods that we don't want
    ANYONE to call.  Useful if you receive a bean
```

Source 13.6 *(continued)*

```
    from someone with methods that you don't need.
    -->
    <exclude-list>
        <description>
            We don't have a 401k plan, so we don't
            support this method.
        </description>
        <method>
            <ejb-name>EmployeeManagement</ejb-name>
            <method-name>modify401kPlan</method-name>
            <method-params>String</method-params>
        </method>
    </exclude-list>

    . . .

</assembly-descriptor>
. . .
```

Source 13.6 *(continued)*

Once defined, the EJB container automatically performs these security checks on your bean's methods at runtime and throws a *java.lang.SecurityException* exception back to the client code if the client identity is not authenticated or authorized.

Step 2: Declare Security Roles

Declaring security roles is a process similar to programmatic security. We need to define our security roles and (optionally) describe each so the deployer can understand them (see Source 13.7).

```
<assembly-descriptor>

    . . .

    <security-role>
        <description>
        System administrators
        </description>
        <role-name>administrators</role-name>
    </security-role>

    <security-role>
        <description>
```

Source 13.7 Declaring security roles for the deployer. *(continued)*

```
            Employees that manage a group
            </description>
            <role-name>managers</role-name>
        </security-role>

        <security-role>
            <description>
            Employees that don't manage anyone
            </description>
            <role-name>employees</role-name>
        </security-role>

        . . .

    </assembly-descriptor>
```

Source 13.7 *(continued)*

The deployer reads in Source 13.7 and, using the container's tools, maps these roles to principals, as shown in Table 13.1.

Declarative or Programmatic?

As with persistence and transactions, security is a middleware service that you should strive to externalize from your beans. By using declarative security, you decouple your beans' business purpose from specific security policies, thus enabling others to modify security rules without modifying bean code. No security role strings are hard-coded in your bean logic, keeping your code simple.

In the ideal world, we'd code all our beans with declarative security. But unfortunately, the EJB specification does not provide adequate facilities for this; specifically, there is no portable way to declaratively perform *instance-level authorization*. This is best illustrated with an example.

Let's say you have an enterprise bean that models a bank account. The caller of the enterprise bean is a bank account manager who wants to withdraw or deposit into that bank account. But this bank account manager is responsible only for bank accounts with balances below $1,000, and we don't want him modifying bank accounts with larger balances. Declarative authorization has no way to declare in your deployment descriptor that bank account managers can modify only certain bean instances. You can specify security roles only on the enterprise bean class, and those security rules apply for all instances of that class. Thus, you would need to create separate methods for each security role, as we did in Source 13.7. This gets hairy and makes your bean's interface dependent on security roles. For these situations, you should resort to programmatic security.

Security Propagation

Behind the scenes, all security checks are made possible due to *security contexts*. Security contexts encapsulate the current caller's security state. You never see security contexts in your application code, because the container uses them behind the scenes. When you call a method in EJB, the container can propagate your security information by implicitly passing your security context within the stubs and skeletons.

For example, let's say a client is authenticated and has associated security credentials. That client calls bean A, which calls bean B. Should the client's security credentials be sent to bean B, or should bean B receive a different principal? By controlling security context propagation, you can specify the exact semantics of credentials streaming from method to method in a distributed system.

You can control the way security information is propagated in your deployment descriptor. The following descriptor snippet takes the client's credentials and propagates them to all other beans you call:

```
...
<enterprise-beans>
      ...
      <session>
            <ejb-name>EmployeeManagement</ejb-name>
            <home>examples.EmployeeManagementHome</home>
            ...
            <security-identity>
               <use-caller-identity/>
            </security-identity>
            ...
      </session>
      ...
</enterprise-beans>
```

In comparison, the following descriptor code ignores the client's credentials and propagates the role *admins* to all other beans you call:

```
...
<enterprise-beans>
      ...
      <session>
            <ejb-name>EmployeeManagement</ejb-name>
            <home>examples.EmployeeManagementHome</home>
            ...
```

```
            <security-identity>
                <run-as>
                    <role-name>admins</role-name>
                </run-as>
            </security-identity>
            ...
        </session>

    <assembly-descriptor>
        . . .
        <security-role>
            <description>
            This role is for personnel authorized
            to perform employee administration.
            </description>

            <role-name>admins</role-name>
         </security-role>
         . . .
    </assembly-descriptor>
    </enterprise-beans>
```

The EJB container is responsible for intercepting all method calls and ensuring that your bean is running in the propagation settings you specify. It does this by generating code that executes at the point of interception (inside the EJB objects and EJB home objects).

Secure Interoperability

Secure interoperability means that EJB containers from different vendors cooperate in protecting EJB invocations that originate in one vendor's product and target EJBs in another. The most important functionality that EJB containers must agree on here is the authentication of principals on one end of the invocation and the propagation of the principal information to the other. In addition, there must be consensus about how confidentiality and integrity protections should be applied on the wire.

For this to happen, any security information that needs to be exchanged must be standardized. Otherwise, one vendor's product would not be able to understand the information sent by its colleague on the other end of the wire.

The general protocol that the EJB specification requires for interoperability is RMI-IIOP. For the additional, security-related interoperability, the EJB specification leverages two more protocols that were originally designed for CORBA:

- IIOP/SSL (IIOP over SSL) for authentication, integrity and confidentiality
- CSIv2 (*Common Secure Interoperability version* 2), for additional authentication capabilities and principal propagation.

You will probably not need to deal with the internal details of either IIOP/SSL or CSIv2 directly in development, but if you are curious about what is under the hood, then the rest of this section provides the background information. Also, when you are responsible for managing large-scale EJB server architectures that involve interoperating with external clients or servers, then you should be aware of the trust relationships that must be established to allow for principal delegation across platforms.

IIOP/SSL

The first part of interoperable security—integrity and confidentiality protections—is actually simple thanks to SSL/TLS, which takes care of all the details of setting up secure transports between endpoints. For deployers, there is nothing left to do but provide proper credentials that SSL/TLS can use during its initial handshake. This is far from trivial, but since credentials are necessary anyway, this adds little complexity.

Internally, the hosting EJB container's CORBA Object Request Broker (ORB) is equipped to insert SSL-level transport information into *EJBObject* and *EJBHome* references. For IIOP/SSL, these references take the format of the CORBA *Interoperable Object References* (IORs), and SSL/TLS-related information is stored in the IOR as *tagged components*. The receiving container's ORB recognizes the IOR and its tagged components and hence knows how to let the SSL/TLS layer open transport connections.

CSIv2

SSL/TLS is not a silver bullet for all your security problems. It does offer interoperable, standardized means for mutual authentication between communicating peers, but it requires public key certificates in X.509 format to do this. While this is a proven mechanism, it requires some form of certificate management infrastructure. Mapping other client authentication mechanisms, such as Kerberos, is hard, and propagating principal information from clients a few hosts up in the invocation chain is not supported at all. Moreover, SSL/TLS is heavy-weight in the sense that the initial handshake required to set up a secure transport adds a significant overhead. In some cases you may want to authenticate a client but don't actually care for the additional integrity and confidentiality protection of SSL.

Common Secure Interoperability version 2 (CSIv2) was specified for CORBA by the Object Management Group (OMG) in 1999 as a successor to earlier secure interoperability protocols. CSIv2 was designed to be used together with transport-level SSL security and to complement it. The *Security Attribute Service* (SAS) protocol in CSIv2 defines additional client authentication functionality that is independent of SSL/TLS and can be used with Kerberos or UserID/Password schemes. Target authentication is not supported in the SAS protocol, so if *mutual* authentication is required, the SAS protocol must be combined with the transport-level target authentication offered by SSL/TLS.

Additionally, the CSI protocol supports *identity assertions* as a means of principal propagation. An identity assertion is sent by the calling client to tell the receiver that it should not consider the client identity (which was established on the transport layer or by the authentication process) for making authorization decisions, but the asserted *identity* instead. An asserted identity is much like a *run-as* statement or a *set-uid* bit in the UNIX file system—with one important difference: it is the client who wants to define a different identity for its own actions.

With identity assertions, a single method call may have as many as three different identities associated with it: the transport-level identity as established by SSL, an additional client identity established through the SAS client authentication, and the asserted identity. Note that any or all of these may be missing. Figure 13.4 illustrates these layers.

What are these many identities good for? An asserted identity is useful when the client is acting on behalf of another principal who should be held responsible, especially when the client cannot re-use the principal's credentials to impersonate it when talking to the target. For example, the client may be a remote servlet container (running in vendor X's application server) calling an EJB container (a product by vendor Y) on a different network, as shown in Figure 13.5. The Web container did authenticate the Web user by using SSL client authentication and established a principal identity. It cannot itself authenticate as the principal to the EJB container, however. Because it does not have access to the client's required private keys, it can authenticate only itself. However, access control and auditing should use the actual user ID, not the servlet container's identity, so the Web container needs to assert the client identity.

Security Attribute Layer	**Identity Assertion**
Client Authentication Layer	**Client Authentication**
Transport Layer (SSL/TLS)	**Client Authentication** **Message Protection** **Target Authentication**

Figure 13.4 Layers in CSIv2.

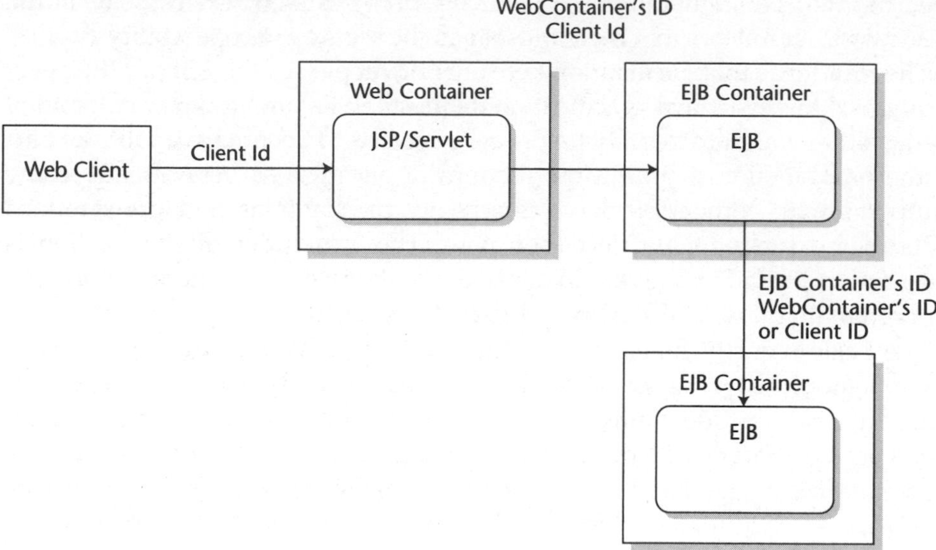

Figure 13.5 Identity assertion in a call chain.

Obviously, accepting an asserted identity that arrives in the security context of a method call is a matter of trust. Trust here means trusting that the JSP files and servlets did not cheat when inserting the identity assertion, and trusting that an attacker did not penetrate the Web container host. Looking closer, we find that this trust actually extends to all predecessors in the call chain, which the target has no secure way of identifying. This is also called *transitive trust*. The EJB specification simply states that identity assertions should be accepted only from containers with predefined trust, which in most practical settings means that containers authenticate each other using public key certificates on the transport layer that were distributed beforehand. A receiving container can then simply accept identities that the sending container asserts.

Note that the problem with transitive trust still exists: the whole trust chain is only as strong as its weakest link. Effectively, this means that deployers should take considerable care when exchanging public key certificates and marking them as trustworthy.

Because no tight control of principal propagation can be enforced by the technology alone, there must be organizational frameworks to support cooperation and trust establishment.

Web Services Security

You may be wondering why, after so much security coverage, there is a need for an extra section on security for Web Services. The simple reason is that Web Services are not just an implementation approach for stateless session beans: they need to interoperate with other, potentially non-EJB Web Services, say, in the .NET world. It follows that there must again be secure interoperability.

The standards that we mention here are not yet part of the EJB or J2EE specifications. However, Java Specification Requests (JSRs) are under way for all of them so that standardized Java APIs are expected to become available as part of the next version of EJB. Most modern application servers already come equipped with some Web Services security mechanisms and pre-standard APIs to the functionality described here. The remainder of this section is intended to provide you with an overview of the relevant standards and concepts so that you will be able to use them successfully.

The basic security functionality that must be provided in a standardized fashion should by now sound familiar to you: authentication, authorization, integrity, and confidentiality. Interestingly, the Web Services security standards go well beyond the traditional approaches in a number of respects. The most important goal that the technologies we are about to meet aim for is true *end-to-end security* for the messages sent to and received from Web Services, such as SOAP messages.

End-to-End Security

Let's consider the scenario where a client uses a Web Service, which behind the scenes delegates some of the functionality to other Web Services, which may do the same with still other services. The original client has no way of knowing who will see which parts of the original request message, nor does it know who will actually create which parts of the result. (See Figure 13.6.)

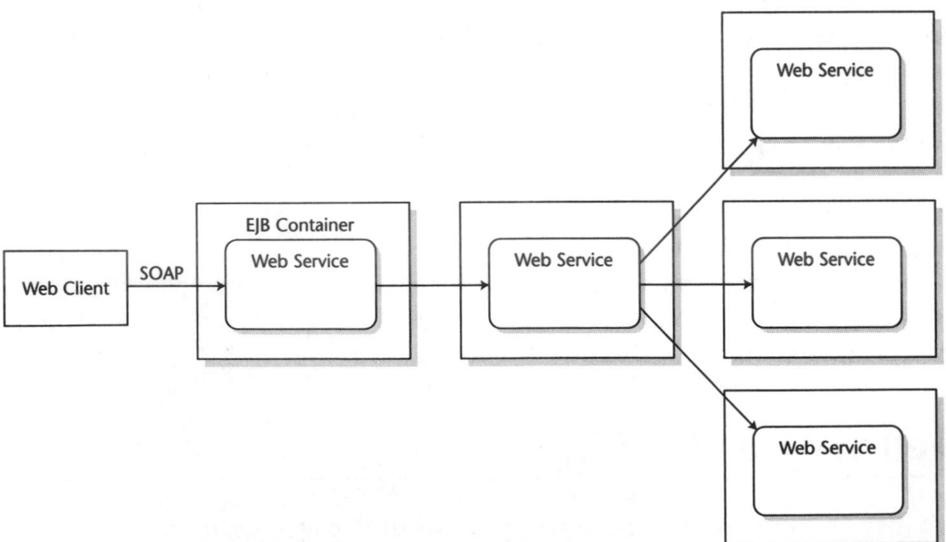

Figure 13.6 End-to-end security.

This functional abstraction is fundamental for making large-scale architectures possible, but from a security standpoint it means that you have to trust a potentially unlimited number of unknown parties to play fair. This may be okay within your own local network where you trust all servers and services, including their administrators, but it is certainly not acceptable in cross-enterprise applications with third- and fourth-party involvement. You don't want records of the hardware that you order to be compiled (and the records potentially disclosed), and you don't want the project schedules and design studies that you exchange with a business partner getting fiddled with.

This is where end-to-end security comes into play. It means control over the security of your messages from the point at which you send them until they reach their final destination, regardless of the number and kind of intermediaries that may get a chance to see your messages. Contrast this with the notion of transitive trust in EJB that we had to accept earlier: with transitive trust, anybody that your partner trusts is implicitly trusted by you, too. Regardless of whether you actually trust them or you even know they exist.

End-to-end security is not possible with a point-to-point technology like SSL/TLS. It is possible to build a long channel out of several short ones, but each hop in such a chain of connections terminates one SSL/TLS connection and starts a new one. When SOAP messages and other EJB requests travel through multiple intermediate hops before they reach their final target, the messages are protected *between* hops, but unprotected *within* each hop. All you can do with point-to-point security is trust that the software in those hops doesn't read or modify your messages where it shouldn't.

Enter two security standards that can protect XML documents (and thus also SOAP messages) independently of the transport layer and in true end-to-end fashion: XML Digital Signature and XML Encryption.

XML Digital Signature and XML Encryption

The names of these two standards certainly imply heavy-duty cryptography but don't worry: there are no new algorithms or protocols that we need to discuss here. Both standards rely on traditional cryptography and don't add any of their own. In fact, these two standards, issued by the World Wide Web Consortium (W3C), simply define XML syntax for encrypted or signed data. The data that is either signed or encrypted can be anything, including of course XML content, but it may also be other documents, or even arbitrary binary data.

As an example, consider the following SOAP message that contains a message body with a single, encrypted data element, the operation. The binary, encrypted data content of the inner *CipherValue* has been base64-encoded, the outer *EncryptedData* element describes the encryption algorithm (triple DES) that was used to create the *CipherValue*. Note that the receiver must know the symmetric key that was used to encrypt the message, otherwise he won't be able to decrypt it. We'll discuss in the next section how information about the key (or even the key itself) can be sent in the message.

```
<soapenv:Envelope
xmlns:soapenv="http://schemas.xmlsoap.org/soap/envelope/">
  <soapenv:Header>
....
  </soapenv:Header>
  <soapenv:Body>
    <EncryptedData xmlns="http://www.w3.org/2001/04/xmlenc#"
      Id="#xdn_id0" Type="http://www.w3.org/2001/04/xmlenc#Element">
      <EncryptionMethod
Algorithm="http://www.w3.org/2001/04/xmlenc#tripledes-cbc"/>
      <CipherData>
        <CipherValue>Vy58P2KaKedALCyZt23Hoi7TSK8ZiZvygWorXUX
        Q56EmS1z5LVp8frzQvivk2iIrrYQI8DSbIG+ywfNnZfoVC0QiTbWE29
       HztGTRUhAE2f/VbRzpMisxe2+/Xc7EZXfurZOVFNR2NjW+Ayiuqd
       W5OxkZi7la6tmQefFFYUSAzsUA6p0nabXOVsNCds8Y7pdZXeJtH+
       lnMpfSCFNbS7R4GhFsZBjNL5Hxqb1vUZlgwcP9Lh6ua1yqi2DgUKvtI1/p
       thPNA/QYj3VfEZzk1sit/A==</CipherValue>
      </CipherData>
    </EncryptedData>
  </soapenv:Body>
</soapenv:Envelope>
```

XML digital signatures can cover data that is completely external to the transmitted document. For example, it may be a signature value over the content of a remote Web site or over a Microsoft Word document in a knowledge base somewhere. An XML message may even contain a signature over parts of itself. The added value here is that this signature data can now be transported within XML documents without having the receiver's XML parser complain about unexpected, non-XML data. To give you an impression, here's an example of an XML digital signature that was taken from another SOAP message.

```
<Signature xmlns="http://www.w3.org/2000/09/xmldsig#">
  <SignedInfo>
    <CanonicalizationMethod
     Algorithm="http://www.w3.org/TR/2001/REC-xml-c14n-20010315"/>
    <SignatureMethod Algorithm="http://www.w3.org/2000/09/xmldsig#rsa-sha1"/>
    <Reference>
      <Transforms>
        <Transform Algorithm="http://www.w3.org/TR/1999/REC-xpath-19991116">
          <XPath
```

```
xmlns:soap="http://schemas.xmlsoap.org/soap/envelope/">ancestor-or-
self::soap:Envelope[1] and ancestor-or-self::soap:Body[1]</XPath>
          </Transform>
          <Transform Algorithm="http://www.w3.org/TR/2001/REC-xml-c14n-20010315"/>
        </Transforms>
        <DigestMethod Algorithm="http://www.w3.org/2000/09/xmldsig#sha1"/>
        <DigestValue>/VYLngXLqJP//BWhmGxVysqlrxw=</DigestValue>
      </Reference>
    </SignedInfo>
    <SignatureValue>J+L8HqI7Q+/u0zuDWZeg5zKkiHRvQqCMZlFkmGn8x+x8KPNqu/j

RpbEvacA1MjIIY00snVIti2yIgDHtfhNTQDa5GludCINbT5sEYeGYjVQwv8nFtwCMX+EmDXig/
        E2JHbQEDT4E02/1MrMV7Mk2cUorqk7bHuEG4wwIGdzqEIk=
    </SignatureValue>
    <KeyInfo>
      <X509Data>
        <X509Certificate>...</X509Certificate>
      </X509Data>
    </KeyInfo>
  </Signature>
```

The *Signature* element has three main elements: the *SignedInfo* that describes the signed data, the *SignatureValue* (a base64 encoding of an encrypted hash value), and the *KeyInfo*, that describes which key was used to create the signature. The *SignedInfo* describes the data that is signed. In this case, it is a SOAP message header body, which is referred to using an XML path expression (XPath). This data was then transformed using a canonicalization algorithm before actually applying the signature algorithm (RSA-SHA1) to the message digest, which was computed using the SHA1 hash algorithm. Canonicalization is necessary for all XML content before signing because XML documents may undergo a number of changes (such as adding or removing whitespace in some places) during transport or other processing that do not change the document structure or content and thus should not cause the signature to break. To allow for these XML modifications, the sender first constructs the canonical form of an XML document and only then applies the signature. The receiver also first constructs the canonical form of the document he just received and then compares the outcome of another signature computation with the signature value that was received.

The two standards discussed in this section support some very important security features:

- **With XML Digital Signature and XML encryption** it is possible to send encrypted XML documents through untrusted channels. Only legitimate receivers that possess the necessary cryptographic keys will be able to decrypt the encrypted parts, and any in-transit modifications of signed parts of the message will be detected by the recipients.

- **With transport-independent protections** it is now possible to persist the signature, meaning that we can store the signature with the message, for example as a signed receipt. This is not possible with SSL/TLS: as soon as the message leaves the secure transport, the signature is gone, so SSL/TLS is not a good tool for application-level cryptography.
- **With the granularity of XML digital signature and XML encryption** it is possible to encrypt or sign only selected parts of a message. With SSL/TLS, in contrast, messages were always signed and/or encrypted completely. It would not be possible to create a controlled document-based workflow where some parts of a message are designed for modifications by processors at different stages in the workflow, whereas others would remain locked.

SAML

The acronym SAML means *Security Assertion Markup Language* and is an open standard ratified by the OASIS consortium. OASIS is short for *Organisation for the Advancement of Structured Information Standards* and is a large industry consortium comparable to the OMG. OASIS is also responsible for WS-Security (see the following section). The two main application areas for SAML are interoperability between security products and single sign-on (SSO). SAML has two main parts: the XML syntax for security assertions, and a simple request/response protocol for requesting assertions from SAML *authorities*. We only cover the assertion syntax here.

Assertion is another word for a security token. Assertions are used by entities that need security information in order to enforce security. In SAML speak, these entities are *Policy Enforcement Points*. The creator or issuer of a SAML assertion is called a SAML *authority*. Obviously, there is no need for SAML if the enforcement point creates all security tokens internally and for its own use and therefore does not need any external information. But if the enforcer is not in a position to authenticate the actual caller of a request and still needs to make an authorization decision, then a SAML assertion made earlier by an authentication service would help a lot. Sounds a lot like principal propagation, doesn't it? Yes, you may think of SAML as the CSIv2 of the Web Services world.

Now for a quick summary of the remaining SAML concepts: a SAML assertion expresses statements by the *issuer* about the *subject* of the assertion, such as "Subject S is authenticated (by me)," or "Subject S is authorized for actions A and B (by me)," or even "Subject S has attribute R," where R may be a role membership. Here is an example of an authentication assertion:

```
<Assertion xmlns="urn:oasis:names:tc:SAML:1.0:assertion"
  MajorVersion="1" MinorVersion="0" AssertionID="4711"
  Issuer="MySecuritySoftware"
  IssueInstant="2003-08-19T14:54:43">
    <Conditions NotBefore="2003-08-19T14:54:43"
                NotOnOrAfter="2003-08-19T15:04:43"/>
    <AuthenticationStatement
       AuthenticationMethod="urn:oasis:names:tc:SAML:1.0:am:unspecified"
       AuthenticationInstant="2003-08-19T14:54:43">
        <Subject>
            <NameIdentifier>Bart</NameIdentifier>
        </Subject>
    </AuthenticationStatement>
</Assertion>
```

The main part of the assertion is the *AuthenticationStatement* element, which states that someone named *Bart* was authenticated at a specific point in time using an unspecified mechanism. The outer *Assertion* element comprises further details, such as a validity condition (*NotBefore* and *NotOnOrAfter*), information about the issuer and issue instant, an assertion ID, and the SAML version used.

These assertions are not just made by anybody, but by authorities that someone inspecting an assertion would trust. In the previous assertion, all we know about the issuer is that she calls herself *MySecuritySoftware*. In an untrusted environment, an assertion would normally be digitally signed by the authority so that trust in the assertion can be established. In the example, this step was skipped to reduce overhead because, presumably, the enforcement point axiomatically trusts the issuer, and forgery of assertions was not assumed to be possible.

WS-Security

WS-Security is another specification ratified by the OASIS consortium. It describes how encryption and signatures should be used on SOAP messages to enable end-to-end security, and defines a SOAP security header element. Moreover, it defines a couple of security tokens, such as a user name and password token, an X.509 token, and a binary token format that can be used to transmit Kerberos tickets. As a standard it is comparatively short and straightforward, at least when compared to the EJB specification or CORBA.

The new security header was defined because the authors of the specification knew that message-oriented, end-to-end security cannot rely on sessions between peers along the way. The security header was therefore designed to contain the complete security information about the message in the message. In other words, the message is its own security context!

Here is an example of a SOAP message with this new WS-Security header element. In fact, this example contains the security information necessary to decrypt the encrypted message shown in the previous section, an encrypted key (a session key). Note how the *EncryptedKey* element's child *ReferenceList* refers to the encrypted data in the SOAP body using a URI reference to the Id attribute:

```
<soapenv:Envelope>
  <soapenv:Header>
    <wsse:Security xmlns:wsse="http://www.docs.oasis-
open.org/wss/2004/01/oasis-200401-wss-wssecurity-secext-1.0.xsd">
      <EncryptedKey xmlns="http://www.w3.org/2001/04/xmlenc#">
        <EncryptionMethod
          Algorithm="http://www.w3.org/2001/04/xmlenc#rsa-oaep-mgf1p"/>
        <KeyInfo/>
        <CipherData>
<CipherValue>jQEtmEsQ9CUUT0CuUM6yKKcpBbGV4psNdYN2o+eaXyAc2D1JM3Zz0xHqKoR
URwy2y13nGv3qzrjbPO55uyTn0KBG6jZRoFi6zsAdw1bJc0qBzDE3ca5LuLTKZ/PEqvtIptm
gQefv80bgXXQjmFTuyOEkOxLLv6uoobDxb29Lkf0=</CipherValue>
        </CipherData>
        <ReferenceList>
          <DataReference URI="#xdn_id0"/>
        </ReferenceList>
      </EncryptedKey>
    </wsse:Security>
  </soapenv:Header>
  <soapenv:Body>
    <EncryptedData Id="#xdn_id0">
....
```

Figure 13.7 illustrates how the different standards can be combined to send a SAML assertion, which is an authentication assertion, with a SOAP message. The SOAP header contains a WS-Security header, which in turn contains the SAML assertion. To prevent any modifications while in transit and to bind the assertion to the message, an XML digital signature is used, which is also contained in the security header. This signature not only guarantees integrity, it also serves to authenticate the SAML assertion in the context of the message: without such a signature, the assertion could have been obtained by someone eavesdropping on the message traffic and then attached to his or her own messages.

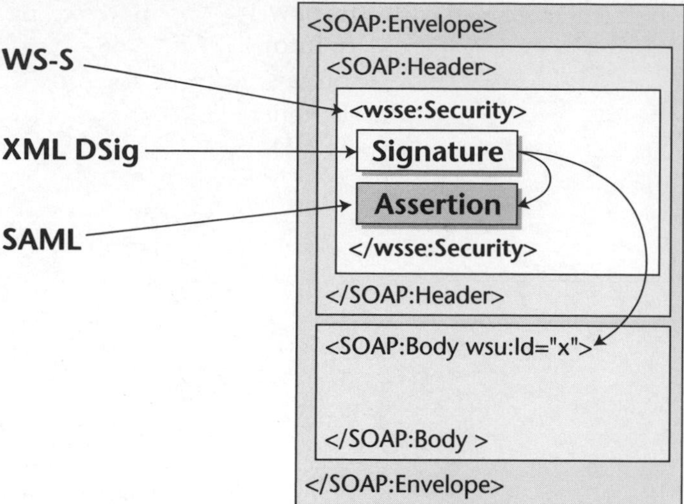

Figure 13.7 Standards in concert.

Summary

For all practical purposes, security should be seen as a trade-off between risks and cost. This chapter has described the most important security standards relevant in the EJB world, including the J2EE view on Web Application security. You have encountered both declarative and programmatic security in EJB, and the security interoperability protocol CSIv2. Moreover, we have presented some important standards in the Web Services security world that will turn into standardized APIs in the near future.

CHAPTER

14

EJB Timers

All these years, what was lacking in the Enterprise JavaBeans standard was a decent scheduling mechanism. EJB 2.1 addresses this requirement by introducing the EJB timer service. In this chapter, we examine how to use the EJB timer service with different types of beans. We also provide a sample to walk you through a typical EJB timer development.

Scheduling

Scheduling functionality is required in many business applications. Various scenarios involving scheduling ensure that certain code gets executed at a given point in time. For instance, imagine a system that handles huge loads during the peak hours and during the off hours wants to run maintenance chores such as cleaning the file system of temporary files, generating the activity reports, cleaning the databases, preparing audit reports of access from various parties to its subsystems, and so on. These tasks can be carried out automatically by scheduling them to run during the off hours. This way your IT professional will not be pressed for resources during the peak traffic hours and also will be able to perform routine maintenance tasks and all around use the resources better.

In many other similar situations scheduling can help—workflows are another example. Simply put, a workflow is a set of activities, each of which is scheduled to run at a specific time or when a conditional criteria is met. For example, consider a reservation workflow rule that ensures that if the customer does not guarantee a reservation with credit card within 24 hours, the reservation is cancelled, and an e-mail notification is sent to the customer's travel agent and also possibly to the customer. There are numerous ways in which scheduling can help you implement such use cases.

Scheduling techniques have been around for many years in the computer science world. UNIX-based operating systems have supported job-scheduling mechanisms through system services such as *Cron* for a long time. Cron is basically a daemon that uses the system clock to facilitate the scheduling of jobs for execution at any given time of day. Scheduled jobs or Cron jobs, as they might be called, are UNIX commands or scripts that you want to run on a particular schedule. These jobs are maintained in Cron tables. Authorized UNIX users create/edit these Cron tables, which are then read by the Cron daemon *almost* every minute to start these jobs. The Cron table is an ASCII text file consisting of entries for Cron jobs, each specified with a UNIX command to execute and its scheduled time of execution in terms of hours and minutes, day of week, day of month, and month. Another variant of the Cron service is the *At* utility. While Cron enables you to schedule a repetitive task, At lets you schedule a one-time task for execution. UNIX also supports another form of scheduling through its *Batch* utility. Batch executes a set of tasks instead of a single task; however, it is similar to At in that it executes only once.

Windows-based operating systems support a similar kind of functionality through the *At* utility, which basically takes the information about the command or batch program to execute, time to execute, and other such parameters, and schedules the job for execution. Linux too offers system-level scheduling capabilities quite similar to those of UNIX.

Hence, almost all the operating-system environments today support sophisticated scheduling mechanisms. It should come as no surprise that developers would want similar scheduling functionality in their programming platforms to be able to exploit scheduling techniques in different applications—EJB developers are no different.

EJB and Scheduling

If you think scheduling operating system commands and programs is powerful, think how powerful it would be to be able to schedule execution of parts of your code or methods on your components. Yes, that is what scheduling with EJB should allow us to do. EJB containers should let us schedule a given method to run at a particular point in time so that the container can call back that method once the scheduled time has elapsed. This capability can open a whole new world of possibilities with EJB.

THE JAVA PLATFORM AND SCHEDULING

The Java language platform has been providing basic scheduling capabilities since J2SE 1.3 via *java.util.Timer* and *java.util.TimerTask* APIs. Together, these are termed as the Java Timer APIs. Java Timer APIs provide a programming model in which your schedulable task, or in other words the worker class, will extend the *TimerTask* abstract class. *TimerTask* implements *Runnable* and it represents a Java class that can be scheduled to run once or repeatedly by a timer. Thus, the action you need to perform when the timer calls your class should be put in the *run()* method of your *TimerTask* implementation.

The *Timer* object provides methods that you can use to schedule *TimerTask* objects for future execution in a background thread. Corresponding to each *Timer* object is a single background thread that is used to execute all the timer's tasks sequentially. Thus, if you used the same *Timer* object to schedule multiple timer tasks and if a certain timer task takes longer than expected to complete, the subsequent timer task will be held up until the previous one completes.

The *Timer* object, and hence the corresponding background thread, is kept alive by the JVM as long as there is an outstanding task to complete. Once all the tasks associated with the given *Timer* object are done executing, the JVM will kill the thread and release the *Timer* object in the subsequent garbage collection cycle. By default, your application could be held up as long as the timer is alive. This means that if you have a repeated timer task, your application can theoretically keep running forever. To get around this, you can create a *Timer* object that uses a daemon thread so that it does not keep the application from terminating.

An important point to understand about scheduling on the Java platform is that due to the inherent nature of Java, it is impossible to guarantee that the timer will execute a given timer task at exactly the specified moment. In other words, Java does not provide us with a consistently met real-time guarantee, the main reason being that the implementation of thread scheduling, on which job scheduling is dependent, is inconsistent across various JVMs. The *Timer* object schedules tasks via the *Object.wait()* mechanism, and so the exact moment at which the JVM wakes up the timer task objects is dependent on JVM's thread scheduling policy and such factors. Garbage collection adds yet another parameter and further makes job scheduling on the Java platform non-deterministic.

Thus, the Java Timer API is more than enough for simple scheduling activities for non-managed Java applications. If you need more sophisticated functionality, you can use scheduling frameworks, such as Quartz, to meet those needs. There is also another timer API in Java: the JMX (Java Management Extensions) timer API. However, it is very tightly coupled with the JMX framework and hence, not suitable for generic purposes.

Unfortunately though, scheduling support for EJB was not available until EJB 2.1. However, the need for this kind of capability was always there and so as a result, there are a variety of non-standard schedulers available for the J2EE platform today. In fact, quite a few projects we have worked on involved the use of these non-standard schedulers, such as the open-source Quartz scheduler or Sims Computing Flux Scheduler, due to lack of standard scheduler support in EJB container at the time.

The EJB Timer Service

EJB 2.1 supports scheduling through the container-managed EJB timer service. Developers interact with the EJB timer service through various timer service APIs. These APIs can be used for creating timers for specified dates and periods. You can also create timers scheduled to expire at recurring intervals. As soon as the date or period specified for the timer is reached, the timer expires and the container notifies your bean of the timer expiration by calling a specific callback method on the EJB. This timer method will implement the logic that you want to execute upon timer expiration(s). Figure 14.1 describes the high-level interaction between the timer service and an EJB interested in receiving timer notifications.

Enterprise beans interested in receiving timer notifications through the callback methods will register themselves to the timer service. Stateless session beans, entity beans, and message-driven beans can all receive timed notifications from the container. Timers cannot be created for stateful session beans; however, future versions of EJB are expected to support stateful session bean timers as well. The timer created for an entity bean is associated with an entity bean's identity and so when the entity bean is removed the container will remove all the timers associated with the bean.

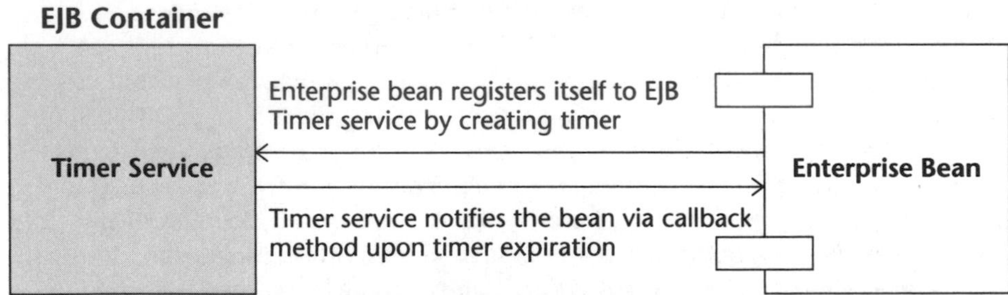

Figure 14.1 Interaction between the timer service and EJB.

Timer Service API

The timer service API consists of four interfaces—*javax.ejb.TimedObject*, *javax.ejb.Timer*, *javax.ejb.TimerHandle*, and *javax.ejb.TimerService*.

javax.ejb.TimerService

This interface provides enterprise bean components access to the container's timer service. It provides various *createTimer()* methods to create timers and thereby register with container timer service for timer notifications. Using these *createTimer()* methods you can create mainly four types of timers, depending on your needs.

- Recurrent expiration timers whose first expiration occurs at a given point in time as specified by the *Date* argument to *createTimer()* method and the subsequent timer expirations occur at interval durations specified in milliseconds.
- One-time expiration timers whose first and only expiration occurs at a given point in time as specified by the *Date* argument to *createTimer()* method.
- Recurrent expiration timers whose first expiration occurs after the specified number of milliseconds has elapsed and the subsequent timer expirations occur at interval durations specified in milliseconds.
- One-time expiration timers whose first and only expiration occurs after the specified number of milliseconds has elapsed.

Apart from various methods for creating timers, *TimerService* has made available a *getTimers()* method which retrieves all the timers associated with the given bean.

Source 14.1 shows the definition of the *TimerService* interface.

```
public interface javax.ejb.TimerService {
     public Timer createTimer(long duration, Serializable info)
          throws IllegalArgumentException, IllegalStateException,
EJBException;
     public Timer createTimer(long initialDuration, long
intervalDuration,
          Serializable info)
          throws IllegalArgumentException, IllegalStateException,
EJBException;
     public Timer createTimer(Date expiration, Serializable info)
          throws IllegalArgumentException, IllegalStateException,
EJBException;
```

Source 14.1 The javax.ejb.TimerService interface. *(continued)*

```
     public Timer createTimer(Date initialExpiration, long
intervalDuration,
          Serializable info)
          throws IllegalArgumentException, IllegalStateException,
EJBException;
     public Collection getTimers()
          throws IllegalStateException, EJBException;
}
```

Source 14.1 *(continued)*

javax.ejb.Timer

This interface represents a timer instance that was created through *TimerService*. Its methods provide information about the timer, such as the point in time when the next timer expiration is scheduled, the number of milliseconds that will elapse before the next scheduled timer expiration, and so on.

Also, this interface provides access to the timer information class through the *getInfo()* method. The timer information class has to be a *Serializable* instance, and it can be used as a means to provide application-specific information corresponding to the timer such as, for example, the actions bean will take upon timer expiration. This information class is written by the application provider and is passed as an argument to the respective *createTimer()* method in *TimerService*. If you do not want to provide a timer information object, pass null while creating the timer.

Finally, the *getHandle()* method retrieves the *Serializable* handle to the timer. This handle can be persisted and retrieved at a later time to obtain reference to the timer instance.

Source 14.2 shows the definition of the *Timer* interface.

```
public interface javax.ejb.Timer {
     public void cancel()
          throws IllegalStateException, NoSuchObjectLocalException,
EJBException;
     public long getTimeRemaining()
          throws IllegalStateException, NoSuchObjectLocalException,
EJBException;
     public Date getNextTimeout()
          throws IllegalStateException, NoSuchObjectLocalException,
EJBException;
     public Serializable getInfo()
```

Source 14.2 The javax.ejb.Timer interface.

```
        throws IllegalStateException, NoSuchObjectLocalException,
EJBException;
    public TimerHandle getHandle()
        throws IllegalStateException, NoSuchObjectLocalException,
EJBException;
}
```

Source 14.2 *(continued)*

javax.ejb.TimedObject

This interface contains a single method: *ejbTimeout()*. The container calls this callback method to notify the EJB of timer expiration. Therefore, for an EJB to receive notification from the container about its timer expiration, it should implement this interface and hence, implement the *ejbTimeout()* method. *ejbTimeout()* contains the logic that you want to execute upon timer expiration. The container passes a corresponding instance of *Timer* associated with the bean to *ejbTimeout()*.

Source 14.3 shows the definition of the *TimedObject* interface.

```
public interface javax.ejb.TimedObject {
    public void ejbTimeout(Timer timer);
}
```

Source 14.3 The javax.ejb.TimedObject interface.

javax.ejb.TimerHandle

This interface contains a single method, *getTimer()*, which retrieves the reference to *Timer* represented by the given handle. This method throws *NoSuchObjectException* if invoked for a timer that has already expired or cancelled.

Source 14.4 shows the definition of the *TimerHandle* interface.

```
public interface javax.ejb.TimerHandle
    extends Serializable {
    public Timer getTimer()
        throws IllegalStateException, NoSuchObjectException,    ⮐
EJBException;
}
```

Source 14.4 The javax.ejb.TimerHandle interface.

Durations in the timer API are specified in milliseconds, taking into consideration that the rest of the J2SE APIs use millisecond as the unit of time. However, do not expect the timers to expire with the millisecond precision given the incapability of the Java platform to support real-time notifications.

Interaction between the EJB and the Timer Service

It is clear that *TimerService* is the top-level API that allows you to create timers. The question is—how to get access to a *TimerService* instance? You can get hold of the *TimerService* instance through *EJBContext*. The *EJBContext* interface has been updated to include the *getTimerService()* method in EJB 2.1. Hence, within any business method in your bean, you can create a timer by getting the timer service instance through the EJB context object.

What happens if you create a timer from one of your EJB methods without implementing the *TimedObject* interface for that EJB? Check it out.

Figure 14.2 shows the sequence diagram of interaction between EJB and timer service.

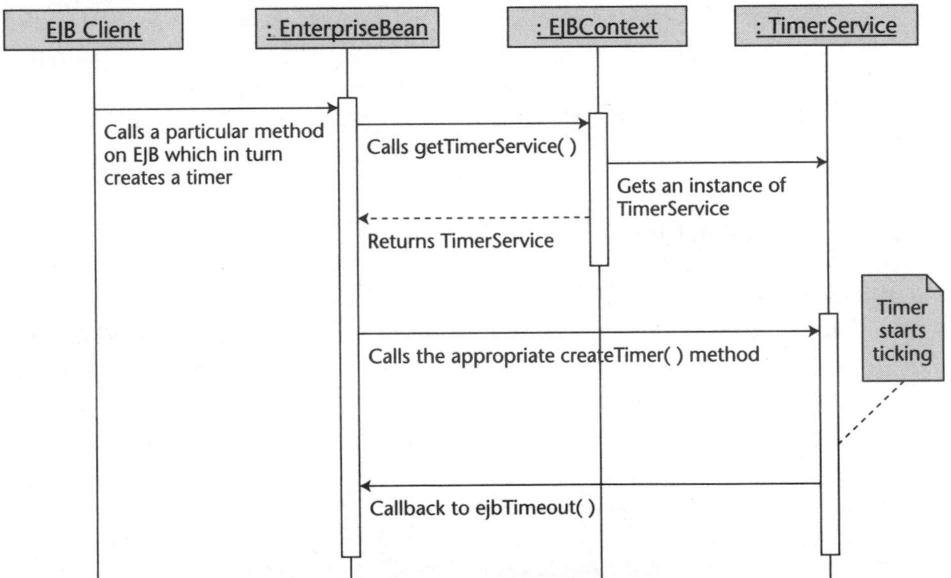

Figure 14.2 Sequence diagram of interaction between EJB and the timer service.

TIMERS AND TRANSACTIONS

The creation of timers is supported within transactions.

Therefore, if an enterprise bean method that creates the timer is executed as part of a transaction and if that transaction is rolled back, the timer creation is rolled back too. Similarly, if an enterprise bean method cancels the timer by calling *cancel()* on the *Timer* interface within a transaction and if that transaction is rolled back, the container rolls back the timer cancellation as well. The container restores the duration of the timer to the duration it would have had, had it not been rolled back.

***ejbTimeout()* can also be called within a transaction. Hence, if the transaction rolls back, the container will call *ejbTimeout()* again.**

Timer Example: CleanDayLimitOrdersEJB

Let us now examine the code for stateless session bean timers. Entity bean and message-driven bean timers are written exactly the same way as stateless session bean timers are. To understand this example, take into consideration an online securities trading system. The system allows the customer to place *limit* orders for a given security, say for example stocks, such that the buy or sell transaction for the given security can be limited to occur anytime during a day or anytime during the trading week or anytime until the end of the current month and so on so long as the buy/sell criteria specified by the customer is met. Limit orders are supported by most of the contemporary online securities trading systems. Now not all limit orders are executed since the criteria, mainly the price criteria, set by the customer could not be met during the specified limit period. Obviously, such limit orders should be removed upon expiration of limit periods.

Our example bean, *CleanDayLimitOrdersEJB*, demonstrates an elegant way of cleaning the trading database by removing all the limit orders that were not executed during the limit period. As per our scenario, a client application, *CleanDayLimitOrdersClient*, will invoke the *cleanPeriodicallyDayLimitOrders()* method on *CleanDayLimitOrdersEJB*. *cleanPeriodicallyDayLimitOrders()* creates a recurrent expiration timer based on the current date such that at the end of every trading day a timer expires and container callbacks to *ejbTimeout()* method takes place. For now, we are least concerned with the database logic and hence, this example code does not elaborate the database part.

Note that the source files for this example are available on the book's accompanying Web site wiley.com/compbooks/roman.

You can also implement the *CleanDayLimitOrdersEJB* functionality on the so-called *Order* entity bean, assuming that you have such an entity bean in your application. Each *Order* entity bean will need to create and associate a one-time expiration timer to itself upon creation. Also your *Order* entity bean class will implement the *TimedObject*. Thus, if the order's limit is day, the entity timer will expire at the market close of the current trading session; similarly, if the order limit is end of week, the timer will expire at the market close of the last trading session of the week, and so on. Once your *Order* entity bean is removed, the timer associated with it will also be removed. Hence, if the object model for such a securities trading system involves an *Order* entity bean, then associating timers with entity bean provides for an elegant solution.

The CleanDayLimitOrders EJB Remote Interface

First let us define our bean's remote interface. The code is shown in Source 14.5. Our remote interface defines a single business method, *cleanPeriodicallyDayLimitOrders()*, which we will implement in the enterprise bean class.

```
package examples;

import javax.ejb.EJBObject;
import java.rmi.RemoteException;

public interface CleanDayLimitOrders extends EJBObject {

   public void cleanPeriodicallyDayLimitOrders () throws 
RemoteException;
}
```

Source 14.5 The examples.CleanDayLimitOrders interface.

The CleanDayLimitOrders EJB Bean Class

Our bean implements *TimedObject* apart from *SessionBean* interface, since it is interested in receiving timer expiration notifications. Our bean class has one business method, *cleanPeriodicallyDayLimitOrders()*, which is responsible for cleaning the trading system database of expired day limit orders. The implementation of this method makes use of *java.util.TimeZone* and *java.util.Calendar* types to manipulate the time. It does various calculations to arrive at the number of milliseconds that should expire until the market close on the current day. This example takes into consideration the U.S. exchanges' market close time, which is 4 PM Eastern. Finally the method creates a recurrent expiration timer, whose subsequent expirations occur at an interval of 86,400,000 milliseconds (24 hours). The idea is that once the first timer is fired off sometime after 4 PM Eastern, the subsequent timers will fire off exactly 24 hours after that instant.

As noted earlier, *ejbTimeout()* has not been implemented in its entirety in that the database code has been omitted for brevity. Source 14.6 shows the *CleanDayLimitOrdersBean.java* code.

```
package examples;

import javax.ejb.*;
import java.util.Calendar;
import java.util.TimeZone;
import java.util.SimpleTimeZone;
import java.util.GregorianCalendar;
import java.util.Date;

public class CleanDayLimitOrdersBean implements SessionBean,
TimedObject {

     private SessionContext context;

     public void cleanPeriodicallyDayLimitOrders() {
          // Get hold of the eastern time zone assuming that the
securities are being
          // traded on NYSE and NASDAQ exchanges.
          String[] timezoneIDs = TimeZone.getAvailableIDs (-5 * 60
* 60 * 1000);

          SimpleTimeZone est = new SimpleTimeZone (-5 * 60 * 60 * 1000,
               timezoneIDs[0]);

          // Provide the rules for start and end days of daylight
savings time.
          est.setStartRule (Calendar.APRIL, 1, Calendar.SUNDAY,
2 * 60 * 60 * 1000);
          est.setEndRule (Calendar.OCTOBER, -1, Calendar.SUNDAY,
2 * 60 * 60 * 1000);

          // Get hold of a calendar instance for the eastern time zone.
          Calendar cal = new GregorianCalendar(est);

          // Set the calendar to the current time.
          cal.setTime (new Date ());

          // Calculate the difference between now and market
close i.e. 4 PM Eastern.
          int hourofday = cal.get (cal.HOUR_OF_DAY);
```

Source 14.6 The examples.CleanDayLimitOrdersBean class. *(continued)*

```
        int minuteofhour = cal.get (cal.MINUTE);

        // If this method is invoked after the market close,
then set the timer
        // expiration immediately i.e. start=0. Otherwise,
calculate the
        // milliseconds that needs to elapse until first timer
expiration.
        long start = 0;
        if (hourofday < 16)
        {
            int hourdiff = 16 - hourofday - 1;
            int mindiff = 60 - minuteofhour;

            start = (hourdiff * 60 * 60 * 1000) +
(mindiff * 60 * 1000);
        }

        // Finally, get hold of the timer service instance from
EJBContext object
        // and create the recurrent expiration timer.
        TimerService timerService = context.getTimerService();
        Timer timer = timerService.createTimer(start, 86400000, null);

        System.out.println("CleanDayLimitOrdersBean: Timer
created to first expire
            after " + start + " milliseconds.");
    }

    public void ejbTimeout(Timer timer) {

        System.out.println("CleanDayLimitOrdersBean: ejbTimeout
called.");

        // Put here the code for cleaning the database of day
limit orders that have
        // not been executed.
    }

    public void setSessionContext(SessionContext sc) {

        System.out.println("CleanDayLimitOrdersBean:
setSessionContext called.");
        context = sc;
    }

    public void ejbCreate() {
```

Source 14.6 *(continued)*

```
            System.out.println("CleanDayLimitOrdersBean: ejbCreate
called.");
      }

      public CleanDayLimitOrdersBean() {}
      public void ejbRemove() {}
      public void ejbActivate() {}
      public void ejbPassivate() {}
}
```

Source 14.6 *(continued)*

When trying this example, you might want to provide smaller values for both start and interval periods to immediately see the timer expiration results.

The CleanDayLimitOrders EJB Home Interface

To complete our timer session bean code, we must define a home interface. The home interface details how to create and destroy our *CleanDayLimitOrders* EJB object. The code for our home interface is shown in Source 14.7.

```
package examples;

import java.io.Serializable;
import java.rmi.RemoteException;
import javax.ejb.CreateException;
import javax.ejb.EJBHome;

public interface CleanDayLimitOrdersHome extends EJBHome {

    CleanDayLimitOrders create() throws RemoteException,
CreateException;
}
```

Source 14.7 The examples.CleanDayLimitOrdersHome interface.

The CleanDayLimitOrders EJB Deployment Descriptor

Now that we have implemented our bean, we need to define the deployment descriptor to let the container know of the requisite settings for our bean. The deployment descriptor settings we use are listed in Source 14.8.

```
<?xml version='1.0' encoding='UTF-8'?>
<ejb-jar
        xmlns="http://java.sun.com/xml/ns/j2ee"
        version="2.1"
        xmlns:xsi="http://www.w3.org/2001/XMLSchema-instance"
        xsi:schemaLocation="http://java.sun.com/xml/ns/j2ee
        http://java.sun.com/xml/ns/j2ee/ejb-jar_2_1.xsd">
    <display-name>CleanDayLimitOrdersEJB</display-name>
    <enterprise-beans>
        <session>
            <ejb-name>CleanDayLimitOrdersBean</ejb-name>
            <home>examples.CleanDayLimitOrdersHome</home>
            <remote>examples.CleanDayLimitOrders</remote>
            <ejb-class>examples.CleanDayLimitOrdersBean</ejb-class>
            <session-type>Stateless</session-type>
            <transaction-type>Bean</transaction-type>
            <security-identity>
                <use-caller-identity>
                </use-caller-identity>
            </security-identity>
        </session>
    </enterprise-beans>
</ejb-jar>
```

Source 14.8 The ejb-jar.xml.

The CleanDayLimitOrders EJB Client

Now that our bean is ready, we need to write the client. Our client is a typical EJB client. It gets a hold of the JNDI initial context, looks up the EJB home object, and creates the EJB remote object thereof. Finally, it invokes the *cleanPeriodicallyDayLimitOrders()* method on the EJB remote object. Source 14.9 shows the code for *CleanDayLimitOrdersClient.java.*

```
package examples;

import java.util.Properties;
import javax.naming.Context;
import javax.naming.InitialContext;
import javax.rmi.PortableRemoteObject;

public class CleanDayLimitOrdersClient {
     public static void main(String[] args) {
          try {
```

Source 14.9 The examples.CleanDayLimitOrdersClient class.

```
            Properties env = new Properties();
            env.put("java.naming.factory.initial",
                "com.sun.jndi.cosnaming.CNCtxFactory");
            env.put("java.naming.provider.url",
"iiop://localhost:3700");
            InitialContext ctxt = new InitialContext(env);

            Object objref = ctxt.lookup("CleanDayLimitOrdersBean");

            CleanDayLimitOrdersHome home = (CleanDayLimitOrdersHome)
                PortableRemoteObject.narrow(objref,
                    CleanDayLimitOrdersHome.class);

            CleanDayLimitOrders cleanDayLimitOrders = home.create();
            cleanDayLimitOrders.cleanPeriodicallyDayLimitOrders();

            System.out.println ("cleanPeriodicallyDayLimitOrders()
returned
                successfully. Take a look at the application
server log or console
                    for messages from bean.");

            cleanDayLimitOrders.remove();
        } catch (Exception ex) {
            System.err.println("Caught an unexpected exception!");
            ex.printStackTrace();
        }
    }
}
```

Source 14.9 *(continued)*

Running the Client

To run the client, look at the Ant scripts bundled along with this example. The following is the client-side output you will get upon running *CleanDayLimitOrdersClient*.

```
C:\MEJB3.0\Timer\CleanDayLimitOrders>asant run_client
cleanPeriodicallyDayLimitOrders() returned successfully.
Take a look at the appl
ication server log or console for messages from bean.
```

On the application server console, you should see the following output. Make sure to run your application server in verbose mode.

```
[#|2004-07-19T15:24:08.918-0400|INFO|sun-appserver-pe8.0.0_01|javax.enterprise.
system.stream.out|_ThreadID=23;|
CleanDayLimitOrdersBean: Timer created to first expire after 2160000
milliseconds.|#]

[#|2004-07-19T16:00:08.724-0400|INFO|sun-appserver-pe8.0.0_01|javax.enterprise.
system.stream.out|_ThreadID=24;|
CleanDayLimitOrdersBean: setSessionContext called.|#]

[#|2004-07-19T16:00:08.724-0400|INFO|sun-appserver-pe8.0.0_01|javax.enterprise.
system.stream.out|_ThreadID=24;|
CleanDayLimitOrdersBean: ejbCreate called.|#]

[#|2004-07-19T16:00:08.724-0400|INFO|sun-appserver-pe8.0.0_01|javax.enterprise.
system.stream.out|_ThreadID=24;|
CleanDayLimitOrdersBean: ejbTimeout called.|#]
```

Take a close look at the highlighted portions. You'll notice that our timer was first created at around 3:24 PM Eastern and the first timer was fired at 4:00:08 PM Eastern time. You should continue to get these notifications for as long as the enterprise bean is deployed and its respective J2EE application is running. Of course, the application server has to be running in order to receive these notifications.

Finally note that this output is for an EJB deployed on the reference implementation of J2EE 1.4.

We can generalize *CleanDayLimitOrdersEJB* further so that it can clean the end-of-week or end-of-month limit orders as well. For this, we can create multiple timers associated with our bean in a way that each of these timers expires at a different interval.

Now that we know how to develop EJB timers, let us take a look at some shortcomings of the EJB timer service.

Strengths and Limitations of EJB Timer Service

The EJB timer service has some obvious strengths with respect to other scheduling utilities and frameworks, in that:

- Scheduling semantics provided by the EJB timer service are platform independent. You can use platform-specific utilities such as Cron or At to schedule calls to an EJB client, which in turn calls a certain EJB method; and this will work just fine. However, there is a caveat to this approach. What do you do if your client needs to run on a different platform? You will now have to learn and work with the scheduling semantics of the new platform, which again may or may not satisfy your requirements.

- The EJB timer service lets you schedule the timers programmatically. Consider a scenario where EJB wants to create timers based on a certain request from a client. Without having a framework API, such as the one provided by the EJB timer service, it is hard to achieve this. More so if you were to use platform-specific utilities for scheduling calls to EJB methods, because then your EJB will require a way to schedule *platform* timers from within the EJB environment.
- Finally, the EJB timer service provides a standard interface to scheduling functionality as opposed to frameworks such as Flux or Quartz. This gives you one less thing to worry about when your application is required to support multiple J2EE platform products.

On the other hand, there is a lot of scope for the EJB timer service to improve further. Currently, it lacks the following two features:

- Support for declaration of timer intervals in the deployment descriptors is not available today. As a result, the developer has to embed the timer expiration period and the subsequent expiration interval information in the EJB bean class. This restricts the ability of the developer to declaratively provide timer-related information at the time of deployment.
- There is not much flexibility in the way the timers could be specified today. Take our example into consideration. Since the only unit of time that the timer APIs accept is milliseconds, we had to write the logic for converting the hours and minutes into milliseconds in order to create the timer for the *CleanDayLimitOrders* EJB. Had the timer API given a provision for creating timers wherein the periods could be specified in terms of hours, days, or months, it would have been much more powerful and simpler to use.

  Also, we cannot create timers that would expire on given days of the week and not on other days. Again, take *CleanDayLimitOrders* EJB into consideration. Here, we actually want a timer that would expire after 4 PM Eastern every day from Monday through Friday. We do not want our timer to expire on Saturdays and Sundays. However, because there is no mechanism to specify this level of finer-grained scheduling information to the EJB timer service right now, we will have to add this logic in our code. Our implementation does not have this but a real trading system should have the logic in place to avoid hitting the database when the timer expiration occurs on Saturdays, Sundays, and other non-trading days (such as public holidays).

Our hope is that in the subsequent EJB specifications, these features will be added.

Summary

In this chapter we provided a complete overview of using the EJB timer service. We learned that although the EJB timer service is simple to use and very helpful for implementing certain scenarios, it has some shortcomings, which should be addressed in the upcoming EJB specifications.

In the next chapter, we discuss an advanced topic—entity bean relationships. So sit up straight and read on!

CHAPTER

15

BMP and CMP Relationships

In previous chapters, we looked at how to build entity beans using BMP and CMP. In this chapter, we'll heat things up and learn about *relationships* between data. Examples of relationships include an order having one or more line items, a student registering for a course, and a person having an address. These relationships need to be defined and maintained for advanced data models.

In this chapter, we'll learn about the following relationship topics:

- Cardinality
- Directionality
- Aggregation versus composition and cascading deletes
- Recursive, circular, and lazily loaded relationships
- Referential integrity
- Accessing relationships from client code through collections
- Implementing each of the preceding topics using *both* CMP and BMP

If these concepts are new to you, don't worry—you'll be an expert on them shortly.

To help you understand the concepts and to keep things brief, we'll use a bit of pseudo-code in this chapter. If you would like a complete example of code that you can copy and paste into your deployment illustrating relationships, download the book's source code from the accompanying Web site at wiley.com/compbooks/roman.

The CMP and BMP Difference

Relationships in EJB are implemented quite differently for CMP and for BMP. BMP entity beans manage relationships explicitly in the bean itself. You need to write a good deal of scaffolding code to maintain the relationship. At the high level, your BMP entity bean looks like this:

```
public class OrderBean implements EntityBean {
 // private fields
 // get/set methods
 // code to manage relationships in ejbXXX methods
}
```

With CMP, you *declare* the way you would like your relationships to work in your deployment descriptor. The container then *generates* all the relationship code you need when the container subclasses your entity bean. At the high level, your deployment descriptor looks like this:

```
<ejb-jar>

<enterprise-beans>
     ... define enterprise beans ...
</enterprise-beans>

<relationships>
     ... define EJB relationships ...
</relationships>

</ejb-jar>
```

Let's explore what goes into the preceding comments by tackling each relationship topic in detail.

Cardinality

Our first relationship topic is *cardinality*. Cardinality specifies how many instances of data can participate in a relationship. There are three flavors of cardinality:

- **One-to-one (1:1) relationships,** such as the relationship between an employee and his home address. Each employee has exactly one home address, and each home address has exactly one employee.
- **One-to-many (1:N) relationships,** such as the relationship between a manager and his employees. Each manager can have many employees working for him, but each employee can have only one manager.
- **Many-to-many (M:N) relationships** such as the relationship between an employee and an e-mail list. Each employee can be subscribed to many e-mail lists, and each e-mail list can have many employees subscribed.

Just to get you thinking: Why don't we talk about many-to-one relationships?

Figure 15.1 illustrates the three flavors of cardinality. Let's look at how to code each type of relationship for both BMP and CMP.

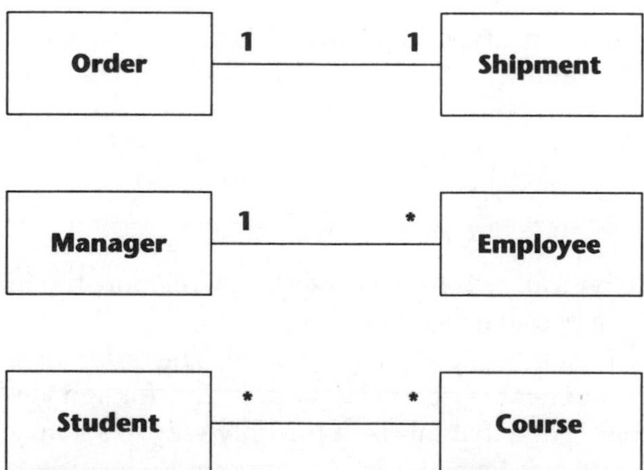

Figure 15.1 The three flavors of cardinality.

IMPLEMENTING RELATIONSHIPS IN SESSION BEANS

Session beans can perform persistence that involves relationships, just like CMP and BMP entity beans can. If you are familiar with traditional procedural programming, programming on the Microsoft platform, or programming that involves servlets or JSP technology talking to a database via JDBC, the session bean approach is quite analogous.

You can use a *stateful session bean* just like an entity bean; the only difference is that with a stateful session bean, you expose methods to a client for loading and storing data, and the client controls when the bean is loaded and stored by calling those methods. In this case, all of the best practices for relationship persistence that apply to BMP entity beans apply to stateful session beans that use JDBC.

You can also use a *stateless session bean* to perform persistence that involves relationships. Stateless session beans do not hold state and therefore do not have an identity, so you can't treat a stateless session bean like an entity bean. You need to use the stateless session bean as a *service* to read and write rows to and from the database, marshaling the state back to the client on each method call. In essence, the stateless session bean serves as a stateless persistence engine, and the relationship code needs to be custom coded.

In general, if you have complex relationships, we do not recommend the session bean approach, due to all the manual coding. The entity bean value proposition really shines through when it comes to relationships.

1:1 Relationships

In a one-to-one relationship, each constituent can have at most one relationship with the other constituent. Examples of one-to-one relationships include:

- Person:Address
- Car:Windshield
- Order:Shipment

One-to-one relationships are typically set up by a *foreign key* relationship in the database. Figure 15.2 shows a possible database setup.

In Figure 15.2, the order has a relationship with a shipment. The order table has a foreign key, which is the shipment table's primary key. This foreign key is the link between the two tables. Note that this isn't the only way to set up a one-to-one relationship. You could also have the shipment point to the order.

OrderPK	OrderName	Shipment ForeignPK
12345	Software Order	10101

ShipmentPK	City	ZipCode
10101	Austin	78727

Figure 15.2 A possible one-to-one cardinality database schema.

Implementing 1:1 Relationships Using BMP

The following code shows how to implement a one-to-one relationship using BMP:

```
public class OrderBean implements EntityBean {
 private String orderPK;
 private String orderName;
 private Shipment shipment; // EJB local object stub

 public Shipment getShipment() {  return shipment; }
 public void setShipment(Shipment s) {  this.shipment = s;}

 ...

 public void ejbLoad() {
  // 1: SQL SELECT Order.  This also retrieves the
  //    shipment foreign key.
  //
  // 2: JNDI lookup of ShipmentHome
  //
  // 3: Call ShipmentHome.findByPrimaryKey(), passing
  //    in the shipment foreign key
 }
 public void ejbStore() {
  // 1: Call shipment.getPrimaryKey() to retrieve
  //    the Shipment foreign key
  //
  // 2: SQL UPDATE Order.  This also stores the
  //    Shipment foreign key.
 }
}
```

As with all BMP entity beans, we must define our SQL statements in our bean. See Chapter 6 for more on this. The special relationship management code is in bold.

The relationship management code is necessary only at the instant we transform our bean to and from relational data. It is necessary because we can't just persist a stub, as we can with our other fields (such as a String). If we did persist a stub, and (by some miracle) that worked, it would look like a bit-blob in the foreign key column. That bit-blob foreign key would not match up to the primary key in the shipment table.

Here is an explanation for what's happening in our bean:

- Our *ejbLoad()* method loads the database data of the order, and part of that data is a foreign key to the shipment. We need to transform that foreign key into a stub to a shipment bean. Therefore we need to perform a JNDI lookup of the shipment home and then call a finder method, passing in the foreign key. This gives us a stub, and we can then call business methods on the shipment.
- Our *ejbStore()* method stores the database data for the order, and part of that data is a foreign key to the shipment. We need to transform the shipment stub into a foreign key. Therefore, we need to call *getPrimaryKey()* on the shipment stub. This gives us our foreign key, and we can then perform the SQL.

Implementing 1:1 Relationships Using CMP

The following code shows how to implement that same one-to-one relationship using CMP:

```
public abstract class OrderBean implements EntityBean {
 // no fields

 public abstract Shipment getShipment();
 public abstract void setShipment(Shipment s);

 ...

 public void ejbLoad() { }     // Empty
 public void ejbStore() { }    // Empty
}
```

As with all CMP entity beans, we define our get/set methods as abstract methods and have no fields. The container implements these methods (and defines the fields) when the container subclasses our bean (see Chapter 7).

What's exciting is that our *ejbLoad()* and *ejbStore()* methods are free of any scaffolding code because the container generates all that scaffolding code for us. We do need to specify the relationship in the deployment descriptor, and we do so as follows:

```
<ejb-jar xmlns="http://java.sun.com/xml/ns/j2ee" version="2.1"
xmlns:xsi=http://www.w3.org/2001/XMLSchema-instance
         xsi:schemaLocation="http://java.sun.com/xml/ns/j2ee
         http://java.sun.com/xml/ns/j2ee/ejb-jar_2_1.xsd">

 <enterprise-beans>
 ...
 </enterprise-beans>

 <relationships>

  <!-- This declares a relationship -->
  <ejb relation>

   <!-- The nickname we're giving this relationship -->
   <ejb-relation-name>Order-Shipment</ejb-relation-name>

   <!--
    This declares the 1st half of the relationship
    (the Order side)
   -->
   <ejb-relationship-role>

    <!-- The nickname we're giving this half of the relationship -->
    <ejb-relationship-role-name>
     order-spawns-shipment
    </ejb-relationship-role-name>

    <!-- The Cardinality of this half of the relationship -->
    <multiplicity>One</multiplicity>

    <!--
     The name of the bean corresponding to this
     half of the relationship
    -->
    <relationship-role-source>
     <ejb-name>Order</ejb-name>
    </relationship-role-source>

    <!--
     Recall that a CMP entity bean has an abstract get/set
     method for the relationship.  We need to tell the
     container which get/set method corresponds to this
     relationship, so that the container can generate the
     appropriate scaffolding code when sub-classing our bean.
     That is the purpose of this element, which is called the
```

```
     container-managed relationship (CMR) field.  The value
     of the CMR field should be the name of your get/set
     method, but without the get/set, and with a slight
     change in capitalization.  getShipment() becomes shipment.
    -->
    <cmr-field><cmr-field-name>shipment</cmr-field-name></cmr-field>
   </ejb-relationship-role>

   <!--
    This declares the 2nd half of the relationship
    (the Shipment side)
   -->
   <ejb-relationship-role>
    <ejb-relationship-role-name>
     shipment-fulfills-order
    </ejb-relationship-role-name>
    <multiplicity>One</multiplicity>
    <relationship-role-source>
     <ejb-name>Shipment</ejb-name>
    </relationship-role-source>
   </ejb-relationship-role>
  </ejb-relation>
 </relationships></ejb-jar>
```

The deployment descriptor should be self-explanatory. After we write the proprietary descriptor that maps CMP fields to columns, we will have supplied enough information to the container that its tools can generate any necessary relationship code, such as the code we saw in the BMP example.

1:N Relationships

A one-to-many relationship is one of the more common relationships you'll see in your object model. This is because one-to-one relationships are often combined into a single data object, instead of having a relationship between two separate data objects. Examples of one-to-many relationships include:

- Order:LineItems
- Customer:Orders
- Company:Employees

One-to-many relationships are also typically set up by a foreign key relationship in the database. Figure 15.3 shows a possible database setup.

In Figure 15.3, the company has a relationship with many employees. The company has a vector of line-item foreign keys stored as a bit-blob in the database. We need a vector because we have a relationship with many employees, not just one employee.

The approach shown in Figure 15.3 is not ideal, because it's very nasty to deal with bit-blobs in the database. Queries and reporting become challenging, as databases were not meant to handle relationships in this way. Figure 15.4 shows an alternative.

In Figure 15.4, each employee has a foreign key, which is the company table's primary key. Thus, the employees are pointing back to their company. This may seem backwards if we want to get from the company to the employees. It works, however, because the database doesn't care—it is a flat structure without a sense of direction. You can still construct queries that get from the company to employees.

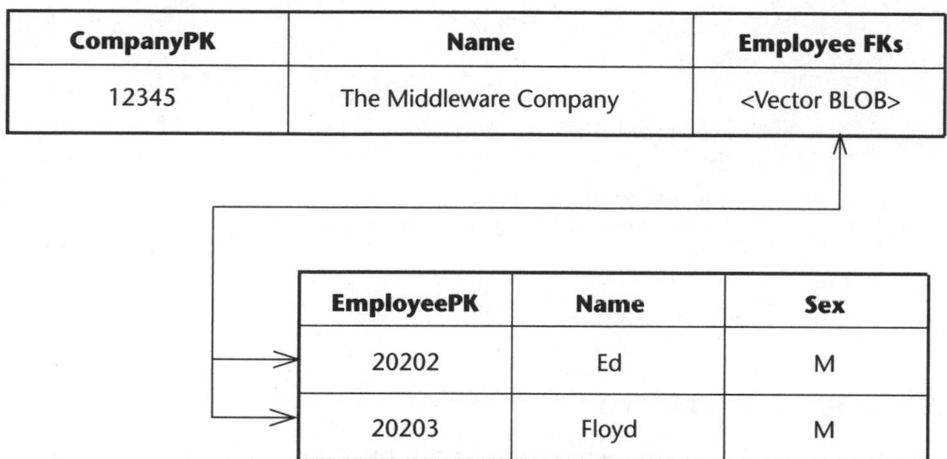

CompanyPK	Name	Employee FKs
12345	The Middleware Company	<Vector BLOB>

EmployeePK	Name	Sex
20202	Ed	M
20203	Floyd	M

Figure 15.3 A possible one-to-many cardinality database schema.

CompanyPK	Name
12345	The Middleware Company

EmployeePK	Name	Sex	Company
20202	Ed	M	12345
20203	Floyd	M	12345

Figure 15.4 Another one-to-many cardinality database schema.

Implementing 1:N Relationships Using BMP

The following code shows how to implement a one-to-many relationship using BMP:

```
public class CompanyBean implements EntityBean {
 private String companyPK;
 private String companyName;
 private Vector employees;      // EJB object stubs

 public Collection getEmployees() {  return employees; }
 public void setEmployees(Collection e) {
  this.employees = (Vector) e;
 }

 ...

 public void ejbLoad() {
  // 1: SQL SELECT Company
  // 2: JNDI lookup of EmployeeHome
  // 3: Call EmployeeHome.findByCompany(companyPK)
 }
 public void ejbStore() {
  // 2: SQL UPDATE Company
}
```

The code works as follows:

- A one-to-many relationship has a Vector of stubs, rather than a single stub. Our get/set method gets and sets this Vector (a Vector is a Collection).
- Our *ejbLoad()* method is responsible for loading the company state, as well as loading the relationships to employees. How can we achieve this? Remember that the employee table contains the foreign key relationships to the company, not the reverse. Therefore it is natural for the employee bean to access that relationship data, not the company bean. Thus, we do not deal with foreign keys in our bean; we let the employee bean deal with them. We do so by calling a finder method on the employee local home object. That finder method locates each employee that is a member of this company and returns a collection of stubs to us. Note that this causes a second SQL statement to be executed.
- Our *ejbStore()* method is extremely straightforward. Since our *ejbLoad()* method is not responsible for dealing with foreign keys, neither is our *ejbStore()* method. It doesn't even know about the relationship. The employee (not the company) has an *ejbStore()* that persists foreign keys to the company.

If you're good at SQL, you might have noticed that in our example, if we really wanted to do so, we could load both the company and the foreign keys for our employee in one SQL statement. But this would not help us, because we would still need to transform those foreign keys into stubs. We'd need to call *EmployeeHome.findByPrimaryKey()* for each found key, which would generate even more SQL.

Implementing 1:N Relationships Using CMP

The following code shows how to implement a one-to-many relationship using CMP:

```
public abstract class CompanyBean implements EntityBean {
 // no fields

 public abstract Collection getEmployees();
 public abstract void setEmployees(Collection employees);

 ...

 public void ejbLoad() { }    // Empty
 public void ejbStore() { }   // Empty
}
```

Our *ejbLoad()* and *ejbStore()* methods are free of any scaffolding code. The relationships are specified in the deployment descriptor as follows:

```
<ejb-jar xmlns="http://java.sun.com/xml/ns/j2ee" version="2.1"
         xmlns:xsi=http://www.w3.org/2001/XMLSchema-instance
         xsi:schemaLocation="http://java.sun.com/xml/ns/j2ee
         http://java.sun.com/xml/ns/j2ee/ejb-jar_2_1.xsd">
 <enterprise-beans>
 ...
 </enterprise-beans>

 <relationships>
  <ejb-relation>
   <ejb-relation-name>Company-Employees</ejb-relation-name>
   <ejb-relationship-role>
    <ejb-relationship-role-name>
     Company-Employs-Employees
    </ejb-relationship-role-name>
    <multiplicity>One</multiplicity>
    <relationship-role-source>
     <ejb-name>Company</ejb-name>
    </relationship-role-source>
    <!--
```

```
     When you have a relationship with more than one object, you
     can use either a java.util.Collection or a java.util.Set.
     We need to identify which one we're using.  How do you choose
     between a Collection and a Set?  A Collection can contain
     duplicates, whereas a Set cannot.  This needs to match up to
     your bean's get/set methods.
    -->
    <cmr-field>
     <cmr-field-name>employees</cmr-field-name>
     <cmr-field-type>java.util.Collection</cmr-field-type>
    </cmr-field>
   </ejb-relationship-role>

   <ejb-relationship-role>
    <ejb-relationship-role-name>
     Employees-WorkAt-Company
    </ejb-relationship-role-name>
    <multiplicity>Many</multiplicity>
    <relationship-role-source>
     <ejb-name>Employee</ejb-name>
    </relationship-role-source>
   </ejb-relationship-role>
  </ejb-relation>
 </relationships>
</ejb-jar>
```

As you can see, this is much simpler than BMP. If you understood the deployment descriptor for a one-to-one relationship described earlier in this chapter, then you should be able to grasp this one fairly easily.

Relationships with CMP can perform much better than their BMP equivalents. To load a one-to-many relationship with BMP, we need to perform two SQL statements: We need to *ejbLoad()* the *"1"* side of the relationship and then *find()* the *"N"* side of the relationship.

This is an inherent downside to BMP; you are limited to performing SQL operations at the granularity of an entity bean. With CMP, if your container is good, you can optimize and tell the container to perform one gigantic SQL statement to load yourself and your relationships.

M:N Relationships

A many-to-many relationship is not as common as a one-to-many relationship but is still important. Examples of one-to-many relationships include the following:

- Student:Course
- Investor:MutualFund
- Stock:Portfolio

Many-to-many relationships are typically set up by an *association* table in the database. An association table contains foreign keys to two other tables. Figure 15.5 shows a possible database setup.

What's interesting about Figure 15.5 is that we've created a third table, called an Enrollment table, which models the relationship between a student and a course. The alternative to an association table is for each half of the relationship to have a vector of foreign keys to the other half, persisted as bit-blobs, which is nasty to deal with.

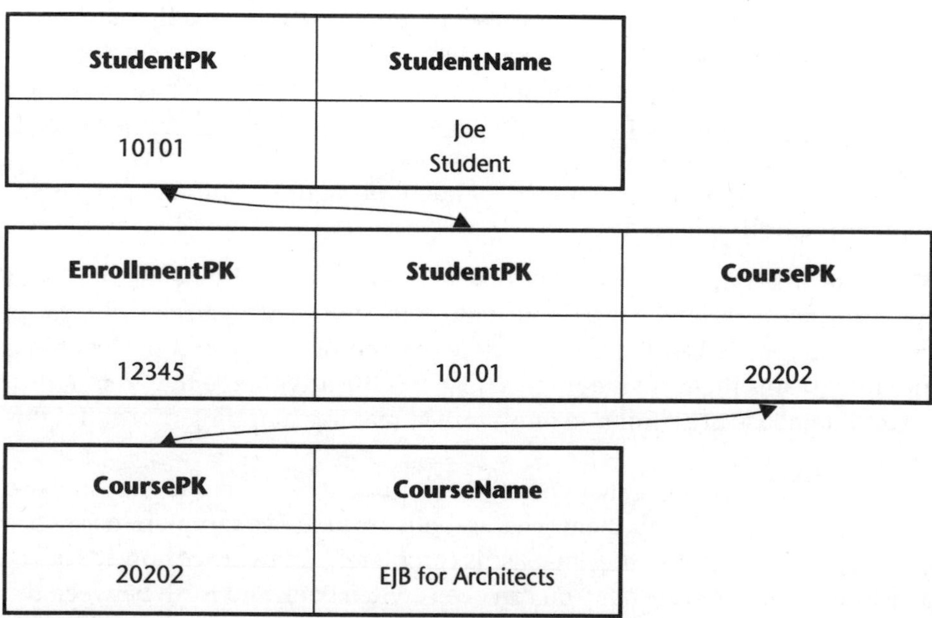

Figure 15.5 A possible many-to-many cardinality database schema.

Two Choices When Implementing M:N Relationships

When you model a many-to-many relationship using entity beans, you have two choices.

- **Fake the many-to-many relationship by introducing a third entity bean.** Our enrollment table could theoretically include other information as well, such as the date when the enrollment was made. It then makes sense to model the many-to-many relationship itself as an entity bean—an enrollment bean. The enrollment bean would map to the association table. This demonstrates a great modeling principle: When you have a many-to-many relationship, consider making the relationship itself a first-class citizen. When you do this, you are introducing an intermediary. That intermediary has two one-to-many relationships. Thus, we have effectively reduced the many-to-many relationship problem into two one-to-many relationship problems!
- **Model the many-to-many relationship as a true many-to-many relationship.** If all you're doing is storing relationship information, you might not need to introduce a third entity bean. In this case, you have only two entity beans, each representing half the relationship. Each entity bean would contain a Collection of the other entity bean. Each entity bean would be persisted to its own table, and each entity bean's Collection would be persisted to the relationships table. With BMP, you are in control of the JDBC, so you can map an entity bean to two tables very easily. With CMP, you're dependent on your container's persistence handling logic.

We prefer the fake approach, because it keeps your entity beans pure and clean. The fewer relationships you code into your entity beans, the more reusable your entity beans are in a variety of circumstances, and the less bloat your entity beans incur. This approach also has the advantage that your entity bean and database are similar to one another, making mapping more straightforward.

What's cool, however, is that your EJB components can map to the database any way you'd like to map them. That is, both approaches can map to association tables. This is because the database is completely unaware of how it's being represented in the middle tier. You can even switch back and forth between the fake and real approach if you'd like. And even if you're not using an association table but some other approach, you can still map your beans any way you'd like, assuming you're good with JDBC (in the BMP case) or assuming your container vendor has a good persistence engine (in the CMP case).

Let's see how to model both fake and real many-to-many relationships with both BMP and CMP.

Implementing Fake M:N Relationships Using BMP

The following code shows how to implement a many-to-many relationship as two one-to-many relationships using BMP:

```
public class StudentBean implements EntityBean {
 private String studentPK;
 private String studentName;
 ...
 public void ejbLoad()  {  // SQL SELECT Student }
 public void ejbStore() {  // SQL UPDATE Student }
}

public class CourseBean implements EntityBean {
 private String coursePK;
 private String courseName;
 ...
 public void ejbLoad()  {  // SQL SELECT Course }
 public void ejbStore() {  // SQL UPDATE Course }
}

public class EnrollmentBean implements EntityBean {
 private String enrollmentPK;
 private Student student;    // EJB local object stub
 private Course course;      // EJB local object stub

 public Course getCourse() {  return course; }
 public void setCourse(Course c) {  this.course = c;}

 public Student getStudent() {  return student; }
 public void setStudent(Student s) {  this.student = s; }

 ...

 public void ejbLoad() {
  // 1: SQL SELECT Enrollment.  This loads both the
  //    Enrollment plus the foreign keys to Student
  //    and Course.
  //
  // 2: JNDI lookup of StudentHome, CourseHome
  //
  // 3: Call findByPrimaryKey() on both the Student
  //    and Course homes, passing the foreign keys
 }
 public void ejbStore() {
  // 1: Call getPrimaryKey() on Student,Course.  This
  //    gives us our foreign keys.
  //
  // 2: SQL UPDATE Enrollment
 }
}
```

As usual, the relationship code is in **bold**. A brand-new entity bean, called enrollment, models the relationship between student and course. The enrollment bean keeps a stub for a course and a stub for a student and has get/set methods for clients to access those stubs. At the point in which object/relational mapping occurs, we transform those stubs to and from their foreign key database representation.

Implementing Fake M:N Relationships Using CMP

The following code shows how to implement a fake many-to-many relationship using CMP:

```
public abstract class StudentBean implements EntityBean {
 // no fields
 ...
 public void ejbLoad() { }     // Empty
 public void ejbStore() { }    // Empty
}

public abstract class CourseBean implements EntityBean {
 // no fields
 ...
 public void ejbLoad() { }     // Empty
 public void ejbStore() { }    // Empty
}

public abstract class EnrollmentBean implements EntityBean {
 // no fields

 public abstract Course getCourse();
 public abstract void setCourse(Course c);

 public abstract Student getStudent();
 public abstract void setStudent(Student s);

 ...

 public void ejbLoad() { }     // Empty
 public void ejbStore() { }    // Empty
}
```

Our *ejbLoad()* and *ejbStore()* methods are free of any scaffolding code. The relationships are specified in the deployment descriptor as follows:

```
<ejb-jar xmlns="http://java.sun.com/xml/ns/j2ee" version="2.1"
        xmlns:xsi=http://www.w3.org/2001/XMLSchema-instance
        xsi:schemaLocation="http://java.sun.com/xml/ns/j2ee
        http://java.sun.com/xml/ns/j2ee/ejb-jar_2_1.xsd">
 <enterprise-beans>
 ...
```

```
  </enterprise-beans>

  <relationships>
   <ejb-relation>
    <ejb-relation-name>Enrollment-Student</ejb-relation-name>
    <ejb-relationship-role>
     <ejb-relationship-role-name>
      Enrollments-AreRegisteredBy-Student
     </ejb-relationship-role-name>
     <multiplicity>Many</multiplicity>
     <relationship-role-source>
      <ejb-name>Enrollment</ejb-name>
     </relationship-role-source>
     <cmr-field><cmr-field-name>student</cmr-field-name></cmr-field>
    </ejb-relationship-role>

    <ejb-relationship-role>
     <ejb-relationship-role-name>
      Student-Has-Enrollments
     </ejb-relationship-role-name>
     <multiplicity>One</multiplicity>
     <relationship-role-source>
      <ejb-name>Student</ejb-name>
     </relationship-role-source>
    </ejb-relationship-role>
   </ejb-relation>

   <ejb-relation>
    <ejb-relation-name>Enrollment-Course</ejb-relation-name>
    <ejb-relationship-role>
     <ejb-relationship-role-name>
      Enrollments-AreRegistrationsFor-Course
     </ejb-relationship-role-name>
     <multiplicity>Many</multiplicity>
     <relationship-role-source>
      <ejb-name>Enrollment</ejb-name>
     </relationship-role-source>
     <cmr-field><cmr-field-name>course</cmr-field-name></cmr-field>
    </ejb-relationship-role>

    <ejb-relationship-role>
     <ejb-relationship-role-name>
      Course-Has-Enrollments
     </ejb-relationship-role-name>
     <multiplicity>One</multiplicity>
     <relationship-role-source>
      <ejb-name>Course</ejb-name>
     </relationship-role-source>
    </ejb-relationship-role>
   </ejb-relation>
  </relationships>
</ejb-jar>
```

As you can see from the preceding deployment descriptor, we model our fake many-to-many relationship as two many-to-one relationships (one for each bean in the relationship). A many-to-one relationship is conceptually the same as a one-to-many relationship, and we learned how to model a one-to-many relationship with CMP earlier.

Implementing True M:N Relationships Using BMP

The following code shows how to implement a true many-to-many relationship using BMP:

```
public class StudentBean implements EntityBean {
 private String studentPK;
 private String name;
 private Vector courses;     // EJB object stubs

 public Collection getCourses() {  return courses; }
 public void setCourses(Collection c) {  this.courses = c;}

 ...

 public void ejbLoad() {
  // 1: SQL SELECT Student
  // 2: JNDI lookup of CourseHome
  // 3: Call CourseHome.findByStudent(studentPK)
 }
 public void ejbStore() {
  // SQL UPDATE Student
}

public class Course implements EntityBean {
 private String coursePK;
 private String name;
 private Vector students;     // EJB object stubs

 public Collection getStudents() {  return students; }
 public void setStudents(Collection s) {  this.students = s;}

 ...

 public void ejbLoad() {
  // 1: SQL SELECT Course
  // 2: JNDI lookup of StudentHome
  // 3: Call StudentHome.findByCourse(coursePK)
 }
 public void ejbStore() {
  // SQL UPDATE Course
 }
```

The relationship code is in **bold**. As you can see, all we've done to model a true many-to-many relationship is to code a one-to-many relationship for each bean in the relationship. This code is similar to the code presented when we discussed one-to-many relationships.

Implementing True M:N Relationships Using CMP

The following code shows how to implement a true many-to-many relationship using CMP:

```
public abstract class StudentBean implements EntityBean {
 // no fields

 public abstract Collection getCourses();
 public abstract void setCourses(Collection courses);

 ...

 public void ejbLoad() { }    // Empty
 public void ejbStore() { }   // Empty
}

public abstract class CourseBean implements EntityBean {
 // no fields

 public abstract Collection getStudents();
 public abstract void setStudents(Collection students);

 ...

 public void ejbLoad() { }    // Empty
 public void ejbStore() { }   // Empty
}
```

Our *ejbLoad()* and *ejbStore()* methods are free of any scaffolding code. The relationships are specified in the deployment descriptor as follows:

```
<ejb-jar xmlns="http://java.sun.com/xml/ns/j2ee" version="2.1"
        xmlns:xsi=http://www.w3.org/2001/XMLSchema-instance
        xsi:schemaLocation="http://java.sun.com/xml/ns/j2ee
        http://java.sun.com/xml/ns/j2ee/ejb-jar_2_1.xsd">
 <enterprise-beans>
 ...
 </enterprise-beans>

 <relationships>
  <ejb-relation>
   <ejb-relation-name>Student-Course</ejb-relation-name>
```

```
    <ejb-relationship-role>
     <ejb-relationship-role-name>
      Students-EnrollIn-Courses
     </ejb-relationship-role-name>
     <multiplicity>Many</multiplicity>
     <relationship-role-source>
      <ejb-name>Student</ejb-name>
     </relationship-role-source>
     <cmr-field>
      <cmr-field-name>courses</cmr-field-name>
      <cmr-field-type>java.util.Collection</cmr-field-type>
     </cmr-field>
    </ejb-relationship-role>

    <ejb-relationship-role>
     <ejb-relationship-role-name>
      Courses-HaveEnrolled-Students
     </ejb-relationship-role-name>
     <multiplicity>Many</multiplicity>
     <relationship-role-source>
      <ejb-name>Course</ejb-name>
     </relationship-role-source>
     <cmr-field>
      <cmr-field-name>students</cmr-field-name>
      <cmr-field-type>java.util.Collection</cmr-field-type>
     </cmr-field>
    </ejb-relationship-role>
   </ejb-relation>
  </relationships>
 </ejb-jar>
```

As you can see, modeling a true many-to-many relationship using CMP is extremely straightforward. We just use the word *many* on each half of the relationship, and state that each half of the relationship has a collection of the other half.

If you've made it this far, congratulations; this concludes our cardinality discussion! Let's move on to directionality.

Directionality

The *directionality* of a relationship specifies the direction in which you can navigate a relationship. There are two flavors of directionality.

- **Bidirectional.** You can get from entity A to entity B, and can also get from entity B to entity A.
- **Unidirectional.** You can get from entity A to entity B, but *cannot* get from entity B to entity A.

Directionality applies to all cardinalities (1:1, 1:N, and M:N). Directionality and cardinality are orthogonal and complementary concepts. You can mix and match them any way you would like.

Let's use our one-to-one relationship example of an order and a shipment to help us figure out directionality.

Implementing Directionality with BMP

The following code is a bidirectional relationship, with the key information in bold:

```
public class OrderBean implements EntityBean {
 private String orderPK;
 private String orderName;

 // EJB local object stub, must be stored/loaded
 private Shipment shipment;

 public Shipment getShipment() {  return shipment; }
 public void setShipment(Shipment s) {  this.shipment = s; }

 ...
}

public class ShipmentBean implements EntityBean {
 private String shipmentPK;
 private String shipmentName;

 // EJB local object stub, must be stored/loaded
 private Order order;

 public Order getOrder() {  return order; }
 public void setOrder(Order o) {  this.order = o; }

 ...
}
```

As you can see, in a bidirectional relationship, each bean in the relationship has a field pointing to the other bean, along with a get/set method.

In comparison, with a unidirectional relationship, we don't allow the user to get from the second bean to the first bean.

```
public class OrderBean implements EntityBean {
 private String orderPK;
 private String orderName;

 // EJB local object stub, must be stored/loaded
 private Shipment shipment;
```

```
  public Shipment getShipment() {  return shipment; }
  public void setShipment(Shipment s) {  this.shipment = s; }

  ...
}

public class ShipmentBean implements EntityBean {
  private String shipmentPK;
  private String shipmentName;

  // No Order stub, no Order get/set method

  ...
}
```

Implementing Directionality with CMP

The following is a bidirectional CMP relationship:

```
public abstract class OrderBean implements EntityBean {
  // no fields

  public abstract Shipment getShipment();
  public abstract void setShipment(Shipment s);

  ...

  public void ejbLoad() { }      // Empty
  public void ejbStore() { }     // Empty
}

public abstract class ShipmentBean implements EntityBean {
  // no fields

  public abstract Order getOrder();
  public abstract void setOrder(Order o);

  ...

  public void ejbLoad() { }      // Empty
  public void ejbStore() { }     // Empty
}
```

As you can see, in a bidirectional CMP relationship, each bean in the relationship has a pair of abstract get/set methods pointing to the other bean. We need to tell the container that these get/set methods are special relationship methods so that the container can generate relationship code. Here is the deployment descriptor that achieves this.

```
<ejb-jar xmlns="http://java.sun.com/xml/ns/j2ee" version="2.1"
         xmlns:xsi=http://www.w3.org/2001/XMLSchema-instance
         xsi:schemaLocation="http://java.sun.com/xml/ns/j2ee
         http://java.sun.com/xml/ns/j2ee/ejb-jar_2_1.xsd">

 <enterprise-beans>
 ...
 </enterprise-beans>

 <relationships>
  <ejb-relation>
   <ejb-relation-name>Order-Shipment</ejb-relation-name>
   <ejb-relationship-role>
    <ejb-relationship-role-name>
     order-spawns-shipment
    </ejb-relationship-role-name>
    <multiplicity>One</multiplicity>
    <relationship-role-source>
     <ejb-name>Order</ejb-name>
    </relationship-role-source>
    <cmr-field><cmr-field-name>shipment</cmr-field-name></cmr-field>
   </ejb-relationship-role>

   <ejb-relationship-role>
    <ejb-relationship-role-name>
     shipment-fulfills-order
    </ejb-relationship-role-name>
    <multiplicity>One</multiplicity>
    <relationship-role-source>
     <ejb-name>Shipment</ejb-name>
    </relationship-role-source>
    <cmr-field><cmr-field-name>order</cmr-field-name></cmr-field>
   </ejb-relationship-role>
  </ejb-relation>
 </relationships>

</ejb-jar>
```

In the deployment descriptor, we set up two container-managed relationship (CMR) fields: one for each bean's abstract get/set method pair that points to the other bean.

To make this into a unidirectional relationship, we simply get rid of an abstract get/set method pair, along with its corresponding CMR field.

Directionality May Not Map to Database Schemas

Note that directionality in entity beans may *not* correspond to the inherent directionality of the database schema. An entity bean can provide for directionality even though the database does not do so easily, and vice versa. For example, Figure 15.6 is a normalized database schema for a Person:Address relationship. Figure 15.7 is a denormalized schema.

Both of these schemas give us enough information to derive relationship information. You can, if you choose to do so, map entity beans to both these schemas and use bidirectional relationships. The difference is that the denormalized schema allows for more efficient SQL. That is the classic computer science space-time tradeoff. If you denormalize the database, you waste space and increase maintenance problems, but you gain speed.

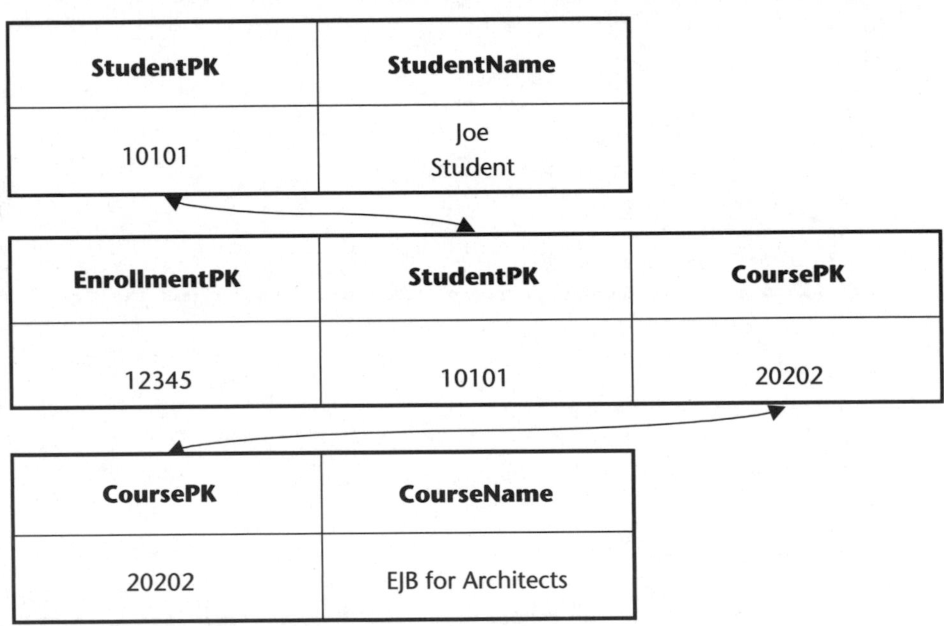

Figure 15.6 A normalized schema.

PersonPK	PersonName	Address
12345	Ed Roman	10101

AddressPK	City	ZipCode	PersonForeignPK
10101	Austin	78727	12345

Figure 15.7 A denormalized schema.

RELATIONSHIPS AND LOCAL INTERFACES

A common theme throughout this book has been to always use local interfaces when possible. This is especially true for entity beans, and has a big impact on relationships.

Specifically, if you decide for some bizarre reason to use remote interfaces with entity beans, then you must adhere to the following rules:

- **You must not expose *get/set* methods for relationship fields to remote clients. Doing so creates problems because, for example, the client does not have access to the container-implemented collection interface.**
- **Your entity bean can only have unidirectional relationships with other entity beans. The lack of a local interface prevents other entity beans from having a relationship with you.**

Bidirectional or Unidirectional?

How do you choose between bidirectional and unidirectional relationships? Here are some questions to ask:

- Should each bean know about the other bean? Would that hamper reuse?
- From the client's perspective, does it make intuitive sense to navigate the relationship from the direction in question?
- Is the database mapping of stubs to foreign keys straightforward, or does adding directionality result in mapping to multiple tables, resulting in inadequate performance?

Lazy Loading

All the relationship code we've discussed so far makes a big assumption: Whenever an entity bean is loaded, all of the other entity beans that it has a relationship with are also loaded. This is called *aggressive loading*. We saw this, for example, with our Order:Shipment relationship at the beginning of this chapter. The order bean looked up the shipment bean in the order bean's *ejbLoad()* method.

Aggressive loading is nice because you can load all database data in a single transaction. However, it does have its downside. Aggressive loading could lead to loading a very large entity bean graph, and you may not need that entire graph.

Lazy loading means to load only related beans when you need to access those beans. For example, with the Order:Shipment relationship using BMP that we presented at the beginning of this chapter, we would rewrite the code to lazy-load as follows:

```
public class OrderBean implements EntityBean {
 private String orderPK;
 private String orderName;

 private String shipmentFK; // Foreign key to shipment
 private Shipment shipment; // EJB local object stub

 public void ejbLoad() {
  // 1: SQL SELECT Order, loading the shipment foreign key
  // 2: Set shipmentFK field to the loaded key
 }

 public Shipment getShipment() {
  // 1: JNDI lookup of ShipmentHome
  // 2: Call ShipmentHome.findByPrimaryKey(shipmentFK)
  return shipment;
 }

 ...

}
```

In the preceding code, we are looking up the shipment *just in time* when the client calls *getShipment()*, rather than in *ejbLoad()*. *ejbLoad()* merely locates the appropriate foreign key, which *getShipment()* uses.

With CMP, lazy loading happens automatically behind the scenes. You are, however, reliant on container-specific flags to enable lazy loading. Most major containers support this, so check your container documentation.

Aggregation Versus Composition and Cascading Deletes

When you have a relationship between two entity beans, you need to think about whether that relationship is an *aggregation* or a *composition* relationship.

An aggregation relationship is a *uses* relationship. For example, students use courses. If you delete a student, you don't delete the courses the student is registered in, because other students are using that course. Similarly, if you delete a course, you don't murder a student!

A composition relationship is an *is-assembled-of* relationship. For example, orders are assembled of line items. Deleting an order deletes all line items. Line items shouldn't be around if their parent order is gone.

DESIGN TIP: AGGRESSIVELY LOAD IN ONE DIRECTION ONLY FOR M:N RELATIONSHIPS

With many-to-many relationships, you need to be careful about how aggressively you load your entity bean graph. For example, assume that Larry lives at addresses A, B, and C; Curly at C and D; Moe at C and E; and E is a commune with 37 people living in it. Larry, Curly, Moe, and everyone in the commune are customers of ours. If we cascade the load across the relationship in both directions when we read in Larry, we would retrieve at least 5 address objects and 40 customer objects, not to mention any other addresses at which the commune people also live and any customers and their addresses that those retrievals would then cascade to. The same problem arises if we also cascade the deletion in both directions. We need to cascade the retrieval and deletion in one direction, or be incredibly smart about how we cascade in both directions. Unless your entity bean graph is small, we recommend you use lazy-loading for at least one direction of the relationship.

After you've figured out whether your relationship is an aggregation or composition, you need to write your entity beans so they model the semantics you desire. This all boils down to a concept called a *cascading delete*. An aggregation relationship does not cause a cascading delete, whereas a composition relationship does.

With BMP, you implement a cascading delete manually in your *ejbRemove()* method. For example, an order bean's *ejbRemove()* method would not only perform a SQL DELETE of the order, but would also call the shipment bean's *ejbRemove()* method:

```
public class OrderBean implements EntityBean {
 private String orderPK;
 private String orderName;
 private Shipment shipment; // EJB local object stub

 public Shipment getShipment() {  return shipment; }
 public void setShipment(Shipment s) {  this.shipment = s;}

 ...

 public void ejbRemove() {
  // 1: SQL DELETE Order
  // 2: shipment.remove();
 }
}
```

With CMP, the container generates cascading delete code for you. If you have a composition relationship, you just need to set up a *<cascade-delete/>* tag in the deployment descriptor, as follows:

```
<ejb-jar xmlns="http://java.sun.com/xml/ns/j2ee" version="2.1"
         xmlns:xsi=http://www.w3.org/2001/XMLSchema-instance
         xsi:schemaLocation="http://java.sun.com/xml/ns/j2ee
         http://java.sun.com/xml/ns/j2ee/ejb-jar_2_1.xsd">

 <enterprise-beans>
 ...
 </enterprise-beans>

 <relationships>
  <ejb-relation>
   <ejb-relation-name>Order-Shipment</ejb-relation-name>
   <ejb-relationship-role>
    <ejb-relationship-role-name>
     order-spawns-shipment
    </ejb-relationship-role-name>
    <multiplicity>One</multiplicity>
    <relationship-role-source>
     <ejb-name>Order</ejb-name>
    </relationship-role-source>
    <cmr-field><cmr-field-name>shipment</cmr-field-name></cmr-field>
   </ejb-relationship-role>

   <ejb-relationship-role>
    <ejb-relationship-role-name>
     shipment-fulfills-order
    </ejb-relationship-role-name>
    <multiplicity>One</multiplicity>
    <cascade-delete/>
    <relationship-role-source>
     <ejb-name>Shipment</ejb-name>
    </relationship-role-source>
    <cmr-field><cmr-field-name>order</cmr-field-name></cmr-field>
   </ejb-relationship-role>
  </ejb-relation>
 </relationships>

</ejb-jar>
```

If you have an aggregation relationship, you just leave the *<cascade-delete/>* tag out.

Relationships and EJB-QL

When setting up CMP relationships, you can also set up special queries using the EJB Query Language (EJB-QL), which we briefly describe in Chapter 7 and fully explain in Appendix D. The following is relevant to our discussion and is excerpted from Appendix D.

The big difference between EJB-QL and SQL is that EJB-QL enables you to traverse relationships between entity beans using a dot notation. For example:

```
SELECT o.customer
FROM Order o
```

In this EJB-QL, we are returning all customers that have placed orders. We are navigating from the order entity bean to the customer entity bean easily using a dot notation. This is quite seamless.

What's exciting about this notation is that bean providers don't need to know about tables or columns; they merely need to understand the relationships between the entity beans that they've authored. The container will handle the traversal of relationships for us because we declare our entity beans in the same deployment descriptor and Ejb-jar file, empowering the container to manage all of our beans and thus understand their relationships.

In fact, you can traverse more than one relationship. That relationship can involve container-managed relationship fields and container-managed persistent fields. For example:

```
SELECT o.customer.address.homePhoneNumber
FROM Order o
```

The restriction on this type of recursive relationship traversal is that you are limited by the *navigatability* of the relationships that you define in the deployment descriptor. For example, let's say that in the deployment descriptor, you declare that orders have a one-to-many relationship with line items, but you do not define the reverse many-to-one relationship that line items have with orders. When performing EJB-QL, you can get from orders to line items, but not from line items to orders.

Recursive Relationships

A recursive relationship is one in which an entity bean instance has a relationship with another instance of the same entity bean class, as shown in Figure 15.8.

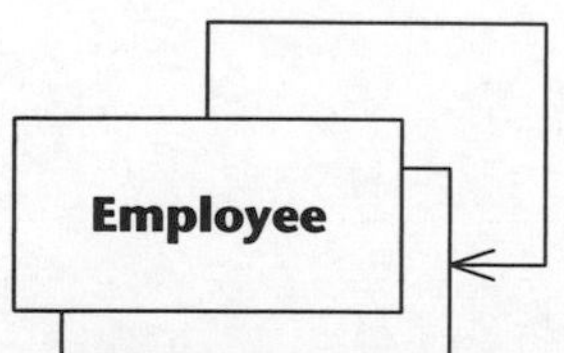

Figure 15.8 A recursive relationship.

Figure 15.8 shows an Employee:Manager relationship. All that this means is that our employee entity bean has a relationship with another employee entity bean.

As you would expect, recursive relationships are implemented exactly as nonrecursive relationships are. All the principles we learned earlier apply, and nothing is new. We just happen to have a relationship with an instance of an entity bean that uses the same class.

Circular Relationships

A circular relationship is similar to a recursive relationship except that instead of involving a single entity bean, it involves several. Figure 15.9 depicts a circular relationship.

The following relationships exist:

- Employees work in a division.
- A division owns one or more workstations.
- An employee has a workstation.

The problem with circular relationships is that if your beans automatically find each other, you will get into an endless circle of finding. The same problem exists for cascading deletes.

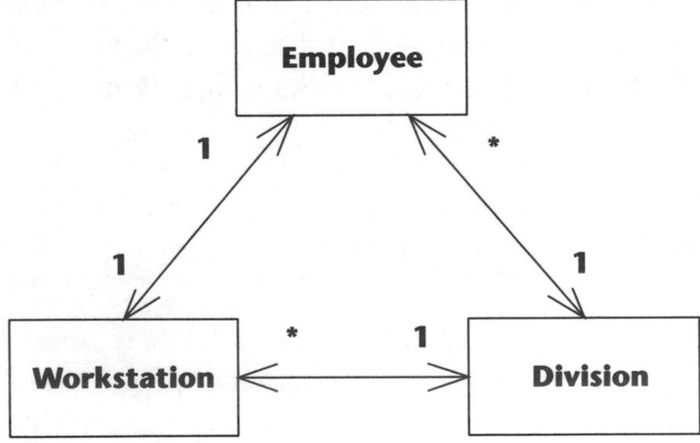

Figure 15.9 A circular relationship.

So how do you implement circular relationships between EJBs appropriately? You have several implementation strategies.

- Some containers enable you to optimize performance and load an entity bean at the same time that it's found. This is where the circularity issue stems from, because the *ejbLoad()* method performs the cascading find. Not loading an entity bean when it's found means no cascading find operation occurs.
- Break the circular relationship by removing one of the relationships altogether. This is a harsh approach to resolving the problem.
- Break the circular relationships within your model by making one or more relationships unidirectional, effectively breaking the circle in both directions. This isn't always an option because your requirements may not permit it.
- Use lazy loading rather than aggressive loading, and do not use cascading deletes.
- Choose an application server with persistence logic that can detect circular relationships. Many persistence administration tools automatically detect and warn you of circular relationships when you define them. This enables you to prevent the problem before it occurs.

Referential Integrity

Referential integrity is the assurance that a reference from one entity to another entity is valid. For example:

- Let's say a company, department, and position each has relationships with an employee. If the employee is removed, all references to it must also be removed, or your system must not allow the removal of employee.
- Let's say an order has a one-to-many relationship with a line item. Someone adding a second order to an order line item is trying to change a one-to-many relationship to a many-to-many relationship. We must therefore break the line item's relationship with the original order so that we maintain our intended one-to-many semantics.

Referential integrity issues arise in both the database (keeping foreign keys correct) and in the application server (keeping stubs correct). So how do you ensure referential integrity within your EJB applications? You have three fundamental options:

- **Enforce referential integrity within your database with triggers.** For example, you could write a trigger that fires when an employee is deleted. This trigger would delete the relationships the employee had with other database tables to preserve referential integrity.
- **Enforce referential integrity within your database with stored procedures.** Your EJB component would call these stored procedures to perform database operations, and the stored procedures would be responsible for preserving referential integrity.
- **Enforce referential integrity within EJB components.**

Implementing referential integrity in your database has the advantage in that other non-EJB applications can take advantage of it, your database being the lowest common denominator within your organization. Relational databases implement triggers for exactly this purpose, and most data modeling tools support the generation of trigger code to simplify this effort for you. The drawback of implementing logic in your database is that it increases the processing burden on your database server(s), running the risk that your database becomes a bottleneck to your application. You can also take a hybrid approach to implementing referential integrity—your EJBs handle the referential integrity for some entities and your database for others.

Of these options, we believe that the EJB approach is the cleanest and easiest to maintain over the long term, because your EJB layer encapsulates all relationships. Here is how you do it with EJB:

- **With BMP** you need to take care of referential integrity on your own. You do so by manually breaking old relationships. If someone tries to assign a second order to your line item, your line item bean should call the order bean and tell the order bean to remove you from its list of line items.
- **With CMP** the container will *automatically* handle referential integrity for you. You never have to worry about these issues. This is one neat feature the container provides that makes CMP a compelling value proposition.

Note that it's not quite this simple. To complicate matters, you might have a farm of EJB application servers, and your component might exist simultaneously on several machines. Furthermore, if you have other applications accessing your database, it is possible that they too have representations of your data in their memory as well. The good news is that *transactions* (see Chapter 12) solve this problem. For example, when you delete an employee and also delete the relationships it has with other entities within a transaction, either all or none of the deletions occur, preserving referential integrity.

Writing code to enforce referential integrity in your EJB components instead of your database works only when all of your applications are written this way (and hopefully they share a common code base). However, this is rarely the case. In many organizations, some or often most applications are written assuming that the database(s) will handle referential integrity. This is clearly an inappropriate layering of these applications because business logic is now implemented on several disparate architectural tiers, making the applications less robust. However, it is a reality that many EJB developers must accept; some of their business logic will be implemented in the database, perhaps through triggers or through Java objects implemented within the database.

Relationships, Referential Integrity, and Client Code

Throughout this chapter, we've seen lots of fascinating relationships. Many of those relationships involved collections. For example, here is our Company:Employee one-to-many CMP relationship again:

```
public abstract class CompanyBean implements EntityBean {
 // no fields

 public abstract Collection getEmployees();
 public abstract void setEmployees(Collection employees);

 ...

 public void ejbLoad() { }     // Empty
 public void ejbStore() { }    // Empty
}
```

This code has methods to get/set entire Collections of employees. But what's interesting is that there is no API for clients to perform operations on *individual* employees.

This is where the Collection Collection comes into play. By using the Collection Collection from client code, you can modify the contents of a one-to-many relationship. For example:

```
// Lookup local home objects
Context ctx = new InitialContext(...);
CompanyHome companyHome = (CompanyHome) ctx.lookup("CompanyHome");
EmployeeHome employeeHome = (EmployeeHome) ctx.lookup("EmployeeHome");

// Make a new employee
Employee employeeA = employeeHome.create("Ed Roman");
```

```
// Find a company
Company company =
 companyHome.findByPrimaryKey("The Middleware Company");
Collection employees = company.getEmployees();

// Add the employee to the company.
// This demonstrates the add() Collection API method
employees.add(employeeA);

// Look at each employee in the company.
// This demonstrates using iterators to loop through collections
Iterator i = employees.iterator();
while (i.hasNext()) {
 Employee emp = (Employee) i.next();
 System.out.println(emp.getName());
}

// Remove the employee from the company.
// This demonstrates the remove() Collection API
employees.remove(employeeA);
```

Since we're using local interfaces, the collection that the client modifies is the same as the collection inside the bean. This is because the get/set methods pass the collection by reference rather than by value. Thus, when the client modifies the contents of the collection, he is actually changing the bean's relationships. If remote interfaces were used, the relationships would not be accessible through the remote interface to begin with, due to the remote interface restrictions discussed earlier in this chapter.

The container is responsible for providing an implementation of the *Collection* interface. This needs to be a *smart* collection that understands how to preserve referential integrity behind the scenes.

Be careful when using iterators and relationships. If you want to modify a relationship while an iterator is at work, use only the *java.util.Iterator .remove()* method. Adding or removing elements from a collection while the iterator is in progress will throw off the iterator.

Table 15.1 lists the effects that client operations have on referential integrity. Note that for the one-to-many and many-to-many rows on the table, we are performing operations on collections and using the collections API for operations such as *add()* and *remove()*.

Table 15.1 Client Operations and Referential Integrity

SITUATION	ORIGINAL RELATIONSHIPS	OPERATION	NEW RELATIONSHIPS
1:1 Relationship Order:Shipment	orderA-shipmentA orderB-shipmentB	orderA.setShipment (orderB.getShipment());	OrderA-ShipmentB, OrderB-NULL
1:N Relationship Company: Employee	companyA-employeeA, companyA-employeeB, companyB-employeeC, companyB-employeeD	CompanyA.set Employees (CompanyB. getEmployees());	NULL-employeeA, NULL-employeeB, companyA-employeeC, companyA-employeeD, companyB-Empty Collection
1:N Relationship Company: Employee	companyA-employeeA, companyA-employeeB, companyB-employeeC companyB-employeeD	EmployeeA.set Company (employeeC.get Company());	companyB-employeeA, companyA-employeeB, companyB-employeeC, companyB-employeeD
1:N Relationship Company: Employee	companyA-employeeA, companyA-employeeB, companyB-employeeC, companyB-employeeD	CompanyB.get Employees().add (employeeA);	companyB-employeeA, companyA-employeeB, companyB-employeeC, companyB-employeeD
1:N Relationship Company: Employee	companyA-employeeA, companyA-employeeB, companyB-employeeC, companyB-employeeD	CompanyA.get Employees().remove (employeeA);	NULL-employeeA companyA-employeeB, companyB-employeeC, companyB-employeeD
M:N Relationship Student:Course	studentA-courseA, studentA-courseB, studentB-courseB, studentB-courseC	studentA.setCourses (studentB.get Courses());	studentA-courseB, studentA-courseC, studentB-courseB, studentB-courseC

(continued)

Table 15.1 *(continued)*

SITUATION	ORIGINAL RELATIONSHIPS	OPERATION	NEW RELATIONSHIPS
M:N Relationship Student:Course	studentA-courseA, studentA-courseB, studentB-courseB, studentB-courseC	studentA.get Courses().add (courseC);	studentA-courseA, studentA-courseB, studentA-courseC, studentB-courseB, studentB-courseC
M:N Relationship Student:Course	studentA-courseA, studentA-courseB, studentB-courseB, studentB-courseC	studentA.get Courses().remove (courseB);	studentA-courseA, studentB-courseB, studentB-courseC

Try to look at only the first three columns of Table 15.1 and see if you can guess what the fourth column should be.

Summary

Still with us? Fantastic! Pat yourself on the back, because you've achieved a great deal in this chapter. You learned about cardinality, directionality, referential integrity, cascading deletes, recursive relationships, circular relationships, lazily loaded relationships, and how to control relationships from client code. You also saw how to implement each of the above topics using both CMP and BMP.

You should be prepared now to go ahead and implement relationships in your own deployments. For concrete examples without pseudo-code that you can use as a basis for your own deployments, see the book's accompanying source code (wiley.com/compbooks/roman).

CHAPTER

16

Persistence Best Practices

Most modern business applications require that you persist data—create, retrieve, update, and delete data. Persisting data from EJB components can be as easy as defining a few simple class-to-table mappings using an EJB container's persistence administration tool, or as difficult as writing sophisticated Java source code.

In this chapter we explore the issues surrounding EJB persistence and explore the various approaches to persistence that you may employ within your EJB applications. We'll cover the following topics:

- Comparing entity beans with other persistence approaches
- How to choose between container-managed persistence (CMP) and bean-managed persistence (BMP)
- A collection of persistence best practices, such as versioning EJB components, and dealing with a legacy data design

This chapter is written with the assumption that you will use one or more relational databases to store your business objects. We are considering only relational databases because that's what most organizations use.

Comparing Entity Beans with Other Persistence Approaches

A fundamental issue that you need to address is how to persist the information encapsulated by your EJBs. There are three approaches to this:

- Session beans plus JDBC. A session bean persists data manually, typically via JDBC.
- Session beans plus O/R persistence frameworks. A session bean can use O/R frameworks such as JDO, Hibernate, OJB, and so on for persisting or accessing domain data.
- Entity beans, either BMP or CMP.

Let's first figure out how entity beans (either CMP or BMP) compare to other persistence approaches such as session beans plus JDBC or session beans plus persistence frameworks. This discussion will help you make the decision of selecting the appropriate persistence option in your projects. Then we'll compare BMP and CMP.

Control

There are significant control differences between performing persistence via session beans and entity beans. Session beans are more of a service-oriented architecture because you call methods explicitly to load and store data. Thus, you are in command of when to use JDBC explicitly. This is very similar to the Microsoft approach to business components. In comparison, with entity beans, the container automatically loads and stores data on your behalf.

This loss of control that entity beans give you can be somewhat disturbing. If you're not careful to tune your container properly using its flags, and to start and end transactions at the right times, operations that require a single SQL statement can take several statements. Proper education of your developers will help solve these problems.

Data retrieval

Another way to compare these persistence options is by understanding how data is retrieved in each of these approaches and understanding their performance impact.

Session Bean Plus JDBC

When you perform a JDBC query from session bean, the session bean gets returned a result set. The result set contains queried data and the session bean traverses through the result set object to access this relational data. Here, since the client makes local method invocations on a result set object to access data to access underlying relational data, the performance is typically very good.

The session bean will require putting the data represented within the result set object into serializable data transfer objects (DTO) so that it can be marshaled to its client across the network. Of course, this chore is not required when using disconnected JDBC rowsets since they can be marshaled to the client directly.

Session Bean Plus O/R Persistence Frameworks

When you do a query using JDO or other non-standard frameworks such as Hibernate, a session bean will get returned a collection of objects mapped to the underlying relational data. The returned collection of objects contains the queried data and session bean traverses through these plain old Java objects (POJO) to access the relational data. Here, since the client makes local method invocations on POJOs to access underlying relational data, the performance is typically very good. The session bean can directly pass the collection of POJOs to its client.

Session Bean Plus Entity Bean

When you do a query using entity bean home, the session bean will get returned a collection of stubs to the server-side entity objects. The returned collection of stubs provides access to the server-side relational data. The session bean uses these stubs to do method invocations, which in turn retrieves the relational data. This will have negative impact on performance when the stubs correspond to remote entity objects, as the client will be required to make remote method invocations to retrieve data. However, if session beans and entity beans are deployed in the same container, and if entity bean supports local interfaces, then there is no negative performance impact because the client now makes local method invocations on the object representations of data to access the underlying relational data.

Here the session bean will require putting the data represented by entity objects into serializable DTOs so that it can be marshaled to the client.

Thus, the point to take away is that there are performance implications of using remote entity beans, especially when entity beans and their clients (session beans, typically) are not co-located within the same virtual machine.

Procedural versus Object-Oriented

Most EJB deployments work with data that is either procedural (tabular) or object-oriented in nature. Session beans that use JDBC for data access work with tabular representation of data. Session beans that use the O/R framework for data access work with object-oriented representation of data. Also, since entity beans are Java objects, session beans that use entity beans for data access work with object-oriented data.

Object-oriented data access is favored over procedural data access simply because they provide benefits such as encapsulation and relationships, which are inherent to object-oriented programming. Object-oriented data access thus helps when working with data that requires encapsulation or relationships with other data.

Caching

Middle-tier data caching is extremely important because it empowers you to reduce database traffic, and your database will most likely be your bottleneck.

Session beans do not represent database data and therefore cannot be cached at all. Hence, when using session beans you will have to rely on the data access mechanism to provide caching. Persistence frameworks such as Hibernate and JDO do support caching. Mostly, the rows they read in are cache-consistent for the duration of a single transaction only. However, Hibernate does support JVM-level or cluster-level cache.

Most of the application servers support entity bean caching across multiple transactions provided application server has exclusive access to that part of the database. You can set this up using container-specific flags.

If data is shared, entity bean caching benefits are more prominent because that data is likely to be viewed many times. An example of shared data is a product catalog, such as the hottest 100 books on Amazon.com.

If your data is exclusive (not shared), caching offers almost no benefits. An example of exclusive data is a personal account, such as your personal account settings on Amazon.com. In the exclusive data case, the extra SQL statements that sometimes occur through entity beans may offset the caching benefits, making entity beans a lower-performing solution. However, in most deployments, most data is shared and read-only, and hence caching is an important performance boost that entity beans provide.

Enforcement of Schema Independence

Schema independence is an extremely important feature of your persistence layer. As a nightmare motivational story, a project for one of our clients took three developers four months to change two columns in a database because of spaghetti SQL all over the place. By encapsulating that data with a layer, we would have avoided those headaches.

Entity beans force developers to go through an entity bean layer, yielding a single entry point to the database. Developers are isolated from the schema, allowing ease of schema evolution and data encapsulation.

In comparison, session beans can also isolate you from the schema, if you use the appropriate data access approach such as an O/R mapping framework like JDO or Hibernate. Most of these O/R mapping frameworks enable you to specify the field-column mappings in configuration files, thereby taking the schema dependence off the code. In the end, if your developers are on top of things, either session beans or entity beans will give you schema independence.

Migration

Most EJB deployments are based on existing databases. These databases are likely to be tabular in nature, and many have SQL code that has been tuned over the years to be high performing. It is a known commodity that works well.

Session bean and JDBC persistence approach is somewhat procedural in nature and is a natural evolution of those legacy procedural systems. For some deployments, application developers can simply copy SQL code from existing solutions into the new EJB system. This eliminates a risk factor in a new EJB architecture.

In comparison, entity beans, or O/R persistence frameworks for that matter, represent data in an object-oriented manner such that the container maps the data objects to the underlying tabular data via its generated SQL code. If the EJB server is good, it will generate optimized SQL for accessing the database. Mostly, the persistence engines of EJB servers are fairly smart in generating optimized SQL. Again, here you do lose some control in that you rely on the SQL code from your container and not your time-tested SQL. But in the long term this will prove to be a better choice, given that server vendors will continue to make their products smarter in terms of accessing data. Hence, once you migrate your data access logic to entity beans you are likely to benefit from EJB server advancements in the future.

Rapid Application Development

When building a new EJB system, using entity beans or an O/R framework will provide a rapid application development advantage over session beans and JDBC. Most popular UML editors (Rational Rose, Borland TogetherJ) enable you to autogenerate framework-based persistence objects, such as Hibernate objects or JDO objects, and entity beans from UML diagrams. Furthermore, tools (such as IDEs or popular code generation tools, such as XDoclet or EJBGen, enable you to generate complete entity bean Ejb-jar files from a few bits of information about the data you're modeling.

Note, however, that developing EJB applications inherently consumes more time because of the overhead involved in writing all the files that comprise a bean. Therefore, if you're not using powerful tools, or at least copying and pasting template code, you may find yourself bogged down.

Choosing Between CMP and BMP

Now that we've compared session beans and entity beans, let's assume we're using entity beans. In Chapter 6, you discovered two approaches for persisting entity beans: With BMP, you are responsible for coding all database logic, while with CMP, the container handles the persistence for you.

The choice between CMP and BMP is not necessarily clear-cut. Both bean-managed and container-managed beans have virtues and drawbacks.

Code Reduction and Rapid Application Development

The promise of CMP is quite compelling. If you tell the EJB container a couple of things about your bean, container-managed persistence can perform all data access logic for you. This reduces the size of your bean tremendously—no more JDBC code in your beans—which reduces overall development time. It also makes code easier to understand and maintain. CMP beans are also fantastic for prototyping. If you need to get something working right away, go with CMP, knowing that you can take a BMP approach later if required.

Know that in reality you still may need to write persistent code with container-managed beans. This could be going through a series of wizards to specify how your entity beans map to an underlying store. You also need to specify the logic behind your finder methods. The difference is that with CMP, your data access logic is now specified declaratively, whereas with BMP, you're writing the logic in Java. To CMP's credit, the amount of programming you're doing is much less.

Performance

CMP entity beans, if tuned properly, are much higher performing than BMP entity beans.

For example, with BMP, it takes two SQL statements to load an entity bean: the first to call a finder method (loading only the primary key) and the second during *ejbLoad()* to load the actual bean data. A collection of *n* bean-managed persistent entity beans requires *n*+1 database calls to load that data (one finder to find a collection of primary keys, and then *n* loads).

With CMP, the container can reduce the *n*+1 database calls problem to a single call, by performing one giant *SELECT* statement. You typically set this up using container-specific flags (which do not affect bean portability). Check your container's documentation to see if this feature is supported.

There is a hack work-around to increase BMP performance. It's called the *fat key pattern* and is explained on the book's companion Web site at wiley.com/compbooks/roman.

Bugs

CMP systems tend to be harder to debug than BMP systems are. The reason is that with BMP, you are in total control of the JDBC code; if something goes wrong, you can debug that code.

With CMP, you are generating code based on deployment descriptor values. While it may be true that user error is reduced at the database level, serious ramifications occur if there *is* some kind of bug. Because the container is performing your persistence for you, it is tough to figure out which database operations the container is really doing. You may need to trace through container-generated code if it's available, decompile the container, or possibly wait on technical support lines, delaying a project.

Furthermore, since we're all human, we make mistakes writing CMP deployment descriptors, such as having values that are incorrect or that do not match up perfectly to our bean files. Often the container's JDBC code generator is too dumb to point out your error and simply generates bad code. At other times, your container's generator tool might even crash, making it even harder to figure out what the problem is. (This is *really* annoying!)

See Chapter 11 for strategies for debugging misbehaving EJB applications.

Control

BMP gives you ultimate control over JDBC, and thus you have unlimited flexibility for the way you map your objects to the database. For CMP, many containers support complex mappings, but some containers don't. For example, if your container-managed persistent entity bean class has a vector of Java objects as a container-managed field, you may need to convert that vector into a bit-blob or other form that the container can handle when mapping to storage.

Application Server and Database Independence

One nice thing about container-managed persistence is that you aren't hard-coding a particular database storage API into your beans, such as JDBC. Because you aren't issuing explicit relational database calls in your persistence layer, you can easily move into a different database, such as Oracle instead of SQL Server. Theoretically, you might even port your beans to use object databases without changing code.

Database independence is important for those who are providing beans to others. Often those beans must be able to work with whatever target database the customer has. Given that enterprise beans represent intellectual property, they most likely will not ship with their source code. This means that if an entity bean uses BMP, the customer cannot easily tweak the data access logic. For these vendors, CMP is the only alternative to shipping multiple versions of the same bean code.

Unfortunately, there is no standard way to specify the actual O/R mapping with CMP. Each container has its own tools, wizards, or mapping files that specify which fields correspond to which database columns. But what if you want to install your bean in a different container? You'll need to re-specify your mappings using the new container's tools. If you have a complex data model, this could become a hefty task. Furthermore, since not all application servers support your complex persistence needs, your beans may not be portable to other containers.

Because of this, sometimes using BMP and allowing your SQL to be hand-tuned through the EJB environment properties (see Chapter 10) is the way to go if you want to be application server- and database-neutral.

Relationships

The EJB 2.*x* CMP model offers many useful relationship features to bean providers. These include referential integrity, cardinality, relationship management, and cascading deletes. The container can take care of all these issues for you.

With BMP, you must write the scaffolding code to manage and persist the relationships between entity beans. This can get very hairy. You'll notice that a big chunk of your BMP code is dedicated to managing these relationships, which decreases time to market and makes your beans more difficult to understand.

Learning Curve and Cost

Most developers already understand how to perform relational database access from Java, and thus BMP does not require much of a learning curve. In comparison, some advanced EJB servers ship with complex O/R mappers for CMP. These mappers provide useful functionality but do require training and ramp-up time. They also might cost some money, depending on your vendor's policy.

Most people would love to go with CMP but are afraid to risk that CMP is not flexible enough. If you're in this category, you have a path to try out CMP before you buy. You can make all your entity beans use CMP, and then *subclass* those beans as necessary if you want to use BMP. This works because CMP entity beans are abstract classes.

Choosing the Right Granularity for Entity Beans

If you do decide to go with entity beans (instead of session beans plus JDBC, or session beans plus Java classes), then you need to decide on the *granularity* of your entity beans. The granularity refers to how big (or small) your entity beans are.

In the past, entity beans were restricted to represent only large chunks of data involving complex joins across multiple tables. Now with the advent of local interfaces and the new CMP model, the container can make many more optimizations. This means the idea of small-grained entity beans is much more viable, if you tune your entity beans properly (see Chapter 18 for tips here).

Another choice you have is to make some of your entity beans be Java classes. These Java classes would hang off other entity beans. For example, you could have an order entity bean that has a vector of line item Java classes. If you're using CMP, the EJB specification refers to these Java classes as *dependent value classes*. Don't be confused by the terminology; this is just the Java Community Process's way of giving a fancy name to Java classes that hang off a CMP entity bean.

For example, here is a dependent value class:

```
package examples;

public class LineItem implements java.io.Serializable {

 private String product;
 private int quantity;

 public void setProduct(String product) {  this.product = product; }
 public String getProduct() {  return product; }
 public void setQuantity(int quantity) {  this.quantity = quantity; }
 public int getQuantity() {  return quantity; }
}
```

If you're going to use them, then you should know that there are a few rules for dependent value classes:

- Dependent value classes are defined as CMP fields, and they work just like CMP fields do. For example, rather than having a *java.util.String* CMP field, you might have a custom class like *examples.LineItem*. Everything we learned about how to use CMP fields in Chapter 8 applies to these custom Java classes too.
- Dependent value classes may not be container-managed relationship (CMR) fields, which we learned about in Chapter 15. Relationships exist only between entity beans, not Java classes.

- Dependent value classes cannot contain references to other entity beans. For example, this sequence of references would be illegal: order (entity bean) points to line item (dependent value class) points to address (entity bean).
- Dependent value classes must be serializable. Getting and setting them are performed by-value rather than by-reference. This hampers performance, but does enable you to access it via the remote interface.

The real value of dependent value classes over entity beans is that they are quick to develop. The downside is that you lose many of the entity bean benefits described earlier in this chapter.

Persistence Tips and Tricks

In this section, we'll present a number of best practices when performing object-to-relational mapping.

Beware the Object-Relational Impedance Mismatch

The object-oriented paradigm, which EJB follows, is based on proven software engineering principles for building applications out of objects that have both data and behavior. The relational paradigm, however, is based on proven mathematical principles for efficiently storing data. Difficulties arise when you attempt to use object and relational technologies together, such as EJBs and relational databases, because of the *impedance mismatch* between the two paradigms. The impedance mismatch becomes apparent when you look at the preferred approach to access: With the object paradigm you traverse objects through their relationships, whereas with the relational paradigm you join the data rows of tables. This fundamental difference results in a less-than-ideal combination of object and relational technologies. Of course, when have you ever used two different things together without a few hitches? To be successful using EJB and relational databases together is to understand both paradigms and their differences, and then make intelligent tradeoffs based on that knowledge.

Hard-Coded versus Soft-Coded SQL

Most developers hard-code SQL into their BMP entity beans. We showed an example of this in Chapter 7. The problem with this approach is that when your data schema changes, you need to update your source code, retest it, compile it, and redeploy it.

Another possibility is to take a soft-coded approach to SQL, where the mapping of your EJB object schema to your database schema is maintained outside your EJBs. You can keep a list of database mappings in a file or a database, or internally as a data collection, or you can use EJB environment properties accessed through JNDI (see Chapter 10 for more details). The advantage of the soft-coded approach is that you need to update only the metadata representing your mappings, not the EJB code itself, along the same lines that CMP works for entity beans.

To implement soft-coded SQL within your session beans, you could either build a mapping facility yourself or adopt one of several Java persistence layers or frameworks. The high-level design of a persistence layer, as well as links to several vendors of commercial and open source products, is provided at www.ambysoft.com/persistenceLayer.html.

When to Use Stored Procedures

Stored procedures are operations that run within a database. A stored procedure typically runs some SQL code, massages the data, and then hands back a response in the form of zero or more records, or a response code, or as a database error message. In the past, stored procedures were written in a proprietary language, such as Oracle PL/SQL, although Java is quickly becoming the language of choice for database programming. You can invoke stored procedures from a J2EE deployment via JDBC.

The following code invokes a stored procedure (thrown exceptions omitted):

```
// Define the code to invoke a stored function
CallableStatement orderCounter = connection.prepareCall(
  "{ call ? = COUNT_CUSTOMER_ORDERS[(?)]} " );

// Invoke the stored function
orderCounter.registerOutParameter(1, java.sql.Types.FLOAT);
orderCounter.setInt(2, customer.getCustomerID() );
orderCounter.execute();

// Get the return value
numberOfOrders = orderCounter.getFloat(2);

// End the transaction and close the connection
connection.commit();
orderCounter.close();
```

Now that you've seen how to call stored procedures, when should you use them in an EJB environment? Here are some good use cases:

1. **Performance.** Often you're performing data-intensive operations with small result sets, and stored procedures then become very appetizing. For example, a good candidate for a stored procedure would be to produce counts listing the number of critical orders (criticality defined by a business rule involving a list of preferred customers, preferred

products, and order total) that have been outstanding for more than 30, 60, or 90 days. This operation is data intensive; it would need to take a pass at every order record that has been outstanding for more than 30 days and run it through the defined business rule to determine if it is critical or not. This involves an amount of data that you wouldn't want to bring across the network to an EJB application server, convert to objects, and then process accordingly. The stored procedure could do all the work on the database server and simply send back the three resulting numbers. Stored procedures are also precompiled, resulting in performance wins.

2. **Shared business rules.** We encourage organizations to strive, first and foremost, towards centralizing on an EJB layer for all their applications. However, due to political reasons, the reality is that this may not be feasible for all organizations. When your application must share a relational database with other non-EJB applications, such as a legacy system or Microsoft-based system, the database becomes an option for implementing your business rules. This is especially true when legacy applications are unable to access better approaches to implementing business rules, such as an EJB application server or a business rules server. As a result, your relational database becomes the most viable option to implement shared business rules because it is the lowest common denominator that your suite of applications can interact with.
3. **Data security access control logic.** If you have external systems touching your database without going through your EJB layer, you can secure your data by configuring access control on the database. For example, you may want to give another department access to view salary data, but not update it.
4. **Legacy database encapsulation.** You often find that you need to write stored procedures to present a clean view of a legacy database to your EJBs. Most legacy designs are completely inappropriate for access by object-oriented code, or non-object code for that matter, yet cannot easily be reworked due to the large number of legacy applications coupled to them. You can create stored procedures to read and write records that look like the objects that you want. Dealing with legacy databases is discussed later in this chapter.
5. **Centralized SQL.** The SQL is kept in the stored procedures and is written by database experts who excel at writing optimized SQL and do not need to know Java.
6. **Easier migration for fast-changing schemas.** If your database schema changes, then compiling a stored procedure will result in a compile-time error. This makes it easy to find out the ripple effect on schema

changes, which is very useful if your schema is being enhanced at a high velocity. SQL code from Java can only be debugged at runtime or by combing through your code.

Note that there are also many reasons to avoid the use of stored procedures:

1. The server can quickly become a bottleneck using this approach. You really need to be careful when moving functionality onto your server: A stored procedure can bring the server to its knees if it is invoked often enough.
2. Stored procedures that are written in a proprietary language can be problematic if you want to be able to port your application to another database vendor in the future. It is quite common to find that you need to port your database to scale it to meet new transaction volumes—don't underestimate the importance of portability. These proprietary languages also increase your learning time before you're productive.
3. You dramatically increase the coupling within your database because stored procedures directly access tables, coupling the tables to the stored procedures. This increased coupling reduces the flexibility of your database administrators. When they want to refactor the database schema, they need to rewrite stored procedures.
4. You increase the maintenance burden for your application because those who maintain your system need to deal with application logic in two places: in your EJBs and in stored procedures. Your system will become messy over time and difficult to deal with.

The following statement sums up our thoughts on stored procedures: Use them only when necessary.

Normalizing and Denormalizing

When building your data model, you'll often be confronted with a space versus time tradeoff. For example, if you have an *order* that uses a *customer*, you can keep the two separate and unique in the database, or you can copy the customer data into the order table. By duplicating the customer information, you may make queries for orders faster, since you don't have to use the *JOIN* statement across several tables. *Data normalization* is the process of eliminating data redundancy in a database, while *denormalization* is the process of increasing redundancy for performance.

The advantage of having a highly normalized data schema is that information is stored in one place and one place only, reducing the possibility of inconsistent data. Furthermore, highly normalized data schemas in general are closer conceptually to object-oriented schemas, such as those you would create for your EJB design because the object-oriented goals of promoting high cohesion and loose coupling between classes results in similar solutions (at least from a data point of view). This generally makes it easier to map your EJBs to your data schema.

The disadvantage of normalized data schemas is that when put into production, they often suffer from performance problems. An important part of data modeling is to denormalize portions of your data schema to improve database access times.

For example, often by analyzing the relationships between data, you will see many opportunities for denormalization. One-to-one relationships, such as those between *customer* and *address*, are often prime candidates for denormalization. Their data may be stored in a single *customer* table to improve performance (the address data would be stored as one or more columns within the *customer* table). This is particularly true of leaf tables, tables that are related to only one other table, a trait that the *address* table also exhibited.

Note that if your initial, normalized data design meets the performance needs of your EJBs, it is fine as is. You should resort to denormalization only when performance testing shows that you have a problem with your beans and subsequent profiling reveals that you need to improve database access time. Enterprise-ready databases, such as Oracle, Sybase, and DB2, include data access monitoring tools that enable you to do exactly this. But if it ain't broke, don't fix it.

Table 16.1 summarizes the three most common normalization rules describing how to put data entities into a series of increasing levels of normalization. Strategies for achieving normalization are classic database challenges that are beyond the scope of this book. *An Introduction to Database Systems, 7th Edition* by C.J. Date (Addison-Wesley, 2000) goes into greater detail.

Table 16.1 Data Normalization Rules

LEVEL	RULE
First normal form	A data entity is in 1NF when it contains no repeating groups of data.
Second normal form	A data entity is in 2NF when it is in 1NF and when all of its non-key attributes are fully dependent on its primary key.
Third normal form	A data entity is in 3NF when it is in 2NF and when all of its attributes are directly dependent on the primary key.

When you are trying to track down the source of an EJB performance problem, you'll often discover that database access is the source of the problem. This is why it is important for your data design to be driven by your EJB design, and for you to be prepared to move away from a pure or normalized database design to one that is denormalized to reflect the actual performance needs of your EJBs.

Use Your EJB Object Model to Drive Your Data Model

For EJB components to map well to a relational database, your EJB schema and relational database schema must reflect one another. This evokes the question should your EJB object model drive your data model or the other way around? Whenever you are given the choice, your EJB object model should drive the development of your data model. Data models take into account only half of the picture (data), whereas object-oriented EJB models take into account the entire picture (data and behavior). By using your EJB models to drive the development of your data models, you ensure that your database schema actually supports the needs of your EJB components.

Note that for this to work, you need to have the freedom to define your data schema, which you will not have if you have to work with a legacy data schema. You also may find that you're not allowed to define the data model; rather, another group at your organization handles that. This approach often proves to be a disaster, resulting in poor performance and significant rework later in the project. In reality, data modeling is an iterative approach. You will likely need to make several iterations of your object model based on feedback from your data modeling efforts, and vice versa.

Follow a Good Data Design Process

Your life as an EJB programmer accessing a relational database will be much saner if you apply a process to object-relational mapping. We recommend the following steps:

1. Develop a data schema based on your object schema. Strip away the operations from each class, declare the classes to be tables, and remove any tables that have no attributes. Associations between classes, including inheritance, simple associations, aggregation, and composition are translated into relationships between tables. It is important to understand that this provides you with a starting point, not a final solution.
2. Apply data naming conventions. Your organization may have naming conventions for the names of tables and columns; if so, apply them as appropriate. For example, the customer table may be called TCustomer and the first name column of that table FIRST_NAME_C.

3. Identify keys for each data entity. Each table should have a primary key, one or more columns that uniquely identify an individual row in the table. Foreign keys need to be introduced to implement relationships between tables, and many-to-many relationships between tables need to be resolved via the introduction of an associative table.
4. Normalize or denormalize your data schema as required. You normalize your data schema to improve the robustness of your design, although you may find that you need to denormalize occasionally.
5. Refactor your object schema and your data schema as required. Performance problems require that your team tune the container, change the EJB object model, or change the relational database schema to improve the data access times of your EJBs.

Use Surrogate Keys

A common challenge in EJB deployments is to generate unique primary keys. You can generate two basic types of keys

- **A natural key** is one or more existing data attributes that are unique to the business concept. For example, a customer table might have two candidate natural keys, *CustomerNumber* and *SocialSecurityNumber*.
- **A surrogate key** is a key that has no business meaning, such as an *AddressID* column of an address table. Addresses don't have an easy natural key because you would need to use all of the columns of the address table to form a key for it. Introducing a surrogate key is therefore a much better option in this case.

The foremost advantage of natural keys is that they already exist; you don't need to introduce a new, unnatural value to your data schema. However, the primary disadvantage of natural keys is that because they have business meaning, they may need to change if your business requirements change. For example, if your users decide to make *CustomerNumber* alphanumeric instead of numeric, in addition to updating the schema for the customer table (which is unavoidable), you would have to change every single table where *CustomerNumber* is used as a foreign key. If the customer table instead used a surrogate key, the change would have been localized to just the customer table itself (*CustomerNumber* in this case would just be a non-key column of the table). Naturally, if you needed to make a similar change to your surrogate key strategy, perhaps adding a couple of extra digits to your key values because you've run out of values, you would have the exact same problem. This points out the need to set a workable surrogate key strategy.

For a key to remain a surrogate, you must never display its value, never allow anyone to edit it, and never allow anyone to use it for anything other than identification. As soon as you display or edit a value you give it business meaning, which effectively makes it a natural key. For example, a *Customer-Number* could have been originally intended to serve as a surrogate key, but if one day a customer number is printed on an invoice, the customer number has effectively evolved into a natural key. Ideally nobody should know that the persistent object identifier even exists, except perhaps the person(s) debugging your data schema during initial development of your application.

It's important that your primary keys are unique. There are dozens of ways to generate unique keys, such as using a database's built-in counter, an entity bean, an RMI-IIOP object, the current System time, and so forth. Each approach has its advantages and disadvantages. This discussion is fully presented in Floyd Marinescu's book *EJB Design Patterns*, published by John Wiley and Sons (2002, ISBN: 0-471-20831-0).

Understand the Impacts of Database Updates

It is important to recognize that changes to database data affect the state of the EJB components that represent that data in your application server. A database should not be updated, either by an EJB or a non-EJB application, if the impact of those changes is not fully understood. You can prevent that from happening by setting an internal policy that all database access should go through a common persistence layer (of either session beans, entity beans, or both) and championing that policy to all developers who access that database.

Versioning EJB Components

Sometimes you might need to track *versions* of an EJB component, which means to access old information that no longer exists in your bean. For example, if a customer suddenly got married, her last name might change. You might want to access her maiden name when trying to get information about her that may be stored in a different system. As another example, the historical titles that an employee has held at your organization might be important data for you to determine the next title in her career path.

To develop a versionable EJB component, you have several strategies at your disposal:

1. As your object changes, record those changes in an audit log. You can store entire objects in the log, or you can store just the deltas (changes) to your objects. You might write to this log by using an XML structure

or serialized string. To restore an object from the log, either read the object of the appropriate version in, or (if you're using deltas) perform a manual merge.

2. Add versioning columns to your tables. Tables representing versionable objects require several columns to be added, as described in Table 16.2. Whenever an object is updated, a new record is inserted into the appropriate table(s) and made the current version. The previously current version is closed, the CurrentVersion column is set to false, and the EffectiveEnd column is set to the current datetime. Note that both of those columns are optional: You can determine which row represents the current version of the object by taking the one with the most recent EffectiveStart value, and a previous version can be restored for a specific point in time by taking the row with the effective start date just previous to the requested point in time. This approach is called the immutable object design pattern.

3. Add historical tables. With this strategy you have one set of operational tables for your system that you use as you normally would, and a corresponding set of historical tables that have the same schemas with the addition of the EffectiveEnd column described in Table 16.2. When an object is updated or deleted, the operational tables are changed in the normal way. In addition, the values that had been initially retrieved into memory are written to the corresponding historical table(s), with the EffectiveEnd value set to the current datetime.

PATTERNS FOR THINGS THAT CHANGE WITH TIME

Martin Fowler has developed a pattern language for the development of versionable objects. Posted online at www.martinfowler.com, the language consists of the following patterns:

1. **Audit log: A simple log of changes, intended to be easily written and non-intrusive.**
2. **Effectivity: Add a time period to an object to show when it is effective.**
3. **Snapshot: A view of an object at a point in time.**
4. **Temporal object: An object that changes over time.**
5. **Temporal property: A property that changes over time.**
6. **Time point: Represents a point in time to some granularity.**

Table 16.2 Potential Table Columns to Support Versioning

COLUMN	TYPE	PURPOSE
CurrentVersion (Optional)	Boolean	Indicates whether the row represents the current version of the object, simplifying retrieval for most business transactions.
EffectiveStart	Datetime	Indicates the beginning of the period when the values contained in the row were valid. Must be set to the current datetime when the row is first inserted.
EffectiveEnd (Optional)	Datetime	Indicates the end of the period when the values contained in the row were valid. The value is set to the current datetime when the replacement version of an object is first inserted.

A few quick observations about making your EJB components versionable:

- The addition of versioning columns is not an option if you are mapping to a legacy database schema.
- For any of these approaches to work, all systems or objects accessing your database must follow them consistently.
- Versioning is performance intensive, requiring additional writes to support updates and deletions as well as more complex retrievals.
- There is no explicit support for versioning with CMP entity beans. If you're using CMP, check your EJB container's documentation to see if it supports versioning.
- If your EJB object model and database schemas vary wildly, the audit log approach is likely your best bet.
- These approaches focus on the versioning of data only, not behavior. To version behavior, you need to support different versions of the same classes or apply the *strategy* or *command* design patterns.
- Avoid versioning if you can because it is complex, error-prone, and it negatively affects performance.

Living with a Legacy Database Design

For the sake of simplicity we have assumed throughout this chapter that you are in a position to define your data schema. If this is actually your situation, consider yourself among the lucky few. The vast majority of EJB developers are often forced to tolerate an existing legacy design, one that is often difficult, if not impossible, to change because of corresponding changes that would be required to the legacy applications that currently access it. The problem presented by your legacy database is often too difficult to fix immediately; you therefore have to learn to work around it.

This section is *not* about general integration with non-RDBMS legacy systems, such as an SAP R/3 system or a CICS/COBOL system. For integration with legacy systems, see Chapter 17.

How do you learn to live with a legacy data design? The first step is to understand the scope of the challenge. Start by identifying and understanding the impact of typical data-related problems that you will encounter with legacy data. Table 16.3 lists the most common data problems and summarizes their potential impact on your application. You will likely experience several of these problems in any given database, and any given table or even column within the database will exhibit these problems.

Table 16.3 is lengthy and intended for reference purposes only—you don't need to read or understand the entire table right now. When you encounter a legacy database and want to migrate that into an EJB environment, return to this table.

Both data and database design problems have a common impact on your EJB components: They make it harder to take advantage of CMP because your EJB container needs the ability to overcome the problems appropriately. For those living with a hairy legacy design, we recommend BMP or session beans plus JDBC.

The good news is that your project team isn't the only one facing these sorts of challenges—almost every organization has these problems. As a result, a large market exists for tools to help deal with legacy databases. A sampling is listed in Table 16.4. The basic features are extraction of legacy data, transformation of the legacy data to cleanse it, and the loading of that data into a new data schema that is more robust. Products that support all of these features are referred to as ETL (extract, transform, load) tools.

Table 16.3 Typical Legacy Data Problems

PROBLEM	EXAMPLE	POTENTIAL IMPACT
A single column is used for several purposes	Additional information for an inventory item is stored in the Notes column	• One or more attributes of your EJB components may need to be mapped to this field, requiring a complex parsing algorithm to determine the proper usage of the column.
	Additional information will be one or more of a lengthy description of the item, storage requirements, or safety requirements when handling the item.	• Your EJB component(s) may be forced to implement a similar attribute instead of implementing several attributes as your design originally described.
The purpose of a column is determined by the value of one or more other columns.	If the value of *DateType* is 17, *PersonDate* represents the date of birth of the person. If the value is 84, *PersonDate* is the person's date of graduation from high school. If the value is between 35 and 48, it is the date the person entered high school.	• A potentially complex mapping is required to work with the value stored in the column.
Incorrect data values	The *AgeInYears* column for a person row is –3 or the *AgeInYears* column contains 7, although the *BirthDate* is August 14, 1967 and the current date is October 10, 2001.	• Your EJB components need to implement validation code to ensure that their base data values are correct. • Strategies to replace incorrect values may need to be defined and implemented. • An error-handling strategy needs to be developed to deal with bad data. This may include logging of the error, attempting to fix the error, or dropping the data from processing until the problem is corrected.

(continued)

Table 16.3 *(continued)*

PROBLEM	EXAMPLE	POTENTIAL IMPACT
Inconsistent/incorrect data formatting	The name of a person is stored in one table in the format Firstname Surname, yet in another table, Surname, Firstname.	• Parsing code will be required to both retrieve and store the data as appropriate.
Missing data	The date of birth of a person has not been recorded in some records.	• See strategies for dealing with incorrect data values.
Missing columns	You need a person's middle name, but a column for it does not exist.	• You may need to add the column to the existing legacy schema. • You might need to do without the data. • Identify a default value until the data is available. • An alternate source for the data may need to be found.
Additional columns	The Social Security number for a person is stored in the database and you don't need it	• For columns that are required for other applications, you may be required to implement them in your EJB components to ensure that the other applications can use the data your application generates. • You may need to write the appropriate default value to the database when inserting a new record. • For database updates, you may need to read the original value, and then write it out again.

Table 16.3 *(continued)*

PROBLEM	EXAMPLE	POTENTIAL IMPACT
Multiple sources for the same data	Customer information is stored in three separate legacy databases.	• Identify a single source for your information and use only that. • Be prepared to access multiple sources for the same information. • Identify rules for choosing a preferred source when you discover the same information is stored in several places.
Important entities, attributes, and relationships hidden and floating in text fields	A Note's text field contains the information Clark and Lois Kent, Daily Planet Publications.	• Develop code to parse the information from the fields. • Do without the information.
Data values that stray from their field descriptions and business rules	The maiden name column is being used to store a person's fabric preference for clothing.	• You need to update the documentation to reflect the actual usage. • Bean providers that took the documentation at face value may need to update their code. • Data analysis should be performed to determine the exact usage in case different applications are using the field for different purposes.
Various key strategies for the same type of entity	One table stores customer information using SSN as the key, another uses the ClientID as the key, and another uses a surrogate key.	• You need to be prepared to access similar data using several strategies, implying the need for similar finder operations in some classes. • Some attributes of an entity bean may be immutable—their value cannot be changed—because they represent part of a key in your relational database. Note that these attributes would not be part of the primary key class for your entity bean.

(continued)

Table 16.3 *(continued)*

PROBLEM	EXAMPLE	POTENTIAL IMPACT
Unrealized relationships between data records	A customer has a primary residence and a summer home. Both of his homes are recorded in your database, but there is no relationship stored in the database regarding this fact	• Data may be inadvertently replicated. Eventually a new address record is inadvertently created (and the relationship now defined) for the summer home even though one already exists. • Additional code may need to be developed to detect potential problems. Procedures for handling the problems will also be required.
One attribute is stored in several fields.	The person class requires a single name field, but is stored in the columns *FirstName* and *Surname* in your database.	• Potentially complex parsing code may be required to retrieve, and then save the data.
Inconsistent use of special characters	A date uses hyphens to separate the year, month, and day, whereas a numerical value stored as a string uses hyphens to indicate negative numbers.	• Complexity of parsing code increases. • Additional documentation is required to indicate character usage.
Different data types for similar columns	A customer ID is stored as a number in one table and a string in another.	• You may need to decide how you want the data to be handled by your EJBs and then transform it to/from your data source(s) as appropriate. • If foreign key fields have a different type than original data they represent, then table joins, and hence any SQL embedded in your EJBs, become more difficult.

Table 16.3 *(continued)*

PROBLEM	EXAMPLE	POTENTIAL IMPACT
Different levels of detail	A bean requires the total sales for the month, but your database stores individual totals for each order; or a bean requires the weight of individual components of an item such as the doors and engine of a car, but your database records only the aggregate weight.	• Potentially complex mapping code may be required to resolve the various levels of detail.
Different modes of operation	Some data is a read-only snapshot of information, but other data is read-write.	• The design of your EJBs must reflect the nature of the data they are mapped to. EJBs based on read-only data, therefore, cannot update or delete it.
Varying timeliness of data	The customer data is current, address data is one day out of date, and the data pertaining to countries and states is accurate to the end of the previous quarter because you purchase that information from an external source.	• Your EJB code must reflect, and potentially report to their clients, the timeliness of the information that they are based on.
Varying default values	Your EJB uses a default of green for a given value, yet another application has been using yellow, resulting in a preponderance (in the opinion of your users) of yellow values stored in the database.	• You may need to negotiate a new default value with your users. • You may not be allowed to store your default value (green is an illegal value in the database).
Various representations	The day of the week is stored as T, Tues, 2, and Tuesday in four separate columns.	• Translation code back and forth between a common value that your EJB(s) use will need to be developed.

(continued)

Table 16.3 *(continued)*

PROBLEM	EXAMPLE	POTENTIAL IMPACT
Database encapsulation scheme exists	Access to the database is provided only through stored procedures; for example, to create a new customer you must invoke a specified stored procedure. Access to views on the database is permitted; direct table access is denied. The database must be accessed via an API implemented by a C or COBOL wrapper that in turn accesses database directly. The database must be accessed via predefined classes/objects.	• To enable CMP the encapsulation scheme must be made to look like a data source that your persistence container recognizes. Otherwise you will be forced to take a Session Beans plus JDBC or BMP approach to persistence. • The encapsulation scheme will likely increase the response time of database access. • The individual components of the encapsulation scheme may not be able to be included as a data step in a transaction.
Naming conventions	Your database(s) may follow different naming conventions from one another and likely do not follow common Java naming conventions.	• The bean deployer(s) will need to understand all relevant naming conventions. • Political pressure may be put on your team to follow inappropriate corporate data naming conventions for use with your EJBs.
Inadequate documentation	The documentation for your database is sparse, nonexistent, or out of date.	• A significant legacy data analysis effort will be required to determine the proper usage of each table, column, and stored procedure within your database.

Table 16.3 *(continued)*

PROBLEM	EXAMPLE	POTENTIAL IMPACT
Original design goals are at odds with current project needs.	The legacy database was built for internal use by data entry clerks to capture customer orders in batch mode, whereas you are building a 24x7 order entry application to be deployed over the Internet.	• Good luck. You'll need it.
Inconsistent key strategy	Your database uses natural keys for some tables, surrogate keys in others, and different strategies for surrogate keys when they are used.	• Bean providers must understand, and then appropriately code support for the various key strategies for their EJBs. • Key generation code increases in complexity to support the various strategies. • Additional source code to validate that natural keys are, in fact, unique will be required. • Relationship management code increases in complexity because you can't code, and then reuse a single approach.

Table 16.4 Sample Legacy Data Integration Tools

TOOL	URL
Informatica PowerCenter	www.informatica.com
ETI*Extract	www.eti.com
Aardvark Knowledge Builder	www.d2k.com
Ascential Software's DataStage	www.ascentialsoftware.com
Trillium Control Center	www.trilliumsoft.com

Once you've identified the challenges in your legacy data integration efforts, the second step is to determine how you will address the problems that you have found with your legacy data and the legacy database design. Table 16.5 compares and contrasts several strategies at your disposal.

Table 16.5 Strategies for Mitigating Legacy Data Problems

STRATEGY	ADVANTAGES	DISADVANTAGES
Create your own private database for new attributes.	• You have complete control over your database. • You may be able to avoid conforming to legacy procedures within your organization, speeding up development	• Replication of common data is likely. • Unable to easily take advantage of the existing corporate legacy data. • May still be required to integrate with the legacy corporate database(s) via triggers, programmed batch jobs, or ETL tools. • Your team must have database expertise. • Your project risks significant political problems because you may be perceived as not being team players.
Refactor your data schema.	• You have a clean database design to work with. • Your database schema can be redesigned to reflect the needs of modern, object-oriented, and component-based technologies, such as EJB.	• This is very difficult to achieve. • Legacy applications will need to be updated to reflect the new data schema. • You will need to identify and fix all of your data-related problems, requiring significant effort.

Table 16.5 *(continued)*

STRATEGY	ADVANTAGES	DISADVANTAGES
		• You need to develop, and then follow, procedures to ensure that your database design remains clean; otherwise you will end up in the same position several years from now.
Encapsulate database access with stored procedures, views classes or objects, or an API.	• A clean access approach to encapsulation can be presented to application developers.	• Legacy applications should be rewritten, to ensure integrity within the database. • Implementing your encapsulation strategy may require significant effort. • Your encapsulation approach may become an architectural bottleneck. • Depending on the range of technologies within your organization, you may not be able to find one strategy that works for all applications.
Design your EJBs to work with the existing design as is.	• Your EJBs work with the legacy database(s).	• Significant redesign and coding is likely to be required for this to work. • The actual problem, a poor database design, is not addressed and will continue to affect future projects. • This may not be feasible, depending on the extent of the mismatch between the legacy database design and the requirements for your application.

(continued)

Table 16.5 *(continued)*

STRATEGY	ADVANTAGES	DISADVANTAGES
Design your EJBs to work with the existing design as is. *(continued)*		• Performance is likely to be significantly impacted because of the resulting overhead of mapping your EJBs to the database and the transformations required to support those mappings. • Common approaches to persistence, such as CMP and the use of a persistence layer or framework, is likely not an option if the mismatch is too great.

Although descriptions of how to implement these three strategies is clearly beyond the scope of this book, we can provide some advice:

1. Do not underestimate the effort required to address this problem. If it can be done at all, data migration or improvement efforts often prove to be a project, or a series of projects, that span several years. This is easily on the order of magnitude of your organization's Year 2000 (Y2K) efforts.
2. Think small. A series of small changes, or refactorings, is often preferable to a single big-bang approach in which you need to re-release all of your organization's applications at once. Martin Fowler's book *Refactoring: Improving the Design of Existing Code* (Addison Wesley, 1999) describes the principles and practices of refactoring. It should provide some insight into how to make incremental changes to your legacy data design (many of his refactorings are geared to changing object-oriented designs, but the fundamentals still apply).
3. Did we mention not to underestimate the effort required?

Handling Large Result Sets

A serious problem when writing finder methods of entity beans (or any relational database code for that matter) is handling larger-than-expected result sets. If you locate too much data, you are causing undue performance issues, because you may not need the entire result set. To handle this situation, you have several strategies at your disposal:

- Add code to estimate the size of the result set, a feature most relational databases support, and throw an exception if it's too big. This works for session beans plus JDBC.
- Learn to live with the large result set. If it doesn't happen very often, it might not be worth your while to write code to deal with this. This works for session beans plus JDBC, BMP, and CMP.
- Write tighter *SELECT* statements by introducing additional parameters to narrow the results. This works for session beans plus JDBC, BMP, and CMP.
- Limit the results of the finder through the SQL bound to the method (a feature of most databases).
- Use a scrollable result set. JDBC 2.0 introduced the ability to access the results of *SELECT* clauses as database cursors, enabling bean providers to write code that brings portions of the result set across the network at a time. This works for session beans plus JDBC.
- Use session beans to control how the result set is handled. For example, you can use a stateful session bean that caches a collection of primary keys. When the client requests data, return only a block (say 20 pieces) of data at a time based on the primary keys.
- Let your persistence container handle it. Some persistence containers, such as Oracle TOPLink, implement strategies for dealing with large result sets. This works for entity beans.

Summary

In this chapter, we touched on a variety of best practices and strategies when performing persistence in an EJB environment. We learned when to (and when not to) use entity beans, and how to choose between BMP and CMP, and we surveyed a large collection of persistence best practices.

In the next chapter, we'll take a look at an advanced EJB topic—integration with legacy systems. Stay tuned!

CHAPTER

17

EJB Integration

In this chapter, we will begin our journey into the world of EJB integration. If you are faced with a situation where you are required to integrate EJB applications with those running on other platforms or legacy applications, this chapter will provide you with a lot of helpful information. Specifically, you'll learn about the following:

- Introduction to integration, including an overview of various styles of integration
- Various approaches to integrate EJB with non-EJB applications
- J2EE connector architecture by example
- Best practices for integrating EJB applications

Why Does Integration Matter?

Integrating applications, services, and data is absolutely critical for streamlining business processes. These processes might run throughout your company or be used by your business partners, suppliers, and customers. Companies with integrated business processes are quick to respond to fluctuating market conditions as compared to those lacking integrated business processes. Also, if the industry you are in is hit by a consolidation wave, it is quite possible for your company to participate in mergers and acquisitions. With every merger or acquisition comes the huge challenge of integrating business processes, mostly electronic, of the two companies. Although, this integration is gradual, it provides a definite value to your company.

Apart from the business imperatives, there are many technical reasons why businesses should take integration seriously. A typical enterprise IT today comprises anywhere from dozens to hundreds of applications. These applications might have been acquired from outside or built in-house. Many times these applications would be developed using legacy technologies or deployed on legacy platforms. It is not uncommon to find an enterprise with silos of applications mostly written using different architectures and potentially maintaining their own instances of domain data. This places huge burdens in terms of resources and time on an enterprise IT.

It is not very hard to see some of the clear-cut benefits of integrating these isolated silos of applications across your IT.

- Integration eliminates the need to build new applications and services every time a new business requirement has to be met. Thereby, it maximizes the use of current IT assets and provides a better return on IT investments.
- Integration makes it possible to optimize resources in terms of storage and processing by taking redundancy out of data and business functions.
- Integration brings together the entire enterprise from back-end transaction processing to front-end customer service. This ultimately increases the value of IT to a business.

These benefits are the core reasons why integration does matter to a CIO, and hence, to us.

Integration Styles

Depending on whether it is being done within or across the enterprise boundary, integration solutions can be categorized as intra-enterprise or inter-enterprise. Integration solutions can be further classified into the following two groups:

- **Application integration** focuses on establishing connectivity between applications. This style forms the basis for enterprise application integration (EAI) solutions. This connectivity can be established through messaging systems such as message-oriented middleware (MOM) or RPC communications such as IIOP, sockets, SOAP RPC, and so on.

- **Business process integration** automates business processes by coordinating and controlling activities that span multiple systems. Process integration middleware can reuse various applications implementing process activities and also can support long-running transactions. Traditionally this style of integration has been achieved using business process management systems (BPMS) from vendors such as Vitria, SeeBeyond, Intalio, TIBCO, Sun Microsystems, IBM, Microsoft, BEA, and so on. Also some BPM vendors provide BPM products that focus exclusively on the target industries. Recently, this sector has seen a lot of standardization in terms of how the processes are described and how their activities are coordinated. BPMI BPML, W3C Choreography, OASIS WS-BPEL, and EbXML BPSS are just a few examples of such standards.

Thus, process integration can be viewed as a business logic layer that determines *what* needs to be done at a given point in a process while application integration can be viewed as a technology layer that determines *how* it gets done. Usually, business process integration is done with the help of business analysts, as opposed to application integration that is done by software architects. As technologists we are best served by focusing on the *how* part of integration, that is application integration.

EJB and Integration

Presently, EJB applications have three technology choices for application integration:

- **JMS and JMS-based message-driven beans** are a foremost technology choice for communicating with message-oriented middleware systems from EJB platform.
- **Java Web Services** is another approach of integration to and from EJB applications, especially with a target platform such as Microsoft .NET, which is also Web Services aware.
- **J2EE Connector Architecture** is a full-fledged enterprise integration framework for building adapters or connectors that can communicate with EJB applications.

We already discussed JMS-based message-driven beans and Java Web Services in Chapters 9 and 5, respectively. In this chapter, we will focus on learning J2EE Connector Architecture and see how it addresses the integration problem.

J2EE Connector Architecture

J2EE Connector Architecture is a standard framework for supporting enterprise application integration for Java platform. Connector architecture defines the notion of a resource adapter (RA) that can be plugged into any J2EE-compliant application server to enable J2EE applications to communicate with the enterprise information system (EIS). The connector specification thus defines a component model for developing and deploying resource adapters.

Why J2EE Connectors?

Even before J2EE Connector Architecture existed, it was possible to communicate with native applications via Java Native Interfaces (JNI). Socket communication presented yet another alternative of integrating with non-Java applications. And don't forget IIOP—using RMI-IIOP it is possible to communicate with any CORBA-IIOP application. So why do we need J2EE connectors?

To understand this, let us first understand various problems pertaining to integration in a connector-less world.

An EIS encompasses all those systems that provide information infrastructure for an enterprise. These EISs provide a well-defined set of information services to their clients through various interfaces. Examples of EISs include ERP systems, transaction processing systems, and database systems. More recently, the term EIS is also used to refer to custom IT applications.

Integrating J2EE Platform with Non-IIOP World

The two most common ways to integrate with non-IIOP applications from the Java platform are to use JNI or sockets. However, if you want to integrate a J2EE application with non-IIOP application you cannot use either of these mechanisms since using both JNI and sockets is taboo in J2EE for security reasons. A safe, robust framework that provides integration with the non-IIOP world of applications is needed. J2EE Connector Architecture is an answer to this need.

The M x N Integration Problem

Prior to J2EE connectors no standard mechanism of integrating J2EE applications with heterogeneous non-J2EE, non-IIOP EIS existed. To integrate J2EE applications with EIS, most EIS vendors and application server vendors had to provide non-standard proprietary solutions. For example, if you had to integrate your J2EE order management application with a SAP inventory management application you had to use proprietary integration adapters to make your application server communicate with SAP. These non-standard adapters could have been provided by your application server vendor or by your EIS vendor, which was SAP in this case. Similarly, if you wanted your J2EE applications to integrate with any other EISs, you needed specific adapters that allowed your application server to talk to your EIS.

This presented a big challenge for the vendors of application servers and EIS—they were required to support and maintain M x N number of proprietary integration solutions to make M number of application servers communicate with N number of EISs. This M x N problem, described in Figure 17.1, was the main motivation for these vendors to create J2EE connector technology that enables building standard adapters (a.k.a. resource adapters/connectors) for specific EISs so that these adapters can plug into any J2EE-complaint application server and communicate with the EIS.

Hence, the M x N problem is now reduced to 1 x N problem, where N adapters are needed to integrate with N number of EIS from *any* J2EE environment as shown in Figure 17.2.

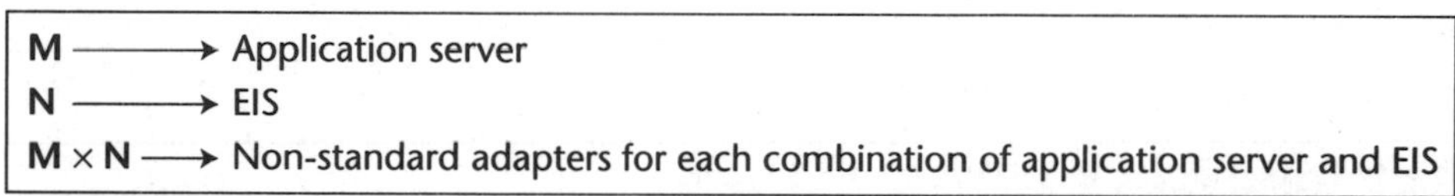

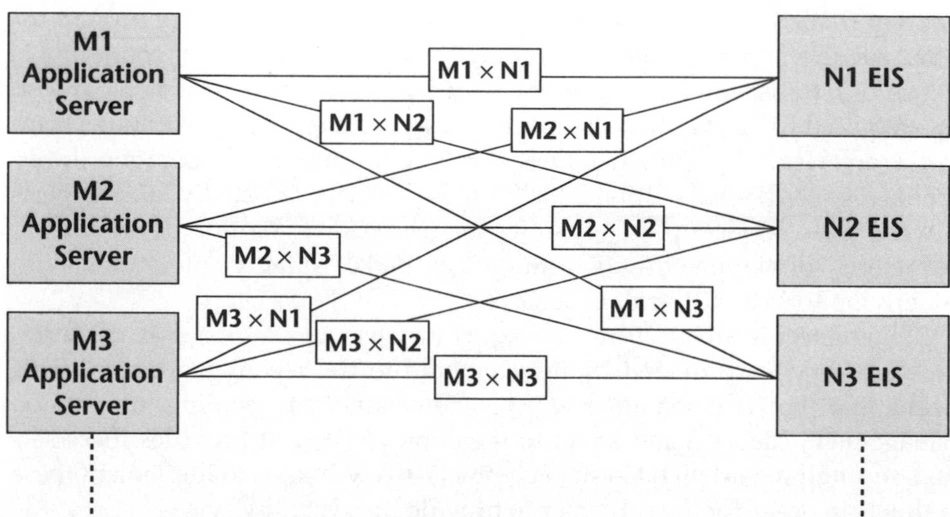

Figure 17.1 The M x N integration problem.

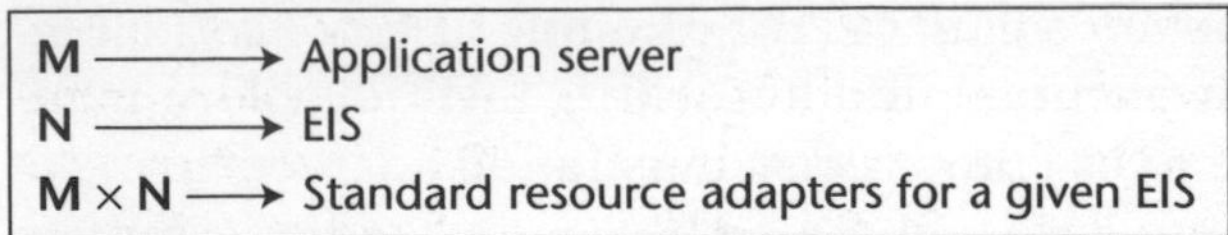

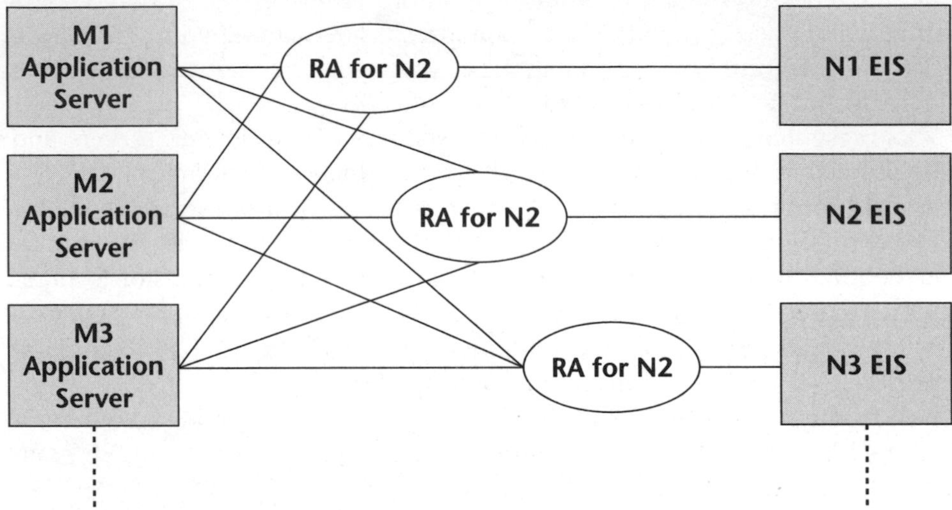

Figure 17.2 Reduction of M x N integration problem to 1 x N.

The Infrastructure Services Problem

Another challenge when building integration solutions is to enable support for infrastructure services—such as resource pooling (for threads, connections, and so on), transaction management, security, life cycle management, and so on—required for transactional, robust, and secure integration. Without a standard framework that provides these services, an integration solution developer is responsible for writing logic for these services. It usually takes experts to write these services plus it requires longer cycle of solution development, debugging, deployment, and testing. This makes quality integration with underlying EIS very difficult to achieve.

J2EE connector architecture solves this problem too—it extends the infrastructure services provided by the container to the resource adapters. This means that the J2EE container will provide connection pooling, transaction management, security, and so on to the deployed RA. It provides these services through well-defined system contracts. RA will need to implement these contracts in order for the container to provide the system services.

Thus, the application server and resource adapter keep the system-level details related to the interaction with the underlying EIS transparent from the application component. This is one of the main reasons for using resource adapters—it keeps the components free from the complexity of having to deal with transactions, security, connections, multithreading, and other such infrastructure details, while communicating with the EIS. This is what we call "integration made simple"!

Resource Adapter Interaction with J2EE Components

When deployed in a managed environment by way of an application server, RA accepts requests from various J2EE components, such as servlets, JSPs, and EJBs, translates those requests into EIS-specific calls, and sends those requests to the EIS. The response that it receives from the EIS is forwarded to the client J2EE components. Application components thus interact with RA through its client contracts. RA can support client contracts in one of the following ways:

- **Common Client Interfaces (CCI)** is a standard set of APIs for interacting with *any* EIS through its respective RA. CCI provides a mechanism for accessing a heterogeneous EIS using the same interface. CCI support is optional although recommended for the RA provider. Especially providers that expect their RA to be used by third-party tools should support CCI to enable tools to communicate with them through the standard CCI.
- **EIS-specific client interfaces** can be supported by the RA provider to make it easier for application components to work with the underlying EIS by using APIs attuned to EIS's inner workings. Most of the EISs have EIS-specific client APIs. For example, the JDBC API is the client API for communicating with RDBMS EIS.

Figure 17.3 shows this interaction between various J2EE components, RA, and EIS.

J2EE CONNECTORS AND NON-MANAGED ENVIRONMENTS

Standalone Java applications run in a non-managed environment since there is no container to provide them with *managed* services such as transactions, security, life cycle management, resource pooling, and so on.

J2EE Connector Architecture supports non-managed environments. This enables Java applications to access the underlying EIS through an RA. In a non-managed scenario, the application client directly uses the RA library. RAs that support non-managed access should expose the low-level APIs for transaction, security, and connection management. The application client will interact with RA and use its low-level APIs. This model is similar to using a resource adapter such as a JDBC driver in a non-managed environment.

Since this chapter is on EJB integration we will discuss connectors only in the context of managed environment.

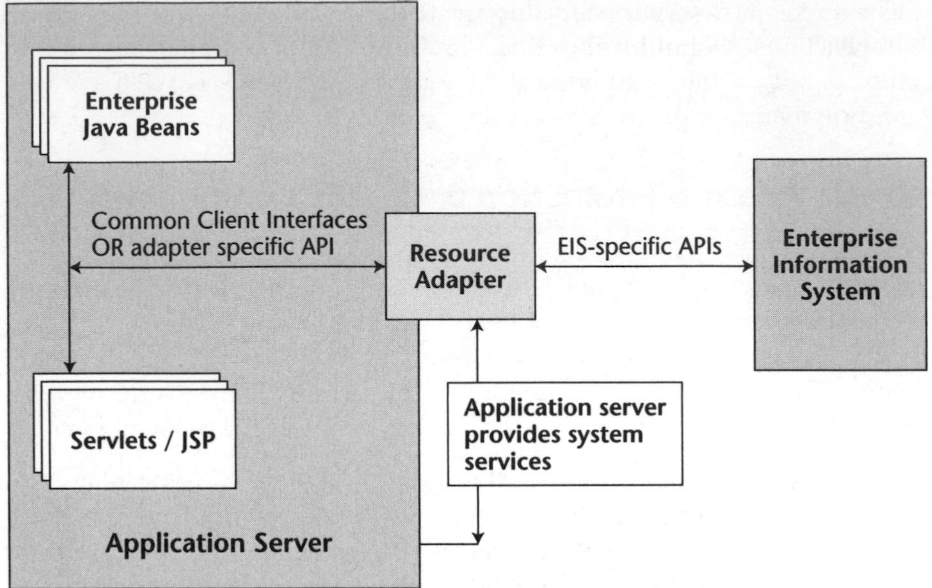

Figure 17.3 Interaction between the J2EE connector, RA, and EIS.

Resource Adapter Interaction with Application Server

To interact with the application server and avail various container services, the RA provider can choose to implement the following system contracts:

- **The connection management contract** enables application components to connect to the EIS so that the application server can pool these connections. Essentially, by implementing this contract your components can connect to the resource adapter, which in turn will establish the connection to the underlying EIS.
- **The transaction management contract** allows transactional access to the EIS from your application components. It enables the application server to leverage the transaction manager for managing global transactions across multiple resource managers, including the EIS resource manager. Also, RA can support local transactions, which do not require coordination from a transaction manager through this contract.
- **The security contract** enables secure access to the EIS from the application component.
- **The life cycle management contract** has been introduced in J2EE Connector Architecture 1.5. It allows the application server to manage life cycle functions, such as bootstrapping the RA upon application server startup or RA deployment and shutting down RA upon application server shutdown or undeployment, on behalf of a resource adapter.

The application server will notify the RA instance of these bootstrapping/shutdown events.

- **The work management contract** was introduced in J2EE Connector Architecture 1.5. By implementing this contract, RA can submit the *work* it needs to perform to the application server, which in turn will spawn a new thread or retrieve a worker thread from its thread pool to execute RA-delegated work. This contract thus enables RA to increase throughput of handling requests from application components without having to spawn or manage threads directly.
- **The transaction inflow contract**, also introduced in J2EE Connector Architecture 1.5, allows the RA to propagate the transaction context imported from EIS to the application server. This contract supplements the transaction management contract, which allowed RA to propagate the transaction context from application server to the underlying EIS. Through this contract, the RA can notify the application server of transaction completion and crash recovery calls initiated by the EIS thereby helping the application server coordinate transactions at its end.

THE GROWING IMPORTANCE OF CONNECTORS IN J2EE

In J2EE 1.4 the application of RA has been extended further in that RA can now be used to provide connectivity for all kinds of EIS applications. Regardless of whether a standard connectivity solution to the EIS from the Java platform exists, vendors are encouraged to provide connectivity to their EIS through RA. Hence, we will eventually see vendors providing RA for connecting to all kinds of EISs—RDBMS, MOM systems, and enterprise applications such as SAP, Siebel, PeopleSoft, and so on.

This is a step in a good direction because:

- **The whole industry can now unify around a single architecture for connectivity regardless of the type of underlying EIS. This will enable tool vendors and system integrators to provide out-of-the-box integration solutions, which in turn will reduce the cost of building integration solutions on J2EE platform.**
- **The industry will not have to spend time defining connectivity per EIS. Connector architecture eliminates the need to define Service Provider Interfaces (SPI) for different EIS connectivity providers. As a result, the Java community is not required to create standard SPIs for writing JMS message providers or JDBC providers in the future. Rather, the vendors will leverage SPI as defined by J2EE connector architecture to interact with the J2EE application server and its container services.**

The fact that vendors are building and shipping RA for connecting to all kinds of EIS—including databases, messaging systems, and enterprise applications—establishes connector architecture as the predominant framework in the J2EE integration space.

- **The message inflow contract**, introduced in J2EE Connector Architecture 1.5, allows RA to asynchronously deliver messages to message endpoints residing in the application server independent of the messaging semantics, style, and infrastructure used to deliver messages. This contract also serves as a standard message provider pluggability contract that allows a wide range of messaging providers to be plugged into any compatible J2EE application server via a resource adapter.

The J2EE Connector API

The Connector API consists of six packages—*javax.resource, javax.resource .cci, javax.resource.spi, javax.resource.spi.endpoint, javax.resource.spi.security,* and *javax.resource.spi.work*. We will take a look at each of these packages and their main interfaces and classes. This overview of connector APIs followed by the description of how RA should implement various system contracts should help you understand the connector architecture.

The javax.resource Package

Table 17.1 discusses the main members of this top-level connector API package.

Table 17.1 The javax.resource Package Members

PACKAGE MEMBERS	DESCRIPTION
javax.resource.Referenceable	The implementation class of RA's connection factory is required to implement *Referenceable* interface to enable its registration in the JNDI namespace.
javax.resource.ResourceException	This is the root interface of the connector exception hierarchy.
javax.resource.NotSupportedException	This class extends *ResourceException* and is thrown to indicate that the RA did not support a particular operation.

The javax.resource.cci Package

This package comprises the APIs that should be implemented by an RA that supports CCI. Table 17.2 discusses the main members of this package.

Table 17.2 The javax.resource.cci Package Members

PACKAGE MEMBERS	DESCRIPTION
javax.resource.cci .Connection	This interface represents a handle that is used by the client to access the underlying physical connection represented by a *ManagedConnection* instance.
javax.resource.cci .ConnectionFactory	Represents a factory interface that is used to obtain the *Connection* handle via *getConnection()* method. The client looks up an instance of *ConnectionFactory* registered with JNDI during deployment. The *ConnectionFactory* implementation class is required to implement *Referenceable* so that it can support registration to JNDI.
javax.resource.cci .ConnectionMetaData	The client can use this interface to get specific information, such as product name and version, about the underlying EIS. Also, *ConnectionMetaData* provides a user name corresponding to the resource principal under whose security context the given connection to the EIS has been established. An instance of *ConnectionMetaData* could be obtained through the *getMetaData()* method on the *Connection* interface.
javax.resource.cci .ConnectionSpec	If supported by RA, the client can use this interface to pass the connection request–specific properties to *ConnectionFactory*. *ConnectionSpec* is a marker interface and the RA should implement this interface as a JavaBean with getters/setters for each connection property. The specification defines standard connection properties, such as *UserName* and *Password*. However, the RA is not required to implement getters/setters for these standard properties if it is not relevant to the underlying EIS.
javax.resource .cci.Interaction	*Interaction* is a representation of the client's interaction with the EIS in terms of executing various functions or procedures on the EIS. The client obtains the *Interaction* instance through the *createInteraction()* method on *Connection.* There are two methods the client can use to interact with the EIS: • *execute (InteractionSpec ispec, Record input)* executes the EIS function as specified by the *InteractionSpec* instance and produces the output *Record* which carries the resulting return value. • *execute (InteractionSpec ispec, Record input, Record output)* executes the EIS function as specified by the *InteractionSpec* instance and updates the output *Record* with the resulting return value.

(continued)

Table 17.2 *(continued)*

PACKAGE MEMBERS	DESCRIPTION
javax.resource.cci .InteractionSpec	This interface represents properties required for driving interaction with the EIS. RA is required to implement *InteractionSpec* as a JavaBean with getters/setters for each of the properties. Connector specification defines the following three standard interaction properties: • *FunctionName* corresponds to the name of the EIS function that the given interaction will execute. • *InteractionVerb* specifies the mode of interaction with EIS. The standard interaction verbs are SYNC_SEND, SYNC_SEND_RECEIVE, and SYNC_RECEIVE. SYNC_SEND specifies that the execution of an *Interaction* will perform only send operation and not receive. SYNC_SEND_RECEIVE specifies that the execution will perform both synchronous send and receive operations. SYNC_RECEIVE specifies that the execution will perform only synchronous receive operations. The last mode is used by an application component to perform a synchronous callback to EIS. Note that CCI does not support asynchronous delivery of messages to the application components. The message inflow system contract should be used for the same, as we will see later in this chapter. • *ExecutionTimeout* specifies the number of milliseconds an *Interaction* will wait for an EIS to execute the specified function. RA is not required to support a standard property if that property does not apply to the underlying EIS. Also, RA can support additional *InteractionSpec* properties if relevant to the EIS.
javax.resource.cci.Record	This interface represents input or output to the *execute( )* methods on *Interaction* object. This is the base interface for *javax.resource.cci.MappedRecord*, *javax.resource.cci.IndexedRecord*, and *javax .resource.cci.Resultset* types of records.
javax.resource.cci .MappedRecord	*MappedRecord* represents input or output in the form of a key-value pair-based collection. Naturally, it extends *java.util.Map*, apart from *javax.resource.cci.Record* interface, to provide this functionality.
javax.resource.cci .IndexedRecord	*IndexedRecord* represents input or output in the form of an ordered and indexed collection. It extends the *java.util.List* interface, apart from *javax.resource.cci.Record*, to enable this searchable and indexed collection of record elements.

Table 17.2 *(continued)*

PACKAGE MEMBERS	DESCRIPTION
javax.resource.cci .ResultSet	This interface represents tabular data that is retrieved from EIS as a result of executing a function on EIS. It extends *java.sql.ResultSet*, apart from the *javax.resource.cci.Record* interface, to provide this functionality. Thus, a CCI *Resultset* has capabilities similar to JDBC *ResultSet* in that it can be scrollable and updatable, can support various Java types and concurrency modes, and so on.
javax.resource.cci .ResultSetInfo	The client application component can get information about the various facilities provided for *ResultSet* by the EIS through this interface. *ResultSetInfo* supports methods such as *supportsResultSetType( )*, *supportsResultTypeConcurrency( )*, and so on, to provide this information. The client can get a hold of the *ResultSetInfo* instance through the *getResultSetInfo( )* method on *Connection*.
javax.resource.cci .RecordFactory	This factory interface allows the clients to create instances of *MappedRecord* and *IndexedRecord*. Note that it is not used for creating *ResultSet* records. The client component gets a hold of *RecordFactory* instance through *getRecordFactory( )* method on *ConnectionFactory*.
javax.resource.cci .LocalTransaction	This represents the transaction demarcation interface to be used by client application components for managing local transactions at the EIS level. If RA supports local transactions, it should implement this interface. The client can get a hold of the *LocalTransaction* instance through the *getLocalTransaction( )* method on the *Connection* object. If RA's CCI implementation does not support local transactions, *getLocalTransaction( )* should throw *javax.resource.NotSupportedException*.
javax.resource.cci .MessageListener	This CCI interface represents a request/response message listener that should be implemented by message endpoints (such as message-driven beans) to enable EIS to communicate with them through the *onMessage( )* method.
javax.resource.cci .ResourceAdapter MetaData	This interface provides information about the capabilities of the RA. The client gets a hold of its instance through the *getMetaData( )* method on *ConnectionFactory*.

Note that the RA is only supposed to implement the type of record that it deems fit for the underlying EIS.

The javax.resource.spi Package

This package consists of APIs corresponding to various system contracts. An RA should implement APIs for system contracts that it chooses to support with the help of the application server. Table 17.3 discusses the main members of this package.

Table 17.3 The javax.resource.spi Package Members

PACKAGE MEMBERS	DESCRIPTION
javax.resource.spi .ConnectionManager	The *allocateConnection()* method on *ConnectionManager* provides a hook to the application server so that it can provide *generic* quality of services such as security, connection pooling, transaction management, logging, and so on, while establishing connection to the EIS.
javax.resource.spi .ManagedConnection	This interface represents a physical connection to the underlying EIS.
javax.resource.spi .ManagedConnection Factory	This acts as a factory for *ManagedConnection*. It also provides methods for matching and creating *ManagedConnection* instances thereby supporting connection pooling. The *ManagedConnectionFactory* instance can support various standard and non-standard connection properties. However, it must support these connection properties through JavaBean style getters/setters.
javax.resource.spi .ManagedConnection MetaData	This interface provides information about the underlying EIS instance. An application server uses *ManagedConnectionMetaData* to get runtime information about the connected EIS instance such as the user associated with the *ManagedConnection* instance, the maximum limit of active connections that an EIS can support, and the EIS product name and version. The application server gets this meta data instance through the *getMetaData()* method on *ManagedConnection*.
javax.resource.spi .ConnectionEventListener	This interface, implemented by the application server, is used by the *ManagedConnection* implementation to send connection events to the application server. The application server registers an instance of *ConnectionEventListener* with *ManagedConnection* through the *addConnectionEventListener()* method on *ManagedConnection*. The application server uses these event notifications to manage connection pools, local transactions, and perform clean-up, and so on.

Table 17.3 *(continued)*

PACKAGE MEMBERS	DESCRIPTION
javax.resource.spi .ConnectionRequestInfo	RA implements this interface to support its own connection request–specific properties. The application server passes these properties to a resource adapter via the *createManagedConnection( )* and *matchManagedConnection( )* methods on *ManagedConnectionFactory* so that RA can use this additional per-request information to do connection creation and matching.
javax.resource.spi .ResourceAdapter	This interface represents an RA instance. It contains various operations for life cycle management and message endpoint setup, provided RA supports life cycle management and message inflow system contract. If RA does not support these contracts, it does not have to implement this interface.
javax.resource.spi .BootstrapContext	The *BootstrapContext* instance is passed by the application server to the RA that implements life cycle system contract through the *start( )* method on *ResourceAdapter*. It allows the RA to use various application server-provided facilities such as the timer service and work manager. Also, it provides an instance of *XATerminator* through the *getXATerminator( )* method.
javax.resource.spi .XATerminator	The application server implements this interface as part of the transaction inflow system contract. The RA uses the *XATerminator* instance to flow-in transaction completion and crash recovery calls from an EIS. *XATerminator* provides methods such as *commit( )*, *prepare( )*, *forget( )*, *recover( )*, and *rollback( )* to communicate with the application server's transaction manager about the state of the incoming global transaction.
javax.resource.spi .LocalTransaction	The RA implements the *LocalTransaction* interface to support transactions local to EIS. The RA provides access to its *LocalTransaction* instance through the *getLocalTransaction( )* method on *ManagedConnection*. The *getLocalTransaction( )* method on the *Connection* interface implementation will call the *getLocalTransaction( )* method on *ManagedConnection* to ultimately provide an instance of *javax.resource.cci.LocalTransaction* to the client application component.

(continued)

Table 17.3 *(continued)*

PACKAGE MEMBERS	DESCRIPTION
javax.resource.spi .ResourceAdapter Association	The RA implements this interface to associate the *ResourceAdapter* object with other objects such as *ManagedConnectionFactory* and *ActivationSpec*. It has *getResourceAdapter( )* and *setResourceAdapter( )* methods that can be used for this purpose.
javax.resource.spi .ActivationSpec	The RA that supports message inflow contract should implement this interface as a JavaBean. The *ActivationSpec* instance can provide connectivity information to enable inbound messaging.

Note once again that the RA should implement only system contracts that are needed. For instance, if the RA does not need help for managing outgoing connections to the EIS, it does not have to implement the various *javax .resource.spi* APIs for connection management. Similarly, if the RA does not need help managing its life cycle it does not need to implement the *javax.resource.ResourceAdapter* interface.

The javax.resource.spi.endpoint Package

This package consists of APIs pertaining to message inflow system contract. Table 17.4 discusses the main members of this package.

Table 17.4 The javax.resource.spi.endpoint Package Members

PACKAGE MEMBERS	DESCRIPTION
javax.resource.spi .endpoint.Message Endpoint	The application server implements this interface. The RA calls various methods on this interface to notify the application server that it is about to deliver a message or that it just delivered a message. The application server uses these notifications to start or stop transactions, provided that message delivery is transactional, that is, the *onMessage( )* method on the message listener interface implemented by MDB is marked as transactional (container managed).
javax.resource.spi .MessageEndpointFactory	When the RA supports message inflow contract it uses an instance of *MessageEndpointFactory* to obtain message endpoint instances for delivering messages. Also, the RA can use this interface to find out if message deliveries to a target method on message listener interface implemented by a given message endpoint is transactional or not. Like *MessageEndpoint*, the application server also implements *MessageEndpointFactory*.

The javax.resource.spi.security Package

This package contains APIs for security system contract. Table 17.5 discusses members of this package.

The RA uses other interfaces and classes as well for implementing security system contract. These are discussed later in this chapter.

The javax.resource.spi.work Package

This package contains APIs for work management system contract. Table 17.6 discusses main members of this package.

Table 17.5 The javax.resource.spi.security Package Members

PACKAGE MEMBERS	DESCRIPTION
javax.resource.spi .security.Password Credential	This class acts as a holder of the user name and password security token. This class enables the application server to pass user's security credentials to the RA.

Table 17.6 The javax.resource.spi.work Package Members

PACKAGE MEMBERS	DESCRIPTION
javax.resource.spi .work.WorkManager	The application server implements this top-level interface for work management contract. The RA gets a hold of *WorkManager* by calling *getWorkManager( )* on *BootstrapContext*. It provides methods used by the RA for submitting *Work* instances for processing.
javax.resource.spi .work.Work	The *Work* interface is implemented by the RA and it represents the logic, such as delivering incoming messages to message endpoints in the application server that the RA wants the application server to execute on a different thread.
javax.resource.spi .work.WorkListener	The RA can implement this interface if it wants to be notified by the application server of various stages, such as work accepted, work completed, work rejected, and so on, in the work processing life cycle. The RA supplies the *WorkListener* instance to the application server via various work submission methods such as *scheduleWork( )*, *startWork( )*, or *doWork( )* on *WorkManager*.

(continued)

Table 17.6 *(continued)*

PACKAGE MEMBERS	DESCRIPTION
javax.resource.spi.work .ExecutionContext	This class models an execution context associated with a given *Work* instance such as transactions, security, and so on. RA can extend this class and override methods of interest to further tune the execution context to the EIS.
javax.resource.spi .work.WorkEvent	This class represents the various events that occur during *Work* processing. the application server constructs the *WorkEvent* instance and passes it to the RA via *WorkListener*.

System Contracts

Now that we know connector APIs, let us understand how the RA implements system contracts so as to enable the application server to provide it with various services. This understanding will prove instrumental while developing RA for your own EIS.

Lifecycle Management

By implementing lifecycle management contract, RA enables application server to manage its lifecycle in terms of:

- **Bootstrapping an RA instance** during RA deployment or application server startup. During bootstrapping, the application server makes facilities such as the timer service and work manager available to the RA.
- **Notifying the RA instance** during its deployment, application server startup, undeployment, and application server shutdown events.

Figure 17.4 shows the object diagram for life cycle management.
Some of the important implementation details for this contract are:

- The RA implements the *ResourceAdapter* interface to receive its life cycle–related notifications from application server.
- If the RA supports inbound communication from EIS in the form of message or transaction inflow, it occurs within the context of a *ResourceAdapter* thread.

- The application server calls the *start()* method on *ResourceAdapter* during which it passes *BootstrapContext* instance. The RA saves this *BootstrapContext* instance for later use. The RA can also perform other initialization routines in *start()*, such as setting up *Work* instances to be executed on multiple threads or preparing to listen incoming messages from the EIS.
- The application server calls the *stop()* method on *ResourceAdapter* in which RA should release its resources.

Connection Management

By implementing a connection management contract, the RA enables the application server to manage connections and provide quality of services on its behalf. The RA provides connection and connection factory interfaces. A connection factory acts as a factory for EIS instances. For example, *java.sql.DataSource* and *java.sql.Connection* act as connection factory and connection interfaces for JDBC databases. If an EIS does not have an EIS-specific API, then it can provide implementations of *javax.resource.cci.ConnectionFactory* and *javax.resource.cci.Connection*.

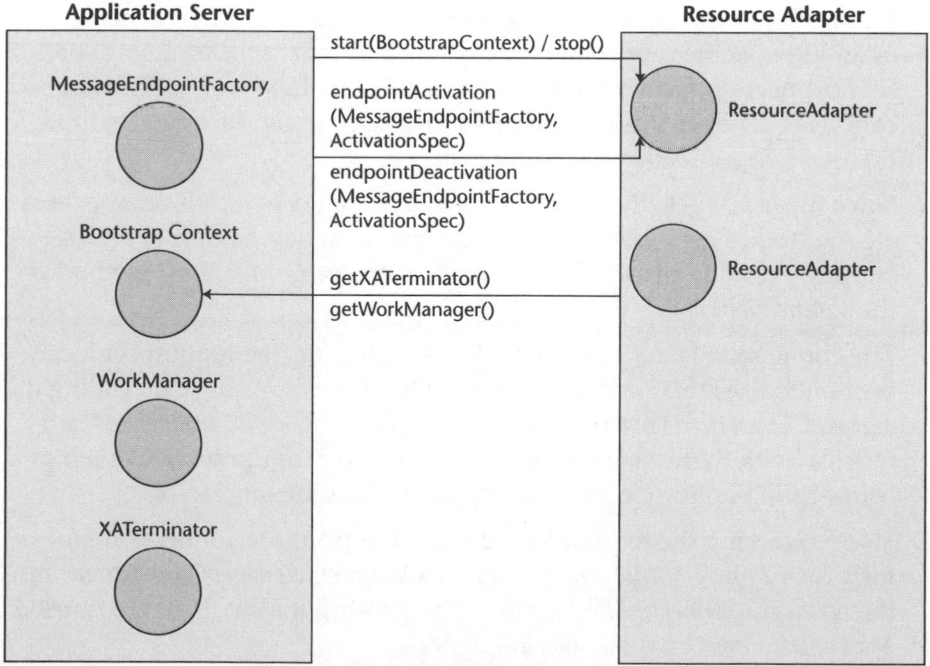

Figure 17.4 Life cycle management object diagram.

The various steps involved during connection management are:

1. When the RA is deployed or the application server is started, an instance of *ManagedConnectionFactory* is created. The application server calls various setters on *ManagedConnectionFactory* instance to set the RA-specific connection properties, if they were provided during RA deployment. For example, if your RA needs to know the EIS URL in order to connect to it, you can provide an *Eis_Url* connection property during RA deployment and implement the respective getter/setter methods for this property in *ManagedConnectionFactory* implementation.
2. The deployer then creates a connection pool for the given RA using the vendor-provided administration tools (such as http://localhost:4848 for J2EE 1.4 RI).
3. When a client application component attempts to create a connection to EIS for the first time after pool creation or after the application server has been started, the application server creates *ManagedConnection* instances by calling *createManagedConnection()* on the *ManagedConnectionFactory* object. The deployer can specify the number of managed connection instances required in the connection pool during the pool creation.
4. The application component then looks up the EIS connection factory in the JNDI namespace. The application server either returns an instance of an EIS-specific connection factory (such as *javax.sql.DataSource*) or CCI connection factory (*javax.resource.cci.ConnectionFactory*). The application server does this by calling the *createConnectionFactory()* method on the *ManagedConnectionFactory* instance.
5. Once the client gets the connection factory instance, it calls an appropriate method to get a hold of the connection instance. In case of an RA supporting CCI, this would mean calling the *getConnection()* method on the *ConnectionFactory* instance.
6. The connection factory implementation delegates the request for a connection to the *javax.resource.spi.ConnectionManager* instance by calling its *allocateConnection()* method. As already noted, *allocateConnection()* provides a hook to the application server for it to provide services such as connection pooling, security, transactions, logging, and so on.
7. Upon receiving the request for a connection from the connection factory, the *ConnectionManager* instance calls *matchManagedConnection()* on the *ManagedConnectionFactory* instance, passing it a set of all the unused *ManagedConnection* instances in the pool.
8. If the *matchManagedConnection()* method determines that a *ManagedConnection* could be used, it returns it to the application server. This

determination is done by matching the connection request properties provided by the client application component, through the *javax.resource.cci.ConnectionRequestInfo* object, with that of the *ManagedConnection* instance.

9. If the *matchManagedConnection()* method does not find a usable instance of *ManagedConnection*, the application server creates a new instance of *ManagedConnection*.
10. The application server calls *getConnection()* on the *ManagedConnection* instance, and returns the connection handle corresponding to *ManagedConnection* (*javax.resource.cci.Connection* in case of CCI) to the client.
11. Once the application component gets a connection handle, it starts interacting with EIS using the appropriate client-side APIs. An application component working with CCI-enabled RA uses the *javax.resource.cci.Interaction* object to do this. It gets a hold of the *Interaction* object by calling the *createInteraction()* method on the *Connection* instance.
12. The client application component uses one of the *execute()* methods on *Interaction* to execute an EIS function. The semantics of EIS function call such as function name, execution timeout, and so on, are provided through the *InteractionSpec* instance. The input and output to the EIS function is provided in terms of *javax.resource.cci.Record* instances.
13. Once the EIS function is executed and the application component receives resultant output, it can close the connection to EIS by calling *close()* on *Connection* instance.
14. By calling the *close()* method, the application server is notified that the managed connection corresponding to the given connection handle is finished servicing the client and that it can be placed back into the pool. At this time, the application server can also call *destroy()* on *ManagedConnection* if it created a new instance of *ManagedConnection* just to satisfy this specific client request. This happens when the application server had to create a new *ManagedConnection* instance in spite of reaching the maximum limit of connections in the pool to satisfy a client request.
15. Finally, when the application server is about to shut down or when the connection pool is undeployed (using the vendor-provided administration tools), the application server will call *destroy()* on each instance of *ManagedConnection* in the pool.

Figure 17.5 shows the interaction between various objects upon receiving connection request from the client application component.

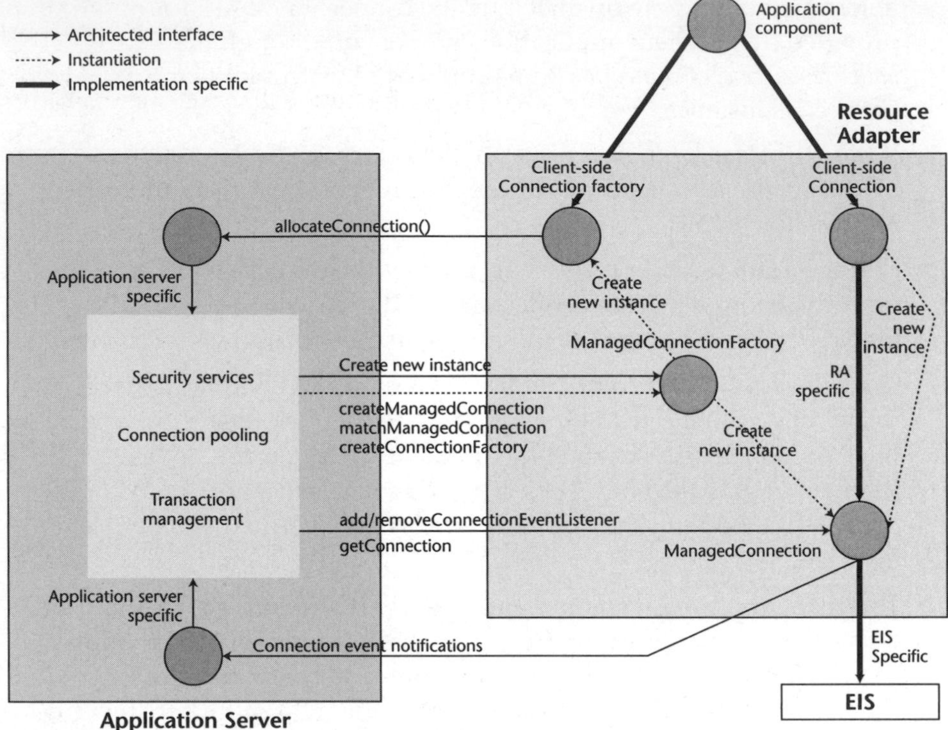

Figure 17.5 Connection management object diagram.

Security Management

The security management contract is an extension of the connection management contract, meaning the RA will have to implement the connection management contract to provide security connectivity to and from the EIS. Connector security architecture extends the security model for J2EE applications, specifically authentication and authorization, to EIS sign-on. The connector architecture specification does not mandate application servers to support specific authentication mechanisms. J2EE 1.4 RI however supports Kerberos v5 and basic password authentication mechanisms.

EIS sign-on can be done programmatically or declaratively. The former is known as component-managed sign-on and the latter is known as container-managed sign-on.

Container-managed Sign-on

In container-managed sign-on, the application server is configured to manage EIS sign-on. When the client application component calls *getConnection()* on *javax.resource.cci.ConnectionFactory* or an equivalent method of the RA client API, it is not required to pass any security information. When the *getConnection()* method invokes the *allocateConnection()* method on *ConnectionManager*, it gives the application server a chance to provide security services. This is when the application server creates the JAAS *Subject* corresponding to the authenticated user. It passes this *Subject* instance to the RA when calling the *createManagedConnection()* method on the *ManagedConnectionFactory* instance. Note that an application server might map the caller principal (principal associated with the application component's security context) to the resource principal (principal under whose security context a connection to EIS is established) or might provide other specific security services before passing the *Subject* to the RA.

The RA uses the security credential(s) information presented within *Subject* to establish a connection to the EIS. Depending on authentication mechanism used by the application server and RA, the credentials can be of type *javax.resource.spi.security.PasswordCredential* or *org.ietf.jgss.GSSCredential*. Thus in container-managed sign-on, the RA is driven by the application server in that it acts based on the security information passed down by the container.

The sequence diagram in Figure 17.6 demonstrates container-managed EIS sign-on.

Refer to Chapter 13 for more on EJB security and JAAS.

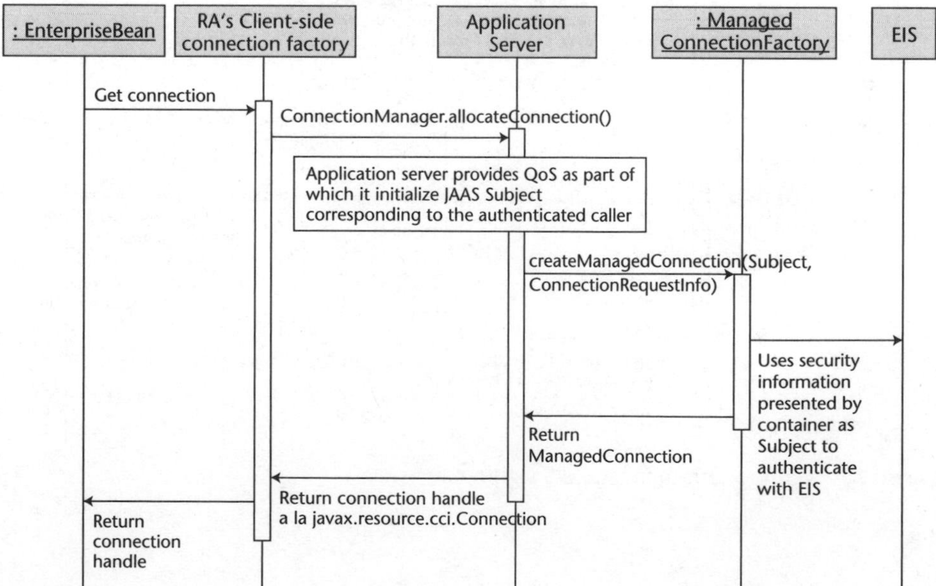

Figure 17.6 Container-managed EIS sign-on.

Component-managed Sign-on

This sign-on requires the client application component to provide security information explicitly through *ConnectionSpec* in *getConnection()* or an equivalent method of the RA client API. The *getConnection()* method on the connection factory instance invokes the *allocateConnection()* method on the *ConnectionManager* instance and passes this security information via the *ConnectionRequestInfo* object. The security information passed this way is opaque to the application server. Hence, when the application server calls *createManagedConnection()* on the *ManagedConnectionFactory* instance, it passes it a null *Subject* instance. However, the security information passed by the client application component is maintained intact in the *ConnectionRequestInfo* object passed to *createManagedConnection()*. The RA uses the security information presented within the *ConnectionRequestInfo* JavaBean to establish a connection to the EIS. Thus in component-managed sign-on, the RA is driven by the client application component, in that it acts based on the security information provided by the component.

The sequence diagram in Figure 17.7 demonstrates container-managed EIS sign-on.

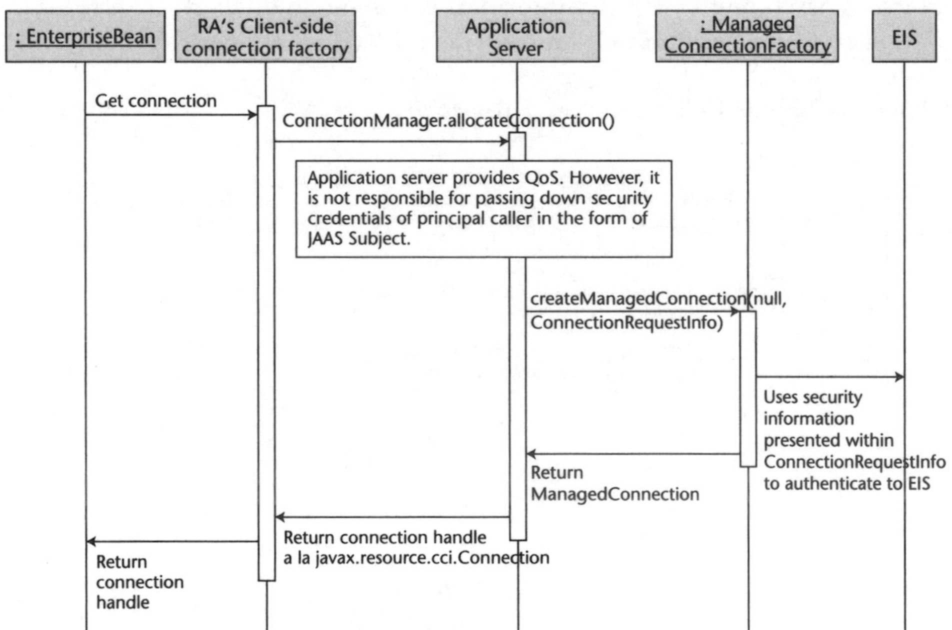

Figure 17.7 Component-managed EIS sign-on.

Transaction Management

The transaction management contract is layered on top of connection management. To support outbound transaction propagation, the RA has to support outbound connections to the EIS. The RA can support either local transactions or global transactions through the transaction management system contracts. A local transaction is managed internal to the EIS and RA, without any help from external transaction managers such as the one provided by J2EE Transaction Service. Global transactions, on the other hand, are controlled and coordinated by an external transaction manager.

Local Transaction Management Contract

A local transaction management contract requires the RA to implement the *javax.resource.spi.LocalTransaction* interface. The *LocalTransaction* implementation will work with the low-level EIS APIs to signal its resource manager about the transaction begin, commit, and rollback events.

The application server uses the instance of *LocalTransaction* to transparently manage local transactions in case of container demarcated transactions. The application server gets a hold of the *LocalTransaction* instance by calling *getLocalTransaction()* on *ManagedConnection*. Figure 17.8 shows how local transaction management is done for container-managed transaction.

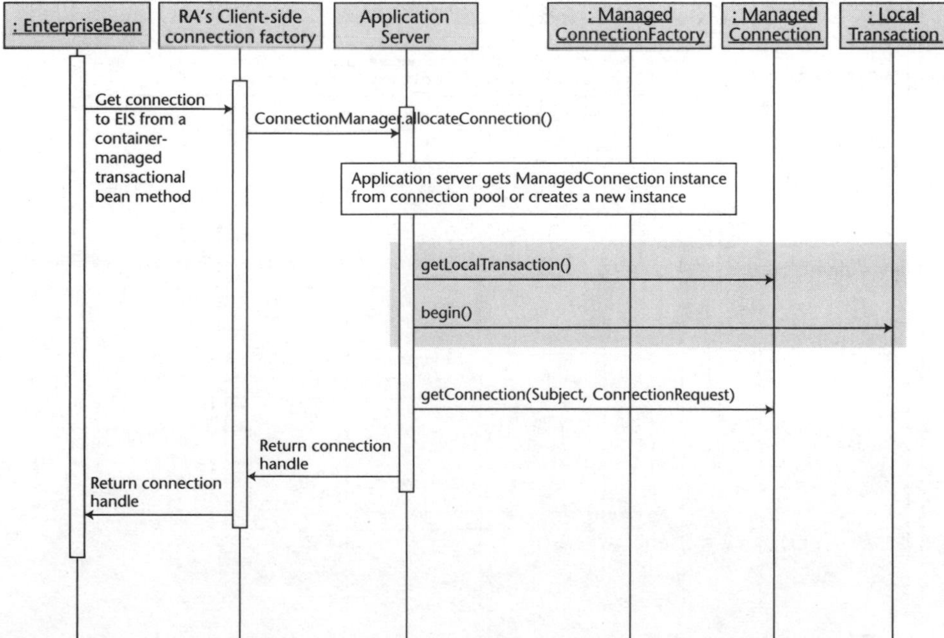

Figure 17.8 Local transaction management for container-managed transaction.

If the client application component chooses to demarcate transactions using an RA-supported client transaction demarcation API (such as *javax.resource .cci.LocalTransaction*), then the RA will be responsible for notifying the application server of the transaction events such as begin, commit, and rollback. The RA does this by calling the *localTransactionStarted()*, *localTransactionCommitted()*, and *localTransactionRolledback()* methods on *javax.resource.spi.ConnectionEvent Listener*. Figure 17.9 shows how local transaction management is done for a client demarcated transaction.

Global Transaction Management Contract

A global transaction management contract requires the RA to provide an implementation for the *javax.transaction.xa.XAResource* interface. The *XAResource* implementation will use low-level libraries to communicate with the EIS resource manager. Implementing *XAResource* will enable the EIS resource manager to participate in transactions that are controlled and coordinated by the application server's transaction manager. The transaction manager communicates transaction association, completion, and recovery signals to the EIS resource manager via *XAResource*.

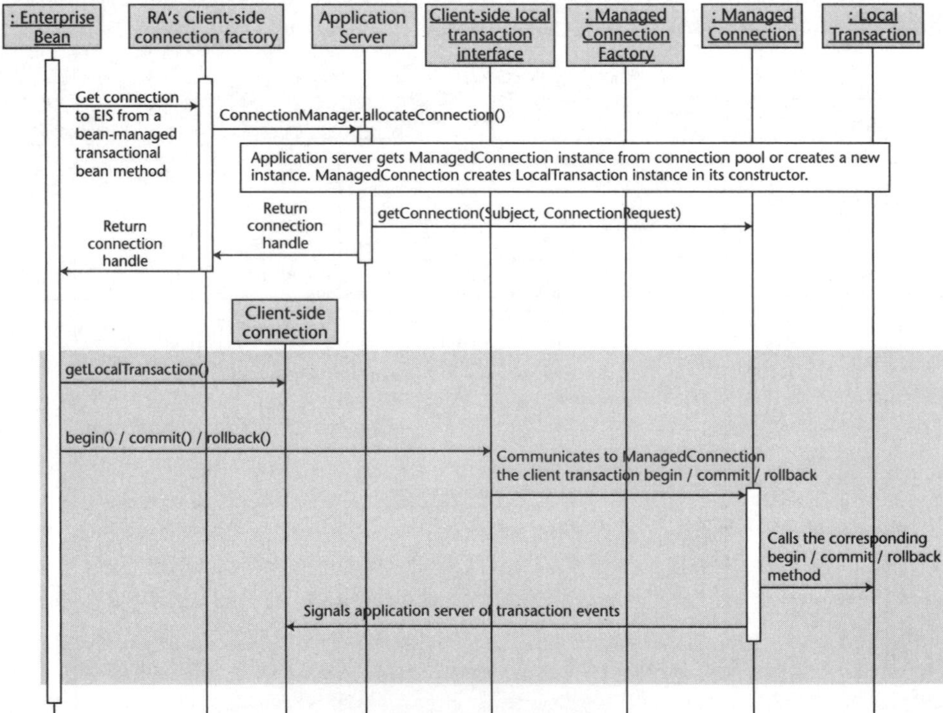

Figure 17.9 Local transaction management for client demarcated transaction.

The application server gets the *XAResource* instance by calling the *getXAResource()* method on *ManagedConnection*. The application server gets the *XAResource* instance when it has to enlist the EIS resource manager in a global transaction. Subsequently when the client application component closes the connection, the application server performs transactional cleanup by de-listing the *XAResource* corresponding to *ManagedConnection* from the transaction manager.

The object interaction diagrams of enlisting and de-listing XAResource are shown in Figures 17.10 and 17.11.

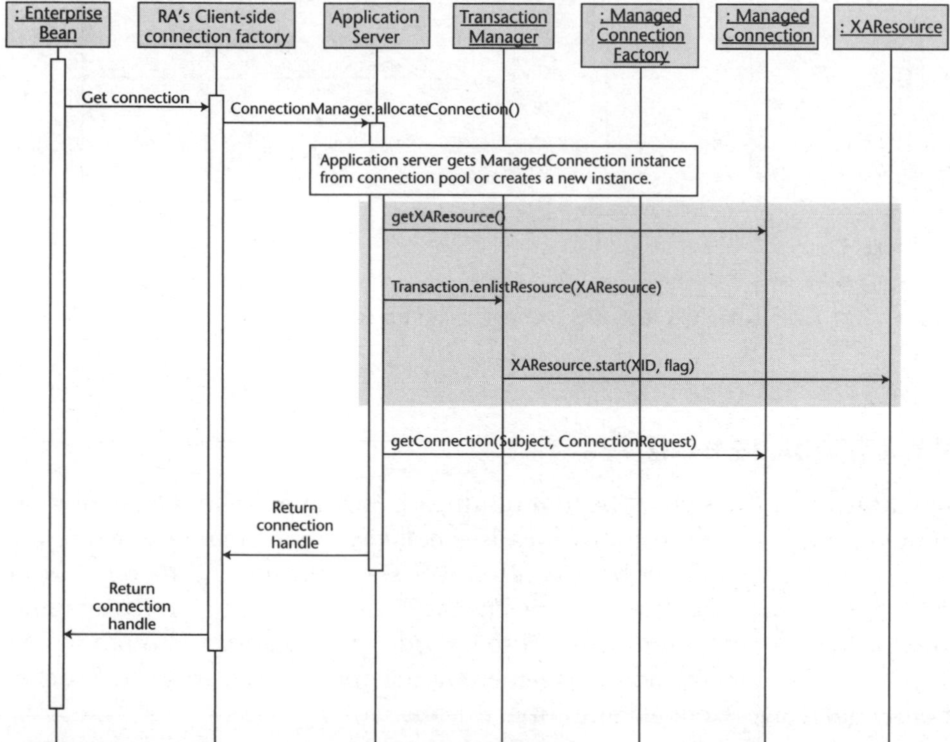

Figure 17.10 Enlisting EIS resource manager with transaction manager.

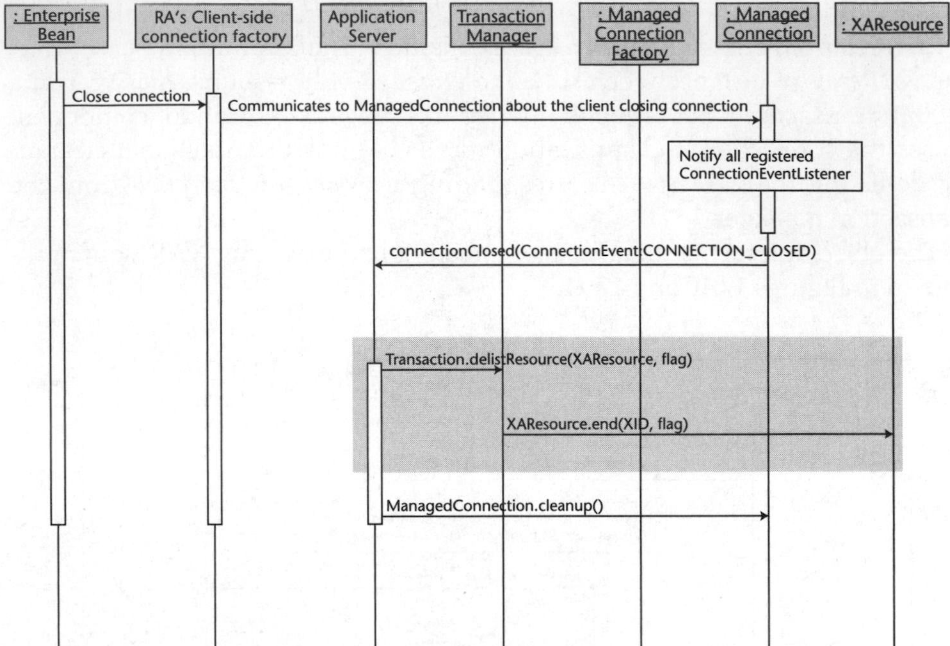

Figure 17.11 De-listing EIS resource manager with transaction manager.

Work Management

Sometimes you need your RA to multithread. However, in a managed environment creating and executing threads is not encouraged mainly because the application server will not have control over such threads and therefore will not be able to manage them. To prevent the RA from creating and managing threads directly, connector architecture provides a mechanism through which the RA can delegate thread management to the application server and consequently get its work done on multiple threads.

Under the work management contract, the RA creates *Work* instances, representing unit of work that the RA wants to execute on a different thread, and submits to the application server. The application server uses the threads from its pool to execute these submitted *Work* instances. *Work* instances can be executed on separately executing threads since they implement *Runnable*.

Figure 17.12 shows the interaction among various objects during work management.

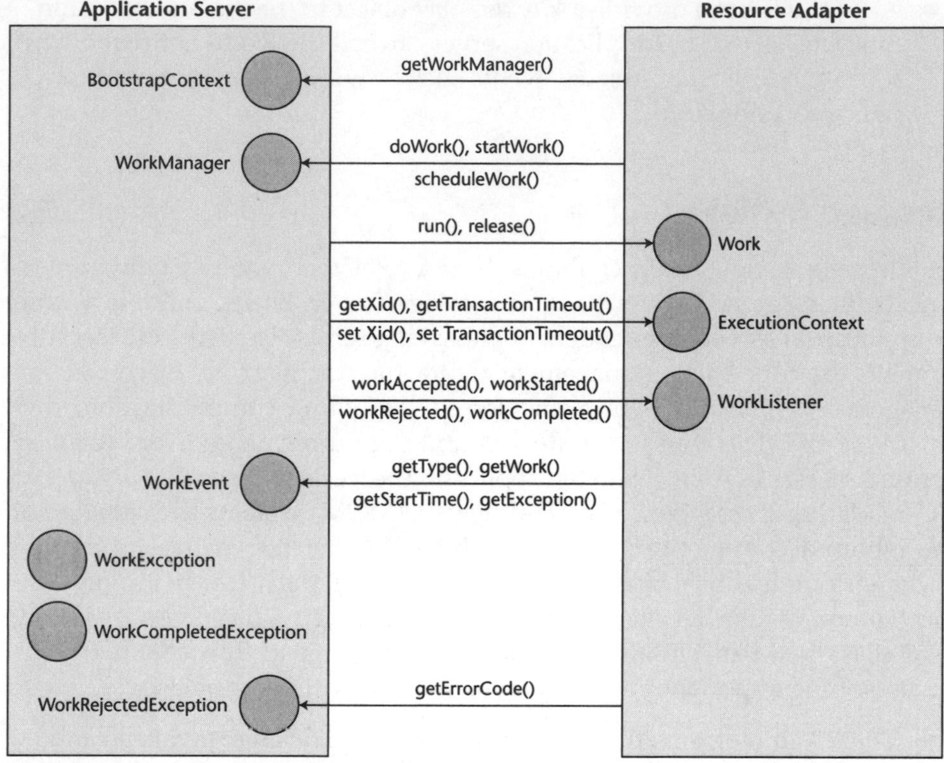

Figure 17.12 Work management object diagram.

Note the following in Figure 17.12:

- The RA gets the *WorkManager* instance by calling the *getWorkManager()* method on the *BootstrapContext* object.
- The RA implements units of work as instances of *Runnable* and submits them for execution on different threads to the application server through the *doWork()*, *startWork()*, or *scheduleWork()* methods. The *doWork()* method blocks the current thread until the *Work* instance completes execution; the *startWork()* method blocks until the *Work* instance starts execution, and the *scheduleWork()* method accepts the *Work* instance for processing and returns immediately.
- After accepting *Work* for processing, the *WorkManager* dispatches a thread that calls the *run()* method to begin execution of *Work*. The *Work* execution completes when *run()* returns. The *WorkManager* can call *release()* to request *Work* instance to complete execution as soon as it can.
- Additionally, the RA can provide *ExecutionContext* within which the *Work* instance will be executed, when submitting work.

- Also, the RA can provide a *WorkListener* object to the work submission methods so that the application server can call the RA to notify it of various work execution-related events such as work acceptance, work rejection, and so on.

Message In-flow

The message in-flow contract allows the RA to asynchronously deliver messages to message endpoints, such as message-driven beans, residing within the application server independent of messaging semantics. This contract supplements the connection management contract in that just like the connection management contract it is implemented for outbound communication from the RA to EIS; the message in-flow contract is implemented for receiving inbound messages from EIS to the application server endpoints.

Considering message-oriented middleware (MOM) systems as a category of EIS, inbound communication from such MOM systems to the application server endpoints can be facilitated by implementing the message in-flow contract. Hence, in J2EE 1.4, all JMS and non-JMS messaging providers are implemented as the RA that in turn implements the message in-flow contract.

Some of the important implementation details for this contract are:

- The RA implements the *javax.resource.spi.ActivationSpec* JavaBean and supplies its class to the application server during its deployment. *ActivationSpec* is opaque to the application server and is used by the RA to establish subscriptions to the requested data from the EIS.
- The RA provides a message listener interface, akin to *javax.jms.MessageListener*, and a message interface, akin to *javax.jms.Message*. The message listener interface will be implemented by message endpoints similar to the way JMS MDB implements *javax.jms.MessageListener*. Also, the message listener interface should have a public method, akin to *onMessage()* of the *javax.jms.MessageListener* interface, that can be invoked by the RA to deliver messages to the endpoint. The deployer will specify the message listener interface class associated with the RA during its deployment.
- The RA also implements the *javax.resource.spi.ResourceAdapter* interface to facilitate message in-flow by implementing the *endpointActivation()* and *endpointDeactivation()* methods.
- The application server calls the *endpointActivation()* method on *ResourceAdapter* to notify the RA when the message endpoint interested in consuming messages from the RA is deployed or when the application server with such a deployed message endpoint is started. The

application server passes *javax.resource.spi.endpoint.MessageEndpointFactory* and *ActivationSpec* instances when calling *endpointActivation()*. The *MessageEndpointFactory* instance is used by the RA to create a *MessageEndpoint* instance later when it has to deliver a message to the endpoint by invoking its *onMessage()* method. *ActivationSpec* represents the deployment properties of the message endpoint. The deployer provides these properties during message endpoint deployment. The application server creates the *ActivationSpec* JavaBean instance and instantiates its properties with values supplied by the deployer. The RA uses the information in the *ActivationSpec* JavaBean to establish subscription to the requested data from the EIS.

- The application server calls the *endpointDeactivation()* method on *ResourceAdapter* to notify the RA when the message endpoint interested in consuming messages from the RA is undeployed or when the application server with such a deployed message endpoint is being shut down. The application server passes *MessageEndpointFactory* and *ActivationSpec* instances when calling *endpointDeactivation()*. The RA uses *MessageEndpointFactory* to retrieve the underlying endpoint consumer and remove it from its list of active message endpoints.

Figures 17.13 shows the object diagram of message in-flow contract.

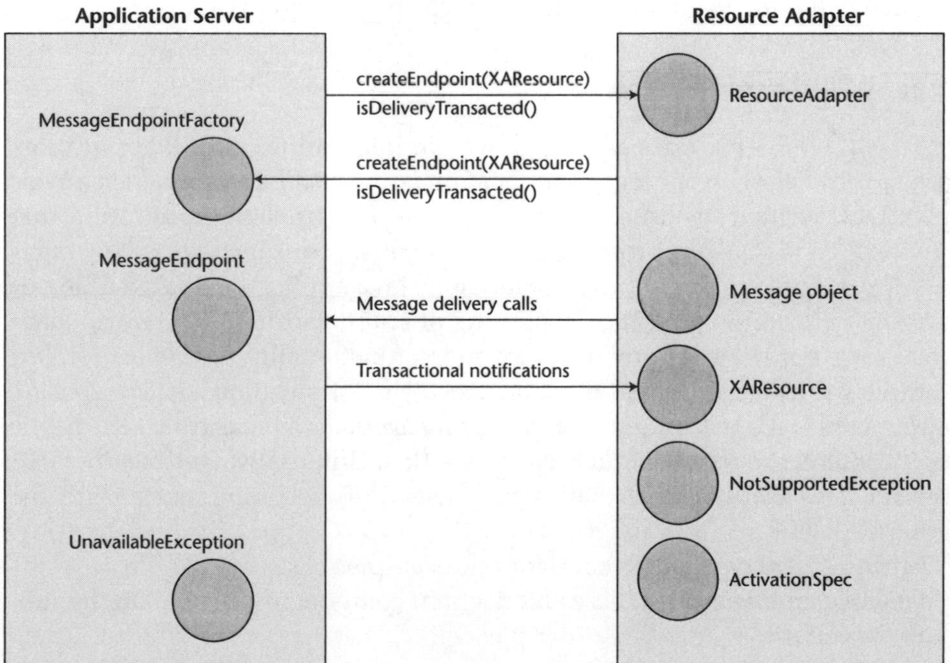

Figure 17.13 Message in-flow object diagram.

J2EE 1.4 RI ships with a sample connector that implements message in-flow contract for Java Mail. Studying this sample will prove very helpful if you want to develop an RA that listens to messages from EIS and delivers those messages to message endpoints in the application server.

Connector Example: OutboundLoanRA

Okay! So we are halfway through our journey of learning about the J2EE Connector Architecture. The remaining half will be more exciting than the previous half because we will now deep dive into developing and deploying our own connector, *OutboundLoanRA*. As is obvious from the name, our RA supports outbound communication from the application server to the EIS. RA development tends to be more complex than that of other J2EE components since the RA developer is responsible for implementing not just client contracts but also system contracts. To keep the complexity manageable, we will implement only the connection management system contract in *OutboundLoanRA*. Even then, you should find this example helpful given that most of the connectors support outbound communication to the EIS, and hence, connection management. Connection management is the most commonly implemented contract.

OutboundLoanRA supports client contracts in the form of CCI.

Example Architecture

OutboundLoanRA provides an elegant way of integrating our EJB application, *LoanApplication*, with our legacy application *LoanApp.dll*. *LoanApp.dll* is a Windows DLL written in Visual C++. *LoanApp.dll* is a backend application that provides typical loan processing functionality. *LoanApplication* leverages *LoanApp.dll* for loan processing. A standalone Java application is a client to our *LoanApplication* EJB application consisting of *LoanRatesEJB*. A real-world loan-processing application provides way more functionality, however, for our example we will assume that our loan processing application, i.e. *LoanApp.dll*, implements just one function: *getHomeEquityLoanRate()*. It basically returns the rate of interest on home equity loans as a float. Internally, *OutboundLoanRA* uses the *JavaLoanApp* class that in turn uses JNI to communicate with the native C++ DLL.

Figure 17.14 shows architecture for our example.

We will examine each of these architectural components in detail in the subsequent sections.

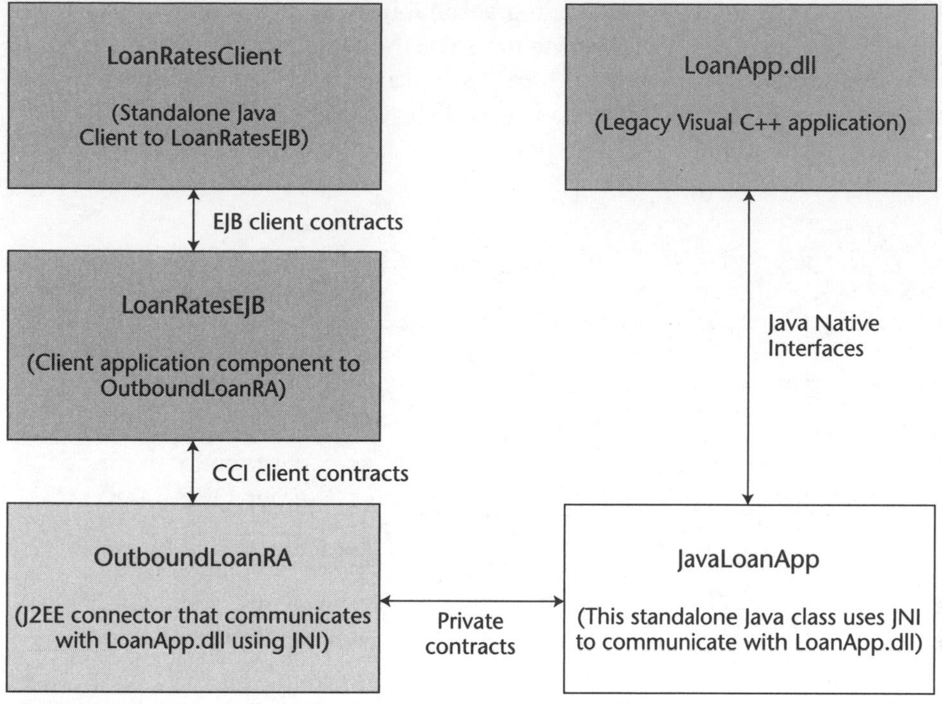

Figure 17.14 Example architecture.

All the source files and setup details for this example are available on the book's accompanying Web site: wiley.com/compbooks/roman.

JavaLoanApp.java

This is a POJO that uses JNI to communicate with *LoanApp.dll*. Here, *getHome EquityLoanRate()* is declared as a native function. Source 17.1 shows *Java LoanApp.java* code.

```
package examples.jni;

public class JavaLoanApp
{
     public JavaLoanApp(String libPath) {
          System.load(libPath);
     }

     // Native method declaration
     public native float getHomeEquityLoanRate();
}
```

Source 17.1 The examples.jni.JavaLoanApp class.

Once we compile the source using a conventional *javac* compiler, we will need to generate a header file containing the JNI function definition so that it can be included by our C++ *LoanApp.dll* application. We can use the *javah* utility that ships with JDK for this. Source 17.2 shows the generated *examples_jni_JavaLoanApp.h* containing JNI exported function *Java_examples_jni_JavaLoanApp_getHomeEquityLoanRate()*.

```
/* DO NOT EDIT THIS FILE - it is machine generated */
#include <jni.h>
/* Header for class examples_jni_JavaLoanApp */

#ifndef _Included_examples_jni_JavaLoanApp
#define _Included_examples_jni_JavaLoanApp
#ifdef __cplusplus
extern "C" {
#endif
/*
 * Class:     examples_jni_JavaLoanApp
 * Method:    getHomeEquityLoanRate
 * Signature: ()F
 */

/* JNI export function definition (generated by javah utility)
 */
JNIEXPORT jfloat JNICALL
Java_examples_jni_JavaLoanApp_getHomeEquityLoanRate
      (JNIEnv *, jobject);
```

Source 17.2 The examples_jni_JavaLoanApp.h header file.

LoanApp.dll

The source code of interest in *LoanApp.dll* is *LoanApp.h*. It implements the JNI exported function, *Java_examples_jni_JavaLoanApp_getHomeEquityLoanRate()*. We have kept the JNI function definition very simple—it always returns 5.64 percent as the home equity loan rate. Source 17.3 shows *LoanApp.h*. Note how we included the *javah* generated *examples_jni_JavaLoanApp.h* header file.

```
// LoanApp.h : main header file for the LoanApp DLL
#pragma once

#ifndef __AFXWIN_H__
     #error include 'stdafx.h' before including this file for PCH
```

Source 17.3 The LoanApp.h header file.

```
#endif

#include "resource.h"              // main symbols

// CLoanAppApp

#include "examples_jni_JavaLoanApp.h"

class CLoanAppApp : public CWinApp
{
public:
     CLoanAppApp();

// Overrides
public:
     virtual BOOL InitInstance();

     DECLARE_MESSAGE_MAP()
};

/* A very simplistic implementation of JNI exported function
 */
JNIEXPORT jfloat JNICALL
Java_examples_jni_JavaLoanApp_getHomeEquityLoanRate(JNIEnv *, jobject) {
     return 5.64;
};
```

Source 17.3 *(continued)*

OutboundLoanRA

Now that we have skimmed through the implementations of *JavaLoanApp* and *LoanApp.dll*, let us examine the source code for *OutboundLoanRA*. We will examine the client contracts first, followed by the system contracts.

OutboundLoanRA Client Contracts

As noted earlier, *OutboundLoanRA* supports client contracts through CCI. We have implemented *javax.resource.cci.ConnectionFactory*, *javax.resource.cci.Connection*, *javax.resource.cci.ConnectionMetaData*, *javax.resource.cci.ConnectionSpec*, *javax.resource.cci.Interaction*, *javax.resource.cci.MappedRecord*, *javax.resource.cci.RecordFactory*, and *javax.resource.cci.ResourceAdapterMetaData* client contracts for this example.

ConnectionFactoryImpl.java

Source 17.4 shows *ConnectionFactoryImpl.java,* which implements the *javax .resource.cci.ConnectionFactory* client contract.

```
package examples.out_loan_ra;

import java.io.*;

import javax.resource.Referenceable;
import javax.resource.*;
import javax.resource.spi.*;
import javax.naming.Reference;
import javax.resource.cci.*;

public class ConnectionFactoryImpl implements ConnectionFactory,
Serializable, Referenceable {

     private ManagedConnectionFactory manConnFactory;
     private ConnectionManager connManager;
     private Reference ref;

     //ManagedConnectionFactory implementation creates
ConnectionFactory instance
     // by calling this constructor. During construction it also
passes an instance
     // of ConnectionManager which ConnectionFactoryImpl will use
to call
     // allocateConnection() method on ConnectionManager later
when client component
     // invokes getConnection() on ConnectionFactory.
     public ConnectionFactoryImpl(ManagedConnectionFactory
manConnFactory,
          ConnectionManager connManager) {

System.out.println("ConnectionFactoryImpl(ManagedConnectionFactory
               manConnFactory, ConnectionManager connManager) called");
          this.manConnFactory = manConnFactory;
          this.connManager = new ConnectionManagerImpl();
     }

     // Client component calls this definition of getConnection() when
     // container manages EIS sign-on.
     public javax.resource.cci.Connection getConnection() throws
ResourceException {
          System.out.println("ConnectionFactoryImpl.getConnection()
called");

          javax.resource.cci.Connection conn = null;
```

Source 17.4 The ConnectionFactoryImpl class.

```
        conn = (javax.resource.cci.Connection)
             connManager.allocateConnection(manConnFactory, null);

        return conn;
    }

    // Client component can call this method to pass ConnectionSpec
containing RA
    // specific security and connection information.
    public javax.resource.cci.Connection getConnection
(ConnectionSpec cSpec)  throws
        ResourceException {
        System.out.println("ConnectionFactoryImpl.getConnection
             (ConnectionSpec cSpec) called");

        javax.resource.cci.Connection conn = null;
        ConnectionRequestInfo connRequestInfo = new
ConnectionRequestInfoImpl();
        conn = (javax.resource.cci.Connection)
             connManager.allocateConnection(manConnFactory,
connRequestInfo);

        return conn;
    }

    public ResourceAdapterMetaData getMetaData() throws
ResourceException {
        return new ResourceAdapterMetaDataImpl();
    }

    public RecordFactory getRecordFactory() throws ResourceException {
        return new RecordFactoryImpl();
    }

   public void setReference(Reference ref) {
        this.ref = ref;
    }

    public Reference getReference() {
        return ref;
    }
}
```

Source 17.4 *(continued)*

Note the following about *ConnectionFactoryImpl*:

- Our class implements *Referenceable* so that the connection factory can be registered with JNDI.

- The application server creates an instance of *ConnectionFactory* using a constructor during which it passes an instance of *ManagedConnection-Factory* for creating physical connections to the EIS.
- One implementation of the *getConnection()* method does not take any arguments and calls *allocateConnection()* on *ConnectionManager* passing it a reference to *ManagedConnectionFactory* and a null *ConnectionRequestInfo* object.
- The other implementation of the *getConnection()* method takes a single argument, a *ConnectionSpec* instance. *ConnectionSpec* is used by an application component to pass connection request–specific properties. However, since we do not have any connection-specific request properties, our *ConnectionSpec* is practically empty. If we had connection request–specific properties (such as user name, password, port number, and so on), the *getConnection()* implementation would be required to populate *ConnectionRequestInfo* with these *ConnectionSpec* properties. Since we do not have any connection request properties, we simply create the *ConnectionRequestInfo* object and pass it as an argument to *allocateConnection()* on *ConnectionManager*.
- The *getMetaData()* method returns an instance of the *ResourceAdapter MetaData*, and *getRecordFactory()* method returns an instance of *RecordFactory*.

ConnectionImpl.java

Source 17.5 shows *ConnectionImpl.java,* which implements *javax.resource.cci .Connection* client contract.

```
package examples.out_loan_ra;

import java.util.*;

import javax.resource.cci.*;
import javax.resource.ResourceException;
import javax.resource.spi.ConnectionEvent;
import javax.resource.spi.IllegalStateException;
import javax.resource.spi.*;
import javax.resource.NotSupportedException;

public class ConnectionImpl implements javax.resource.cci.Connection {

     private ManagedConnectionImpl manConn;

     // RA creates an instance of Connection using this constructor from
     // getConnection() method of ManagedConnection.
```

Source 17.5 The ConnectionImpl class.

```
    ConnectionImpl(ManagedConnectionImpl manConn) {
        System.out.println("ConnectionImpl(ManagedConnectionImpl)
called");

        this.manConn = manConn;
    }

    public Interaction createInteraction() throws ResourceException {
        return new InteractionImpl(this);
    }

    public javax.resource.cci.LocalTransaction
getLocalTransaction() throws
    ResourceException {
        throw new NotSupportedException("Local transactions are
not supported.");
    }

    public ResultSetInfo getResultSetInfo() throws ResourceException {
        throw new NotSupportedException("ResultSet records are
not supported.");
    }

    // This method called by client component should be used to
signal to the
    // underlying physical connection of client's intent to close
the connection.
    // How client-side connection handle signals these (and other
events such as
    // transaction begin, commit, and rollback in case of client
demarcated local
    // transactions), is left up to RA to decide. In our
implementation we make
    // our ManagedConnection implementation provide a private
contract method named
    // sendEvent() that our ConnectionImpl will call to signal
it of various
    // connection related events. Since this is a
Connection.close() method imple-
    // mentation, we will signal a CONNECTION_CLOSED event.
    public void close() throws ResourceException {
        System.out.println("ConnectionImpl.close() called");

        if (manConn == null)
            return;

        manConn.sendEvent(ConnectionEvent.CONNECTION_CLOSED,
null, this);
        manConn = null;
```

Source 17.5 *(continued)*

```
    }

    public ConnectionMetaData getMetaData() throws ResourceException {
        return new ConnectionMetaDataImpl(manConn);
    }
}
```

Source 17.5 *(continued)*

Note the following about our implementation:

- It throws *javax.resource.NotSupportedException* if someone tries to call the *getLocalTransaction()* and *getResultSetInfo()* methods. It does so because it does not implement the transaction management system contract and it does not support *ResultSet* type of *Record.*
- In the implementation for *close(),* it sends a CONNECTION_CLOSED event notification to *ManagedConnection.* The application server uses this event notification to either destroy the underlying *ManagedConnection* or to put the *ManagedConnection* instance back into the pool.

ConnectionMetaDataImpl.java

Source 17.6 shows *ConnectionMetaDataImpl.java,* which implements the *javax.resource.cci.ConnectionMetaData* client contract. *ConnectionMetaDataImpl* simply provides information about the underlying EIS connected through the given *Connection* handle.

```
package examples.out_loan_ra;

import javax.resource.ResourceException;
import javax.resource.cci.*;
import javax.resource.spi.*;

public class ConnectionMetaDataImpl implements ConnectionMetaData {

    private ManagedConnectionImpl manConn;

    public ConnectionMetaDataImpl (ManagedConnectionImpl manConn) {
        this.manConn = manConn;
    }

    public String getEISProductName() throws ResourceException {
        return "Loan Application DLL";
    }
```

Source 17.6 The ConnectionMetaDataImpl class.

```
    public String getEISProductVersion() throws ResourceException {
        return "1.0";
    }

    public String getUserName() throws ResourceException {
        return null;
    }
}
```

Source 17.6 *(continued)*

ConnectionSpecImpl.java

Source 17.7 shows *ConnectionSpecImpl.java,* which implements the *javax.resource.cci.ConnectionSpec* client contract. This is the minimal implementation of *ConnectionSpec,* given that we do not support any connection request–specific properties. If we did support connection request–specific properties then we would have to provide getters and setters for those properties.

```
package examples.out_loan_ra;

import javax.resource.cci.*;

public class ConnectionSpecImpl implements ConnectionSpec {

    public ConnectionSpecImpl() {
    }
}
```

Source 17.7 The ConnectionSpecImpl class.

InteractionImpl.java

Source 17.8 shows *InteractionImpl.java,* which implements the *javax.resource.cci.Interaction* client contract.

```
package examples.out_loan_ra;

import examples.jni.JavaLoanApp;

import java.util.*;
import javax.resource.ResourceException;
import javax.resource.spi.ConnectionEvent;
```

Source 17.8 The InteractionImpl class. *(continued)*

```
import javax.resource.spi.IllegalStateException;
import javax.resource.cci.*;
import java.lang.reflect.*;
import java.lang.*;

public class InteractionImpl implements Interaction {

     Connection conn = null;

     public InteractionImpl(Connection conn) {
          System.out.println("InteractionImpl(Connection conn) called");

          this.conn = conn;
     }

     public javax.resource.cci.Connection getConnection() {
          return conn;
     }

     public void close() throws ResourceException {
          conn = null;
     }

     public boolean execute (InteractionSpec iSpec, Record in, Record out)
throws
          ResourceException {
          System.out.println ("InteractionImpl.execute(InteractionSpec
iSpec, Record
               in, Record out) called");

          out = exec((MappedRecord)in,(MappedRecord)out);

          if (out != null) {
               return true;
          } else {
               return false;
          }
     }

     public Record execute (InteractionSpec iSpec, Record in) throws
ResourceException
     {
          System.out.println ("InteractionImpl.execute(InteractionSpec
iSpec, Record
               in) called");

          MappedRecord out = new MappedRecordImpl();
          return exec((MappedRecord)in, out);
     }

     Record exec(MappedRecord in, MappedRecord out) throws ResourceException {
```

Source 17.8 *(continued)*

```
        try {
            System.out.println("InteractionImpl.exec(MappedRecord in,
MappedRecord
                out) called");

            Set keys = in.keySet();
            Iterator iterator = keys.iterator();
            while (iterator.hasNext()) {
                String key = (String)iterator.next();
                if (key.equalsIgnoreCase("HomeEquityRate")) {
                    JavaLoanApp jlaObj = new
JavaLoanApp("C:\\LoanApp.dll");
                    float equityRate = jlaObj.getHomeEquityLoanRate();
                    System.out.println ("JNI Call Returned: " +
equityRate);
                    out.put(key, new Float(equityRate));
                }
            }
            return out;
        }
        catch(Exception e) {
            throw new ResourceException(e.getMessage());
        }
    }

    public ResourceWarning getWarnings() throws ResourceException {
        return null;
    }

    public void clearWarnings() throws ResourceException {
    }
}
```

Source 17.8 *(continued)*

This is the crux of *OutboundLoanRA*. *InteractionImpl* contains the logic required for communicating with the EIS. It is *InteractionImpl* that creates an instance of *JavaLoanApp* and calls its native method. Note the following about our implementation:

- We support both the *execute()* methods; the one that takes input and output records as well as the one which takes only input and returns output record.
- Both the *execute()* methods call the *exec()* method, which in turn takes the input *Record*, gets the name of the EIS function to execute, instantiates *JavaLoanApp*, and finally calls the *getHomeEquityLoanRate()* native method on *JavaLoanApp*. The result of this invocation is put into the output *Record* and returned back to the client application component, which is *LoanRatesEJB* in this case.

MappedRecordImpl.java

Source 17.9 shows *MappedRecordImpl.java,* which implements the *javax.resource .cci.MappedRecord* client contract. *MappedRecordImpl* implements both the *java.util.Map* and *javax.resource.cci.Record* interfaces. As shown in Source 17.10, implementing *MappedRecord* is fairly simple.

```
package examples.out_loan_ra;

import java.util.*;

public class MappedRecordImpl implements javax.resource
.cci.MappedRecord {

     private String recordName;
     private String recordDescription;
     private HashMap mappedRecord;

     public MappedRecordImpl() {
          mappedRecord = new HashMap();
     }

     public MappedRecordImpl (String recordName) {
          mappedRecord = new HashMap();
          this.recordName = recordName;
     }

     public String getRecordName() {
          return this.recordName;
     }
     public void setRecordName(String recordName) {
          this.recordName = recordName;
     }

     public String getRecordShortDescription() {
          return recordDescription;
     }

     public void setRecordShortDescription(String recordDescription) {
          this.recordDescription = recordDescription;
     }

     public boolean equals(Object object) {
          if(!(object instanceof MappedRecordImpl))
               return false;

          MappedRecordImpl mappedRecordObject =
(MappedRecordImpl)object;
```

Source 17.9 The MappedRecordImpl class.

```
        return (recordName == mappedRecordObject.recordName) &&
            mappedRecord.equals(mappedRecordObject.mappedRecord);
    }

    public int hashCode() {
        return (new String("MappedRecordImpl")).hashCode();
    }

    public Object clone() throws CloneNotSupportedException {
        return this.clone();
    }

    public void clear() {
        mappedRecord.clear();
    }

    public boolean containsKey(Object key) {
        return mappedRecord.containsKey(key);
    }

    public boolean containsValuc(Object value) {
        return mappedRecord.containsValue(value);
    }

    public Set entrySet() {
        return mappedRecord.entrySet();
    }

    public Object get(Object object) {
        return mappedRecord.get(object);
    }

    public boolean isEmpty(){
        return mappedRecord.isEmpty();
    }

    public Set keySet(){
        return mappedRecord.keySet();
    }

    public Object put(Object key, Object value) {
        return mappedRecord.put(key, value);
    }

    public void putAll(Map map) {
        mappedRecord.putAll (map);
    }

    public Object remove(Object object) {
```

Source 17.9 *(continued)*

```
            return mappedRecord.remove(object);
        }

        public int size() {
            return mappedRecord.size();
        }

        public Collection values() {
            return mappedRecord.values();
        }
    }
```

Source 17.9 *(continued)*

RecordFactoryImpl.java

Source 17.10 shows *RecordFactoryImpl.java,* which implements the *javax .resource.cci.RecordFactory* client contract. Since *OutboundLoanRA* supports only the *MappedRecord* client contract, we throw *NotSupportedException* if somebody tries to create an indexed record.

```
package examples.out_loan_ra;

import javax.resource.cci.*;
import java.util.Map;
import java.util.Collection;
import javax.resource.ResourceException;
import javax.resource.NotSupportedException;

public class RecordFactoryImpl implements
javax.resource.cci.RecordFactory{

        public MappedRecord createMappedRecord(String recordName) throws
            ResourceException {
            return new MappedRecordImpl(recordName);
        }

        public IndexedRecord createIndexedRecord(String recordName) throws
            ResourceException {
            throw new NotSupportedException("IndexedRecords are not
supported.");
        }
}
```

Source 17.10 The RecordFactoryImpl class.

ResourceAdapterMetaDataImpl.java

Source 17.11 shows *ResourceAdapterMetaDataImpl.java*. In our implementation of the *javax.resource.cci.ResourceAdapterMetaData* client contract, we provide not only general information about the RA but also information about specific capabilities of the RA such as the system contracts it supports.

```
package examples.out_loan_ra;

import java.io.*;

import javax.resource.Referenceable;
import javax.resource.*;
import javax.resource.spi.*;
import javax.naming.Reference;
import javax.resource.cci.*;

public class ResourceAdapterMetaDataImpl implements
ResourceAdapterMetaData {

     private String adapterName;
     private String adapterShortDescription;
     private String adapterVendorName;
     private String adapterVersion;
     private String[] interactionSpecsSupported;
     private String specVersion;
     private boolean supportsExecuteWithInputAndOutputRecord;
     private boolean supportsExecuteWithInputRecordOnly;
     private boolean supportsLocalTransactionDemarcation;

     // Additional properties
     private boolean supportsGlobalTransactions;
     private boolean supportsLifecycleManagement;
     private boolean supportsMessageInflow;
     private boolean supportsTransactionInflow;
     private boolean supportsConnectionManagement;
     private boolean supportsSecurityManagement;

     public ResourceAdapterMetaDataImpl() {
          adapterName = "Loan Application Resource Adapter";
          adapterShortDescription = "Loan Application Resource
Adapter provides
               connectivity to Loan Application DLL";
          adapterVendorName = "Connectors Inc.";
          adapterVersion = "1.0";
          interactionSpecsSupported[0] = "InteractionImpl";
          specVersion = "1.5";
          supportsExecuteWithInputAndOutputRecord = true;
          supportsExecuteWithInputRecordOnly = true;
```

Source 17.11 The ResourceAdapterMetaData class. *(continued)*

```
        supportsLocalTransactionDemarcation = false;
        supportsGlobalTransactions = false;
        supportsLifecycleManagement = false;
        supportsMessageInflow = false;
        supportsTransactionInflow = false;
        supportsConnectionManagement = true;
        supportsSecurityManagement = false;
    }

    public String getAdapterName() {
        return adapterName;
    }

    public String getAdapterShortDescription() {
        return adapterShortDescription;
    }

    public String getAdapterVendorName() {
        return adapterVendorName;
    }

    public String getAdapterVersion() {
        return adapterVersion;
    }

    public String[] getInteractionSpecsSupported() {
        return interactionSpecsSupported;
    }

    public String getSpecVersion() {
        return specVersion;
    }

    public boolean supportsExecuteWithInputAndOutputRecord() {
        return supportsExecuteWithInputAndOutputRecord;
    }

    public boolean supportsExecuteWithInputRecordOnly() {
        return supportsExecuteWithInputRecordOnly;
    }

    public boolean supportsLocalTransactionDemarcation() {
        return supportsLocalTransactionDemarcation;
    }

    public boolean supportsGlobalTransactions() {
        return supportsGlobalTransactions;
    }
```

Source 17.11 *(continued)*

```
        public boolean supportsLifecycleManagement() {
            return supportsLifecycleManagement;
        }

        public boolean supportsMessageInflow() {
            return supportsMessageInflow;
        }

        public boolean supportsTransactionInflow() {
            return supportsTransactionInflow;
        }

        public boolean supportsConnectionManagement() {
            return supportsConnectionManagement;
        }

        public boolean supportsSecurityManagement() {
            return supportsSecurityManagement;
        }
    }
```

Source 17.11 *(continued)*

OutboundLoanRA System Contracts

Now let us examine the connection management–related system contracts for *OutboundLoanRA*. We implemented *javax.resource.spi.ManagedConnectionFactory*, *javax.resource.spi.ManagedConnection*, *javax.resource.spi.ConnectionRequestInfo*, and *javax.resource.spi.ManagedConnectionMetaData* system contracts for this example.

ManagedConnectionFactoryImpl.java

Source 17.12 shows *ManagedConnectionFactoryImpl.java*, which implements the *javax.resource.spi.ManagedConnectionFactory* system contract.

```
package examples.out_loan_ra;

import java.io.*;
import java.util.*;

import javax.resource.*;
import javax.resource.spi.*;
import javax.resource.spi.security.PasswordCredential;
import javax.resource.spi.SecurityException;
import javax.security.auth.Subject;
```

Source 17.12 The ManagedConnectionFactoryImpl class. *(continued)*

```
import javax.naming.Context;
import javax.naming.InitialContext;

public class ManagedConnectionFactoryImpl implements
ManagedConnectionFactory, Serializable {

     private PrintWriter manConnLogWriter;

     public ManagedConnectionFactoryImpl() {
          System.out.println("ManagedConnectionFactoryImpl() called");
     }

     // This method is called by application server and is a hook for RA to
     // to create the client-side connection factory interface instance.
Application
     // server passes an instance of ConnectionManager to this method, which is
     // passed forward to the client-side connection factory instance.
The connection
     // factory instance on the client-side will use ConnectionManager to call
     // allocateConnection().
     public Object createConnectionFactory(ConnectionManager connManager) throws
          ResourceException {
          System.out.println
("ManagedConnectionFactoryImpl.createConnectionFactory
               (ConnectionManager) called");

          return new ConnectionFactoryImpl(this, connManager);
     }

     // This method will never be called in a managed environment because
     // in a managed environment application server is required to provide
     // an implementation of ConnectionManager such that its
allocateConnection()
     // method provides all the QoS necessary. Hence, application server
     // will never call this version of createConnectionFactory().
This method is
     // part of ManagedConnectionFactory interface only to
accommodate non-managed
     // environments.
     public Object createConnectionFactory() throws ResourceException {
          throw new ResourceException ("How can you call this method in a
managed
               environment?");

     }

     // This method is called by application server to create an instance of
     // ManagedConnection. It passes an instance of Subject representing
authenticated
     // user's principal in case of container-managed EIS sign-on. In case of
     // component-managed EIS sign-on, application component can pass
```

Source 17.12 *(continued)*

```
    // connection request properties including username/password (or other form
    // of security credential information) through ConnectionSpec JavaBean
    // when it calls getConnection() on ConnectionFactory.
ConnectionFactory impl-
    // mentation will take ConnectionSpec property information and populate
    // ConnectionRequestInfo JavaBean, and pass it down to
application server as
    // an argument to allocateConnection() on ConnectionManager.
When application
    // server calls createManagedConnection(), it passes this very instance of
    // ConnectionRequestInfo so that ManagedConnectionFactory can get access to
    // connection request properties, including security information.
    public ManagedConnection createManagedConnection (Subject subject,
        ConnectionRequestInfo connRequestInfo) {
        System.out.println
("ManagedConnectionFactoryImpl.createManagedConnection
            (Subject, ConnectionRequestInfo) called");

        return new ManagedConnectionImpl (this);
    }

    // This method is called by application server and is a hook for RA to
    // implement the connection matching logic. If the EIS connection have
    // connection properties, then the match logic should also compare the
    // property values of ConnectionRequestInfo structure with those of
    // the available connections to determine the correct match.
    public ManagedConnection matchManagedConnections(Set connSet,
Subject subject,
        ConnectionRequestInfo connRequestInfo)
        throws ResourceException {
        System.out.println
("ManagedConnectionFactoryImpl.matchManagedConnections
            (Set, Subject, ConnectionRequestInfo) called");

        Iterator iterator = connSet.iterator();
        while (iterator.hasNext()) {
            Object object = iterator.next();
            if (object instanceof ManagedConnectionImpl) {
                ManagedConnectionImpl manConn =
(ManagedConnectionImpl) object;
                ManagedConnectionFactory manConnFactory =
                    manConn.getManagedConnectionFactory();

                if (manConnFactory.equals(this)) {
                    System.out.println("From ManagedConnectionFactoryImpl.
                        matchManagedConnections() -> Connection matched");
                    return manConn;
                }
            }
        }
        System.out.println("From ManagedConnectionFactoryImpl.
```

Source 17.12 *(continued)*

```
                matchManagedConnections() -> Connection did not match");

            return null;
        }

        public void setLogWriter(PrintWriter manConnLogWriter) {
            this.manConnLogWriter = manConnLogWriter;
        }

        public PrintWriter getLogWriter() {
            return manConnLogWriter;
        }

        public boolean equals(Object object) {
            if (object == null) return false;
            if (object instanceof ManagedConnectionFactoryImpl) {
                return true;
            } else {
                return false;
            }
        }

        public int hashCode() {
            return (new String("ManagedConnectionFactoryImpl")).hashCode();
        }
    }
```

Source 17.12 *(continued)*

Note the following about our implementation:

- In the *createManagedConnection()* method, had we implemented the security system contract, we would have been required to get the caller principal credentials from the *Subject*, in case of container-managed EIS sign-on, or from the *ConnectionRequestInfo* JavaBean, in case of component-managed EIS sign-on.
- Had we used connection request–specific properties, in *matchManagedConnection()* method we would have been required to match the properties as well as determine the matching connection from the pool.

ManagedConnectionImpl.java

Source 17.13 shows *ManagedConnectionImpl.java*, which implements the *javax.resource.spi.ManagedConnection* system contract.

```
package examples.out_loan_ra;

import java.io.*;
import java.util.*;

import javax.resource.*;
import javax.resource.spi.*;
import javax.resource.spi.security.PasswordCredential;
import javax.resource.spi.IllegalStateException;
import javax.resource.spi.SecurityException;
import javax.resource.NotSupportedException;
import javax.security.auth.Subject;
import javax.transaction.xa.XAResource;

public class ManagedConnectionImpl implements ManagedConnection {

      private ConnectionEventListener connEventListener;
      private ManagedConnectionFactory manConnFactory;
      private boolean isDestroyed;
      private PrintWriter manConnLogWriter;

      // This method is called by createManagedConnection() of
      // ManagedConnectionFactory.
      ManagedConnectionImpl (ManagedConnectionFactory manConnFactory) {
           System.out.println("ManagedConnectionImpl(ManagedConnectionFactory)
                called");

           this.manConnFactory = manConnFactory;
      }

      // This method is called by application server to obtain the client-side
      // connection handle for this physical connection. If you want to share
      // a physical connection to the EIS among various clients, you can use
      // caller security information represented in Subject or
ConnectionRequestInfo
      // objects to authenticate each client that shares this physical
connection
      // to the backend EIS.
      public Object getConnection(Subject subject, ConnectionRequestInfo
           connectionRequestInfo) throws ResourceException {
           System.out.println("ManagedConnectionImpl.getConnection(Subject,
                ConnectionRequestInfo) called");

           ConnectionImpl conn = new ConnectionImpl(this);
           return conn;
      }

      // This method is called by application server to explicitly destroy the
      // physical connection to the EIS.
      public void destroy() throws ResourceException {
```

Source 17.13 The ManagedConnectionImpl class. *(continued)*

```
        System.out.println("ManagedConnectionImpl.destroy() called");

        isDestroyed=true;
        cleanup();
    }

    // The cleanup method is called by application server when it has to
    // put the ManagedConnection instance back in pool. In this method's
    // implementation you should release all the client-specific
associated with
    // ManagedConnection instance.
    public void cleanup() throws ResourceException {
        System.out.println("ManagedConnectionImpl.cleanup() called");
    }

    // RA should implement this method if it supports physical
connection sharing
    // such that it can associate a different client-side connection
handle with
    // the Managedconnection instance. Application server will call
this method
    // based on its criteria of connection sharing.
    public void associateConnection(Object connection) throws
ResourceException {
        throw new NotSupportedException
            ("ManagedConnectionImpl.associateConnection() not supported.");
    }

    // Application server calls this method to associate
ConnectionEventListener
    // object with this managed connection.
    public void addConnectionEventListener(ConnectionEventListener
        connEventListener){
        System.out.println("ManagedConnectionImpl.addConnectionEventListener
        (ConnectionEventListener) called");

        this.connEventListener = connEventListener;
    }

    public void removeConnectionEventListener (ConnectionEventListener
        connEventListener) {
    }

    public XAResource getXAResource() throws ResourceException {
        throw new NotSupportedException("Global transactions are not
supported");
    }

    public LocalTransaction getLocalTransaction() throws ResourceException {
        throw new NotSupportedException("Local transactions are not
supported");
```

Source 17.13 *(continued)*

```
    }

    public ManagedConnectionMetaData getMetaData() throws ResourceException {
        if (isDestroyed)
            throw new ResourceException ("Managed connection has already been
                closed.");

        return new ManagedConnectionMetaDataImpl (this);
    }

    public void setLogWriter(PrintWriter manConnLogWriter) {
        this.manConnLogWriter = manConnLogWriter;
    }

    public PrintWriter getLogWriter() {
        return manConnLogWriter;
    }

    // This method is implemented as part of private contract between RA and
    // the client-side connection API, so that client-side connection can
    // communicate with ManagedConnection instance various connection related
    // events such as connection close, transaction begin / commit /
rollback, and
    // so on. Once we determine the type of client-side connection
event, we call
    // the appropriate method on ConnectionEventListener object to provide
    // a hook to application server to add its own container services.
    void sendEvent(int eventType, Exception e, Object connHandle) {
        System.out.println("ManagedConnectionImpl.sendEvent(int, e,
connHandle)
            called");

        ConnectionEvent connEvent = null;
        if (e == null)
            connEvent = new ConnectionEvent(this, eventType);
        else
            connEvent = new ConnectionEvent(this, eventType, e);

        connEvent.setConnectionHandle(connHandle);
        switch (connEvent.getId()) {
            case ConnectionEvent.CONNECTION_CLOSED:
                this.connEventListener.connectionClosed(connEvent);
                break;
            case ConnectionEvent.LOCAL_TRANSACTION_STARTED:
                this.connEventListener.localTransactionStarted(connEvent);
                break;
            case ConnectionEvent.LOCAL_TRANSACTION_COMMITTED:
                this.connEventListener.localTransactionCommitted(connEvent);
                break;
            case ConnectionEvent.LOCAL_TRANSACTION_ROLLEDBACK:
```

Source 17.13 *(continued)*

```
this.connEventListener.localTransactionRolledback(connEvent);
                    break;
                case ConnectionEvent.CONNECTION_ERROR_OCCURRED:
                    this.connEventListener.connectionErrorOccurred(connEvent);
                    break;
                default:
                    throw new IllegalArgumentException("Unsupported event: " +
                        connEvent.getId());
            }
        }

        ManagedConnectionFactory getManagedConnectionFactory() {
            return manConnFactory;
        }
}
```

Source 17.13 *(continued)*

Note the following about our implementation of *ManagedConnection*:

- The application server registers a *ConnectionEventListener* with the *ManagedConnection* instance. We maintain this *ConnectionEventListener* for later use.
- We implement a *sendEvent()* method so that the client contract's connection implementation, *ConnectionImpl*, can notify the underlying managed connection instance when it is about to close the connection, and other such events. The *sendEvent()* method in turn calls the appropriate event notification method such as *connectionClosed()*, *connectionErrorOccured()*, and so on, on the *ConnectionEventListener* object.
- Since we do not support transaction management system contract, calls to the *getXAResource()* or *getLocalTransaction()* methods throw *NotSupportedException*.
- We do not support the sharing of *ManagedConnection* instances among connection handles and therefore the *associateConnection()* implementation throws *NotSupportedException*.

ConnectionRequestInfoImpl.java

Source 17.14 shows *ConnectionRequestInfoImpl.java*, which implements the *javax.resource.spi.ConnectionRequestInfo* system contract. As can be seen from Source 17.15, *ConnectionRequestInfoImpl* is a very simple implementation of *ConnectionRequestInfo* since our RA does not have any connection request–specific properties.

```
package examples.out_loan_ra;

import javax.resource.spi.ConnectionRequestInfo;

public class ConnectionRequestInfoImpl implements
ConnectionRequestInfo {

    public ConnectionRequestInfoImpl() {
    }

    public boolean equals(Object object) {
        if (object == null) return false;
        if (object instanceof ConnectionRequestInfoImpl) {
            return true;
        } else {
            return false;
        }
    }

    public int hashCode() {
        return (new String("ConnectionRequestInfoImpl")).hashCode();
    }
}
```

Source 17.14 The ConnectionRequestInfoImpl class.

ManagedConnectionMetaDataImpl.java

ManagedConnectionMetaDataImpl implements the *javax.resource.spi .ManagedConnectionMetaData* system contract. Since its implementation is quite similar to that of *ConnectionMetaData,* we will skip listing its source code.

Deploying OutboundLoanRA

During RA deployment, deployer will specify the interface and implementation classes for various client and system contracts supported by RA.

- **If RA supports the connection management system contract,** then the deployer will have to provide interface and implementation classes for connection factory and connection. In our case, these will be *javax.resource.cci.ConnectionFactory / example.out_loan_ra .ConnectionFactoryImpl* and *javax.resource.cci.Connection / example_out_loan_ra.ConnectionImpl*, respectively. Also, the deployer will have to provide the implementation class for *ManagedConnectionFactory,* which is *ManagedConnectionFactoryImpl* in our case.

If RA supports configuration properties for connection factories, that will be specified during deployment. In our case, we do not have any connection factory configuration properties.

- **If RA supports transaction management system contract**, the deployer will have to specify whether it supports local or global transactions.
- **If RA supports security management system contract**, you can also specify the authentication mechanism used during deployment.
- **If RA supports the message in-flow contract**, the deployer will need to provide the message listener interface class and activation specification JavaBean class.
- **If RA supports message in-flow or life cycle contract**, the deployer will need to specify the *ResourceAdapter* implementation class.

Apart from bundling the system and client contract classes, the deployer will also bundle the libraries that the RA uses to handle communication with EIS. For our example, this would be the *JavaLoanApp* Java class. Hence, we also bundle the *JavaLoanApp* class with *OutboundLoanRA*.

Also, if your RA loads native libraries or does socket communication, or any such activity that warrants explicit permissions, you must set the right runtime permissions for the application server's JVM instance. Since *OutboundLoanRA* uses a Java class that loads the system library, we will have to explicitly permit the underlying JVM instance to do so. One of the ways to achieve this is by directly modifying the *java.policy* file in *<JDK_HOME>/jdk/lib/security* folder to grant runtime permission to load native libraries.

Once the RA is deployed, the deployer will create a connection pool and associate it with the RA's connection factory. The deployer will use vendor-provided administration tools for creating a connection pool. Finally, the deployer will bind the connection pool to JNDI so that client application components can retrieve the underlying connection factory instance from JNDI and create the connection to the EIS.

OutboundLoanRA Deployment Descriptor

Source 17.15 shows deployment descriptor for *OutboundLoanRA*. Note that connectors do not have application server–specific deployment descriptors.

```
<?xml version='1.0' encoding='UTF-8'?> <connector
     xmlns="http://java.sun.com/xml/ns/j2ee"       version="1.5"
     xmlns:xsi="http://www.w3.org/2001/XMLSchema-instance"
     xsi:schemaLocation="http://java.sun.com/xml/ns/j2ee
     http://java.sun.com/xml/ns/j2ee/connector_1_5.xsd">
```

Source 17.15 The ra.xml.

```
    <display-name>OutboundLoanRA</display-name>
    <vendor-name>Vendor Name</vendor-name>
    <eis-type>EIS Type</eis-type>
    <resourceadapter-version>1.5</resourceadapter-version>
    <license><license-required>false</license-required></license>
    <resourceadapter>
      <outbound-resourceadapter>
        <connection-definition>
          <managedconnectionfactory-class>
            examples.out_loan_ra.ManagedConnectionFactoryImpl
          </managedconnectionfactory-class>
          <connectionfactory-interface>
            javax.resource.cci.ConnectionFactory
          </connectionfactory-interface>
          <connectionfactory-impl-class>
            examples.out_loan_ra.ConnectionFactoryImpl
          </connectionfactory-impl-class>
          <connection-interface>
            javax.resource.cci.Connection
          </connection-interface>
          <connection-impl-class>
            examples.out_loan_ra.ConnectionImpl
          </connection-impl-class>
        </connection-definition>
        <transaction-support>LocalTransaction</transaction-support>
        <reauthentication-support>false</reauthentication-support>
      </outbound-resourceadapter>
    </resourceadapter>
  </connector>
```

Source 17.15 *(continued)*

Now that we have developed and deployed the RA as well as the RA connection pool and JNDI resources associated with it, our RA is all set to receive requests from client application components, such as *LoanRatesEJB*.

LoanRatesEJB

LoanRatesEJB is a stateless session bean that uses *OutboundLoanRA* to communicate with backend loan processing application, *LoanApp.dll*.

Developing LoanRatesEJB

LoanRatesEJB's remote interface has a single method, *getHomeEquityRate()*. The *getHomeEquityRate()* method implementation uses the CCI client contracts supported by *OutboundLoanRA*. Source 17.16 is a partial listing of the *LoanRatesEJB* bean class, *LoanRatesBean.java*.

```
package examples;

import javax.ejb.CreateException;
import javax.ejb.SessionBean;
import javax.ejb.SessionContext;
import javax.naming.InitialContext;
import javax.naming.NamingException;

public class LoanRatesBean implements SessionBean {

     // SessionBean methods

     // Business method
     public float getHomeEquityRate() {
          float retVal=0;
          System.out.println("LoanRatesBean.getHomeEquityRate() called");
          InitialContext initCtx = null;
          try {
               // Lookup the CCI ConnectionFactory instance
               initCtx = new InitialContext();
               javax.resource.cci.ConnectionFactory connFactory =
                    (javax.resource.cci.ConnectionFactory)
                         initCtx.lookup("java:comp/env/eis/LoanAppAdapter");

               // Get CCI Connection handle
               javax.resource.cci.Connection myCon =
connFactory.getConnection();

               // Prepare for interaction with EIS
               javax.resource.cci.Interaction interaction =
myCon.createInteraction();
               javax.resource.cci.MappedRecord recordIn =
                    connFactory.getRecordFactory().createMappedRecord("");

               // Provide the EIS function name that you would like to execute
               recordIn.put("HomeEquityRate","");

               // Execute the EIS function
               javax.resource.cci.MappedRecord recordOut =
               (javax.resource.cci.MappedRecord) interaction.execute(
                    null, (javax.resource.cci.Record)recordIn);

               // Close CCI Connection
               myCon.close();

               // Return the rate of home equity loan returned by EIS
to EJB client
               Object result = recordOut.get("HomeEquityRate");
               retVal = ((Float)result).floatValue();
          } catch(Exception e) {
               e.printStackTrace();
```

Source 17.16 The LoanRatesBean class.

```
            }
            return retVal;
        }
}
```

Source 17.16 *(continued)*

Deploying LoanRatesEJB

LoanRatesEJB should be deployed like a regular stateless session bean. The only additional deployment configuration required is mapping the resource reference in our code, *java:comp/env/eis/LoanAppAdapter*, to the actual JNDI resource. This mapping can be done using deployment tools provided by your application server.

Source 17.17 is a partial listing of the *LoanRatesEJB* standard deployment descriptor and Source 17.18 is a partial listing of the *LoanRatesEJB* application server–specific deployment descriptor. Source 17.18 shows the mapping of coded resource reference to the actual JNDI resource.

```
<?xml version='1.0' encoding='UTF-8'?>
<ejb-jar ...>
   <display-name> LoanRatesEJB</display-name>
   <enterprise-beans>
     <session>
         <ejb-name> LoanRatesBean</ejb-name>
         ...
         <resource-ref>
            <res-ref-name> eis/LoanAppAdapter</res-ref-name>
            <res-type> javax.resource.cci.ConnectionFactory</res-type>
            <res-auth> Container</res-auth>
            <res-sharing-scope> Shareable</res-sharing-scope>
         </resource-ref>
         ...
     </session>
   </enterprise-beans>
</ejb-jar>
```

Source 17.17 The ejb-jar.xml.

```
<?xml version="1.0" encoding="UTF-8"?>
<!DOCTYPE sun-ejb-jar PUBLIC "-
//Sun Microsystems, Inc.//DTD Application Server 8.0 EJB 2.1//EN"
"http://www.sun.com/software/appserver/dtds/sun-ejb-jar_2_1-0.dtd">
<sun-ejb-jar>
  <enterprise-beans>
    <name> LoanRatesEJB</name>
      <ejb>
        <ejb-name>LoanRatesBean</ejb-name>
        <jndi-name> LoanRatesBean</jndi-name>
         <resource-ref>
         <res-ref-name>eis/LoanAppAdapter </res-ref-name>
         <jndi-name>OutboundLoanJNDIName </jndi-name>
       </resource-ref>
      </ejb>
    </enterprise-beans>
</sun-ejb-jar>
```

Source 17.18 The sun-ejb-jar.xml.

LoanRatesClient

LoanRatesClient standalone Java application is a client to *LoanRatesEJB*. Like a typical EJB client, it looks up the EJB home object and creates the EJB remote object, followed by an invocation to EJB remote method *getHomeEquityRate()*. Source 17.19 shows *LoanRatesClient.java*.

```
package examples;

import java.util.Properties;
import java.rmi.RemoteException;
import javax.ejb.CreateException;
import javax.naming.Context;
import javax.naming.InitialContext;
import javax.naming.NamingException;
import javax.rmi.PortableRemoteObject;

public class LoanRatesClient {
     public static void main(String[] args) throws RemoteException,
CreateException,
          NamingException {
          Properties env = new Properties();
          env.put("java.naming.factory.initial",
               "com.sun.jndi.cosnaming.CNCtxFactory");
          env.put("java.naming.provider.url", "iiop://localhost:3700");
```

Source 17.19 The LoanRatesClient class.

```
            InitialContext ctxt = new InitialContext(env);

            Object objRef = ctxt.lookup("LoanRatesBean");

            LoanRatesHome home = (LoanRatesHome)
PortableRemoteObject.narrow
                  (objRef, LoanRatesHome.class);

            LoanRates loanRatesObj = (LoanRates)
PortableRemoteObject.narrow
                  (home.create(), LoanRates.class);

            System.out.println("getHomeEquityRate() returned: " +
                  loanRatesObj.getHomeEquityRate() + ". Take a look at
                  application server log or console for messages
from LoanRatesEJB and
                  OutboundLoanRA.");
      }
}
```

Source 17.19 *(continued)*

Running the Client

To run the client, look at the Ant scripts bundled along with this example. The following is the client-side output you will get upon running the *LoanRatesClient*.

```
C:\MEJB3.0\Integration>asant run_client
getHomeEquityRate() returned: 5.64. Take a look at application server
log or console for messages from LoanRatesEJB and OutboundLoanRA.
```

On the application server console, you should see the following output. Make sure to run your application server in verbose mode. Note that this output is for J2EE 1.4 reference implementation.

```
[#|2004-08-09T15:03:29.813-0400|INFO|sun-appserver-pe8.0.0_01|javax.enterprise.
system.stream.out|_ThreadID=12;|
LoanRatesBean.getHomeEquityRate() called|#]

[#|2004-08-09T15:03:29.813-0400|INFO|sun-appserver-pe8.0.0_01|javax.enterprise.
system.stream.out|_ThreadID=12;|
ManagedConnectionFactoryImpl.createConnectionFactory(ConnectionManager)
called|#]

[#|2004-08-09T15:03:29.813-0400|INFO|sun-appserver-pe8.0.0_01|javax.enterprise.
```

```
system.stream.out|_ThreadID=12;|
ConnectionFactoryImpl(ManagedConnectionFactory manConnFactory, ConnectionManager
 connManager) called|#]

[#|2004-08-09T15:03:29.813-0400|INFO|sun-appserver-pe8.0.0_01|javax.enterprise.
system.stream.out|_ThreadID=12;|
ConnectionFactoryImpl.getConnection() called|#]

[#|2004-08-09T15:03:29.823-0400|INFO|sun-appserver-pe8.0.0_01|javax.enterprise.
system.stream.out|_ThreadID=12;|
ManagedConnectionFactoryImpl.matchManagedConnections(Set, Subject,
ConnectionRequestInfo) called|#]

[#|2004-08-09T15:03:29.823-0400|INFO|sun-appserver-pe8.0.0_01|javax.enterprise.
system.stream.out|_ThreadID=12;|
From ManagedConnectionFactoryImpl.matchManagedConnections() -> Connection
matched|#]

[#|2004-08-09T15:03:29.823-0400|INFO|sun-appserver-pe8.0.0_01|javax.enterprise.
system.stream.out|_ThreadID=12;|
ManagedConnectionImpl.getConnection(Subject, ConnectionRequestInfo) called|#]

[#|2004-08-09T15:03:29.823-0400|INFO|sun-appserver-pe8.0.0_01|javax.enterprise.
system.stream.out|_ThreadID=12;|
ConnectionImpl(ManagedConnectionImpl) called|#]

[#|2004-08-09T15:03:29.823-0400|INFO|sun-appserver-pe8.0.0_01|javax.enterprise.
system.stream.out|_ThreadID=12;|
InteractionImpl(Connection conn) called|#]

[#|2004-08-09T15:03:29.823-0400|INFO|sun-appserver-pe8.0.0_01|javax.enterprise.
system.stream.out|_ThreadID=12;|
InteractionImpl.execute(InteractionSpec iSpec, Record in) called|#]

[#|2004-08-09T15:03:29.823-0400|INFO|sun-appserver-pe8.0.0_01|javax.enterprise.
system.stream.out|_ThreadID=12;|
InteractionImpl.exec(MappedRecord in, MappedRecord out) called|#]

[#|2004-08-09T15:03:29.823-0400|INFO|sun-appserver-pe8.0.0_01|javax.enterprise.
system.stream.out|_ThreadID=12;|
JavaLoanApp Constructor called|#]

[#|2004-08-09T15:03:29.823-0400|INFO|sun-appserver-pe8.0.0_01|javax.enterprise.
system.stream.out|_ThreadID=12;|
Library loaded successfully.|#]

[#|2004-08-09T15:03:29.833-0400|INFO|sun-appserver-pe8.0.0_01|javax.enterprise.
system.stream.out|_ThreadID=12;|
JNI Call Returned: 5.64|#]

[#|2004-08-09T15:03:29.833-0400|INFO|sun-appserver-pe8.0.0_01|javax.enterprise.
system.stream.out|_ThreadID=12;|
ConnectionImpl.close() called|#]
```

```
[#|2004-08-09T15:03:29.833-0400|INFO|sun-appserver-pe8.0.0_01|javax.enterprise.
system.stream.out|_ThreadID=12;|
ManagedConnectionImpl.sendEvent(int, e, connHandle) called|#]

[#|2004-08-09T15:03:29.843-0400|INFO|sun-appserver-pe8.0.0_01|javax.enterprise.
system.stream.out|_ThreadID=12;|
ManagedConnectionImpl.cleanup() called|#]
```

Carefully study the highlighted portions in the output. This will further clear up the sequence of interactions among various objects in our integration solution.

Extending OutboundLoanRA

Before ending our discussion of the example application, let us briefly go through possible extensions to *OutboundLoanRA*.

Implementing additional system contracts can certainly augment the current capabilities of *OutboundLoanRA*. A good starting point for this exercise will be to add security management. Try component-managed EIS sign-on. *LoanApp.dll* currently does not authenticate access. However, you can improve *LoanApp.dll* by adding a *signOn()* native method. The *signOn()* method implementation could be as simple as logging the user name/password security credentials received from the client. At the RA end, you will be required to implement the *ConnectionSpec* and *ConnectionRequestInfo* JavaBeans so that they reflect the user name/password connection properties.

Another possible extension could be to augment the current outbound connection management contract of *OutboundLoanRA* with inbound messaging contract. Imagine a scenario in which a user submits a loan application to our loan processing. Since it can take days to make a decision on loan application, we want our loan application to send a message to the RA when the loan approval decision is ready. This could be done very simply: The loan application can create a simple text file containing the loan approval decision in a file system location that is continuously monitored by the RA. The RA will pick up the loan approval decision's text file, parse it, and create an *examples.out_loan_ra.LoanApprovalMessage* instance. Finally it sends this message to the endpoint that implements *examples.out_loan_ra.LoanApprovalMessageListener* within application server. You can extend this one step further by allowing the RA to do file system monitoring with the help of *Work* instance!

Integration Best Practice: When to Use Which Technology

Now that we know all the technologies for integrating EJB applications, the question is how to decide which one to use in a given scenario. The following guidelines should help you determine the right technology for your application integration problem on the EJB platform.

When to Use JMS and JMS-Based MDB

Java Message Service is a Java abstraction to MOM systems. All application servers support a JMS service that listens to a messaging provider (an RA, actually) and delivers messages from the messaging provider to JMS messaging endpoints a.k.a. JMS-based MDB. Decoupled communication along with reliable and asynchronous messaging forms the basis of this approach.

Use JMS and JMS-based MDB for application integration when:

- You are integrating Java application endpoints; for example, consider a scenario where a Java application wants to integrate with your EJB application in an asynchronous yet reliable manner. Here, your Java application can simply create and send a JMS message to the MDB, and it is all set.
- You are integrating non real-time applications. For example, processing inventory and shipping or communication with suppliers.
- You need reliability and transaction support for integrating application endpoints.

The only disadvantage to this approach is that because JMS does not define a wire protocol, out-of-the-box integration across various JMS products is difficult and almost impossible without using MOM bridges. As a result, if your scenario involves using different JMS products, this approach might not work without using a bridge to translate your JMS product's protocol to that of the target application endpoint's JMS product protocol.

When to Use J2EE Connectors

Use J2EE connectors for application integration when:

- You want to integrate with backend EIS applications without modifying them.
- The quality of services is a prerequisite for integration. For example, if you need transactional and secure access to the EIS, connectors can be the way to go. If you want the application server to pool your outbound connections, connector architecture can enable that. Again, if you want the application server to host message endpoints so that they can consume messages from your EIS, connector architecture is the answer.
- You are integrating with a widely used EIS because you are likely to find off-the-shelf connectors for most of these. This greatly reduces the time it takes to integrate with the EIS.

When to Use Java Web Services

Web Services are becoming a predominant choice for application integration, both within and outside the enterprise boundaries. The main reason behind this is the ubiquitous support for Web Services protocols found in most of the modern programming platforms and languages. The interoperability guidelines from organizations such as Web Services Interoperability (WS-I) further increase the applicability of Web Services in integration space.

Think of using Web Services when:

- You need to quickly integrate application endpoints.
- The target applications for integration exist on disparate platforms.
- The target application endpoints are deployed behind the demilitarized zone (DMZ) thereby requiring access through the firewalls.

Web Services provide a quick fix to the integration problem. However, they are far from providing a robust solution for integration because of the lack of quality of services support in the Web Services protocols. The good news is that industry is working hard to define security, transactions, and other such semantics for Web Services.

Summary

In this chapter we introduced integration and presented an overview of various styles of integration. We learned how J2EE connectors provide an excellent framework for integrating EJB with non-IIOP applications. We then learned various best practices related to choosing appropriate technology for application integration on the EJB platform.

In the next chapter, we learn about various performance optimizations you can implement to boost the performance of session beans, entity beans, and message-driven beans.

CHAPTER

18

EJB Performance Optimizations

In this chapter, we will discuss *EJB best practices*—tried-and-true approaches relevant to EJB performance optimization. By being aware of these best practices, you will be able to architect for good performance right from the beginning so that you will not be required to retrofit your design and code to achieve the performance numbers during load/performance testing.

Let's begin now with our collection of best practices, optimizations, tips, and techniques for performance.

This chapter does *not* cover low-level EJB design patterns. We started to put those together but realized that those patterns deserved a book of their own. That's what gave birth to Floyd Marinescu's book *EJB Design Patterns*, published by John Wiley & Sons and a companion to this book.

It Pays to Be Proactive!

The most important requirement for building highly optimized applications is to specify clearly performance requirements right in the design stages. Defining performance requirements basically means outlining your performance needs from various points of views: determining user experience under varying loads, the percentage of the system resources used, the allocation of system resources to achieve the desired performance, and so on. Many times we see these requirements defined after the system is developed and is about to be deployed—most often, on the night of load testing. QA calls the development manager to discuss a JVM "out-of-memory" error with a concurrent load of 20 users! And more often than not, the crash takes place because some developer forgot to release a Java container object, such as a collection, containing hundreds of instances of data transfer objects returned from a stateful session bean, after displaying its contents to the client.

To avoid this nightmare, we suggest the following:

- **Be proactive in defining your performance expectations.** This is the only way you will know what you want from your application and hence, how you should plan, design, and develop your application right from the start.
- **Design applications with performance in mind**. The most effective way to do this is by making use of the right architecture and design patterns, which are not anti-performance. Hire architects with sound knowledge of these patterns and their implications on performance (and simplicity and code maintenance). If you do not have this expertise in-house then hire competent consultants for architecting and designing your applications. The investment required to put in place a performance-friendly skeleton of your application at the architecture level would pay you back later.
- **Be proactive in educating your developers to write optimized code**. Even though you might have the best software architects or consultants in the world to design your application, if the developers implementing the design do not understand how to write optimized code, the cost you incurred in hiring these architects would be in vain. Therefore we suggest, conduct regular code reviews and find coding bottlenecks.
- **Master the science of tuning.** The first step towards mastering tuning is to understand that tuning can and should be done at multiple levels to achieve the highest levels of performance. In a typical J2EE enterprise application, you can ideally tune all the layers right from the network communications and operating system level to JVM to J2EE application server to your application code to your database to your cluster. Thus, the scope for tuning is much wider. If your performance requirements are extremely stringent, we suggest you tune all the layers of this stack. For most of the business applications, however, we have observed that tuning J2EE application server (both Web/EJB containers), the JVM used by the application server and Java application (in case of a Swing client), and the database is sufficient for a tuning exercise. You can actually define a tuning methodology so that everyone can become aware of all the steps involved in tuning all new development your organization.

With this in mind, let us see which best practices and optimizations lead us towards better EJB performance.

The Stateful Versus Stateless Debate from a Performance Point of View

Lately there's been a lot of fuss over statelessness. The limitations of statelessness are often exaggerated, as are its benefits. Many statelessness proponents blindly declare that statelessness leads to increased scalability, while stateful backers argue about having to rearchitect entire systems to accommodate statelessness. What's the real story?

Designed right, statelessness has two virtues:

- With stateless beans, the EJB container is able to easily pool and reuse beans, allowing a few beans to service many clients. While the same paradigm applies to stateful beans, if the server is out of memory or has reached its bean instance limit, then the bean state may be passivated and activated between method calls, possibly resulting in I/O bottlenecks. So one practical virtue of statelessness is the ability to easily pool and reuse components at little or no overhead.
- Because a stateful session bean caches a client conversation in memory, a bean failure may entail losing your conversation. This can have severe repercussions if you don't write your beans with this in mind or if you don't use an EJB container that provides stateful recovery. In a stateless model, the request could be transparently rerouted to a different component because any component can service the client's needs.

The largest drawback to statelessness is that you need to push client-specific data into the stateless bean for each method invocation. Most stateless session beans need to receive some information that is specific to a certain client, such as a bank account number for a banking bean. This information must be resupplied to stateless beans each time a client request arrives because the bean cannot hold any state on behalf of a particular client.

One way to supply the bean with client-specific data is to pass the data as parameters into the bean's methods. This can lead to performance degradation, however, especially if the data being passed is large. This also clogs the network, reducing available bandwidth for other processes.

Another way to get client-specific data to a stateless bean is for the bean to store data persistently on behalf of a client. The client then does not need to pass the entire state in a method invocation but simply needs to supply an identifier to retrieve the data from persistent storage. The tradeoff here is, again, performance; storing conversations persistently could lead to storage I/O bottlenecks, rather than network I/O bottlenecks.

Yet another way to work around the limitations of statelessness is for a bean to store client-specific data in a directory structure using JNDI. The client could later pass the bean an identifier for locating the data in the directory structure. This is quite similar to storing data in a database. The big difference is that a JNDI implementation could be an in-memory implementation such as the one from the SourceForge.net Tyrex project—an effect similar to a shared property manager, familiar to COM+ readers. If client data is stored in memory, there is no database hit.

When choosing between stateful and stateless, you should ask if the business process spans multiple invocations, requiring a conversation. Since most business processes are stateful anyway, you would quite probably need to retain state on behalf of clients. So the guideline to follow is if you are short of resources to spare on the server, choose stateless session beans and maintain the conversation in a database or an in-memory directory. If you have enough resources on the server system so that you would not need to passivate or activate the stateful bean instances frequently under average to high loads, then go for stateful session beans.

Note that if you are going to maintain state, and if you're building a Web-based system, you may be able to achieve what you need with a servlet's *HttpSession* object, which is the Web server equivalent to a stateful session bean and is easier to work with because it does not require custom coding. We have found that a stateful session bean should be used over an *HttpSession* object in the following situations:

- You need a stateful object that's transactionally aware. Your session bean can achieve this by implementing *SessionSynchronization*, described in Chapter 12.
- You have both Web-based and non–Web-based clients accessing your EJB layer, and both need state.
- You are using a stateful session bean to temporarily store state for a business process that occurs within a single HTTP request and involves multiple beans. To understand this point, consider that you are going through a big chain of beans, and a bean deep in the chain needs to access state. You could marshal the state in the parameter list of each bean method (ugly and could be a performance problem if you're using remote interfaces). The better solution is to use a stateful session bean and just pass the object reference through the stack of bean calls.

In summary, most sophisticated deployments are likely to have a complex and interesting combination of the stateless and stateful paradigm. Use the paradigm that's most appropriate for your business problem. If you are on the fence about stateful versus stateless, you may find that stateful session beans are not your primary issue—until you test your code, you're just shooting in

WHAT IF MY STATEFUL BEAN DIES?

Bean failure is an important factor to consider. Because a stateful session bean caches a client conversation in memory, a bean failure may entail losing your conversation. This was not a problem with statelessness—there was no conversation to be lost. Unless you are using an EJB product that routinely checkpoints (that is, persists) your conversations, your conversations will be lost if an application server fails.

Losing a conversation has devastating impacts. If you have large conversations that span time, you've lost important work. And the more stateful session beans that you use in tandem, the larger the existing network of interconnected objects that each rely on the other's stability. Many EJB servers today do offer stateful recovery of Enterprise Java Beans. However, if yours does not then your code will need to be able to handle the fail-over gracefully. Here are some of the guidelines you can use while designing your stateful beans to enable them to handle stateful recovery:

- **Keep your conversations short.**
- **If the performance is feasible, consider checkpointing stateful conversations yourself to minimize the impacts of bean failure.**
- **Write smart client code that anticipates a bean failure and reestablishes the conversational state with a fresh stateful session bean.**

the dark. It would help to do a proof of concept for stateful session beans. However, shooting down stateful session beans blindly is not advisable. Don't forget that they exist for a good reason—to take the load of managing client-related state off your shoulders and thereby make your life easier.

How to Guarantee a Response Time with Capacity Planning

Many types of business problems are trivial, such as basic Web sites or non-mission critical applications. But then there are those that *must not fail* and must *guarantee* a certain response time. For example, a trading application needs to guarantee a response time because stock market conditions might change if the trade is delayed. For those serious deployments, capacity planning is essential for your deployment.

The specific amount of hardware that you'll need for your deployment varies greatly depending on the profile of your application, your anticipated user load, your performance requirements, and the EJB server you choose. Most of the major EJB server vendors have strategies for capacity planning that they can share with you.

One strategy, however, works with all EJB server vendors. The idea is to *throttle*, or limit, the amount of work any given EJB server instance can process at any one time. Why would you ever want to limit the amount of work a machine can handle? A machine can only guarantee a response time for the clients it serves and be reliable if it isn't using up every last bit of system resources it has at its disposal. For example, if your EJB server runs out of memory, it either starts swapping your beans out to disk because of passivation/activation, or it uses virtual memory and uses the hard disk as swap space. Either way, the response time and reliability of your box is jeopardized. You want to prevent this from happening at all costs by limiting the amount of traffic your server can handle at once.

You can throttle (or limit) the amount of traffic your machine can handle using a variety of means. One is by limiting the *thread pool* of your EJB server. By setting an upper bound on the number of threads that can execute concurrently, you effectively limit the number of users that can be processed at any given time. Another possibility is to limit the *bean instance pool*. This lets you control how many EJB components can be instantiated at once, which is great for allowing more requests to execute with lightweight beans and fewer requests to execute with heavyweight beans.

Once you've throttled your machine and tested it to make sure it's throttled correctly, you need to devise a strategy to add more machines to the deployment in case your cluster-wide capacity limit is reached. An easy way to do this is to have a standby machine that is unused under normal circumstances. When you detect that the limit is reached (such as by observing message queue growth, indicating that your servers cannot consume off the request queue fast enough), the standby machine kicks in and takes over the excess load. A system administrator can then be paged to purchase a new standby machine.

This algorithm guarantees a response time because each individual server cannot exceed its limit, and there's always an extra box waiting if traffic increases.

Use Session Façade for Better Performance

Consider the following scenarios:

- A bank teller component performs the business process of banking operations, but the data used by the teller is the bank account data.
- An order-entry component performs the business process of submitting new orders for products, such as submitting an order for a new computer to be delivered to a customer. But the data generated by the order-entry component is the order itself, which contains a number of order line-items describing each part ordered.

- A stock portfolio manager component performs the business process of updating a stock portfolio, such as buying and selling shares of stock. But the data manipulated by the portfolio manager is the portfolio itself, which might contain other data such as account and stock information.

In each of these scenarios, business process components are manipulating data in some underlying data storage, such as a relational database. The business process components map very well to session beans, and the data components map very well to entity beans. The session beans use entity beans to represent their data, similar to the way a bank teller uses a bank account. Thus, a great EJB design strategy is to wrap entity beans with session beans. This design pattern is generally referred to as session façade.

Another benefit of this approach is performance. Accessing an entity bean directly over the network is expensive, due to:

- The stub
- The skeleton
- Marshaling/demarshaling
- The network call
- The EJB object interceptor

You can minimize these expensive calls to entity beans by wrapping them with session beans. The session beans perform bulk create, read, update, delete (CRUD) operations on behalf of remote clients. The session bean also serves as a transactional façade, enforcing that transactions occur on the server, rather than involving a remote client. This makes entity beans into an implementation detail of session beans. The entity beans are never seen by the external client; rather, entity beans just happen to be the way that the session bean performs persistence.

A final benefit of this approach is that your entity beans typically achieve a high level of reuse. For instance, consider an order entry system, where you have an order submission session bean that performs operations on an order entity bean. In the next generation of your application, you may want an order fulfillment session bean, an order reporting session bean, and so on. That same order entity bean can be reused for each of these session beans. This approach enables you to fine-tune and change your session bean business processes over time as user requirements change.

Thus, in practice you can expect the reuse of entity beans to be high. Session beans model a current business process, which can be tweaked and tuned with different algorithms and approaches. Entity beans, on the other hand, define your core business. Data such as purchase orders, customers, and bank accounts do not change very much over time.

There are also a few caveats about this approach:

- You can also wrap entity beans with other entity beans, if you have a complex object model with relationships.
- The value of session beans as a network performance optimization goes away if you do not have remote clients. This could occur, for example, if you deploy an entire J2EE application into a single process, with servlets and JSPs calling EJB components in-process. However, the session façade could still be used for proper design considerations and to isolate your deployment from any particular multitier configuration. If you're lazy, an alternative is to use an entity bean's home business methods, which are instance-independent business methods that act effectively as stateless session bean methods, except they are located on the entity bean.
- Note that what we've presented here are merely guidelines, not hard-and-fast rules. Indeed, a session bean can contain data-related logic as well, such as a session bean performing a bulk database read via JDBC. The key is that session beans never embody permanent data, but merely provide access to data.

Choosing Between Local Interfaces and Remote Interfaces

Local interfaces, a feature since EJB 2.0, enable you to access your EJB components without incurring network traffic. They also allow you to pass nonserializable parameters around, which is handy. So what is the value of a remote interface? Well, there really isn't a value, unless:

- You need to access your system remotely (say from a remote Web tier).
- You are trying to test EJB components individually and need to access them from a standalone client to perform the testing.
- You need to allow your containers more choices for workload distribution and fail-over in a clustered server environment.

For optimal performance, we recommend that you build your system using all local interfaces, and then have one or more session bean wrappers with remote interfaces, exposing the system to remote clients.

Note that the problem with local and remote interfaces is that the code is slightly different for each paradigm. Local interfaces have a different interface name and do not use *PortableRemoteObject.narrow()*, and there are no *RemoteExceptions* thrown. Because of this, you need to recode your clients when switching between the two paradigms. This is an unfortunate consequence of having a programmatic approach to better performance.

To limit the amount of recoding you'll need to do, decide whether the clients of your beans are going to be local or remote *before you start coding*. For example, if you're building a Web-based system, decide whether your system will be a complete J2EE application in a single process, or whether your Web tier will be split off from your EJB tier into a separate process. We discuss the tradeoffs of these approaches in Chapter 19.

As a final note, if you are connecting to your EJB deployment from a very distant client (such as an applet or application that gets downloaded by remote users), consider exposing your EJB system as an XML-based Web service, rather than a remote interface. This will be slower than a straight RMI/IIOP call, but is more appropriate for WAN clients.

Partitioning Your Resources

When programming with EJB, we've found it very handy to separate the kinds of resources your beans use into two categories: *bean-specific resources* and *bean-independent resources*.

- **Bean-specific resources** are resources your bean uses that are tied to a specific data instance in an underlying storage. For example, a socket connection is a bean-specific resource if that socket is used only when particular bank account data is loaded. That is, the socket is used only when your bean instance is bound to a particular EJB object. Such a resource should be acquired when a bean instance is created in *ejbCreate()* or when activated in *ejbActivate()* and released when the instance is removed in *ejbRemove()* or passivated in *ejbPassivate()*.
- **Bean-independent resources** are resources that can be used over and over again, no matter what underlying data your instance represents. For example, a socket connection is a bean-independent resource if your bean can reuse that socket no matter what bank account your bean represents (that is, no matter what EJB object your bean instance is assigned to). Global resources like these should be acquired when your bean is first created, and they can be used across the board as your bean is assigned to different EJB objects. When the container first instantiates your bean, it associates you with a context object (such as the *setEntityContext()* method); that is when you should acquire your bean-independent resources. Similarly, when you are disassociated with a context object (such as the *unsetEntityContext()* method), you should release bean-independent resources.

Because acquiring and releasing resources may be costly operations, categorizing your resources as outlined is a vital step. Of course, the stingiest way to handle resources is to acquire them on a *just-in-time* basis and release them directly after use. For example, you could acquire a database connection only when you're about to use it and release it when you're done. Then there would be no resources to acquire or release during activation or passivation. In this case, the assumption is that your container pools the resource in question. If not, just-in-time acquisition of resource might prove expensive because every time you request to acquire a resource, its handle is actually being created and every time you request to release the resource, the underlying object is actually being destroyed. To get around this, you will need to write your own implementation that can pool the resource in question. You will then need to use this pool manager abstraction to acquire or release the resource. The slight disadvantage to just-in-time resource acquisition or release is that you need to code requests to acquire or release resources over and over again in your bean.

Tuning Stateless Session Beans

Taking into consideration the life cycle of stateless session beans, as discussed in Chapter 4, these tuning techniques should be examined closely to achieve best performance:

- **Tune pool size.** The pool size-related settings are made available by your EJB server vendor and hence, you will need to specify them in the vendor-specific deployment descriptor. It controls the number of stateless session bean instances in the pool. Some products will enable you to specify a range for pool size. In this case, mostly, you would also be able to specify the resize quantity of your pool. When the server runs out of pooled bean instances to service further client requests, resize quantity will specify the number of new instances a server should create at a time, until the maximum of the pool size range is reached.

  For example, consider the range for pool size is *initial=50* and *maximum=100*, and the resize quantity is *10*. Now if at a given point in time all 50 instances are busy servicing client requests, then when the 51st request comes for that stateless session bean, the EJB container will create 10 more instances of the bean, make available one of these newly created instances to the client and pool the remaining 9 instances for future requests. This resizing of the pool will continue happening until the maximum pool size range is reached, that is 100. So then what happens when at a given point in time all 100 instances are servicing requests? The 101st client request will have to wait for one of the previous 100 clients to release the bean so that the container can make this underlying bean instance available to our 101st client. The client request thus will have to be queued by the container.

Also some containers will provide you with a pool idle timeout setting. It basically specifies the maximum time that a stateless session bean is allowed to be idle in the pool before removing it from the pool. Pool resize quantity setting will play a role here too. It will specify the number of beans that the server will destroy once they have reached idle time limit. Hence, an increase or decrease in the maximum limit of the pool size should mean an appropriate change in the resize quantity too to maintain a good balance.

Make sure that you set the initial and maximum values for the pool size such that they are representative of the normal and peak loads on your system. Setting a very large initial or maximum value is an inefficient use of system resources for an application that does not have much concurrent load under normal and peak conditions, respectively. Also this will cause large garbage collection pauses. At the same time, setting a very small initial or maximum value compared to the typical loads is going to cause a lot of object creation and object destruction.

- **Efficient resource caching.** As discussed earlier, it is a good practice to cache bean-independent resources in *setEntityContext()* and release the cache in *unsetEntityContext()* methods of the bean life cycle. However, if you cache a resource, such as a database, connection in the previous methods within a stateless session bean deployment with large pool size and heavy concurrent client access, chances are that container will run out of free connection instances in the connection pool very soon; the container might need to queue the request for connection resource. To avoid this, it is better to obtain connection resources from the connection pool *just-in-time* in such situations.

Tuning Stateful Session Beans

Taking into consideration the life cycle of stateful session beans as discussed in Chapter 4, these tuning techniques should be examined closely to achieve best performance:

- **Tune cache size.** The stateful session bean life cycle as defined by the EJB standard is such that stateful session beans are cached but not pooled. Beans are cached when the number of concurrent users requesting the services of stateful session bean exceeds that of the maximum allowable number of stateful session bean instances. During caching the state of the bean is stored in the disk (a.k.a. passivation) for later use by its client and the bean instance is made available for use to another client. The cache and other stateful session bean–related tuning settings are EJB server specific and so they will go in the vendor-specific deployment descriptor. Most of the vendors allow you to specify the maximum cache size for stateful session beans.

Some vendors will allow you to specify cache resize quantity that works similar to the pool resize quantity for stateless session beans. The container can use a variety of algorithms to select beans for passivation, and if the container is good enough, it will let you choose the algorithm for passivation. These algorithms could be the least recently used (LRU), first in first out (FIFO), or not recently used (NRU) techniques.

The cache idle timeout setting will let you specify the time interval after which an idle bean will be passivated. Some containers will also let you specify the removal timeout value, which sets the time interval after which the passivated state of the bean is removed from the disk thereby freeing the disk resources. A good coding practice is for your client code to explicitly remove the bean instance by calling *remove()* on EJB object. This way the state, on behalf of your client, will not unnecessarily be maintained on the server until the container passivates it and finally removes it.

Again, tune the cache, taking into consideration the number of concurrent users that will access your stateful session bean under typical and peak conditions. Setting a large maximum value for cache size in comparison to the typical loads and peak loads of concurrent users respectively will lead to inefficient usage of memory resources; whereas setting a small maximum value for cache size will lead to a lot of passivation and activation of bean instances and hence serialization and deserialization, thereby straining on the CPU cycles and disk I/O.

- **Control serialization.** Serialization consumes CPU cycles and I/O resources. More serialization leads to more consumption of resources. The same is the case for deserialization, which takes place during the activation of stateful session beans. It is a good practice to keep the amount of serialization and deserialization to a minimum. One way to achieve this is by explicitly instructing the container to not serialize the state that you would not need after activation. You can do so by marking such objects as *transient* in your stateful session bean class.

Tuning Entity Beans

Taking into consideration the life cycle of entity beans as discussed in Chapter 6, the following tuning techniques and best practices should be examined closely to achieve best performance:

- **Use CMP.** Again we want to reiterate our stand of considering the use of CMP 2.*x*. If you have had bad memories of using CMP in the EJB 1.*x* days, reconsider their use again. They have totally changed! They are not just easy to use, but also offer a lot of avenues for boosting performance. Most of the CMP implementations today provide various options for tuning the performance of CMP by enabling lazy loading of entity data, lazy loading of relationship data, and so on, which we will discuss in the points to follow. To gain the most from CMP, choose an EJB server that provides a wide array of CMP tuning parameters.
- **Provide a local interface for entity beans.** Avoid calling entity beans, especially the ones that return lots of data via finder methods say, directly from remote clients. The reason is that all the data returned from such entity beans will have to be marshaled to the remote client. Design so that entity beans are called by clients, session beans preferably, from within the same JVM. Also, colocating entity beans with their callers enables calling via their local interfaces and hence, pass-by-reference semantics.
- **Tune pool size.** Entity bean life cycle, as defined by EJB standard, is such that they are pooled as well as cached. The pooling of entity beans is quite similar to that of stateless session beans. Most of the EJB servers have a provision to specify vendor-specific pool settings, such as initial pool size (also known as steady pool size in some products), maximum pool size, pool resize quantity, and pool idle timeout. The best practices for tuning the entity bean pool are the same as discussed previously for stateless session beans.
- **Tune cache size.** The caching of entity beans is similar to the caching of stateful session beans in that the tuning settings for stateful session beans and entity beans for a given vendor are the same. Most of the EJB servers will provide some common cache tuning options such as maximum cache size, cache resize quantity, cache idle timeout, removal timeout, and so on. Apart from the best practices for tuning cache that we discussed for stateful session beans, you should also:
  - **Provide a bigger cache** for entities that are used a lot and provide a smaller cache for entities that are not used very much.
  - **Keep the maximum** limit of the pool size the same as the maximum cache size, because while associating data to the entity bean instance, the container brings the entity bean instance from the pool. Hence, a pool smaller than cache can lead to a situation where clients are waiting on the container to get ahold of the entity bean which in turn is waiting on the entity bean pool queue for its turn to get ahold of a bean instance.

While tuning the entity bean pool and cache, always keep in mind that in most of the deployments the number of entities is mostly going to be larger than the number of session beans taking into consideration finder methods that return large numbers of entity stubs. Hence, pool and cache sizes of entity beans are usually much larger than that for stateless and stateful session beans.

- **Use lazy loading.** If you do not need all the data of your entity the first time you access it, choose to lazy load the unneeded data upon request from the client. This will optimize memory consumption on your system as well as the use of network bandwidth. If you are using BMP then you will need to code for lazy loading in your bean class by putting relevant SQLs in the appropriate *getXXX()* methods. If you are using CMP, your container will have to support lazy loading for your entity beans.

  Lazy loading helps a lot when accessing relationship data. For example, you can load the data for an Employee:Paychecks one-to-many relationship only when the client actually wants the paycheck information of that given employee and not when a client is just interested in getting the basic employee information. We discuss the implementation of lazy loading of relationship data for BMP in Chapter 15. For CMP, you will have to depend on a container to enable lazy loading of relationship data.

  Remember though that there is always a tradeoff when using lazy loading for core entity data—your bean can end up accessing the database quite a number of times if the client requests data chosen for lazy loading often. To get around this issue, you need to closely observe the way client applications use your entity bean and then select the less frequently requested data for lazy loading.

- **Mark entity beans as read-only, read-mostly, or read-write.** If your entity bean is used only for viewing the underlying database data but never used for changing the database data, then you should consider marking them *read-only*. This way you avoid using the unnecessary calls to *ejbStore()* on your bean at the end of each transaction. Note that if a method on such a read-only bean is accessed within a transaction, *ejbLoad()* is always called to synchronize the state with the underlying database. If you are very sure that the data for your entity will never change or if you do not care much about displaying up-to-date data to the client, you should access the methods on read-only entity beans outside the transaction.

  On the other hand, if your entity beans change less frequently, you can set a refresh timeout value on such beans by marking them *read-mostly*. Here, *ejbLoad()* on your beans would be called any time a client accesses the bean at the end of the refresh timeout period.

Thus, marking the entity beans as read-only, read-mostly, or read-write, you can control if and when the *ejbLoad()* and *ejbStore()* methods get called. Of course, the container has to allow these settings.

- **Choose the right semantics for transactions.** Be sure your transactions run on the server, are as short as possible, and encapsulate all the entity bean operations you'd like to have participating in that transaction. This is important because the synchronization with underlying database occurs at the beginning and end of transactions. If you have a transaction occurring for each entity bean get/set operation, you are performing database hits on each method call. The best way to perform transactions with entity beans is to wrap all your entity bean calls within a session bean method and mark that session bean method as transactional. Here you will also have to mark the entity bean methods with the container-managed transaction attribute of *Required*. This creates a transaction in the session bean that encapsulates all entity beans in the same transaction.
- **Choose the right transaction isolation level.** Isolation levels are explained with a lot of details in Chapter 12. In short, isolation levels help maintain integrity of concurrently accessed data. You should choose an optimum isolation level for your application. Isolation levels are set at the database connection (or connection pool) level and not in your entity bean deployment descriptor. Hence, the chosen isolation level will apply for all database access—from a single bean, multiple beans, one J2EE application, or multiple J2EE applications—via that connection pool. Some of the best practices for selecting the right isolation level are:
  - **Use the lowest** possible isolation level, for example *READ_UNCOMMITTED* for beans that represent operations on data that is not critical from a data integrity standpoint. If you do not care about reading uncommitted data or others updating the rows that you are reading or inserting new data into the data set you are accessing, go for this isolation level.
  - **Use *READ_COMMITTED*** for applications that intend to always read the data that is committed. However, your applications still have to be prepared to live with unrepeatable read and phantom read problems.
  - **Use *REPEATABLE_READ*** for applications that intend to always read and reread the same data. However, your applications still can get newly created rows when they try to reread the same data. Understand that your database achieves this behavior by locking the rows you are reading so that nobody else can update these rows. However, other users can still read your data.

- Use *SERIALIZABLE* for applications that want to hold exclusive access to data. The cost of using this isolation mode is that all requests to read and modify this data will be serialized by your database. Hence, others will have to wait to read/update the data that you are accessing. You should only use this isolation level in cases that warrant for single user data access.
- **Finally, set transaction** isolation levels only when you are fully aware of your application's semantics. Also note that not all databases support all the transaction isolation levels.

- **Use the appropriate commit option.** Commit options enable you to specify what the container should do to a bean after the transaction in which the bean participates is completed. EJB standard defines three commit options, for example, A, B, and C. In commit option A, when a transaction completes, the bean is kept in the ready state, meaning the bean has its identity intact. This means that the next request to the container for the same primary key will not require the container to do anything since the corresponding bean is already in the ready state. In commit option B, when a transaction completes, the bean is cached; however, the bean's identity is retained. Thus, the next request to the container for the same primary key will not require the container to associate a bean instance with the primary key since a bean corresponding to the primary key is already available. However, the *ejbLoad()* method would be called to synchronize the data from the database. In commit option C, when a transaction completes, the bean is passivated, meaning the bean state is serialized and the bean instance is returned to the pool. Hence, the next invocation for the same primary key will require the container to take a free bean instance from the pool and associate it with the primary key and then associate (deserialize) the bean's state. Also, the bean's *ejbLoad()* method will be called to synchronize the bean's state with the database.

  Hence, in commit option A no *ejbLoad()*, *ejbActivate()*, or *ejbPassivate()* methods are executed during a subsequent client request given that the bean is kept in the ready state. This is the fastest way to service client requests. However, you should not set this commit option for entity beans bound to tables with a large number of records. Also, don't use this option if data is a candidate for concurrent access. This commit option requires exclusive access to data and so for concurrent environments this commit option might not work.

  In commit option B, no *ejbActivate()* or *ejbPassivate()* methods are executed during a subsequent client request given that the bean's state is maintained across the transactions. However, *ejbLoad()* is required to synchronize the state with the database since the bean does not have exclusive access to the underlying data. In deployments where entity caching is used a lot, commit option B works much better. It is much more efficient.

In commit option C, all three methods—*ejbActivate()*, *ejbPassivate()*, and *ejbLoad()*—are called by a container upon the next client request for the same primary key. This adds to some latency while servicing client requests since the container puts back the beans into the pool after transaction completion or method invocation on the bean. This way instances are used better. This option works the best in environments where caching is not a requirement. Caching of entities is not required for deployments where different clients work with different pieces of data.

- **Use JDBC access when retrieving large amounts of data.** Entity beans work very well when working with small to medium-sized data sets. But in our experience, when working with larger data sets, for example, working in use cases where a single *SELECT* statement is going to retrieve thousands of records, it is better not to use entity beans. Code such data access by using JDBC from session beans. You can use a Data Access Object (DAO) abstraction in between to place all the JDBC code. Again, using JDBC has another benefit. If you were to use JDBC 3.0, you could make use of a *CachedRowSet* implementation to get disconnected rowset functionality. This boosts performance by not maintaining a connection to the database while you are traversing the large set of data.
- **Use JDBC optimizations for BMP.** There are quite a few JDBC optimizations that you can employ to obtain improved performance when working with BMP.
- **Choose the optimal database driver for accessing data.** This applies also when working directly with data from session beans or other J2EE components. Know the differences between the four types of JDBC drivers. Most importantly, avoid using type 1 JDBC drivers a.k.a. JDBC-ODBC drivers. They tend to give the least performance because of the fact that all the JDBC calls are translated twice—JDBC to ODBC and ODBC to database-specific calls. Use type 1 drivers only when your database does not support a JDBC driver, which is an unlikely situation. Today, you can find various types of JDBC drivers for almost all major databases. Another criterion for selecting JDBC driver is to get a driver that supports the latest JDBC standard. This is because with each version of the JDBC standard, the sophistication of its SPI keeps increasing, thereby providing better performing data access to the database. For example, all JDBC 2.0 and above drivers provide connection pooling support. Hence, if you are using a driver below 2.0 you will not gain the performance enhancement due to connection pooling. Another example—JDBC 3.0 driver supports *PreparedStatement* object pooling.

Anybody who has worked with JDBC would know that prepared statements are pre-compiled SQL statements and so they boost performance dramatically especially when the same pre-compiled SQL is used multiple times. However, creating the *PreparedStatement* object imposes some overhead. To avoid incurring this overhead each time you use the prepared statement, you can pool it using a JDBC 3.0 driver.

- **Use batch updates**. If your BMP entity bean method issues multiple updates to the database by calling *executeUpdate()* methods, then you should explicitly turn the automatic commit option off by calling *setAutoCommit()* method. By doing this your transaction is committed only when the *commit()* method is called. Not doing so will result in database roundtrips for each *executeUpdate()* call.
- **Use batch retrievals.** If your BMP entity bean issues SQLs that will eventually fetch large amounts of data, you should optimize the data retrieval by using the batch retrieval feature of *Statement*. By setting fetch size on the *Statement* interface to a large number, the driver will not have to go to the database frequently to fetch the data. You should set the fetch size taking into consideration your system resources also.
- **Choose the right *Statement* interface.** JDBC provides three main types of statement abstractions: *Statement*, *PreparedStatement*, and *CallableStatement*. *Statement* is to execute SQL statements with no input and output parameters. *PreparedStatement* should be used when you want pre-compilation of SQL statement that accept input parameters. *CallableStatement* should be used when you need pre-compilation of SQL statements that support both input and output parameters. You should use *CallableStatement* for most of your stored procedures.
- **Use other CMP optimizations.** Remember—one of the main reasons to use CMP besides ease of development is to leverage performance enhancement techniques implemented by the container for entity beans. Apart from those discussed previously, following are the two other tips that you can employ while using CMP, given that your container supports them.
  - **Instruct your container** to persist fields in bulk. For example, WebLogic has the notion of field groups. This empowers you to define groups of fields (even across relationships) that persist together, reducing the number of database roundtrips required.
  - **Instruct your container** to have your finder methods automatically load your bean, rather than having finding and loading functions happen separately, requiring two database roundtrips. The only time you should not use this option is if you're not going to read data from your entity bean (for example, setting fields, but not getting fields).

Tuning Message-Driven Beans

Now let us examine some best practices and techniques to boost message-driven bean performance:

- **Tune pool size.** MDB is essentially a stateless session bean whose *onMessage()* method is invoked by the container upon arrival of a message. Hence, to reduce the overhead of creation (and the release) of MDB bean instances upon each message arrival, the container pools them. The pool tuning settings are pretty much the same as stateless session bean. A container can let you specify one or all of the initial pool size, maximum pool size, resize quantity, and pool idle timeout settings.

  Use these settings to match the message processing loads under typical and peak conditions. For better throughput under high traffic conditions, maintain a large pool of MDB bean instances. Needless to say, these settings go into the vendor specific deployment descriptor.

- **JMS-specific tuning.** If your MDB consume JMS messages, one important performance tuning you can do is select the right acknowledgment mode. You set the acknowledgment mode in the MDB deployment descriptor. Chapter 9 discusses the various acknowledgment modes in detail. Use *Auto_acknowledge* mode when you do not want to receive duplicates and thereby avoid inefficient use of network bandwidth. Note that here the JMS engine makes sending the acknowledgment top priority. Hence, throughput might suffer in scenarios where a lot of JMS messages arrive and need to be processed by the MDB. On the other hand, if you want your JMS engine to leave everything in order to send acknowledgment, you should consider *Dups_ok_acknowledge* mode.

Tuning Java Virtual Machine

Don't ignore the impact of a nicely tuned JVM on which your EJB server is running. Each application server comes with a different JVM and hence, different tuning parameters. However, some of the settings remain common across most of the JVMs. In our experience, 95 percent of the JVM tuning exercise involves tuning the garbage collector. The garbage collector is a piece of code within the JVM that releases the memory claimed by objects whose references have gone out of scope or for objects whose references are explicitly set to null. Understand that you have no control over when the garbage collector runs—it will run when the JVM thinks it should and when your underlying OS schedules the GC thread to run. There are two things you should do to work well with the JVM: make your code JVM friendly, and use JVM proprietary switches to further tune the garbage collector and set the heap space related settings. Let us examine both of these:

- **Write JVM friendly code.** This entails writing Java code that releases objects in a timely manner by setting their references to null. By setting the references to null, you are declaring to the JVM that you no longer need the object and so the garbage collector should reclaim its memory allocated in the JVM heap space. Also, you should refrain from implementing *final()* methods on your Java objects, because finalizers might not be called before the object reference goes out of scope and hence, the object might never get garbage collected (because the finalizer hasn't been executed).

  Also, do not use *System.gc()* if you can avoid it, because it does not guarantee that the garbage collector would be executed upon your request. If you understand the semantics of *System.gc()* you know that it is basically meant to *request* the JVM to run the garbage collector and thereby reclaim the memory; at the end of the call, however, your request may or may not have been granted; it all depends on whether JVM thinks that it is time to run the garbage collector. We are amazed to see developers with many years of Java experience putting *System.gc()* calls all over in their code.

  Yet another example of writing JVM-friendly code is the use of weak references when writing implementations for caching or similar functionality. Weak references allow your code to maintain references to an object in a way that does not prevent the object from being garbage collected if need be. You can also receive notifications when an object to which you hold a weak reference is about to be garbage collected. Thus, if the JVM is running very low on memory, your weak reference to the live object will not stop the JVM from garbage collecting the object.

  These are just a few examples of writing JVM friendly code. If you read some of the classic Java performance books, you can find many more techniques.

- **Tune the JVM via switches.** Each JVM implementation, and there are about a dozen of them, provides vendor-specific switches to further tune the virtual machine. To effectively use these switches though, you will need to understand the implementation of the JVM. For example, all recent Sun JVMs support a technology, called HotSpot, which employs a concept termed *generational garbage collection* to effectively garbage collect the memory without introducing huge garbage collector caused pauses in the application. Ultimately the goal of garbage collection is to reduce those inevitable system pauses during the period when the garbage collector is running. So in order to efficiently work with a Sun JVM, you should understand how generational garbage collection works, various algorithms for garbage collection supported by the Sun JVM, when to use which algorithm for garbage collection, and so on. The same holds true for most of the other JVMs. For example, BEA WebLogic products use the BEA JRockit JVM. Thus, if you are a BEA shop, you should understand how JRockit works in order to be able to tune it properly.

Most of the JVM implementations also allow setting the heap memory size available to the virtual machine. The heap requirements for server applications obviously would be more than that of client applications. You should tune the heap size so that it is not too small or too large for your application. A small JVM heap would cause the JVM to run garbage collection more frequently thereby introducing unexpected pauses, albeit short, in your application. On the other hand, a large JVM heap will not cause frequent garbage collection but whenever garbage collection happens it takes a good while for it to scour through the large heap space and reclaim the memory, thereby introducing a longer pause.

Bottom line—thou must know thy JVM!

Miscellaneous Tuning Tips

Now let us see some other miscellaneous tips to further help your optimization exercises:

- **Send output** to a good logging/tracing system, such as a logging message-driven bean. This enables you to understand the methods that are causing bottlenecks, such as repeated loads or stores.
- **Use a performance-profiling tool**, OptimizeIt or JProb, to identify bottlenecks. If your program is hanging on the JDBC driver, chances are the database is your bottleneck.
- **Tune the JDBC connection pool** using various options provided by your EJB server. Some servers provide options to specify initial pool size, maximum pool size, pool resize quantity, maximum wait time the caller will have to wait before getting a connection timeout, idle timeout period, transaction isolation level, and so on. A larger connection pool will provide more connections to fulfill requests although it would consume more resources on the EJB server and also on the database server. On the other hand, a smaller connection pool will provide a fewer number of connections to fulfill requests, but it also consumes fewer resources on database and EJB servers. Also some EJB servers can enable you to specify a connection validation option, which, if set to true, essentially checks whether the connection instance is a valid

instance, at the time of the request. Remember that setting this option to true will add some latency during the *getConnection()* method.

- **Avoid putting unnecessary** directories in the CLASSPATH. This will improve the class loading time.
- **Utilize the RMI-IIOP** protocol specific tuning settings. Also, many servers provide a means to tune the thread pool of server. You can use these settings to have better control on the overall number of threads in your EJB server.

DON'T FORGET TO TUNE THE WEB SERVER

Most of the time, EJBs sits behind Web applications. Hence, it is important to tune the Web applications accessing your EJB application since an under-performing Web application can lead to bad user experience as well. Although Web application tuning entails a lot more details, following are some of the common and useful tips that you should use to boost performance:

- **Explicitly turn HTTP session support off for stateless Web applications. Session management does add to overhead and so you should turn it off when not using it. Use the JSP directive *<%page session="false"%>* to turn session off. Also don't store very large objects in HTTP session. Also release sessions when you are done using them by calling *HTTPSession.invalidate()*.**
- **Set optimal values for various HTTP keep-alive settings. The HTTP 1.1 protocol refers to the keep-alive connections as persistent connections. Keep-alive connections are essentially long-lived connections that allow multiple requests to be sent over the same TCP connection. In some cases, enabling keep-alive connections has produced a good reduction in latency.**
- **Turn off JSP recompilation, especially if your JSPs are not changing frequently.**
- **Use JSP and servlet caching techniques made available by your Web server. Also cache servlet instance independent resources in *Servlet.init()* method for efficient utilization of resources.**
- **Don't use the single thread model for servlets, because they have been deprecated. This means that all servlets are designed to be multi-threaded. Hence, you should carefully avoid using class-level shared variables. If you do have to, synchronize the access to these class-level object references for ascertaining integrity.**

Choosing the Right EJB Server

Finally, you need to choose an EJB server that offers the best performance numbers and optimization techniques. The following list details the criteria through which you should evaluate the performance and tuning support provided by your EJB server:

- **CMP Support.** Make sure CMP optimizations, such as lazy loading, entity fail-over recovery, various pooling and caching strategies, and so on, are supported by your EJB server. This is relevant, of course, when you are planning to use CMP.
- **Load balancing and clustering.** Most of the EJB servers provide clustering support for session beans and entity beans, whereas only some servers provide clustering and stateful recovery for stateful beans and entity beans. Also, not every application server provides load balancing, especially for message-driven beans. This could be an important consideration for high-throughput message consumption as well as fail-over support for message-driven beans.
- **Throttling of resources.** Throttling capabilities can help a great deal during capacity planning. Most of the high-traffic deployments do throttle resources. If you are one of such deployments, check with the vendors about whether their product provides throttling support. The more types of resources you throttle, the better tuning you will have.
- **Various types of tuning facilities.** Tuning options for various types of beans are not the only thing you should seek. You should make sure that your vendor provides comprehensive tuning options for your Web server (if you are using a Web server from the same vendor), thread management, CPUs, resources such as connection pools, JMS connections, topics/queues, IIOP tuning, JVM tuning, and so on.
- **Good SPECjAppServer numbers.** There is a bit of history behind SPECjAppServer benchmarks; for example, they are based on the ECPerf benchmark standard created by the Java community. SPECjAppServer benchmark is from the reputed Standard Performance Evaluation Corporation (SPEC) performance benchmarking organization. SPECjAppServer benchmark is for measuring performance of J2EE application servers. It is a great tool for gauging the performance of your EJB product. You should always insist to see SPECjAppServer numbers for the version of EJB server that you are buying. They will give you a very good idea about the price/performance of the EJB server in question. Refer to specbench.org/jAppServer/ for further information on these benchmark numbers.

Summary

In this chapter, we reviewed a series of performance optimizations and best practices when working on an EJB project. We hope that you refer back to these strategies while working with EJB—after all, an ounce of prevention is worth a pound of cure.

CHAPTER 19

Clustering

In this chapter, we'll talk about *clustering* technology, which addresses many of the challenges faced by large, high-capacity systems. This chapter also explores many issues relating to EJB and large systems and provides you with a broad understanding of the issues as well as solutions.

Specifically, we'll cover the following topics:

- Approaches and characteristics of large-scale systems with J2EE application servers
- Approaches to instrumenting clustered EJBs
- Issues related to designing clustered EJB systems
- Issues that impact EJB performance in a clustered system.

Clustering can be a very involved technology, encompassing network components such as load balancers and traffic redirectors at different layers in the protocol stack. The technologies that we will look at here are the ones that EJB developers may have to be aware of, that is, application-level techniques.

Overview of Large-Scale Systems

The number of systems being developed is rapidly increasing year after year. Some of these systems are small, targeted at a specific, well-defined user group that is understood when development of the system begins. Other systems are large, targeted at a diverse, massive user group that evolves over time. Given the variety of systems that can be designed, what makes a system large scale? And, more importantly, how can EJB technology operate in a large-scale system?

This section discusses some of the principles behind large systems and defines terminology that will be used throughout the chapter. This section also provides some background and history of theories applicable to large-scale systems in the past.

What Is a Large-Scale System?

Unfortunately, there is no complete computer science definition of a large-scale system. Since requirements for systems vary wildly, what may be considered large for one project is insignificant for another project.

For the purposes of this book, we will define a large-scale system as one that requires the use of more than one application server that typically operates in a *cluster*. A cluster is a loosely coupled group of servers that provide unified services to their clients. Clients that use services deployed into a cluster are typically unaware that their requests are being serviced by a cluster and typically have no control over deciding which servers in the cluster process their requests. Servers in a cluster may operate on one or more computers, each of which may have one or more processors. Additional, typical features of large-scale systems that are not considered here include the use of multiple databases, firewalls, or Web servers.

Many organizations fail to estimate the load that their systems will require and so design their system with only small-scale characteristics in mind. While current project schedules may not leave room for planning far into the future, we recommend that you always assume that you will need a large-scale system eventually. With this in mind, you should anticipate ways of scaling up the system and always have a path to follow if your user load increases, due to future business forces that may be out of your control.

Essential requirements on large-scale systems are often summarized by the following three properties (collectively called RAS):

- **Reliability** gauges whether the system performs at a constant level, even if the stresses on that system change. While this may sound a lot like scalability at first, reliability is *not* the same as performance or scalability. The most important word of this definition is *constant*. For example, if the simplest request takes 10 ms to complete with one user, the system is reliable if the same request takes 10 ms with 1,000,000 concurrent users. The measure of reliability can take many different forms:

It can be as broad as supporting a certain number of registered users, or as specific as requiring the round-trip time for a single method invocation to be within a discrete range. For every component added to a system, the number of scenarios that can cause a disruption in reliable service increases and thus makes reliability of the overall system harder to ensure. Depending on the type of architecture employed, a cluster may improve reliability; for example clustering might scale up better to increasing demands, or reduce reliability through adding extra complexity that may turn out to make behavior less consistent.

- **Availability** measures the percentage of time that your system is available for use by its clients. A measurement of availability is not related to the effectiveness of servicing those requests; rather, it focuses on whether the services are accessible. A system may be unavailable for a variety of reasons, such as network blockage, network latency, maintenance downtimes, or total system failure. The principle of availability states that if the probability of a single application server being unavailable is $1/m$, the probability an application server will be available is $1-1/m$. If there are n application servers in a cluster, the probability of the system being available is $(1-1/m)^n$. The value of $(1-1/m)^n$ decreases as n increases, implying that a cluster will always be more available than a single server. A popular way of phrasing how available a system is to its clients is to count the number of nines: A system has an availability of *five nines* if it is available 99.999 percent of the time, whereas four nines means 99.99 percent of the time. With four nines, a system is unavailable no more than 52 minutes throughout the year. This time is reduced to just 5 minutes with five nines. (How often can you restart an application server in this time?)
- **Serviceability** measures how manageable your system is. System management occurs at a variety of levels, including runtime monitoring, configuration, maintenance, upgrades, and so on. The principle of serviceability states that two application servers are more complex to service than a single application server. This implies that a cluster is inherently more difficult to service than a non-clustered system.

The reason we talk about clustering so prominently here is that clustering addresses two of these issues at the same time: availability and load balancing, which addresses the scalability-related part of reliability. The underlying principle is that of *redundancy*. If you have many redundant copies of a resource you can spread the load between them. At the same time, redundant resources enable you to lose one or more and still be able to operate. Clustering is the prime technology to provide redundancy.

An important takeaway point of the preceding discussion is that *increasing the reliability of a system impacts its availability and serviceability. A similar argument can be made for attempting to improve the availability or serviceability of a system.* It is important to appreciate that there is no such thing as a perfect system. Any system that has a high level of availability will likely not have a high level of reliability and serviceability. You just need to be aware of the trade-offs.

Basic Terminology

When working on large-scale projects, engineers and developers tend to use a variety of terms freely in relation to clusters and large-scale system without always using those terms precisely. Here are definitions for terms used in this chapter:

- **A cluster** is a loosely coupled group of servers that provide a unified, simple view of the services that they offer individually. Servers in a cluster may or may not communicate with one another. Generally, the overall goal of employing a cluster is to increase the availability or reliability of the system.
- **A node** is a single server in the cluster.
- **Load balancing** distributes the requests among cluster nodes to optimize the performance of the whole system. A load-balancing algorithm can be systematic or random.
- **A highly available system** can process requests even in the face of failing nodes.
- **Fail-over** lets another node in the cluster continue processing when the original node cannot process the request due to failures. Failing over to another node can be coded explicitly. Alternatively, it can be performed automatically by the underlying platform, which transparently reroutes communication to another server.
- **Request-level fail-over** occurs when a request that is directed to one node for servicing cannot be serviced and is subsequently redirected to another node. This may not be sufficient if session state is shared between clients and servers. In this case, the session state must also be reconstructed at the server node.
- **Single access point simplicity** is the idea that clients generate requests to the cluster rather than individual nodes of the cluster. The requests are transparently directed to a node in the cluster that can handle the request. The client's view of the cluster is a single, simple system, not a group of collaborating servers.

- **Transactions per second (TPS)** measures the number of transactions executed by a system in a second. A single request can cause zero, one, or more transactions to occur. TPS is a measure of how well the system's transaction management performs and is commonly used to compare the performance of different systems or algorithms.
- **Requests per second (RPS)** measures how many requests can be processed and responded to in a second. In a typical system, a number of threads are responsible for processing messages arriving into the system and placing those messages into a *processing queue*. A separate pool of threads is responsible for taking messages off the processing queue and actually executing the appropriate service. RPS is a measure of how many messages can be serviced off of the *processing queue* in a second.
- **Arrivals per second (APS)** measures how many incoming messages from clients can be taken from a connection and placed onto a processing queue in a second.
- **Throughput** measures how many requests can be fully serviced in a given time period. This measure includes the processing of arrivals and the handling of requests. If the throughput of a system is high, the system is capable of processing many requests in a given amount of time. Throughout can be measured in the number of requests for an application server, but is sometimes also given as a data rate, for example in MByte per second.
- **Invocations per second (IPS)** measures how many component invocations can be made in a second. IPS usually applies to the number of EJB invocations that can be made in a second.

Partitioning Your Clusters

Now that we've gotten the definitions out of the way, let's look at the different choices you have for clustering a J2EE system.

Modern J2EE servers contain a Web server and an application server. This means that in a Web-based system, the following configurations are possible:

- **A collocated architecture** runs the Web server components (servlets and JSP files) and application server components (EJBs) on the same machine.
- **A distributed architecture** separates the Web server components and application server components onto different physical machines.

The differences between the two architectures are shown in Figure 19.1.

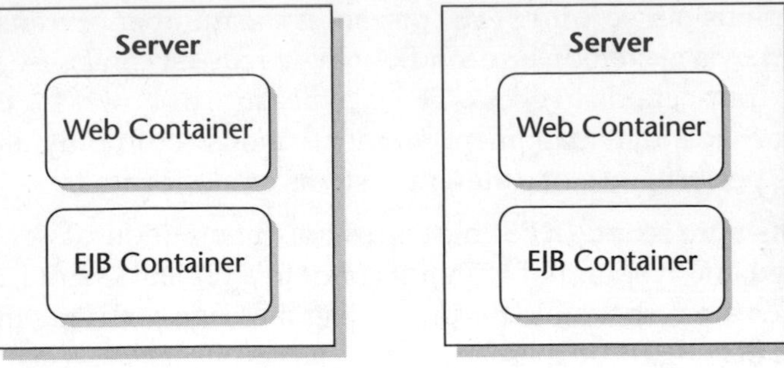

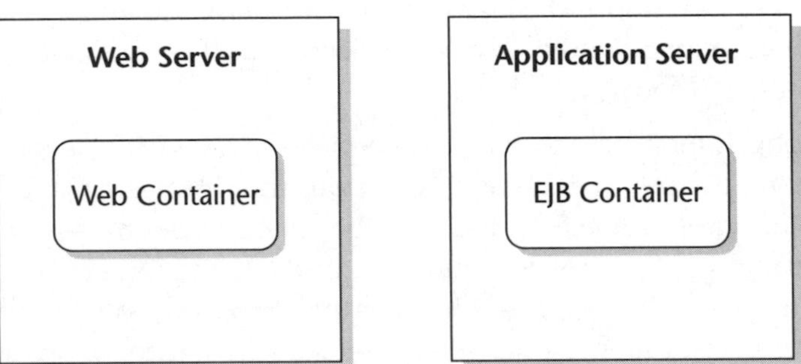

Figure 19.1 Collocated versus distributed server architecture.

The collocated versus distributed server debate is important as the chosen architecture has many ramifications. A distributed architecture is invariably more complex to set up and maintain because distribution introduces new classes of problems such as increased latency and additional failure modes. It can also give more flexibility in certain areas, such as scalability and security, as we discuss below. Whether this flexibility is worth the added complexity must be carefully evaluated. A collocated architecture is sufficient and simpler to operate in many situations—and hence recommended whenever applicable.

The pros and cons of collocated versus distributed servers are listed in Table 19.1.

Table 19.1 Collocated Versus Distributed Server Architecture

FEATURE	COLLOCATED	DISTRIBUTED	WINNER?
Reliability	High, because there is no remote inter-process communication. Everything is in a single process, so there are few factors that can cause unpredictable behavior.	Low, because there are more machines involved with a single request. Hence, there are more factors that can cause unpredictable behavior, such as network connections	Collocated
Availability	High, because any machine can fail-over to any other machine. When the whole cluster fails, the entire site is down.	Higher than no cluster at all, but lower than in the collocated setting, because there are typically fewer machines that can provide for fail-over in a given tier (assuming we have the same absolute number of machines as in the collocated case). Because we actually have a cluster for each tier, failure of a complete cluster for one tier may still leave the other tier intact.	Collocated
Serviceability	High, because each box is identical (simpler), and there is no network connection between the Web servers to bother with.	Low, because the Web server cluster must be maintained differently than the application server cluster. There is also a network connection between the tiers.	Collocated
Network efficiency	The Web server components can call EJB local interfaces. Local communication means no sockets to traverse between the Web servers and application servers.	The Web server components must call the EJB remote interfaces, which means more marshaling overhead. Remote inter-process communication between Web servers and application servers slows things down significantly.	Collocated

(continued)

Table 19.1 *(continued)*

FEATURE	COLLOCATED	DISTRIBUTED	WINNER?
Efficient use of hardware	High, because a J2EE server can be used for whatever purposes it is needed at a given point in time (Web server tasks or application server tasks).	Low, because you need to predetermine how many machines to devote to Web server tasks, and how many machines to devote to application server tasks. This may not be exactly optimal, and your load characteristics may change over time.	Collocated
Security	You cannot place a firewall between your Web server and application server because they are in-process. Therefore, your EJB components are more exposed than in the distributed case.	You can place a firewall between the Web servers and application servers to further restrict accesses from Web components to EJBs.	Distributed
Serving quick static data, or simple Web requests that do not involve EJB components	If the application servers are overloaded, static data (such as HTML and images) are served up slowly because the Web servers are competing for hardware resources with the application servers.	If the application servers are overloaded, static data (such as HTML and images) can be served up quickly because the Web servers are dedicated.	Distributed
Conflicts over ownership and management responsibility	High because the Web team and EJB team use the same boxes, which could mean conflicts if you're in a political environment.	Low, because the Web team and EJB team use different boxes. They don't interfere with each other as much.	Distributed
Load balancing	You need to set up a separate load-balancing box in front of the J2EE *servers*. Examples include a software load-balancer running on a cheap Linux box, or a hardware load-balancer such as a local director.	You need to set up a separate load-balancing box in front of the *Web servers*. Examples include a software load-balancer running on a cheap Linux box, or a hardware load-balancer such as a local director.	Equal

To determine which architecture is most appropriate you have to consider a large number of factors. We generally favor the collocated approach because it is simpler. However, the arguments for a distributed server architecture tend to become more important the larger your system is.

- **Static data.** Static data can be served faster in a distributed architecture, but this is not an issue for companies that actually run a separate Web server box just for static data. That static Web page server could also make use of a Storage Area Network (SAN), a network of hard drives to increase throughput.
- **Scalability.** The separation between Web and EJB servers enables you to fine-tune each set of servers separately and more precisely to the actual requirements of the applications. For example, you may have applications that use servlets and JSP files only sparingly, but create significant load on EJB servers so that adding to the number of EJB servers more directly enhances the overall performance. This argument tends to be less important in smaller systems where the differences among the interaction patterns between clients and Web components and EJBs may not be significant.
- **Security.** The fact that you can have a firewall in distributed server systems (between the Web servers and application servers) is important. It may seem difficult to create a malicious RMI-IIOP request that targets exposed EJBs, but it really is not difficult for anyone who really tries. Hence, your beans, especially entity beans that represent persistent data, should never be directly reachable without first passing through security controls. A firewall is a necessary first line of defense at the perimeter, but it is not sufficient. (See Chapter 13 for details on additional security controls.) Moreover, a separation of the Web and EJB servers reduces the chance that an attacker can exploit weaknesses, such as buffer overflows, in server implementations and thereby gain control of the entire server machine. Such vulnerabilities are frequently found in Web Server implementations. The captured server would then be used to stage additional attacks, for example on your databases, because internal firewalls allow traffic from the server. Again, these considerations become more important the larger your system is, as the business value of your assets tends to increase as well.

Remember that we recommended you always keep the option of scaling your systems up, so when choosing the collocated approach, you should be prepared to switch to a distributed architecture later when it becomes necessary.

Instrumenting Clustered EJBs

Although the actual technology that your J2EE server uses is proprietary, most application servers have similar approaches to clustering. Let's look at the possible options that application server vendors have for clustering EJBs of all types. We'll then look at the specifics of clustering stateless session, stateful session, entity, and message-driven beans.

How EJBs Can Be Clustered

There are many places in the system where vendors can provide *clustering logic* (such as load balancing or fail-over logic):

- **JNDI.** A vendor could perform load balancing logic in the JNDI contexts that are used to locate home objects. The JNDI context could have several equivalent home objects for a given name and spread traffic across numerous machines. Some vendors let you deploy an application to all machines in the cluster at the same time.
- **Container.** A vendor could provide clustering logic directly within the container. The containers would communicate with one another behind the scenes using an interserver communication protocol. This protocol could be used to exchange state or perform other clustering operations. For example, if a ShoppingCart stateful session bean container has filled up its cache and is constantly activating and passivating EJBs to and from secondary storage, it might be advantageous for the container to send all *create()* invocations to another container in a different server that hasn't reached its cache limit. When the container's burden has been reduced, it can continue servicing new requests.
- **Home stub.** This is the first object accessed by remote clients and runs locally on a client's virtual machine. Since stub code is generated by a vendor tool, the underlying logic in a stub can be vendor-specific so that the stub knows about multiple equivalent copies of the home. Vendors can instrument method-level load balancing and fail-over schemes directly in a smart stub. Every *create()*, *find()*, and home method invocation can have its request load balanced to a different server in the cluster; it doesn't matter which machine handles each request.
- **Remote stub.** This object is the client's proxy representing a specific enterprise bean instance. It can perform the same types of load balancing and fail-over as a home stub can, but vendors have to be careful about when they choose to do so. Remote stubs must load balance and fail-over requests to instances that can properly handle the request *without disrupting the system.*

The most common scenario is for stubs to be generated at development time through a utility, such as a vendor-specific EJB compiler. This isn't the only option, however. Some application servers can use interception technology, such as the JDK 1.3 Proxy class, to automatically generate remote home and remote stub logic dynamically at runtime. The JBoss application server is an example of a server that has an EJB container using this approach.

Whether an application server uses interception technology or creates custom classes for the stubs and skeletons does not alter the places where cluster-based logic can be inserted. In the following discussions, we continue to reference home stubs, remote stubs, or containers irrespective of how or when these pieces are generated.

One potential drawback of vendor-specific logic on the client side is the loss of portability: When moving clients to a different vendor's products, even standalone RMI-IIOP clients need to be redeployed using the new vendor's tools. Porting applications to a different server creates significant amount of work on the server side, however, so this issue is a comparatively minor one.

The different options that are available to developers and vendors provide a vast array of configurations with which clusterable EJB may be instrumented. By now, you must be thinking, "How do I know what to use, when, and where?" The answer lies within the capabilities of any single application server. The rest of this chapter discusses the various issues that application-server vendors face when attempting to provide a clusterable infrastructure for stateless session, stateful session, entity, and message-driven EJBs.

Load balancing and fail-over logic doesn't exist for local interfaces. Remember that local interfaces do not receive traffic from the network. Parameters must be marshaled by reference rather than by value serialization. If the client is local to the bean, then any failure of either component will likely cause the other to fail, too. Nothing can be done to save such a situation. Thus, our discussion applies only to remote clients.

The Concept of Idempotence

An *idempotent* (pronounced *i-dim-po-tent*, not *i-dimp-uh-tent*) method is one that can be called repeatedly with the *same* arguments and achieve the *same* results.

An idempotent method in a distributed system doesn't impact the state of the system. It can be called repeatedly without worry of altering the system so that it becomes unusable or provides errant results. Generally any methods that alter a persistent store are not idempotent since two invocations of the same method will alter the persistent store twice. For example, if a sequencer is stored in a database and *m1()* increments the sequencer, two calls to *m1()* will leave the sequencer at a different value than if *m1()* was invoked a single time. An idempotent method leaves the value in the persistent store the same no matter how many invocations of *m1()* occur.

Remote clients that witness a failure situation of a server-side service are faced with a perplexing problem: Exactly how far did the request make it before the system failed? A failed request could have occurred at one of three points:

- After the request has been initiated, but *before* the method invocation on the server has begun to execute. Fail-over of the request to another server should always occur in this scenario.
- After the method invocation on the server has begun to execute, but before the method has completed. Fail-over of the request to another server should occur only if the method is idempotent.
- After the method invocation on the server has completed, but before the response has been successfully transmitted to the remote client. Fail-over of the request to another server should occur only if the method is idempotent.

Why is this important? A remote stub that witnesses a server failure *never* knows which of the three points of execution the request was in when the failure occurred. Even though failures of requests that haven't even begun method execution should always fail-over, a client can never determine when a failed request is in this category.

Thus, remote stubs can automatically fail-over only requests that were sent to methods flagged as idempotent. In comparison, fail-over of non-idempotent methods must occur programmatically by the client that originated the request. If your EJB server vendor is a major player, it will likely give you the ability to mark an EJB component's method as idempotent or nonidempotent using proprietary container descriptors.

You might think that all methods that are marked to require a new transaction are idempotent. After all, if failure happens, the transaction will roll back, and all transactional state changes (such as transactional JDBC operations) will be undone. So why can't the stub fail-over to another bean to retry the operation?

The answer is that container-managed transactions have an inherent flaw, which we first discussed in Chapter 12. What if the transaction commits on the server, and the network crashes on the return trip to the stub? The stub would then not know whether the server's transaction succeeded and would not be able to fail-over.

Stateless Session Bean Clustering

Now, let's take a look at how we can cluster each type of EJB component. We begin with stateless session beans.

Load Balancing

All Java object instances of a stateless session bean class are considered identical. There is no way to tell them apart, since they do not hold state. Therefore all method invocations on the remote home stub and remote stub can be load balanced. Some EJB servers also give you flexibility here, and allow you to *pin* stubs so that they direct requests to a single server only. Some vendors even allow you to configure subsets of methods on a single stub to be pinned or load balanced. This flexibility in load balancing stateless session bean instances is what drives the perception that stateless session EJBs are the most scalable types of synchronous EJB components.

Fail-Over

For stateless session beans, automatic fail-over on *remote home stubs* can always occur. Recall that stateless session bean home stubs have only one method, which is an empty *create()* method. This corresponds to the bean's *ejbCreate()* method. But your container does not call *ejbCreate()* when the client calls *home.create()*—the container can call *ejbCreate()* whenever it feels like kicking beans into the pool, as we saw in Chapter 4. Therefore, your *ejbCreate()* methods should not modify your system's state and should be coded as idempotent.

Automatic fail-over on *remote stubs* can occur only if the called method is idempotent. If your method is nonidempotent, or if your vendor does not support automatic fail-over, you might be able to fail-over *manually* by writing code to retry the method. You need to be careful, however, and factor business rules and other logic into the decision as to whether a fail-over request should be made.

For example, the following pseudo-code manually fails-over any method invocation that is not automatically done so by the remote home or remote stub.

```
InitialContext ctx = null;
SomeHomeStub home = null;
SomeRemoteStub remote = null;

try {
  ctx = ...;
  home = ctx.lookup(...);

  // Loop until create() completes successfully
  boolean createSuccessful = false;
  while (createSuccessful == false) {
```

```
      try {

        remote = home.create();

      }  catch (CreateException ce) {
        // Handle create exception here.
        // If fail over should occur, call continue;
        continue;

      }  catch (RemoteException re) {
        // Handle system exception here.
        // If fail over should occur, call continue;

      }  catch (Exception e) {
        // Home stub failure condition detected.
        // If fail over should occur, call continue;
        continue;

      }

      // If processing gets here, then no failure condition detected.
      createSuccessful = true;

    }

    boolean answerIsFound = false;
    while (answerIsFound == false) {

      try {

        remote.method(...);

      }  catch (ApplicationException ae) {
        // Handle application exception here.
        // If fail over should occur, call continue.

      }  catch (RemoteException re) {
        // Handle server-side exception here.
        // If fail over should occur, call continue.

      }  catch (Exception e) {
        // Failure condition detected.
        // If fail over should occur, call continue.
        continue;

      }

      // If processing gets here, then no failure condition detected.
      answerIsFound = true;

    }  // while
  }  catch (Exception e) { }
```

If we wanted it to do so, our EJB component could also assist with this fail-over decision by checking the system state before continuing.

Stateful Session Bean Clustering

Stateful session beans are clustered a bit differently than their stateless cousins. The major EJB server vendors support *replication* of state. It works like this: When a stateful session bean is created, the state must be copied to another machine. The back-up copy isn't used unless the primary fails. The bean is routinely synchronized with its backup to ensure that both locations are current. If the container ever has a system failure and loses the primary bean instance, the remote stub of the bean fails-over invocations to another machine. That other machine can use the back-up state and continue processing. A new backup is then nominated, and the state begins to replicate to that new backup. This all occurs magically behind the scenes after you configure your EJB server to replicate state, using your EJB server's proprietary descriptors or administrative console.

Stateful replication should be used with caution. It will limit your performance. Instead, you may want to consider placing critical, transactional, and persistent data in a database via session beans plus JDBC or entity beans. Stateful session beans should be used for session-oriented (conversational) data that would not adversely impact the system if the data were lost.

Replication of stateful data typically occurs at one of two points:

- **At the end of every method.** This is not ideal since unnecessary replication of unmodified data can frequently occur.
- **After the commit of a transaction.** For reasons touched upon in Chapter 12, this is ideal. Transactions give you an all-or-nothing fail-over paradigm. By replicating on transactional boundaries, your stateful session bean state is consistent in time with other changes to your system state (such as performing JDBC work).

Most EJB servers perform stateful fail-over in one of two ways:

- **In-memory replication.** The state could be replicated in-memory across the cluster. In-memory replication is fast. The downside is that most EJB servers limit the replication to only two machines, since memory then becomes a scarce resource.
- **Persistent storage to a shared hard drive or database.** This approach is slower than in-memory replication, but every server in the cluster has access to the persistent state of the replicated bean.

Load Balancing

With stateful session beans, *remote home stubs* can freely load balance *create()* requests to different servers in the cluster. These factory methods do not apply to an individual instance in a container but can be serviced by any container in the cluster.

However, *remote stubs* cannot load balance as easily. Your client requests can be sent only to the server that has your state. Note that if your stateful session bean is *replicated* across multiple servers, a remote stub could conceivably load balance different requests to different servers. This wouldn't be ideal, however, since most vendors have a designated *primary* object that requests are sent to first. The effort involved with load balancing requests in this scenario outweighs any benefits.

Fail-Over

You might think that fail-over can always occur with stateful session beans if the state is replicated across a cluster. After all, if something goes wrong, we can always fail-over to the replica.

However, this is *not* the case. If your bean is in the *middle of a method call,* we still need to worry about idempotency. Your bean might be modifying the state elsewhere, such as calling a database using JDBC or a legacy system using the J2EE Connector Architecture. Your stub can fail-over to a backup only if the method is idempotent. The only time your EJB server can disregard idempotency is if your container crashed when nobody was calling it, either between method calls or between transactions, depending on how often you replicate.

For stateful session beans, automatic fail-over on a *remote stub* or *remote home stub* can occur only if your methods are idempotent. Most methods are not idempotent, such as a *create()* method, which performs JDBC work, or a *set()* method. However, stateful session beans *can* have some idempotent methods! Any method that does not alter the state of the system or alters the value of the state stored in the stateful session EJB is an idempotent method. For example, if a stateful session EJB has a series of *get()* accessor methods to retrieve the values of state stored in the server, these *get()* accessor methods would be idempotent.

If your method is not idempotent, or if your container does not support replication, you can manually fail-over, similar to our approach to stateless session beans.

Entity Bean Clustering

Now that we've seen session beans, let's see how entity beans are clustered.

Load Balancing

If you're coding your EJB deployments correctly, you will wrap entity beans with a session bean façade. Therefore, most access to entity EJBs should occur over local interfaces by in-process session beans, rather than remote clients. Thus, the need for load balancing goes away. Note that most containers do support load-balancing for entity beans through stubs, which is similar to the way it works for session beans. But you'll probably never take advantage of it.

Some container vendors provide a means for declaring a BMP entity bean as read-only in the vendor-specific deployment descriptor. If the container finds a read-only entity bean, it can load balance each and every call as no updates to a persistent state will ever occur. This is a proprietary feature, however.

Fail-Over

Since you should always access entity beans using local interfaces, fail-over makes little sense. Consider this: If you called an entity bean using a local interface and that failed-over to another machine, you'd suddenly be using its remote interface, changing the client API and entailing pass-by-value rather than pass-by-reference.

If you are accessing entity beans remotely, then as with all other bean types, you can automatically fail-over entity beans only if the methods are idempotent. This usually means *get()*, *finder()*, and possibly some *ejbHome()* business methods.

Entity beans don't have the same replication needs as stateful session beans. This is because entity beans are routinely synchronized with a database via its store and load operations. Thus, an entity bean *is* backed up on a regular basis by design. From this perspective, you can think of an entity bean as a stateful session bean that is always replicated by the container on transactional boundaries through store and load operations. Those automatic load and store operations are the most important differences between stateful session beans and entity beans.

Since entity beans are backed up on transactional boundaries, transparent fail-over can only occur in-between transactions (and not between methods that are part of a larger transaction). If you have a transaction committing on every method call (for example, through the *Requires New* transaction attribute), fail-over can occur at the method granularity. However, this is not a recommended approach, since your session beans should initiate the transaction and serve as a transactional façade.

Caching

Because entity beans are basically Java objects that represent database data, they are in themselves a middle tier cache for that database. It is a tricky and technically complicated task for an application server to support this cache well. It is also a common misperception that caching always improves the performance of a system. Caching makes a system perform better only when the average overhead associated with updating the cache is less than the overhead that would be needed to access individual instances repeatedly between cache updates. Since the amount of synchronization needed to manage a cache in a cluster is high, a cache generally needs to be accessed three or four times between updates for the benefits of having the cache to outweigh not having it.

Containers provide many different types of caching algorithms. Each of these algorithms has the same principle behind it: to reduce the frequency of *ejbLoad()* and *ejbStore()* methods, which are normally called on transactional boundaries.

You set up these caches using proprietary container tools or descriptors. No Java coding should be required.

Read-Only Caches

A *read-only cache* contains a bunch of read-only entity beans. This is a very useful cache because most enterprise data *is* read-only. This type of caching has enormous benefits.

Since read-only entity beans never change, their *ejbStore()* methods are never called, and they are never called with a transactional context. If your entity bean methods are participating in a read-only cache, they need to have *Never* or *Not Supported* as their transactional attribute.

Read-only caches implement an *invalidation strategy* that determines when the data in the read-only instance is no longer valid and should be reloaded from the persistent store. Common algorithms include:

- **Timeout.** Every *X* seconds, the cache is invalidated and the read-only entity bean is reloaded immediately or upon the next method invocation. You set the time-out interval based on your tolerance for witnessing stale data.
- **Programmatic.** Your vendor provides a home stub or remote stub with *invalidate()* or similar methods that allow a client to programmatically invalidate entity beans.
- **System-wide notification.** When someone changes entity beans in a read/write cache, the container invalidates those entity beans that also reside in a read-only cache elsewhere.

It doesn't take long for you to perform operations on a read-only entity bean. The lock on the entity bean needs to be held just long enough to perform the method call that gets you the data you need. Thus, each server's read-only cache typically keeps a single entity bean instance in memory for each primary key. This saves overhead involved with creating multiple instances and managing the concurrent access.

Distributed Shared Object Caches

A *distributed shared-object cache* is an advanced EJB server feature that few vendors provide today. It is a cluster-wide cache for read/write data. This immediately introduces an obvious problem: *cache consistency*. How does the container stay in sync with the database? What if someone updates the database behind your back? You'll need to refresh your cache.

A distributed shared object cache could theoretically detect collisions at the database level. This might be detected through database triggers, although this gets very hairy. The idea is that when someone updates the database behind your back, a trigger is fired. The cache is notified by this trigger and updates its contents so that read-only clients can access the latest data. Because each of the servers receives the notification, updating of the data can occur concurrently across the cluster.

A distributed shared object cache also needs to stay in sync with other caches in the cluster. It needs to replicate itself to other nodes on regular intervals, similar to the concept of stateful session bean replication. It also needs to implement a distributed *lock manager* that locks objects in memory, similar to how a database locks database rows. Additionally, if a nonreliable messaging infrastructure, such as IP multicast, is used to send notification messages between servers, a system runs the risk of having two caches trying to lock the same data concurrently; their notification messages might cross in mid-air! An algorithm that allows the pausing of other systems during the period where critical events and notification messages are generated needs to be implemented. As you can see, this convergence of state across multiple nodes is very difficult to implement.

Because of these issues, we do not recommend using a distributed shared object cache for most systems. However, if you'd like to give it a shot, we recommend strongly testing your system for a variety of failure conditions before going live.

Read-Mostly Caches

Some application servers provide an exciting *read-mostly* algorithm. This powerful idea allows you to have read-only entity beans that are also updated every now and then, without having the burden of a true distributed shared object cache. The idea is that for any given entity bean class, some instances will be read-only, and some will not be cached at all (read/write).

- **When you perform a read operation,** you use a cached, read-only entity bean for performance.
- **When you perform a write operation,** you use a regular, noncached entity bean. When you modify a regular entity bean and a transaction completes, all of the read-only entity bean caches become invalidated. When the read-only entity beans are next used, they need to reload from the database.

This *read-mostly* pattern has some interesting characteristics:

- **Each cache uses a different JNDI name.** For example, a read-only cache might have RO appended to the JNDI name, while a read/write cache might have RW appended to the JNDI name. This is somewhat annoying.
- **This pattern requires only the use of a read-only cache,** which almost all application servers have. You don't need to deal with the complexity of a true distributed shared object cache.

When using a read-mostly algorithm, be sure that your container uses a reliable communications protocol when invalidating the read-only cache. If a message is accidentally lost, you could be working with stale data.

Message-Driven Bean Clustering

Message-driven beans behave differently than session and entity beans do and thus have different implications in a cluster. Since message-driven beans do not have home or remote interfaces, they don't have any remote stubs or skeletons that can perform load balancing and fail-over logic on their behalf.

Message-driven beans are consumers of messages; they behave in a pull scenario grasping for messages to consume, rather than a push scenario in which a remote client sends invocations directly to the consumer. See Chapter 9 for a full discussion of this behavior.

Message-driven bean clustering is really about JMS clustering. A message-driven bean is dependent upon the clusterable features of the JMS server and destinations that it binds itself to. Message-driven beans achieve load balancing by having multiple EJB servers of the same type bound to a single JMS queue for message consumption. If four messages arrive concurrently at the queue and four containers of the same message-driven bean type are bound to the destination, each container is delivered one of the messages for consumption. Each container consumes its message concurrently, achieving a pseudo-load-balancing effect.

Fail-over of message-driven beans is integrated into the very nature of the beans themselves. Fail-over occurs any time a message that is being processed is acknowledged as *unsuccessful* to the JMS server. An unacknowledged message is placed back on the destination for reconsumption. The message-driven bean that consumes the message a second (or third, fourth, and so on) time need not be the one that consumed it the first time.

In some advanced JMS server implementations, JMS destination replication allows nonpersistent messages to be replicated across servers in a cluster. Message-driven beans that bind to a replicated destination detect any server failures and automatically rebind themselves as a consumer to the server hosting the replicated destination.

Other EJB Clustering Issues

This final section discusses some miscellaneous issues about J2EE clustering that can impact the behavior of a system.

First Contact

When a client wants to use an EJB component, whether it is a session, entity, or message-driven bean, the client must always first connect to the JNDI tree:

- Clients that want to use a session or entity bean look up their home stub.
- Clients that want to send a JMS message to be consumed by a message-driven bean must look up a JMS *ConnectionFactory* and *Destination* object.

Since all EJB clients use JNDI, naming server clustering ultimately has an impact on the behavior of EJB components in a cluster, too. What kind of clustering enhancements can be made to naming servers, and how does this impact EJBs? There are two types of clustered naming servers:

- **Centralized.** The naming server is hosted on a single server. All EJB servers register their same EJB components on the single naming server, and all clients look up EJB components on the single naming server. The naming server can even distribute clients to the identical servers in the cluster.
- **Shared, replicated.** Each node in a cluster hosts its own JNDI naming server that contains replicated objects hosted on other servers in the cluster. The naming servers replicate their contents—including home stubs, JDBC *DataSource* objects, JMS *ConnectionFactory* object, JMS *Destination* objects—to the other naming servers in the cluster. Thus, every naming server has a copy of every other naming server's objects in the tree. In a scenario in which the same EJB component is deployed on

every server in the cluster, each naming server has a copy of the home stub representing each server. If a server in the cluster crashes, all of the other naming servers that are still active merely have to remove from their naming server the objects hosted on the other machine.

Initial Access Logic

When an application server provides a *centralized naming server*, the logic that clients use to get access to the cluster is simple: They hard-code the DNS name or IP address of the centralized naming server into all of their *InitialContext* creation calls.

But what about J2EE vendors that support a shared, replicated naming server? Clients can connect to any server in the cluster and make a request for a service hosted anywhere else in the cluster. Architects have a variety of options available to them.

- **DNS load balancing.** This allows multiple IP addresses to be bound to a single name in a network's *Domain Name Service* (DNS). Clients that ask for an *InitialContext* pass in a DNS name in the URL of the naming server. Every translation of the DNS name results in the generation of a different IP address, which is part of a round-robin list for that name in the DNS server. Using this technique, every client *InitialContext* request is transparently directed to a different server. Networks support this feature or they do not—it is *not* dependent upon the capabilities of your application server. Generally, this is a low-level technique that can cause difficult network problems and needs to be well understood and implemented. We do not recommend it for your average network.
- **Software proxies.** Software proxies maintain open connections to a *list of servers* that are preconfigured in a descriptor file. Software proxies can maintain keep-alive TCP/IP connections with each of the servers to provide better performance instead of attempting to reconnect every request. These software proxies immediately detect any server crash or unresponsiveness because its link is immediately lost. Software proxies can also support a wider range of load balancing algorithms including round-robin, random, and weight-based algorithms.
- **Hardware proxies.** Hardware proxies have capabilities similar to software proxies but often can outperform their software counterparts. Hardware proxies can also double as firewalls and gateways.

Summary

In this chapter, we discussed the major challenges and solutions for working with EJB in a clustered system. We discussed what makes a system large and the major characteristics that large systems exhibit. We then compared the collocated and distributed approaches to clustering. We analyzed the type-specific behavior that can be exhibited by stateless session, stateful session, entity, and message-driven beans in a cluster. And finally, we discussed cluster deployments of EJB, clustered naming servers, and initial access logic to naming servers. So pat yourself on the back! You've just learned a great deal about clustering. Stay with us now and we'll learn all about how to get your EJB project started the right way.

CHAPTER

20

Starting Your EJB Project on the Right Foot

To be successful with an EJB/J2EE project, you must plan and understand a great deal beyond the technologies themselves. You must overcome a wealth of project management challenges, including designing the object model, dividing up your team, and educating your team.

This chapter is a guide for how to get started on your EJB project; it has links to external resources that you should consider in your project. They are taken from real-world experiences and intended to help you build enterprise Java systems. As you read the chapter, you may find project management issues that you have not considered. If this happens, consider weaving these issues into your project plan, or highlight the issues for future reference when you begin an enterprise Java project. While we may not answer every question for each issue, we will point you towards external resources to help you find your own answers.

Get the Business Requirements Down

Before embarking on a J2EE project, try to lock down as many of the business requirements as possible. Your approach might look as follows:

1. Build a complete list of requested features. This is the phase in which you ask questions about user interface requirements, legacy integration

requirements, use-case analysis, and so on. If your feature list is incomplete, you should consult with any subject matter experts you can access.

2. Weigh each feature based on corporate and business goals, as well as the time anticipated for its implementation. Prioritize the list by feature weight.
3. Gain stakeholder support for the feature list to avoid future bickering.
4. Secure a committed project budget from stakeholders.

You should now have a fairly complete basis for designing an object model.

Decide Whether J2EE Is the Right Choice

Once you have the business requirements, you need to settle on a platform for development and deployment. This is a big decision and depending on the size and scope of the project, mostly this decision is made at CIO/CTO level. Making a wrong choice here can very easily lead to project failures. Platform selection depends on many factors—scalability requirements, available system infrastructure, project timelines, project budget, and most importantly, platform technologies. For your project you should evaluate J2EE platform with the criteria. J2EE may be appropriate, but then again, it may not. Spend the time for the appropriate research on the various alternatives up front and see what best suits your requirements. But to select J2EE, or any platform for that matter, for the sake of it might not prove to be the right choice.

The software development world is clearly divided into two camps: Java and .NET. Both, the Sun Microsystems–led Java community and the Microsoft-led .NET community, have accepted this reality of bipolar world, and yet both are trying hard to outperform each other in terms of the facilities they provide to the developers. This competition can only be good for us. We believe neither J2EE nor .NET is going to serve as panacea to all the problems experienced in software development. At the end of the day, understanding a project's architectural or platform requirements is what is going to help you make the right choice between the two.

To help you with this decision, we will outline some of the areas where J2EE clearly wins and others where .NET, the most concrete alternative to the J2EE platform available today, wins. Let us first discuss the areas where J2EE has a clear lead.

- **Availability of choices.** J2EE is a set of openly developed specifications that are available free for anyone to implement on any platform. As a result, an ecosystem comprising hundreds of vendors is thriving on J2EE platform today. You can choose any of these vendors to provide you with J2EE middleware; a vendor that best matches your needs of scalability, high-availability, management or administration tools, licensing cost or lack thereof. This is one of the main reasons for the wide success of the J2EE platform in enterprise computing.

  The strength of J2EE is actually the biggest weakness of .NET platforms. The core .NET framework minus C# and Common Language Runtime/Common Language Interfaces (CLR/CLI), is not available for anyone to implement but Microsoft. Microsoft submitted C# and CLR/CLI to ECMA and later to ISO for standardization. Hence, a vendor wanting to implement C# CLR/CLI-based virtual machine on another platform can do so. However, .NET, the way we all know it and use it, is much more than just C# and CLR/CLI. It is a set of enterprise services, libraries, and object models, including ADO.NET, ASP.NET, managed components, security services, directory services, transaction services, and much more; and these are not available for infrastructure vendors to implement on other operating environments such as UNIX, Linux, and so on. So you do not have the choice to run a full-fledged .NET application on a highly available UNIX system or a "good enough" Linux system, unless you think C# is .NET in which case you can use Mono or the dotGNUs C# CLR/CLI-based virtual machines on a variety of UNIX and Linux systems.

- **Ecosystem.** Multiple vendors providing J2EE middleware has another benefit too: faster innovation. All vendors contribute their technological ideas to the Java Community Process (JCP), a sanctuary that furthers the J2EE platform through standardization. As a result, you are not dependent on a single vendor for thought leadership. Also, this ecosystem of J2EE vendors makes your investment in J2EE much safer. In case your vendor falters financially, you can always switch to another vendor's J2EE product. This switch may not be easy, but it at least is an alternative in the J2EE world.

  Ecosystem, or lack thereof, is yet another weakness of the .NET platform, where you depend on Microsoft for innovation and for the safety of your infrastructure investment. If for some reason Microsoft stops supporting a given technology (case in point, COM), you are left with only one option—migrate your applications to the new technology that it is planning to support.

- **The open source factor.** J2EE and Java in general are open source, friendly platforms. Most of the open source projects use Java as a language and platform for development and deployment. This is no small strength. Open source, as we are witnessing today, is changing the conventional software industry very rapidly. It is no longer a phenomenon involving a bunch of geeks and academics. Today, many corporations are considering open source product deployment in their IT infrastructures. Some choose open source because it is free, as in "free beer"; whereas many choose open source to increase their control over the code they are deploying. The numerous Java- and J2EE-based open source projects are a definite plus. If you ever decide to develop a full-fledged J2EE application and deploy it on an open source J2EE platform, you have not just one but multiple choices today, including JBoss and Apache Geronimo. Both of these should be J2EE 1.4–certified from Sun Microsystems. Hence, you get not just the benefits of an open source model but also J2EE compliance.

  Although, in the past year or so, we are starting to see an increasing number of open source developments for the .NET platform, the open source–led innovation in .NET still lags behind that in Java and J2EE. Some of the notable .NET-based open source projects are the Novell-led Mono, Free software dotGNU, NAnt hosted at sourceforge.net, and NHibernate, also hosted at sourceforge.net.

  Both Mono and dotGNU projects are backed by enthusiastic software developers who want to provide an alternative to the Microsoft .NET implementation in an open source way. The only shortcoming of these projects is that they are *not* really .NET. Other than the fact that Mono and dotGNU provide CLR/CLI-based C# virtual machine, there is not much similarity between them and the Microsoft implementation of .NET. As a result, companies planning to implement an enterprise application on the Microsoft .NET platform by using Mono or dotGNU, experience vast differences in terms of platform semantics and APIs. Switching from one to another would be similar to learning a whole new platform. Nonetheless, the Mono and dotGNU efforts are interesting and worth following if you are interested in the Microsoft .NET implementation alternatives.

- **Performance and scalability.** J2EE is a platform-agonistic industry standard. As a result, you find implementations of J2EE on multiple hardware and software platforms. Some of these hardware and software platforms have been quite successful in high-performance and throughput systems space. Most of the UNIX-based systems fall into this category. Hosting J2EE applications on such systems inherently makes J2EE applications highly scalable and fast. Besides this, pretty much all the leading players in high-performance space have some or the other J2EE offering. As a result, their J2EE products reflect the years of experience they have had with high-performance and high throughput systems.

The Middleware Company recently did a study comparing the performance of various J2EE application servers with Microsoft .NET. The results of this study are documented extensively and are available for free at *middlewareresearch.com/endeavors/030730J2EEDOTNET/endeavor.jsp*, for your use.

The following list details some of the areas that .NET handles better than J2EE:

- **Great tools.** Tools have always been a forte of Microsoft and will remain so for a considerable amount of time. J2EE industry does have many tools to offer; however, Microsoft surpasses these offerings, mostly. Good tools enable the faster development of applications. In our experience, typical development times for Microsoft .NET applications tend to be less than for J2EE applications of equal complexity. J2EE vendors are realizing this shortcoming and are changing it by continuously updating their tool sets. Also, open source Java-based development tools such as Eclipse and Netbeans are providing good alternatives in this space.
- **Time to market.** Ease of development coupled with support for better tools amounts to a shorter time to market for your .NET-based application or product. This is an important consideration, especially for projects with time constraints. However, you always have to balance faster development with better scalability and potentially better performance. J2EE makes simple development more complex and complex developments simpler. The converse of that is quite true for .NET, meaning, .NET makes simple development simpler and complex developments more complex.
- **Support for multiple languages.** Believe it or not, this is a plus for Microsoft .NET in certain situations. Especially when you have to port legacy code to managed environments, such as the one provided by .NET, multiple language support can come quite handy. Although this port is not very straightforward, Visual Studio .NET supports many tools and add-ons that can simplify porting, for example, legacy code to .NET.
- **Simplicity.** One of the recurring complaints we keep hearing from J2EE as well as the Java community is that J2EE is gradually turning into a behemoth. With each passing day, some new Java Specification Request (JSR) is initiated in the JCP. It is quite impossible for developers, mostly busy in day-to-day development activities, to follow up with all these actions in the J2EE and Java space. From this standpoint, the .NET platform is easier to live with. Developers mostly need to keep track of upcoming .NET products and their features, and they are all set with the latest and the greatest in the .NET world!

Table 20.1 Resources to Help You Decide If J2EE Is Appropriate

RESOURCE	DESCRIPTION
TheServerSide.com (www.TheServerSide.com)	Keeps you up-to-date with various news bulletins and articles about the J2EE space.
J2EE and .NET Application Server and Web Services Performance Comparison (middlewareresearch.com/endeavors/030730J2EEDOTNET/endeavor.jsp)	A number of studies and resulting research reports comparing performance of J2EE application servers with Microsoft .NET. The Middleware Company did these studies.
"J2EE vs. Microsoft.NET" whitepaper by Roger Sessions (www.objectwatch.com)	Whitepaper comparing J2EE and Microsoft.NET. Microsoft.NET wins.
"J2EE and .NET" article by Rima Patel Sriganesh	An article by one of the authors providing various perspectives.

As you may have realized by now, choosing between J2EE and .NET is not a simple task by any means. The safest route is to diversify your investments in both these IT infrastructures. That way you will not have to depend on either of these two camps alone. However, we do believe that both J2EE and .NET are going to coexist as viable platform choices for a foreseeable period. Table 20.1 lists external resources to further help you make a sound decision.

Staff Your Project

If your CIO decides to do project development in-house, then you will need to staff the J2EE project. With the limited resources of a typical IT organization these days, you will often not find a sufficient number of people available for the project and even if there are people available, they might not have enough experience developing with J2EE technology. Don't despair; many organizations are in the same position. You have several options:

- **Hire full-time experienced J2EE employees.** Full-time experienced employees are the most cost-effective way to staff a development team. Especially if you foresee a lot of new in-house J2EE development in the near to mid-term future, it is advisable to build the required J2EE expertise within the organization. One of the ways to build this expertise is to hire new people. However, candidates for full-time employment, particularly those with significant J2EE skills, are often difficult to find. You must have a solid recruiting process.

- **Educate existing developers on J2EE.** For organizations with existing development teams, a much easier alternative to hiring full-time J2EE experts is to educate your existing staff on Java and J2EE through training provided by firms. You can fill in holes in your staff by hiring Java developers or computer science graduates who are eager to learn J2EE.
- **Hire short-term consultants.** Consultants hired for several days or weeks can help you with specific issues such as choosing a J2EE application server; selecting tools, standards, and guidelines; resolving internal debates; providing an unbiased architectural review of your project; aiding project initiation and planning; and mentoring in a specific technology. Short-term consultants are a bit pricey but provide significant benefit to your project when used effectively for that expertise. Because of their cost, engage these experts for short-term use only. All project teams can benefit from bringing in one or more consultants at the onset of a project.
- **Hire long-term contractors.** Long-term contractors are a happy medium between full-time employees and consultants. They're paid more than employees but often significantly less than consultants. They are often easier to hire because most developers perceive contracting as high paying yet low risk, therefore more people choose this career path and typically have the experience that you require. (Today's J2EE contractor was yesterday's full-time J2EE employee somewhere else.) Using contractors is an effective way to fill out your project team when you don't have enough full-time employees with J2EE experience and don't want to pay consulting rates for a significant portion of your staff. Skills that you should demand of your contractors include expertise in the specific application server that you are using, experience on one or more projects of similar scope, and ideally, experience on one or more projects of a similar nature.

If you decide to go the training or contracting route, the authors of this book may be able to help you. See Table 20.2.

Table 20.2 J2EE-Related Service Vendors

VENDOR	SERVICE FOCUS
The Middleware Company (www.middleware-company.com)	Provides training, consultants, and contractors for Java, EJB, J2EE, and XML projects.
Ronin International (www.ronin-intl.com)	Provides consultants and contractors for object-oriented and component-based architecture and software process development.

Design Your Complete Object Model

Once your team is assembled and has a good level of J2EE understanding, you are empowered to flesh out your object model. Ideally you should minimize risk by working hand-in-hand with an external J2EE expert who has built such systems in the past.

Whenever you inject a new object into this object model, all layers should be considered. Ignoring the user interface, the business layer, or the data layer could lead to false assumptions that bite you down the line.

See Table 20.3 for suggested resources when building a J2EE object model.

Table 20.3 Resources for Building Your J2EE Object Model

RESOURCE	DESCRIPTION
TheServerSide.com (www.TheServerSide.com)	Design Patterns section is invaluable resource for building J2EE systems.
Chapters 11, 16, 18, and 22 of this book	Chapter 11 discusses various EJB design and development best practices. Chapter 16 discusses various persistence-related best practices. Chapter 18 discusses best practices relevant to performance optimizations. Chapter 22 is a sample design and development for a complete EJB/J2EE system.
"EJB Design Patterns" by Floyd Marinescu, published by John Wiley & Sons	Patterns for building EJB object models.
"Core J2EE Patterns" by John Crupi, et al. published by Addison-Wesley	Patterns for building J2EE systems (includes Web tier and EJB tier patterns).
J2EE Blueprints (http://java.sun.com/j2ee/blueprints)	Best practices guide for J2EE systems.

REUSE OF J2EE COMPONENTS

In our experience, it is a myth that J2EE components achieve high reuse across projects. Components are often copied-and-pasted, but not reused in the true O-O sense.

For large organizations building complex J2EE systems, we recommend investing in a J2EE best practices task force. This task force enforces coding standards across all projects, such that all teams speak the same vocabulary for objects in their system, and that correct design patterns are applied in projects. The benefits of this task force include easing communication between projects and enabling developers to easily transition between projects with minimal ramp-up time.

If you choose the path of reuse, we recommend using the best practice specified in Chapter 11 to achieve your goal.

Implement a Single Vertical Slice

After you have defined an initial architecture, you need to start building to that architecture. We recommend implementing an *initial vertical slice* of the system. A vertical slice is a subset of the use-cases in your system. For example, if you're putting together an e-commerce site, you might have the vertical slice be the search engine or the product catalog. A vertical slice should demonstrate usage of all the relevant J2EE technologies in tandem—you would want to show that a browser can connect to a Web server running servlets, which in turn interacts both with EJBs that access your back-end database and with JSPs to generate HTML to return to the browser. A vertical slice is *not* just EJBs. Developing an initial vertical slice offers several benefits:

- **Provides experience developing J2EE software.** By developing an end-to-end vertical slice, you learn how to work with all of the technologies, tools, and techniques that you are going to apply on your project. You have to start somewhere, and it's better to discover and address any problems as early in your project as possible.
- **Provides experience deploying J2EE software.** The first time you deploy a J2EE application can be confusing. You have several types of nodes to potentially install and configure Web servers, application servers, database servers, security gears, and so on. You can safely gain this experience by internally deploying your initial vertical slice into your staging area.
- **Reduces unsoundness risk.** By developing an initial vertical slice, you show that the technologies you have chosen all work together, thereby eliminating nasty integration surprises later in your project. Remember the old cliché: Everything works well in management presentations, but not necessarily in reality.

- **Proves to your project stakeholders that your approach works.** At the beginning of a project, your stakeholders may support you because they have faith that your team can deliver what you have promised; but their support will be even stronger if you show that you can actually deliver. Furthermore, developing and then deploying (at least internally) an initial vertical slice can be incredibly important to your project politically because your detractors can no longer claim that it isn't going to work.
- **Answers the question: Will it scale?** The vertical slice is a real working piece of your system and should demonstrate how well your design scales under load. You can stress test this slice before building the rest of your system. This reduces risk, especially in situations where you may have questions about whether your object model will work (for example, will EJB entity beans scale?).
- **Gets the design patterns right early on.** Building the vertical slice gives you experience with what works and what doesn't work with J2EE. For example, you'll have an opportunity to compare and contrast different model-view-controller (MVC) implementation paradigms. This leads to the discovery of a common technical vision. Once you've locked down that implementation paradigm, you can apply those best practices to other vertical slices and enable developers to implement them faster.

DO YOU START FRESH OR EVOLVE YOUR INITIAL SLICE?

Once you have developed your initial vertical slice, you need to make an important decision: Do you throw it away to start fresh on future vertical slices, or do you continue to evolve it into your system? The answer depends on the quality of your work. If it is of poor quality—either because you rushed or simply because you were new to the technologies or techniques and made some fundamental mistakes—you should consider starting afresh. There's absolutely nothing wrong with starting fresh because you still would gain all the benefits. On the other hand, if the quality of your initial vertical slice is good enough, you can and should consider keeping the code (or at least applicable portions of it) and use it as a base from which to develop your system. This is something that the rational unified process refers to as building the skeleton first. Also, XP refers to this technique of developing vertical slices and then expanding upon it famously as iterative programming.

Choose an Application Server

The choice of an application server is important to your project. Although your J2EE applications may be portable between vendors, the differences make it painful to switch vendors.

Companies that are eager to get started with their EJB development should go with one of the current market leaders. But companies who want to reduce risk before jumping into purchasing a J2EE server should spend the time to research whether the vendor they're thinking about using is right for them. This is applicable for both large and small projects. Our recommended process is as follows:

1. List the features you want in an application server. A consultant can help you build this list.
2. Weigh and prioritize the feature list.
3. Eliminate all vendors that don't meet the majority of your criteria.
4. With the two or three vendors left, download and deploy your initial vertical slice into those application servers. You can then measure how well these application servers handle your specific business problem, as well as their general usability.

In all cases, we recommend you do not purchase your application server *until* you've deployed your vertical slice into the application server. You may find the application server does not behave as the vendor's marketing propaganda promised. Download that free evaluation copy and deploy that real, working slice of your system into the server to see for yourself.

The following are suggested resources for choosing an application server:

- Chapter 21 of this book provides a guide to choosing an EJB server.
- TheServerSide.com application server matrix (theserverside.com/reviews/matrix.tss).
- Research reports from various analyst firms. We recommend you own an updated copy of Gartner's Application Server Evaluation Model (ASEM) and Server Magic Quadrant report.

Divide Your Team

Dividing your J2EE team is one of your most critical decisions. When assembling a J2EE project team, you have two basic choices:

- **Horizontal approach.** Have folks specialize in different technologies. For example, you'd have a JSP team, a servlets team, an EJB session beans team, and an EJB entity beans team. Members of your team become specialists in specific technologies.
- **Vertical approach.** Have folks specialize in vertical business use cases. For example, you'd have a search engine team, a product catalog team, and a payment processing team. Team members become *generalists* and gain experience with all the J2EE technologies involved in that domain, such as servlets, JSP, and EJB.

You can also use a hybrid approach, which is a combination of the two. Table 20.4 describes the horizontal, vertical, and hybrid approaches to team organization with their advantages and disadvantages. Table 20.5 lists several recommended resources for building project teams.

Table 20.4 Team Organization Strategies

STRATEGY	ADVANTAGES	DISADVANTAGES
Horizontal—Your team is composed of *specialists* in particular J2EE APIs.	• The same team uses the same API across all vertical use cases. This ensures consistency in design patterns, paradigms, and frameworks used. • Specialists become proficient with their API, yielding rapid application development.	• Specialists do not gain exposure to other APIs, resulting in disconnects between layers. • Requires strong planning to achieve parallel development. Need to define rock-solid interfaces between layers. • Retention issues arise. Specialists do not have a concept of ownership of a use case. They only understand only a single part of J2EE, and so their skills grow more slowly.
Vertical—Your team is composed of *generalist* developers who gain experience with every J2EE technology. They focus on a specific problem domain or use case.	Smooth end-to-end development on an individual use-case basis. • Parallel development is easy if use cases are separated well. Each developer works on his own use case. Developers have a concept of ownership of a use case. They gain a wider range of skills. Good for retention.	• Generalists need to know many technologies and are typically highly paid and difficult to find. • Generalists typically do not have the specific technical expertise required to quickly solve detailed problems. • Subject matter experts must work with several developer groups, increasing their burden.

Table 20.4 Team Organization Strategies

STRATEGY	ADVANTAGES	DISADVANTAGES
	• Good for educating developers on different technologies used in your system to give them a broader picture.	• Design patterns, paradigms, and frameworks used may change between use cases. • If use cases are interdependent, it is difficult to partition the team.
Hybrid—Your team is made up of both generalists and specialists. The generalists have authority over one or more use-cases. They support API specialists who work on many use cases within a particular API.	• The same team uses the same API across all vertical use cases. This ensures consistency in design patterns, paradigms, and frameworks used. • Specialists become proficient with their API, yielding rapid application layers for specialists to develop in parallel.	• Requires planning and structure early on in the project. • Requires an understanding and buy-in from the team that the generalists have authority within their use cases. • Must still spec out interfaces between developments. • Individual use cases are implemented consistently.

Table 20.5 Recommended Resources for Building a Project Team

RESOURCE	DESCRIPTION
Peopleware: Productive Project and Teams, 2nd Edition, Tom Demarco and Timothy Lister, 1999, Dorset House Publishing	This book is the de facto classic within the information technology industry for how to build and manage a software project team.
Constantine on Peopleware, Larry L. Constantine, 1995, Yourdon Press	This book presents a collection of writings about the software aspects of software development, including developer productivity, teamwork, group dynamics, and developer personalities. This is a good book to read for anyone trying to understand how to organize and then manage a bunch of software "geeks."

(continued)

Table 20.5 *(continued)*

RESOURCE	DESCRIPTION
Organizational Patterns for Teams, Neil B. Harrison, 1996, Pattern Languages of Program Design 2, pages 345–352, Addison-Wesley Publishing Company	The paper describes a collection of patterns for building a software development team, including Unity of Purpose, Diversity of Membership, and Lock 'Em Up Together.
The Unified Process Inception Phase, Scott W. Ambler & and Larry L. Constantine, 2001, CMP Books, www.ambysoft.com	This book describes a collection of activities and best practices for the Rational Unified Process (RUP) Inception phase, including advice for building your project team.
ExtremeProgramming.Org	A Web site that discusses how to start working on new projects that follow XP methodology.

So which approach is better? The answer depends on the goals for your project:

- **If your goal is to get your project completed quickly and in a consistent manner,** our experience has shown us that the horizontal or hybrid approach is superior. Design patterns, paradigms, and frameworks are kept consistent across the board. Specialists build a core competency in their API, yielding rapid application development.
- **If your goal is to invest in the education of your developers** to reduce retention issues or to give them a broader long-term skill set, the vertical approach works well. Developers gain experience with every technology in J2EE. The downside is consistency of design patterns across use cases. In a day and age when good software professionals are hard to find, let alone keep, this is an important consideration.

Invest in Tools

A number of tools are worth a look when building your EJB/J2EE deployment. These include testing tools (JUnit, MockObjects, and so on), profiling tools (JProbe or OptimizeIt), UML modeling tools (Borland Together J or IBM Rational Rose), IDEs (Eclipse, NetBeans, IBM Websphere Studio, Sun Microsystems Java Studio Enterprise, Oracle JDeveloper, or Borland JBuilder), and more. Chapter 11 discusses the subject of tools further.

Rather than describe each and every tool that's out there, we are providing a resource that is updated very frequently by the users of TheServerSide.com who post reviews of various tools and other J2EE products at theserverside.com/reviews/index.tss.

Invest in a Standard Build Process

An easy choice when picking tools is a tool to help you with a standard build process. If you decide to use a standard build process, you must use some sort of build scripts, written in some scripting language. The build tool does not take the place of your build process—it only acts as a tool to support it. What characteristics would you like to have in this scripting language?

- **Widely understood.** It would be nice if your developers (who are more often than not doing the builds) already understood the technology behind the language.
- **Functional.** The scripting language needs to support a wide array of functionality out of the box, especially for Java features.
- **Extensible.** Since no two projects are the same, and projects use all sorts of different technology, it would be useful if you could add functionality to the scripting language to handle your particular needs.
- **Cross-platform.** In an enterprise environment, you usually are developing on a Windows machine and doing testing and quality assurance on a non-Windows box. You want your build scripts to be as cross-platform as your code.

The Apache group's Ant build tool (http://jakarta.apache.org) combines ideas from Java and XML to achieve these goals. Many of our clients are using Ant successfully, and we highly recommend it. Chapter 11 discusses various best practices that involve usage of Ant tool.

Next Steps

With your initial vertical slice in place, you are in a position to continue your construction efforts by developing additional slices of your system. For each vertical slice, you effectively run through a miniature project life cycle—fleshing out its requirements, modeling it in sufficient detail, coding it, testing it, and internally deploying it. This approach reduces your project risk because you deliver functionality early in the project; if you can deploy your system internally, you can easily make it available to a subset of your users to gain their feedback. Furthermore, your development team gains significant lifecycle experience early in the project, giving developers a better understanding of how everything fits together.

Summary

In this chapter, we gained greater insight into how to start our EJB projects on the right foot. We learned about a time-tested process that has worked for other organizations to reduce risk and lead to a win-win situation for all parties involved. Armed with this knowledge, you should be able to confidently begin work on your EJB project.

CHAPTER

21

Choosing an EJB Server

Throughout this book, we've explained the concepts behind EJB programming and put the concepts to practice in concrete examples. But perhaps an even more daunting task than learning about EJB is choosing from the legion of container/server product vendors out there—currently more than 30 such products. For the uninformed, this is a harrowing task. What should you be looking for when choosing an EJB product? That is the focus of this chapter.

To make the best use of this chapter, first ask which application server features are most important to you in your deployment, including specific features that you need (such as support for a particular database). Once you've listed your requirements, assign a weight to each feature. For example, if transparent fail-over is important in your deployment, you might rank it a 7 of 10. Once you've weighed each feature, you can begin evaluating application server products and create a scorecard for each product.

Once you've reduced your list of servers to two or three, we recommend that you deploy code into those servers and test them for yourself. You should measure both quantitative data (how many transactions per second can the server support?) as well as qualitative data (how easy is the server to use?). See Chapter 20 for more details on how choosing an EJB server fits into a larger EJB development process.

The remainder of this chapter discusses our criteria for choosing an EJB server.

This chapter *does not* recommend a particular EJB server. Why not? Because by the time this book fell into your hands, the information would already be out of date. Instead, we are hosting a complete review section on application servers and other J2EE products at theserverside.com/reviews/index.tss that contains a lot of useful information.

J2EE Standard Compliance

Perhaps the most important issue to think about when choosing an EJB container/server product is compatibility. When you make your purchase decision, you need to write code and purchase beans that are compatible with your container/server product. If in the future you decide to switch to a different vendor's product, the transition will surely not be free and it will always involve some migration headaches. While the EJB standard defines the interfaces that should make products compatible, realistically, every vendor's product will differ from the next in some semantic ways, which will impact your deployment. Ideally, you want to make the right choice on your first purchase.

J2EE v1.4 ships with a compatibility test suite, which verifies that a particular vendor's product is indeed compatible with the J2EE 1.4 specifications, including EJB 2.1. You can verify compatibility by looking for a J2EE seal of approval, which Sun Microsystems stamps on J2EE-compliant products.

Pluggable JRE

Some containers are hard-coded to a specific version of the Java Runtime Environment (JRE). Other vendors are more flexible, supporting many different JREs. This may be important to you if you have existing applications that depend on specific JRE versions.

Conversion Tools

Does the EJB server ship with tools to migrate old J2EE code into the latest version? Consider that even though J2EE 1.4 sounds new today, it won't be new tomorrow. You may need to upgrade your application in the future to a new version of J2EE, and your vendor's historical support of migration tools is most indicative of whether it will support such migration in the future.

Complex Mappings

Be sure your EJB server enables you to perform any complex database mappings that you may need, such as mapping to stored procedures and mapping to complex *JOIN* statements across a relational database, as well as the ability to write custom SQL if necessary.

Third-Party JDBC Driver Support

Some servers do not allow the substitution of JDBC drivers—or if they do, they may disable features, such as connection pooling. Be sure your vendor supports your database connection needs.

Lazy Loading

Lazy loading means to load entity bean data on demand. This is important for large object graphs where the user may only need access to a small portion of the graph. Note, however, that your EJB server should allow you to tune lazy loading on a per-bean basis, so that you can load an entire object graph if you know you need that entire graph.

Deferred Database Writes

A deferred database write means to defer JDBC write operations until transaction commit time. This is important, because if you have a transaction involving many EJB components and thus many database writes, it is counterproductive to perform many network roundtrips to the database. The superior approach is to perform one large write at transaction commit time.

Pluggable Persistence Providers

Some EJB containers provide proprietary APIs for plugging in third-party persistence modules, such as a module that persists your entity beans to an object database rather than a relational database. Other possibilities include persisting to a file, persisting to a relational database using a simple object-relational mapping, persisting to a relational database using a complex object-relational mapping, or persisting using user-defined persistence routine (which may implement persistence through a legacy application).

If you're planning on plugging in a third-party persistence engine into your container, be sure that you can gain transactions and connection pooling.

In-Memory Data Cache

If you are using entity beans (and many deployments will, now that they can be accessed in a high-performance way through local interfaces), be aware that entity bean performance is not equal between application servers.

Some application servers work in a *pass-through* mode, which means that any entity bean operations are passed through to the database, resulting in a low-level database transaction. Other vendors implement smart caching of entity beans, allowing some operations to occur in memory rather than at the database level. For example, if you're merely reading the same data over and over again from an underlying storage, you should not need to hit the database on every method call. The difference between pass-through and caching application servers is tremendous. Some vendors have reported a 30-fold or more performance increase over the pass-through application server.

There is even a third-party marketplace for such caching providers. For example, Javlin is a product that plugs into an EJB server to add caching support.

Integrated Tier Support

Throughout this book, we've concentrated on EJB as a server-side component model. Now in many deployments, Web components written with servlet and JSP technology need to access the EJB layer. Some EJB servers offer the ability to run servlets and JSPs in the same JVM that you run your enterprise beans. If you want this style of deployment, look for this feature.

Scalability

Your EJB server should scale linearly with the amount of resources thrown at it. If you add extra machines with equal power (memory, processor power, disk space, and network bandwidth), the number of concurrent users your server-side deployment can support and the number of transactions your system can execute per second should increase linearly. Be sure to ask your EJB server vendor for case studies and customer references to back up its scalability story.

Other questions to ask include:

- How long does it take for the EJB server to start up or restart? This is important for development as well as for production deployment. If the restart cycle is long, it makes it inconvenient to develop and debug with the EJB server. In production, a slow startup cycle affects the availability of the application to the clients.
- Can the EJB server recover from backend database loss and restart? For example, if the EJB server temporarily loses connectivity to the database, does it need to be restarted to reestablish connectivity to the database, or can it do so automatically?

High Availability

High availability is critical for server-side deployments. You want the highest level of confidence that your EJB server won't come down, and you can look for a number of things to increase your confidence. Your EJB server vendor should have compelling numbers indicating the availability of its product and backed up by existing customers. Realize, too, that your EJB server is only as available as the operating system and hardware that it's deployed on. Be sure to ask your EJB server vendor which operating systems and hardware configurations they support. See Chapter 19 for further discussion on this subject.

Security

A typical EJB deployment leverages predefined security schemes that are already available in existing systems. For example, an IT shop may store user information in an LDAP server, in which case you should be able to use this LDAP user information (credentials, and so on) in your EJB deployment. Many EJB products offer assistance with importing and exporting user data from existing data stores such as directories, databases, and so on. Thus you won't have to write code from scratch for migrating this data into your data repository, thereby saving you time when deploying EJB products. Some systems can even tap into existing security systems—they get the user and authorization information from the existing security service.

Standardized support for the Java Authentication and Authorization Service (JAAS) will enable you to plug in different security providers.

Other questions include:

- Can the server integrate with LDAP in real-time for authentication and authorization?
- Does the security system support SSL?
- Can a firewall be placed between the servlet container and the EJB container? Between a third-party Web server and the servlet container? Can it be an application proxy-type firewall or only a packet filtering firewall?

See Chapter 13 for further discussion on securing EJB applications.

IDE Integration

An essential component of any development is an easy-to-use *Integrated Development Environment* (IDE), such as IBM Websphere Studio, BEA WebLogic Workshop, Sun Microsystems Java Enterprise Studio, or Oracle Jdeveloper. IDEs can assist in code management, automate programming tasks, and aid in debugging, among many other things. Some IDEs also help in modeling EJB applications.

Most of the IDE vendors these days are also EJB container/server vendors—examples are IBM, BEA, Sun, and Oracle. As a result, IDEs from such vendors are often well integrated with their server products, enabling seamless development and deployment experience. The end result is compelling: The IDE can aid in coding, debugging, and deploying your beans by working together with the application server. Other EJB server vendors who do not have their own IDE are forming strategic alliances with IDE vendors to gain a competitive edge in the marketplace.

Some useful EJB specific features to look for in IDEs include:

- Automatic creation of home and remote interfaces from bean
- Automatic identification of business methods
- Creation and editing of deployment descriptors
- Construction of Ejb-jars, Web archives (.wars), and enterprise archives (.ears) from within the IDE
- Direct deployment from the IDE to the J2EE server
- Debugging into the container via the Java remote debug protocol

See Chapter 11 for more discussion on tools.

UML Editor Integration

The diagrams in this book were drawn using the Unified Modeling Language (UML), the de facto standard for communicating development architectures between programmers. A number of visual UML editors are on the market, such as IBM Rational Rose and Borland Together J. Many of these UML editors enable you to visually design EJB components, and then automatically generate and deploy those components into the EJB server of your choice, yielding rapid application development. Be sure to ask your EJB server vendor about which UML editors support their servers.

Intelligent Load Balancing

A common deployment scenario involves a set of machines, all working together to provide an *n*-tier solution.

The variety of ways to *load balance* requests across a set of machines include random, round-robin, active load balancing, weighted load balancing, and custom algorithms (see Chapter 19 for more on this).

In the long run, if you have many requests hitting your servers, the particular load-balancing algorithm that you choose will likely not matter, as long as your server supports some algorithm. Load-balancing algorithms become particularly important in two cases: if you have a heterogeneous hardware situation and need to skew the load to one machine; or if you only have a few, heavy-duty requests coming into your system. If you're among these cases, be sure that your EJB server supports the load-balancing algorithms you require.

Stateless Transparent Fail-over

When your application server crashes, there should be a transparent rerouting of all requests to a different application server. The natural place to put this process is in intelligent client-side proxies, which intercept all network-related problems and retry methods on alternative application servers or in the object request broker runtime. Transparent fail-over is fairly easy to implement if you restrict the client to invoke only on a stateless server and assume that all transactional resource updates can be rolled back.

Clustering

A more advanced level of transparent fail-over is a stateful transparent fail-over or clustering. With clustering, your application server is replicating a conversational state across servers. If an application server crashes, another server can pick up the pieces since it has replicated state. If your application server supports clustering for Web components (servlets, JSP scripts) and for enterprise beans, you can completely eliminate single points of failure from your deployment, ensuring uninterrupted business processes.

An extension of clustering is application partitioning—configuring components to run only on particular nodes within a cluster. High-end servers provide tools for managing this complexity. Chapter 19 discusses this subject further.

Java Management Extension (JMX)

JMX is a J2EE API for monitoring a deployment. If your EJB server supports JMX, you can write an application that monitors your EJB server. Your application could set properties in your EJB server as well; for example, it could modify the current thread pool, redeploy an EJB component, and so on. If you want to write an application that performs advanced monitoring or control over your EJB deployment, JMX is the way to go.

Administrative Support

A Web-based administrative console allows system administrators to monitor your deployment from afar. Web-based consoles are superior to thick client administrative consoles because you can easily access your system from any machine, and firewalls don't get in the way.

Command line–based administration is also important. It is necessary to allow the automation of deployment and management. After all, your automated testing process will need to deploy beans quickly into a server. It is inappropriate to require a human to click a Web-based console to achieve this. Common tasks that need to be automated from the command line include:

- Start, stop, and restart the EJB server
- Deploy, redeploy, and undeploy an application
- Configure other EJB server resources such as connection pools

Hot Deployment

Hot deployment means *redeploying* EJB components into a running EJB server without shutting down the EJB server. This feature may be necessary if you are in a 24x7 environment where even a small amount of downtime during scheduled maintenance is unacceptable.

Instance Pooling

Instance pooling is the pooling and reuse of EJB components. Advanced EJB servers can pool and reuse any type of component, be it a stateful or stateless session bean, CMP or BMP entity bean, or message-driven bean. Look for flexibility in configuring this pool size, including configurable rules for dynamically increasing and decreasing its size under various load conditions.

Automatic EJB Generation

Some EJB servers ship with wizard-like or command line tools to automatically generate EJB components for you. For example, you could supply the name of an entity bean, along with the names and types of its persistent fields. From this, the tool should be able to generate your bean class, component interfaces, home interfaces, deployment descriptor, and Ejb-jar file. If EJB servers do not support this feature natively, you should see if a popular code generation utility, such as XDoclet, supports the generation of code and deployment descriptors for your specific EJB server. Refer to Chapter 11 for more on code generation for EJB.

Clean Shutdown

What happens when you want to take down an application server for maintenance for rebooting the machine the application server is installed on, upgrading the application server, or installing some software on the machine? In this situation, if you simply kill the process, any connected clients' work would be lost, potentially resulting in critical errors.

This leads to another area of value that EJB products can provide: a clean way to shut the application server down without having a gross impact on clients. For example, the EJB application server may simply have a routine that refuses to accept connections from new clients and instead reroutes these requests to other application server instances and waits for all existing clients to gracefully disconnect.

Real-Time Deployment

Starting up and shutting down an EJB application server is usually a fairly heavyweight operation. If you're debugging an EJB application, having to restart the EJB application server each time you regenerate your beans is a hassle. Having to shut down an application server to deploy new beans has an even greater impact, because that application server cannot service clients when it is down.

An enhanced value that some EJB products can provide above and beyond the EJB specification is a mechanism for deploying enterprise beans in real time. This means the ability to deploy and redeploy beans without shutting down a running application server.

Distributed Transactions

In Chapter 12, we examined transactions in depth and noted how multiple processes on different physical machines could participate in one large transaction. This is known as a *distributed transaction*, and it is a fairly heavyweight operation. It necessitates the use of the *distributed two-phase commit protocol*, a reliable but cumbersome dance that transaction participants must take part in for a distributed transaction to succeed.

If you require distributed transactions, make sure your EJB server supports them, and also supports a clean recovery in case of transactional failure. For a two-phase commit transaction to work, you also need to have the same transaction service deployed on all participant machines or to have interoperable transaction services.

Superior Messaging Architecture

If you are using messaging in your system, realize that not all messaging architectures were created equal. Some messaging architectures do not enable you to cluster your JMS destinations, which creates single points of failure. Other messaging architectures cannot support as many messages per second as others. Be sure to get these statistics from your EJB server vendor.

You also might want to look for additional quality of services (if you need them) such as synchronous and asynchronous delivery, publish/subscribe and point-to-point, acknowledgment (ACK) and negative acknowledgment (NACK) guaranteed message delivery, certified delivery, and transactional delivery.

Provided EJB Components

Some EJB servers ship EJB components as optional packages with their servers. This can include personalization components, marketing components, e-commerce components, vertical industry specific components, and many more. Making use of any of these components may help shorten your development cycle.

If, on the other hand, you plan to use a third-party bean provider's components, you should ask if the components are certified on the EJB servers you have chosen. If not, you run the risk of incompatibility.

Web Services

Web Services technologies (SOAP, WSDL, and UDDI mainly) enable you to integrate with existing systems seamlessly. Evaluate the support for these Web Service protocols in terms of SOAP performance, tools support, and so on from your vendors.

Workflow

Advanced EJB servers, as well as third-party independent software developers, are shipping J2EE-based workflow engines. A workflow engine enables you to model business processes. A business process could span EJB components, existing enterprise systems, partner facing systems, and more. A workflow engine typically has a flow of control that can change depending on the state of the current system. These flows are designed visually using a graphical workflow design GUI. This is extremely useful for involving business analysts in the development of business processes.

Currently the standard framework for supporting workflow protocols on J2EE platform, Java Business Integration (JBI), is a work in progress within the Java Community Process. JBI is expected to release in around spring of 2005. Until then, any workflow solution you find will remain proprietary. When shopping for a workflow engine, ask your vendor the following:

- Does the workflow engine integrate with J2EE?
- Is the workflow engine itself written in J2EE, so that you are not injecting foreign technology into your deployment?
- Does the workflow engine integrate with your existing infrastructure such as message-oriented middleware or does it require you to buy new infrastructure?

- Does the workflow engine allow for long-lived business processes that may take days, weeks, or even months? One example is a workflow that begins with purchasing a book on a Web site, then leads to fulfilling that book, and finally handles a possible return shipment of the book. That business process could span quite some time.

Open Source

Some EJB servers are open source code servers, similar to Linux, in that anyone can contribute to their development. Examples are JBoss, OpenEJB, and Apache Geronimo.

If you choose an open source code EJB server, be sure you choose one for the right reasons—you'd like more fine-grained control over the code base, you are running a nonmission critical deployment, or you'd like to foster the open source code community.

The wrong reason is usually price. Realize that the total cost of ownership of your deployment includes far more than just the licensing cost of the application server. The total cost of ownership includes hardware costs, software costs, costs to employ developers, costs to train developers, and opportunity costs if your system is not ideal. Unless you are strapped for cash, we recommend you take price out of the equation.

Specialized Services

EJB vendors provide numerous other features to differentiate their products. Some of these features do not impact your code at all. For instance, your bean code should always remain the same no matter what load-balancing scheme your application server uses. Other features may require explicit coding on your part, such as ERP integration. When choosing a product, ask yourself how much explicit coding you would need to write to a particular vendor's proprietary API. The more of these APIs you use, the less portable your EJB code becomes.

Some examples of special features offered in EJB products are:

- Optimized mechanisms for pooling and reusing sockets, multiplexing many clients over a single socket
- Specialized JVM switches for added performance
- Advanced systems management integration to professional monitoring tools

As you can see, the emergence of these services becomes one of the chief advantages of EJB as a competitive playing field that encourages vendors to provide unique qualities of service.

Nontechnical Criteria

There are a host of nontechnical criteria to consider as well:

- **Reputable vendor.** Does the vendor have a brand name and a history in distributed transaction processing systems space? How large is the firm? How many years has it been in operation?
- **High-quality technical support available after hours.** If a crisis situation ensues in the middle of the night, will your vendor be available to resolve problems?
- **Verifiable customer success stories.** Look for large, well-known (ideally Fortune 500) companies implementing solutions with the vendor's product. Don't hesitate to ask tough questions to get beyond the marketing hype.
- **Training and consulting services available.** The company should have its own internal training and consulting services or should have channel partnerships with other firms to provide those services to you. Be sure that the vendor's training or consulting department is adequately staffed to provide the care you need, and that the vendor is not overburdened with other projects.
- **Historical velocity to meet standards.** Looking back in time, how close has the vendor's release cycle been to the J2EE specifications' release cycle? The shorter, the better.
- **Free evaluation copy.** Any deserving vendor should let you evaluate a product free of charge for either a limited time period or as a stripped-down product version. Otherwise, rule that vendor out immediately.

Summary

In this chapter, you've surveyed the criteria for making an EJB application server purchase decision. The EJB specifications (as well as the products that implement it) are evolving rapidly. The features offered in the marketplace are likely to change over time. For the latest information about EJB products and news, check out the following resources:

- **TheServerSide.com.** TheServerSide.com maintains an application server comparison matrix, a very useful tool for evaluating application servers (theserverside.com/reviews/matrix.tss). There are also ECPerf/SPECjAppServer benchmark results to compare the performance of different application servers available on middlewareresearch.com.
- **Online whitepapers.** Some research firms offer reviews they have performed on EJB products. An example of such a site is TechMetrix.com.
- **The Sun Microsystems Web site.** The http://java.sun.com/j2ee/licensees.html page has a list of current J2EE licensees that you can refer to, to find out whether your vendor is one of them. J2EE licensees are the ones to provide J2EE standard compliant application server.
- **Magazine article reviews.** Some Java-based print magazines offer comparisons of EJB products as well. Examples here include *Java Developer's Journal* and *JavaPro.*

CHAPTER

22

EJB-J2EE Integration: Building a Complete Application

In this chapter, we will show you how to design and build a complete EJB/J2EE system. In particular, you'll learn how to use entity beans, session beans, and message-driven beans *together*, and how to call EJB components from Java servlets and JavaServer Pages (JSP). We will use container-managed persistence (CMP) and also expose a stateless session bean as a Web Service for integration with other applications.

We will first motivate our deployment by describing the business problem. We'll then design the example system. The complete source code is available on the book's accompanying Web site at www.wiley.com/compbooks/roman. The code is fully commented and ready to run. As we go through the design, we will point out implementation alternatives that you can use for your own experiments.

The Business Problem

Jasmine's Computer Parts, Inc. is a fictitious manufacturing company that makes a wide variety of computer equipment, including motherboards, processors, and memory. Jasmine, the company's owner, has been selling her products using direct mail catalogs, as well as a network of distributors and resellers.

Jasmine wants to lower the cost of doing business by selling her computer parts directly to the end customer through a Web-based sales model. Jasmine has given us a high-level description of the functionality of the e-commerce solution. She'd like the following features in the system we provide for her:

- **User authentication.** Registered users would first log in to the Web site to access the complete catalog. Only registered users should be able to browse and purchase from her online store.
- **An online catalog.** Users should be able to browse her complete product line on the Web and view details of each product.
- **Shopping cart functionality.** While browsing the catalog, a user should be able to choose the products he or she wants. The user should be able to perform standard shopping cart operations, such as viewing the current shopping cart or changing quantities of items already picked out.
- **Specialized pricing functionality.** Users who order items in bulk should get a percentage discount. For example, if I order five memory modules, I get a 10 percent discount on that memory. In addition, registered users who frequent the store should get additional discounts.
- **Order generation.** Once the user is happy with his or her selections and has committed to ordering the products, a permanent order should be generated. A separate fulfillment application (which we won't write) would use the data in the orders to manufacture the products and ship them. The user would be able to return to the Web site later to view the status of current orders.
- **Billing functionality.** Once the user has placed the order, we should bill it to him or her. If the user does not have enough funds to pay, the order should be cancelled.
- **E-mail confirmation.** After the order has been placed and the credit card debited, a confirmation e-mail should be sent to the user.

This is definitely going to be a full-featured deployment!

A Preview of the Final Web Site

To give Jasmine an idea of what the final product should be like, our sales team has put together a series of screenshots. The screenshots show what the e-commerce system will look like when an end user hits the Web site. These example screens do not yet contain any artwork or corporate design items because we focus on functionality here.

Figure 22.1 shows a user logging into the system initially. Our authentication will be through login names and passwords.

When the user has been recognized, he or she is presented with a Web storefront. The Web storefront is the main page for Jasmine's online store (see Figure 22.2). From the Web storefront, the user can jump to the catalog of products that Jasmine offers (see Figure 22.3). A user who wants to view details about a product can check out the product detail screen (see Figure 22.4). The user can also add the product to the current shopping cart—a temporary selection of products that the user has made but has not committed to purchasing yet.

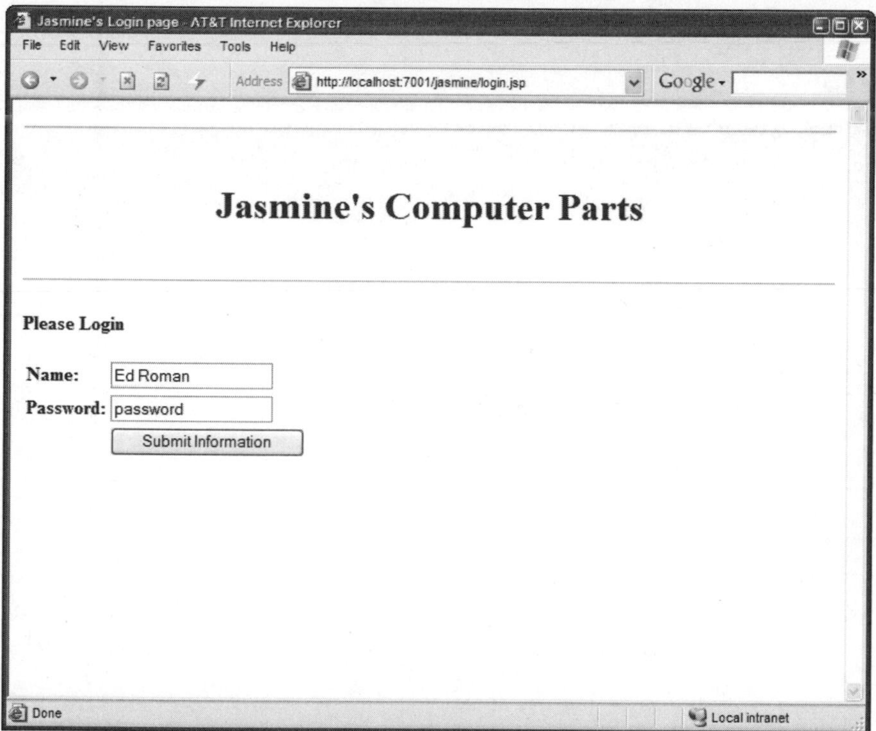

Figure 22.1 A user logging into Jasmine's Computer Parts.

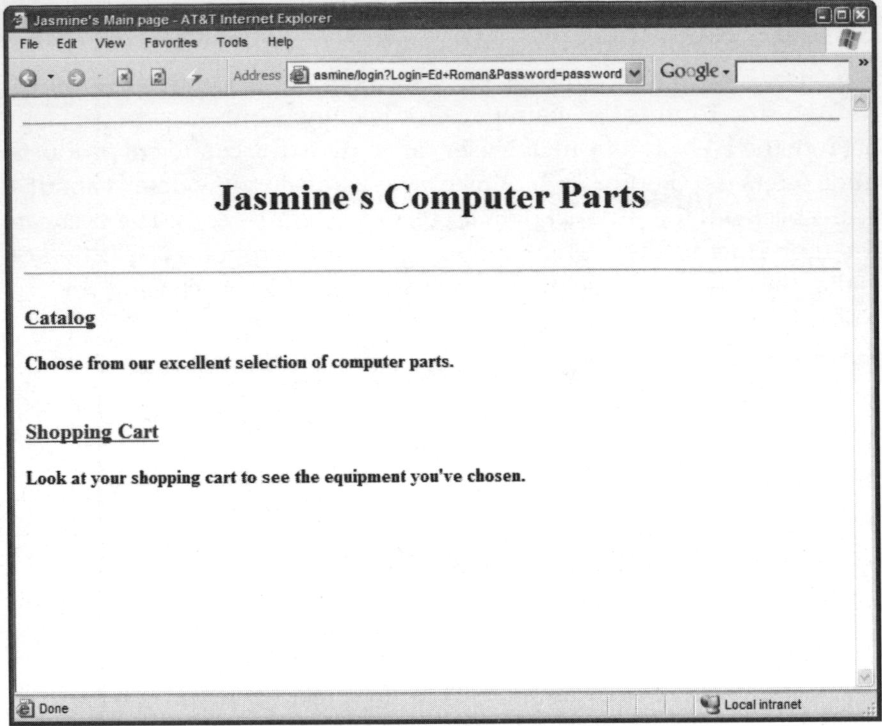

Figure 22.2 The Web storefront for our online store.

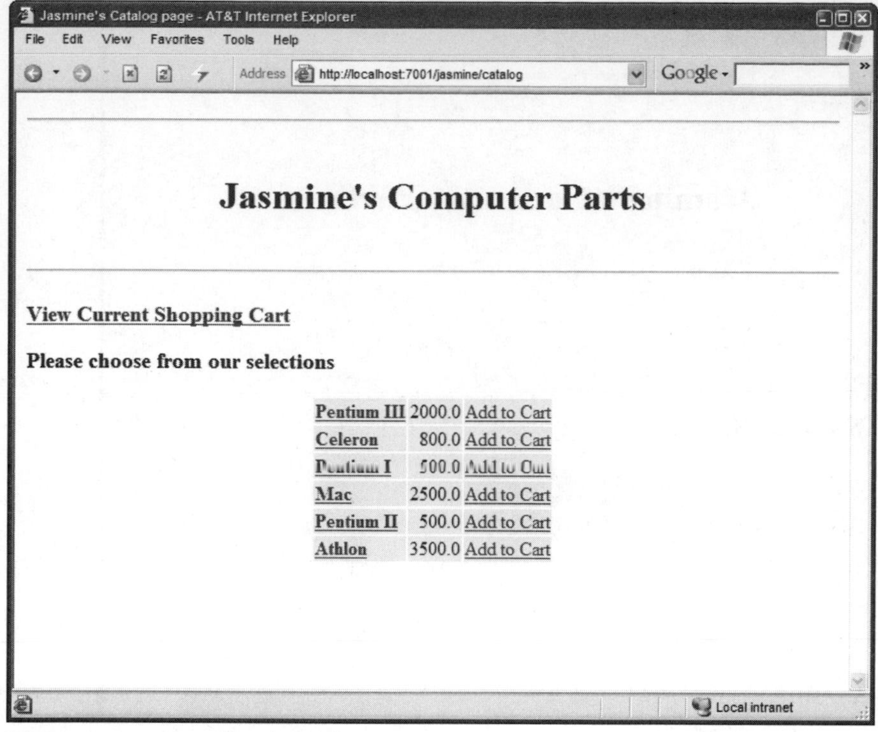

Figure 22.3 Browsing the online catalog.

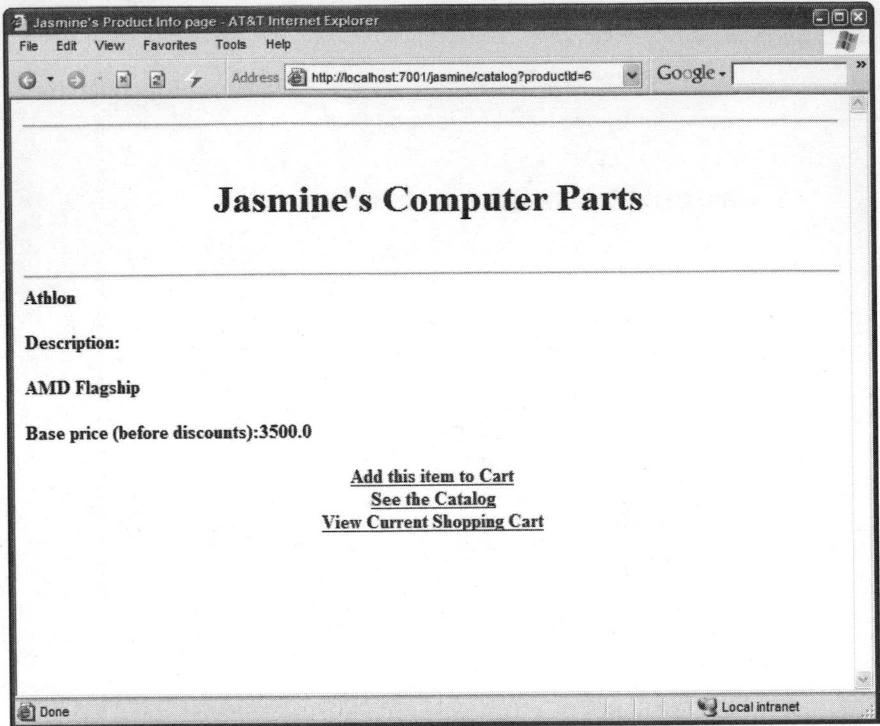

Figure 22.4 Viewing a particular product.

Once the user has made product choices, the user can view a cart for the current selections (and make any last-minute changes), as shown in Figure 22.5. When the user clicks the button to purchase the selection, he or she is billed and a new order is generated. Finally, the user is given the order number for future reference (see Figure 22.6).

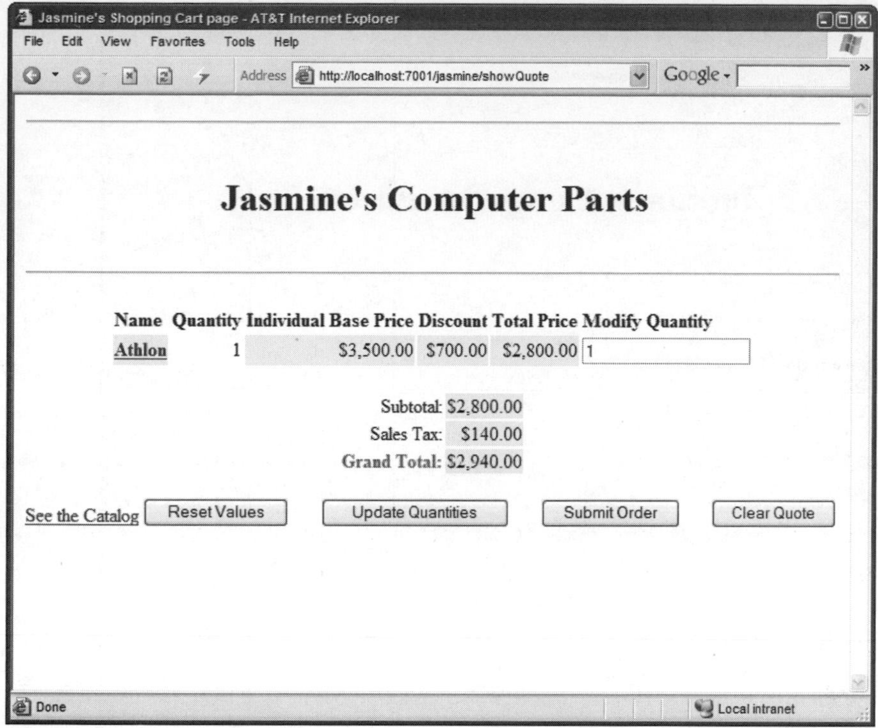

Figure 22.5 Viewing and modifying a cart.

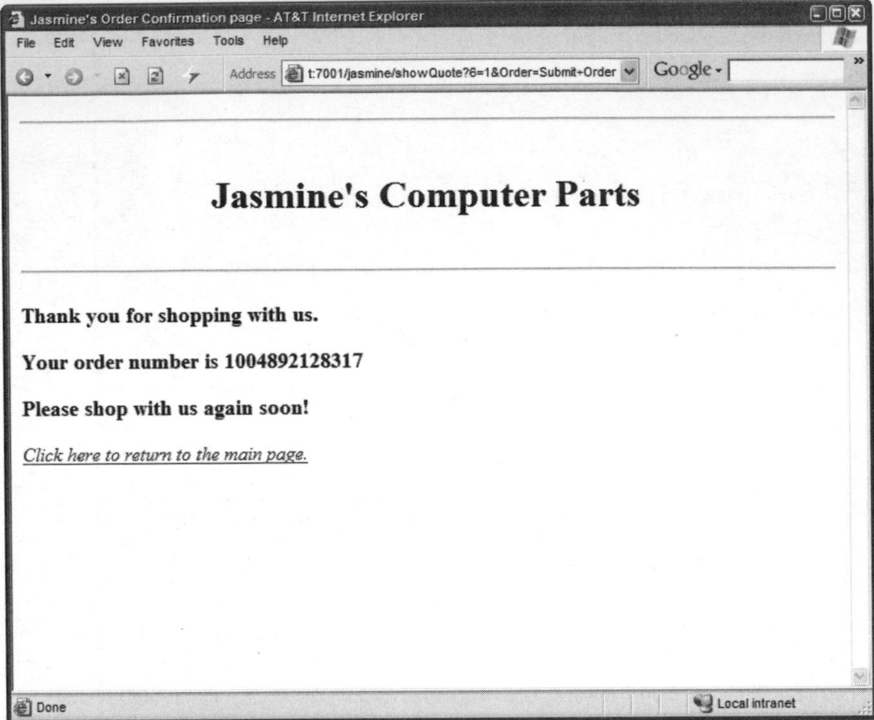

Figure 22.6 Making a purchase.

Scoping the Technical Requirements

While meeting Jasmine's requirements, we'd like to develop an extensible infrastructure that she can add to in the future. That means making the right abstractions to loosen the coupling between our components. Ideally, Jasmine should be able to plug in a different implementation of any part of the system with very few modifications.

Our deployment will be partitioned into three tiers:

- **The presentation tier** involves one or more Web servers, each responsible for interacting with the end user. The presentation tier displays the requested information in HTML to the end user; it also reads in and interprets the user's selections and makes invocations to the business tier's EJB components. The implementation of the presentation tier uses *servlets* and *JSP technology*.
- **The business logic tier** consists of multiple EJB components running under the hood of an EJB container or server. These reusable components are independent of any user interface logic. We should be able to,

for example, take our business tier and port it to a different presentation tier (such as a disconnected salesforce's laptop) with no modifications. Our business tier is made up of session beans, entity beans, and message-driven beans. To allow Jasmine to integrate the pricing functionality with other applications, we will additionally expose this bean as a Web Service.

- **The data tier** is where our permanent data stores reside. The databases aggregate all persistent information related to the e-commerce site. Jasmine has relational databases already in place, so we need to map any persistent data to relational tables.

The Business Logic Tier

Let's begin designing our EJB model. The major beans are shown in Figure 22.7. We'll explain this UML diagram as we go.

We will co-locate our servlets and JSP files in the same process as our EJB components, allowing us to exclusively use efficient local interfaces. As you can see from this diagram, we are following the design strategy of hiding all entity beans behind a session bean façade as recommended multiple times in this book.

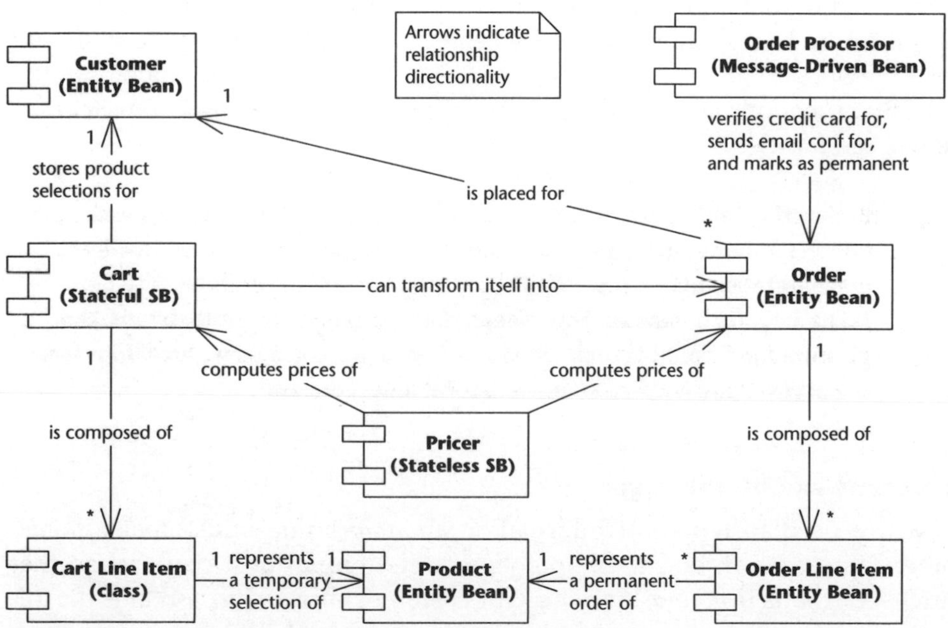

Figure 22.7 The major EJB components in our system.

Entity Beans

We will begin the explanation of our system design with the persistent data and the entity beans that we will create to access this data. We will also mention the session beans that we provide as façades for the entities. Internally, all entity beans use container-managed persistence (CMP) for storage and rely on container-managed relationships (CMR).

Products and Catalog

First, we need to model the products that Jasmine is selling. A product could be a motherboard, a monitor, or any other component. Products should be persistent parts of the deployment that last forever. Our product abstractions should represent the following data:

- The unique product ID
- The product name
- A description of the product
- The base price of the product (indicating the price of the product, with no discounts or taxes applied)

Jasmine should be able to add and delete products from the system using a separate tool that connects to the database; we don't provide this functionality in our Web shop. Because products are permanent, persistent parts of the system, they are best modeled as entity beans. Our product entity bean should have methods to get and set the above fields. We also have a catalog session bean that functions as a façade for this entity bean, serving as a transactional networked façade.

Rather than entity beans, we could have used Java classes to represent the entities in our system, such as products, customers, and so on. However, many of these nouns (especially products) are prime candidates to be cached by the container. This means that by going with entity beans, our performance would actually improve. Because we are using local interfaces, the access time is comparable to a local object access.

Customers and UserManager

Next, we need to represent information about Jasmine's customers. A customer represents an end user—perhaps an individual or a corporation that purchases goods from our Web site. Our customer abstraction contains the following data:

- Customer ID
- The customer's name (also used as the customer's login name for our Web site)

- The customer's address
- The customer's password (used to verify the customer's identity)

We also have a UserManager session bean that wraps this entity bean, again serving as a transactional networked façade that allows us to retrieve user names and compare passwords that users supply with those that we have on record.

New customers, products, and so on can be added to the system in many ways. Jasmine could have users log in through a separate Web site and input their name, address information, password, and other profile data. We could also develop a custom maintenance tool (standalone or Web-based) for adding new products. To keep this example simple, we'll manually insert direct database data, but feel free to extend this for your purposes.

Orders

Next, we need to model a permanent order for goods. We'll define an order abstraction for this purpose. An order is a shopping cart that has been converted into a work request. Shopping carts are explained in this section and are the session bean access points for orders. An order represents a real business action that needs to take place, such as the production of goods. Generating an order and billing a customer go hand in hand.

An order contains the following information:

- The ID of this order (which the user can use to check on order status)
- The customer for which this order is generated (used for shipping address information)
- The products and quantities that should be ordered (as with carts, best represented as separate information; contained in order line items, described shortly)
- The subtotal and taxes on the order
- The date the order was placed

Orders are permanent, persistent objects. You want an order's state to be around even if your deployment crashes for any reason because an order means money. Therefore, orders are best depicted as entity beans. In comparison, carts are not permanent—they represent temporary interactions with the customer. You don't want to write a cart's data to a database during a customer interaction, but you do want to keep track of the user's information—hence the stateful session bean is best applied for carts.

Order Line Items

For convenience of manipulation, we break up our notion of an order into individual line items, where each line item represents data pertaining to a single product the user has ordered. An order has a one-to-many relationship with its constituent line items. Our order line item abstraction contains the following data:

- The ID of this order line item
- The product that this order line item represents (used by manufacturing to reveal which product to make)
- The quantity of the product that should be manufactured
- The discount that the customer received on this product

Because order line items are permanent, persistent objects, they are best represented as entity beans. At first, you might think an order line item is too small and fine-grained to be an entity bean and might better be represented as Java classes for performance. However, with EJB 2.0 local interfaces and by properly tweaking your EJB server, it is possible to have both fine-grained and large-grained entity beans. Chapter 18 has more detail about how to optimize such entity beans for performance.

Session Beans

You have seen the central entities that make up our domain model, but so far there has not been much activity in our Web shop. The actual shopping functionality that our Web shop provides is accessed through the shopping cart session bean, with which users interact. The business function of calculating the prices for carts by adding up the individual items and applying personal and bulk discounts is modeled in a separate Pricer session bean.

Carts

We need to keep track of the selections a customer has made while navigating our catalog by modeling a shopping cart. Each customer who has logged in should have his or her own temporary and separate cart in which to work. Therefore, our carts need to hold client-specific state in them. They should not be persistent, because the user can always cancel the cart.

This naturally lends itself to the stateful session bean paradigm. Each cart stateful session bean holds conversational state about the user's current cart. It enables us to treat the entire cart as one coarse-grained object. A new cart needs to be generated every time a user logs in. Each cart bean contains the following information:

- The customer we authenticated at the login screen. We need to store customer information so that we know who to bill, what discounts to apply, and where to ship the manufactured products.
- The products and quantities that the customer currently has selected. This data is best represented in its own separate bean, called a *Cart Line Item,* described later in this chapter.
- The subtotal for the cart, taking into account all the prices of the products the user wants as well as any discounts the user gets.
- The taxes charged. This is added to the subtotal for the final grand total.

In addition to this data, the cart beans will be smart and will know how to generate permanent orders from themselves. We describe orders a bit later.

When making shopping cart-like functionality, you have several choices. You can use session beans (as we are) for temporary shopping carts. You can also use servlets or JSP session objects, which is appropriate if your shopping cart is primitive in functionality and shouldn't be reused for other graphical user interfaces.

A final choice is to use entity beans and to keep the shopping cart data in the database. The entity bean approach is appropriate for persistent shopping carts, where you'd like the user to retrieve the shopping cart when returning later. This might be useful if it requires complex configuration to get an item into a shopping cart, such as custom configuring a laptop computer. The downside to the entity bean approach is you need to write a shopping cart cleaning program that routinely sweeps abandoned shopping carts from the database.

Cart Line Items

As the user navigates the Web site, he or she will add products to the cart. For convenience of manipulation, we'd like to separate a cart into individual line items, where each line item represents data pertaining to a single product the user has currently selected. A cart has a one-to-many relationship with its constituent line items.

Cart line items contain the following data:

- The ID of the line item
- The product that the user wants to buy
- The quantity of that product
- Any discounts the customer gets from the base price of the product

The cart line item is specific to one customer and is not persistent. It is best modeled as either a stateful session bean or a Java class that hangs off the cart. We'll choose to make it a Java class because there is no middleware that we need when a cart calls a line item. Furthermore, we may need to marshal the line item out to a servlet or JSP so that the contents can be displayed to a user. By modeling our line items as classes to begin with, we can achieve this easily.

Pricer

Because Jasmine wants customized pricing, we need the concept of a pricer—a component that takes a cart as input and calculates the price of that cart based on a set of pricing rules. A pricing rule might be, "Customer X gets a 5 percent discount" (a frequent-buyer discount) or, "If you purchase 10 motherboards, you get a 15 percent discount" (a bulk discount). These pricing rules could be read in from a database or set via EJB environment properties (see Chapter 10). The implementation on the companion Web site uses this latter approach. It is a useful exercise to move the frequent buyer discount information to the customers database instead.

Our pricer takes a cart as input and computes the subtotal (before taxes) of that cart. It figures out the subtotal by computing a discount for each cart line item in that bean and subtracting the discounts from the total price.

Our pricer works on any cart and holds no client-specific state. Once the pricer has computed a price on a cart, it is available to perform another computation on a different cart. It is also not a persistent object—it would not make sense to save a price, because a pricer simply performs logic and holds no state. This means our pricer fits into the EJB world best as a stateless session bean.

Finally, Jasmine considers reusing the pricing logic in other applications, such as in her mail order processing system. Consequently, we need to plan in advance for integrating this component with other, potentially non-EJB systems. We therefore also expose the pricer stateless session bean as a Web Service to allow for easy integration.

Order Processor

The last challenge we face is how to *generate* orders in our system. We'd like for the user to continue browsing the Web site when he has placed the order, rather than waiting to see if his credit card is approved. This is similar to the Amazon.com one-click functionality. We'd also like to e-mail the user afterwards indicating whether the order was successfully placed.

The best paradigm to achieve this is messaging. When the user wants to order the shopping cart, we could send a JMS message containing the shopping cart reference. Then later, the message will be processed off the queue by an *order processor* message-driven bean. This order processor is responsible for querying the shopping cart, checking the user's credit card, checking inventory, e-mailing the user a confirmation, and creating the order (entity bean).

The challenge of sending data through JMS is that we cannot marshal EJB stubs in a JMS message. Thus, we couldn't send a shopping cart stub as a serialized bit-blob in a JMS message. This is a fundamental problem with message-driven beans: It's very challenging to send data into a message-driven bean that comes from another bean.

An alternative is to use *EJB object handles* (described in Chapter 10), which are serializable stubs. However, this might not work either, since the stateful session bean cart might time-out before the JMS message was processed.

Another alternative is to create a custom, serializable representation of the shopping cart, perhaps by using serializable Java objects. The problem here is we'd need to create all these extra Java classes, which is very annoying.

The best solution for us is to submit the order *before* sending a JMS message. We'd then mark the order status as *unverified*. The order processor receives the primary key of the order, retrieves the order entity bean from the database, checks the credit card, sends the confirmation e-mail, and then changes the order status to *submitted*.

Our notion of an order can be easily extended to include order status, such as *Manufacturing* or *Shipping* and other order fulfillment information. It would also be interesting to e-mail the order status to the end user at regular intervals using the *JavaMail* API. Since we do not fulfill orders, we leave this as an exercise to the reader.

The Presentation Tier

Our next task is to design our presentation tier, which displays the graphical user interface to the end user. For our presentation tier, we will use a few Java servlets and JSP files to interact with a client over HTTP. The following sections contain a brief introduction to servlets and JSP technologies. You can safely skip this if you are already familiar with these technologies.

What Are Servlets?

A *servlet* is a Java object that runs within a Web container and reacts to Hypertext Transfer Protocol (HTTP) requests by sending HTTP responses. Requests contain data that the client wants to send to the server. A *response* is data that the server wants to return to the client to answer the request. A servlet is a Java object that takes a request as input, parses its data, performs some logic, and issues a response back to the client (see Figure 22.8).

Figure 22.9 illustrates an HTTP servlet running inside a J2EE server, and Source 22.1 shows an example of an HTTP servlet.

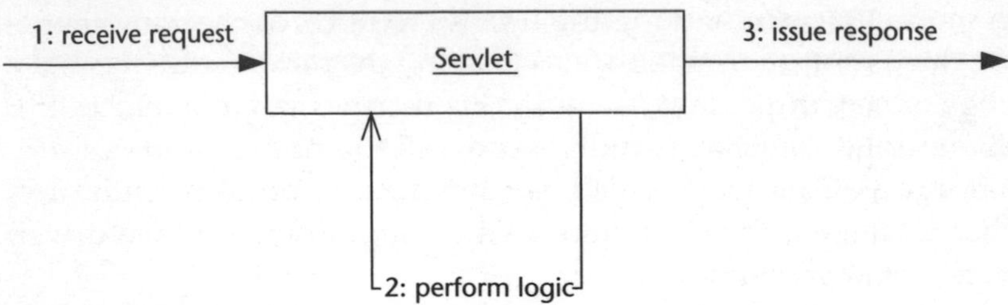

Figure 22.8 The basic servlet paradigm.

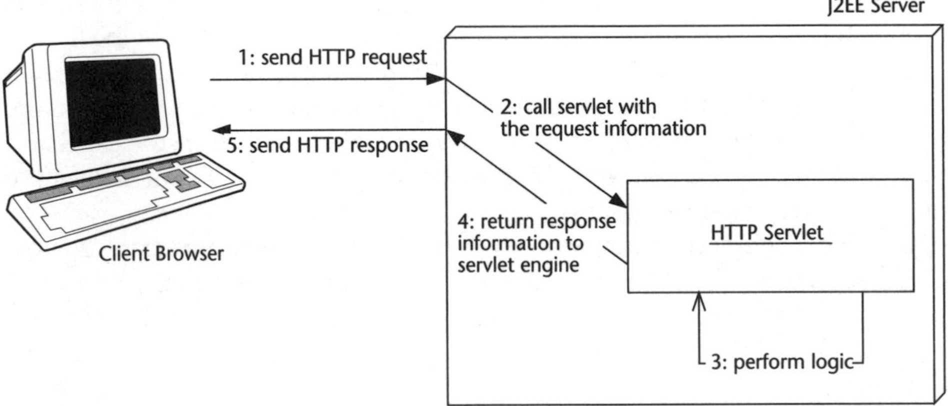

Figure 22.9 HTTP servlets.

```
import javax.servlet.*;
import javax.servlet.http.*;
import java.io.*;

public class HelloWorld extends HttpServlet
{
  public void service(HttpServletRequest req, HttpServletResponse rsp)
     throws ServletException, IOException
  {
     PrintWriter out = rsp.getWriter();
     out.println("<H1>Hello World</H1>");
  }
}
```

Source 22.1 A sample HTTP servlet.

As you can see, HTTP servlets are very straightforward. They have a simple method called *service()* that responds to HTTP requests. In that method, we write some HTML back to the browser. If properly configured, the J2EE server will pool and reuse this servlet to service many HTTP requests at once.

We can also do trickier things—respond differently to different types of HTTP requests, maintain user sessions, read input parameters from Web forms (using the *HttpServletRequest* object), and call EJB components.

The great thing about servlets is that they are written in Java and therefore can be debugged just like any other Java code. The downside to servlets is that they require Java knowledge. It is therefore inappropriate to use servlets to write large amounts of HTML back to the user, because that HTML is interlaced with Java code, as we saw in Source 22.1. This makes it very challenging for Web designers to get involved with your deployment.

What Are JavaServer Pages?

A JavaServer Page (JSP) is a flat file that is translated at runtime into a servlet. JSP files are generally useful for presentation-oriented tasks, such as HTML rendering. You don't need to know Java to write a JSP file, which makes JSP files ideal for Web designers. A sample JSP is shown in Source 22.2.

```
<!doctype html public "-//w3c/dtd HTML 4.0//en">
<html>
<body>
<H1>Hello World</H1>
</body>
</html>
```

Source 22.2 A sample JSP.

As you can see, this just looks like HTML and is easily maintained by a graphic designer. You can do fancy things as well, such as interlacing Java code with JSP, managing user sessions, and so on. Just about anything you can do in a servlet can be done with JSP. The difference is that a JSP file is a flat file that is translated into a servlet later. The code in Source 22.2 would be translated into a servlet with *out.println()* statements for the HTML code.

How Do I Combine Servlets, JSP, and EJB Components?

You have several choices when architecting your Web-based system. Here are just a few examples.

- **The JSP files can have embedded Java code that calls EJB components.** For example, we could interlace the following code into a JSP file:

```
<html>
<H1>About to call EJB...</H1>
<%
javax.naming.Context ctx = new javax.naming.InitialContext();
Object obj = ctx.lookup("MyEJBHome");
...
%>
</html>
```

When this JSP is translated into a servlet, the Java code would be inserted into the generated servlet. This is a bad idea, because the JSP files cannot be easily maintained by a graphic designer due to the large amount of Java code in the JSP file.

- **The JSP files can communicate with EJB components via custom tags.** You can design custom JSP tags that know how to interact with EJB components, called *JSP tag libraries*. Tag libraries are appealing because once you've designed them, graphic designers can call EJB components by using familiar tag-style editing rather than writing Java code. The tags then call Java code that understands how to invoke EJB components.
- **Servlets can call EJB components and then call JSP files.** You can write one or more Java servlets that understand how to call EJB components and pass their results to JSP files. This is a Model-View-Controller (MVC) paradigm, because the EJB layer is the model, the JSP files are the view, and the servlet(s) are the controller—they understand which EJB components to call and then which JSP files to call (see Figure 22.10). The advantage of this paradigm is that it pushes most of the Java code into servlets and EJB components. The JSP files have almost no Java code in them at all and can be maintained by graphic designers.
- **You can go with an off-the-shelf Web framework.** Several off-the-shelf Web frameworks aid in building Web-based systems, such as Jakarta Struts.

JSP Files in Our E-Commerce Deployment

We will choose an MVC paradigm for our e-commerce deployment. We will have servlets that perform the controller processing, call our EJB components, and select the appropriate JSP file based on the results of the EJB layer processing.

To fulfill Jasmine's requirements, we'll define the following servlets and JSP files:

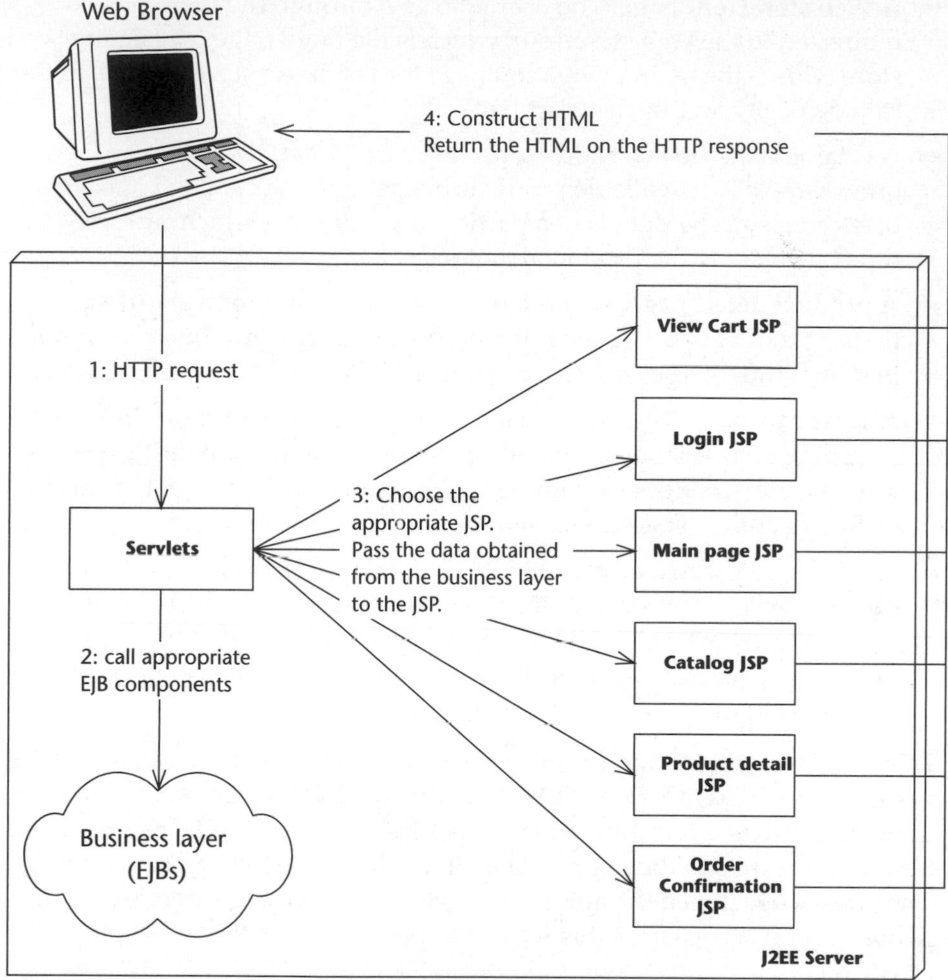

Figure 22.10 The EJB-JSP-Servlet Model-View-Controller paradigm.

- **A login page.** The login page will be the first page that the user deals with when going to Jasmine's Web site. It is responsible for reading in the user's name and then retrieving the appropriate customer entity bean that matches that name. It compares the user's submitted password with the permanent password stored with the customer entity bean. If the passwords match, a new cart stateful session bean is created for this customer. The customer information is stored in the cart so the cart contains the user's billing and shipping information. If the passwords don't match, an error is displayed and the user is given another chance to enter a password.

- **A Web storefront page.** The user who gets through the login page is redirected to the Web storefront, which is the main page for Jasmine's store. This is the main navigation page for Jasmine's store. It links to the catalog page and the view cart page.
- **A catalog page.** To start adding products to the cart, the user can browse the list of available products by going to the catalog page. The user can also view details of a particular product, in which case we direct the user to the product detail page.
- **A product detail page.** When the user wants information about a particular product in the catalog, the product detail page shows that information. From this screen, the user can add the product to his or her cart.
- **A view cart page.** This page enables the user to view and modify the shopping cart. This means deleting items or changing quantities. Every time the user changes something, we recalculate the price of the cart by calling the pricer stateless session bean.
- **An order confirmation page.** Finally, when the user is happy, he or she can convert the cart stateful session bean into an order entity bean. The user is then shown his or her order number, which is extracted from the order bean. We then send a JMS message to the *OrderProcessor* bean, which asynchronously processes the order.

This completes the design for our presentation tier. The flow of control for our pages is depicted in Figure 22.11. Note that the JSP files do not directly call each other: servlets receive all requests, call the appropriate EJB components, and route the results to the appropriate JSP file for the HTML to be rendered.

Once we've developed the application, we need to package and deploy it. A J2EE application is packaged this way:

- **An Ejb-jar file (.jar)** contains EJB components.
- **A Web archive file (.war)** contains Web components, such as servlets, JSP files, HTML, images, and JSP tag libraries.
- **An enterprise archive file (.ear)** is a J2EE application that contains a .jar file and a .war file. This is the unit of deployment you care most about, because it represents a J2EE application.

Each of these files follows the ZIP rules for compression. The idea is that you first create the Ejb-jar file, then the Web archive, and then zip them up together into an enterprise archive. You deploy the enterprise archive into your application server using its tools, or perhaps by copying it into the appropriate folder. For code examples of how to build and deploy these archives, see the book's accompanying source code.

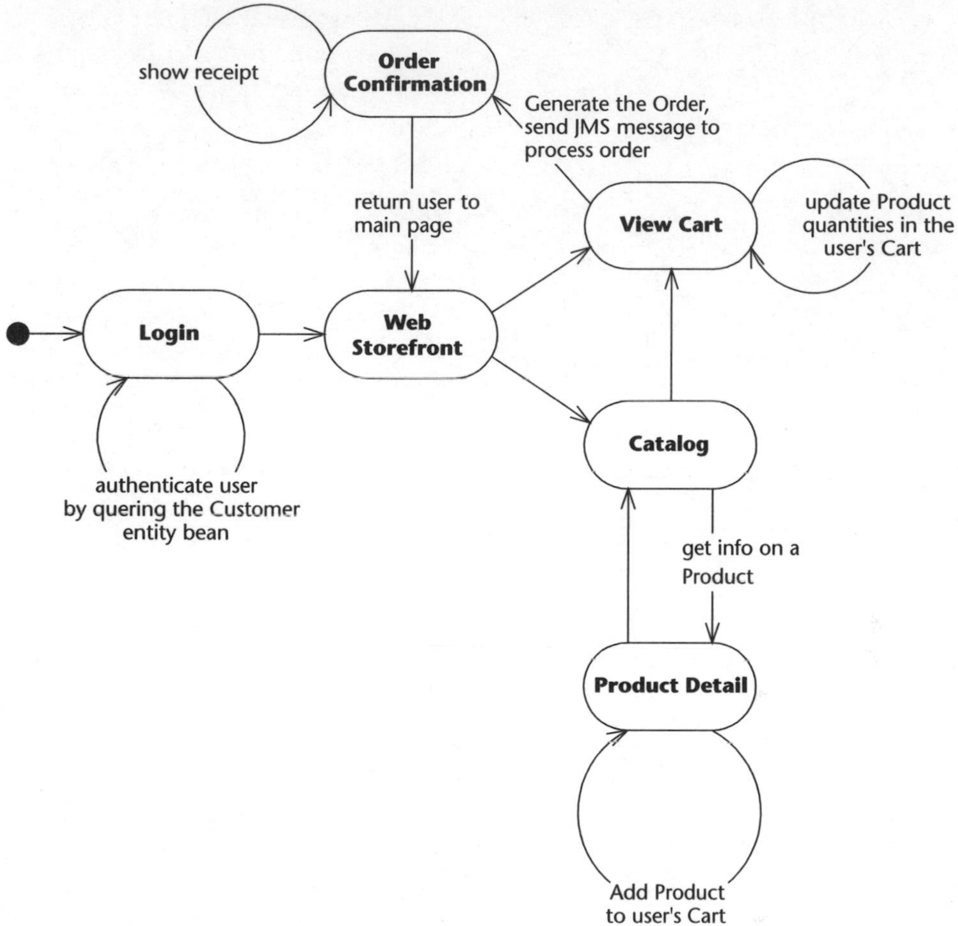

Figure 22.11 State diagram for our Web shop.

Example Code

Before concluding this chapter, let's look at an example of a servlet calling EJB components and then calling a JSP file, so that you can grasp how this MVC paradigm is achieved. As a final piece of code, we will also look at the pricer Web Service and bean interfaces.

We'll take the example of logging into our site. Source 22.3 shows the login JSP code.

```
<%--
 This JSP displays a login screen.  When the user fills out
 the login screen, it will submit it to the Login Servlet,
 which will verify the user's credentials by calling
 EJB components.

 if verification is unsuccessful, the login servlet will return
 the user to this page to re-enter his credentials.

 if verification is successful, Jasmine's main page will be
 displayed.
--%>

<html>
<head>
 <title>Jasmine's Login page </title>
</head>

<body>

<%-- Include the title, which is "Jasmine's Computer Parts"--%>
<jsp:include page="title.jsp" />

<%-- Indicate the error page to use if an error occurs --%>
<jsp:directive.page errorPage="error.jsp" />

<%-- Display the login form --%>
<h4>Please Login<h4>
<p>
<form action="/jasmine/login" method="get">
 <table>
  <tr>
   <td><b>Name:</b></td>
   <td>
    <input type="text" name="Login" value="Ed Roman" size="19">
   </td>
  </tr>
  <tr>
   <td><b>Password:</b></td>
   <td>
    <input type="text" name="Password" value="password" size="19">
   </td>
  </tr>
  <tr>
   <td></td>
   <td>
    <input type="submit" value="Submit Information">
   </td>
  </tr>
```

Source 22.3 The login JSP.

```
  </table>
 </form>

 <%
  // get whether the person logged in successfully
  Boolean failed = (Boolean) request.getAttribute("loginFailed");
  if (failed != null) {
   if (failed.booleanValue() == true) {
 %>
   <p>
   <strong>Could not log in!  Please try again.</strong>
   <p>
 <%
   }
  }
 %>

 </body>
 </html>
```

Source 22.3 *(continued)*

Source 22.4 shows our login servlet.

The login servlet is self-documenting. It cracks open the request, figures out which EJB components to call, and selects the appropriate JSP file.

```
package examples;

import java.io.*;
import java.util.*;
import javax.servlet.*;
import javax.servlet.http.*;
import javax.naming.*;

/**
 * This is the very first servlet the client deals with.
 * It's a Login authentication servlet. It asks the user
 * for his name and password, and passes it to the UserManager
 * stateless session bean for verification.
 * If the user authenticates properly, reference to a new
 * Cart is saved in his HttpSession object, and the user can
 * begin to add items to his cart and shop around.
 */
public class LoginServlet extends HttpServlet {

 /*
  * UserManager home object for authenticating user
```

Source 22.4 The login servlet. *(continued)*

```
 */
private UserManagerHome userManagerHome;

/*
 * Cart home object for creating a new cart when
 * the user logs in.
 */
private CartHome cartHome;

/**
 * The servlet engine calls this method once to
 * initialize a servlet instance.
 *
 * In the body of this method, we acquire all the
 * EJB home objects we'll need later.
 */
public void init(ServletConfig config) throws ServletException {

 super.init(config);

 try {
  /*
   * Get the JNDI initialization parameters.
   * We externalize these settings to the
   * servlet properties to allow end-
   * users to dynamically reconfigure their
   * environment without recompilation.
   */
  String initCtxFactory =
   getInitParameter(Context.INITIAL_CONTEXT_FACTORY);

  String providerURL =
   getInitParameter(Context.PROVIDER_URL);

  /*
   * Add the JNDI init parameters to a
   * properties object.
   */
  Properties env = new Properties();
  env.put(Context.INITIAL_CONTEXT_FACTORY, initCtxFactory);
  env.put(Context.PROVIDER_URL, providerURL);

  /*
   * Get the initial JNDI context using the above
   * startup params.
   */
  Context ctx = new InitialContext(env);

  /*
```

Source 22.4 *(continued)*

```
     * Look up the UserManager and Cart Home Objects
     * we need via JNDI
     */
    userManagerHome = (UserManagerHome)
     ctx.lookup("UserManagerHome");

    cartHome = (CartHome) ctx.lookup("CartHome");
   }
   catch (Exception e) {
    log(e);
    throw new ServletException(e.toString());
   }
  }

  /**
   * The servlet engine calls this method when the user's
   * desktop browser sends an HTTP request.
   */
  public void service(HttpServletRequest request,
                      HttpServletResponse response)
                      throws ServletException, IOException {

   /*
    * Set up the user's HttpSession
    */
   HttpSession session = request.getSession(true);

   /*
    * Retrieve the login name / password from the
    * URL string.
    */
   String loginName = request.getParameter("Login");
   String password = request.getParameter("Password");
   boolean isLogin=false;

   /*
    * If user has not tried to log in yet, present
    * him with the login screen.
    */
   if ((loginName == null) || (password == null)) {
    writeForm(request, response, false);
   }

   /*
    * Otherwise, the user has been to this screen
    * already, and has entered some information.
    * Verify that information.
    */
   else {
```

Source 22.4 *(continued)*

```
/*
 * Uses the UserManager Stateless Session bean to
 * authenticate the user credentials.
 */
try {
 UserManager  userManager=userManagerHome.create();
 isLogin= userManager.validateUser(loginName,password);
}
catch (Exception e) {
 writeForm(request, response, true);
 e.printStackTrace();
 return;
}
/*
 * If the passwords match, make a new Cart Session
 * Bean, and add it to the user's HttpSession
 * object.  When the user navigates to other
 * servlets, the other servlets can access the
 * HttpSession to get the user's Cart.
 */
if (isLogin) {
 try {
  Cart cart = cartHome.create(loginName);
  session.setAttribute("cart", cart);

  /*
   * Call the main page
   */
  RequestDispatcher disp =
   this.getServletContext().getRequestDispatcher("/wsf.jsp");
  disp.forward(request, response);

  return;
 }
 catch (Exception e) {
  log(e);
  throw new ServletException(e.toString());
 }
}
}

/*
 * If there was no match, the user is
 * not authenticated.  Present another
 * login screen to him, with an error
 * message indicating that he is not
 * authenticated.
 */
writeForm(request, response, true);
```

Source 22.4 *(continued)*

```
}

/**
 * Writes the Login Screen (private use only)
 *
 * @param showError true means show an error b/c client
 *        was not authenticated last time.
 */
private void writeForm(HttpServletRequest request,
                       HttpServletResponse response,
                       boolean showError)
                       throws ServletException, IOException {

  /*
   * Set a variable indicating whether or not we failed to
   * log-in.  The JSP will read this variable.
   */
  request.setAttribute("loginFailed", new Boolean(showError));

  /*
   * Forward the request to the login JSP
   */
  RequestDispatcher disp =
   this.getServletContext().getRequestDispatcher("/login.jsp");
  disp.forward(request, response);
}

private void log(Exception e) {
  e.printStackTrace();
}

public String getServletInfo() {
  return "The Login servlet verifies a user.";
}
}
```

Source 22.4 *(continued)*

As a final code example, let's look at the two interfaces that the Pricer component exposes: the Web Service interface and the remote bean interface. The Web Service interface is shown in Source 22.5.

```
package examples;

/**
 * This is the Pricer Web Service's remote interface (the service
 * endpoint interface)
```

Source 22.5 The Pricer Web Service interface. *(continued)*

```
 */
public interface PricerInterface
    extends java.rmi.Remote
{
    /**
     * @return the applicable tax rate
     */
    double getTaxRate()
        throws java.rmi.RemoteException;

    /**
     * @return the current discount rate for buying lots of items
     */
    double getBulkDiscountRate()
        throws java.rmi.RemoteException;

    /**
     * @return the discount rate for a given user in percent
     */
    double getPersonalDiscountRate(String userName)
        throws java.rmi.RemoteException;

    /**
     * This method computes the applicable discount in absolute
     * figure, based on bulk and personal discounts that may apply.
     *
     * @param quantity the number of items that a user intends to buy
     * @param basePrice the overall, non-discounted volume of the
     *        purchase (individual price times quantity)
     * @param the user name
     * @return the subTotal for the line item after applying any
     *         applicable discounts, excluding taxes
     */
    double getDiscount(int quantity, double basePrice, String user)
        throws java.rmi.RemoteException;

}
```

Source 22.5 *(continued)*

In the same manner as in Chapter 5, we can generate a WSDL file from this Java interface using container tools, and then generate SOAP stubs and a JAX-RPC mapping file from theWSDL. The pricer bean exposes a remote interface that extends the Web Service interface in Source 22.5. The rationale here is that other applications at Jasmine's, such as a mail order application, do not use the shopping cart abstraction that our Web shop uses. These applications do need the discount calculation operations, however. Source 22.6 shows the remote interface of the pricer bean, which adds a single operation that performs price calculations for carts.

```
package examples;

import javax.ejb.*;
import java.rmi.RemoteException;
import java.rmi.Remote;

/**
 * These are the business logic methods exposed publicly by the
 * PricerBean. This interface extends the service endpoint interface
 * for the pricer web service.
 */
public interface Pricer
    extends EJBObject, PricerInterface
{
    /**
     * Computes the price of a set of goods
     */
    public void price(Cart cart) throws RemoteException,
PricerException;
}
```

Source 22.6 The remote interface of the pricer bean.

If you're curious to see how the other use cases are implemented, see the book's accompanying source code. And as a reminder, this is just one of many ways to implement a Web architecture.

As an alternative, we could have also chosen a single-servlet architecture with only one servlet and many JSP files. This single servlet would call Java classes, and each Java class would represent a Web use-case and understand the EJB components to call. For example, we could have a Java class that understood how to verify login credentials. The advantage of this paradigm is we could reuse these Web use-case classes in several pages, and our servlet layer would be completely decoupled from our EJB components.

Summary

In this chapter, we've painted a picture of how our e-commerce system should behave. Now that we've made the proper abstractions, our components should fall into place easily. By performing this high-level analysis, we can be confident that our final product will be extensible and reusable for some time to come.

We strongly encourage you to compile and run the example code that we have provided for you. You can use this code as the basis for doing you own experiments with a shopping-style application and for exploring other options. Some of the directions that we encourage you to take with the example is to try a different persistence framework instead of CMP, play with global distributed transactions, devise your own graphic design for the JSP files, let the *Order-Processor* send e-mail notifications to customers, and perhaps try a different, non-JMS messaging style for the *OrderProcessor* message-driven bean.

APPENDIX

A

RMI-IIOP and JNDI Tutorial

To help you to truly understand EJB, this appendix explains the technologies that EJB depends upon—Java RMI-IIOP and the Java Naming and Directory Interface (JNDI).

The goal of this appendix is to teach you enough about RMI-IIOP and JNDI to be productive in an EJB environment. This tutorial will cover the basics, but is by no means a complete RMI-IIOP and JNDI tutorial, and for good reason—most organizations will not need to use these technologies beyond the extent we describe in this appendix, and your reading time is valuable.

Readers who want to learn more about RMI-IIOP and JNDI should consult the following references:

- **The RMI-IIOP and JNDI tutorials.** These are available for free on the Sun Microsystems Web site at http://java.sun.com.
- **The RMI-IIOP and JNDI specifications.** The specifications define the core of RMI-IIOP and JNDI. They are a bit more technical but should not be tough to understand after reading this appendix. They are also downloadable from http://java.sun.com.

Your J2EE server implementation ships with RMI-IIOP and JNDI implementations. It is generally a bad idea to mix and match implementations, like combining the Sun Microsystems RMI-IIOP package with a BEA JNDI implementation. For the easiest development path, stick with a single-vendor solution.

Java RMI-IIOP

Java RMI-IIOP (which stands for Java Remote Method Invocation over the Internet Inter-ORB Protocol) is J2EE's de facto mechanism for performing simple, powerful networking. Using RMI-IIOP you can write distributed objects in Java, enabling objects to communicate in memory, across Java Virtual Machines and physical devices.

RMI-IIOP is not your only choice for performing remote method invocations in Java. You can also use Java Remote Method Invocation (RMI). RMI was the original way to perform remote method invocations in Java and uses the *java.rmi* package. RMI-IIOP is a special version of RMI that is compliant with CORBA and uses both *java.rmi* and *javax.rmi*.

RMI has some interesting features not available in RMI-IIOP, such as distributed garbage collection, object activation, and downloadable class files. But EJB and J2EE mandate that you use RMI-IIOP, not RMI. Therefore we will not cover RMI.

If you want to learn more about why RMI-IIOP was invented as an extension of RMI and also survey the CORBA compatibility features of RMI-IIOP, read Appendix B.

Remote Method Invocations

A *remote procedure call (RPC)* is a procedural invocation from a process on one machine to a process on another machine. RPCs enable traditional procedures to reside on multiple machines, yet still remain in communication. They provide a simple way to perform cross-process or cross-machine networking.

A *remote method invocation* in Java takes the RPC concept one step further and allows for distributed *object* communications. RMI-IIOP enables you to invoke not merely procedures, but also methods on objects remotely. You can build your networked code as full objects. This yields the benefits of object-oriented programming, such as inheritance, encapsulation, and polymorphism.

Remote method invocations are by no means simple mechanisms. These are just some of the issues that arise:

- **Marshalling and unmarshalling.** RMIs (as well as RPCs) enable you to pass parameters, including Java primitives and Java objects, over the network. But what if the target machine represents data differently than the way you represent data? For example, what happens if one machine uses a different binary standard to represent numbers? The problem becomes even more apparent when you start talking about objects. What happens if you send an object reference over the wire? That pointer is not usable on the other machine because that machine's memory layout is completely different from yours. *Marshalling* and *unmarshalling* is the process of massaging parameters so that they are usable on the machine on which they are invoked remotely. It is the packaging and unpackaging of parameters so that they are usable in two heterogeneous environments. As we shall see, this is taken care of for you by Java and RMI-IIOP.
- **Parameter passing conventions.** There are two major ways to pass parameters when calling a method: *pass-by-value* and *pass-by-reference* (see Figure A.1). When you use the pass-by-value parameter, you pass a copy of your data so that the target method is using a copy, rather than the original data. Any changes to the argument are reflected only in the copy, not the original. Pass-by-reference, on the other hand, does not make a copy. With pass-by-reference, any modifications to parameters made by the remote host affect the original data. The flexibility of both the pass-by-reference and pass-by-value models is advantageous, and RMI-IIOP supports both. We'll see how in the following pages.
- **Network or machine instability.** With a single JVM application, a crash of the JVM brings the entire application down. But consider a distributed object application, which has many JVMs working together to solve a business problem. In this scenario, a crash of a single JVM should not cause the distributed object system to grind to a halt. To enforce this, remote method invocations need a standardized way of handling a JVM crash, a machine crash, or network instability. When some code performs a remote invocation, the code should be informed of any problems encountered during the operation. RMI-IIOP performs this for you, abstracting out any JVM, machine, or network problems from your code.

As you can see, there's a lot involved in performing RMIs. RMI-IIOP contains measures to handle many of these nasty networking issues for you. This reduces the total time spent dealing with the distribution of your application, allowing you to focus on the core functionality.

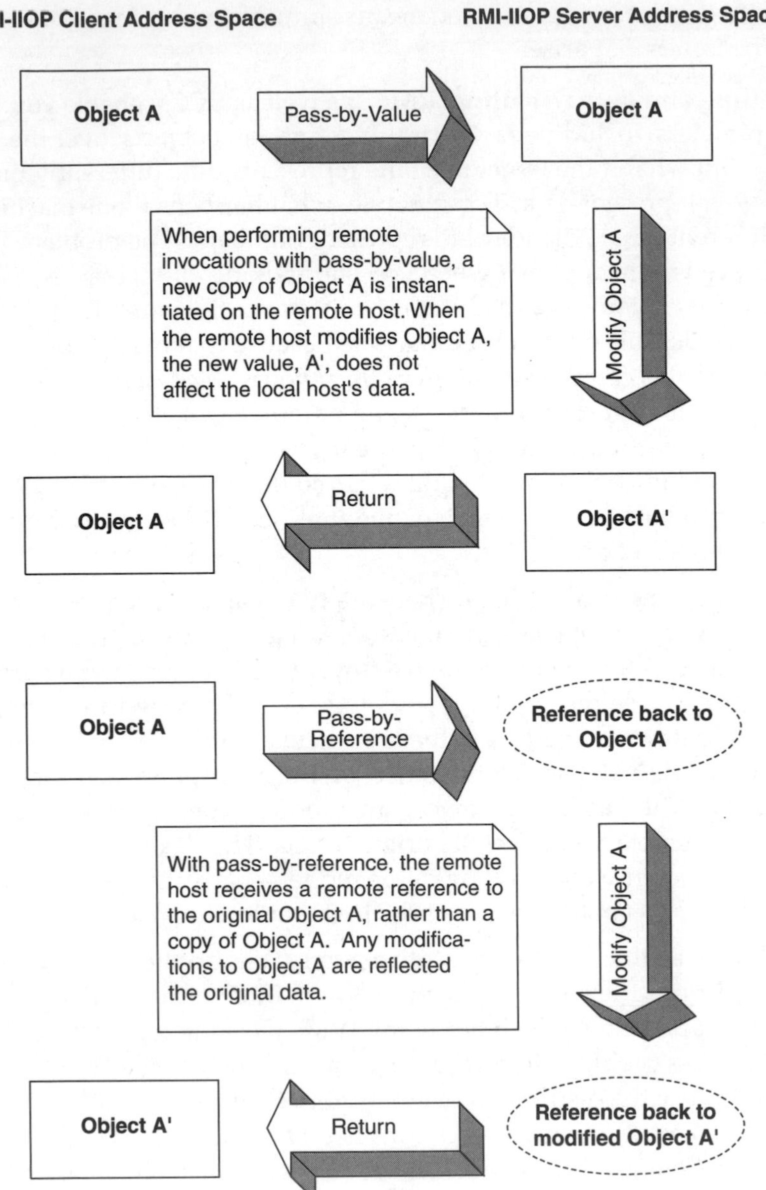
RMI-IIOP Client Address Space
RMI-IIOP Server Address Space
Object A
Pass-by-Value
Object A
When performing remote invocations with pass-by-value, a new copy of Object A is instantiated on the remote host. When the remote host modifies Object A, the new value, A', does not affect the local host's data.
Modify Object A
Object A
Return
Object A'
Object A
Pass-by-Reference
Reference back to Object A
With pass-by-reference, the remote host receives a remote reference to the original Object A, rather than a copy of Object A. Any modifications to Object A are reflected the original data.
Modify Object A
Object A'
Return
Reference back to modified Object A'

Figure A.1 Pass-by-value versus pass-by-reference.

J2EE-compliant servers are required to ship RMI-IIOP implementations to enable you to perform networking. Your RMI-IIOP code is then portable to any hardware or operating system on which these implementations execute. Contrast this with proprietary, platform-dependent RPC libraries, and you can see some real value in RMI-IIOP.

The Remote Interface

We begin our exploration of RMI-IIOP by reviewing one of object-oriented design's great programming practices—the separation of the interface of code from its implementation.

- **The interface** defines the exposed information about an object, such as the names of its methods and what parameters those methods take. It's what the client works with. The interface masks the implementation from the viewpoint of clients of the object, so clients deal only with the end result: the methods the object exposes.
- **The implementation** is the core programming logic that an object provides. It has some very specific algorithms, logic, and data.

By separating interface from implementation, you can vary an object's proprietary logic without changing any client code. For example, you can plug in a different algorithm that performs the same task more efficiently.

RMI-IIOP makes extensive use of this concept. All networking code you write is applied to interfaces, *not* implementations. In fact, you *must* use this paradigm in RMI-IIOP—you do not have a choice. It is impossible to perform a remote invocation directly on an object implementation. You can operate solely on the interface to that object's class.

Therefore, when using RMI-IIOP, you must build a custom interface, called a *remote interface*. This remote interface *extends* the interface *java.rmi.Remote*. Your interface provides all methods that your remote object exposes.

We'll now begin to build a simple example illustrating the basics of RMI-IIOP. In this example, a remote object exposes one method: *generate(). generate()* returns a new, unique long number each time it's called. This is useful, for example, when generating primary keys for data, such as entity beans (discussed in Chapter 6).

Source A.1 is a valid remote interface.

```
import java.rmi.Remote;
import java.rmi.RemoteException;

/**
 * The remote interface for the remote object.  Clients use this
 * remote interface to perform any operations on the remote object.
 */
public interface IPKGenerator extends Remote {
     public long generate() throws RemoteException;
}
```

Source A.1 IPKGenerator.java.

Client code that wants to call methods on your remote object must operate on *IPKGenerator*. Notice that each method must also throw a *java.rmi.RemoteException*. A *RemoteException* is thrown when there is a problem with the network, such as a machine crashing or the network dying.

With RMI-IIOP, you can never fully separate your application from the network. At some point, you'll need to deal with remote exceptions being thrown due to networking issues. Some may consider this a limitation of RMI-IIOP because the network is not entirely transparent: Remote exceptions force you to differentiate a local method from a remote method. But in some ways, this is an advantage of RMI-IIOP as well. Interlacing your code with remote exceptions forces you to think about the network and encourages distributed object developers to consider issues such as the network failing, the size of parameters going across the network, and more.

The Remote Object Implementation

Remote objects are networked object implementations that can be called by another JVM. They *implement* a remote interface and thus expose methods that can be invoked by remote clients.

The physical locations of remote objects and the clients that invoke them are not important. For example, it is possible for a client running in the same address space as a remote object to invoke a method on that object. It's also possible for a client across the Internet to do the same thing. To the remote object, both invocations appear to be the same.

To make your object available as a remote object and allow remote hosts to invoke its methods, your remote class must perform *one* of the following steps:

- **Extend the class *javax.rmi.PortableRemoteObject*.** *PortableRemoteObject* is a base class from which you can derive your remote objects. When your remote object is constructed, it automatically calls the *PortableRemoteObject* constructor, which makes the object available to be called remotely.
- **Manually export your objects as remote objects.** Perhaps your remote object class needs to inherit implementation from another custom class. In this case, because Java does not allow for multiple implementation inheritance, you cannot extend *PortableRemoteObject*. If you do this, you must manually export your object so that it is available to be invoked on by remote hosts. To export your object, call *javax.rmi.PortableRemoteObject.exportObject()*.

Now let's create the remote object class. This class implements the *IPKGenerator* interface, and it is shown in Source A.2.

```
import java.rmi.RemoteException;
import javax.rmi.PortableRemoteObject;

/**
 * The remote object which generates primary keys
 */
public class PKGenerator
     extends PortableRemoteObject
     implements IPKGenerator {

     /*
      * Our remote object's constructor
      */
     public PKGenerator() throws Exception, RemoteException {

          /*
           * Since we extend PortableRemoteObject, the super
           * class will export our remote object here.
           */
          super();
     }

     /*
      * Generates a unique primary key
      */
     public synchronized long generate() throws RemoteException {
          return i++;
     }

     private static long i = System.currentTimeMillis();
}
```

Source A.2 PKGenerator.java.

Extending *javax.rmi.PortableRemoteObject* makes our object available to be called remotely. Once the remote object's constructor is complete, this object is available forever for any virtual machine to invoke on; that is, until someone calls *unexportObject()*.

This primary key generator has its own shortcoming as well: to generate a primary key, someone needs to invoke a remote method, which could be a performance bottleneck.

If you need to generate primary keys in production, see the companion book to this book, Floyd Marinescu's *EJB Design Patterns*, published by John Wiley & Sons.

ISSUES WITH OUR PRIMARY KEY GENERATION ALGORITHM

Our primary key generation algorithm is to simply increment a number each time someone calls our server. This generator overcomes two common challenges when writing an RMI implementation:

- ***Threading.*** **RMI-IIOP allows many clients to connect to a server at once. Thus, our remote object implementation may have many threads running inside of it. But when generating primary keys, we never want to generate a duplicate key because our keys are not unique and thus would not be good candidates to use in a database. Therefore, it is important to have the synchronized block around the** ***generate()*** **method, so that only one client can generate a primary key at a time.**
- ***JVM crashes.*** **We must protect against a JVM crash (or hardware failure). Thus, we initialize our generator to the current time (the number of milliseconds that have elapsed since 1970). This is to ensure that our primary key generator increases monotonically (that is, primary keys are always going up in value) in case of a JVM crash. Note that we haven't considered daylight savings time resulting in duplicate keys. If we were to use this code in production, we would need to account for that.**

Stubs and Skeletons

Now that we've seen the server code, let's look at the architecture for networking in RMI-IIOP. One of the benefits of RMI-IIOP is an almost illusionary, transparent networking. You can invoke methods on remote objects just as you would invoke a method on any other Java object. In fact, RMI-IIOP completely masks whether the object you're invoking on is local or remote. This is called *local/remote transparency*.

Local/remote transparency is not as easy as it sounds. To mask that you're invoking an object residing on a remote host, RMI-IIOP needs some way to simulate a local object that you can invoke on. This local object is called a *stub*. It is responsible for accepting method calls locally and *delegating* those method calls to their actual object implementations, which are possibly located across the network. This effectively makes every remote invocation appear to be a local invocation. You can think of a stub as a placeholder for an object that knows how to look over the network for the real object. Because you invoke methods on local stubs, all the nasty networking issues are hidden.

Stubs are only half of the picture. We'd like the remote objects themselves—the objects that are being invoked from remote hosts—to not worry about networking issues as well. Just as a client invokes methods on a stub that is local to that client, your remote object needs to accept calls from a *skeleton* that is local to that remote object. Skeletons are responsible for receiving calls over the network (perhaps from a stub) and delegating those calls to the remote object implementation (see Figure A.2).

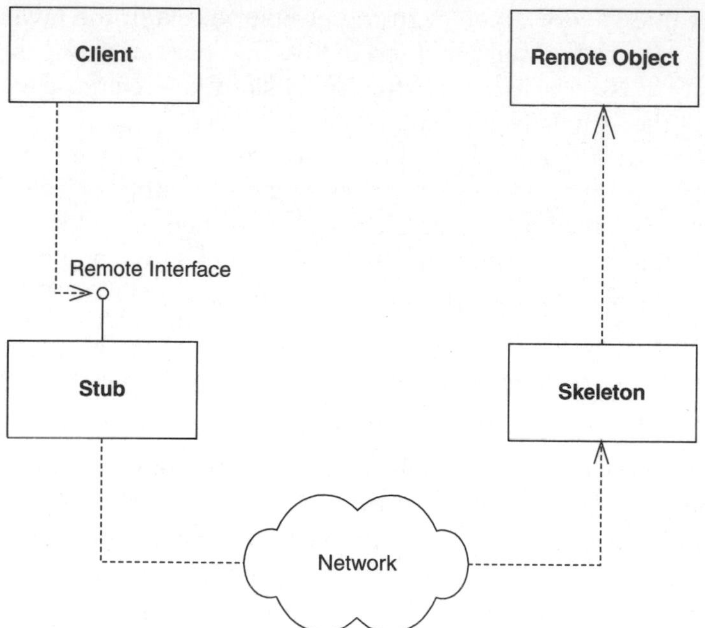

Figure A.2 Stubs and skeletons.

Your RMI-IIOP implementation (that is, your J2EE server) should provide a means to *generate* the needed stubs and skeletons, thus relieving you of the networking burden. Typically, this is achieved through command line tools. For example, the Sun Microsystems J2EE reference implementation ships with a tool called *rmic* (which stands for the RMI compiler) to generate stub and skeleton classes. As you can see from Figure A.2, you should deploy the stub on the client machine and the skeleton on the server machine.

Object Serialization and Parameter Passing

One of the more interesting responsibilities of stubs and skeletons is to handle your parameters. The following section discusses how parameters are passed in Java RMI-IIOP. We also explore the role of *object serialization* in parameter passing.

Passing By Value

When invoking a method using RMI-IIOP, all parameters to the remote method are passed *by value*. This means that when a client calls a server, all parameters are copied from one machine to the other.

Passing objects by value is very different from passing objects in the Java programming language. When you call a method in Java and pass an object as a parameter, that object is passed *by reference*. More specifically, the reference to the object is copied, but the actual object's data is not.

There's a big problem with passing by value. If you're trying to pass an object over the network and that object contains references to other objects, how are those references resolved on the target machine? A memory address on one machine does not map to the same memory address on another machine. Also, the referenced object may not even exist on the target machine. How do we get around this?

Object Serialization

Java introduces the concept of *object serialization* to handle this problem. *Serialization* is the conversion of a Java object into a bit-blob representation of that object. You can send bit-blobs anywhere. For example, you can use object serialization as an instant file format for your objects and save them to your hard disk. RMI-IIOP also uses object serialization to send parameters over the network. When you're ready to use the object again, you must deserialize the bit-blob back into a Java object. Then it's magically usable again.

The Java language handles the low-level details of serialization. In most cases, you don't need to worry about any of it. To tell Java that your object is serializable, your object must implement the *java.lang.Serializable* interface. That's all there is to it: Take this one simple step, and let Java handle the rest. *java.lang.Serializable* defines no methods at all—it's simply a *marker interface* that identifies your object as something that can be serialized and deserialized.

You can provide your own custom serialization by implementing the *writeObject()* method on your object, or provide custom deserialization by implementing *readObject()*. This might be useful if you'd like to perform some sort of compression on your data before your object is converted into a bit-blob and decompression after the bit-blob is restored to an object.

Figure A.3 shows the serialization/deserialization API, where *writeObject()* is responsible for saving the state of the class, and *readObject()* is responsible for restoring the state of the class. These two methods will be called automatically when an object instance is being serialized or deserialized. If you choose not to define these methods, then the default serialization mechanisms will be applied. The default mechanisms are good enough for most situations.

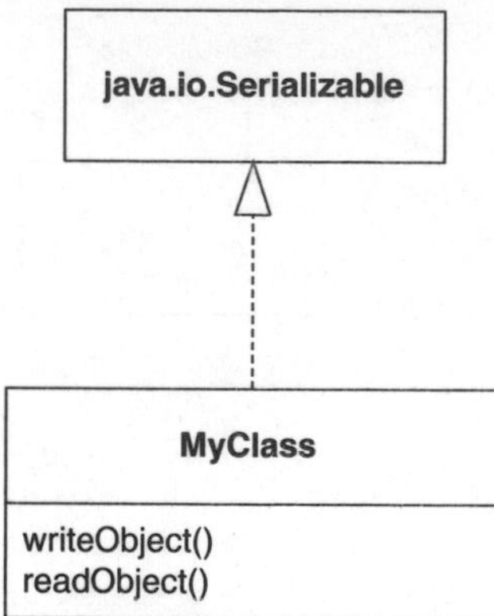

Figure A.3 The Java serialization API.

Rules for Serialization

Java serialization has the following rules for member variables held in serialized objects:

- Any basic primitive type (*int*, *char*, and so on) is serializable and will be serialized with the object, unless marked with the *transient* keyword. If serialized, the values of these types are available again after deserialization.
- Java objects can be included with the serialized bit-blob or not; it's your choice. The way you make your choice is as follows:
  - Objects marked with the *transient* keyword are not serialized with the object and are not available when deserialized.
  - Any object that is not marked with the *transient* keyword must implement *java.lang.Serializable*. These objects are converted to the bit-blob format along with the original object. If your Java objects aren't transient and don't implement *java.lang.Serializable*, a *NotSerializable* exception is thrown when *writeObject()* is called.

Thus, when you serialize an object, you also serialize all nontransient subobjects as well. This means you also serialize all nontransient sub-subobjects (the objects referenced from the subobjects). This is repeated recursively for every object until the entire reference graph of objects is serialized. This recursion is handled automatically by Java serialization (see Figure A.4). You simply need to make sure that each of your member objects implements the *java.lang.Serializable* interface. When serializing *MyClass*, object serialization will recurse through the dependencies shown, packaging the entire graph of objects as a stream. In Figure A.4, everything will get serialized except for transient long b, since it is marked as transient.

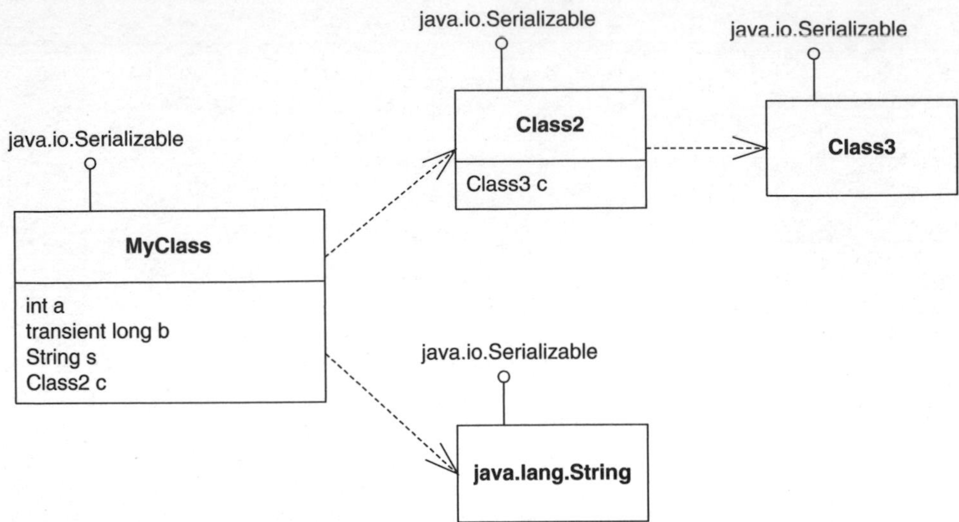

Figure A.4 Object serialization recursion.

What Should You Make Transient?

How do you know which member variables should be marked transient and which should not? Here are some good reasons to mark an object as transient:

- The object is large. Large objects may not be suitable for serialization because operations you do with the serialized blob may be very intensive. Examples here include saving the blob to disk or transporting the blob across the network.
- The object represents a local resource that cannot be reconstructed on the target machine. Some examples of such resources are thread objects, database connections, and sockets.
- The object represents sensitive information that you do not want to pass in a serialized stream.

Note that object serialization is not free—it is a heavyweight operation for large graphs of objects. Make sure you take this into account when designing your distributed object application.

Object Serialization and RMI-IIOP

Java RMI-IIOP relies on object serialization for passing parameters via remote method invocations. Figure A.5 shows what the *MyObject* object graph could look like. Notice that every field and subfield is a valid type for Java serialization.

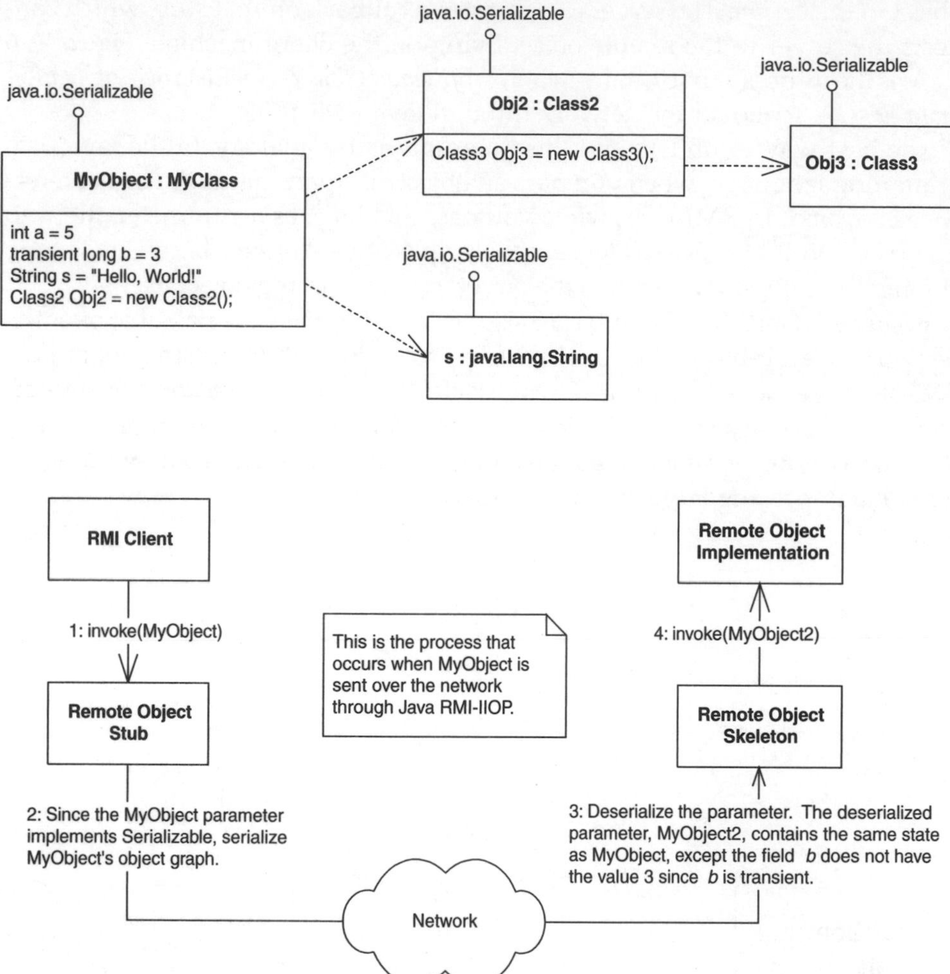

Figure A.5 Java RMI-IIOP and object serialization.

Figure A.5 shows how RMI-IIOP handles pass-by-value, where an entire graph of objects is serialized into a bit-blob, sent across the network, and then deserialized on the target machine. But passing parameters by value can lead to inefficiencies. What if your referenced graph of objects is very large? What if you have lots of state to send across the network? The ensuing network lag from performing the invocation may be unacceptable.

There is another way to pass arguments. RMI-IIOP *simulates* a pass-by-reference convention, which means the arguments are not copied over. Rather, the server modifies the client's copy of the parameter.

If you want to pass a parameter by reference, the parameter must itself be a remote object. The parameter is thus an object that is callable remotely. When the client calls the server, the RMI-IIOP runtime sends a stub to that remote object to the server. The server can perform a callback on that stub, which connects the server to the remote object living on the client machine. Figure A.6 shows the process that occurs when *MyRemoteObject*, an instance of *MyRemoteClass*, is sent over the network through Java RMI-IIOP.

The best way to understand this paradigm is by analogy. In the Java programming language, when you pass an object as a parameter, the object reference is copied. In RMI-IIOP, when you pass an object as a parameter, the stub is copied. Both of these strategies achieve pass-by-reference because they are cloning the thing that points to the object, rather than the object itself.

Because Java RMI-IIOP stubs are also serializable, they are passable over the network as a bit-blob. This is why earlier we said that *all* parameters in Java RMI-IIOP are passed by value. Thus, Java RMI-IIOP only *simulates* pass-by-reference by passing a serializable stub, rather than serializing the original object. By making your parameters remote objects, you can effectively avoid the network lag in passing large objects.

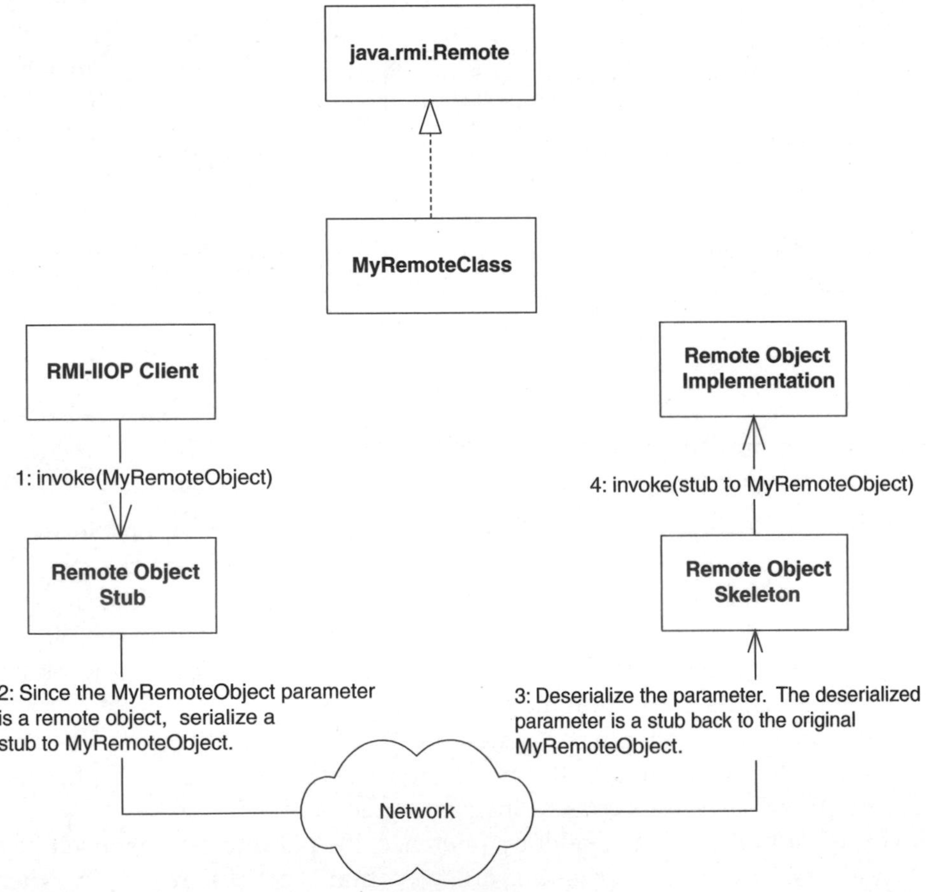

Figure A.6 Pass-by-reference with Java RMI-IIOP.

In summary, we have the following rules for passing objects using Java RMI-IIOP:

- All Java basic primitives are passed by value when calling methods remotely. This means copies are made of the parameters. Any changes to the data on the remote host are not reflected in the original data.
- If you want to pass an object over the network by value, it must implement *java.lang.Serializable*. Anything referenced from within that object must follow the rules for Java serialization. Again, any changes to the data on the remote host are not reflected in the original data.
- If you want to pass an object over the network by-reference, it must be a remote object, and it must implement *java.rmi.Remote*. A stub for the remote object is serialized and passed to the remote host. The remote host can then use that stub to invoke callbacks on your remote object. There is only one copy of the object at any time, which means that all hosts are calling the same object.

Now that you understand parameter passing, let's move on. For us to complete our RMI-IIOP sample application, we need some way to publish the server and have the client locate that server. This process, called *bootstrapping*, is achieved via the JNDI. Let's put our RMI-IIOP example on hold while we learn about JNDI. We'll return later to complete the example.

The Java Naming and Directory Interface

The Java Naming and Directory Interface (JNDI) is a J2EE API that provides a standard interface for locating users, machines, networks, objects, and services by name. For example, you can use JNDI to locate a printer on your corporate intranet. You can also use it to locate a Java object or connect with a database. JNDI is used in EJB, RMI-IIOP, JDBC, and more. It is the standard J2EE way of looking up things by name over the network.

Naming and Directory Services

To understand JNDI, we must first understand the concept of naming and directory services.

A *name* is like a reference in that it denotes an entity, for example an object or a person. The name is not the same as the referenced thing and has no meaning by itself ("What's in a name?"). Names are often preferred over other kinds of references because they are easier to use and remember than unwieldy references like phone numbers, SSNs, IP addresses, or remote object references.

A *naming service* is analogous to a telephone operator. When you want to call someone over the phone and you don't know that person's phone number, you can call your telephone company's information service operator to *look up* the person you want to talk with. You supply the telephone operator with the name of the person. The operator then looks up the phone number of the person you want to speak with and returns it to you. (The operator can even dial the number for you, connecting you to that person, but that is beyond what a pure naming service will do for you.)

A naming service is an entity that performs the following tasks:

- It associates names with objects. We call this *binding* names to objects. This is similar to a telephone company's associating a person's name with a specific residence's telephone number.
- It provides a facility to find an object based on a name. We call this looking up an object, or resolving a name. This is similar to a telephone operator finding a person's telephone number based on that person's name.

Naming services are everywhere in computing. When you want to locate a machine on the network, the *Domain Name System (DNS)* is used to translate a machine name to an IP address. If you look up www.wiley.com on the Internet, the name www.wiley.com is translated into the object (which happens to be a String) *208.215.179.146* by the DNS.

Another example of naming occurs in file systems. When you access a file on your hard disk, you supply a name for the file such as c:\autoexec.bat or /etc/fstab. How is this name translated into an actual file of data? A file system naming service can be consulted to provide this functionality.

In general, a naming service can be used to find any kind of generic object by name, like a file handle on your hard drive or a printer located across the network. But one type of object is of particular importance: a *directory object* (or *directory entry*). A directory object differs from a generic object because you can store *attributes* with directory objects. These attributes can be used for a wide variety of purposes.

For example, you can use a directory object to represent a user in your company. You can store information about that user, like the user's password, as attributes in the directory object. If you have an application that requires authentication, you can store a user's login name and password in directory object attributes. When a client connects to your application, the client supplies a login name and password, which you can compare with the login name and password that are stored as a directory object's attributes. If the data matches, the user is authenticated. If the data doesn't match, your application can return an error. You can store other attributes besides a login name and password, including a user's e-mail address, phone number, and postal address.

A *directory service* is a naming service that has been extended and enhanced to provide directory object operations for manipulating attributes. A directory is a system of directory objects that are all connected. Some examples of directory products are Netscape Directory Server and Microsoft Active Directory. Your company probably uses a directory to store internal company information (locations of computers, current printer status, personnel data, and so on).

What does a directory look like internally? The directory's contents—the set of connected directory objects—usually forms a hierarchical tree-like structure. Why would you want a tree-like structure? A tree's form suggests the way a real-world company is organized. For example, the *root* (or top node) of your directory tree can represent your entire company. One branch off the root could represent people in the company, while another branch could represent network services. Each branch could have subtrees that decrease in granularity more and more, until you are at individual user objects, printer objects, machine objects, and the like. This is illustrated in Figure A.7.

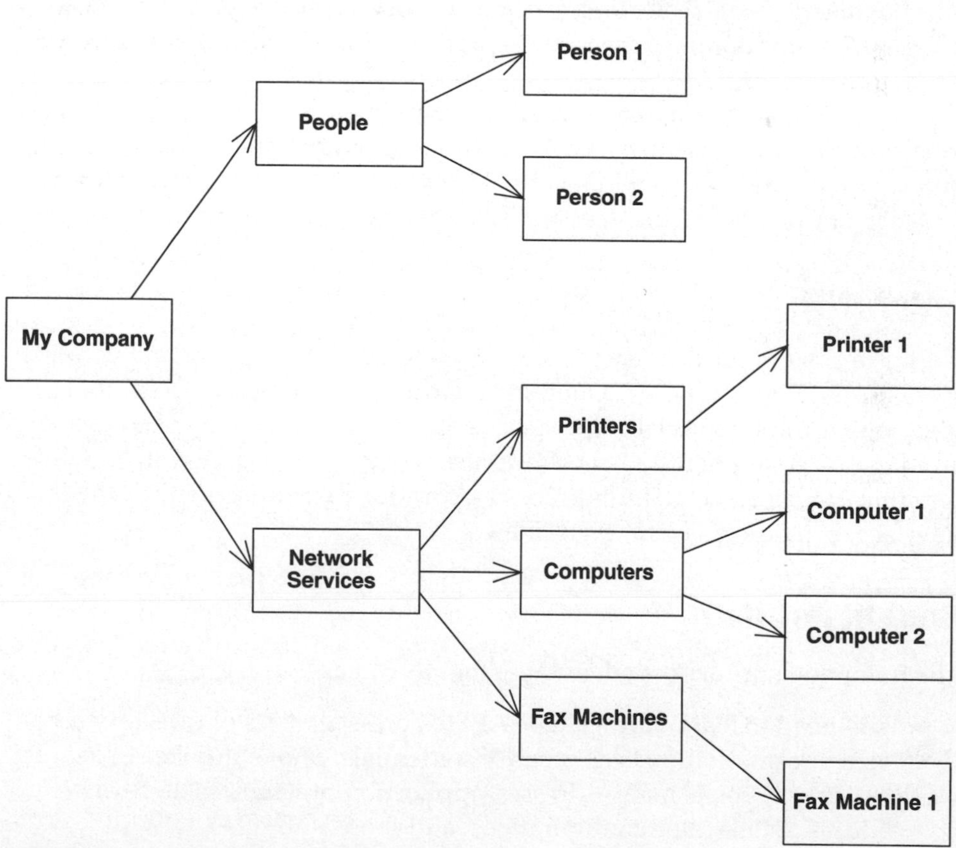

Figure A.7 A hierarchical directory structure.

All in all, directories are not very different from databases. A database can store arbitrary data, just like a directory can. Databases provide query operations to look up items in a database, just like directories do. You can think of a directory as a scaled-down, simplified database. In fact, most directories are implemented by a database behind the scenes.

Problems with Naming and Directories

There are many popular naming and directory products out today. Directory vendors differentiate their product lines by offering different types of services. Unfortunately, this leads to different naming and directory standards. And each directory standard has a different protocol for accessing the directory. For example, directories based on the *Lightweight Directory Access Protocol* (LDAP) are accessed differently than those based on the *Network Information System* (NIS) or Novell's *Network Directory System* (NDS).

This means that if you want to switch directory vendors, you need to rewrite all your client code that accesses the directory. It also means you need to download a new library, learn a new API, and test new code each time you use a different directory.

Initially, LDAP was meant to resolve this problem by becoming *the* ubiquitous protocol for directories. LDAP is straightforward and is being adopted quickly by the industry—IBM's Lotus Notes and Microsoft's Active Directory both are LDAP-based. However, not all directory products are LDAP-based.

Enter JNDI

JNDI is a system for Java-based clients to interact with naming and directory systems. JNDI is a *bridge* over naming and directory services, a beast that provides one common interface to disparate directories. Users who need to access an LDAP directory use the same API as users who want to access an NIS directory or a Novell directory. All directory operations are done through the JNDI interface, providing a common framework.

Benefits of JNDI

The following surveys the advantages that JNDI has to offer:

- You need to learn only a single API to access all sorts of directory service information, such as security credentials, phone numbers, electronic and postal mail addresses, application preferences, network addresses, machine configurations, and more.
- JNDI insulates the application from protocol and implementation details.

- You can use JNDI to read and write whole Java objects from directories.
- You can link different types of directories, such as an LDAP directory with an NDS directory, and have the combination appear to be one large, federated directory. The federated directory appears to the client to be one contiguous directory.

In J2EE, you can use JNDI for many purposes. These include:

- Using JNDI to acquire a reference to the *Java Transaction API* (JTA) *UserTransaction* interface
- Using JNDI to connect to resource factories, such as JDBC drivers or Java Message Service (JMS) drivers
- Using JNDI for beans to look up other beans

See Chapters 10 and 11 for examples of achieving these operations.

The JNDI Architecture

JNDI is made up of two halves: *the client API* and the *Service Provider Interface* (SPI). The client API allows your Java code to perform directory operations. This API is uniform for all types of directories. You will spend the most time using the client API.

The JNDI SPI is a framework for JNDI implementors: an interface to which naming and directory service vendors can plug in. The SPI is the converse of the API: While the API allows clients to code to a single, unified interface, the SPI allows naming and directory service vendors to fit their particular proprietary protocols into the system, as shown in Figure A.8. This allows for client code to leverage proprietary naming and directory services in Java while maintaining a high level of code portability.

The JNDI architecture is somewhat like the Java Database Connectivity (JDBC) package:

- In JDBC, one uniform client API performs database operations. In JNDI, naming and directory service clients invoke a unified API for performing naming and directory operations.
- In JDBC, relational database vendors provide JDBC drivers to access their particular databases. In JNDI, directory vendors provide *service providers* to access their specific directories. These providers are aware of specific directory protocols, and they plug in to the JNDI SPI.

For example, Sun Microsystems gives away an LDAP service provider for free. The LDAP service provider knows how to map a JNDI client API operation into an LDAP operation. It then executes the LDAP operation on an LDAP directory, using the specific LDAP protocol.

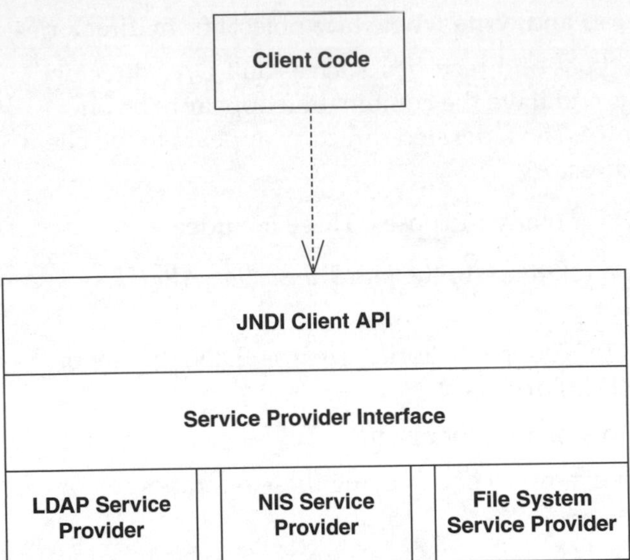

Figure A.8 The JNDI architecture.

A number of JNDI service providers are available today, including LDAP, NIS, Novell NDS, SLP, CORBA Naming Service, File System, RMI-IIOP, and many more. The JNDI homepage (http://java.sun.com/products/jndi) has a list of service providers.

J2EE servers *bundle* a JNDI implementation with their product. Typically this is a custom implementation provided by the J2EE server vendor. JNDI then just becomes another service provided by the server, along with RMI-IIOP, JMS, and so on. Many servers ship JNDI implementations that are fault tolerant, providing a high level of availability. These JNDI implementations are intended to integrate with the other J2EE services, such as RMI-IIOP, JDBC, EJB, and JMS.

JNDI Concepts

We begin our JNDI exploration with naming concepts. There are several kinds of names in JNDI:

- An *atomic name* is a simple, basic, indivisible name. For example, in the string */etc/fstab*, *etc* and *fstab* are atomic names.
- A *compound name* is zero or more atomic names put together using a specific syntax. In the previous example, the entire string */etc/fstab* is a compound name formed by combining two atomic names with a slash.

A *binding* is an association of a name with an object. For example, the file name *autoexec.bat* in the Windows file system has a binding to the file data on your hard disk. Your *c:\windows* folder is a name that is bound to a folder on your hard drive. Note that a compound name such as */usr/people/ed/.cshrc* consists of multiple bindings, one to *usr*, one to *people*, one to *ed*, and one to *.cshrc*.

A *context* is a set of zero or more bindings. Each binding has a distinct atomic name. So for example, in the UNIX file system, let's consider a folder named */etc* that contains files named *mtab* and *exports*. In JNDI, the */etc* folder is a context containing bindings with atomic names *mtab* and *exports*. Each of the *mtab* and *exports* atomic names is bound to a file on the hard disk.

To expand this further, consider a folder named */usr* with subfolders */usr/people*, */usr/bin*, and */usr/local*. Here, the */usr* folder is a context that contains the *people*, *bin*, and *local* atomic names. Each of these atomic names is bound to a subfolder. In JNDI terms, these subfolders are called *subcontexts*. Each subcontext is a full-fledged context in its own right, and it can contain more name-object bindings, such as other files or other folders. Figure A.9 depicts the concepts we have learned so far.

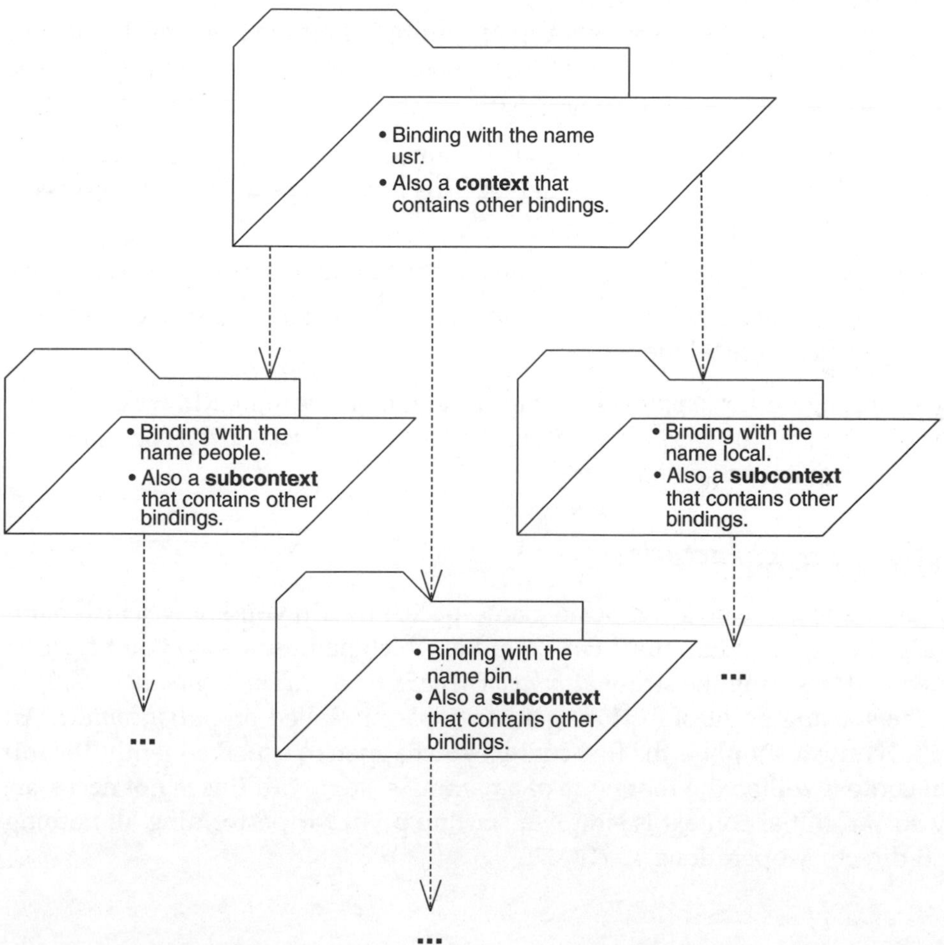

Figure A.9 JNDI naming concepts.

Naming Systems, Namespaces, and Composite Names

A *naming system* is a connected set of contexts that use the same name syntax. For example, a branch of an LDAP tree could be considered a naming system, as could a folder tree in a file system. Unfortunately, naming systems each have a different syntax for accessing contexts. For example, in an LDAP tree, a compound name is identified by a string such as cn=Ed Roman, ou=People, o=Middleware-Company.com, c=us, whereas a file system compound name might look like *c:\java\lib\tools.jar*.

A *namespace* is the set of names contained within a naming system. Your hard drive's entire collection of file names and directories or folders is your hard drive file system's namespace. The set of all names in an LDAP directory's tree is an LDAP server's namespace. Naming systems and namespaces are shown in Figure A.10. This branch of a hard disk is an example of a naming system because it's a connected set of contexts. Within this naming system, the namespace is every name shown.

A *composite name* is a name that spans multiple naming systems. For example, on the Web, the URL http://java.sun.com/products/ejb/index.html is composed of the following namespaces:

- *http* comes from the *URL scheme-id* namespace. You can use other scheme-ids, such as ftp and telnet. This namespace defines the protocol you use to communicate.
- *java.sun.com* uses the DNS to translate machine names into IP addresses.
- *products, ejb,* and *index.html* are from the file system namespace on the Web server machine.

By linking multiple naming systems as in the preceding URL, we can arrive at a unified *composite namespace* (also called a *federated namespace*) containing all the bindings of each naming system.

Initial Context Factories

If you are to traverse a composite namespace, how do you know which naming system to look into first? For example, which namespace do you first look in when traversing the string *http://www.TheServerSide.com/events/index.jsp*?

The starting point of exploring a namespace is called an *initial context*. An initial context simply is the first context you happen to use. Frequently, the initial context will be the root node of a naming system, but this is not necessarily so. An initial context is simply a starting point for performing all naming and directory operations.

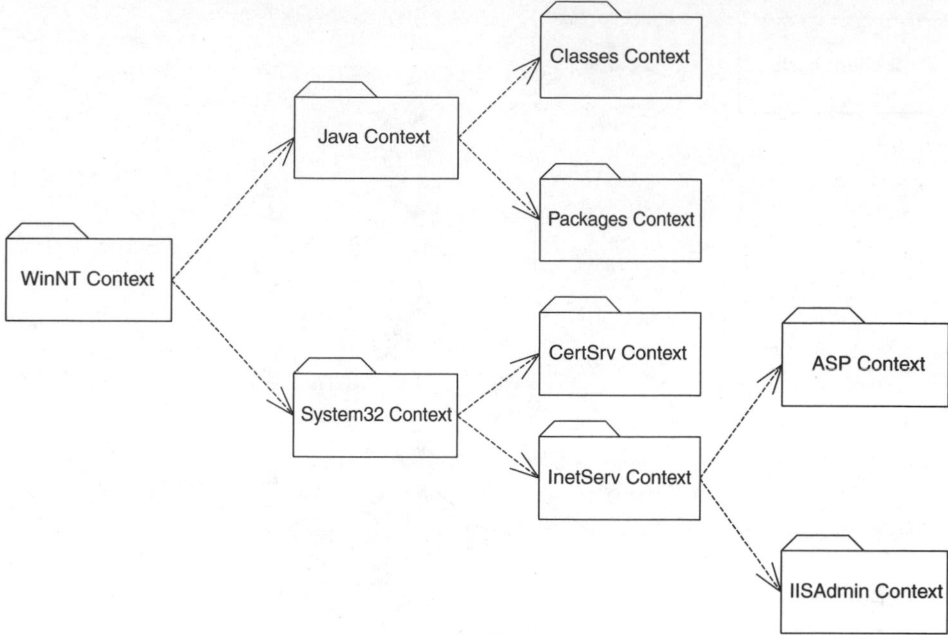

Figure A.10 Naming systems and namespaces.

To acquire an initial context in JNDI, you use an *initial context factory*. An initial context factory is responsible for churning out initial contexts and is implemented by your JNDI driver. For example, there is an LDAP initial context factory, as well as a file system initial context factory. These initial context factories know the specific semantics of a particular directory structure. They know how to acquire an arbitrary context that you can use as an initial starting context for traversing a directory structure.

When you acquire an initial context, you must supply the necessary information for JNDI to acquire that initial context. For example, if you're trying to access a JNDI implementation that runs within a J2EE server, you might supply:

- The IP address of the J2EE server
- The port number that the J2EE server accepts requests on
- The starting location within the JNDI tree
- Any user name and password combination necessary to use the J2EE server

You could use this same paradigm to access an LDAP server—just substitute *LDAP server* for *J2EE server* in the preceding list.

Initial contexts and composite namespaces are illustrated in Figure A.11.

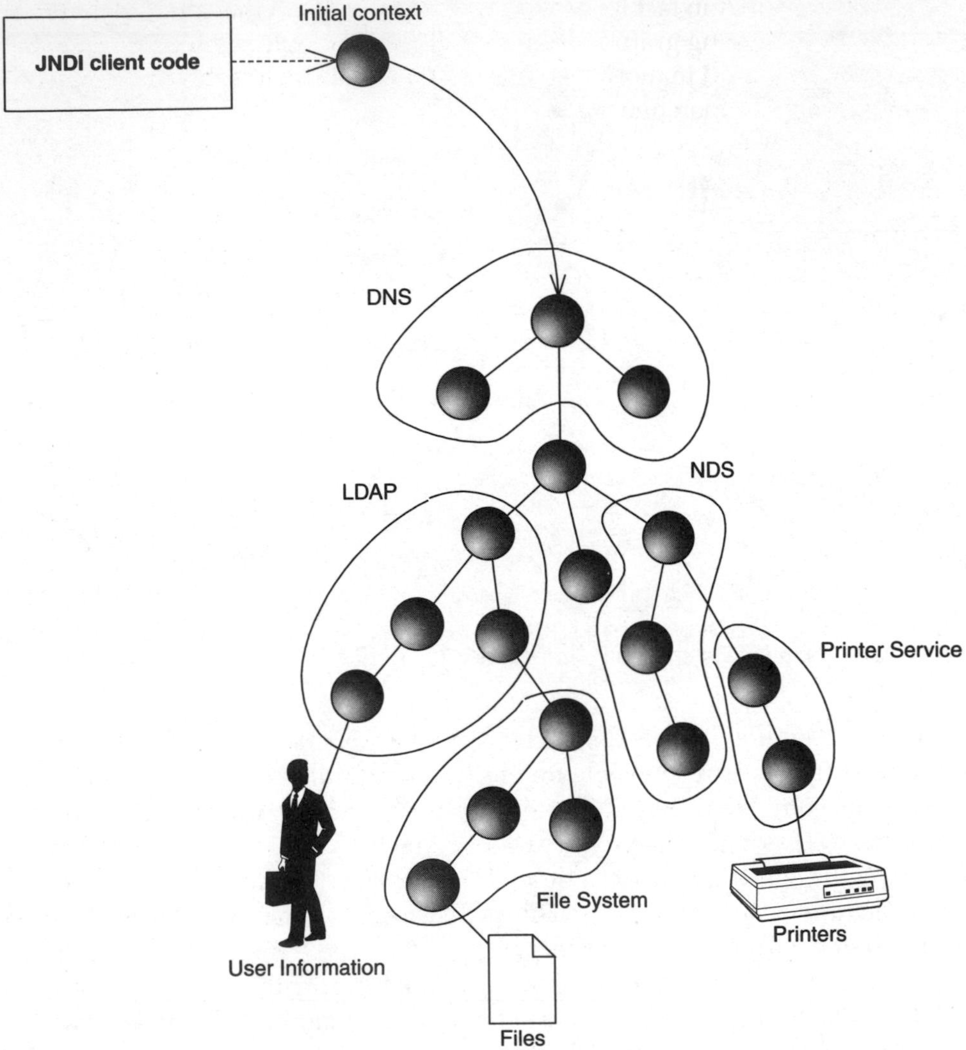

Figure A.11 A federated namespace with an initial context.

A quick performance tip for you: some J2EE servers take a long time to create an initial context. If this is the case, we strongly recommend caching an initial context for future use. Create it once, and then reuse it when needed later.

The naming contexts and subcontexts in Figure A.11 form a directed graph that you can navigate. In the figure as in most practical scenarios, these naming graphs are acyclic, but this is not required. An example of a cycle in a naming graph is a symbolic link in a subdirectory of the UNIX file system that links to a directory closer to the root. JNDI naming graphs are often referred to as

JNDI trees. Note that in fact there is no restriction in JNDI that ensures that the graph is a tree. Naming graphs also need not have a single root node, and subcontexts can be bound in more than one context, so a single subcontext may be known under more than one name.

Programming with JNDI

Now that you've seen the concepts behind JNDI, let's put our theory into concrete use. Source A.3 shows a simple JNDI example.

```
package examples;

public class InitCtx {

     public static void main(String args[]) throws Exception {
       // Form an Initial Context
          javax.naming.Context ctx =
               new javax.naming.InitialContext(System.getProperties());
       System.err.println("Success!");
     }
}
```

Source A.3 InitCtx.java.

The code simply acquires an initial context, and then the program completes. The specific JNDI driver that we use is based on the system properties passed in at the command line. For example, to connect to your file system, you would use the Sun Microsystems *file system* JNDI service provider, which is a driver that connects you to your own hard disk to browse the file system. You would then run the program as follows:

```
java
  -Djava.naming.factory.initial=
     com.sun.jndi.fscontext.RefFSContextFactory
  -Djava.naming.provider.url=file:c:\  examples.InitCtx
```

The *java.naming.factory.initial* parameter identifies the class of the JNDI driver. Then we identify the starting point on the file system that we want to begin navigating; specifically, the c:\ folder. This starting point is structured in the form of a Uniform Resource Locator (URL). In JNDI, it is called the *provider URL* because it is a URL that the service provider accepts for bootstrapping.

We can reuse this same code to connect to an LDAP server as follows:

```
java
  -Djava.naming.factory.initial=com.sun.jndi.ldap.LdapCtxFactory
  -Djava.naming.provider.url="ldap://ldap.funet.fi:389/c=fi"
  examples.InitCtx
```

As you can see, this data-driven mechanism of performing JNDI has its advantages. It enables you to avoid recompiling your Java code. It also enables non-Java-savvy users to customize the behavior of your programs without modifying source code, which is important if you ship your products only as *.class* files.

OTHER JNDI OPERATIONS

After acquiring the initial context, you could begin to execute JNDI operations, such as reading or writing data to and from the JNDI tree by using the other API calls available in JNDI. Here is a brief list of available operations that you can call on the context:

- ***list()* retrieves a list of bindings available in the current context. This typically includes names of objects bound in the JNDI graph, as well as subcontexts. In a file system, this might be a list of file names and folder names. If you're connecting to a proprietary J2EE server's JNDI implementation, you might see a list of bound objects as well as subcontexts to which you can navigate.**
- ***lookup()* resolves a name binding in the context, meaning that the operation returns the object bound to a given name in the context. The operation can also be used to move from one context to another context, such as going from c:\ to c:\ windows. The return type of *lookup()* is JNDI driver specific. For example, if you're looking up RMI-IIOP objects, you would receive a *java.rmi.Remote* object; if you're looking up a file in a file system, you would receive a *java.io.File*.**
- ***rename()* gives a context a new name, such as renaming c:\ temp to c:\ tmp.**
- ***createSubcontext()* creates a subcontext from the current context, such as creating c:\ foo\ bar from the folder c:\ foo.**
- ***destroySubcontext()* destroys a subcontext from the current context, such as destroying c:\ foo\ bar from the folder c:\ foo.**
- ***bind()* creates a new name binding in the current context. As with *lookup()*, JNDI drivers accept different parameters to *bind()*.**
- ***rebind()* is the same operation as bind, except it forces a bind even if there is already something in the JNDI tree with the same name.**

Integrating RMI-IIOP and JNDI

Now that you've seen both RMI-IIOP and JNDI, let's see how to combine them and complete our RMI-IIOP example. There are essentially two uses of JNDI with RMI-IIOP:

- An RMI-IIOP server first binds a reference to one or more of its object in a JNDI context using the JNDI API.
- A client then uses JNDI to look up an RMI-IIOP server.

This process is shown in Figure A.12.

Your JNDI implementation is typically bundled with the J2EE server runtime. Therefore, when you start up your J2EE server, the JNDI service runs in-process to the J2EE server and starts up as well. J2EE servers also ship with a JNDI driver that can connect to that JNDI implementation, which clients call.

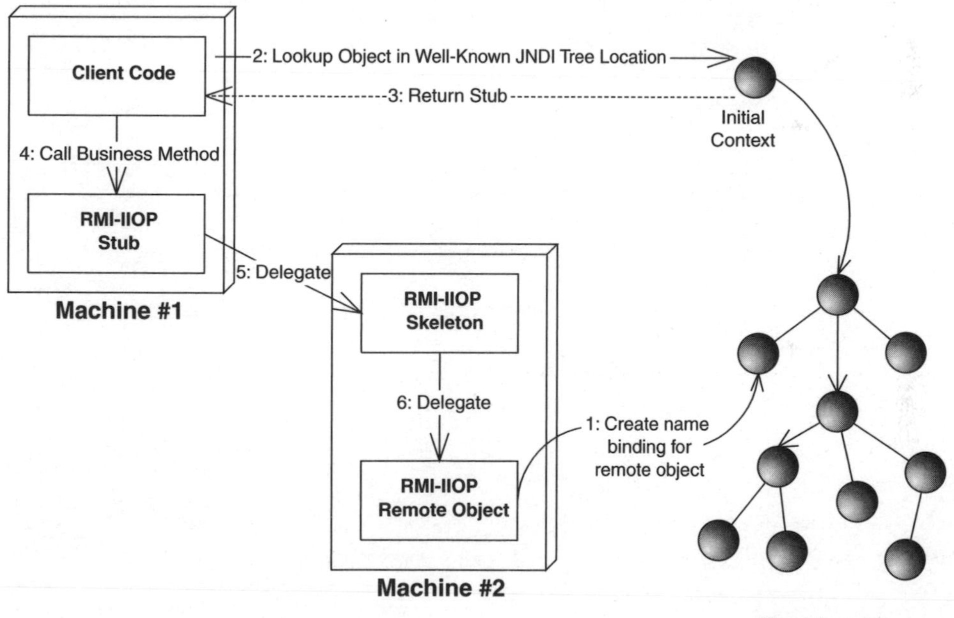

Figure A.12 Bootstrapping with JNDI.

Binding an RMI-IIOP Server to JNDI

The source code for binding the RMI-IIOP server to a JNDI name is in Source A.4.

```
import javax.naming.*;

/**
 * A helper class which starts our RMI-IIOP server
 */
public class Startup {

     /**
      * Our main() method starts things up
      */
     public static void main(String args[]) throws Exception {

          /*
           * Start up our PKGenerator remote object.  It will
           * automatically export itself.
           */
          PKGenerator generator = new PKGenerator();

          /*
           * Bind our PKGenerator remote object to the JNDI tree
           */
          Context ctx = new InitialContext(System.getProperties());
          ctx.rebind("PKGenerator", generator);
          System.out.println("PKGenerator bound to JNDI tree.");

          synchronized (generator) {
            generator.wait();
          }
     }
}
```

Source A.4 Startup.java.

The *Startup* class instantiates a remote object, acquires an initial context, binds the remote object to a name in the context, and then waits for a client to call. It assumes that your J2EE server's JNDI implementation is already up and running. Note that you must supply your J2EE server's JNDI driver initialization parameters via the command line, as we showed earlier in this chapter when we ran our JNDI initial context example. Check your server's documentation or see the book's accompanying source code for this.

Looking up an RMI-IIOP Server with JNDI

Our client code that looks up the RMI-IIOP object via JNDI is shown in Source A.5.

```
import javax.naming.*;
import java.rmi.*;

public class Client {

    public static void main (String[] args) throws Exception {

        // Lookup the remote object via JNDI
        Context ctx = new InitialContext(System.getProperties());
        Object remoteObject = ctx.lookup("PKGenerator");

        // Cast the remote object, RMI-IIOP style
        IPKGenerator generator = (IPKGenerator)
            javax.rmi.PortableRemoteObject.narrow(
                remoteObject, IPKGenerator.class);

        // Generate a PK by calling the RMI-IIOP stub
        System.err.println(generator.generate());
    }
}
```

Source A.5 Client.java.

Our client code is self-explanatory, with one exception. After looking up our remote object, we perform the operation *javax.rmi.PortableRemoteObject.narrow()*. This is a static method on an RMI-IIOP class called *PortableRemoteObject*. This method casts the generic object that we looked up via JNDI to our RMI-IIOP interface type. This *narrow()* operation is required whenever you look up an RMI-IIOP object via JNDI. Why do we need it, and why don't we just cast it using a regular Java cast? The short answer is CORBA interoperability. And if you're *really* curious, the long answer is in Appendix B.

As with the server, to run the client, you must supply your J2EE server's JNDI driver initialization parameters via the command line, as we showed earlier in this chapter when we ran our JNDI initial context example. Check your server's documentation or see the book's accompanying source code for this.

Summary

In this appendix, we've discussed how Java RMI-IIOP and JNDI are fundamental underlying technologies in an EJB deployment. We looked at the RMI-IIOP architecture, comparing it to traditional RPCs. We examined stubs and skeletons, parameter passing, and object serialization. We concluded our RMI-IIOP discussion by introducing a sample primary key generator RMI-IIOP server.

Next, we delved into JNDI. We looked at the basics of naming and directory concepts, and saw how to acquire an initial context. We then investigated how to bind and look up an RMI-IIOP object using JNDI.

In the next appendix, we'll delve into RMI-IIOP at a deeper level, by examining how it can be used for CORBA interoperability. This topic is important for anyone who has existing CORBA systems, or existing systems written in other languages that they'd like to bridge into their EJB system.

APPENDIX

B

CORBA Interoperability

EJB would not be complete without a way to integrate with CORBA. CORBA enables EJB applications to communicate with existing CORBA applications, as well as to integrate with existing investments written in non-Java languages, such as C11 and COBOL. Indeed, CORBA and EJB are related—many of the concepts in Java 2 Platform, Enterprise Edition came from CORBA.

In this appendix, we'll learn the high-level concepts behind CORBA. We'll then see how J2EE can integrate with CORBA via RMI-IIOP. Finally, we'll look at how to use CORBA clients to access EJB systems.

What Is CORBA?

The *Common Object Request Broker Architecture* (CORBA) is a unifying standard for writing distributed object systems. The standard is completely neutral with respect to platform, language, and vendor. CORBA incorporates a host of technologies and is very broad in scope.

The Object Management Group (OMG), a consortium of companies that began in 1989, invented CORBA. CORBA itself is simply a standard, just like EJB. CORBA-compliant products implement the CORBA specification, just as EJB-compliant servers implement the EJB specification.

As one of the key parts of the CORBA specification, the OMG has defined a protocol called *Internet Inter-ORB Protocol* (IIOP, pronounced "eye-op"). IIOP is the standard Internet protocol for CORBA. You never see IIOP directly in your applications; it is used behind the scenes for distributed object communications.

CORBA as the Basis for EJB

Many of the concepts in EJB came out of CORBA. In a sense, you can think of EJB as CORBA with a new hat. EJB and J2EE bring a Java-centric, component-based approach to traditional middleware programming—an architecture suitable for rapid application development. CORBA, on the other hand, offers a much broader suite of middleware features to work with. This includes a time service, a distributed locking service, a relationship service, a notification service, and more. Moreover, CORBA has a large number of domain-specific specifications, for example, in the telecommunications or health care sector. The primary advantage of EJB over CORBA is that EJB has more industry momentum; indeed, the very middleware vendors who offered CORBA implementations in the past are now focused on their EJB implementations.

Just like EJB, CORBA was jointly developed by a large group of companies. This prevents CORBA from becoming a standard that's specific to one product or architecture (in the way that Microsoft .NET, for example, is specific to Windows).

Why Should I Care about CORBA?

Why would you want to use CORBA? There are several reasons:

- **You can use CORBA for legacy integration.** If you have an existing investment, such as a legacy banking application, you can leverage that investment today using CORBA. For example, let's say you have a banking application written in COBOL or C++. CORBA gives you the ability to preserve and reuse it. You can wrap your existing investment as a CORBA object, allowing it to be called from any application. As we'll find out, CORBA is a language-neutral standard and allows code written in several languages to communicate. Thus, CORBA is an ideal platform for code written in different languages to cooperate.
- **CORBA allows for advanced middleware development.** Remember that EJB is not supposed to be an end-all to every problem. But if there is a middleware service that can be generalized, you're likely to find it standardized as a CORBA service. For those who need it, CORBA gives great functionality.

- **CORBA has a large installed basis of mission-critical systems.** Especially in the banking and telecommunications industries, you are likely to find large installations of CORBA applications, some in highly critical, real-time operation scenarios. While CORBA is no longer receiving much interest in developer magazines, the installed basis of (and the market for) CORBA systems is still growing while you are reading these lines.
- **CORBA and EJB have hooks connecting them.** Some EJB products will allow your enterprise beans to be called from two different kinds of clients: clients written to use the J2EE suite of APIs and clients written to use CORBA APIs. This means that code written in C11 or Smalltalk can call your enterprise beans.

Drawbacks of CORBA

As usual, the world isn't perfect. Using CORBA has disadvantages as well as advantages:

- **CORBA is slow-moving.** All standards committees are bureaucratic and slow to make decisions. This is because the standards committee itself is not driven by revenues, but rather by individual interests from participating companies. CORBA experiences benefits from not being owned by one company, but its openness is also a drawback. The cycle time for the OMG to adopt a new CORBA feature is on the order of years.
- **CORBA has a steep learning curve.** As CORBA has evolved over the years, it has undergone *feature creep.* More and more features have been added, which makes CORBA a robust standard but also increases the learning curve. Indeed, the specifications that define the whole of CORBA are thousands of pages long and are quite challenging to master. The nice thing about CORBA is that you don't have to learn it all to use it—you can learn optional CORBA *services* as you need them.
- **Products developed under CORBA may have incompatible features.** It's great that CORBA is a unifying standard. Because no single company controls the standard, it levels the playing field for companies competing to build CORBA products. But there remain the problems of multivendor solutions. As with EJB products, if you mix and match CORBA products, you will inevitably run into assumptions that vendors have made but that are specific to their own products. This is the tradeoff between a one-vendor solution, such as Microsoft, and an open standard, such as CORBA or EJB. The price of freedom is eternal vigilance.

Understanding How CORBA Works

Before we delve into CORBA/EJB interoperability, we'll cover the core CORBA fundamental concepts. This will lay the groundwork for us to discuss how CORBA and EJB are compatible.

Object Request Brokers

An *Object Request Broker* (ORB) facilitates network communication. ORBs enable disparate applications to communicate without being aware of the underlying communications mechanism. They are responsible for finding objects to service method calls, handling parameter passing, and returning results. Whenever you have multiple objects interacting in a CORBA environment, ORBs facilitate the communications. This is shown in Figure B.1.

Numerous commercial and Open Source CORBA ORBs for different platforms and programming languages are available on the market. Some examples are Iona Orbix, Borland VisiBroker, and the Open Source ORBs TAO and JacORB. Each vendor offers various qualities of service that differentiate that vendor's product from those of other vendors in the marketplace.

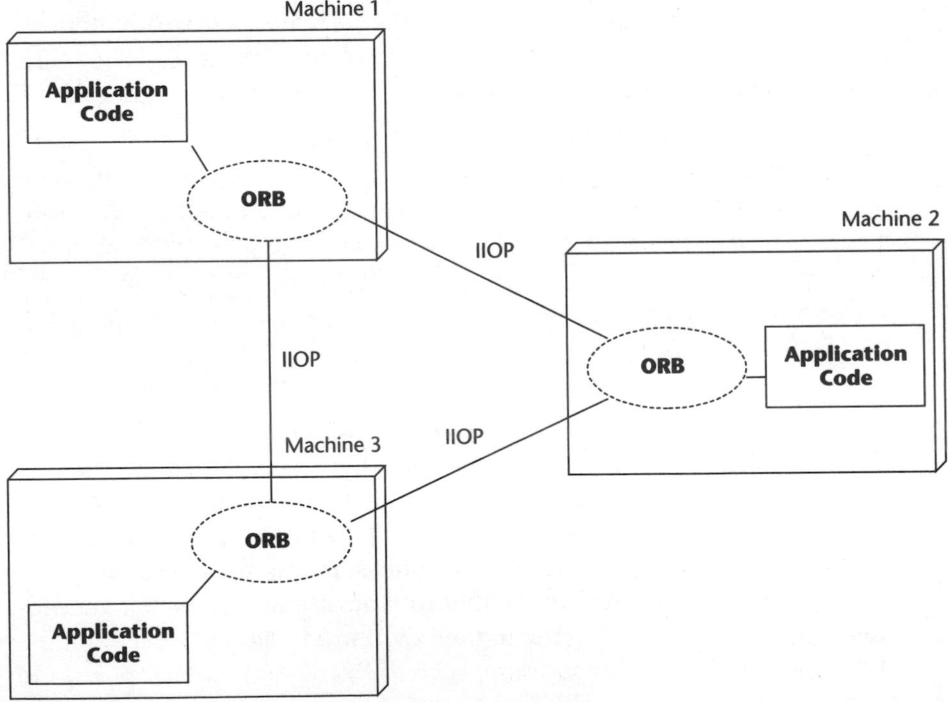

Figure B.1 The ORB facilitates your networking needs.

The concept of an ORB is not specific to CORBA. J2EE implementations and Microsoft .NET contain ORB functionality as well because both architectures facilitate network communications and hence, serve as object request brokers. For the rest of this chapter, however, we'll assume we're dealing with CORBA ORBs.

The OMG Interface Definition Language

The cornerstone of CORBA is the OMG *interface definition language* (OMG IDL). OMG IDL is a language that CORBA uses to define the interfaces between clients and the objects they call. When you write a CORBA object implementation, that object implementation must have a corresponding IDL that defines the interface for that object implementation. By programming with OMG IDL, you force a clear distinction between interface and implementation; you can vary your implementation without changing the interface your clients use. The IDL concept is shown in Figure B.2.

Another great benefit to OMG IDL is that it is a *language-neutral* interface for object implementations. You can write your IDL once and then define your object implementations in any language that CORBA supports, such as C++ or Smalltalk. And because IDL is language-neutral, client code that calls your object implementations can be written in any language that CORBA supports as well. Thus, IDL enables you to have a deployment mixing heterogeneous languages.

IDL is also inherently *platform-neutral,* allowing clients and object implementations to be deployed in different platforms. For example, your clients can exist on a Windows box and talk to business objects deployed on a Sun Solaris box.

You should think of IDL as a middleman language—a common ground that in theory is independent of language change. IDL allows you to write a distributed application with the illusion that it's all written in one language.

Here is a sample snippet of IDL:

```
module examples {
     interface HelloWorld {
        string sayHello(in string myName);
     }
}
```

As you can see, IDL is very similar to C++ and Java.

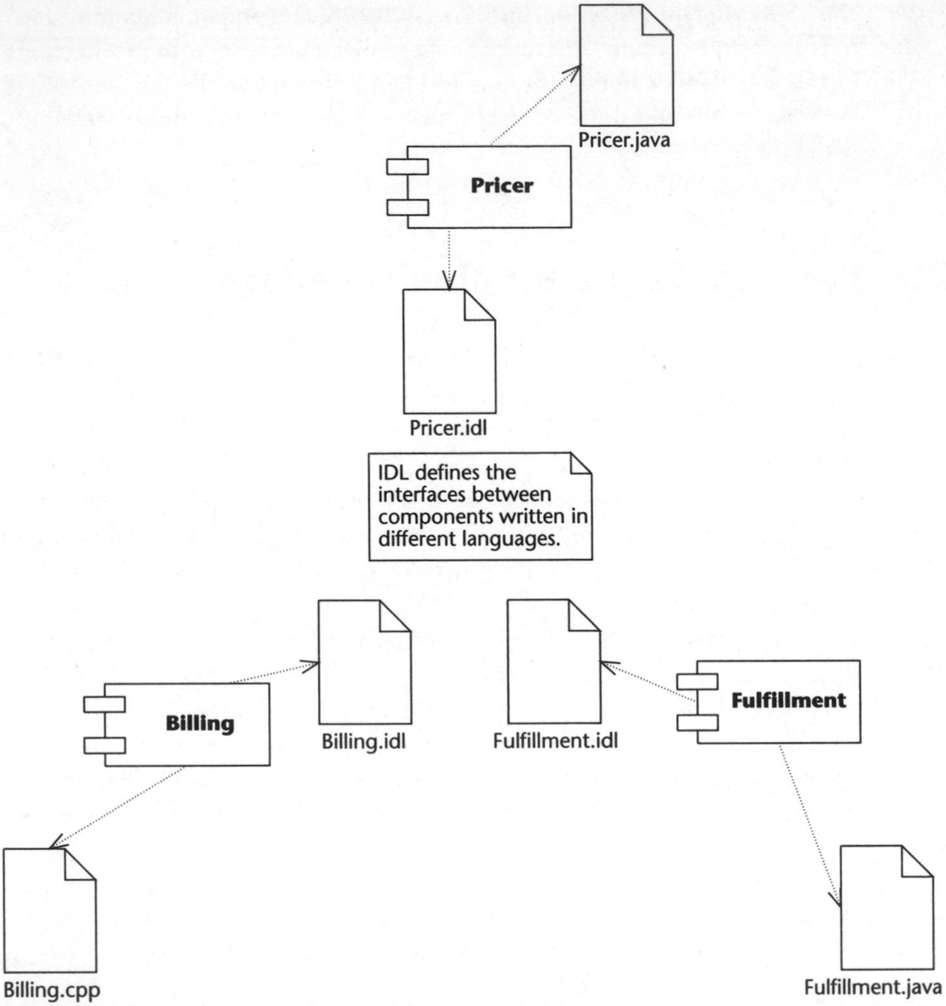

Figure B.2 The interface definition language concept.

There are many different types in IDL, including basic types (such as *short* and *float*) and constructed types (such as *struct* and *enumeration*). You'll find that if you know C++, learning to use OMG IDL is pretty straightforward. If you're a Java programmer, you should not have too much difficulty using IDL to define your object's interfaces either, because Java's syntax is similar to C++.

We only briefly describe IDL in this chapter. Most CORBA books will have a section explaining IDL fully. For more details, see Brose, Vogel, and Duddy, *Java Programming With CORBA* (ISBN 0-471-37681-7). And if you're serious about CORBA, take a look at the specifications on the OMG Web site (www.omg.org), which detail OMG IDL rigorously.

OMG IDL Maps to Concrete Languages

IDL is only a descriptive language in that it describes the interfaces to your objects. You cannot execute IDL. Neither your CORBA object implementations nor your CORBA clients ever see IDL. You program your clients and object implementations in whatever language you're using, such as Java or C++. But how, then, do you refer to CORBA objects? The answer is the OMG IDL *maps* to specific languages, such as Java or C++. If you go to the OMG Web site (www.omg.org), you'll see that there are specifications detailing how OMG IDL maps to various languages. For instance, there is an IDL-to-Java mapping specification that defines how IDL maps to Java. With the IDL-to-Java mapping, the *string* type in OMG IDL maps to the *java.lang.String* object in Java.

It is important to realize that, although IDL is a language, it is more of an abstraction because you never write client code or object implementations that use IDL files. Rather, you use IDL to define the interfaces to your objects and then *map* that IDL into your particular language using an *IDL compiler*. For example, an IDL-to-Java compiler would take as input an IDL file and generate Java interfaces for your object implementations. Once this is done, you can implement those interfaces in Java. You could then map the IDL to a different language, such as C++, by using an IDL-to-C++ compiler. This would allow you to write client code in C++ that calls your Java object implementations.

For the sake of brevity, we do not cover the IDL-to-Java mapping here. You can download the complete IDL-to-Java mapping specification for free from the OMG Web site.

CORBA Static Invocations

As we've mentioned, the ORB facilitates client/server communications, simplifying client networking needs. But how does a client invoke a method on a remote CORBA object? The answer is via a local method call, which gets translated into a remote method call across the network. This is quite analogous to how networking is accomplished in Java RMI.

The conventional way to perform distributed computing in CORBA is to have the client invoke locally on a pregenerated *stub*. The stub is a proxy for the real object implementation, which exists elsewhere on the network. The stub is responsible for going through the client-side ORB runtime, which channels the request over the network via IIOP.

The receiving server-side ORB runtime receives the IIOP request, then calls a *skeleton* to handle the request. The server-side skeleton is a pregenerated file, just like the stub. The skeleton is responsible for delegating the invocation to the actual server-side CORBA object implementation (also called a *servant*) that will service the request. The skeleton is also responsible for coordinating with an *object adapter*. This object adapter performs many tasks, such as mapping object references to servants, activating servants in case they don't exist already, housekeeping of threads, and more. Modern ORB implementations have object adapters coded to the CORBA *Portable Object Adapter* (POA) specification.

The CORBA invocation process is shown in Figure B.3.

Both the stub and skeleton are pregenerated files. They are usually generated from the IDL file that defines the server-side CORBA object's method signatures. This invocation mechanism is called a *static invocation*, because you're statically binding your client code to stubs at compile time. CORBA also provides an alternative invocation mechanism called *dynamic invocation* that does not rely on type-safe, pregenerated stubs. CORBA has a special API, the dynamic invocation interface (DII) that enables programmers to create special request objects, insert parameters, make the invocation, and then extract the results or exceptions. We do not cover dynamic invocations here because it is an untyped, error-prone way to make remote invocations that is usually avoided except for specific applications that must deal with interfaces that are not known at compile time.

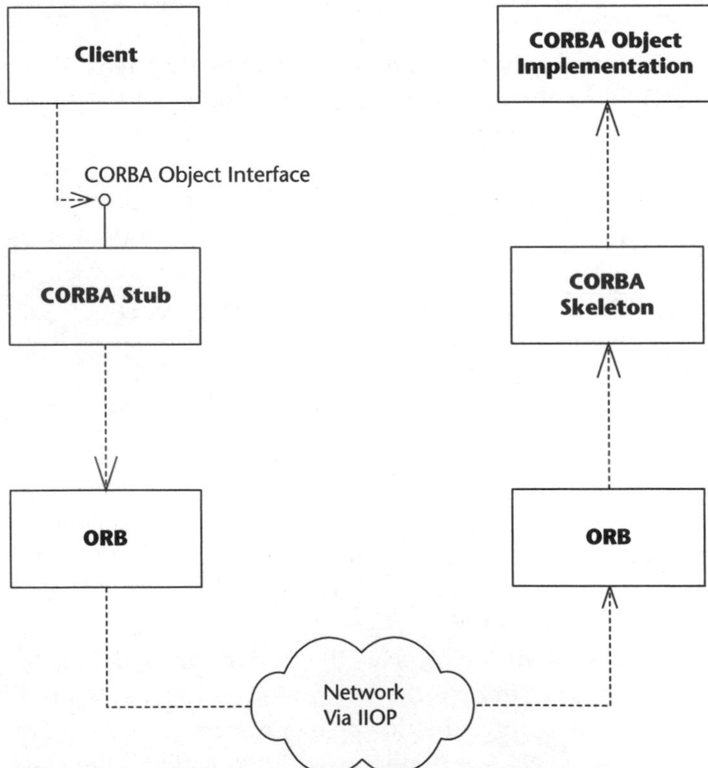

Figure B.3 Calling a method in CORBA.

CORBA's Many Services

In addition to enabling objects to communicate over the network, the OMG has published a set of CORBA Object Services (known as CORBA Services [COS]) that give your networked objects additional capabilities. These services are optionally provided by CORBA vendors. Most serious CORBA products give you one or more services to aid development. These include:

- The *CORBA Naming Service* (COS Naming) is a CORBA service that enables you to look up CORBA objects by name, a technology similar to the Java Naming and Directory Interface (JNDI).
- The CORBA Notification Service allows for asynchronous communications between CORBA objects.
- The CORBA Object Transaction Service (OTS) enables CORBA objects to perform transactions.
- The Concurrency Control Service allows for multiple clients to concurrently interact with a resource.
- The *CORBA Security Service* adds secure functionality to your CORBA system.

A final specification, called *CORBA Component Model (CCM)*, adds component features to CORBA objects, allowing them to function similarly to enterprise beans. This means that CORBA now has a proposal that allows for true components to be developed in the CORBA world. CORBA Components is very similar to Enterprise JavaBeans, although broader in scope and more powerful. You can think of CCM as a superset of EJB. This was done intentionally so that CORBA Components and enterprise beans can reside together. One goal of CORBA Components is to integrate with enterprise beans. Thus, it should be possible to do either of the following:

- Make a CORBA Component appear as though it were an enterprise bean.
- Make an enterprise bean appear as though it were a CORBA Component.

For now, there is very little industry momentum for CORBA Components. This will definitely be an interesting standard to keep an eye on as EJB and CORBA evolve.

The Need for RMI-IIOP

Now that you've seen the basics of CORBA, let's compare Java RMI to CORBA. We'll first discuss why people use RMI and CORBA. Next, we'll explore the semantic differences that must be overcome to merge CORBA and

RMI. Finally, we'll look at how the industry merged RMI and CORBA with RMI-IIOP. This standard is the key to EJB-CORBA compatibility.

The Need for RMI-CORBA Interoperability

RMI and CORBA are similar technologies with slightly different goals. One technology is not better than the other—it all depends on what kind of development you're doing.

CORBA is a robust distributed object standard that allows for language interoperability. RMI, on the other hand, was built for very simple distributed object communications in Java. While RMI does not contain CORBA's cross-language support, it is well-suited for pure Java development due to Java-specific features, such as distributed garbage collection, object activation, and downloadable class files.

While both RMI and CORBA are intended for distributed object communications, neither technology contains high-end middleware services, such as persistence or transactions. CORBA programmers can gain those middleware services by leveraging CORBA's optional services that we described earlier. RMI programmers can gain those middleware services by leveraging the Java 2 Platform, Enterprise Edition suite.

Unfortunately, although RMI and CORBA are similar in nature, they historically have been incompatible technologies. When you program code with Java RMI, you need to write your code to the RMI API. Similarly, when you program code with CORBA, you need to write your code to the CORBA API. This is terrible for code reuse: If you write code in either RMI or CORBA, you'll need to rewrite major pieces of your code if you want to switch networking technologies.

Ideally, we'd like a world where we could perform the following:

- **Combine client-side Java RMI with server-side CORBA.** We should be able to write an object implementation to the CORBA API and write client code to the Java RMI API that calls that CORBA object. This is shown in Figure B.4.
- **Combine client-side CORBA with server-side Java RMI.** We should be able to write a remote object implementation with the RMI API and have a client written to the CORBA API call that object. This is shown in Figure B.5.

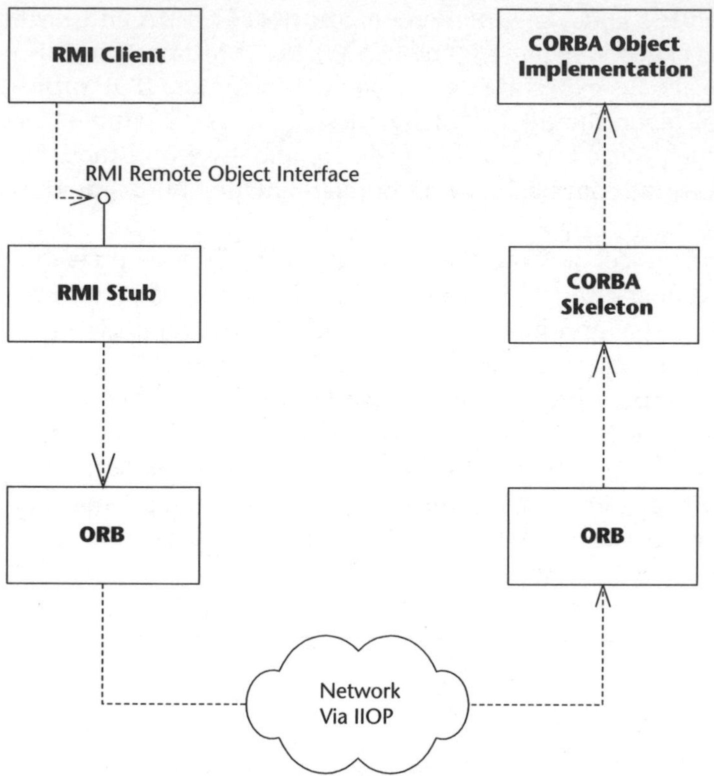

Figure B.4 An RMI client calling a CORBA object implementation.

Combining RMI with CORBA

What strategy should we use to combine the CORBA world with the Java RMI world? To begin to answer this question, let's compare how CORBA and RMI work behind the scenes:

- Both CORBA (except in its dynamic invocation mechanism) and RMI use pregenerated stubs and skeletons to perform network communications.
- Behind the scenes, CORBA uses IIOP as the protocol to perform client/server communications. This occurs beneath the stub/skeleton layer.
- Behind the scenes, Java RMI uses the Java Remote Method Protocol (JRMP) protocol for performing client/server communications. This occurs beneath the stub/skeleton layer as well.

The protocol being used is the key to interoperability of CORBA and RMI. RMI skeletons always expect a request to come in via the JRMP protocol, and CORBA skeletons are always expecting data to come in using the IIOP protocol. But this protocol layer should be totally pluggable. For example, we should be able to switch out the RMI JRMP protocol and switch in the IIOP protocol. If we did this, we could achieve the implementations illustrated in Figures B.4 and B.5.

So why is IIOP our protocol of choice, rather than JRMP? The reason is that IIOP is a much more robust protocol than JRMP. IIOP is supported by numerous vendors in the industry and has been designed with interoperability of heterogeneous distributed objects in mind.

The scheme we've just presented is the basis for the unification of CORBA and RMI, and it is called RMI-IIOP (pronounced RMI over IIOP). RMI-IIOP allows for CORBA clients, RMI clients, CORBA object implementations, and RMI object implementations to be mixed and matched. This accomplishes our goal of creating a bridge between RMI and CORBA. Table B.1 shows the RMI-IIOP combinations that are possible.

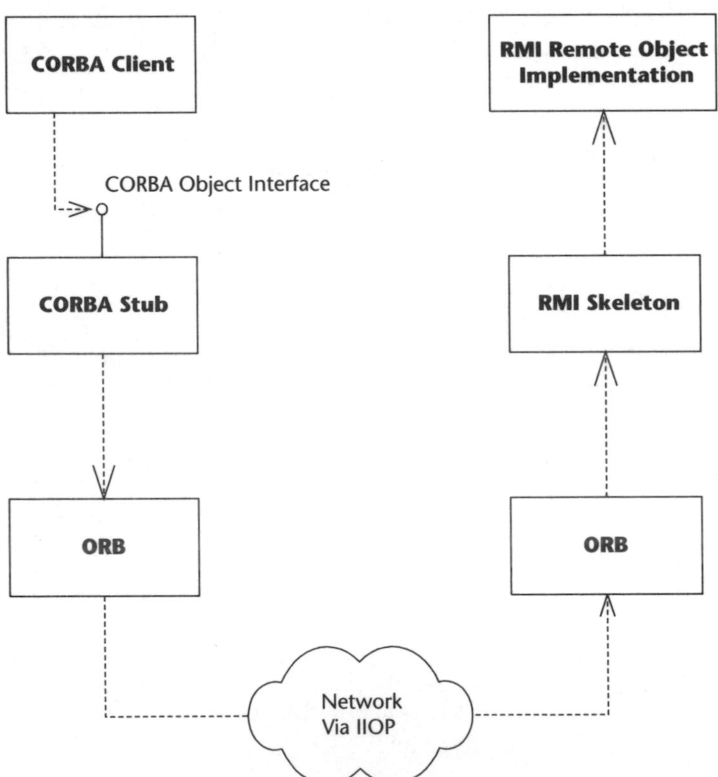

Figure B.5 A CORBA client calling an RMI remote object implementation.

Table B.1 Combinations Possible Using RMI-IIOP

CLIENT	SERVER
RMI-IIOP client	RMI-IIOP server
RMI-IIOP client	CORBA server
CORBA client	RMI-IIOP server
CORBA client	CORBA server

Resolving the Differences between RMI and CORBA

Combining Java RMI with CORBA was not a straightforward task. There were incompatibilities. For example, in RMI you can pass parameters by-value using serialization (see Appendix A). Initially, there was no way in CORBA to marshal parameters by-value. Thus, a new CORBA specification called *objects-by-value* was developed and adopted as part of CORBA to address this. The CORBA ORB you use with RMI-IIOP must implement this specification if you want to marshal objects by value. All modern ORBs support the objects-by-value part of the CORBA specification.

Parameter passing conventions were not the only differences between RMI and CORBA. There are other semantic differences as well. Let's take a look at the major concerns:

- **Distributed garbage collection.** RMI gives you an automatic way of cleaning up objects over the network with a distributed garbage collector. CORBA, on the other hand, has no such mechanism. Why? Because not every language that CORBA maps to has the concept of even regular in-process garbage collection.
- **Narrowing.** When you receive an object using Java RMI, you can simply cast it into the desired object using a Java cast. This is possible because RMI automatically downloads the appropriate stub for the object you're dealing with. CORBA, however, does not have a mechanism for automatic stub downloading.
- **Java RMI programmers don't want to learn OMG IDL.** One of the niceties of Java RMI is that it's all Java, which means you don't need to learn a separate interface definition language (such as OMG IDL) to handle your networking needs. But with RMI-IIOP, you can mix CORBA clients with RMI server object implementations. Those CORBA clients are pure CORBA clients (with pure CORBA stubs), and they need to work with some IDL. That IDL needs to come from somewhere. Should we force Java RMI programmers to churn out an IDL file? If we make Java RMI coders learn OMG IDL, a large benefit of RMI has been lost.

A separate OMG specification called the *Java-to-IDL Mapping* specification resolves the semantic differences between RMI and CORBA. This document details all of the subtleties of combining the RMI API with the IIOP protocol. It addresses issues such as distributed garbage collection and inheritance, as well as the resolution of the differences between RMI and CORBA. In essence, the Java-to-IDL Mapping document is the complete specification for RMI-IIOP.

Let's take a look at how Java-to-IDL solves some of the semantic differences between RMI and CORBA.

- **Distributed garbage collection (DGC).** RMI-IIOP does not propose to accomplish distributed garbage collection. And rightfully so—DGC is in general a hard problem to solve. Instead, the Java-to-IDL specification mandates that RMI coders cannot rely on distributed garbage collection when using RMI-IIOP.
- **Narrowing.** When using RMI-IIOP, you cannot simply cast an object you receive over the network, because the stub class file may not exist on the client machine. RMI-IIOP does not allow downloadable class files because CORBA does not mandate support for this feature. Thus, you must perform a *safe cast* by explicitly calling the *javax.rmi.PortableRemoteObject.narrow()* method. This static method converts an object into the desired remote interface type for you. You pass *narrow()* the object you desire to cast, and the class to which you wish to cast it. The *narrow()* method returns the resultant object or throws an exception if the narrow is not possible, perhaps because the class does not exist.
- **Java RMI programmers don't want to learn OMG IDL.** One great benefit of Java RMI is that you don't need to learn a separate interface definition language to perform remote computing. We'd like to preserve this feature. RMI-IIOP therefore defines a mapping from RMI IDL types to OMG IDL types. This mapping provides a well-defined way for Java language types used by RMI-IIOP to be automatically mapped into OMG IDL. Once we have this, a vendor can write a tool that automatically performs this mapping. Such a tool is called a *java-to-idl compiler*. It takes in code written in Java and spits out OMG IDL. This IDL can be used by CORBA clients when calling your RMI remote object implementations. The IDL can also be used by CORBA object implementations that your RMI clients call.
- **Java-to-IDL allows you to build complete distributed applications in Java and then use apps written in other languages to invoke on your distributed application.** The Java-to-IDL mapping simplifies your network programming tremendously. No longer do you have to write IDL

and then translate that into Java. Java-to-IDL compilers allow you to write your Java application as you normally would; yet they allow for CORBA interoperability by generating IDL for you. This is a great convenience—Java RMI programmers gain the benefits of CORBA-IIOP interoperability, such as cross-language support, at a very low cost.

THE IIOP DEBATE

The IIOP standardization solution that the J2EE and CORBA communities reached was not the only possible solution. In fact, this solution was heavily debated and highly political. Here are the dirty details.

The problem here is that originally not all J2EE server vendors based their servers on CORBA. BEA WebLogic, for example, built its server from scratch with a custom RMI implementation, as did many other server vendors. These vendors did not want to standardize on IIOP, because that meant they had to rewrite their server to use CORBA instead. This added up to increased development time and loss of control over what happened at the network level, which could introduce performance or functionality constraints.

To understand a possible alternative solution, you must understand the concept of context propagation. Let's say your code is involved in a transaction or has security credentials associated with it. Most systems (including EJB) manifest transaction and security data in *contexts*. These contexts are invisible to you and are passed along transparently. Typically they are kept in *Thread Local Storage*, which is a pocket of memory associated with each thread. When you perform an invocation, you want this context information to be *propagated* automatically to the receiving system so the object implementation can execute its business logic for you within the same contexts. RMI-IIOP standardizes the way contexts are propagated, which achieves interoperability.

But there is another solution as well. Imagine if you have two EJB servers talking to one another—say, Weblogic calling WebSphere. Weblogic is invoking on a Websphere stub (not Weblogic stub) that has been deployed on the Weblogic machine. That Websphere stub understands how to talk to a Websphere skeleton. Therefore it should not be necessary to standardize on a protocol such as IIOP. Rather, there should be a standard mechanism for a stub to retrieve transaction and security contexts from the EJB server's thread local storage.

In the end, a compromise was reached. J2EE server vendors are allowed to use other protocols besides IIOP. However, they need to *support* IIOP in case interoperability is required with CORBA systems. That is the irony of the phrase RMI-IIOP—it does not necessarily mean usage of the IIOP protocol. Rather, it means standardizing on the *PortableRemoteObject.narrow()* method.

Steps to Take for RMI and CORBA to Work Together: An Overview

Now that you've seen the theory of combining RMI with CORBA, let's see exactly what steps you need to take for interoperability.

RMI-IIOP Client with a CORBA Object Implementation

Our first scenario depicts an RMI-IIOP client with a CORBA object implementation. To develop such a system, perform the following steps:

1. **Write your RMI-IIOP remote interface.** You write the remote interface in Java. The remote interface is the RMI-IIOP client/server contract for distributed objects.
2. **Generate the needed client-side RMI-IIOP stubs.** The RMI-IIOP client will use the stubs to invoke on the CORBA object implementation. You can generate these stubs using your J2EE server's RMI-IIOP compiler (rmic).
3. **Generate the OMG IDL.** When you define your CORBA object implementations, you're going to need IDL. This IDL must match your RMI-IIOP remote interface if you want RMI-IIOP clients to be able to invoke your CORBA object implementations. Rather than laboriously writing it yourself, you can automatically generate it through a Java-to-IDL compiler. The Java-to-IDL compiler takes in your RMI-IIOP remote interface and spits out OMG IDL. Where do you get a Java-to-IDL compiler? It typically ships with your container's tools. For example, most J2EE servers have a flag on their RMI-IIOP compiler (rmic) to spit out IDL. In most cases, steps 2 and 3 will be performed in a single run of the RMI-IIOP compiler rmic.
4. **Generate the needed server-side CORBA files.** You're going to need some helper code, such as skeletons for your CORBA object implementations. And remember that this helper code can be in any CORBA-compliant language in which you choose to implement your CORBA object implementations. This is where the IDL you generated in step 3 comes into play. When you define your CORBA object implementations, you can use any language to which IDL maps. You then use an IDL compiler to take in your IDL and produce network management code in the language in which you're implementing your objects. For example, if you use Java, you'll need an IDL-to-Java compiler. All ORB vendors that support Java include an IDL-to-Java tool with their products and J2EE servers that bundle ORBs should do so as well.

5. **Write the client and the server.** You can now write your RMI-IIOP client in Java and your CORBA object implementations in whichever programming language you prefer for the task at hand.

CORBA Client with an RMI-IIOP Object Implementation

The second scenario depicts a CORBA client with an RMI-IIOP object implementation. To achieve this, you perform the following steps:

1. **Write your RMI-IIOP remote interface.** You write the remote interface in Java. The remote interface is the RMI-IIOP client/server contract for distributed objects.
2. **Generate the needed server-side RMI-IIOP skeletons.** The skeletons will be used to receive invocations and delegate them to your RMI-IIOP remote object implementations. You can generate these skeletons using your J2EE server's RMI-IIOP compiler (rmic).
3. **Generate the OMG IDL.** When you define your CORBA clients, you're going to need IDL. This IDL must match your RMI remote interface if you want CORBA clients to call your RMI-IIOP object implementations. Rather than laboriously writing it yourself, you can automatically generate it through a Java-to-IDL compiler. The Java-to-IDL compiler takes in your RMI-IIOP remote interface and spits out OMG IDL, and ships with your ORB or J2EE server.
4. **Generate the needed client-side CORBA files.** As in the previous section, you need to generate helper code, such as stubs for your CORBA clients. Thus, you need to generate these network plumbing classes from the IDL with an IDL compiler, such as an IDL-to-Java compiler that ships with your ORB or J2EE server.
5. **Write the client and the server.** You can now write your CORBA client and your RMI-IIOP object implementations.

As you can see, mixing and matching RMI-IIOP and CORBA requires a number of non-trivial code generation steps that involve different code generator tools. Different J2EE servers may behave differently here, so be prepared to spend some time experimenting to get RMI-IIOP and CORBA working together.

Bootstrapping with RMI-IIOP and CORBA

Recall from earlier in this appendix that CORBA has its own built-in naming service, called the CORBA Naming Service (or COS Naming). COS Naming is the standard way CORBA clients look up remote CORBA objects. But again, this is simply looking up an arbitrary resource over the network; the resource just happens to be CORBA objects rather than printers or RMI-IIOP objects. Therefore, COS Naming is a perfect fit for JNDI. You can look up CORBA objects using JNDI by using a special CORBA-compatible JNDI driver. One such driver is the COS Naming service provider, downloadable for free from http://java.sun.com. Note that you should check your J2EE server's documentation for the specific driver they recommend.

What's great about this paradigm is that our RMI-IIOP client code can access both RMI-IIOP servers and CORBA servers without changing code, but rather by merely plugging in a different JNDI driver.

The Big Picture: CORBA and EJB Together

CORBA and EJB have an interesting relationship. They compete with one another in some respects (due to CORBA Components), and at the same time, they complement each other. This is because CORBA is often the enabling technology that resides beneath the EJB level. Many EJB server vendors layer their EJB products on top of an existing CORBA infrastructure, and RMI-IIOP allows just this to happen.

CORBA-EJB interoperability is a solid technology by now, and it provides several benefits. The biggest benefit is that CORBA clients written in any language (that OMG IDL maps to) can call your enterprise beans.

Another benefit of CORBA-EJB interoperability is at the transaction and security level. Clients can mix calls to both CORBA objects and enterprise beans under the hood of the same transaction. Similarly, you should be able to construct a distributed transaction that spans heterogeneous EJB servers. And finally, you should eventually be able to propagate security contexts from one EJB server to another, allowing for single sign-on between different EJB server vendors. The specifications are maturing slowly but are sure to make this a reality in the future.

What You Don't Get from CORBA-EJB Interoperability

We want to make it clear that there is one benefit that you do *not* get from CORBA-EJB interoperability. CORBA-EJB interoperability is for connecting a CORBA *client* to an enterprise bean written in *Java*. You *cannot* write your enterprise beans in any language but Java. If you want to write your server-side components using another language, see Chapter 17 for legacy integration strategies.

Sample Code

Now let's write some sample code to illustrate how to use CORBA to call an EJB component. We'll use the "Hello, World" bean developed in Chapter 3. The key thing to notice is that we are taking a bean that we called using RMI-IIOP in Chapter 3, and are reusing the bean without modification and accessing it from a CORBA client.

We'll use the following to access our bean:

- COS Naming to look up the home object
- OTS to demarcate transaction boundaries
- The Java language to write our CORBA client

Source B.1 shows the implementation.

```
package examples;

import java.util.*;
import org.omg.CosNaming.*;

// if your ORB does not support CosTransactions, comment
// out this line:
import org.omg.CosTransactions.*;

public class CORBAClient
{
    public static void main(String[] args)
        throws Exception
    {
        /*
         * Initialize the ORB.
         */
        org.omg.CORBA.ORB orb = org.omg.CORBA.ORB.init(args, null);

        /*
         * Get a reference to a naming context
         */
        NamingContext context = NamingContextHelper.narrow
            (orb.resolve_initial_references("NameService"));

        /*
         * Look up the home object using COS Naming
         */
        NameComponent[] names = { new NameComponent("HelloHome", "") };
        HelloHome helloHome = HelloHomeHelper.narrow
            (context.resolve(names));
```

Source B.1 Example CORBA EJB client. *(continued)*

```
        /*
         * Get the CORBA OTS Current interface for controlling
         * transactions.  If your ORB does not support
         * CosTransactions, comment out the following line:
         */
        Current currentTX = CurrentHelper.narrow
            (orb.resolve_initial_references("TransactionCurrent"));

        /*
         * Begin the transaction.
         * If your ORB does not support CosTransactions, comment
         * out the following line:
         */
        currentTX.begin();

        /*
         * Use the home object to create an EJB object
         */
        Hello hello = helloHome.create();

        /*
         * Call a business method. Note trailing '_' in the method name,
         * which was introduced by the Java-to-IDL mapping rules:
         */
        System.out.println(hello.hello_());

        /*
         * Remove the EJB object
         */
        hello.remove();

        /*
         * Commit the transaction
         * If your ORB does not support CosTransactions, comment
         * out the following line:
         */
        currentTX.commit(true);
    }
}
```

Source B.1 *(continued)*

As you can see, initializing CORBA clients is a bit more complex than with RMI-IIOP clients. We first need to initialize the ORB before beginning any CORBA operations. Next we get a reference to a naming context via COS Naming, which we use to look up home objects. Once we've retrieved the home object, calling methods on enterprise beans is syntactically similar to calling them on RMI-IIOP. We also get a reference to the OTS *Current* interface, which is used to demarcate transactional boundaries, analogous to the Java Transaction API (JTA) described in Chapter 12. The *begin()* and *commit()* calls have the same semantic meaning as their JTA equivalents.

Summary

In this appendix, you've experienced a whirlwind tour of CORBA and IIOP. We've displayed CORBA's advantages and the reasons that CORBA is a useful technology. We then delved into the inner workings of CORBA and explored its architecture. We also glanced at CORBA's services and touched on the IDL-to-Java mapping.

We then compared RMI to CORBA and explained why the two worlds need cohesion. We designed the requirements for RMI-IIOP interoperability and dove into several scenarios illustrating RMI and CORBA working in unison. We wrapped up our discussion of RMI-IIOP by illustrating the steps necessary for you to write RMI-IIOP code.

In the last section of this appendix, we caught a glimpse of the future—EJB and CORBA interoperability—and showed some example code.

APPENDIX

C

Deployment Descriptor Reference

This appendix is a reference guide for building XML deployment descriptors. You do not need to read this appendix front-to-back; rather, you should use it as a reference guide when you have questions about deployment descriptors. This is a handy reference when working with deployment descriptors, because you can quickly look up the structure in question.

How to Read the XML Schema

This appendix is a consolidated view of the EJB 2.1 deployment descriptor XML Schema definitions (XSD). An XSD provides schema for an XML document. It constrains how you can form your XML-based deployment descriptor so that a computer program, such as an EJB compiler tool, can interpret the resulting document.

The tables in this appendix use the following syntax:

ELEMENT	DESCRIPTION
element?	A question mark (?) indicates this element is optional.
element*	An asterisk (*) indicates zero or more of these elements may exist.
element+	A plus sign (+) indicates one or more of these elements may exist.
elementA | elementB	This means you can have either elementA or elementB, but not both.
Element	No punctuation means there must be exactly one element.

Note that the ordering of elements in the tables is important. Your deployment descriptor will not be valid unless you follow the exact ordering. For example, it would be invalid to define a local home interface before defining a home interface. Elements are also case sensitive. Be sure you use the correct capitalization.

The Header and Root Element

All EJB deployment descriptors should be named *ejb-jar.xml* and be located in the *META-INF* folder of your Ejb-jar file. The XML file is a flat text file that begins with the following declaration:

```
<ejb-jar xmlns=http://java.sun.com/xml/ns/j2ee version="2.1"
         xmlns:xsi=http://www.w3.org/2001/XMLSchema-instance
         xsi:schemaLocation="http://java.sun.com/xml/ns/j2ee
         http://java.sun.com/xml/ns/j2ee/ejb-jar_2_1.xsd">
```

The *ejb-jar* element is the root element of all deployment descriptors. Table C.1 provides information about the header and root elements.

Table C.1 Header and Root Elements

ELEMENT	DESCRIPTION	WHERE TO GO FOR MORE INFORMATION
description?	A text description of this Ejb-jar file.	
display-name?	A short name of this Ejb-jar file, to be displayed by tools.	

Table C.1 *(continued)*

ELEMENT	DESCRIPTION	WHERE TO GO FOR MORE INFORMATION
small-icon?	The relative path within the 16 × 16 icon image (either JPEG or GIF) to be displayed by tools when manipulating this Ejb-jar file.	
large-icon?	Same as small icon, except a 32 × 32 image.	
enterprise-beans	Defines one or more enterprise beans.	See *session, entity,* or *message-driven* later in this appendix.
relationships?	Defines CMP relationships.	See *relationships* later in this appendix.
assembly descriptor?	Defines application assembly information, such as transactions *descriptor* and security.	See *assembly* later in this appendix.
ejb-client-jar?	Specifies an optional JAR file that contains classes that remote clients use to access beans, such as stubs and interfaces. Only useful if you have remote clients.	Chapter 3

Here is an example of high-level structure of *ejb-jar* element:

```
<ejb-jar xmlns=http://java.sun.com/xml/ns/j2ee version="2.1"
         xmlns:xsi=http://www.w3.org/2001/XMLSchema-instance
         xsi:schemaLocation="http://java.sun.com/xml/ns/j2ee
         http://java.sun.com/xml/ns/j2ee/ejb-jar_2_1.xsd">
 <description>E-Commerce System</description>
 <display-name>E-Commerce EJB-JAR file</display-name>
 <small-icon>small.gif</small-icon>
 <large-icon>large.gif</large-icon>

 <enterprise-beans>
  ... One or more session, entity, and message-driven ...
 </enterprise-beans>

 <relationships>
  ... Define relationships ...
 </relationships>
```

```
  <assembly-descriptor>
   ... Define application assembly information ...
  </assembly-descriptor>

  <ejb-client-jar>ECommerceClient.jar</ejb-client-jar>
</ejb-jar>
```

Defining Session Beans

The following is an example of how to set up a session bean. Descriptions follow.

```
<ejb-jar xmlns=http://java.sun.com/xml/ns/j2ee version="2.1"
         xmlns:xsi=http://www.w3.org/2001/XMLSchema-instance
         xsi:schemaLocation="http://java.sun.com/xml/ns/j2ee
         http://java.sun.com/xml/ns/j2ee/ejb-jar_2_1.xsd">
  <enterprise-beans>
    <session>
      <ejb-name>Count</ejb-name>
      <home>examples.CountHome</home>
      <remote>examples.Count</remote>
      <ejb-class>examples.CountBean</ejb-class>
      <session-type>Stateful</session-type>
      <transaction-type>Container</transaction-type>
    </session>
  </enterprise-beans>
</ejb-jar>
```

<session>

The *session* element defines a session bean. Used in *ejb-jar*. (See Table C.2.)

Table C.2 The <session> Element

ELEMENT	DESCRIPTION	WHERE TO GO FOR MORE INFORMATION
description?	A text description of this bean.	
display-name?	A short name of this bean, to be displayed by tools.	

Table C.2 *(continued)*

ELEMENT	DESCRIPTION	WHERE TO GO FOR MORE INFORMATION
small-icon?	The relative path within the Ejb-jar file that you can find a 16 × 16 icon image (either JPEG or GIF) representing this bean, to be displayed by tools.	
large-icon?	Same as small icon, except a 32 × 32 image.	
ejb-name	The nickname that you want to give this bean. The ejb-name can be referenced later in the deployment descriptor.	Chapters 3, 4
home?	Home interface class. Remember to include the package too!	Chapters 3, 4
remote?	Remote interface class. Remember to include the package too!	Chapters 3, 4
local-home?	Local home interface class. Remember to include the package too!	Chapters 3, 4
local?	Local interface class. Remember to include the package too!	Chapters 3, 4
ejb-class	Session bean class. Remember to include the package too!	Chapters 3, 4
session-type	For a stateful session bean, set this to *Stateful*. For a stateless session bean, set this to *Stateless*.	Chapters 3, 4
transaction-type	For declarative transactions, set this to *Container*. For bean-managed transactions, set this to *Bean*.	Chapter 12
env-entry*	Declares environment properties for this bean.	Chapter 10

(continued)

Table C.2 *(continued)*

ELEMENT	DESCRIPTION	WHERE TO GO FOR MORE INFORMATION
ejb-ref*	Declares references to other beans.	Chapter 10
ejb-local-ref*	Declares local references to other beans.	Chapter 10
security-role-ref*	Declares security role references.	
security-identity?	Declares how to perform security context propagation.	Chapter 13
resource-ref*	Declares resource factory references (such as JDBC driver used in bean).	Chapter 10
resource-env-ref*	Binds resource factories to JNDI nicknames.	Chapter 10

Note that you must define home/remote or local-home/local in pairs. For example, it would be invalid to define a home interface without a remote interface. You must also define at least one pair, meaning you must either use remote interfaces, local interfaces, or both.

Defining Entity Beans

The following is an example of how to set up an entity bean. Descriptions follow in Table C.3.

```
<ejb-jar xmlns=http://java.sun.com/xml/ns/j2ee version="2.1"
        xmlns:xsi=http://www.w3.org/2001/XMLSchema-instance
        xsi:schemaLocation="http://java.sun.com/xml/ns/j2ee
        http://java.sun.com/xml/ns/j2ee/ejb-jar_2_1.xsd">
  <enterprise-beans>
    <entity>
      <ejb-name>Product</ejb-name>
      <local-home>examples.ProductHome</local-home>
      <local>examples.Product</local>
      <ejb-class>examples.ProductBean</ejb-class>
      <persistence-type>Container</persistence-type>
      <prim-key-class>java.lang.String</prim-key-class>
      <reentrant>False</reentrant>
      <cmp-version>2.x</cmp-version>
      <abstract-schema-name>Product</abstract-schema-name>
```

```
        <cmp-field><field-name>productID</field-name></cmp-field>
        <cmp-field><field-name>name</field-name></cmp-field>
        <primkey-field>productID</primkey-field>
        <query>
          <query-method>
            <method-name>findByName</method-name>
            <method-params>
             <method-param>java.lang.String</method-param>
            </method-params>
          </query-method>
          <ejb-ql>SELECT OBJECT(a) FROM Product AS a WHERE name = ?1</ejb-
ql>
        </query>
      </entity>
    </enterprise-beans>
  </ejb-jar>
```

<entity>

The *entity* element defines an entity bean. Used in *ejb-jar*. (See Table C.3.)

Table C.3 The <entity> Element

ELEMENT	DESCRIPTION	WHERE TO GO FOR MORE INFORMATION
description?	A text description of this bean.	
display-name?	A short name of this bean, to be displayed by tools.	
small-icon?	The relative path within the Ejb-jar file that you can find a 16 × 16 icon image (either JPEG or GIF) representing this bean, to be displayed by tools.	
large-icon?	Same as small icon, except a 32 × 32 image.	
ejb-name	The nickname that you want to give this bean. This Ejb-name can be referenced later in the deployment descriptor.	Chapters 7, 8

(continued)

Table C.3 *(continued)*

ELEMENT	DESCRIPTION	WHERE TO GO FOR MORE INFORMATION
home?	Home interface class. Remember to include the package too! We don't recommend you use this, because entity beans should always be accessed via their local interfaces.	Chapters 7, 8
remote?	Remote interface class. Remember to include the package too! We don't recommend you use this, because entity beans should always accessed via their local interfaces.	Chapters 7, 8
local-home?	Local home interface class. Remember to include the package too!	Chapters 7, 8
local?	Local interface class. Remember to include the package too!	Chapters 7, 8
ejb-class	Entity bean class. Remember to include the package too!	Chapters 7, 8
session-type	For a CMP entity bean, set this to *Container*. For a BMP entity bean, set this to *Bean*.	Chapters 7, 8
prim-key-class	Primary key class (if you have one). Remember to include the package too!	Chapters 7, 8
reentrant	Set to *True* or *False* depending on whether you want to be able to call yourself through another bean.	Chapters 7, 8
cmp-version?	Set to *1.x* or *2.x* depending on whether you're using the old EJB 1.1 style of entity bean programming, or the new EJB 2.*x* style.	Chapters 7, 8 The book's accompanying source code has EJB 1.1, EJB 2.0, and EJB 2.1 style examples.

Table C.3 *(continued)*

ELEMENT	DESCRIPTION	WHERE TO GO FOR MORE INFORMATION
abstract schema-name?	Declares a nickname for this bean's CMP field definition. Used within EJB-QL queries.	Chapters 8, 15, Appendix D
cmp-field*	Defines a container-managed persistent field for a CMP entity bean.	Chapter 8
primkey-field?	If you're not using a primary key class, declares one of your CMP fields to be a primary key.	Chapter 8
env-entry*	Declares environment properties for this bean.	Chapter 10
ejb-ref*	Declares references to other beans.	Chapter 10
ejb-local-ref*	Declares local references to other beans.	Chapter 10
security-role-ref*	Declares security role references.	
security-identity?	Declares how to perform security context propagation.	Chapter 13
resource-ref*	Declares resource factory references (such as JDBC driver used in bean).	Chapter 10
resource-env-ref*	Binds resource factories to JNDI nicknames.	Chapter 10
query*	Defines a CMP EJB-QL query for a finder or select method.	Chapters 8, 15, Appendix D

<cmp-field>

The *cmp-field* element defines a CMP field within an entity bean definition. Used in *entity*. (See Table C.4.)

Table C.4 The <cmp-field> Element

ELEMENT	DESCRIPTION	WHERE TO GO FOR MORE INFORMATION
description?	A text description of this CMP field.	
field-name	The name of the get/set method corresponding to this CMP field. Leave off t he get/set prefix, and make sure the first letter is lowercase.	Chapter 8

<query>

The *query* element defines an EJB-QL query for a finder or a select method. Applies only to CMP entity beans. Used in *entity*. (See Table C.5.)

Table C.5 The <query> Element

ELEMENT	DESCRIPTION	WHERE TO GO FOR MORE INFORMATION
description?	A text description of this query.	Chapter 8, Appendix D
query-method	The finder or select method that will be associated with this EJB-QL query.	Chapter 8, Appendix D (see later table)
ult-type-mapping?	Maps the return results of the EJB-QL query to either remote interfaces (set to *Remote*) or local interfaces (set to *Local*). The default is *Local.*	Chapter 8, Appendix D
ejb-ql	The actual EJB-QL formatted string to query the storage.	Chapter 8, Appendix

<query-method>

The *query-method* element declares a finder or a select method that will be associated with this EJB-QL query. Applies only to CMP entity beans. Used in *query*. (See Table C.6.)

<method-params>

The *method-params* element declares a list of fully qualified Java types that are parameters to this method. Applies only to CMP entity beans. Used in *query-method*. (See Table C.7.)

Table C.6 The <query-method> Element

ELEMENT	DESCRIPTION	WHERE TO GO FOR MORE INFORMATION
method-name	The name of this method. Leave off the get/set and make sure the first letter is lowercase.	Chapter 8, Appendix D
method-params	A list of fully qualified Java types that are parameters to this method.	Chapter 8, Appendix D (see later table)

Table C.7 The <method-params> Element

ELEMENT	DESCRIPTION	WHERE TO GO FOR MORE INFORMATION
method-param*	Zero or more fully qualified Java types for method parameters that this query accepts.	Chapter 8, Appendix D

Defining Message-Driven Beans

The following is an example of how to set up a message-driven bean. Descriptions follow. See Chapter 9 for complete documentation.

```
<ejb-jar xmlns=http://java.sun.com/xml/ns/j2ee version="2.1"
        xmlns:xsi=http://www.w3.org/2001/XMLSchema-instance
        xsi:schemaLocation="http://java.sun.com/xml/ns/j2ee
        http://java.sun.com/xml/ns/j2ee/ejb-jar_2_1.xsd">
 <enterprise-beans>
    <message-driven>
      <ejb-name>Hello</ejb-name>
      <ejb-class>examples.HelloBean</ejb-class>

      <messaging-type>javax.jms.MessageListener</messaging-type>
      <transaction-type>Container</transaction-type>
      <message-destination-type>javax.jms.Queue</message-destination-
type>

    </message-driven>
 </enterprise-beans>
</ejb-jar>
```

<message-driven>

The *message-driven* element defines a message-driven bean. Used in *ejb-jar*. (See Table C.8.)

Table C.8 The <message-driven> Element

ELEMENT	DESCRIPTION	WHERE TO GO FOR MORE INFORMATION
description?	A text description of this bean.	
display-name?	A short name of this bean, to be displayed by tools.	
small-icon?	The relative path within the Ejb-jar file that you can find a 16 × 16 icon image (either JPEG or GIF) representing this bean, to be displayed by tools.	
large-icon?	Same as small icon, except a 32 × 32 image.	

Table C.8 *(continued)*

ELEMENT	DESCRIPTION	WHERE TO GO FOR MORE INFORMATION
ejb-name	The nickname that you want to give this bean. This Ejb-name can be referenced later in the deployment descriptor.	Chapter 9
ejb-class	Message-driven bean class. Remember to include the package too!	Chapter 9
transaction-type	For declarative transactions, set this to *Container.* For bean-managed transactions, set this to *Bean.*	Chapter 12
messageSelector?	Filters for messages based on a special JMS selector string.	Chapter 9
acknowledge Mode?	If you perform bean-managed transactions, you must specify how to acknowledge messages when your *onMessage()* method is called. Set this to either *Auto-acknowledge* or *Dups-ok-acknowledge*.	Chapter 9
message-destination- type?	Specifies the type of destination that you want to listen for messages.	Chapter 9
env-entry*	Declares environment properties for this bean.	Chapter 10
ejb-ref*	Declares references to other beans.	Chapter 10
ejb-local-ref*	Declares local references to other beans.	Chapter 10
security-role-ref*	Declares security role references.	
security-identity?	Declares how to perform security context propagation.	Chapter 13
resource-ref*	Declares resource factory references (such as JDBC driver used in bean).	Chapter 10
resource-env-ref*	Binds resource factories to JNDI nicknames.	Chapter 10

Table C.9 The <message-destination-type> Element

ELEMENT	DESCRIPTION	WHERE TO GO FOR MORE INFORMATION
subscriptionDurability?	Indicates durability of messages, either *Durable* for durable messages, or *NonDurable* for nondurable messages.	Chapter 9

<messaging-type>

The *messaging-type* element defines the type of message-driven bean as in the message listener interface it implements. Used in *message-driven.*

<message-destination-type>

The *message-destination-type* element specifies the destination that you want to listen for messages. Used in *message-driven.* (See Table C.9.)

Defining Timer Beans

The deployment descriptor for a bean that uses timer service is not any different than the bean that does not use the timer service because there is no timer-specific deployment information. The following example shows deployment descriptor of a session bean that has implemented *javax.ejb.TimedObject* interface. See Chapter 14 for a complete description on using EJB timer service.

```
<ejb-jar xmlns=http://java.sun.com/xml/ns/j2ee version="2.1"
         xmlns:xsi=http://www.w3.org/2001/XMLSchema-instance
         xsi:schemaLocation="http://java.sun.com/xml/ns/j2ee
         http://java.sun.com/xml/ns/j2ee/ejb-jar_2_1.xsd">
 <enterprise-beans>
   <session>
     <ejb-name>SessionTimerEJB</ejb-name>
     <home>examples.SessionTimerHome</home>
     <remote>examples.SessionTimer</remote>
     <ejb-class>examples.SessionTimerBean</ejb-class>
     <session-type>Stateless</session-type>
     <transaction-type>Bean</transaction-type>
   </session>
 </enterprise-beans>
</ejb-jar>
```

Defining J2EE Web Service

As we learned in Chapter 5, a stateless session bean can support Web service protocols, namely WSDL and SOAP. Such a stateless session bean that supports Web service(s) is deployed with an additional deployment descriptor, which is always named as *webservices.xml* and is placed in the META-INF directory of the Web service's JAR file. It contains the service-related deployment information. The following example shows a Web Services deployment descriptor implemented as a stateless session bean endpoint.

```
<webservices xmlns="http://java.sun.com/xml/ns/j2ee"
      xmlns:xsi="http://www.w3.org/2001/XMLSchema-instance"
      xsi:schemaLocation="http://java.sun.com/xml/ns/j2ee
      http://www.ibm.com/webservices/xsd/j2ee_web_services_1_1.xsd"
version="1.1">
 <webservice-description>
   <webservice-description-name>HelloWorldWS</webservice-description-
name>
   <wsdl-file>META-INF/wsdl/HelloWorldWS.wsdl</wsdl-file>
   <jaxrpc-mapping-file>META-INF/mapping.xml</jaxrpc-mapping-file>
   <port-component>
     <description>HelloWorldWS Port Description</description>
     <port-component-name>HelloWS</port-component-name>
     <wsdl-port xmlns:wsdl-port ns="urn:examples">wsdl-port ns
:HelloInterfacePort </wsdl-port>
     <service-endpoint-interface>examples.HelloInterface</service-
endpoint-interface>
     <service-impl-bean>
       <ejb-link>HelloBean</ejb-link>
     </service-impl-bean>
   </port-component>
 </webservice-description>
</webservices>
```

<webservices>

The *webservices* element is the root element of all service deployment descriptors. It describes J2EE Web Service descriptions and the dependencies they have on container resources and services.

<webservice-description>

This element carries information about the Web Service's WSDL file and the set of *port-component* elements associated with the WSDL ports defined in the WSDL file. (See Table C.10.)

Table C.10 The <webservice-description> Element

ELEMENT	DESCRIPTION	WHERE TO GO FOR MORE INFORMATION
webservices	Root element for the Web Service deployment descriptor.	Chapter 5
webservice-description+	Information about WSDL document and a set of port components associated with WSDL-defined ports.	Chapter 5

<jaxrpc-mapping-file>

This element points to the file containing mappings between Java interfaces and WSDL definition. Each WSDL should have a corresponding JAX-RPC mapping file. This information helps in the generation of stubs and TIEs for the services. (See Table C.11.)

Table C.11 The <jaxrpc-mapping-file> Element

ELEMENT	DESCRIPTION	WHERE TO GO FOR MORE INFORMATION
webservice-description-name	Identifies a collection of port components associated with a WSDL and the JAX-RPC mapping.	Chapter 5
wsdl-file	Contains the name of the WSDL file for the Web Service.	Chapter 5
jaxrpc-mapping-file	Specifies the name of the file which contains JAX-RPC mappings between Java interfaces and WSDL.	Chapter 5
port-component+	Associates a WSDL port with the Web Service interface and implementation.	Chapter 5

Table C.12 The <port-component> Element

ELEMENT	DESCRIPTION	WHERE TO GO FOR MORE INFORMATION
description?	Description of port component.	Chapter 5
port-component-name	This name is assigned by the bean provider to name the service implementation bean.	Chapter 5
wsdl-port	Defines the namespace and local name par of the WSDL port QName.	Chapter 5
service-endpoint-interface	Port component's service endpoint interface.	Chapter 5
service-impl-bean	Port component's service implementation bean specification.	Chapter 5
ejb-link|servlet-link	Can refer to existing EJB implementations through this element. Note: You can also refer to beans in a different JAR file, by using a syntax such as *../products/product.jar#ProductEJB*.	Chapter 10

<port-component>

This element associates a WSDL port with the Web Service interface and implementation by defining the name of the port as a component, description, WSDL port name, service endpoint interface and a link to service implementation bean. (See Table C.12.)

Defining Environment Properties

The following is an example of how to set up environment properties. Descriptions follow. See Chapter 10 for complete documentation.

```
<enterprise-beans>
 <session>
  <ejb-name>Pricer</ejb-name>
  <home>examples.PricerHome</home>
  <remote>examples.Pricer</remote>
  <ejb-class>examples.PricerBean</ejb-class>
  <session-type>Stateless</session-type>
```

```
    <transaction-type>Container</transaction-type>
    <env-entry>
     <description>
      The algorithm for this pricing engine.
     </description>
     <env-entry-name>Pricer/algorithm</env-entry-name>
     <env-entry-type>java.lang.String</env-entry-type>
     <env-entry-value>NoTaxes</env-entry-value>
    </env-entry>
   </session>
  </enterprise-beans>
```

<env-entry>

The *env-entry* element defines an environment property that the bean can access via JNDI to customize its functionality at runtime. Used in *session, entity,* and *message-driven.*

Defining EJB References

The following is an example of how to set up references from one bean to another. This is useful because beans can look up each other without needing to initialize JNDI to any particular driver. Descriptions follow in Table C.13. See Chapter 10 for complete documentation.

```
<ejb-jar xmlns=http://java.sun.com/xml/ns/j2ee version="2.1"
         xmlns:xsi=http://www.w3.org/2001/XMLSchema-instance
         xsi:schemaLocation="http://java.sun.com/xml/ns/j2ee
       http://java.sun.com/xml/ns/j2ee/ejb-jar_2_1.xsd">
 <enterprise-beans>

  <session>
   <ejb-name>Catalog</ejb-name>
   ... define a catalog session bean ...
  </session>

  <session>
   <ejb-name>Pricer</ejb-name>
   <home>examples.PricerHome</home>
   <remote>examples.Pricer</remote>
   <ejb-class>examples.PricerBean</ejb-class>
   <session-type>Stateless</session-type>
   <transaction-type>Container</transaction-type>
   <ejb-ref>
    <description>
     This reference is from the Pricer to the Catalog
    </description>
```

```
      <ejb-ref-name>ejb/CatalogHome</ejb-ref-name>
      <ejb-ref-type>Session</ejb-ref-type>
      <home>CatalogHome</home>
      <remote>Catalog</remote>
      <ejb-link>Catalog</ejb-link>
    </ejb-ref>
  </session>
 </enterprise-beans>
</ejb-jar>
```

<ejb-ref>

The *ejb-ref* element defines a remote reference from one bean to another. This should be used sparingly, since local interfaces are the superior way to call from one bean to another. Used in *session, entity*, and *message-driven*. (See Table C.14.)

Table C.13 EJB References

ELEMENT	DESCRIPTION	MORE WHERE TO GO FOR INFORMATION
description?	A text description for this environment property.	Chapter 10
env-entry-property name.	The JNDI name relative to java:comp/env where the bean can lookup this environment.	Chapter 10
env-entry-type	The fully qualified Java type of this environment property (such as *java.lang.String* or *java.lang.Integer*).	Chapter 10
env-entry-value?	The text value of this environment property.	Chapter 10

Table C.14 The <ejb-ref> Element

ELEMENT	DESCRIPTION	WHERE TO GO FOR MORE INFORMATION
description?	A text description of this EJB reference.	Chapter 10
ejb-ref-name	The JNDI name relative to *java:comp/env* that will be used to lookup this EJB reference. Recommended: prefix with *ejb/.*	Chapter 10

(continued)

Table C.14 *(continued)*

ELEMENT	DESCRIPTION	WHERE TO GO FOR MORE INFORMATION
ejb-ref-type	The type of the bean we have a reference to. Could be either *Session* or *Entity.* (Message-driven beans are not referred to directly because they have no home and are accessed via JMS.)	Chapter 10
home	The home interface class being referred to Remember to include the package too!	Chapter 10
remote	The remote interface class being referred to Remember to include the package too!	Chapter 10
ejb-link?	The Ejb-name of the bean we're referring to. Note: You can also refer to beans in a different jar file, by using a syntax such as *../products/product.jar#ProductEJB.*	Chapter 10

<ejb-local-ref>

The *ejb-local-ref* element defines a local reference from one bean to another. We recommend you use these types of references when your beans are co-located, since local interfaces are the superior way to call from one bean to another. Used in *session*, *entity*, and *message-driven*. (See Table C.15.)

Table C.15 The <ejb-local-ref> Element

ELEMENT	DESCRIPTION	WHERE TO GO FOR MORE INFORMATION
description?	A text description of this EJB reference that will be used to look up this EJB reference. Recommended: prefix with *ejb/.*	Chapter 10
ejb-ref-name	The JNDI name relative to *java:comp/env.*	Chapter 10
ejb-ref-type	The type of the bean we have a reference to. Could either be *Session* or *Entity* (message-driven beans are not referred to directly because they have no home, and are accessed via JMS.)	Chapter 10

Table C.15 *(continued)*

ELEMENT	DESCRIPTION	WHERE TO GO FOR MORE INFORMATION
local-home	The local home interface class being referred to. Remember to include the package too!	Chapter 10
local	The local interface class being referred to. Remember to include the package too!	Chapter 10
ejb-link?	The Ejb-name of the bean we're referring to. *Note:* You can also refer to beans in a different JAR file, by using a syntax such as *../products/product.jar#ProductEJB*.	Chapter 10

Defining Security

Security is a bit difficult to explain. See Chapter 13 for complete documentation.

<security-role-ref>

The *security-role-ref* element defines a security role that your bean depends upon. Used in *session, entity,* and *message-driven*. (See Table C.16.)

Table C.16 The <security-role-ref> Element

ELEMENT	DESCRIPTION	WHERE TO GO FOR MORE INFORMATION
description?	A text description of the security role.	Chapter 13
role-name	A text string for the security role that this bean references and depends upon.	Chapter 13
role-link?	Maps the above role-name abstract security role to a real security role defined in the assembly descriptor.	

Table C.17 The <security-identity> Element

ELEMENT	DESCRIPTION	WHERE TO GO FOR MORE INFORMATION
description?	A text description.	Chapter 13
use-caller-identity | run-as	If you want to use the caller's identity when executing, set to the empty element *<use-caller-identity/>*. If you want to run as another security identity, define the *<run-as>* element.	Chapter 13

<security-identity>

The *security-identity* element defines whether the caller's security identity is to be used when this bean executes, or whether another security identity should be used. Used in *session*, *entity*, and *message-driven*. (See Table C.17.)

<run-as>

The *run-as* element allows your bean to run as a specified identity. Used in *security-identity*. (See Table C.18.)

Table C.18 The <run-as> Element

ELEMENT	DESCRIPTION	WHERE TO GO FOR MORE INFORMATION
description?	A text description.	Chapter 13
role-name	The name of the security role you wish to run as.	Chapter 13

Defining Resource Factories

The following is an example of how to set up resource factories, which are drivers to external systems. Descriptions follow. See Chapter 10 for complete documentation.

```
<ejb-jar xmlns=http://java.sun.com/xml/ns/j2ee version="2.1"
        xmlns:xsi=http://www.w3.org/2001/XMLSchema-instance
        xsi:schemaLocation="http://java.sun.com/xml/ns/j2ee
      http://java.sun.com/xml/ns/j2ee/ejb-jar_2_1.xsd">
 <enterprise-beans>
  <entity>
   <ejb-name>Account</ejb-name>
   <home>examples.AccountHome</home>
   <remote>examples.Account</remote>
   <local-home>examples.AccountLocalHome</local-home>
   <local>examples.AccountLocal</local>
   <ejb-class>examples.AccountBean</ejb-class>
   <persistence-type>Bean</persistence-type>
   <prim-key-class>examples.AccountPK</prim-key-class>
   <reentrant>False</reentrant>

   <resource-ref>
    <res-ref-name>jdbc/ejbPool</res-ref-name>
    <res-type>javax.sql.DataSource</res-type>
    <res-auth>Container</res-auth>
    <res-sharing-scope>Shareable</res-sharing-scope>
   </resource-ref>
  </entity>
 </enterprise-beans>
```

<resource-ref>

The *resource-ref* element defines a reference to a resource factory. Used in *session, entity,* and *message-driven.* (See Table C.19.)

Table C.19 The <resource-ref> Element

ELEMENT	DESCRIPTION	WHERE TO GO FOR MORE INFORMATION
description?	A text description.	Chapter 10
res-ref-name	The JNDI name to which you wish to bind the resource factory, referenced off of *java:comp/env.*	Chapter 10
res-type	The fully qualified Java type of the resource factory, such as *javax.jms. ConnectionFactory.*	Chapter 10
res-auth	Set to *Application* if you are providing your own security to access this resource factory. Set to *Container* if the container is handling security access to this resource factory.	Chapter 10
res-sharing-scope?	Specifies whether connections obtained from this resource factory are shareable. Must be either *Shareable* or *Unshareable*.	Chapter 10

<resource-env-ref>

The *resource-env-ref* element defines a reference to an administered object. Used in *session, entity,* and *message-driven*. (See Table C.20.)

Table C.20 The <resource-env-ref> Element

ELEMENT	DESCRIPTION	WHERE TO GO FOR MORE INFORMATION
description?	A text description.	Chapter 10
resource-env-ref-name	The name of the administered object.	Chapter 10
env-ref-type	The fully qualified type of the administered object.	Chapter 10

Defining Relationships

The following is an example of how to set up relationships. Descriptions follow. See Chapter 15 for complete relationships documentation.

```
<ejb-jar xmlns=http://java.sun.com/xml/ns/j2ee version="2.1"
         xmlns:xsi=http://www.w3.org/2001/XMLSchema-instance
         xsi:schemaLocation="http://java.sun.com/xml/ns/j2ee
       http://java.sun.com/xml/ns/j2ee/ejb-jar_2_1.xsd">

 <enterprise-beans>
 ...
 </enterprise-beans>

 <relationships>
  <ejb-relation>
   <ejb-relation-name>Order-Shipment</ejb-relation-name>
   <ejb-relationship-role>
    <ejb-relationship-role-name>
     order-spawns-shipment
    </ejb-relationship-role-name>
    <multiplicity>One</multiplicity>
    <relationship-role-source>
     <ejb-name>Order</ejb-name>
    </relationship-role-source>
    <cmr-field>
     <cmr-field-name>shipment</cmr-field-name>
    </cmr-field>
   </ejb-relationship-role>

   <ejb-relationship-role>
    <ejb-relationship-role-name>
     shipment-fulfills-order
    </ejb-relationship-role-name>
    <multiplicity>One</multiplicity>
    <cascade-delete/>
    <relationship-role-source>
     <ejb-name>Shipment</ejb-name>
    </relationship-role-source>
    <cmr-field>
     <cmr-field-name>order</cmr-field-name>
    </cmr-field>
   </ejb-relationship-role>
  </ejb-relation>
 </relationships>
</ejb-jar>
```

Table C.21 The <relationships> Reference

ELEMENT	DESCRIPTION	WHERE TO GO FOR MORE INFORMATION
description?	A text description of the relationships.	Chapter 15
ejb-relation+	Defines one or more relationships.	Chapter 15, Table C.19

<relationships>

The *relationships* element defines CMP relationships. Used in *ejb-jar*. (See Table C.21.)

<ejb-relation>

Each *ejb-relation* defines a single CMP relationship. Used in *relationships*. (See Table C.22.)

<ejb-relationship-role>

Each *ejb-relationship-role* defines half of a CMP relationship. Used in *ejb-relation*.

Table C.22 The <ejb-relation> Element

ELEMENT	DESCRIPTION	WHERE TO GO FOR MORE INFORMATION
description?	A text description of this relationship.	Chapter 15
ejb-relation name?	A unique nickname for this relationship.	Chapter 15
ejb-relationship?	The first half of the relationship.	Chapter 15
ejb-relationship?	The second half of the relationship.	Chapter 15

Table C.23 The <ejb-relation-role> Element

ELEMENT	DESCRIPTION	WHERE TO GO FOR MORE INFORMATION
description?	A text description of this half of the relationship.	Chapter 15
ejb-relationship-role-name?	A unique nickname for this half of the relationship.	Chapter 15

Table C.23 *(continued)*

ELEMENT	DESCRIPTION	WHERE TO GO FOR MORE INFORMATION
multiplicity	Relationships can be *One:One*, *One:Many*, *Many:One*, or *Many:Many*. This element declares this half of the relationship to either be *One* or *Many*.	Chapter 15
cascade-delete?	By declaring this empty element, when the other half of the relationship is removed, so is this half. *Note:* The other half of the relationship must have a One multiplicity, because otherwise you could get into an infinite cascading deletion loop.	Chapter 15
relationship-role-source	Identifies which bean is participating in this relationship.	Chapter 15
cmr-field?	Identifies the get/set method that will be located on this bean and will access the other half of the relationship.	Chapter 15

<relationship-role-source>

A *relationship-role-source* identifies which bean is participating in a relationship. Used in *ejb-relationship-role*. (See Table C.24.)

<cmr-field>

A *cmr-field* identifies the get/set method that will be associated with a bean to access the other half of a relationship. Used in *ejb-relationship-role*. (See Table C.25.)

Table C.24 The <relationship-role-source> Element

ELEMENT	DESCRIPTION	WHERE TO GO FOR MORE INFORMATION
description?	A text description of this bean participating in the relationship.	Chapter 15
ejb-name	The Ejb-name of the bean participating in this relationship.	Chapter 15

Table C.25 The <cmr-field> Element

ELEMENT	DESCRIPTION	WHERE TO GO FOR MORE INFORMATION
description?	A text description of this container-managed relationship field.	Chapter 15
cmr-field-name	The name of the get/set method associated with accessing the other half of this relationship. *Note:* Leave off the get/set prefix, and make sure the first letter is lowercase.	Chapter 15
cmr-field-type	If the other half of the relationship has a multiplicity of *Many* then you need to choose either: *java.util.Collection* (can contain duplicates) *java.util.Set* (cannot contain duplicates). This needs to match up to your get/set methods.	Chapter 15

Defining the Assembly Descriptor

The following is an example of how to set up an assembly descriptor. Descriptions follow.

```
<ejb-jar xmlns=http://java.sun.com/xml/ns/j2ee version="2.1"
         xmlns:xsi=http://www.w3.org/2001/XMLSchema-instance
         xsi:schemaLocation="http://java.sun.com/xml/ns/j2ee
      http://java.sun.com/xml/ns/j2ee/ejb-jar_2_1.xsd">
 ...
 <assembly-descriptor>

    <security-role>
      <description>
        Personnel authorized to perform employee administration
      </description>
      <role-name>admins</role-name>
    </security-role>

    <method-permission>
      <role-name>administrators</role-name>

      <method>
```

```
        <ejb-name>EmployeeManagement</ejb-name>
        <method-name>*</method-name>
      </method>
    </method-permission>

    <container-transaction>
      <method>
        <ejb-name>EmployeeManagement</ejb-name>
        <method-name>*</method-name>
      </method>
      <trans-attribute>Required</trans-attribute>
    </container-transaction>

    <exclude-list>
      <description>
        We don't have a 401k plan, so we
        don't support this method.
      </description>
      <method>
        <ejb-name>EmployeeManagement</ejb-name>
        <method-name>modify401kPlan</method-name>
        <method-params>String</method-params>
      </method>
    </exclude-list>

  </assembly-descriptor>
</ejb-jar>
```

<assembly-descriptor>

The *assembly-descriptor* element is the root of the assembly descriptor. Used in *ejb-jar*. (See Table C.26.)

Table C.26 The <assembly-descriptor> Element

ELEMENT	DESCRIPTION	WHERE TO GO FOR MORE INFORMATION
security-role*	Identifies zero or more security roles that the application uses. This corresponds to the *role-link* element defined earlier in this appendix.	See later table
method-permission*	Sets up permissions for specific methods on your bean.	See later table

(continued)

Table C.26 *(continnued)*

ELEMENT	DESCRIPTION	WHERE TO GO FOR MORE INFORMATION
container-transaction*	Sets up transactions associates with specific methods on your bean.	Chapter 12, Table C.24
exclude-list? callable.	A list of methods that should never be. Useful if you acquire a bean from a third party and don't want to make use of all its functionality.	

<security-role>

The *security-role* element defines a security role that the application uses. This corresponds to the *role-link* element defined earlier in this appendix. Used in *assembly-descriptor*. (See Table C.27.)

<method-permission>

The *method-permission* element sets up permission on a specific method in your bean. Used in *assembly-descriptor*. (See Table C.28.)

Table C.27 The <security-role> Element

ELEMENT	DESCRIPTION	WHERE TO GO FOR MORE INFORMATION
description?	A text description of this security role.	Chapter 10
role-name	The text string naming this security role.	Chapter 10

Table C.28 The <method-permission> Element

ELEMENT	DESCRIPTION	WHERE TO GO FOR MORE INFORMATION
description?	A text description of this method permission.	
role-name+ | unchecked	The names of one or more security roles that can call these methods. Or, alternatively, you can specify the *<unchecked/>* empty element to disable security checks on these methods.	
method+	A list of one or more methods that these security permissions apply to.	Table C.27

<container-transaction>

The *container-transaction* element associates one or more methods with a container-managed (declarative) transaction. Used in *assembly-descriptor*. (See Table C.29.)

<exclude-list>

The *exclude-list* element is a list of methods that should never be callable. This is useful if you acquire a bean from a third party and don't want to make use of all its functionality. Used in *assembly-descriptor*. (See Table C.30.)

Table C.29 The <container-transaction> Element

ELEMENT	DESCRIPTION	WHERE TO GO FOR MORE INFORMATION
description?	A text description of this transaction.	Chapter 12
method+	A list of one or more methods that this transaction applies to.	Chapter 12
trans-attribute	The style of transaction you'd like, either *NotSupported, Supports, Required, RequiresNew, Mandatory,* or *Never.*	Chapter 12

Table C.30 The <exclude-list> Element

ELEMENT	DESCRIPTION	WHERE TO GO FOR MORE INFORMATION
description?	A text description of why we are excluding these methods.	Chapter 10
method+	A list of one or more methods to exclude clients from being able to call.	Chapter 10, see later table

<method>

The *method* element specifies a method on a bean. Used in *method-permission, container-transaction,* and *exclude-list*. (See Table C.31.)

Table C.31 The <method> Element

ELEMENT	DESCRIPTION	WHERE TO GO FOR MORE INFORMATION
description?	A text description.	
ejb-name	The ejb-name of the bean we're interested in.	
method-intf?	Optionally identifies the interface name that we're specifying the method for, either *Home*, *Remote*, *LocalHome*, or *Local*. Useful if there is a naming conflict between two interface method signatures.	
method-name	The name of the method, capitalized properly. Can also use an asterisk (*) to specify all methods.	
method-	An optional list of parameters.	Table C.29
params?	Useful for disambiguating methods with the same signature.	

<method-params>

The *method-params* element is useful for disambiguating methods with the same signature Used in *method*. (See Table C.32.)

Table C.32 The <method-parems> Element

ELEMENT	DESCRIPTION	WHERE TO GO FOR MORE INFORMATION
method-param*	Zero or more fully qualified Java types of parameters.	

APPENDIX

D

The EJB Query Language (EJB-QL)

This appendix will help you fully understand the syntax and semantics of the *EJB Query Language* (EJB-QL), the language used to describe query methods for container-managed persistent entity beans in EJB 2.*x*. To understand this appendix, you should first be familiar with the chapters on entity beans—Chapters 6, 7, and 8. Chapter 15 will also help.

You can begin coding with EJB without fully understanding EJB-QL. We recommend that you read this appendix if you are struggling with understanding the basics of EJB-QL, or if you are doing EJB-QL coding and need a guide.

EJB-QL Overview

EJB-QL is a standard and portable language for expressing container-managed persistent entity bean query operations. These entity bean query operations can include finder methods (used by external entity bean clients), as well as select methods (used internally by the entity bean itself). EJB-QL is not necessary for bean-managed persistence because the bean provider writes the database access code, which is integrated into the entity bean class itself.

EJB-QL was a new addition to EJB 2.0. Before EJB 2.0, you needed to explain to the container how to implement your query operations in a proprietary way. For example, you might bundle a container-specific flat file with your bean. This flat file would not be portable to other containers, which was annoying for bean providers who wished to write container-agnostic components were.

Throughout this appendix, we use an e-commerce object model for the most part to illustrate EJB-QL, using entity beans such as orders, line items, products, and customers. We designed that object model in Chapter 22.

A Simple Example

Let's kick things off with a simple EJB-QL example. Take the following entity bean remote finder method:

```
public java.util.Collection findAvailableProducts() throws
FinderException, RemoteException;
```

This finder method means to find all products that are currently in stock. The following EJB-QL in the deployment descriptor instructs the container about how to generate the database access code that corresponds to this finder method:

```
...

<entity>
 <ejb-name>Product</ejb-name>
 <home>examples.ProductHome</home>
 <remote>examples.Product</remote>
 <ejb-class>examples.ProductBean</ejb-class>
 <persistence-type>Container</persistence-type>
 <prim-key-class>examples.ProductPK</prim-key-class>
 <reentrant>False</reentrant>

 <cmp-version>2.x</cmp-version>
 <abstract-schema-name>Product</abstract-schema-name>

 <cmp-field>
  <field-name>inventory</field-name>
 </cmp-field>
 ...more container-managed persistent fields...

 <query>
  <query-method>
   <method-name>findAvailableProducts</method-name>
   <method-params>
   </method-params>
```

```
    </query-method>
    <ejb-ql>
     SELECT OBJECT(p) FROM Product AS p WHERE p.inventory > 0
    </ejb-ql>
   </query>

   ...
</ejb-jar>
```

In the preceding code, we put together a query that resembles SQL or OQL. See Chapter 6 for more on Object Query Language (OQL). We can refer to entity beans inside of the EJB-QL by using that entity bean's *abstract-schema-name* defined earlier in the deployment descriptor. We can also query its container-managed fields or container-managed relationships, or other entity beans.

In fact, if we're using a relational database, the container will translate this EJB-QL code into SQL code in the form of JDBC statements. The following SQL is an example of what might be generated depending on your container implementation:

```
SELECT DISTINCT p.PKEY
FROM PRODUCT p
WHERE p.INVENTORY > 0
```

This SQL code returns primary keys (not rows) to the container. The container then wraps those primary keys in EJB objects and returns RMI-IIOP stubs to the client that called the finder method. When the client calls business methods on those stubs, the EJB objects intercept the call, and the *ejbLoad()* method is called on the entity beans. The container then loads the actual rows from the database. Note that this process may be optimized depending on your container implementation.

EJB-QL is useful for home and local home interfaces. A single EJB-QL definition will inform the container about how to implement the SQL code for any home and local home objects that have identically named finder methods.

The Power of Relationships

The big difference between EJB-QL and SQL is that EJB-QL allows you to traverse relationships between entity beans using a dot-notation. For example:

```
SELECT o.customer
FROM Order o
```

In this EJB-QL, we are returning all customers that have placed orders. We are navigating from the order entity bean to the customer entity bean easily using a dot-notation. This is quite seamless.

What's exciting about this notation is that bean providers don't need to know about tables or columns; they merely need to understand the relationships between the entity beans that they've authored. The container handles the traversal of relationships for us because we declare our entity beans in the same deployment descriptor and Ejb-jar file, empowering the container to manage all of our beans and thus understand their relationships.

In fact, you can traverse more than one relationship. That relationship can involve container-managed relationship fields and container-managed persistent fields. For example:

```
SELECT o.customer.address.homePhoneNumber
FROM Order o
```

The restriction on this type of recursive relationship traversal is that you are limited by the *navigatability* of the relationships that you define in the deployment descriptor. For example, let's say that in the deployment descriptor, you declare that orders have a one-to-many relationship with line items, but you do not define the reverse many-to-one relationship that line items have with orders. When performing EJB-QL, you can get from orders to line items, but not from line items to orders. Even though the database is directionally neutral, the line items entity bean should have no knowledge of orders, and thus this traversal cannot take place. For more about how to define these types of relationships, see Chapter 15.

EJB-QL Syntax

An EJB-QL query can contain four parts:

- A required SELECT clause
- A required FROM clause
- An optional WHERE clause
- An optional ORDER BY clause

We now discuss the details of each of these clauses. We'll do the SELECT and ORDER BY clauses later because they deal with the return results of a query.

The FROM Clause

The FROM clause *constricts* the *domain* of a query. It indicates which part of the data storage you are querying—that is, what entity beans you are going to look at. In the case of a relational database, the FROM clause typically restricts which tables you are querying. For example, the following FROM clause means we are looking only at order entity beans:

```
SELECT OBJECT(o)
FROM Order AS o
```

What we're doing here is *declaring a variable* in the FROM clause. We are creating a variable, *o*, which can be used later in the query. In this case, we are reusing that variable in the SELECT clause. You can also reuse that variable in the WHERE and ORDER BY clauses.

Note that declaring variables will restrict your queries even if you don't use the variables. For example:

```
SELECT OBJECT(o)
FROM Order AS o, Customer AS c
```

The previous query finds all orders if and only if there are any customers that do *not* need to be related to the *Order* objects. Even though we aren't using the variable *c* anywhere else, we are still excluding orders if there are no customers. By declaring a variable, you are constraining the domain of the query. This is similar to the following SQL statement that returns all orders so long as there are one or more records in the Customer table:

```
SELECT o.*
FROM Order o, Customer c
```

Finally, you should note that the phrase *AS* is optional and is merely syntactic sugar to help make the query look better. This query produces the same result as the previous EJB-QL statement:

```
SELECT OBJECT(o)
FROM Order o, Customer c
```

Declaring Collection Variables

Sometimes, in the FROM clause, you need to declare variables that represent a collection of values. For example, let's say we want to find all of the line items that are attached to orders. The following query achieves that:

```
SELECT OBJECT(l)
FROM Order AS o, IN(o.lineItems) l
```

The preceding EJB-QL declares two variables:

- The phrase *Order AS o* declares a variable *o*, which represents any order entity bean.
- The phrase *IN(o.lineItems) l* declares a variable *l*, which represents any line item from any order bean's collection of line items.

As you can see, since the evaluation order is left to right, you can use variables on the right that were declared on the left.

Thus, you use the *AS* syntax when declaring a variable representing a single value and the *IN* syntax when declaring a variable representing a collection of values. Note that both *AS* and *IN* queries can return multiple values from the EJB-QL query — the difference is that the *IN* syntax is necessary when traversing an underlying entity bean relationship that uses a *java.util.Collection*, such as an order that points to a collection of line items.

Variables Represent Only One Value at a Time

Next, consider the following query, which returns all line items that are attached to orders that are attached to customers:

```
SELECT OBJECT(l)
FROM Customer AS c, IN(c.orders) o, IN(o.lineItems) l
```

Notice the phrase *o.lineItems*. Although *o* is a collection variable, it represents only one element of that collection at a time. Thus, it is perfectly legal to use the phrase *o.lineItems* because in that phrase, *o* represents an individual order, not a collection of orders.

The WHERE Clause

The EJB-QL WHERE clause restricts the *results* of a query. It is where you choose the values you want from the declared variables in the FROM clause. The general syntax of the WHERE clause is *WHERE conditional expression*. For example:

```
SELECT OBJECT(o)
FROM Order o
WHERE o.lineItems IS NOT EMPTY
```

The query finds all orders that have line items.

Handling Input Parameters

When performing a query, you'll often want to query based upon parameters supplied by the client. For example, to implement the following finder method that finds a product based on a description:

```
findProductByDescription(String s)
```

A WHERE clause can be used as follows:

```
SELECT OBJECT(p)
FROM Product p
WHERE p.description = ?1
```

Here, *?1* represents the first parameter passed in. Additional parameters would be numbered as *?2*, *?3*, and so on. Note that you don't need to use all variables declared in the finder or select method.

Conditional Expressions

Many conditional expressions are built-in to EJB-QL. The complete list is in Table D.1.

Note that you can have more than one conditional expression and use parentheses to denote the order of execution. Your container may provide proprietary extensions to these conditional expressions as well, perhaps in a separate deployment descriptor.

EJB-QL also contains the following built-in functions:

- **CONCAT(String, String)** combines two strings into one and returns a String.
- **SUBSTRING(String, start, length)** cuts a String into a smaller String, beginning at *start* and being *length* long.
- **LOCATE(String, String [, start])** returns an *int* denoting where a String is located within another String. You can use the optional *start* parameter to indicate where to begin locating the search string.
- **LENGTH(String)** gives you a string's length, returned as an *int*.
- **ABS(number)** returns the absolute value of a number, which can be an *int*, *float*, or *double*.
- **SQRT(double)** takes the square root of a number and returns it as a *double*.
- **MOD(int, int)** returns the remainder as *integer* after dividing first integer by second integer.

Table D.1 EJB-QL Conditional Expressions

CONDITIONAL EXPRESSION	EXAMPLE	NOTES
Mathematical operations: 1, -, *, / Comparison operations: =, >, >=, <, <=, <> (not equal) logical operators: NOT, AND, OR	Find all products that are computer chips and whose profit margin is positive: SELECT OBJECT(p) FROM Product p WHERE (p.description = 'chip') AND (p.basePrice - p.cost > 0)	• Two entity beans are equal if and only if they share the same primary key value. • You cannot compare two different entity bean classes.
Between expressions	Find all products whose price is at least 1000 and at most 2000: SELECT OBJECT(p) FROM Product p WHERE p.basePrice BETWEEN 1000 AND 2000	Can also use NOT BETWEEN to return all data that is not between two values.
In expressions	Find all products whose manufacturer is either Intel or Sun: SELECT OBJECT(p) FROM Product p WHERE p.manufacturer IN ('Intel', 'Sun')	Can also use NOT IN to return all data that is not in a range.
Like expressions	Find all products with ids that begin with 12 and end with 3. For example, 123 or 12993 qualifies, but not 1234: SELECT OBJECT(p) FROM Product p WHERE product.productID LIKE '12%3' Find all products with ids that begin with 123 and are a total of four characters long. For example, 123c qualifies, but not 14 nor 12345: SELECT OBJECT(p) FROM Product p WHERE product.productID LIKE '123_'	• % stands for any sequence of zero or more characters. • _ stands for a single character. • You can represent the literal % or character by using special escape sequences (see the EJB spec for more). • You can also use NOT LIKE to achieve the opposite effect.

Table D.1 *(continued)*

CONDITIONAL EXPRESSION	EXAMPLE	NOTES
Null comparison expressions	Find all products that have NULL descriptions: SELECT OBJECT(p) FROM Product p WHERE product.description IS NULL	You can also use NOT NULL to find all data that has non-NULL values.
Empty collection comparison expressions	Find all orders that have no line items: SELECT OBJECT(o) expressions FROM Order o WHERE o.lineItems IS EMPTY	• You can also use IS NOT EMPTY to find valid collections. •In this special case, you can declare collections in the WHERE clause rather than declaring them as variables first in the FROM clause.
Collection member expressions	Find all line items that are attached to orders: SELECT OBJECT(l Order o, LineItem l WHERE l MEMBER OF o.lineItems	• The word OF is optional. In this special case, you can declare collections in the WHERE clause rather than declaring them as variables first in the FROM clause. • Can also use NOT MEMBER OF to locate data where elements are not members of collections.

Dealing with Collections

Normally if you want to use collections in the WHERE clause, you should declare those collections as variables in the FROM clause. For example, the following is invalid:

```
SELECT OBJECT(l)
FROM Order AS o
WHERE o.lineItems.product.name = 'chip'
```

This query is invalid because we are trying to reference a variable from a collection. The following is the correct way to write this EJB-QL:

```
SELECT OBJECT(l)
FROM Order AS o, IN(o.lineItems) l
WHERE l.product.name = 'chip'
```

The two special exceptions to this rule are when you use the EMPTY or MEMBER conditional expressions, shown in Table D.1. In these cases, you can use collections in the WHERE clause.

Performing Comparisons

Sometimes you may need to declare more than one variable that represents the same entity bean. When you are performing comparisons, this comes in very handy. For example:

```
SELECT OBJECT(p1)
FROM Product p1, Product p2
WHERE p1.quantityInStock > p2.quantityInStock AND
      p2.name='Pentium 866'
```

The preceding query finds all products that have a greater quantity in stock than a Pentium 866 chip.

The SELECT Clause

The EJB-QL SELECT clause specifies the return results of a query. To understand why we need the SELECT clause, consider the following query, which returns all orders that contain line items:

```
SELECT OBJECT(o)
FROM Order AS o, IN(o.lineItems) l
```

In this query, we have defined two variables in the FROM clause: *o* and *l*. The SELECT clause is necessary because it affirms that we want to return *o* (and not *l*) to the client that called the query.

How to Traverse Relationships

The SELECT clause can traverse relationships. For example, the following query returns all the products in all the orders that contain line items:

```
SELECT l.product FROM Order AS o, IN(o.lineItems) l
```

As you can see, we can use the convenient dot-notation to traverse relationships in the SELECT clause. Behind the scenes, a SQL JOIN statement might occur.

If you've been paying careful attention, you may have noticed that in the earlier example we wrapped a variable *o* with the phrase *OBJECT()*, but in this example, we didn't use the phrase *OBJECT()* at all. The EJB-QL rule is that you wrap your return result with the phrase *OBJECT()* only if you are returning a standalone variable that does not traverse a relationship using the dot-notation.

How to Deal with Collections

Let's say we want to find all line items on all orders. We are thus asking for a collection of return results. Unfortunately, the following SELECT clause will not work:

```
SELECT o.lineItems
FROM Order AS o
```

The reason this doesn't work is that SELECT clauses may return only single variables, not collections. To get around this restriction, you need to define a variable in the FROM clause. The following demonstrates this as a legal way to find all line items on all orders:

```
SELECT OBJECT(l)
FROM Order AS o, IN(o.lineItems) l
```

How to Filter for Duplicates

You can control whether SELECT clauses return duplicates. For example, take our previous EJB-QL query that finds all products in all order line items:

```
SELECT l.product FROM Order AS o, IN(o.lineItems) l
```

The previous query may return duplicate products because two different people may have ordered the same product. To get a unique list, you must apply the DISTINCT filter, as follows:

```
SELECT DISTINCT l.product FROM Order AS o, IN(o.lineItems) l
```

Another choice is to declare your finder or select method to return a *java.util.Set*, which may not contain duplicates compared to a *java.util.Collection*. If you use a *java.util.Set*, both of the preceding EJB-QL statements would return the same unique results.

How to Control What Gets Returned in Finders

EJB-QL queries return results differently depending on how the client initiates the query. For example, take the following finder queries (thrown exceptions omitted):

```
// declared on the home interface
public java.util.Collection findAllProducts();

// declared on the local home interface
public java.util.Collection findAllProducts();
```

We want EJB objects to be returned for the first query and EJB local objects to be returned for the second query. The EJB-QL code in the deployment descriptor for both of these query methods could be:

```
<query>
 <query-method>
  <method-name>findAllProducts</method-name>
  <method-params>
  </method-params>
 </query-method>
 <ejb-ql>
  SELECT OBJECT (p) FROM Product AS p
 </ejb-ql>
</>
```

What's great here is that we wrote our EJB-QL once, yet we can reuse it for the home and local home interfaces. The container will automatically wrap the return results in an *EJBObject* or *EJBLocalObject* (or collections of *EJBObjects/EJBLocalObjects*). These are the only possible types you can return from a finder query.

How to Control What Gets Returned in Selects

With finder methods, the container knows whether the results of a finder should be EJB objects or EJB local objects, because the container could look at whether the query was defined on the home interface or local home interface, respectively. But what about *ejbSelect()* methods (see Chapter 8)? Consider the following *ejbSelect()*:

```
public abstract java.util.Collection ejbSelectAllProducts();
```

Here, we define the *ejbSelect()* method on the entity bean class, which doesn't give the container any information about whether our query should return EJB objects or EJB local objects. How does the container know which objects to wrap around the results?

To get around this, EJB requires that you set up a special stanza in the deployment descriptor to inform the container about whether the results should be local or remote objects:

```
<query>
 <query-method>
  <method-name>ejbSelectAllProducts</method-name>
  <method-params>
  </method-params>
 </query-method>
 <result-type-mapping>Local</result-type-mapping>
 <ejb-ql>
  SELECT OBJECT (p) FROM Product AS p
 </ejb-ql>
</>
```

The preceding code will cause the *ejbSelect()* method to return a collection of EJB local objects. If you want the results to be a collection of EJB objects, change the *result-type-mapping* element to have the value *Remote*.

Finally, note that *ejbSelect()* methods can also return container-managed fields. For example:

```
public abstract java.lang.String ejbSelectProductName();
```

Finder methods cannot return container-managed fields because finder methods can operate remotely and at the granularity of entity beans, not parts of entity beans.

Using Aggregate Functions

Aggregate functions were not supported in EJB 2.0 EJB-QL. With EJB 2.1, containers now support five widely used aggregate functions:

- **The AVG aggregate function** returns the average value of the numeric cmp-field specified as the function argument. The following EJB-QL returns average order quantity.

  ```
  SELECT AVG(o.quantity) FROM Order o
  ```

- **The COUNT aggregate function** returns the total number of results in the final result set. The following query returns total number of customers holding VISA credit or debit cards.

  ```
  SELECT COUNT(c) FROM Customers c WHERE c.merchanttype = 'VISA'
  ```

- **The MAX aggregate function** returns the largest value in a given *cmp-field*. The *cmp-field* argument to this function must be an orderable cmp-field type such as string, numeric, character, or date types. The following query returns maximum salary among all the employees in a specific salary grade level.

```
SELECT MAX(e.salary) FROM Employees e WHERE e.salarygrade = 'Z12'
```

- **The MIN aggregate function** returns the smallest value in a given *cmp-field*. The following query returns the minimum salary among all the employees in a specific salary grade level.

```
SELECT MIN(e.salary) FROM Employees e WHERE e.salarygrade = 'Z12'
```

- **The SUM aggregate function** returns the sum of all the values of a given *cmp-field* of numeric type. The following example query returns the total salary paid by a given company to its employees.

```
SELECT SUM(e.salary) FROM Employees e
```

Although the EJB 2.1 specification does not specifically restrict the use of aggregate queries with finder methods, it is obvious that aggregate queries should not be used with finder methods because finder methods are allowed to return only reference(s) to entity *EJBObject* or *EJBLocalObject* and aggregate queries return values representing mathematical calculations that cannot be represented as *EJBObject* or *EJBLocalObject*. Hence, use aggregate functions only for queries underlying *ejbSelect* methods.

The ORDER BY Clause

The ORDER BY clause has been newly introduced in the EJB 2.1 specification. It allows the objects or values returned by the query to be ordered. The EJB-QL ORDER BY clause works similarly to SQL ORDER BY clause. The following example returns an alphabetical list of all customers:

```
SELECT OBJECT(c) FROM Customers c ORDER BY c.name
```

You can also specify whether you want to order in ascending or descending fashion by using ASC and DESC keywords. For example, the following query returns an alphabetical list of all customers in a descending order:

```
SELECT OBJECT(c) FROM Customers c ORDER BY c.name DESC
```

The following example returns the list of orders ordered by quantity and total costs such that multiple orders with the same quantity are further sorted by the total cost of the order:

```
SELECT OBJECT(o) FROM Order o ORDER BY o.quantity, o.totalcost
```

When ordering string values using an ORDER BY clause, be aware that not every database supports case-sensitive strings and hence, case-sensitive string ordering. Thus, by changing your EJB application to use a different database, you might be returned differently ordered string values by the EJB-QL ORDER BY clause.

Truth Tables

Let's wrap up our EJB-QL lesson with a look at the truth tables for the way the operations AND, OR, and NOT evaluate (see Tables D.2, D.3, and D.4). To read these tables, combine the column header with the row header using the operator in the upper-left corner. That should give you the result in the cell located at the intersection of the column and row. Note also that in the tables, the case of *unknown* means expressions that produce an unknown result, such as the clause:

```
WHERE NULL IN ('Intel', 'Sun')
```

Table D.2 The AND Truth Table

AND	TRUE	FALSE	UNKNOWN
True	True	False	Unknown
False	False	False	False
Unknown	Unknown	False	Unknown

Table D.3 The OR Truth Table

OR	TRUE	FALSE	UNKNOWN
True	True	True	True
False	True	False	Unknown
Unknown	True	Unknown	Unknown

Table D.4 The NOT Truth Table

True	False
False	True
Unknown	Unknown

In the final section of this appendix, you can test your knowledge of EJB-QL. Here is a list of queries that we'd like to implement. Try to figure out the EJB-QL without looking at the description, or try to figure out the description by looking at the EJB-QL. (Answers at the end of this appendix.)

1. **Find all line items.**
2. **Find all customers' home addresses.**
3. **Find all customers' home addresses without duplicates.**
4. **Find all line items that are attached to orders.**
5. **Find all orders that contain line items.**
6. **Find all orders that do not contain line items.**
7. **Find all products whose descriptions are either chip or motherboard.**
8. **Find all products that have a zero inventory.**
9. **Find all products with inventory greater than a parameter passed in.**
10. **Find all products with inventory between 10 and 20.**
11. **Find all products whose remaining inventory is greater than the remaining inventory for products manufactured by Intel.**
12. **Find the names of all customers whose names begin with A.**
13. **Find the total amount for orders from a certain customer 'John Doe'.**
14. **Find all customers whose names begin with A in ascending order.**

Final Note

Be forewarned that while EJB-QL is a convenient layer of indirection that isolates you from the database, a danger lurks under the covers. The danger is that your generated SQL code could perform poorly because you are not hand-tuning SQL code but rather, you are dealing with high-level EJB-QL code.

Standard performance best practices of optimizing SQL still apply with EJB-QL. Check and recheck the optimization of the container-generated SQL by examining your generated helper files or your database log. Here are some possible ways to optimize your queries:

- Optimize your entity beans using specific container flags such as lazy loading flags (check your container documentation).
- If available, use your container tools to help generate more optimal SQL from EJB-QL.
- Redesign your EJB-QL.
- Rewrite some of your finder or select methods.
- Redesign or denormalize your database schema.
- Rethink your entity bean design.
- Manually write your SQL.

Summary

In this appendix, we've discussed EJB-QL. EJB-QL is a great advancement in EJB because it allows bean providers to ship code that contains queries that are portable across containers. We introduced the syntax of EJB-QL, including the SELECT, FROM, WHERE, and ORDER BY clauses. We then went through several EJB-QL examples. You should now be empowered to try writing your own EJB-QL and begin experimenting with container-managed persistent entity beans.

Following are the answers to the quiz:

1. SELECT OBJECT(l) FROM LineItem l
2. SELECT c.homeAddress FROM Customer c
3. SELECT DISTINCT c.homeAddress FROM Customer c
4. SELECT OBJECT(l) FROM Order o, IN(o.lineItems) l
5. SELECT OBJECT(o) FROM Order o, IN(o.lineItems) l
6. SELECT OBJECT(o) FROM Order o WHERE o.lineItems IS EMPTY
7. SELECT OBJECT(p) FROM Product p WHERE p.description IN ('chip', 'motherboard')
8. SELECT OBJECT(p) FROM Product p WHERE p.inventory = 0
9. SELECT OBJECT(p) FROM Product p WHERE p.inventory > ?1
10. SELECT OBJECT(p) FROM Product p WHERE p.inventory BETWEEN 10 AND 20

11. SELECT OBJECT(p1) FROM Product p1, Product p2 WHERE p1.inventory > p2.inventory AND p2.manufacturer = 'Intel'
12. SELECT c.name FROM Customer c WHERE c.name LIKE 'A%'
13. SELECT SUM(l.price) FROM Order o, IN(o.lineItems) l WHERE o.customer.name = 'John Doe'
14. SELECT OBJECT(c) FROM Customer c WHERE c.name LIKE 'A%' ORDER BY c.name ASC

APPENDIX

E

EJB Quick Reference Guide

This appendix is a quick reference for programmers to use during EJB development. In the first section, you'll find Figures E.1 through E.13 illustrating what's really going on in an EJB system. These were taken directly from the EJB specification; we have condensed the diagrams and commented on them to clarify their meaning. You'll also find summaries and explanations of each method in the EJB architecture, as well as a transaction reference.

Session Bean Diagrams

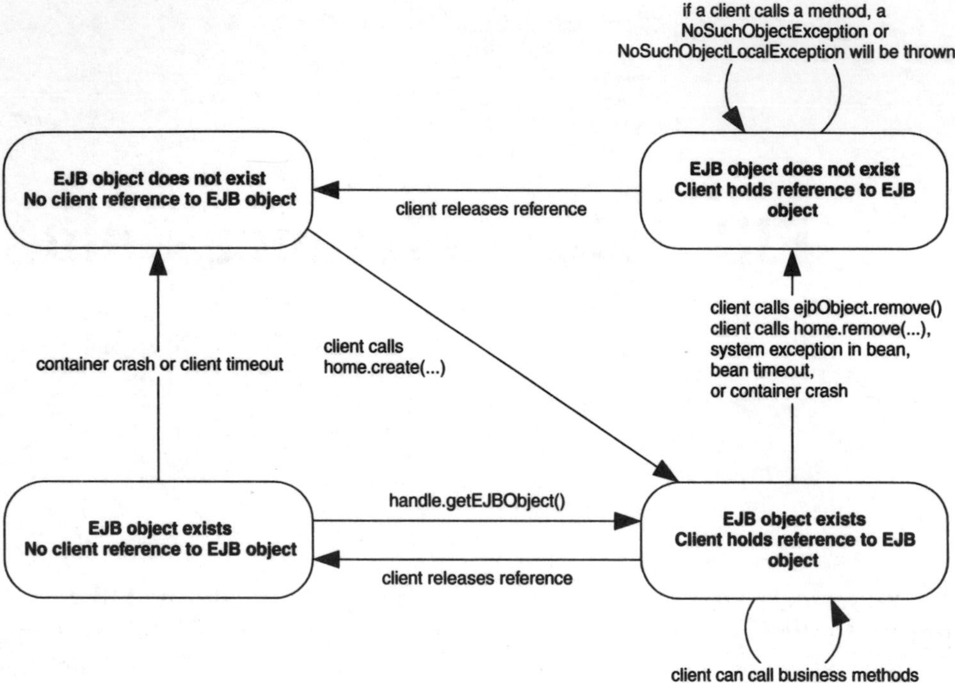

Figure E.1 The client's view of a session bean object life cycle.

Stateless Session Bean Diagrams

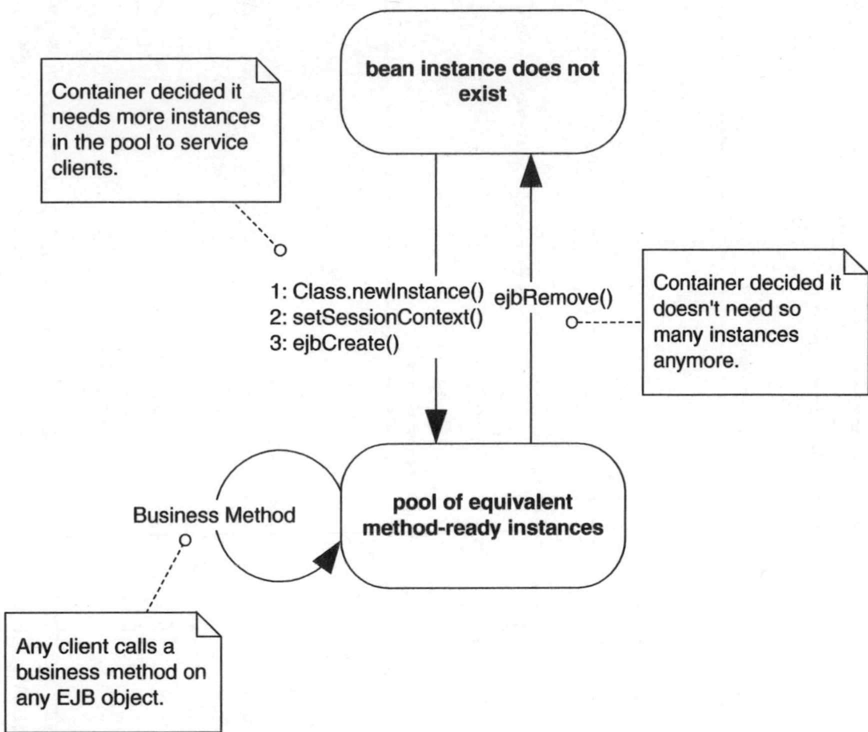

Figure E.2 The life cycle of a stateless session bean. Each method call shown is an invocation from the container to the bean instance.

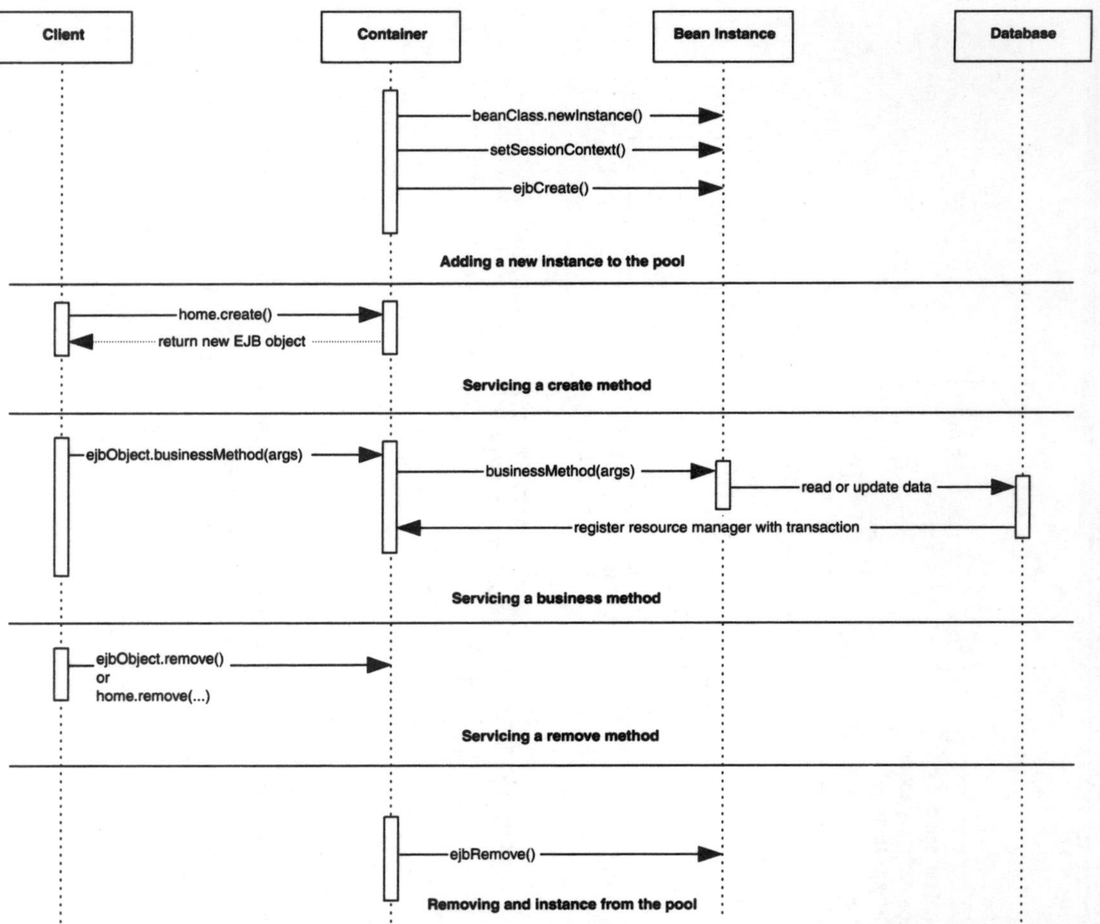

Figure E.3 Sequence diagram for stateless session beans. For simplicity, the Container object represents all container subsystems, including EJB objects, home objects, transaction services, and so on.

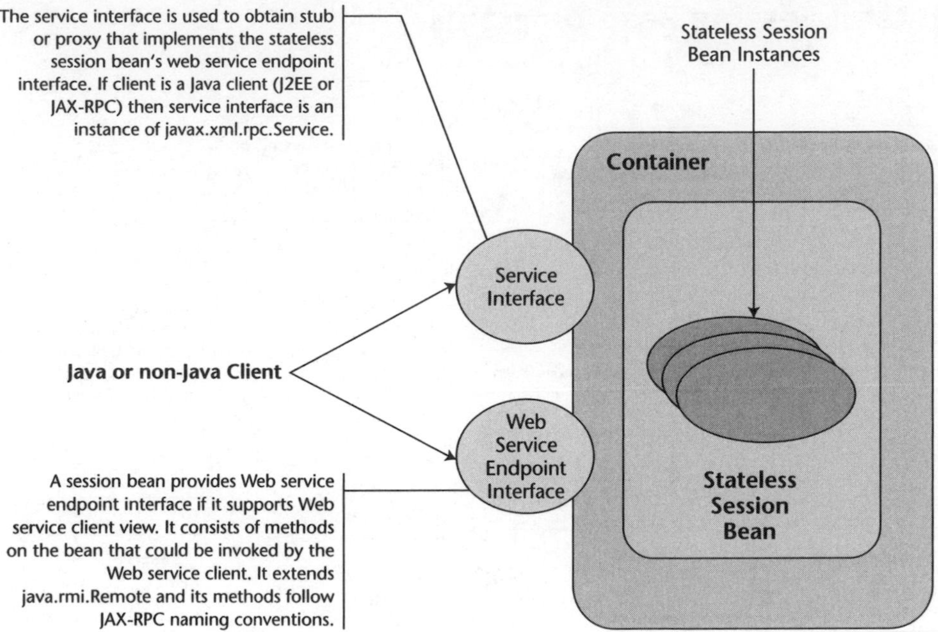
The service interface is used to obtain stub or proxy that implements the stateless session bean's web service endpoint interface. If client is a Java client (J2EE or JAX-RPC) then service interface is an instance of javax.xml.rpc.Service.
Stateless Session Bean Instances
Container
Service Interface
Java or non-Java Client
Web Service Endpoint Interface
A session bean provides Web service endpoint interface if it supports Web service client view. It consists of methods on the bean that could be invoked by the Web service client. It extends java.rmi.Remote and its methods follow JAX-RPC naming conventions.
Stateless Session Bean

Figure E.4 The Web services client view of a stateless session bean. The client can be a Java or non-Java client.

Stateful Session Bean Diagrams

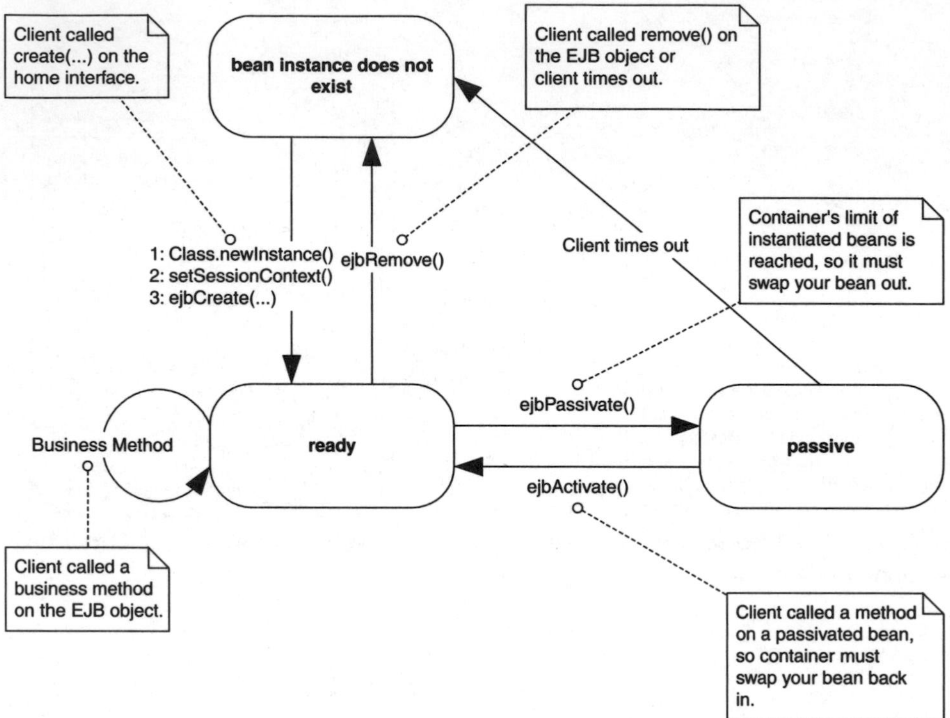

Figure E.5 The life cycle of a stateful session bean (does not implement *javax.ejb .SessionSynchronization*). Each method call shown is an invocation from the container to the bean instance.

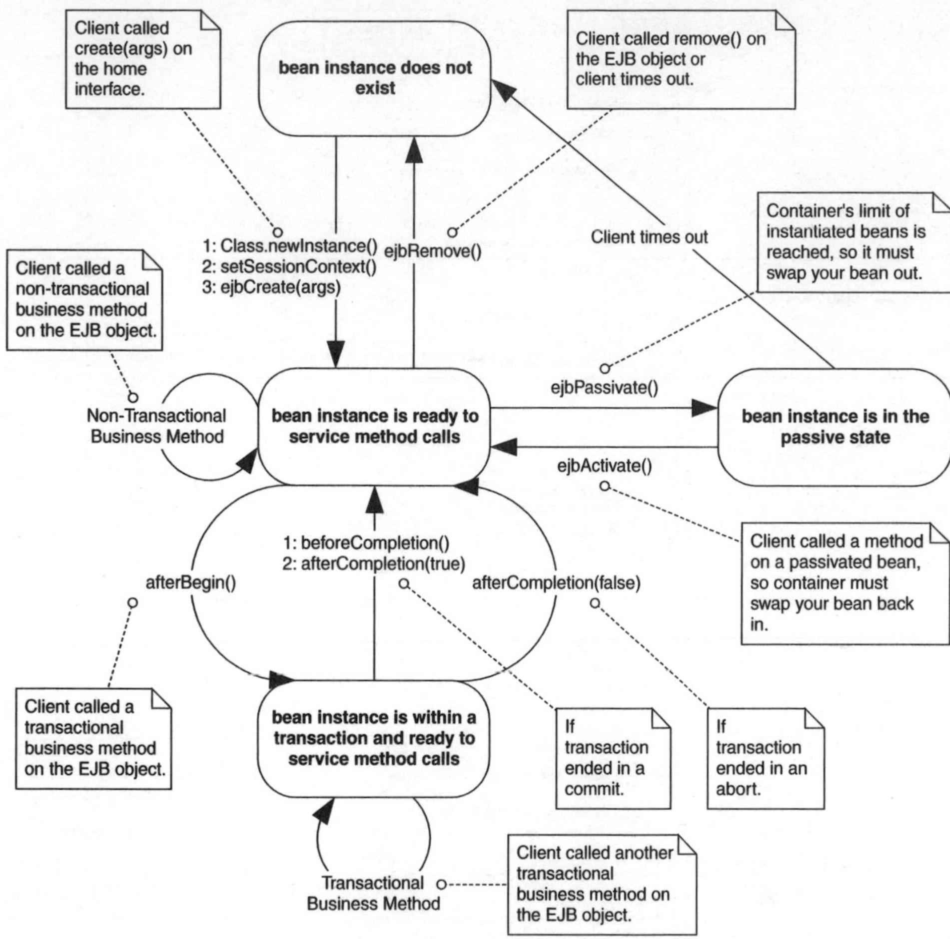

Figure E.6 The life cycle of a stateful session bean (implements *javax.ejb.Session Synchronization*). Each method call shown is an invocation from the container to the bean instance.

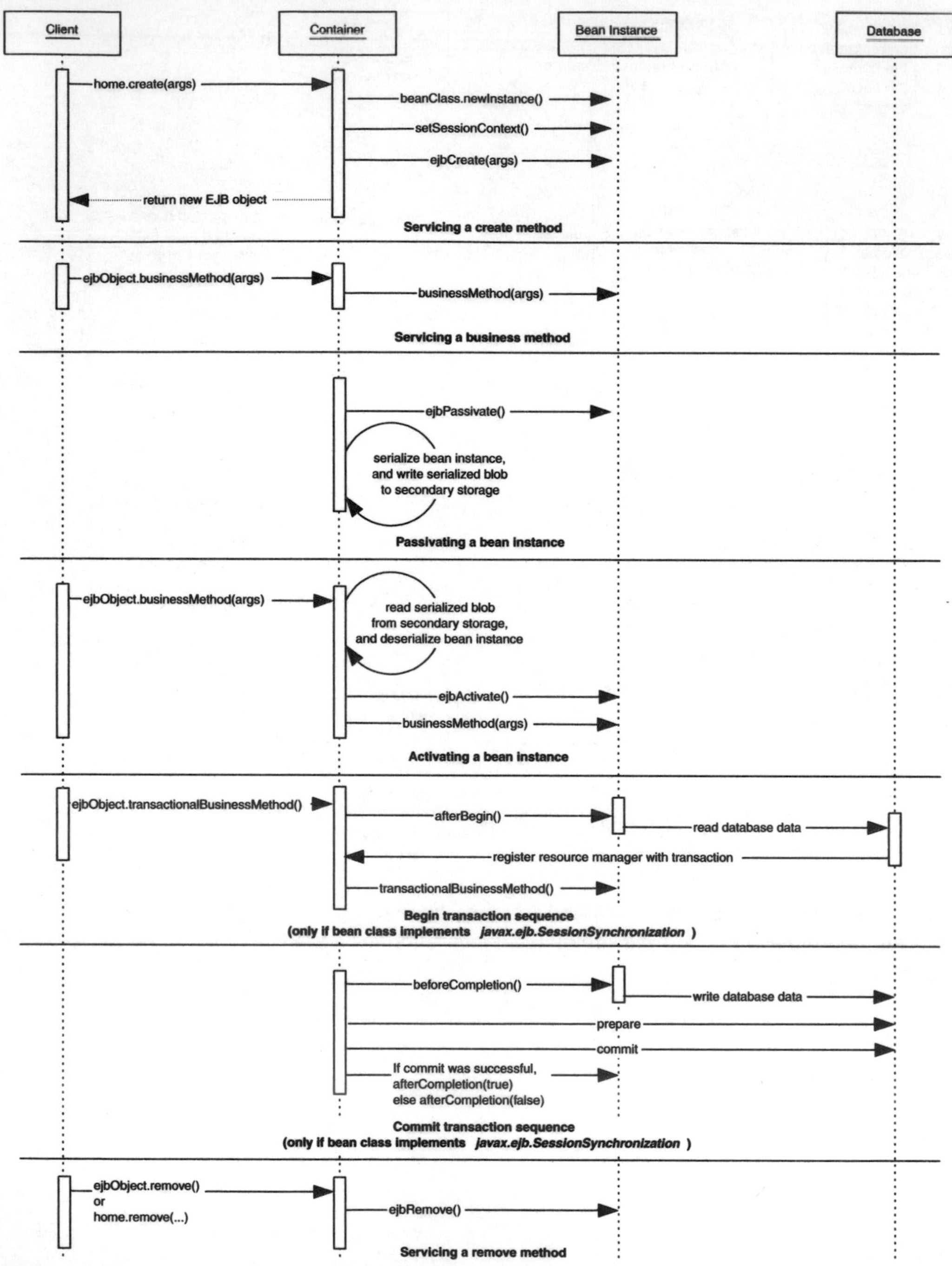

Figure E.7 Sequence diagram for stateful session beans. For simplicity, the Container object represents all container subsystems, including EJB objects, home objects, transaction services, and so on.

Entity Bean Diagrams

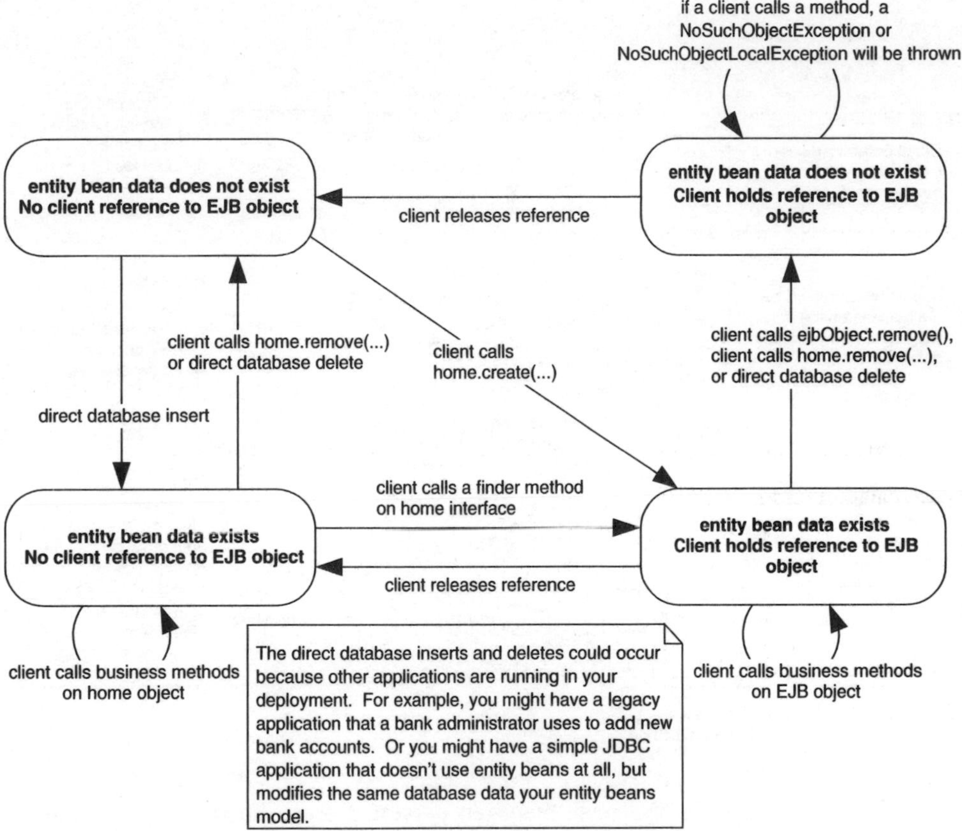

Figure E.8 The client's view of an entity bean object life cycle.

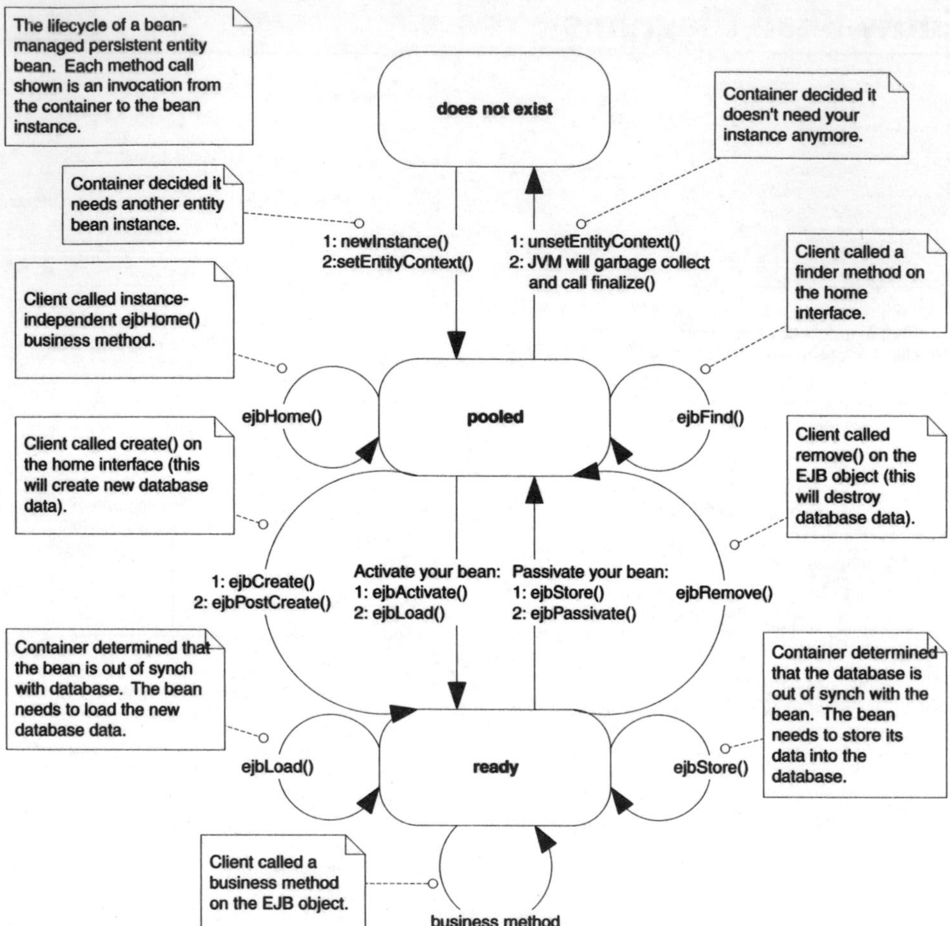

Figure E.9 The life cycle of a bean-managed persistent entity bean. Each method call shown is an invocation from the container to the bean instance.

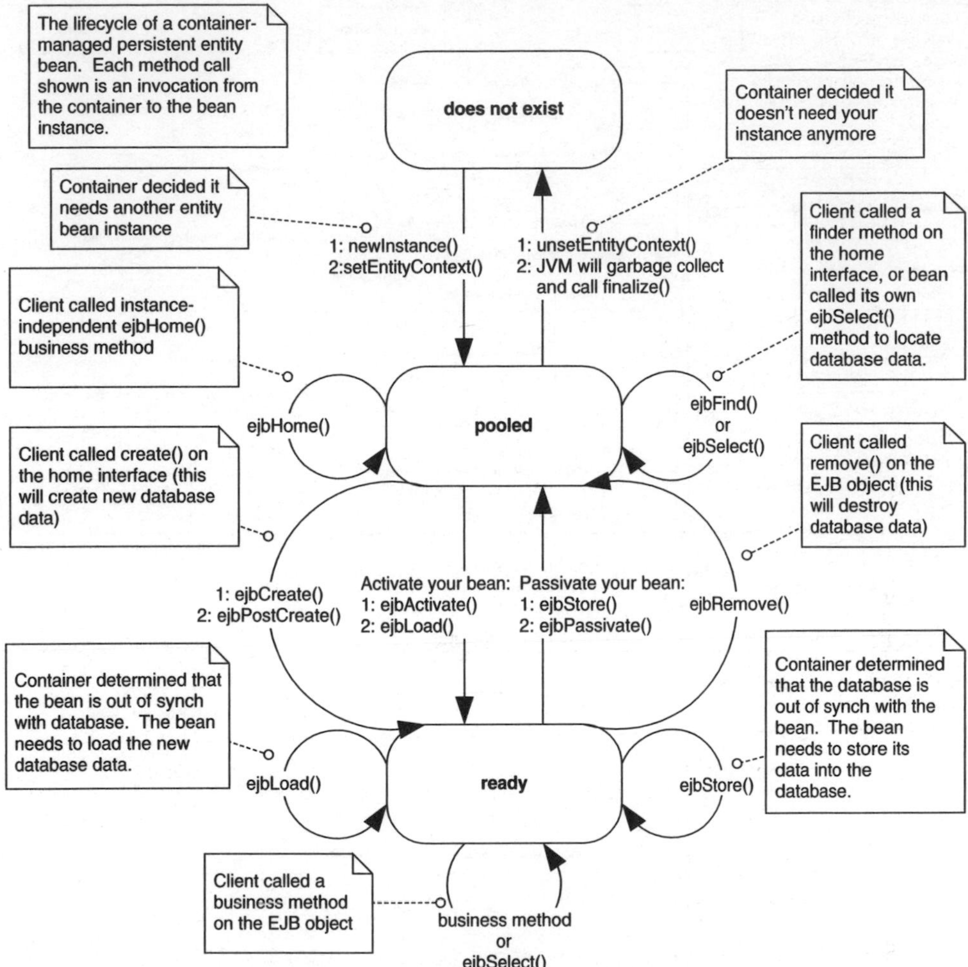

Figure E.10 The life cycle of a container-managed persistent entity bean. Each method call shown is an invocation from the container to the bean instance.

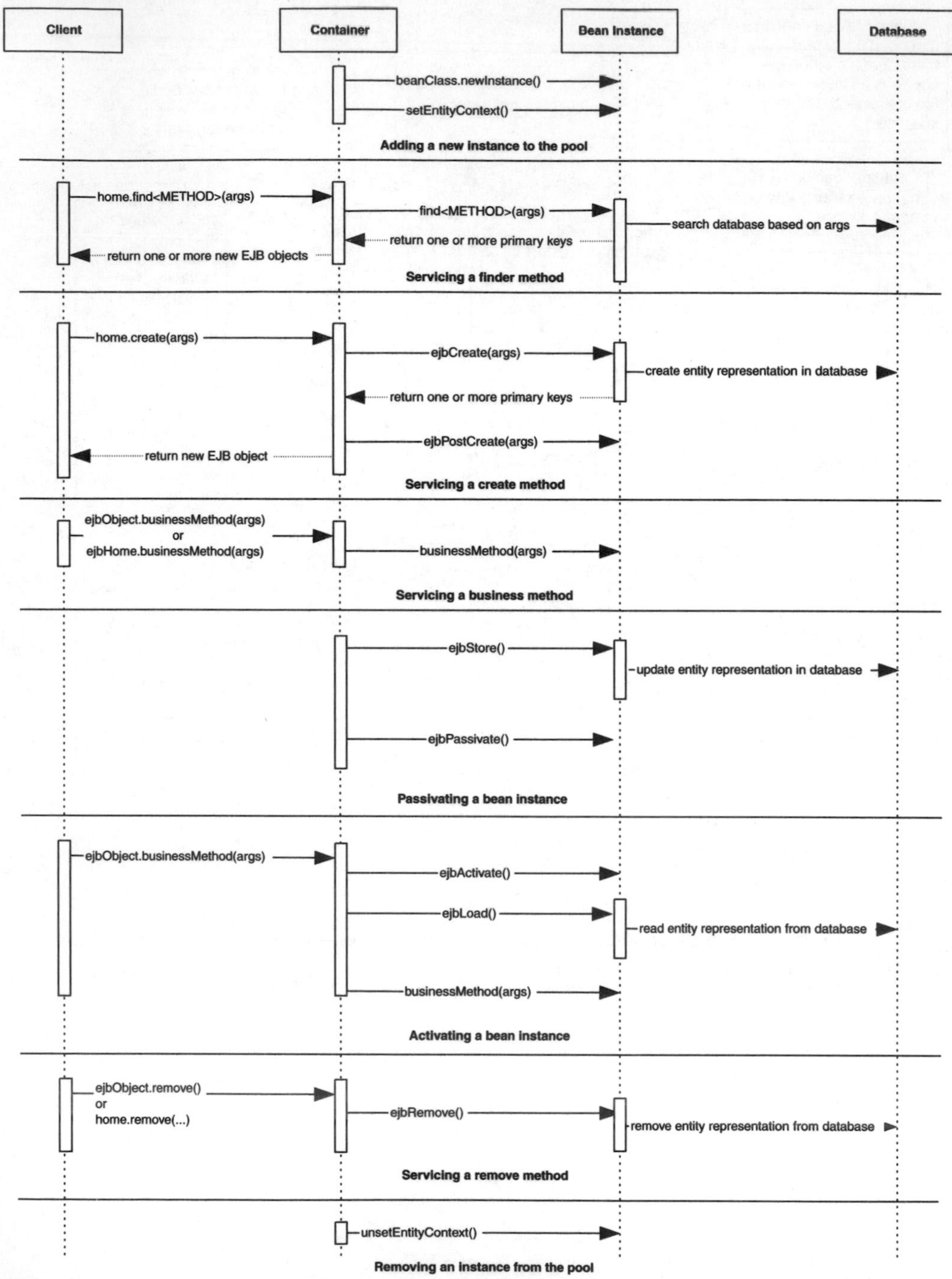

Figure E.11 Sequence diagram for bean-managed persistent entity beans. For simplicity, the Container object represents all container subsystems, including EJB objects, home objects, transaction services, and so on.

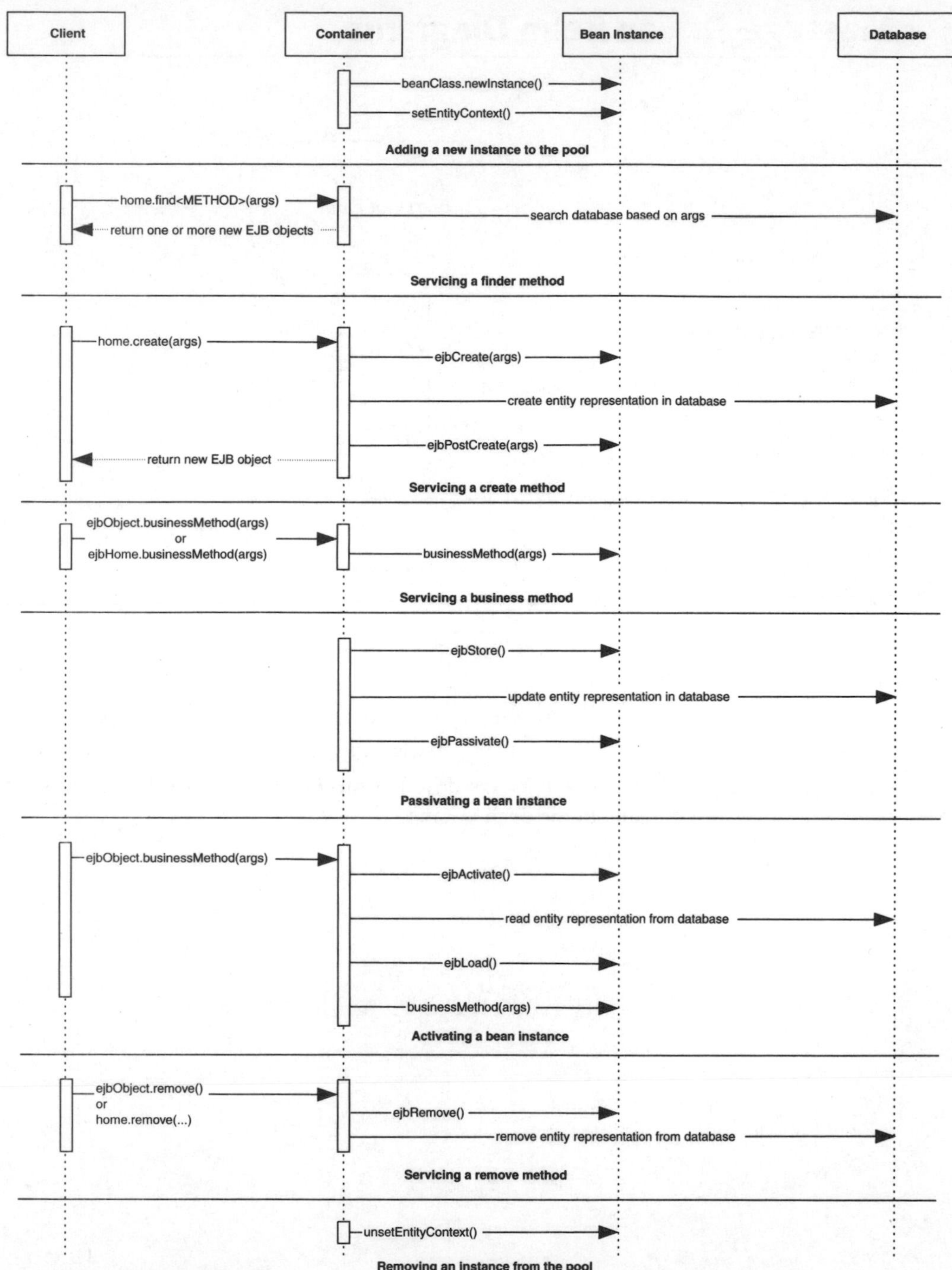

Figure E.12 Sequence diagram for container-managed persistent entity beans. For simplicity, the Container object represents all container subsystems, including EJB objects, home objects, transaction services, and so on.

Message-Driven Bean Diagrams

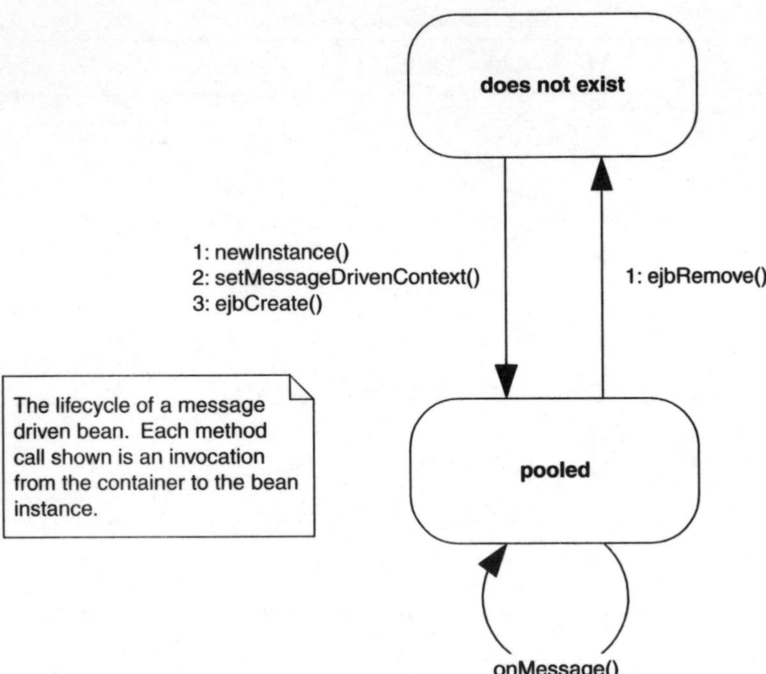
does not exist
1: newInstance()
2: setMessageDrivenContext()
3: ejbCreate()
1: ejbRemove()
The lifecycle of a message driven bean. Each method call shown is an invocation from the container to the bean instance.
pooled
onMessage()

Figure E.13 The life cycle of a message-driven bean. Each method call shown is an invocation from the container to the bean instance.

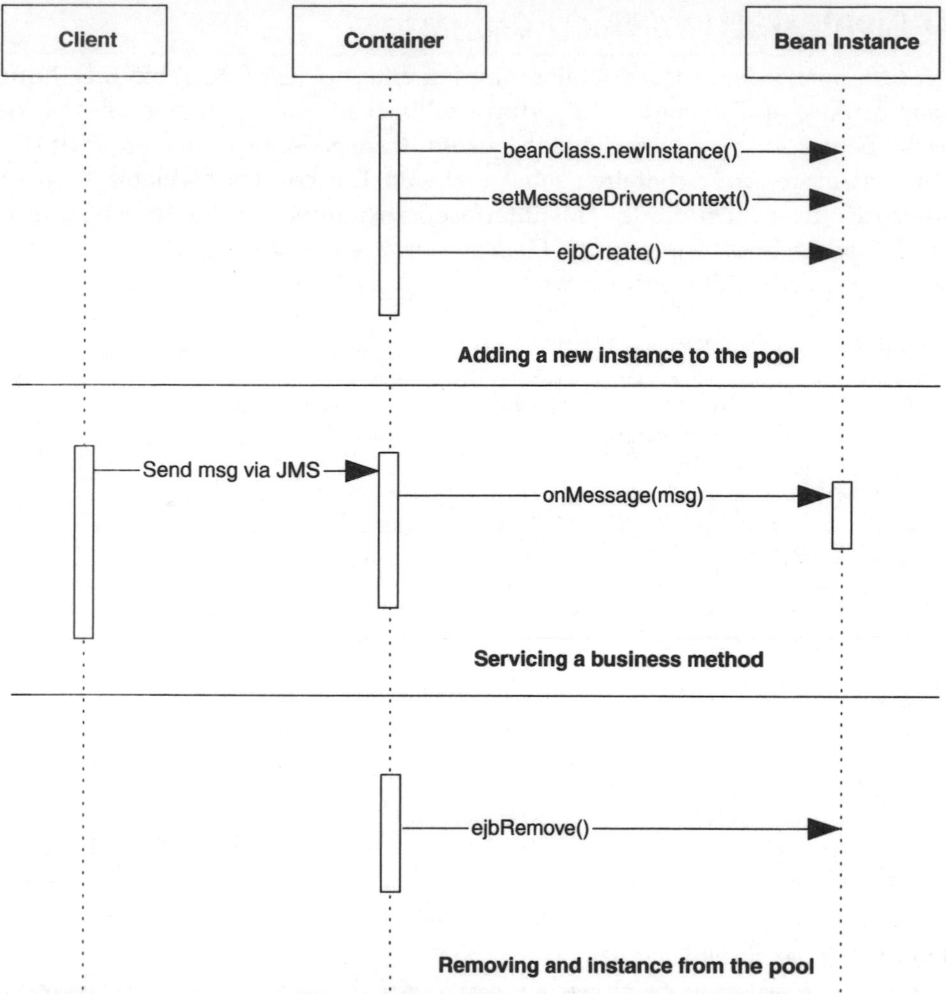

Figure E.14 Sequence diagram for message-driven beans. For simplicity, the Container object represents all container subsystems, including home objects, transaction services, and so on.

EJB API Reference

The following section explains the Enterprise JavaBeans API, which is the *javax.ejb* package. This API is the essence of EJB and defines the specific signature contracts between clients, enterprise beans, and containers.

EJBContext

An *EJBContext* object is a container-implemented object (see Table E.1). Your bean can use an EJB context to perform callbacks to the container. These callbacks help your bean determine its current transactional status, security status, and more. Your container must make an EJB context available to your enterprise bean at runtime. This interface is extended by the *SessionContext*, *EntityContext*, and *MessageDrivenContext* interfaces to provide additional functionality specific to those bean types.

```
public interface javax.ejb.EJBContext
{
 public javax.ejb.EJBHome getEJBHome();
 public javax.ejb.EJBLocalHome getEJBLocalHome();

 public boolean getRollbackOnly()
      throws java.lang.IllegalStateException;
 public void setRollbackOnly()
      throws java.lang.IllegalStateException;
 public javax.transaction.UserTransaction getUserTransaction()
      throws java.lang.IllegalStateException;

 public boolean isCallerInRole(java.lang.String);
 public java.security.Principal getCallerPrincipal();

 public TimerService getTimerService()
      throws java.lang.IllegalStateException;
}
```

Table E.1 javax.ejb.EJBContext

METHOD	EXPLANATION
getEJBHome()	Call this from within your bean to access your own home object. You can use this home object to create, destroy, or find EJB objects of your own bean class type. This method is not used very often.
getEJBLocalHome()	Same as *getEJBHome()* except this retrieves the local interface version.
getRollbackOnly()	Asks the container if the transaction is doomed to rollback. If it's doomed, you can avoid performing computer-intensive operations (see Chapter 12).
setRollbackOnly()	If something goes horribly wrong inside your bean, you can call this method to force the current transaction to rollback (see Chapter 12).

Table E.1 *(continued)*

METHOD	EXPLANATION
getUserTransaction()	Retrieves the JTA *UserTransaction* interface to perform programmatic transactions (see Chapter 12).
isCallerInRole(String)	Asks the container if the current logged-in user is in the proper security role to perform a desired operation. Useful for programmatic security (see Chapter 13).
getCallerPrincipal()	Retrieves the current logged-in user's security principal. You can use this principal to query a database or perform other operations (see Chapter 13).
getTimerService()	Gets access to the EJB timer service (see Chapter 14).

EJBHome

Remote clients create, find, and remove EJB objects through home interfaces. Your home interfaces extend *javax.ejb.EJBHome*. The container will implement the methods in *javax.ejb.EJBHome* when it implements your home interface as a concrete home object (see Table E.2).

```
public interface javax.ejb.EJBHome
    extends java.rmi.Remote
{
    public EJBMetaData getEJBMetaData()
        throws java.rmi.RemoteException;

    public void remove(Handle handle)
        throws java.rmi.RemoteException,
            javax.ejb.RemoveException;

    public void remove(Object primaryKey)
        throws java.rmi.RemoteException,
            javax.ejb.RemoveException;

    public javax.ejb.HomeHandle getHomeHandle()
        throws java.rmi.RemoteException;
}
```

Table E.2 javax.ejb.EJBHome

METHOD	EXPLANATION
getEJBMetaData()	Returns metadata about the enterprise bean you're working with. Useful if your client code is written in a scripting language, or if you're writing EJB development tools.
getHomeHandle()	Retrieves a serializable handle to the bean's home object. You can tuck this handle away somewhere (such as writing it to disk) and then use it again later to retrieve the home without performing a JNDI lookup.
remove()	This method destroys an EJB object based on an EJB object handle or primary key you pass in.

Note: These methods are called by remote clients; for entity beans, *remove()* also deletes the bean from the underlying persistent store.

EJBLocalHome

Local clients create, find, and remove local EJB objects through local home interfaces. Your local home interfaces extend *javax.ejb.EJBLocalHome*. The container will implement the methods in *javax.ejb.EJBLocalHome* when it implements your local home interface as a concrete local home object (see Table E.3).

```
public interface javax.ejb.EJBLocalHome
{
    public void remove(Object primaryKey)
        throws javax.ejb.EJBException,
            javax.ejb.RemoveException;
}
```

Table E.3 javax.ejb.EJBLocalHome

METHOD	EXPLANATION
remove()	This method destroys an EJB local object based upon a primary key you pass in. Applies only to entity beans. This will also delete the bean data from the underlying persistent store.

Note: These methods are called by local clients.

EJBLocalObject

A local client accesses a bean through an EJB local object, which implements a local interface. Your local interface must extend *javax.ejb.EJBLocalObject*. The container will implement the methods in *javax.ejb.EJBLocalObject* when it implements your local interface as a concrete EJB local object (see Table E.4).

```
public interface javax.ejb.EJBLocalObject
{
    public javax.ejb.EJBLocalHome getEJBLocalHome()
        throws javax.ejb.EJBException;

    public java.lang.Object getPrimaryKey()
        throws javax.ejb.EJBException;

    public void remove()
        throws javax.ejb.EJBException;
        javax.ejb.RemoveException;

    public boolean isIdentical(javax.ejb.EJBObject)
        throws java.rmi.RemoteException;
}
```

EJBMetaData

This interface encapsulates metadata about an enterprise bean. Metadata is not very useful for typical client code; it is better suited to clients that need to discover information dynamically about an enterprise bean, such as scripting language environments or EJB development tools. Your client code can retrieve this metadata by calling *homeObject.getEJBMetaData()*. The client code will get back a serializable implementation of *javax.ejb.EJBMetaData*.

Table E.4 javax.ejb.EJBLocalObject

METHOD	EXPLANATION
getEJBLocalHome()	Gets the local home object for this EJB local object.
getPrimaryKey()	Returns the primary key for this EJB local object. A primary key is only used for entity beans (see Chapter 6).
remove()	Destroys this EJB local object. When your client code is done using an EJB local object, you should call this method. The system resources for the EJB local object can then be reclaimed.
isIdentical()	Tests whether two EJB local objects are identical.

Note: For entity beans, *remove()* also deletes the bean from the underlying persistent store.

```
public interface javax.ejb.EJBMetaData
{
    public javax.ejb.EJBHome getEJBHome();
    public java.lang.Class getHomeInterfaceClass();
    public java.lang.Class getPrimaryKeyClass();
    public java.lang.Class getRemoteInterfaceClass();
    public boolean isSession();
    public boolean isStatelessSession();
}
```

EJBObject

A remote client accesses a bean through an EJB object, which implements a remote interface. Your remote interface must extend *javax.ejb.EJBObject*. The container will implement the methods in *javax.ejb.EJBObject* when it implements your remote interface as a concrete EJB object (see Table E.5).

```
public interface javax.ejb.EJBObject
    extends java.rmi.Remote
{
    public javax.ejb.EJBHome getEJBHome()
        throws java.rmi.RemoteException;

    public java.lang.Object getPrimaryKey()
        throws java.rmi.RemoteException;

    public void remove()
        throws java.rmi.RemoteException,
            javax.ejb.RemoveException;

    public javax.ejb.Handle getHandle()
        throws java.rmi.RemoteException;

    public boolean isIdentical(javax.ejb.EJBObject)
        throws java.rmi.RemoteException;
}
```

Table E.5 javax.ejb.EJBObject

METHOD	EXPLANATION
getEJBHome()	Gets the home object for this EJB object.
getPrimaryKey()	Returns the primary key for this EJB object. A primary key is used only for entity beans (see Chapters 6–8).
remove()	Destroys this EJB object. When your client code is done using an EJB object, call this method. The system resources for the EJB object can then be reclaimed.

Table E.5 *(continued)*

METHOD	EXPLANATION
getHandle()	Acquires a *handle* for this EJB object. An EJB handle is a persistent reference to an EJB object that the client can stow away somewhere. Later, the client can use the handle to reacquire the EJB object and start using it again.
isIdentical()	Tests whether two EJB objects are identical. Should be used instead of *equals()* or the == operator, since those test whether two stubs are the same—stubs are not EJB objects.

Note: For entity beans, *remove()* also deletes the bean from the underlying persistent store.

EnterpriseBean

This interface serves as a marker interface; implementing this interface indicates that your class is indeed an enterprise bean class. You should not implement this interface; rather, implement either *javax.ejb.EntityBean*, *javax.ejb.SessionBean*, or *javax.ejb.MessageDrivenBean*, each of which extends this interface.

```
public interface javax.ejb.EnterpriseBean
    extends java.io.Serializable
{
}
```

EntityBean

To write an entity bean class, your class must implement the *javax.ejb.EntityBean* interface. This interface defines a few required methods that you must fill in. These are management methods that the EJB container calls to alert your bean to life cycle events. Clients of your bean will never call these methods, because these methods are not made available to clients via the EJB object (see Table E.6). Each of the following methods can throw a *java.rmi.RemoteException* or *javax.ejb.EJBException*.

```
public interface javax.ejb.EntityBean
    implements javax.ejb.EnterpriseBean
{
    public void setEntityContext(javax.ejb.EntityContext)
         throws javax.ejb.EJBException,
              java.rmi.RemoteException;

    public void unsetEntityContext()
```

```
            throws javax.ejb.EJBException,
                java.rmi.RemoteException;

        public void ejbRemove()
            throws javax.ejb.RemoveException,
                javax.ejb.EJBException,
                    java.rmi.RemoteException;

        public void ejbActivate()
            throws javax.ejb.EJBException,
                java.rmi.RemoteException;

        public void ejbPassivate()
            throws javax.ejb.EJBException
                java.rmi.RemoteException;

        public void ejbLoad()
            throws javax.ejb.EJBException
                java.rmi.RemoteException;

        public void ejbStore()
            throws javax.ejb.EJBException
                java.rmi.RemoteException;
}
```

EntityContext

An entity context is a specific EJB context used only for entity beans (see Table E.7).

```
public interface javax.ejb.EntityContext implements
    javax.ejb.EJBContext
{
    public javax.ejb.EJBObject getEJBLocalObject()
        throws java.lang.IllegalStateException;

    public javax.ejb.EJBObject getEJBObject()
        throws java.lang.IllegalStateException;

    public java.lang.Object getPrimaryKey();
        throws java.lang.IllegalStateException;
}
```

Table E.6 Required Methods for Entity Bean Classes

METHOD	DESCRIPTION	TYPICAL IMPLEMENTATION (BEAN-MANAGED PERSISTENT ENTITIES)	TYPICAL IMPLEMENTATION (CONTAINER-MANAGED PERSISTENT ENTITIES)
SetEntityContext (EntityContext ctx)	Associates your bean with an entity context. You can query the entity context about your current transactional state, your current security state, and more. Store the context away in a member variable so the context can be queried later.	Store the context away in a member variable so the context can be queried later.	Store the context in a member so the context can be queried later.
ejbFind...(...) *Note: You only use ejbFind() methods with bean-managed persistent entity beans.*	Finds an existing entity bean in storage. You can have many different finder methods, which all perform different operations.	Search through a data store using a storage API such as JDBC or SQL/J. For example, you might perform a relational query such as *SELECT id FROM accounts WHERE balance> 0*. Return the resulting primary key set.	Do not implement these methods for container-managed persistent entity beans. The EJB container will handle *all* issues relating to finding data for you. Use your container tools to describe your finder method needs.
ejbSelect...(...) *Note: You only use ejbSelect() methods with container-managed persistent entity beans.*	*ejbSelect()* methods are CMP helper methods that perform queries internally by your bean but that are not accessible to clients of your bean.	There are no *ejbSelect()* methods for BMP entity beans. You can write your own helper methods and name them whatever you wish.	Define this method as abstract. Then write EJB-QL in the deployment descriptor to set up the query.

(continued)

Table E.6 *(continued)*

METHOD	DESCRIPTION	TYPICAL IMPLEMENTATION (BEAN-MANAGED PERSISTENT ENTITIES)	TYPICAL IMPLEMENTATION (CONTAINER-MANAGED PERSISTENT ENTITIES)
ejbHome...(...)	Sometimes you need methods on an entity bean that are not specific to any given data instance (or row)—for example, counting the total number of accounts in a table. You can write *ejbHome* methods to perform these operations. The *ejbHome* methods are special business methods because they are called from a bean in the pool before the bean is associated with any specific data. Clients call these methods from the home interface or local home interface.	Perform your global operations, as counting the rows in a database and returning the results to the client. The fast-and-easy way to achieve this is to use JDBC. The cleaner (but lower-performing way if you're notcareful) is to call *ejbSelect()* and perhaps other entity bean methods entity bean methods.	Perform your global operations, such as counting the rows in a database and returning the results to the client. The fast-and-easy way to achieve this is to use JDBC. The cleaner (but lower-performing way if you're not careful) is to call *ejbSelect()* and perhaps other entity bean methods.
ejbCreate...(...)	Initializes a bean for a particular client and creates underlying database data. Each *ejbCreate()* method you define gives clients a different way to create your entity beans.	Validate the client's initialization parameters. Explicitly create the database representation of the data via a storage API such a JDBC or SQL/J.	Validate the client's initialization parameters. Call your abstract *set()* methods to initialize the generated bean subclass to the parameters passed in. The container will then use these values in the subclass to create the database data for you.

Table E.6 *(continued)*

METHOD	DESCRIPTION	TYPICAL IMPLEMENTATION (BEAN-MANAGED PERSISTENT ENTITIES)	TYPICAL IMPLEMENTATION (CONTAINER-MANAGED PERSISTENT ENTITIES)
ejbPostCreate...(...)	Your bean class must define *ejbPostCreate()* for each *ejbCreate()*. Each pair must accept the same parameters. The container calls *ejbPostCreate()* right after *ejbCreate()*.	Perform any initialization you need to that requires a reference to your own EJB object, such as passing your bean's EJB object reference to other beans. You can get your EJB object via *EntityContext.getEJBObject()*.	Perform any initialization you need that requires a reference to your own EJB object, such as passing your bean's EJB object reference to other beans. You can get your EJB object via *EntityContext. getEJBObject()*.
ejbPassivate()	Called immediately before your bean is passivated (swapped out to disk because too many beans are instantiated).	Release any resources your bean may be holding.	Release any resources your bean may be holding.
ejbStore()	Called when the container needs to update the database with your bean's state. The current transactional state dictates when this method is called. This method is also called during passivation, directly before *ejbPassivate()*.	Explicitly update the database representation of the data via a storage API such as JDBC Typically, you'll write a number of your member variable's fields to disk.	*Do not update the database in this method.* Rather, the EJB container will update the database for you automatically right *after* calling your *ejbStore()* method. It does this in the subclass by taking your bean state and writing it to the database. Thus, you should prepare your state to be written to the database, such as compressing fields, by calling your abstract get/set methods.

(continued)

Table E.6 *(continued)*

METHOD	DESCRIPTION	TYPICAL IMPLEMENTATION (BEAN-MANAGED PERSISTENT ENTITIES)	TYPICAL IMPLEMENTATION (CONTAINER-MANAGED PERSISTENT ENTITIES)
ejbLoad()	Called when the container needs to update your bean with the database's state. The current transactional state dictates when this method is called. This method is also called during activation, directly before *ejbActivate()*.	First your bean instance must figure out which data to load. Call the *getPrimaryKey()* method on the entity context; that will tell your bean what data it should load. Next read database data into your bean via a storage API such as JDBC or SQL/J.	*Do not read data from the database in this method.* The EJB container will read in data from the database for you automatically right *before* calling your *ejbLoad()* method. It does this in the subclass by querying the database and populating your bean state. Thus, you should perform any necessary post-load operations, such as decompressing fields, by calling your abstract get/set methods.
ejbActivate()	Called immediately before your bean is activated (swapped in from disk because a client needs your bean).	Acquire any resources your bean needs, such as those released during *ejbPassivate()*.	Acquire any resources your bean needs such as those released during *ejbPassivate()*.

Table E.6 *(continued)*

METHOD	DESCRIPTION	TYPICAL IMPLEMENTATION (BEAN-MANAGED PERSISTENT ENTITIES)	TYPICAL IMPLEMENTATION (CONTAINER-MANAGED PERSISTENT ENTITIES)
ejbRemove()	To destroy an entity bean's data in a database, the client must call *remove()* on the EJB object or home object. This method causes the container to issue an *ejbRemove()* call on the bean. *ejbRemove()* is a required method of all beans and takes no parameters. *Note: ejbRemove() does not mean* the in-memory entity bean instance is going to be destroyed. *ejbRemove()* destroys only database data. The bean instance can be recycled to handle different database data, such as a bank account bean representing different bank accounts.	First figure out what data you should destroy via *getPrimaryKey()* on the *EntityContext*. Then explicitly delete the database representation of the data via a storage API such as JDBC or SQL/J.	*Do not destroy database data in this method.* Simply perform any operations that must be done before the data in the database is destroyed. The EJB container will destroy the data for you right after *ejbRemove()* is called.
unsetEntityContext()	Called right before your entity bean instance is destroyed (when the container wants to reduce the pool size).	Release any resources you allocated during *setEntityContext()* and get ready for garbage collection.	Release any resources you allocated during *setEntityContext()*, and get ready for garbage collection.

Table E.7 javax.ejb.EntityContext

METHOD	DESCRIPTION	USEFULNESS
getEJBLocalObject()	Returns a reference to your bean's own local EJB object.	Useful if your bean needs to call another local bean and you want to pass a reference to yourself.
getEJBObject()	Returns a reference to your bean's own remote EJB object.	Useful if your bean needs to call another remote bean and you want to pass a reference to yourself.
getPrimaryKey()	Retrieves the primary key that is currently associated with this entity bean instance.	Call to determine what database data your instance is associated with. You need to use this in *ejbLoad()* to determine what database data to load and in *ejbRemove()* to determine what database data to remove.

Handle

An EJB object handle is a persistent reference to an EJB object. Handles enable you to disconnect from your EJB server, shut down your application, and later resume your application while preserving the conversational state in the beans you've been working with. Handles are also useful when your client code needs to store a reference to an EJB object in stable storage and reconnect to that EJB object later.

```
public interface javax.ejb.Handle
     extends java.io.Serializable
{
    public javax.ejb.EJBObject getEJBObject()
         throws java.rmi.RemoteException;
}
```

HomeHandle

Just as an EJB object handle is a persistent reference to an EJB object, a home handle is a persistent reference to a home object. Home handles are useful when your client code needs to store a reference to a home object in stable storage and reconnect to that home object later. Home handles allow you to avoid doing a JNDI lookup when reconnecting to a home object.

```
public interface javax.ejb.HomeHandle
     extends java.io.Serializable
{
    public javax.ejb.EJBHome getEJBHome()
         throws java.rmi.RemoteException;
}
```

MessageDrivenBean

To write a message-driven bean class, your class must implement the *javax.ejb.MessageDrivenBean* interface. This interface defines a few required methods that you must fill in. These are management methods that the EJB container calls to alert your bean about life cycle events. Clients of your bean will never call these methods because clients do not call message-driven beans directly; rather, they send messages to application server, which in turn delivers them to message-driven beans. Each of these methods can throw a *javax.ejb.EJBException* (see Table E.8).

```
public interface javax.ejb.MessageDrivenBean
    extends javax.ejb.EnterpriseBean,
{
    public void setMessageDrivenContext(MessageDrivenContext ctx)
         throws javax.ejb.EJBException;

    public void ejbRemove()
         throws javax.ejb.EJBException;
}
```

Table E.8 Required Methods for Message-Driven Bean Classes

METHOD	DESCRIPTION	TYPICAL IMPLEMENTATION
SetMessage DrivenContext (MessageDriven Context ctx)	Associates your bean with a message-driven context. Your bean can query the context about its current transactional state, retrieve its own home object, and more.	Store the context away in a member variable so the context can be queried later.

(continued)

Table E.8 *(continued)*

METHOD	DESCRIPTION	TYPICAL IMPLEMENTATION
ejbCreate()	Initializes your message-driven bean. You can only define a single *ejbCreate()* method that takes no parameters. This is called directly by the container after the message-driven bean is associated with a context object.	Perform any initialization your bean needs, such as locating external resources or looking up other EJB home objects to be used later.
onMessage (message)	Your bean has received a new message.	Crack open the message, figure out what it means to you, process the message, and perform any logic you desire.
ejbRemove()	Called by the container immediately before your bean is removed from memory.	Prepare your bean for destruction. Free all resources you may have allocated.

MessageDrivenContext

A message-driven context is a specific EJB context used only for message-driven beans. This interface serves as a marker interface. There are no specific additional methods that message-driven beans get on their context objects.

```
public interface javax.ejb.MessageDrivenContext
    extends javax.ejb.EJBContext
{
}
```

SessionBean

To write a session bean class, your class must implement the *javax.ejb.SessionBean* interface. This interface defines a few required methods that you must fill in. These are management methods that the EJB container calls to alert your bean about life cycle events. Clients of your bean will never call these methods because these methods are not made available to clients via the EJB object (see Table E.9). Each of these methods can throw a *java.rmi.RemoteException* or *javax.ejb.EJBException*.

```
public interface javax.ejb.SessionBean
    extends javax.ejb.EnterpriseBean
{
    public void setSessionContext(SessionContext ctx)
         throws javax.ejb.EJBException,
              java.rmi.RemoteExeption;

    public void ejbPassivate()
         throws javax.ejb.EJBException,
              java.rmi.RemoteException;

    public void ejbActivate()
         throws javax.ejb.EJBException,
              java.rmi.RemoteException;

    public void ejbRemove()
         throws javax.ejb.EJBException,
              java.rmi.RemoteException;
}
```

SessionContext

A session context is a specific EJB context used only for session beans (see Table E.10).

```
public interface javax.ejb.SessionContext
    extends javax.ejb.EJBContext
{
    public javax.ejb.EJBLocalObject getEJBLocalObject()
        throws java.lang.IllegalStateException;

    public javax.ejb.EJBObject getEJBObject()
        throws java.lang.IllegalStateException;

    public javax.xml.rpc.handler.MessageContext getMessageContext()
        throws java.lang.IllegalStateException;
}
```

Table E.9 Required Methods for Session Bean Classes

METHOD	DESCRIPTION	TYPICAL IMPLEMENTATION (STATEFUL SESSION BEANS)	TYPICAL IMPLEMENTATION (STATELESS SESSION BEANS)
setSession Context(Session Context ctx)	Associates your bean with a session context. Your bean can query the context about its current transactional state, current security state, and more.	Store the context away in a member variable so the context can be queried later.	Store the context away in a member variable so the context can be queried.
ejbCreate...(...)	Initializes your session bean.	Perform any initialization your bean needs, such as setting member variables to the argument values passed in. Note: You can define several *ejbCreate...(...)* methods, and each can take different arguments. You must provide at least one *ejbCreate...(...)* method in your session bean.	Perform any initialization your bean needs, such as setting member variables to the argument values passed in. *Note:* You can only define a single empty *ejbCreate()* method with no parameters. After all, if it had parameters and the bean initialized itself to those parameters, the bean would never remember what it initialized itself to upon subsequent calls, since it is stateless!
ejbPassivate()	Called immediately before your bean is passivated (swapped out to disk because there are too many instantiated beans).	Release any resources your bean may be holding.	Unused because there is no conversational state; leave empty.
ejbActivate()	Called immediately before your bean is activated (swapped in from disk because a client needs your bean).	Acquire any resources your bean needs, such as those released during *ejbPassivate()*.	Unused because there is no conversational state; leave empty.
ejbRemove()	Called by the container immediately before your bean is removed from memory.	Prepare your bean for destruction. Free all resources you may have allocated.	Prepare your bean for destruction. Free all resources you may have allocated.

Table E.10 javax.ejb.SessionContext

METHOD	DESCRIPTION	USEFULNESS
getEJBLocalObject()	Returns a reference to your bean's own local EJB object.	Useful if your bean needs to call another local bean and you want to pass a reference to yourself.
getEJBObject()	Returns a reference to your bean's own EJB object.	Useful if your bean needs to call another bean, and you want to pass a reference to yourself.
getMessageContext()	Returns a reference to a JAX-RPC message context.	Can be used by your stateless session bean instance invoked through its Web Service endpoint interface to get JAX-RPC/SOAP message-related information via properties.

SessionSynchronization

If your stateful session bean is caching database data in memory or needs to roll back in-memory conversational state upon a transaction abort, you should implement this interface (see Table E.11). The container will call each of the methods in this interface automatically at the appropriate times during transactions, alerting you to important transactional events. Each of these methods can throw a *java.rmi.RemoteException* or *javax.ejb.EJBException*.

```
public interface javax.ejb.SessionSynchronization
{
    public void afterBegin()
          throws javax.ejb.EJBException,
              java.rmi.RemoteException;

    public void beforeCompletion()
          throws javax.ejb.EJBException,
              java.rmi.RemoteException;

    public void afterCompletion(boolean)
          throws javax.ejb.EJBException,
              java.rmi.RemoteException;
}
```

Table E.11 javax.ejb.SessionSynchronization

METHOD	DESCRIPTION
afterBegin()	Called by the container directly after a transaction begins. You should read in any database data you want to cache in your stateful session bean during the transaction. You should also create a backup copy of your state in case the transaction rolls back.
beforeCompletion()	Called by the container right before a transaction completes. Write out any database data you've cached during the transaction.
afterCompletion(boolean)	Called by the container when a transaction completes either in a commit *or* an abort. True indicates a successful commit; false indicates an abort. If an abort happened, revert to the backup copy of your state to preserve your session bean's conversation.

TimedObject

If your session, entity or message-driven beans want to implement timer expiration notification methods so that containers can call back *ejbTimeout()* on *javax.ejb.TimedObject* after a certain period of time has elapsed, you should implement this interface (see Table E.12).

```
public interface javax.ejb.TimedObject
{
    public void ejbTimeout (javax.ejb.Timer timer);
}
```

Table E.12 javax.ejb.TimedObject

METHOD	DESCRIPTION
ejbTimeout(Timer)	Called by container upon timer expiration. You should implement the bean logic that you want to execute periodically in this method.

Timer

This interface provides information about the timer created with the help of EJB timer service, such as the next point in time when the timer expiration is scheduled to occur, the number of milliseconds that will elapse before the next scheduled timer expiration occurs, and much more (see Table E.13). An instance of *javax.ejb.Timer* is initialized by the container and passed to your bean as an argument when it calls *ejbTimeout()* on the *javax.ejb.TimedObject* interface.

```
public interface javax.ejb.Timer
{
    public void cancel()
         throws java.lang.IllegalStateException,
              javax.ejb.NoSuchObjectLocalException,
                   javax.ejb.EJBException;

    public long getTimeRemaining()
         throws java.lang.IllegalStateException,
              javax.ejb.NoSuchObjectLocalException,
                   javax.ejb.EJBException;

    public java.util.Date getNextTimeout()
         throws java.lang.IllegalStateException,
              javax.ejb.NoSuchObjectLocalException,
                   javax.ejb.EJBException;

    public java.io.Serializable getInfo()
         throws java.lang.IllegalStateException,
              javax.ejb.NoSuchObjectLocalException,
                   javax.ejb.EJBException;

    public javax.ejb.TimerHandle getHandle()
         throws java.lang.IllegalStateException,
              javax.ejb.NoSuchObjectLocalException,
                   javax.ejb.EJBException;
}
```

Table E.13 javax.ejb.Timer

METHOD	DESCRIPTION
cancel()	Call this method if you want to cancel all the expiration notifications associated with the given timer instance.
getTimeRemaining()	Returns the number of milliseconds that will elapse before the next scheduled timer expiration.

(continued)

Table E.13 *(continued)*

METHOD	DESCRIPTION
getNextTimeout()	Returns the future point in time at which the next timer expiration is scheduled to occur.
getInfo()	Returns the information associated with the given timer at the time of its creation. If no *Serializable* information object was provided at the time of creation, then this method returns null.
getHandle()	Returns the *Serializable* timer handle that can be persisted by your bean for later reuse.

TimerHandle

A timer handle is a persistent reference to an EJB timer object. All EJB timers implement this interface (see Table E.14). Timer handles allow your beans to persist the timer object for later reuse so that the bean does not have to create a new timer object.

```
public interface javax.ejb.TimerHandle
     extends java.io.Serializable
{
    public javax.ejb.Timer getTimer()
         throws java.lang.IllegalStateException,
              javax.ejb.NoSuchObjectLocalException,
                   javax.ejb.EJBException;
}
```

Table E.14 javax.ejb.TimerHandle

METHOD	DESCRIPTION
getTimer()	Returns the reference to the timer object represented by the given handle. Use this method to retrieve the timer object reference from a persisted timer object.

TimerService

This interface provides your enterprise beans access to EJB timer service implemented by your EJB container (see Table E.15). See Chapter 14 for information on how to create and use EJB timers.

```
public interface javax.ejb.TimerService
{
    public javax.ejb.Timer createTimer (long duration,
java.io.Serializable info)
          throws java.lang.IllegalArgumentException,
               java.lang.IllegalStateException,
                    javax.ejb.EJBException;

    public javax.ejb.Timer createTimer (long initialDuration, long
intervalDuration,
    java.io.Serializable info)
          throws java.lang.IllegalArgumentException,
               java.lang.IllegalStateException,
                    javax.ejb.EJBException;

    public javax.ejb.Timer createTimer (java.util.Date expiration,
    java.io.Serializable info)
          throws java.lang.IllegalArgumentException,
               java.lang.IllegalStateException,
                    javax.ejb.EJBException;

    public javax.ejb.Timer createTimer (java.util.Date
initialExpiration,
    long intervalDuration, java.io.Serializable info)
          throws java.lang.IllegalArgumentException,
               java.lang.IllegalStateException,
                    javax.ejb.EJBException;

    public java.util.Collection getTimers()
          throws java.lang.IllegalStateException,
                    javax.ejb.EJBException;
}
```

Table E.15 javax.ejb.TimerService

METHOD	DESCRIPTION
createTimer (long, Serializable)	Creates a one-time expiration timer, which becomes inactive after the first (and last) expiration. Second argument represents a *Serializable* object containing application specific information. If you do not have any information to associate with the given timer then pass null as the second argument.
createTimer (long, long, Serializable)	Creates a recurrently expiring timer whose first expiration occurs after a given duration (in milliseconds) specified in the first argument has elapsed and subsequent expirations occur after the duration (in milliseconds) specified in the second argument elapses. Subsequent expirations are scheduled relative to the time of the first expiration. If expiration is delayed for some reason, two or more expiration notifications may occur in close succession.
createTimer (Date, Serializable)	Creates a one-time expiration timer that expires at a given point in time.
createTimer (Date, long, Serializable)	Creates a recurrently expiring timer whose first expiration occurs at the point in time specified by the first argument, and subsequent expirations occur after the duration (in milliseconds) specified in the second argument elapses. Subsequent expirations are scheduled relative to the time of the first expiration. If expiration is delayed for some reason, two or more expiration notifications may occur in close succession.
getTimers()	Retrieves a collection of all the timers associated with the given bean.

Exception Reference

Table E.16 describes the purpose of each exception class in EJB.

Table E.16 EJB Exception Explanations

EXCEPTION	DESCRIPTION
AccessLocalException	Indicates the client does not have permission to call this method. Used only for local clients.
CreateException	This exception type indicates failure to create an enterprise bean. You should throw this exception in your home interface's *create(.)* methods.

Table E.16 *(continued)*

EXCEPTION	DESCRIPTION
DuplicateKey	This exception type indicates failure to create an entity bean Exception because an entity bean with the same primary key already exists. This is a subclass of *CreateException* and is thrown in an entity bean home interface's *create(.)* methods.
EJBException	Your enterprise bean class should throw this exception to indicate an unexpected error, such as a failure to open a database connection, or a JNDI exception. Your container treats this exception as a serious problem and may take action such as logging the event or paging a system administrator, depending upon your container's policy. The container then rethrows a *java.rmi.RemoteException* if the client is remote, or a *javax.ejb.EJBException* if the client is local. Since *EJBException* is a *RuntimeException,* it does not need to be declared in *throws* clauses.
FinderException	This exception indicates a failure to locate an existing entity bean. You should throw this method from your home interface's finder methods.
NoSuchEntityException	Your entity bean class should throw this exception to indicate that the database data corresponding to the in-memory entity bean instance has been removed. You can throw this exception from any of your entity bean class' business methods, and from your *ejbStore()* and *ejbLoad()* methods.
NoSuchObjectLocal Exception	Thrown when a client tries to call a method on a bean that has been destroyed.
ObjectNotFound Exception	When you're writing finder methods in your entity bean's home interface, throw this exception to indicate that the specified EJB object was not found. You should use this exception only when your finder method is returning a single EJB object. If you're returning more than one EJB object, a null collection is returned instead.
RemoveException	Your enterprise bean should throw this exception when an error occurs during *ejbRemove()*. The container will re-throw this exception back to the client. This is considered a normal, run-of-the-mill application-level exception and does not indicate a system-level problem. When your client code receives this exception, you do not know for sure whether the entity bean has been removed or not.

(continued)

Table E.16 *(continued)*

EXCEPTION	DESCRIPTION
TransactionRequired LocalException	Indicates the receiving object needed a transaction to run but was not supplied with a transaction context.
TransactionRolled BackLocalException	Indicates the request's transaction was rolled back or marked for rollback. Thus, the request could not be completed.

Transaction Reference

The following section offers reference information on transactions as outlined in Tables E.17 through E.22.

Table E.17 The Effects of Transaction Attributes

TRANSACTION ATTRIBUTE	CLIENT'S TRANSACTION	BEAN'S TRANSACTION
Required	None T1	T2 T1
RequiresNew	None T1	T2 T2
Supports	None T1	None T1
Mandatory	None T1	Error T1
NotSupported	None	None
	T1	None
Never	None T1	None Error

Table E.18 Transaction Attributes

CONSTANT	MEANING
NotSupported	Your bean *cannot* be involved in a transaction at all. When a bean method is called, any existing transaction is suspended.
Never	Your bean *cannot* be involved in a transaction at all. When a bean method is called, if a transaction is in progress, an exception is thrown back to the client (*java.rmi.RemoteException* if remote, *javax.ejb.EJBException* if local).

Table E.18 *(continued)*

CONSTANT	MEANING
Required	Your bean must *always* run in a transaction. If a transaction is already running, your bean joins that transaction. If no transaction is running, the EJB container starts one for you.
RequiresNew	Your bean must always run in a *new* transaction. Any current transaction is suspended.
Supports	If a transaction is already under way, your bean joins that transaction. Otherwise, the bean runs with no transaction at all.
Mandatory	Mandates that a transaction must be already running when your bean method is called, or a *javax.ejb.TransactionRequired* exception is thrown back to the caller.

Table E.19 Permissible Transaction Attributes for Each Bean Type

TRANSACTION ATTRIBUTE	STATELESS SESSION BEAN	STATEFUL SESSION BEAN IMPLEMENTING SESSION SYNCHRONIZATION	ENTITY BEAN	MESSAGE-DRIVEN BEAN
Required	Yes	Yes	Yes	Yes
RequiresNew	Yes	Yes	Yes	No
Mandatory	Yes	Yes	Yes	No
Supports	Yes	No	No	No
NotSupported	Yes	No	No	Yes
Never	Yes	No	No	No

Table E.20 Transaction Isolation Levels

ISOLATION LEVEL	DIRTY READS?	UNREPEATABLE READS?	PHANTOM READS?
READ UNCOMMITTED	Yes	Yes	Yes
READ COMMITTED	No	Yes	Yes
REPEATABLE READ	No	No	Yes
SERIALIZABLE	No	No	No

Table E.21 The javax.transaction.Status Constants for Transactional Status

CONSTANT	MEANING
STATUS_ACTIVE	A transaction is currently happening and is active.
STATUS_NO_TRANSACTION	No transaction is currently happening.
STATUS_MARKED_ROLLBACK	The current transaction will eventually abort because it's been marked for rollback. This could be because some party called *setRollbackOnly()*.
STATUS_PREPARING	The current transaction is preparing to be committed (during Phase One of the two-phase commit protocol).
STATUS_PREPARED	The current transaction has been prepared to be committed (Phase One is complete).
STATUS_COMMITTING	The current transaction is in the process of being committed right now (during Phase Two).
STATUS_COMMITTED	The current transaction has been committed (Phase Two is complete).
STATUS_ROLLING_BACK	The current transaction is in the process of rolling back.
STATUS_ROLLEDBACK	The current transaction has been rolled back.
STATUS_UNKNOWN	The status of the current transaction cannot be determined.

Table E.22 The javax.transaction.UserTransaction Methods for Transactional Boundary Demarcation

METHOD	DESCRIPTION
begin()	Begin a new transaction. This transaction becomes associated with the current thread.
commit()	Run the two-phase commit protocol on an existing transaction associated with the current thread. Each resource manager will make its updates durable.
getStatus()	Retrieve the status of the transaction associated with this thread.
rollback()	Force a rollback of the transaction associated with the current thread.
setRollback Only()	Call this to force the current transaction to roll back. This will eventually force the transaction to abort. One interesting use of this is to test out what your components will do without having them perform any permanent resource updates.
set Transaction Timeout(int)	The *transaction timeout* is the maximum amount of time that a transaction can run before it's aborted. This is useful to avoid deadlock situations, when precious resources are being held by a transaction that is currently running.

Index

C

D

E

L

T